The Apocalyptic Year 1000

The Apocalyptic Year 1000

Religious Expectation and Social Change, 950–1050

EDITED BY

RICHARD LANDES

ANDREW GOW

DAVID C. VAN METER

OXFORD

UNIVERSITY PRESS

2003

OXFORD
UNIVERSITY PRESS

Oxford   New York
Auckland   Bangkok   Buenos Aires   Cape Town   Chennai
Dar es Salaam   Delhi   Hong Kong   Istanbul   Karachi   Kolkata
Kuala Lumpur   Madrid   Melbourne   Mexico City   Mumbai   Nairobi
São Paulo   Shanghai   Taipei   Tokyo   Toronto

Copyright © 2003 by Oxford University Press, Inc.

Published by Oxford University Press, Inc.
198 Madison Avenue, New York, New York 10016

www.oup.com

Oxford is a registered trademark of Oxford University Press

Library of Congress Cataloging-in-Publication Data
The apocalyptic year 1000 : religious expectation and social change, 950–1050 / edited by
Richard Landes, Andrew Gow, and David C. Van Meter.
    p. cm.
Papers delivered at a conference held at the end of 1996.
Includes bibliographical references and index.
ISBN 0-19-511191-5; 0-19-516162-9 (pbk.)
1. Second Advent—History of doctrines—Middle Ages, 600–1500—Congresses.
2. Christianity and culture—Europe—History—To 1500—Congresses.   3. One thousand,
A.D.—Congresses.   I. Landes, Richard Allen.   II. Gow, Andrew Colin.   III. Van Meter,
David C.
BT886.3 .A66 2003
940.1'46—dc21   2002042550

9 8 7 6 5 4 3 2 1

Printed in the United States of America
on acid-free paper

Preface

The "Terrors" of the Year 1000:
Une Question Mal Posée

The theme of this volume, the apocalyptic climate around the year 1000 in Europe, is one of the oldest and most well-worn topics of debate among medievalists. The passions and the intransigence on both sides of the debate concerning "les terreurs de l'an mil" are astounding. The traditional Augustinian position on the Last Days and their advent counsels patient watchfulness rather than excited expectation and interpretation of "signs" and portents—in line with Jesus' admonition in the Gospel of Matthew. In the course of refuting the Romantic myth of a Europe paralyzed by fear at the approach of the year 1000 (Michelet), historians since Burr have made a fatal error by assuming that the attitude of their learned counterparts in the distant past was not only correct but also representative of contemporary opinion. Cultural historians in the third millennium will not, one hopes, take twentieth-century scholars' healthy skepticism about the existence of UFOs as representative of common beliefs in Western society as a whole.

The question as to whether or not large numbers of European Christians were panicked by the approach of the year 1000 as a millennial anniversary, as the end of the thousand years of Satan's bondage as mentioned in the Book of Revelation, is almost precisely analogous in its original functions and in its contemporary persistence to the obsolete question that animated another hoary historical debate, that concerning the nature of the Protestant Reformation: was it or was it not the end of the Middle Ages and the beginning of modernity? Almost no Reformation scholar alive today would agree to debate the significance or import of the Reformation in those terms. The question itself is gravely misleading.

Similarly, the question as to whether or not the broad masses in western Europe were afflicted by fear or terror at the approach of the year 1000 is an irrelevant artifact of nineteenth-century debates. Richard Landes, Johannes Fried, and others show very clearly in their essays in this volume that the debate over "les terreurs de l'an mil" (see, most recently, the rather facile polemic by Sylvain Gouguenheim) has become a waste of time. If, however, we ask about the apocalyptic, even chiliastic *hopes* and expectations of western Europeans in the years leading up to and after 1000, we will come much closer, as Johannes Fried argues, to making sense of the dozens of sources that point unambiguously to a heightened and tense apocalyptic climate in the half century or so on either side of the turn of the millennium. We are so used to understanding the end of the world, its Last Judgment, as its *destruction* that we are blind to the strong tradition that focused both on the persecution of the true Church by Antichrist and on the rewards and cessation of suffering to be enjoyed just beyond the end of earthly time.

Rather than conceiving of apocalyptic expectation as a fear that paralyzed (see Ferdinand Lot's attempt to refute the Terrors thesis—they cannot have been all that afraid, because they were clearly not prevented from effective action, such as instituting the Peace of God, by fear), Fried sees it as a spur to action, to repentance, to belief and hope in a final end to suffering and misery. This reformulation helps refocus the question in terms of Landes's shift of emphasis away from fear and toward hopes for a final, lasting, peaceful transformation of this world into a more perfect one. As many readers of this volume will know, Landes has long argued that the Peace of God movement was intimately connected with hopeful, meliorist, even millenarian apocalypticism. If, as Guy Lobrichon and others have argued, the tenth century was the watershed that divided the relative stagnation of the early Middle Ages from a new, meliorist mentality that spread from the monasteries and then the cathedral schools to western European society, along with new forms of clerical learning and the basis of a relatively orderly, peaceful civil society, parallel to the rise of towns and urban culture, then hopeful apocalyptic beliefs may be of crucial import in deciphering the processes whereby rural, baronial Carolingian Europe gradually gave way to an urban, civic, and finally "civil" Europe. Fried argues that a new system of rational inquiry developed in the ninth and tenth centuries in the monasteries of the West Frankish Kingdom, and he argues implicitly that this system helped to conquer apocalyptic fear and convert it into an impetus to concrete, even social action.

Learned contemporaries were well aware of the inexactitude of current year reckoning, and thus we must broaden the search for millennial dates, which contemporary preachers and theologians did not scruple to set, even in defiance of the injunctions of Jesus and St. Augustine not to seek to know the day or the hour, to the period 979 to 1033/34, and perhaps even into the 1040s. As Fried points out, Adso's famous letter to Queen Gerberga in response to a number of lost questions was used extensively during this period for homiletic purposes. In numerous copies, extracts, and versions, it penetrated the porous divide between clerks and layfolk, such that "the tenth century belonged, not to the learned exegetes, but to the frightened and worried shepherds of souls." The mass of evidence adduced by Fried and the other contributors to this volume must now be taken seriously by all those who dismiss or downplay apocalyptic hope and fear as the exclusive province of those few intellectuals wayward enough to ignore injunctions not to speculate, and learned or influential enough for their writings to have survived. The traditional Augustinian perspective may well have been "correct," but it is now clear that it was not at all unanimous and may have been much less effective than the antiTerrors school maintains.

The public consensus projected by the senior professoriate now—for example, Jacques Le Goff in the December 1998 issue of *En Route*, Air Canada's inflight magazine, or Thomas Bisson at the Harvard History colloquium of 1999—is that a few learned exceptions and fanatics were frightened of the year 1000, but it was not a widespread concern. Not only do such statements replicate the conceptual flaws of the Terrors debate, but they are clearly made in ignorance of much of the material presented in this volume, from sources and genres as diverse as imperial documents, chronicles, histories, exegetical and pastoral writings, liturgical texts, episcopal and royal correspondence, wall paintings, imperial visual propaganda, drama, poetry, legal and constitutional theory, and, of course, apocalyptic prophecy and commentary. A particularly important example can be drawn from three separate essays printed here that come to parallel conclusions, from a multitude of different sources, regarding the apocalyptic beliefs, activities, self-image, self-representation, and plans of Emperor Otto III.

The main conclusions to be drawn from this volume are that in the later ninth and early tenth centuries, large numbers of learned people lived in a heightened atmosphere of mingled hope and fear; that their ideas both influenced and reflected the concerns of larger circles; and that the traditional Augustinian position (the eschatological position which is to await the final events in patience) of many other learned commentators was a deliberate and active response to the imminentist hopes of a large and vocal millenarian party.

Such millenarian voices do not bulk as large in our sources, but their echoes can be heard constantly, for example, in Abbo of Fleury's famous comment that he had in his youth heard a sermon in a Paris church foretelling the arrival of Antichrist when a thousand years had passed, which he resisted, citing Daniel and Revelation; he also relates how a rumor had filled "almost the entire world" that when the Annunciation fell on Good Friday, it would be the end of the world. We have ample evidence for widespread rumors and beliefs concerning the imminent end—in the testimony of learned clerics who rejected them. These examples (and most of the others) do not, of course, show that tenth-century Christians lived in paralytic dread of the year 1000, only that they were acutely aware of the coming end, and of 1000 (along with many others, including 1033) as its potential date. William Prideaux-Collins argues that, in Anglo-Saxon England, learned, elite refutation of apocalyptic imminentism, chiliasm, and millenarianism suggests the existence of strong popular belief in just these things. As Richard Landes notes, when the bishop of Auxerre wrote to the bishop of Verdun in the late tenth century to decry the apocalyptic fervor of the masses who saw in the Northmen and Magyars the legendary apocalyptic destroyers Gog and Magog, he was not trying to persuade his ecclesiastical colleague to follow Jerome's injunction not to identify Gog and Magog with particular peoples (Jerome saw them as code for the collective body of all evil in the world); rather, the bishop of Auxerre was pointing to a widespread and dangerous error and urging his colleague to do his best to suppress it.

As many contributors to this volume believe, it is apposite to cite Stephen O'Leary's work on apocalyptic rhetoric. He argues that such rhetoric is neither hysterical nor the result of panic but rather is a discourse of action, one that urges specific kinds of action, depending on the context, in response to belief in the imminent end. In our schemes of explanation, concrete goals and actions seem to call out for "rational" explanation. But apocalyptic movements and action defy rational explanation, because when such actions are motivated by reasons that lie outside the observer's worldview, only analysis that is both very detailed and highly imaginative can unite actions with motivations, by an in-depth examination of the sources, mentalities, beliefs, and circumstances that produced first the ideas, then their expression. The anti-Terrors party's rejection of so-called hysteria, that is, of les terreurs, is therefore, on the one hand, a serious attempt to come to grips with medieval sources on their own terms and, on the other, a rationalist attempt to make sense of apocalyptic belief in nonapocalyptic terms. It misses the point. If we turn away from the Terrors thesis, we might be spared further aggravation by the Romantic/rationalist dichotomy that has hindered, for most of the twentieth century and for the first years of the twenty-first, serious research into the fraught climate of apocalyptic ideas, beliefs, hopes, and action around the year 1000.

The reader should know that this volume began as a book project that eventually evolved into a conference (held in Boston on November 4–6, 1996). Most of the contributors, having already written papers suitable for publication, came to the conference extraordinarily well prepared to debate the merits of arguments for an apocalyptic or not-too-apocalyptic year 1000. For this reason, the panel discussions were unusually dense and well prepared. The real surprise for many of us, however, was the way in which our very hermeneutic was challenged by the international assembly of scholars representing a great many disciplines, ranging from history to musicology to literature to semiotics. It is customary to revise conference papers for publication; in this case, many of our contributors remarked that the vibrant discussions of the conference prompted substantial rethinking of methods and findings, not to mention a reweighing of a great many of the facts.

We acknowledge with gratitude Umberto Eco's keynote address to the conference. He delighted the audience with his extraordinary ability to present great insights with charming wit. More significantly still, he also challenged those present—and now the reader—to enter the dizzying, labyrinthine, interlaced hermeneutic by which the intellectuals of the year 1000 perforce approached both the Apocalypse and the prospect of an apocalyptic reconfiguration of their own world. Even though this address touches cursorily upon ideas and events that are sometimes far removed from the year 1000, the reader will be none the worse for it. Indeed, the buzz of excitement that ensued from Professor Eco's challenge to immerse oneself fully in the symbolical discourse of early medieval exegesis contributed immensely to the creativity of the conference panel discussions. We are confident that, as an orientation to the problem of thinking in terms of the richly symbolic hopes (and fears!) of the medieval understanding of the Apocalypse, the reader will find the text of his address, reprinted here with only minor changes as chapter 6, to be a sure gate by which to enter the multifaceted debate on the year 1000 contained in the present volume.

Acknowledgments

The editors would like to thank Oxford University Press, especially our editor, Cynthia Read, and the contributors to this volume for their patience in the long delay before publication. Hopefully, as delineated in the introduction to this book, that delay will have served a longer-term purpose. We would also like to thank the president of Boston University, Jon Westling, and the provost, Dennis Berkey, for giving us financial support when the National Endowment for the Humanities, after receiving glowing recommendations for our proposed conference, closed down the division for lack of funds; Beth Forrest for her enduring logistic support at the Center for Millennial Studies (Boston University) since 1996; Linda Bridges for her careful work during revisions; Mandy Batke for making the index; and all those scholars who have, despite the strong current of disapproval that accompanies any investigation of the apocalyptic year 1000, continued to follow the trail when it did not lead where it was supposed to go.

Contents

Abbreviations

AASS	Acta Sanctorum
AASS OSB	Acta Sanctorum, Ordinis Sancti Benedicti
Bibl. Capit.	Biblioteca Capitolana (Vatican)
BM	British Museum
BN (BnF)	Bibliothèque nationale de France
CC	Corpus Christianorum
CCCM	Corpus Christianorum, Continuatio Mediaevalis
CCSL	Corpus Christianorum, Series Latina
CSEL	Corpus Scriptorum Ecclesiasticorum Latinorum
Leiden UB	University Library, Leiden
Mansi	Gian Domenico Mansi, *Sacrorum Conciliorum nova et amplissima collectio*
MGH	Monumenta Germaniae Historica
MGH, DD	Monumenta Germaniae Historica, Diplomata
MGH, SS	Monumenta Germaniae Historica, Scriptores
MGH, Schol.	Monumenta Germaniae Historica, Scriptores rerum Germanicarum in usum scholarum separatim editi
MS	manuscript
PG	Patrologia Graeca
PL	Patrologia Latina
RHEF	Revue d'histoire de l'église de France
SC	Sources chrétiennes
UB	Mittelrheinisches Urkundenbuch
Vat. Reg.	Reginae (manuscript collection in the Biblioteca Apostolica Vaticana)

The Apocalyptic Year 1000

Introduction:
The *Terribles espoirs* of 1000
and the Tacit Fears of 2000

Richard Landes

The approach of 2000 proved fairly unfriendly to those historians who saw apocalyptic themes at work in the culture of the period around 1000. Indeed, in France, the modern culture that first produced the reading of 1000 as a moment of intense apocalyptic expectation produced a spate of books and articles by French historians that either explicitly or implicitly rejected the thesis outright,[1] and two of those books explicitly sought to reject any suggestion that significant apocalyptic activities marked the turn of the first Christian millennium. One of them, Sylvain Gouguenheim's *The False Terrors of the Year 1000: Expectation of the End of the World or Deepening of the Faith?* represented a high point in historiographical polemic: an entire book dedicated to dismissing, often at the cost of misrepresenting, the arguments of other historians.[2] Beyond this field of active opposition, one found, at least in French scholarship, a broad consensus. Books on the period, or on major figures from the period, either failed to even mention the issue or cited Gouguenheim as a "good summary" of the argument.[3] One might say that the profession, at least the most vocal representatives of the profession, came down squarely on the side of the positivists of the late nineteenth century against the Romantics of the mid–nineteenth century.[4]

For a variety of reasons, this volume, which presents papers delivered at a conference at the end of 1996, regrettably did not appear in time to contribute to this debate. Thus, any historians who suspected, almost instinctively, that the "anti-Terrors" position was seriously overstated and somewhat obtuse were nonetheless not in a position to contest it, because they lacked the proper documentation. Perhaps, though, that was for the best. Perhaps these essays would have made little difference in the years immediately preceding 2000 precisely because the voices of opposition were expressing their opinion not so much about the year 1000 as about the year 2000. Indeed, as early as the late 1980s and early 1990s, major French historians weighed in on the subject of 1000 before the "grand publique" with strong *partis pris*: "It [the belief that the people of 1000 thought it marked the apocalypse] is a legend whose neck must be wrung," contended Jean Delumeau, historian of high medieval *mentalités*, including a book on medieval fears, in *Le Nouvel Observateur* in 1989. A couple of years later, Jacques Le Goff, another great historian of *mentalités*, and author of the best four pages on apocalyptic and millenarian beliefs in French historiography, explained to an interviewer from *Télérama* that not only were there no fears in 1000 but that meant there would be none in 2000.

Could the insistence that we need fear nothing in 2000, intensified by the dire prophecies surrounding the Y2K computer problem, have produced a "climate of opinion" that fostered a particularly antiapocalyptic reading of the documentation from 1000?[5] Could the antiapocalyptic reading of the documents from the eleventh century have reflected a kind of exorcism of current concerns through a reading of the past that silenced those very voices one feared in the present? Such a perspective might explain a wide range of strange phenomena:

- Why a self-styled "scientific" historian like Gouguenheim would insist on a theological analysis of the documentation, interpreting every text in light of Augustine's antiapocalyptic reading, thus, for example, viewing a preacher in Paris as an isolated case because he had "insufficiently understood Augustine," and a historian from Burgundy as *non*apocalyptic because he was "too lettered not to understand [and hence agree with] Augustine."[6]
- Why an otherwise perceptive historian would make a blanket statement asserting the absence or passivity of crowds at Peace assemblies that contradicts dozens of documents.[7]
- Why still other historians would hasten to "reassure" their readers that they do not believe a major thinker from the period was millenarian,[8] or would dismiss historiographical work to which they have published no answer as fantasy.[9]
- Why some would insist that they cannot find evidence of apocalyptic *terrors*, when even Michelet (and certainly the modern argument for an apocalyptic year 1000) has emphasized the centrality of *hope* to all millennial expectations.[10]
- Why all the historians who have published arguments *against* an apocalyptic year 1000 have neither defined their terms nor shown any awareness of a large anthropological literature on the subject.[11]
- Why historians continue to invoke the presence of apocalyptic fears *after* 1000 as somehow proof that there were no fears before, when the sociological literature on apocalyptic expectations clearly indicates that disappointment rarely leads to abandoning, but rather most often leads to redating, such expectations?[12]

- Why historians slide effortlessly from claiming there is no evidence of apocalyptic expectations to claiming, when presented with evidence, that such expectations were so pervasive as to be "as common as lice."[13]

"Normal" historiographical reasoning and rhetoric rarely make such sweeping and ill-considered claims; and normally such claims, essentially replicating a positivist historiography first worked out in the later nineteenth century, do not now get the widespread approval these arguments have so recently received. No wonder so many historians dealing with the significant cultural transformations of the period preferred not to deal with these issues at all.[14]

So, had this book appeared before 2000, it might well have suffered the fate that the work of historians already published on the subject suffered: a systematic misrepresentation of their argument, permitting a sweeping dismissal. But now that Y2K has passed without (too much) damage, now that the terrors of the year 2000 have been safely transferred to the somewhat less apocalyptic date of September 11, 2001, now that medievalists no longer have journalists calling them up to find out about the year 1000, perhaps these articles can receive the kind of attention they so richly deserve. When historians no longer need to read their Augustinian concerns into the subjects they study, they may have a better chance of hearing how these people read their own texts, how they read the signs of their own times, and how their own historians refracted these discussions in their tempered, retrospective prose.

The problem, however, does go beyond the cultural atmosphere at the approach of 2000. The problem represents a widespread difficulty that historians have in dealing with apocalyptic beliefs. Generally, modern historians have difficulty with religious ideas. Those who take them seriously have a tendency toward apologetic thinking, defending some orthodoxy or other (largely Protestant and Catholic historiographies); those who might be free of such denominational concerns tend to ignore religious beliefs or else treat them as epiphenomena. Both approaches tend to find apocalyptic beliefs particularly difficult to deal with because they have always proven wrong. No person who believed that his or her own day represented either the end of the world or the advent of the Millennium has ever been right. Indeed, one might even argue that no apocalyptic believer enters the historical record until time has proven him wrong. In a sense, apocalyptic beliefs operate on a Doppler effect: as they approach their climax, they get louder and shriller, and after the disappointment, they rapidly drop in volume and pitch. And, to continue the analogy, the scribes who set down the echo of these sounds on parchment "turn on their recorders" after the moment has passed, after "normal time" has returned and "revealed" these beliefs to be empty. All our narratives about apocalyptic movements—about the "false Christ" of Bourges or the "pseudoprophetess" Thiota—are composed *ex post defecto*.

Thus, naturally, in terms of human psychology, the written record gives us a skewed recording of apocalyptic beliefs in the imminence of the end, however conceived, and heavily favors the perspective of those who "always already" knew that such beliefs were wrong, thereby muting the deeply embarrassing perspective of those—possibly the same people—who had previously believed that apocalypse loomed imminent. We see this in our own day in the resounding silence that followed the passage of the Y2K scare.[15] In addition to this social embarrassment lies the political danger that comes to those who embrace beliefs tied to the most radical and subversive of all eschatological scenarios: the millennial expectation that the evil people who now rule this world will receive their just punishment and a peaceful egalitarian reign of God's elect will ensue. Given such strong long-term (i.e., *ex post defecto*) negatives, one can well understand that a lively oral discourse about such matters might not leave much of a trace in the written record, and certainly not in a clerical written discourse dominated, as Gouguenheim points out so extensively, by an Augustinian teaching that forbids both a millennial reading (the Millennium is already in progress) and an apocalyptic one (no one may read current events as signs of the end).

The issue the historian must consider then is whether the rather limited evidence of apocalyptic beliefs that finds expression in writing (our only detailed source) represents so much flotsam and jetsam of a ship that Augustine sank back in the fifth century or the tip of an iceberg of a widespread oral debate during moments of apocalyptic time (in which, as one monastic historian put it with characteristic regret, even clerics "put aside their ecclesiastical doctrines") that has been muffled by a retrospectively correct revisionism that can, in normal time, reassert Augustinian orthodoxy.[16] The contention of the editors of this volume is not that historians must choose beforehand. On the contrary, historians need to test both ideas extensively to find out whether they "fit" the larger pattern of evidence or not. It will not help to approach the evidence with an a priori assumption that apocalyptic beliefs were either not present or omnipresent, thus either minimizing or exaggerating whatever evidence appears. Rather, we need to approach the evidence with these two proposals as working hypotheses.

Let us take two extreme cases as examples: Radulfus Glaber and Gerbert/ Sylvester II. The first case, that of the Burgundian monastic historian, represents exhibit A for the apocalyptic reading of 1000. While we have over a dozen texts that highlight anno Domini 1000 as a significant date, no one attributes more importance to that date or comes back to the subject more often than Glaber. His multiple references to the wonders and prodigies and great events that occurred around the year 1000 confound any historian who wants to argue that no one cared about that date or that the social and economic changes that occurred at that time were too small for people to notice. And his remark that the year 1000 marked the fulfillment of the prophecy in Revelation that after one thousand years Antichrist would be released, the most staunchly *anti-*Augustinian historical statement made in the six centuries separating the two writers, has even driven historians as scrupulous as Ferdinand Lot to claim he never made it. How do we read Glaber and his reflections on his age: as a good Augustinian whose contemporaries all followed the same nonapocalyptic approach to the events of their lives (Gouguenheim) or as a headstrong individual who, despite the pressure from his superiors to toe such a line, managed to convey some fraction of the widespread apocalyptic beliefs that moved great masses of people to attend Peace assemblies and take the pilgrim's route to

Jerusalem not only at the approach of 1000 but at the approach of the millennium of the Passion, 1033 (Landes)? It is for historians who carefully study the material to decide which reading accords better with the evidence.

On the other extreme, we find Gerbert, the most brilliant man of his generation and the pope of the year 1000, Sylvester II (999–1003), and exhibit A for the "antiapocalyptic" school. In his extensive writings, Gerbert never once mentioned the year 1000, only once used apocalyptic rhetoric, and generally seems completely uninterested in the kinds of matters that the apocalyptic school of the year 1000 suggests obsessed everyone. For some, this vast silence indicates Gerbert's indifference. He, and the other great men of his day, lived in normal time and had other, more important issues to confront than nonsense about the year 1000 and the end of the world. For the millennial reading, however, this silence might indicate the presence of apocalyptic time and derive from a wide consensus among the leaders of Christendom that discussing apocalyptic beliefs at the approach of 1000 could only encourage dangerous ideas. After all, these were the very concerns that drove Augustine to articulate his antiapocalyptic and antimillennial teachings in the first place and drove two earlier generations who had arrived at the "end of the millennium"—500 and 801—to bury the apocalyptic date in a new "corrected" and nonapocalyptic chronology. In this reading, Gerbert becomes pope in 1000 precisely because he is perhaps the only individual capable of making it through 1000 without becoming drawn in by the magic number, the only one who could be counted on *not* to abandon the ecclesiastical teachings of Augustine. The former reading of indifference seems, a priori, simpler and more obvious. But the latter explains certain anomalies about Gerbert, including how a French peasant could become pope and how someone with so extraordinary a destiny and so acute a sense of time did not find, in his unprecedented and astounding promotion to the papacy, any coincidence with so magic a number as 1000.

Such hypotheses naturally make historians uncomfortable. They do not like "conspiracies of silence" and either reject them outright, often mockingly, grant them without taking them seriously,[17] or lump them together with the anti-Semitic and anti-Masonic conspiracy theories of the nineteenth and twentieth centuries.[18] But the argument here is not for a conspiracy of silence but for a consensus of silence, a widespread understanding among a key constituency—the small group who composed our texts—that the less said about apocalyptic beliefs the better. Such tacit consensuses are all around us. When Foucault died of AIDS in 1984, the only French paper to mention the cause of death was the often-scurrilous *Canard Enchâiné*. Was this because the more respectable editors got together the night before in the smoke-filled back room of a Masonic Lodge and decided not to mention it? Or because none of them needed a direct reminder about what the profession considered good taste? Was Glaber the *Canard Enchâiné* of his day? And Gerbert and Odilo, the staid *Figaro* and the reliable *Le Monde*?

To assist the historian interested in such questions, let us turn to certain critical issues of definition, issues notably absent from the writings of "anti-Terrors" historians. The historian's difficulty in finding evidence of millennial phenomena, inherently problematic given the nature of his recording devices, becomes still more difficult when he or she has a limited grasp of the phenomena in question. For the interested investigator, then, let us briefly lay out some basic definitions.

- *Eschatology* represents a notion that *at the end* of time God will judge the living and the dead (hence the resurrection of the latter), rewarding the good and punishing the bad. As most historians will agree, Christianity, Judaism, and Islam are eschatological religions that expect a Day of Judgment at some time in the future. Eschatology represents a collective, public, and total answer to the problem of theodicy, of why God permits the evil to flourish and the good to suffer.
- *Apocalyptic* designates the belief that such a day is near, and one can functionally define "apocalyptic time" as a sense of proximity great enough to lead the believer to change his or her behavior in anticipation (e.g., "repent for the Kingdom of Heaven is at hand"). Almost all eschatological phenomena become visible to societies (and hence their historians) when they enter apocalyptic time. Before then, such beliefs are recessive or dormant, and one might not even detect their presence among people operating in "normal time." Apocalyptic can take a number of forms, some focusing on the catastrophic violence that necessarily accompanies the elimination of evil from the world, some on more peaceful conversions on the part of the evildoers to a new way of life ("they shall beat their swords into plowshares").
- Finally, *millennialism* represents that eschatological scenario that foresees the rewards of the saved in terms of a perfected earthly society, one in which fellowship, peace, and abundance have replaced the oppression, violence, and suffering of this current evil world. Millennial scenarios can envision either a radical egalitarianism, for example, a world without aristocrats, in which commoners enjoy the fruits of their honest labor undisturbed (Mic. 4:1–4); or a triumphant hierarchy in which a great and conquering emperor subdues all evildoing under his just rule ("Last Emperor"). Millennial beliefs are inherently political, viewing the current "powers that be" as a triumph of evil, and their overthrow and replacement *in this world* as decreed by God. When millennialists believe that God wants them to bring about this transformation (active apocalypticism), then we have the foundations of revolutionary behavior.

One of the first issues that will strike the analyst who views millennial beliefs from the perspective of the participant rather than that of its opponents is the enormous place one must give to hope. Hope far more than fear drives the millennial beliefs in "normal time"—the hope for a release from the sufferings of this world, the hope for a place in the coming millennial kingdom—and apocalyptic expectations represent above all, and in the face of all (retrospective) evidence, the triumph of hope over reason. The millennial enthusiast looks forward eagerly to Judgment Day as a day of *pleasure*.[19] Why then do historians seem so fixated on fear as the distinguishing characteristic of apocalyptic time? It must be partly because our ecclesiastical sources emphasize the "terrors" of the Day of Judgment as a way to discourage the faithful from apocalyptic hopes—better to die in "normal time" and meet Judgment along with the other resurrected dead than live in the time of Antichrist, when "even the saints will be tempted." But also, when apocalyptic notions spread from the enthusiastic who look forward to the "pleasures" of that day to those who fear Judgment (primarily but not exclusively those in positions of power), we are dealing not with an apocalyptic movement but with a culture-wide apocalyptic "moment."

But the analyst needs to distinguish the two phenomena: millennial hopefuls who welcome apocalyptic time view its advent (the early stages of the Doppler effect) with hope and its passage with disappointment; opponents of millennialism, who fear the disruptions of apocalyptic time—and, still worse, their possible condemnation at the Last Judgment—view the approach of the apocalypse with fear and its passage with relief. Jules Michelet understood this distinction well and placed it at the heart of his analysis of the apocalyptic year 1000. Michelet focused on the "terrible hopes" of the *impotents* at the approach of the millennium:

> The prisoner awaited in the dark dungeon, the serf waited in his furrow in the shadow of the odious tower; the monk waited in the abstinences of the cloister . . . all hoped to be released from their terrible sufferings . . . [finding] a certain charm in the moment when the sharp and piercing sound of the trumpet of the archangel would pierce the heart of the tyrants. Then from the dungeon, from the cloister, from the furrow, a terrible laugh would explode from amid the tears. This terrible hope of the Last Judgment grew in the calamities that preceded and followed close behind the year 1000.[20]

The *potentes* were the ones paralyzed by the approach of that day, who "sheathed their swords, trembling themselves before the sword of God." The result: the Peace of God, when, for the first time, the voices of the commoners were heard in the land, and the *potentes* publicly accepted unprecedented limitations to their exercise of violence.

Such a reading apparently escaped the attention of historians eager to minimize the effects of both an apocalyptic 1000 and a (possibly) millennial Peace of God. From Michelet's dramatic polychrome reading we move to the monochrome characterization of the modern historian who rejects the picture of a western Christendom "frozen in the total paralysis described by Michelet [sic]" or one who dismisses the reconsideration of recent historians as resurrecting the old Romantic chestnut of "fears and terrors of the year 1000."[21] Ironically, we witness here an (unconscious?) identification of these modern historians with Augustinian clerics, who feared apocalyptic expectations: these historians perceive the phenomenon in the same way as the threatened elites of yesteryear, both groups having every reason to view the advent of an apocalyptic date—1000 or 2000—as a danger and source of anxiety, and every reason to greet its passage with a triumphalist relief.[22] They read the texts the way an orthodox Augustinian should, forgiving those who can, thanks to their ambiguities, slip under the threshold (Glaber) and isolating the rest (the Parisian preacher opposed by Abbo).

The very same people who deny that a small (and largely self-selected) group of clerical writers might have exercised extensive pressure both on others (e.g., William of Volpiano on Glaber) and on themselves (e.g., Ademar) repeatedly give evidence of the pressures under which they write and wish others to write by seeking to wring the neck of this lamentably long-lived *credo*, reassuring their readers that they have not departed from the historiographical orthodoxy, or avoiding the topic entirely. Such an understandable, if one-sided, identification with the theological concerns of the class of people who produce our documentation may serve to reassure us in the present (Augustine's advice on how to think about the end remains, after all, valuable to this day), but it hardly helps us understand the past (just because Augustine was theologically correct does not mean people followed his advice). It seems particularly strange that so theological an approach would claim to wrap itself in the cloak of "scientific method."[23]

The issues involved here go far beyond the question of identifying the presence of apocalyptic expectations and extend to the crucial problem of historical causation. Even if we acknowledge the presence of apocalyptic hopes and fears, what difference does it make if they "failed"? Here we confront the hardest problem for historians, one that goes to the heart of the problem of anachronism and functionalist analysis. If we project back *pre-defecto* an awareness that the prophecies will fail, we miss not only the behavior of those in the grip of belief in the prophecies but the struggles they go through to deal with their errors. In millennial studies the axiom runs "wrong does not mean insignificant." On the contrary, many a religion first began in expectation of the apocalyptic resolution to history, whether the advent of the "Kingdom of Heaven" (Christianity)[24] or the "Day of Judgment" (Islam).[25] Indeed, the ways in which the profound hopes and disappointments of such expectations stir the soul and produce lasting and powerful religions of salvation are the very stuff of religious history. From this perspective, a question like "1000: expectation of the end or deepening of the faith?" is a little like asking, "Dawn: end of the night or beginning of the day?"

The issue here is not what people intended and accomplished but what they intended (the Millennium) and failed to achieve, and in that failure what they accomplished nonetheless. It may seem logical to project back onto the bishops and counts who called Peace assemblies the results they produced over the long run.[26] It makes them seem at once rational and dominant. But it fails to even consider what the other participants in these assemblies may have believed (the millennial kingdom of "sword into plowshare") or the unintended consequences that may have ensued from the failure (communes and Crusades,[27] to name only the most conspicuous candidates). No wonder anti-Terrors historians find it so important to minimize at once the excitement of these moments of public assembly[28] and their overall impact.[29] And, of course, as long as one views apocalyptic expectations as fears that one gladly leaves behind like a bad dream, then one cannot begin to notice the ways that disappointed hopefuls tried to salvage what they could from their failed efforts.

This brings us back to our evidence and the people and conversations that stand behind it. Until historians become familiar with the nature of millennial hopes and the dynamics of apocalyptic excitation and disappointment, until their radar screens have been adjusted to pick up certain kinds of data and to follow its effects past the period when it is most visible, they may most resemble some hypothetical nuclear scientists who deny the existence of subatomic particles by dismissing the shadowy traces of their trails as smudges on paper. But such a conclusion we must leave to the next generation. In the meantime, the historian confronting the evidence must carry both hypotheses with him throughout: that these are mere traces of little significance or that they are the tips of icebergs of a much larger oral culture that lay behind the composition of the texts upon which we modern historians depend so fundamentally. When Abbo tells us briefly of a public debate with a preacher in Paris around 970 about the apocalyptic significance of the year 1000, was that part of a lively and widespread debate that we can reconstruct with the help of our wider knowledge of the phenomenon, including other apocalyptic prophecies that were then circulating?[30] Or should we dismiss it as insignificant because quantitatively it represents only a small fraction of the letter?[31] The decision will favor, not necessarily the scholar who has the most evidence, but the one who makes the most sense of the evidence we have and can connect that evidence to other phenomena.[32] And in order to make such a decision, it behooves the reader to approach the material without *parti pris*, to be familiar with both approaches and capable of trying them both out.

But in order to do so, in order to read the arguments *for* an apocalyptic year 1000, historians need to free themselves of the urge, so strong at the approach of 2000, to *negate* the argument, to "wring the legend's neck." Any intelligent analyst can, if sufficiently motivated, find the flaws in an argument. The easiest thing to do is say no. One cannot possibly understand an argument like this one without a sympathetic effort, especially when the argument deals with so complex a phenomenon—hopes and fears, relief and disappointment—and demands both a constant effort of empathetic imagination and a constant attention to the primacy of perspectives formed *ex post defecto* in the narratives to which we historians have access. Perhaps now, in the aftermath of 2000, historians can begin to give the argument the hearing it deserves. And there is no better place to start than this collection of essays.

NOTES

Editors' note: Richard Landes is Associate Professor of History and Director of the Center for Millennial Studies at Boston University.

1. Pierre Riché, *Les grandeurs de l'an mil* (Paris, 1999); Claude Carozzi, *La fin des temps: Terreurs et prophéties au Moyen Age* (Paris, 1999); Laurent Theis, *Robert le Pieux: Le roi de l'an mil* (Paris, 1999); Dominique Barthélemy, *L'an mil et la Paix de Dieu: La France chrétienne et féodale* (Paris, 1999); Monique Bourin and Michel Parisse, *L'Europe de l'an mil* (Paris, 1999); Sylvain Gouguenheim, *Les fausses terreurs de l'an mil: Attente de la fin du monde ou approfondissement de la foi?* (Paris, 1999).

2. For a detailed response to Gouguenheim, see Johannes Fried, forthcoming in Historische Zeitschrift; for a response to both Barthélemy and Gouguenheim in the notes of an article already published, see Richard Landes, "The Historiographical Fear of an Apocalyptic Year 1000: Augustinian History, Medieval and Modern," *Speculum* 75 (2000): 97–145.

3. ". . . et surtout Gouguenheim . . .": Theis, *Robert le Pieux*, p. 201, n. 1 (note the citation of a book appearing in the same year as the author's). "Bonne mise en point . . .": Jean Flori, *La guerre sainte: La formation de l'idée de croisade dans l'Occident chrétien* (Aubier, 2001), p. 62, n. 3. Among the many cases where such conclusions are either explicitly or tacitly recorded, Jean Flori is the most curious since he is one of the rare French historians of the period who have a sense of how apocalyptic beliefs work (see his treatment of the "First" Crusade and Guibert's attribution of Antichrist beliefs to Urban II [pp. 350–52]) and his approach cannot be farther from the kind of approach that Gouguenheim takes. Yet he, like many other historians, has no problem with identifying apocalyptic in a later period but denying its presence in 1000.

4. Many historians explicitly frame the issue in these terms, arguing that the newer historical arguments in favor of an apocalyptic year 1000 are essentially neo-Romantic (Riché, *Les grandeurs de l'an mil*, pp. 11–23; Gouguenheim).

5. For the expression "climate of opinion," see Carl Becker, *The Heavenly City of the Eighteenth-Century Philosophers* (New Haven, 1932), chap. 1.

6. Gouguenheim's chapter 2 (*Les fausses terreurs*, pp. 65–92) presents an extensive articulation of the Augustinian theology that Gouguenheim insists dominated the age. He then dismisses the Parisian preacher (p. 133) and Radulfus Glaber's explicit invocation of the year 1000 as the year of Antichrist's release as nonapocalyptic because Glaber "could not have ignored this [i.e., Augustine's] framework of exegesis" (p. 170).

7. "The people are outside. . . . This is, *let us not doubt*, the way in which *all the other* 'assemblies of peace' operated. In rural or suburban councils, there was *always* a church, a basilica, for the statutory reunions of the clergy, opened to laity of high rank . . . from which the decrees, sentences, and formulas of oath taking issued. The peace of God is *never* the Constituant Assembly of 1789 or the meeting of Charléty (1968). One speaks of the 'people,' the 'poor,' *but they do not speak themselves*" (Barthélemy, *L'an mil*, p. 370, italics mine). Thus, in one paragraph we find broad generalizations that contradict the texts and a presentist discourse that seeks to eliminate any historical parallels between the Peace movement and modern phenomena. Interestingly enough, Barthélemy places these broad generalizations on the back of Ademar's account of the 1031 council, an account that shows every sign of being not only Ademar's personal invention but also the result of a process of mythomania due specifically to his humiliation before a loud and active crowd of people. Barthélemy, intent on using the material, dismisses the critical analysis as "the very model of hypercriticism" and then asks rhetorically: "should we deprive ourselves of so precious and dense a document?" Note that when Barthélemy has to deal with an account that places the crowds at center stage (Glaber on the Peace assemblies of the millennial year 1033), he has no hesitation in dismissing the text (p. 30). See my arguments and uses of Ademar's forgeries, as well as a detailed explanation of how he entered this period of "mythomania," in my *Relics, Apocalypse, and the Deceits of History: Ademar of Chabannes, 989–1034* (Cambridge, Mass., 1995), pp. 228–85.

8. "Nous tenons a rassurer nos lecteurs . . . : nous n'avons jamais taxé Raoul Glaber de millénarisme" (Carozzi, *La fin des temps*, p. 45).

9. According to Bernard McGinn, the notion of a "subterranean millenarianism [in the early Middle Ages] is a figment of [Landes's] imagination," quoted by Patricia Bernstein, "Terror in A.D. 1000," *Smithsonian* 30 (1999): 119. The argument for this tradition, which I argue is not subterranean but subtextual and clearly marked by the *reactive* nature of the texts to it—that is, the "official" shifts in the accepted chronology from annus mundi I (Incarnation = 5500) and annus mundi II (Incarnation = 5199) in precisely the century before their apocalyptic term (500 and 801)—was laid out in 1988 (Richard Landes, "Lest the Millennium Be Fulfilled: Apocalyptic Expectations and the Pattern of Western Chronography, 100–800 C.E.," *The Use and Abuse of Eschatology in the Middle Ages*, ed. Werner Verbeke, Daniel Verhelst, and Andries Welkenhuysen [Leuven, 1988], pp. 141–211). McGinn has never offered a refutation or even an alternative explanation for the detailed analysis of the chronological material laid out therein.

10. On hope, see below. On the assumption, despite these arguments, that the apocalyptic year 1000 meant "craintes et frayeurs," see Riché, *Les grandeurs de l'an mil*, p. 13; Gouguenheim, *Les fausses terreurs*, pp. 199–202; Carozzi, *La fin des temps*, pp. 45 passim.

11. Gouguenheim and Barthélemy have no anthropological literature in their extensive bibliographies, never define their terms, and never bother to define what they argue doesn't exist, despite the availability of definitions tailor-made for the medievalist as early as 1991 (Richard Landes, "*Millenarismus absconditus*: L'historiographie augustinienne et l'An Mil," *Le Moyen Age* 98, nos. 3–4 [1992]: 355–56). Even historians with an apparent interest in anthropological issues, like R. I. Moore, show no interest in the literature on millennialism (R. I. Moore, *The First European Revolution, c. 970–1215* [Oxford, 2000]). For a survey of the issues concerning millennialism and a more extensive bibliography, see R. Landes, *Encyclopedia of Millennial Movements* (New York, 2000).

12. Riché, *Les grandeurs de l'an mil*, p. 23.

13. Frederick Paxton, paraphrasing Bernhard Töpfer, called apocalypticism "as common as lice" in the Middle Ages ("History, Historians, and the Peace of God," in *The Peace of God: Social Violence and Religious Response in France around the Year 1000*, ed. T. Head and R. Landes [Ithaca, 1992], p. 28), an image taken up by Janet Nelson in her review of the volume (*Speculum* 69 [1994]: 165).

14. Most notably, Robert Bartlett, *The Making of Europe* (Princeton, 1993), seems to leave the creation of the cultural "blueprint" whose astounding career he analyzes at the periphery of Europe to a kind of "post-Carolingian" black box; and R. I. Moore does not even mention apocalyptic expectations as a possible issue in a chapter entitled "The Approach of the Millennium," in his *First European Revolution*, pp. 7–29, and, despite an ample discussion of the Peace of God movement (pp. 7–11), makes no reference to it when he analyzes the social and cultural changes.

15. At the approach of 2000, the Y2K bug provoked major anxieties: virtually no one flew on a plane that day and many "chose" to stay home; businesses, at the very moment that they assured the public there was nothing to fear, had teams of computer specialists on alert throughout the night; over $300 *billion* was spent worldwide on avoiding the problem. It was the first global managerial project based on a catastrophic prediction about the impact of technological mishaps, a prelude to the even more expensive prophecies about the impact of global warming. And yet since virtually no one has mentioned these "fears of 2000," no risk management think tank has done a postmortem to analyze how much of the hundreds of billions was well spent, whether the laissez-faire approach of most governments was a good

idea, and so on. No one seems eager to find out what happened, despite how useful that might be for dealing with similar situations in the future. Fears that do not pan out—something true of *all* apocalyptic ones—invariably produce embarrassment in their aftermath. Few of those who stockpiled food and water will, *ex post defecto*, admit that they did.

16. For the most elaborate arguments in this regard, see Landes, "Lest the Millennium Be Fulfilled," pp. 104–10; and Andrew Gow, *The Red Jews: Antisemitism in an Apocalyptic Age, 1200–1600* (Leiden, 1995). Gow examines a subtheological tradition about the role of Jews at the end of time that left *no* trace in Latin documents but an extensive one in German vernacular sources.

17. "Doubtless there was a Raoul Glaber, but frankly the traces are slim, even admitting that the church tried to deny the existence of such things" (Bourin and Parisse, *L'Europe de l'an mil*, p. 205).

18. Gouguenheim, *Les fausses terreurs*, p. 201; see also his longer analysis, which misrepresents and misunderstands the argument, on pp. 56–63.

19. As one black slave in the American South cried out in her despair at watching her child whipped: "There's a day a-coming! I hear the rumbling of the chariots, I see . . . white folks' blood a-running on the ground like a river and the dead heaped up that high! O Lord! Hasten the day when the blows and the bruises and the aches and the pains shall come to the white folks. . . . O Lord! Give me the pleasure of living to that day" (quoted in Mary Livermore, *My Story of the War* [Hartford, 1889]), cited in James C. Scott, *Domination and the Arts of Resistance: Hidden Transcripts* (New Haven, 1990), p. 5. For a medieval expression of similar sentiments written in 1011, see *Byrhtferth's Manual*, ed. S. J. Crawford, Early English Text Society, Original Series, vol. 177 (London, 1972), p. 242, ll. 3–9.

20. Jules Michelet, *L'histoire de France*, vol. 2 (Paris, 1835), p. 132, cited from *Le moyen âge*, ed. Claude Mettra (Paris, 1981), p. 230.

21. Carozzi, *La fin des temps*, p. 45; Riché, *Les grandeurs de l'an mille*, p. 13.

22. See the reaction of the chronicler from Anchin after the astrological prophecy of catastrophes in 1186 was unfulfilled: Continuation of Anchin of Sigebert de Gembloux, *Chronica* ad an. 1186, *MGH, SS* 6:424; discussion in Richard Landes, "Terreurs apocalyptiques et mutations personelles et sociales: Sur les dynamiques psychologiques de l'attente eschatologique," in *Avoir Peur*, special issue of *Le Fait de l'Analyse* 3 (1997): 167–68.

23. "The myth of the conspiracy [of silence in the texts] comes to the aid of the myth of the terrors, but to the detriment of history and science, which find no advantage therein" (Gouguenheim, *Les fausses terreurs*, p. 201). See also Barthélemy, *L'an mil*, pp. 12–24.

24. Among the immense bibliography in this still highly contested (because highly theological) field, see Bart Ehrman, *Jesus: Apocalyptic Prophet of the New Millennium* (Oxford, N.Y., 1999).

25. Michael Cook and Patricia Crone, *Hagarism: The Making of the Islamic World* (Cambridge, 1977); David Cook, "The Beginnings of Islam in Syria during the Umayyad Period" (Ph.D. diss., University of Chicago, 2002).

26. See the analysis elaborated by Hans Werner Goetz, "Protection of the Church, Defense of the Law and Reform: On the Purposes and Character of the Peace of God, 989–1038," in *Peace of God*, ed. Head and Landes, pp. 259–79.

27. Communes: A. Vermeesch, *Essai sur les origines et la signification de la commune dans le nord de la France (XIe et XIIe siècles)* (Heule, 1966); Crusades: Carl Erdmann, *The Origins of the Crusading Idea*, tran. M. Baldwin and W. Goffart

(Princeton, 1977); for a discussion of the larger historiographical issues, see Paxton, "History, Historians, and the Peace of God," pp. 21–40.

28. Dominique Iogna-Pratt, "Consistances et inconsistances de l'an mil," *Médiévales* 37 (1999): 92, who objects to the citation of Abbo of Fleury's account of a public debate, *coram populo*, about the apocalyptic meaning of 1000, as "cited ad nauseam."

29. Marcus Bull, *Knightly Piety and the Lay Response to the First Crusade: The Limousin and Gascony, c. 970–c. 1130* (Oxford, 1993).

30. Landes, "The Fear of an Apocalyptic Year 1000," pp. 123–30.

31. "The text is brief and represents in total only one paragraph in the entire *opera* of Abbo" (Gouguenheim, *Les fausses terreurs*, p. 132).

32. See the debate between R. I. Moore and Landes on the popular heresy around 1000 in the *Journal of Religious History* 24, 1 (2000): Moore, "The Birth of Popular Heresy: A Millennial Phenomenon? pp. 8–25; and Landes, "The Birth of Heresy: A Millennial Phenomenon," pp. 26–43.

I

Awaiting the End of Time around the Turn of the Year 1000

Johannes Fried

It comes, it comes, the Day of the Lord, like a thief in the night.
—the second visionary of St. Vaast (cf. 2 Peter 3:10)

I

A rain of blood had fallen for three days in Aquitaine in 1027, covering men's heads, their clothes, and the stones themselves. Only from wood could it be washed off. The duke of Aquitaine was appalled and immediately informed the king.

"What does this event mean?" a greatly agitated Robert the Pious wrote to his adviser, Gauzlin, archbishop of Bourges and abbot of Fleury. "I bid you look into your histories and see whether anything like it has ever happened before, and what followed it. Give me an answer quickly, with this same messenger."

Why the excitement? Why the haste? The king did not say, but the answer is obvious: the rain of blood was clearly a sign from Heaven. Did this portent herald the end of the world?

Only the "histories"—the chronicles and annals—could promise a precise answer. This rain of blood was so obviously a sign of the end times that Gauzlin himself became fearful. Almost automatically, words from the apocalyptic sermons of Gregory the Great found their way into his answer. Gregory himself was echoing the twenty-fourth chapter of the Gospel of Matthew and the twenty-first chapter of the Gospel of Luke: Blood meant the sword, civil war, and nation rising up against nation. The church would be threatened with tribulation, and the people would lack the means of sustenance. Gauzlin's explanation of the meaning of history and time implied that the rain of blood proclaimed civil war at the very least, and perhaps even the end of the world. Instead of a clear answer to comfort the king's uncertain fear, Scripture states, "No one knows the day and the hour, not even the angels in the heavens, but the Father alone knows" (Matt. 24:36). Gauzlin concluded his letter with the benediction "May almighty God extend your rule, may his law protect you, may he give you a long life for the peace of the holy church," but his good wishes for the king did nothing to reduce the apocalyptic tension.

The next generation of clerics was more sure of itself. Into his otherwise verbatim transcription of Gauzlin's response, Andrew of Fleury, Gauzlin's biographer, inserted one sentence that "completed" Gauzlin's answer and, at the same time, removed any apocalyptic element from it. According to Andrew, the space of three days meant three years (referring to the years from 1027 to 1029), during which the inhabitants of Aquitaine would be chastised by divine punishment, and "[s]o it really happened." The signs had pertained only to local Aquitanian circumstances.

The response of Fulbert of Chartres has also come down to us. He explores the future, "by the authority of his religious orders," with a single example from Gregory of Tours. The rain of blood promised a "large-scale catastrophe"; the stone, flesh, and wood that the rain covered signified the three kinds of men: the godless, the fornicators, and those "who are neither godless nor fornicators." Blood anticipates war and plague: "Whoever was previously hard or weak in the flesh and does not change himself for the better will die eternally in his own blood. Those who stand in the middle, however, can be delivered by their fear of death or by some other means in accordance with the will of the most secret and most powerful Judge."

Like his predecessors, Fulbert intimates the Last Judgment, but he also questions whether it is imminent, or if there yet remains some time before it arrives. Perhaps the learned bishop leaves the question only explicitly unanswered. The textual tradition of his letters offers some instructive variants. Fulbert recalls the judgment, not of the "best Judge" (*praestantissimi iudicis*), as an eleventh-century manuscript reads (Paris, BN lat. 2872), but instead "a most immediately present Judge" (*presentissimi iudicis*), as the best manuscript of the letters (Paris, BN lat. 14167) and a later manuscript of the twelfth century (Vat. Reg. lat. 278) read. Following the principle of *lectio difficilior*, one should logically choose the latter reading. Be that as it may, the preserved variant readings demonstrate how Fulbert's answer might have been understood (or misunderstood) in the eleventh century and indicate anew the widespread expectation of the Last Judgment.

Like Gregory the Great, Gauzlin also knows a means of salvation. One may be sure "that through penances and alms, and through the fruit of penance, which will ripen in the womb of Mother Church, the anger and fearsomeness of God, the righteous Judge, which pertains to sinners, can be turned to mildness." There is no trace of that blind terror and witless flight or of lethargic indolence in the face of impending catastrophe that the historians of later centuries attributed to the contemporaries of the turn of the year 1000. Instead, Gauzlin recommends redemptive measures. As the signs of God's anger increase, Gauzlin appeals to the urgency of repentance and good works. If the end of time threatens, the "fruits of penance" may awaken God's mercy. What Gauzlin meant by this is made clear by the projects which his biographer has established as contemporary to the exchange of letters: church building, church decoration (Gauzlin had obtained Byzantine mosaic workers), and the formation of prayer brotherhoods.

The Romantic and realist nineteenth century loved to paint those "terrors of the year 1000" in gaudy colors, but were apocalyptic expectations really fear inducing, or is this depiction merely modern legend? One may argue that since the examples cited derive from the period after the foreboding year 1000, they therefore fail to convey true premillennial fear. Did the same fear compel the faithful *after* the year 1000 as it did before?

A single document that is comparable to the previously mentioned sources but dates from an earlier period survives. This document, a letter by a monk of Saint-Germain to a bishop of Verdun, indicates no fundamental change in behavior that might have resulted in the staying of a millennial judgment. Numerous contemporary commentators in the Burgundian-Lotharingian area around 960 understood the approaching, biblically significant interval of a thousand years since the birth of Christ as important and predictably identified the hitherto unknown Hungarians as the apocalyptic peoples of Gog and Magog. Their missives conclude: "Now the last time of the world has dawned, and the end of the world is at hand." The early Christian certainty of living at the end of time did not impress these Lotharingians, but rather the new quality of the signs that the end was coming in the present.

"Now!" is what concerns the bishop of Verdun, who can perhaps be identified as Berengar (940–60) or his successor Wicfred (962–72). He has read the signs and now wants to interpret their meaning. He is troubled by the misery of Christians, the serious calamities besetting the church, and the imminent sword. To him, everything appears monstrous and new. He fears openly that current events could, in fact, indicate the arrival of the Last Days. For this reason, he seeks more precise information about the passage in Ezekiel (38:8) concerning the promise of the people of the Last Days. Is the biblical prophecy now to be fulfilled?

His correspondent, a rather straightforward monk living at a comfortable distance from the Hungarian incursions, does his best to calm the anxious prelate. The situation is clearly not a new one. The blessed Gregory, in his Ezekiel commentary, had already described similar things about his own time and had asked whether or not to anxiously await the end of the world. The monk is ashamed at having to write to so great a lord in such a manner: "I know," he excuses himself, "that I am a little presumptuous, since I speak in a daring and improper way, and without shame, to my lord, as if I wished to console him, who is himself, by God's will, the fullness of consolation and wisdom." The argument of the prophet of doom is frivolous and false. The Hungarians are a perfectly ordinary people from the east or north, who do not appear in histories simply because they have changed their name. They may have been drawn from the Maeotian swamps by hunger, and by hunger they have since become known as *Hungri*.

The apocalyptic argument is false but sensible. The monk's response, at its heart, is about differences between methods of knowing. The Apocalypse, with its one thousand years and the appearance of the two peoples of the end times, is a mystical book and thus may be read only in a "mystical," not a historical, manner. Gog and Magog are to be identified not with real peoples but, as St. Jerome and the Donatist Tyconius taught, with the "furious persecution by the heretics."

If the unknown monk actually wrote, as we think he did, from the monastery of Saint-Germain in Auxerre, then he and his letter are not exactly isolated voices. A little later, in the same monastery, Abbot Hedricus (989–1009) copied and illustrated with his own hands the single surviving manuscript of Haimo's Ezekiel commentary (Paris, BN lat. 12302), and between 1035 and 1041, the Cluniac monk Radulfus Glaber, the great collector of portents, signs, and meanings, also lived in Saint-Germain. Auxerre, where Haimo himself lived and where his writings were certainly available in the tenth century, has proven to be a center of eschatology from the ninth to the eleventh century. This was a widely known and appreciated fact, and numerous anxious questions were asked of the learned monks who lived there. They also provided answers, albeit qualified ones.

The anonymous monk of Saint-Germain also appears to stand in the exegetical tradition of Haimo. The "mystical" interpretation of apocalyptic writings, a practice established in the Carolingian period by Ambrosius Autpertus, allowed the monk of Saint-Germain to criticize every error made by those following the "historical" method that Bede had practiced. However, all enlightenment is constrained by its boundaries, for our fearless monk did not free the concerned bishop of Verdun from his belief about the imminent end of the world. On the contrary, he separated the Hungarians from their eschatological role and transformed the thousand years of the Apocalypse into an irresolvable secret, requesting the prelate to be courageous and calm at the prospect of the coming event. Mysticism may release the present, but it binds the future. The possibility of the coming end of the world is not in any sense dismissed, and in fact, the learned monk also had to reckon with it.

The wisdom of Haimo and his adherents proved to be rich soil from which future millennial fears could sprout. These apprehensions did not end with the passing of the tenth century. The terrors of the year 1000 are clearly the result of the ordinary fears of people in the decades before the end of the millennium, intensified by a new monastic scholarship that strengthened the current and widespread belief in the possibility of the imminent and unexpected end of the world. Its mystical meaning asserted that its continuing actuality and apocalyptic immediacy resided in the "historical" exegesis. It remains to test this argument more exactly. These monastic letters help to clarify certain aspects of belief in the end of the world during the decades around the turn of the year 1000.

1. In Lotharingia, at the Aquitanian ducal court, at the French royal court, in the circle around Gauzlin of Bourges and Fleury, and in learned Chartres in the early eleventh century, one learned to pay particular attention to the "signs" by which the beginning of the end of time could be ascertained. Though this was indeed the work of learned Christian scholars, it was not confined exclusively to esoteric circles of learned clerics, however tradition oriented and topically bound

medieval eschatology might be. Rather, attentiveness to signs made its way into wider circles of society, where it took on a rich life of its own. Individual preparatory signs—a darkening of the sun, monstrous births, and celestial light phenomena—had always announced famine, war, disease, or death. Now, however, there was a compelling tendency to see individual signs in terms of an ensemble of signs, to systematize them, and to compare their statements (with help from the chronicles) in order to scrutinize them and to transfer them into the present. Past history was seen to provide measurable knowledge of what course future history would take. Apocalyptic signs could serve as models for the analysis of the contemporary and as chronological place markers.

No completely new apocalyptic signs appeared, but different questions were asked about the familiar ones. Thus, their study acquired the air of a discipline. The sure knowledge of the imminent end of the world, the unsettling ignorance of the exact time of its arrival, and the new competence of contemporary exegetes required that certainty be found in the sign-filled present, not the uncertain future. Contemporary political and ecclesiastical leaders analyzed time and the meaning of signs and let themselves be terrified or comforted as a result. Thus, not only the "uneducated mass of the people" was troubled by beliefs of doom. The search for certainty, which excited even the ruling segment, assumes theological or speculative training. One would therefore expect a changed attitude among the learned to "time" and "eternity."

2. Expecting the end of the world in the near future and anticipating the signs of its arrival are not confined to the year 1000 of our reckoning. Rather, we can observe this phenomenon occurring over a very large frame of time. Through all of our period, we consistently observe that since "no one knows the day or the hour," it is all the more necessary for the intelligentsia to counsel penance and reply "not yet" or "there is time" to anxious questioners. The letters to King Robert reflect the attitude one would expect of responsible clerics. Their authors, under the unmediated impression of the preliminary signs but without knowledge of the coming events, avoid making a definitive answer and simply leave open the possibility of an arriving end. Later readers of the texts, recognizing their concerns as premature, removed all double meanings from them by using either more or less strong inference.

This presents us with some serious methodological consequences. Every potentially eschatological sign, even when it does not express itself as such in our written sources, can reflect fears of the end of time on the part of the writer. Without supporting documentation, however, one can therefore barely determine the corresponding spread of concern. In the search for pertinent witnesses and events to look at as models, it is certainly a mistake to fix our eyes only on the epoch just before the year 1000 and then abruptly avert them as soon as the calendar reaches January 1, 1001, as such scholars as H. von Eicken and Ferdinand Lot did. Learned contemporaries were very well aware of the inaccuracy of the Christian reckoning of the year and of the difficulties inherent in correcting it.

Even this certain knowledge compelled scholars around the year 1000 into a very specialized kind of research. Abbo of Fleury, who was led to computistical studies through the eschatological speculations of his contemporaries, complains about the obscurity of the question. In which year did Christ die? When would a thousand years have passed since that time? The question possesses an apocalyptic immediacy, since the last span of human history begins with Christ's sacrificial death. Abbo posited a chronology divergent by twenty-one years from the reckoning of Dionysius Exiguus, which quickly spread among learned circles. Meanwhile, Heriger of Lobbes (d. 1053) dated the Passion to the year 42 of our era, while Siegbert of Gembloux turned back to Abbo, who had fixed the corrected "one thousand years after the birth of Christ" in the year 979 of our era (which means that "one thousand years after Christ's death" would not occur until the year 1012). Other computists still reckoned differently. One must broaden the search for potentially millennial dates, as Daniel Verhelst has clearly shown, to at least the period from 979 to 1033/34. Because of the uncertainty of practically all contemporaries in computistical questions, we might also look at an even larger period, one that lasts perhaps as late as 1042.

3. Letters of the kind so far discussed have seldom come down to us. Only Adso's somewhat different letter to the West Frankish queen Gerberga, and its recopying by Albuin for Archbishop Heribert of Cologne, could be added. These writings, their number increased by some sermons of Wulfstan of York and Aelfric of Eynsham, are virtually our only indications of contemporaries known by name who, however weakly or strongly, dealt at all with the end of the world. All other sources are anonymous, satisfying themselves with unspecific references to "this one and that one" or "many." Hagiographical and historical works from the period of the year 1000, with the exception of the writings of Radulfus Glaber, reveal scarcely any traces of anxiety. What prevented this from being written of?

4. The letter to the bishop of Verdun cited above may give an indication. People were ashamed of their anxiety. It is natural to conceal shame and prefer that anxiety not become evident. Wazo of Liege (a decade later and at a safe distance) ridicules the victorious troops of Emperor Otto I because they became terrified at an eclipse of the sun, hiding themselves under barrels and carts and believing that the end of the world was at hand. Meanwhile, the learned cleric himself triumphed over all fear, "because he knew the natural laws that governed eclipses."

A second indication concerns the thousand-year period allowed for in Holy Scripture, such as the Apocalypse of John (chap. 20). To be sure, people had long since grown accustomed to relativizing its assertions of a particular time and most often interpreted them, as St. Augustine did, as "the totality of the years of the last world" (*De civitate Dei*, 27.7.2) or as the last scrap of these last times before the world-Sabbath. This does not, however, entail abandoning scriptural interpretation in a literal, historical sense. The letter to the bishop of Verdun demonstrates this. Of course, as Matt. 24:36 states, no man can reckon "the day and hour" or otherwise clarify it. If he assumes himself capable of doing so, he makes himself not only susceptible to a shameful, if not unforgivable, error, but also guilty of hubristic sacrilege by his very act of exceeding human standards. The learned monk admonishes the anxious bishop of Verdun with the words of Gregory the Great: "To grieve over the end of the world is the business only of him who plants the roots of his heart in the love of the world," and "whoever lets himself be convulsed by the troubles of the world is an enemy of God." Under these circumstances, why should one be concerned with the beliefs and fears for the world's downfall held by the great names of one's own time? It is not the number of signs that is important but their quality and the context from which they emerge.

5. The belief in the approaching end of the world derives from, and is strengthened and confirmed by, a magical worldview shared without differentiation by all social strata, noble and nonnoble, by both "literate people" and "illiterate people." Nature and history compose a unity, and natural signs reveal future human destiny. They must be observed, collected, compared with each other, and interpreted. The responsibility for doing this falls to a Christian king, who is responsible not only for the preservation of peace and law but also for the means of interpreting the present and examining the future, in order to arrive at a course of action. From his learned men, the king expects observations, tests, and advice. Their recommendations become part of the political and ecclesiastical elite's plan of action. Such insight is not, however, easily obtained, since different models for the explanation of signs—in principle, each of equal validity—must compete with each other. Which model should one rely on?

6. This immediate expectation of the world's end, stronger at some times, weaker or even imperceptible at others, is couched in a widespread knowledge of the Last Things, such as the end of the present eon, the return of Christ, and the Last Judgment. These beliefs are inherent in the nature of Christianity, but irritating in their contradictory traditions. As a social phenomenon, they can be understood only against, and in the context of, a reciprocal relationship with this eschatological backdrop. The currency of the imminent end depends directly upon the momentary intensity and coloring of that eschatology. In this manner, biblical exegesis takes on existential significance.

Methods of scriptural interpretation take their existential importance from their removal of fear of the threatening end. By this, they gain legitimacy, channeling anxiety and thus gaining their justification. Traditional knowledge offers binding rules for action that cannot avert the imminent end but can educate the believer on the proper way in which to meet it. The historian who pays attention only to the analysis of expressions of anxiety at the prospect of the end of the world chooses far too narrow a field of vision from which to take evidence to arrive at an appropriate interpretation of the phenomenon.

7. It is not crippling anxiety that accompanies the urgent questioning, awaiting, and consoling but rather a call to penance and the prayer of monks. The historical record is filled with reference to the "fruits of penance" and the doing of good works. This factor has not been considered up till now. Could it be that the increasingly and threateningly expressed expectation of the end of the world was one of many motivating factors in what recent research has termed the "awakening of the tenth century"? Did expectation of the end nourish monastic and church reform, increase readiness to build, enlarge, or decorate churches, or lead directly to the persecution of heretics and Jews? Unfortunately, the impetus to change in

the world of agricultural and early urban work and to a complete revolution in society cannot be pursued here. The objective of my study, rather, is to widen our consideration of piety in the context of the Last Judgment.

II

The Carolingian period, which cannot be left out of our consideration, sowed the seeds of multiple traditions with its ecclesiastical, liturgical, theological, and general cultural reform. "Renaissance" movements, while not entirely unknown in the earlier church or in Byzantium, were by no means widespread. The Carolingian breakthrough, however, produced the prerequisites for sustained success. The ninth century set impulses in motion without experiencing all of their consequences itself. One of these themes was teaching about the end of the world and the Last Judgment. Since Charlemagne, the Latin church was reminded of its eschatological roots in the strongest terms. Preachers were expected to teach the people about the coming terrors and urge them to good works in fear of the impending event.

This preaching influenced not only "naive" and "credulous" folk. The pathless maze that constitutes all the thought about the end of time, built of belief and knowledge, dark misgivings and erroneous interpretations, fears, taboos, and contradictory traditions, all obfuscated by a magical worldview and uncertain means of knowing, misleads anyone who wanders into it and causes all kinds of uncertainty and fear. It has little to do directly with folk beliefs. The "knowing" and the "learned," who incline toward reflection, are more at risk of confusion. The clearest heads of their age were challenged: drawing upon their own capacities and traditional knowledge, they had to sort through the contradictory exegetical traditions, establish an orientation, and establish persuasive grounds for action.

This pattern should be kept in mind during the following discussion. We will first pursue the spread of applicable knowledge (section II), then contemporary reactions to it (section III), and, last, their consequences for belief (section IV). We must, unfortunately, omit from our discussion the different exegetical traditions that these authors followed.

"Since you ask about the Day of Judgment and the Antichrist, go and read the book of St. Augustine, *The City of God*, and the exposition of St. Jerome on the prophet Daniel, and also the Apocalypse with its commentaries" (*PL* 145:838). This syllabus of readings comes from Peter Damian, who was consoling a soul anxious about the end of the world. Knowledge improves and clarifies. What does the diffusion of eschatological knowledge—and its intensity and its treatment—reveal about attitudes toward the turn of the year 1000? What does a consideration of the tradition of biblical and nonbiblical visions, the commentaries on Ezekiel, Daniel, and the Apocalypse, the treatise on Antichrist, and the like in their manuscripts and illuminations lead us to understand?

Some manuscripts allow us to directly see an apocalyptic religiosity on the part of those who commissioned or wrote them. An example of this is an illustration in Bede's Apocalypse commentary (Einsiedeln [Stiftsbibliothek MS 176], tenth century) of Christ, treading the beasts underfoot, and the names Heto and Adelheit, with the words "the highest judge rules all of your acts." The Bamberg Apocalypse (Staatsbibliothek Bamberg Bibl. 140) shows Otto III or Henry II (fol. 59v) witnessing the events of the end of time, since on the facing folio (fol. 60r), the illuminator sets the victory of the virtues over the vices:

> Iussa dei complens, mundo sis corpore splendens.
> Poeniteat culpae, quid sit patientia, disce.

Men were not indifferent to what was written out or illuminated; rather, they were affected by those things that should be read or considered. The well-documented eschatological tradition might, without demanding too much of the "statistical" argument, reflect the spatially and temporally varying intensity of millennial expectations, even when the transcription and availability of the texts in and of themselves do not allow for interpretation.

Here is surely not the place to undertake an examination of the whole corpus of manuscripts of the Apocalypse of John or other texts concerning the end of time (like that of Pseudo-Methodius), or of the commentaries belonging to them. This tradition begins with the Apocalypse exposition of Victorinus and its reworking by Jerome, and thence the commentaries of Jerome and others on Daniel and Ezekiel, and includes the writing of Ambrosius Autpertus, Beatus of Liebana, Alcuin, Haimo, and Adso of Montier-en-Der. Because of this enormous legacy of texts, we can here only begin a preparatory work, restricting ourselves to a few examples.

Be that as it may, the rich and complex tradition of one of the most effective prophetic works, the four recensions of the Latin Pseudo-Methodius, may be thoroughly grasped even if its analysis still remains incomplete. Thus, the following scenario, without considering the question of recension, must be given consideration. The five oldest manuscripts belong to the eighth century; but the Carolingian Renaissance reveals itself to be less interested in the Pseudo-Methodius's *Novissima tempora*: two codices date from the ninth century, while the *Saeculum obscurum*, written in the tenth century and little copied, produces at least the fragments of five manuscripts. The period around the year 1000 adds two, and the later eleventh century adds five further manuscripts. The remaining 182 codices currently known date from later periods.

The same principle applies for the learned Haimo. His commentary on the Apocalypse was copied frequently in the period under discussion here, but no evidence exists in the circumstances of transmission to determine to what extent the tenth century demonstrated an increased interest in him. Tyconian-influenced homilies of a Pseudo-Augustine were transcribed in the ninth and tenth centuries, just as was the *Liber de septem regulis*, which is immensely important for containing the apocalyptic comments of the Donatist exegete himself. The commentary of Victorinus of Pettau is seldom transmitted as a whole, although two tenth-century manuscripts of its reworking by Jerome survive.

We know much more about Ambrosius Autpertus of the eighth century. Alcuin, Hrabanus Maurus, Haimo, and the much later Berengaudus made use of him. The thirty-three known manuscripts or fragments of manuscripts with his commentary spread themselves out across the centuries in revealing ways. The oldest codex dates to around 800, and two further codices originate in the Carolingian period. The "dark" tenth century shows itself to have been sufficiently receptive and leaves six manuscripts. Another is added around the year 1000, as were six more in the following century.

The relationship between a work's content and its frequency of transmission shows a considerable interest in apocalyptic on the part of the generations around the turn of the year 1000. The manuscript tradition of Adso of Montier-en-Der's letter to Queen Gerberga on the Antichrist also appears to bear this out. At least 171 manuscripts containing the letter or its derivatives survive. Of these, at least eight, and perhaps nine, belong to the period around the year 1000. This is an astoundingly small number of copies. The secure provenances are from Chalons-sur-Marne, Troyes, Metz, and Regensburg. Nonetheless, the oldest textual witnesses, written exactly around the turn of the year 1000, certainly did not disappear into libraries. They transmitted Adso's booklet, along with collections of preaching texts, and reveal substantial information concerning the spread of millennial knowledge. In addition, not much later, Adso's clear and concise booklet found a grateful reception among a series of theologians and specialists in pastoral care. Even one of the earliest copies shows an independent treatment of the text: Wulfstan of York alone produced not only a complete text that he had translated into his own vernacular and modified for homiletic purposes but also one in Latin, much revised and, again, translated and abbreviated so as to serve vernacular instructional purposes.

Albuin sent Adso's text unabbreviated or as a comprehensive verbal extract to his patrons three or four times. Among the recipients was Archbishop Heribert of Cologne. Peter Damian, too, had read his Adso, or at least one of the texts deriving from Adso. The manuscript tradition alone shows a most incomplete picture, since Adso's work was more widely known and distributed around the turn of the year 1000 than the actual number of surviving codices indicates. Above all, these documents direct attention to the problems of pastoral care and illustrate both the deep needs of contemporaries and the method by which knowledge of the end of time was expanded, and the accompanying anxiety fed.

Art also reflects this development, suggesting the accents and understanding with which the texts treating the end of time should be read. Of course, illuminations and wall paintings demonstrate apocalyptic themes at different times. Depictions in books of the Last Judgment and the apocalypse began in late antiquity. However, there is no single direct line from the early Christian to the early medieval period. Carolingian pictorial creations represent a new beginning that reaches back to antique pictorial elements but first appears in its totality only in the Carolingian period. The conceptions of reward and punishment are equally important. "Evil supports its forms"; in this period, the depiction of the Last Judgment becomes essentially narrative, as painters represent scenes of damnation and the torments of Hell for the first time.

In the sixth century, probably in Rome, an entire pictorial cycle of the Apocalypse takes shape and is soon broken up into a multiplicity of traditional lines. Its earliest traces are few, but they increase around the time of Charlemagne and migrate from Italy into Francia. The following century reveals a distinctive presence north of the Alps, although its intensity is not exactly measurable today.

Only two manuscripts with closed pictorial cycles are known from this period: an Apocalypse from Trier (Trier Stadtsbibliothek Codex 31) and one from Valenciennes (Bibliothèque municipale MS. 99). Both of these date from the early ninth century. The "dark" tenth and early eleventh centuries have left five manuscripts of this type. In chronological order they are the Apocalypses of Paris (BN Nouv. acq. lat. 1132), Cambrai (Bibl. mun. MS. 386), Einsiedeln (Stiftsbibl. MS. 176), Bamberg (Staatsbibl. MS. Bibl. 140), and Munich (frag. in clm. 29159). The manuscripts thus seem to be divided into an older group around 800 and a more recent group in the tenth century. Does this perhaps indicate a wave movement in early medieval eschatology? Did the minor crest of the wave occur in the late eighth century, followed shortly thereafter by a trough that, in turn, gave way to a new crest around the turn of the year 1000? This impression is confirmed by the documents discussed below.

One quite distinctive group out of these is the Beatus Apocalypses, whose "smooth and linear illustrations" have been the subject of analysis by Spanish scholars. The known manuscripts, most of which come from northern Iberian monasteries and cathedral chapters, began to be produced for the first time around the middle of the tenth century. Their impressive miniatures show clear Arabic and Carolingian influences. Eleven of the known codices were produced between ca. 850 and the middle of the following century, though the tradition continues until the sixteenth century. Save for two of their number, they offer an additional "end of time" text, the (illuminated) commentary of St. Jerome on the Book of Daniel. However, the more recent codices, those produced since the late eleventh century, came to omit the latter.

Northern Iberia in the decades around the year 1000 showed a considerable interest in the illustration of the Apocalypse. The Beatus texts are an example of, and may have influenced, this interest. Although the Mozarabic liturgy contained many readings from the Apocalypse between Easter and Pentecost, this does not explain the complete absence of earlier Beatus manuscripts and the clear predilection for their pictorial commentary during the latter part of our period.

Also, the manuscripts did not circulate only within the orbit of the Mozarabic liturgy. Beatus had come to represent all the teachings concerning the end of the world after 6,000 years, and he fixed the point of time with breathtaking accuracy: "Since the creation of the world until the present time, 824 (that is, until A.D. 786), 5,986 years have passed; until the end of the sixth millennium there remain fourteen years; and the sixth millennium will end in the year 838 (thus, A.D. 800); only within this brief period of fourteen years, that is but an hour, may no man know the exact hour, which God alone knows" (*In Apocalipsin*, 4.5.31, ed. Sanders, p. 371). The Beatus Commentator, placed under the pressure of a world that will end in only a few years, preaches to his contemporaries and writes to his readers in order to prepare them for the terrible event. Until it can be proven otherwise, I would like to believe that the eschatological reasoning of the author is the explanation for the success of his work before and around the year 1000.

The conditions for the transmission of wall paintings are less ideal than for manuscripts. To use only the surviving examples, there is no congruence between the development of the image of the Last Judgment and the Apocalypse cycles. The former seldom appears in early Christian art and only becomes more detailed in late antique triumphal arches. However, it appears regularly during the Carolingian and Ottonian periods in churches, where it was often preserved. Around the turn of the year 1000, depictions of the Last Judgment undergo a change. The documented alfresco Apocalypse cycles first appear around the year 1000, with the oldest examples of this type appearing on the baptistery of the cathedral of Novara and Saint-Michel-d'Aguihle. The apocalypse had already become a favorite subject by the eleventh century, and its popularity continued through the twelfth.

There is a literary example that highlights this. Gauzlin of Fleury, having had a monastic church erected, decorated it with pictures of the apocalypse. Here, for once, is clear proof as to when interest in these depictions began, initiated by those whose millennial concerns are documented elsewhere. Church walls begin to remind the collective body assembled for prayer of coming events, not only of the Judgment. The pictorial visions are no longer only for those few owners who can look at them in their decorated books. Clearly, a new and widespread need for the presence of this theme in the collective awareness and imagination developed in the period around the turn of the year 1000, standing as the natural central point of the religious life. The "wonderful, unique spectacle" of the Last Judgment acquires for itself a spirit filled with holiness: "In meditation, allow this terrifying image of the coming Judgment to unfold itself before your eyes," Peter Damian counsels those who would reject the world (PL 145:288). Pictures on church walls may help them in this.

However incomplete the earlier survey may have been up to now, it is at least clear that the publicized knowledge of the end of the world in text and pictures spread quickly and that the need to know more exactly increased in the course of the ninth and tenth centuries. Not only were men around the turn of the year 1000 better informed, but their interest in secret things that, up until then, had stood as the central theme of evangelization grew enormously in comparison with preceding epochs and continued to increase. The immediacy of the Last Judgment for those whose lives were full of sin, the anxiety in the face of damnation in the flaming sea of Hell, and the call to repentance in the face of the powerful, terrifying decision of the Last Judge, all radiated from the expectation of this upcoming event. The daily approaching deadline itself demanded heightened awareness.

If the discussion up to now has not so far demonstrated an "immediate expectation" of the Last Days, it has at least described the "spiritual state" of the time, whose highest ethic was bound to the view toward the end of time and the Judgment following it. During the later Carolingian period, churchmen reflected more strongly on the Judgment, whereas the tenth century concentrated additionally and above all else on the earthly "end time" as the preparation for the Judgment and disregarded the appearance of preceding signs. The tension increased in the face of the question, "When does the Redeemer come?"

III

To compare the Carolingian period and the tenth century vis-à-vis the Last Things, we should begin with the older writers. Ambrosius Autpertus warns urgently against a literal reading of the Apocalypse and follows his own advice. The millennium during which Satan will be bound signifies the entire span of time that the church (*pro perfectione sua*) is expecting, and "how great it also is." Autpertus strikes out on a tangent from this, in the context of the incursion of the Saracens, to a notable self-examination in which he asks what the present "bursting forth of the heathen" with the help of the Devil means. The learned man knows, as Beatus of Liebana had known shortly before, how to calm himself: "While that temptation [at the end of time] is no less real than all other [earlier] ones, so, what is now can, in comparison, by no means be a temptation." In the empire of Charlemagne, there were not many thinkers particularly concerned with the end of time.

The Spaniard Claudius of Turin, temporarily working at the court at the beginning of the ninth century, clarified this attitude: he collected no "signs." "If someone asks me how long a time or how many years this present passing world will continue to exist, I simply say, 'I don't know.'" This ignorance did not disturb him at all; he neither harbored nor propagated an immediate expectation of the end of the world, and he rejected any eschatology that had this as its goal. Such ideas did not interest this staunch opponent of theological speculation.

In contrast, Agobard of Lyons had advised his emperor to collect everything in Holy Scripture that had anything to do with the Antichrist. As far as we know, Louis the Pious did not take this advice to heart. Both instances are revealing of their age, the former for its glimpse into the eschatological thematic around the year 800 and the latter for the general attitude of the Carolingian period. The poet of the Old Saxon *Heliand* dwells revealingly on the announcement "that no child of man may know when that wondrous time of judgment of this world will be." Dhuoda, the literary noblewoman, does not devote one line to the "apocalypse," but she does admit her fear of the "judgment." Even Otfrid of Weissenburg closes his *Evangelienbuch*, not with a look ahead to the apocalypse and its horrors, but with a mere warning of this "judgment."

Dies irae, dies illa—the day of wrath, the Judgment Day alone, commands the attention of the Carolingian prophets. *Luctu plena, dies illa*. Although the *Muspilli* poem, with its Bavarian coloring, proclaims the destruction of the world, its author takes as his predominant theme, not this destruction and its premonitory signs, but rather the "judgment." Within this context the poet agrees with his contemporaries who write in Latin:

> Libri dantur in medio
> Et erit memoratio
> Ab angelis recitantur peccata nostra
> Initio congregata
> In tremendo die (*MGH, Poetae* 4, p. 647)

The Latin writers of this century continually concern themselves with the *dies iudicii*, the Day of Judgment. However, the signs which announce and accompany this Judgment Day remain for them removed from time and therefore do not take on any earthly, realistic actuality:

> Cum ab igne rota mundi
> Tota coeperit ardere
> Sive flamma concremare
> Caelum ut liber plicare
> Sidera tota cadere
> Finem seculi venire (*MGH, Poetae* 4, pp. 521n22, no. 23)

Or

> Adpropinquat finis seculi, declinatur tempora
> Turbabuntur omnes gentes ante conspectum domini (*MGH,*
>   *Poetae* 4, p. 601, no. 64)

Even the appearance of Enoch and Elijah, who also prophesy concerning the apocalypse, do not force the Carolingians to adopt realistic expectations. The expiration of the one-thousand-year period is simply the *dies illa*. The actual end of the world appears to be relegated to an imaginary time.

Haimo's commentaries on 2 Thessalonians and the Apocalypse are characteristic of biblical exegesis in the ninth century. This exegete, whose sources must remain unexamined here, offers few explanations of signs and concerns himself mostly with allegorical interpretation. Only the *discessio* occurs at the present time, but this has been ongoing for a long time and therefore is without a particularly alarming significance for the present era. Haimo offers not one line of commentary on his own century. The Antichrist will come "in his own time," not necessarily now, but only then, "when all realms have fallen away from the Roman *imperium*," and even then not "immediately" (*statim*) but rather "afterward" (*deinde*). Haimo the theologian does not speculate further concerning an exact point in time, since it lies in the uncertain future. The riddle of the one thousand years of the apocalypse is not in any sense solved. The expiration of the one thousand years signifies *omnia futura tempora*, either the arrival of the Antichrist or the end of the three and one-half years of his rule, *usque ad finem seculi*, and therefore the beginning of the next life of the sanctified.

The protocols of the West Frankish imperial synod at Trosly in the year 909 may serve as a last example of Carolingian eschatology. The synodal patriarchs register the dire moral decay of their own era in tedious detail, but their criticism of this decay, free from any apocalyptically tinged analysis, remains firmly in the tradition of the ninth century. The moral decay they comment upon is not the harbinger of a Last Judgment that has arrived "now." The criticism does not occur because of any one event or because of a sudden upheaval of the times or elements; rather, it is a call for correction and a return to proper conduct. To be sure, "the return of the eternal Shepherd and His horrific Majesty stand before us, at which time all shepherds with their flocks must appear before Him" (Mansi 18:264–66), but this observation is not arrived at by any interpretation of increasingly manifested "signs." Rather, as in centuries before, it is considered a self-explanatory certainty.

If the artists of the period portray the Last Judgment and the punishments of Hell in a literal and concrete way, the Carolingian theologians moralize. They know that the world will be destroyed, but they make no attempt to interpret historical events, let alone to analyze the events in their own times. When a poet like Theodulf of Orléans mentions the evidence of the approaching end of the world, he offers only the most general of observations: the sun and the moon will shine more weakly, and the fruitfulness of the earth will decrease. Human morals will decline, and only evil will increase. Of course, a solar eclipse can routinely inspire millennial fears, but only in the rarest of instances does one find statements such as those in the *Chronicon Vulturnense* of the year 880, which predicts that the end of the world is near, but against a backdrop of the intrusion of the Saracens into southern Italy (*PL* 151:1273).

Conversely, the authors of the Ottonian era transfer the traditional imagery onto the concrete events of their times, using the tradition as a benchmark to measure their own era, which has become unbalanced. One text declaims: "Calamitous events, which are the result of penal judgment, are increasing, signaling that the end of the human race is approaching. Therefore, all mortals everywhere must ponder the way to Eternity, so that they may obtain the Kingdom of Heaven and eternal salvation" (Mittelrheinisches UB 2, p. 17, no. 32). The theology of the end of the world avails itself of temporal events.

Although the Carolingian artistic tradition portrayed the fallen human race appearing before the face of God, it is only in the tenth century that the earthly era is seen as hurtling toward its inevitable end. That which, in the preceding epoch, had been seen only as occurring in the distant future is seen in the *saeculum obscurum* to be fulfilling itself. However, it is not as if the interpretation of signs had not occurred at all in the past. The ninth century is also "full of the expectation of the Antichrist," as Josef Ademek puts it. However, the ninth century's understanding of chronology differed from that of the tenth. Despite the numerous incursions of foreign peoples into France in the ninth century, the immediate expectation of the end of the world was not at all as common as it was in the decades around the turn of the millennium.

Mundus senescit, and sometime "at the end," the horrors of the Last Judgment threaten. Though this had long been common knowledge, the ninth century was not too concerned with going beyond this general acceptance. It was content with fear-inspiring, realistic depictions of the world's destruction, the Judgment, and its consequences. Only later generations felt that these events pertained directly to them in their own times. They thought in terms of actual reality, connecting the eschatological "revelations" with their own horror-filled times. The fear became ever more realistic. The verbal and imaginary scenes of horror are such that everyone confronted with them becomes, to follow Hugo of Farfa, "immediately filled with unbelievable fear and dread and for days at a time cannot but think about death." It is now, also, that the fearful question, to which no one knows or may offer an answer, is asked: "When will it occur?" Let us recall Adamek, who surmises: "So much is certain: especially in the second half of the tenth century and the first half of the eleventh century, the question of the end of the world aroused people's thoughts more than at any other time of the medieval period" (*Vom römischen Endreich der mittelalterichen Bibelerklärung* [Munich, 1838], p. 79).

Whereas the Carolingian era had collected the received eschatological knowledge and produced commentaries on the Apocalypse and the other visionary books of the Bible and the church fathers, the tenth century harvests the fruits of these labors. It adopts the theology and pictorial imagery of the preceding era, propagates it, and expands upon it in revealing ways. Very little that is truly new is added. With the exception of Adso's tract on the Antichrist, the West produces no additional "textbook" on the theme.

However, though new material was added onto this corpus only in exceptional cases, the quantitative judgments had an outcome in qualitative change. The writings of the earlier authors were brought into the present and transformed into hortatory sermons or, especially, into images and prayers. They were internalized for a transformed religious life in which one attempted to orient himself or herself using the received tradition. The tenth century belonged, not to the learned exegetes, but to the frightened and worried shepherds of souls.

A strengthened apocalyptic feeling, increasingly applied to interpret the events of the present, did indeed characterize the period around the year 1000. Its presence was felt everywhere to some degree, although its influence was certainly stronger in some regions or settings than in others. It was located at diverse points in time and space, and even then not necessarily set in writing. Rather, it usually remained imprecise and vague, thereby possessing a most unsettling effect. It was not a discrete fear that affected the activities of people in the tenth century but a tormenting apprehensive expectation, full of repeated questioning: Is now the time? Not yet? Perhaps now? Or now?

It is exactly the evidence of this chronic apprehension, accompanied by an interpretive method different from that taken to heart by the writers of the Carolingian period, that we must pursue. None other than Fulbert of Chartres lends it his pen: "Since the birth of Our Lord, the envy of Satan rages all the more strongly against man, because Satan sees that already the end of his raging stands directly (*iamiamque*) before him" (*PL* 141:283). The increasing calamities signal the imminent end, an end that, it was thought, everyone would experience.

Such concerns course through Aquitaine and the area of influence around Cluny and, as we observe from the above-mentioned letter to the bishop of Verdun, also in Burgundy and Lotharingia. Early on, Abbot Odo provides them with nourishment: "The waves of evil are breaking ever higher . . . dangerous times are upon us, the world is threatened with its end" (*PL* 133:585C). The Cluniac prophets do not tire of asserting "tempora iam venisse" and so also "instante iam tempore Antichristi" (*PL* 133:676C). This "now," repeatedly hammered home, separates the tenth from the ninth century. Only lamentations remain for the current era, which, Odo bemoans, "sees everywhere not the signs of truth but much more the signs of futility and luxury washing over everything." *Sunt . . . omnia confusa.* It is the experience of his own era, the constant pervasion of violence, injustice, and the triumph of evil, that compels the tenth-century monk to these conclusions as the church fathers had been compelled in their own times. It is an increased consciousness of sin, in and of itself not foreign to the Carolingian period, that bathes these events in an apocalyptic light. Hence, Odo has it that "[t]he time is already fulfilled, the rumored enemy already is revealing the *mysterium* of evil, since all the order of religion and Christianity is dissolved," and also that "Behemoth, the King of Evil, holds his triumphal entry."

> Post modicum cunctam mundi transire figuram,
> Quod veniet subitus iudex in carne choruscus (*PL* 133:581–82)

Odo's belief in the imminent end of the world increases the persuasive force of his moral and religious message. He points out the thousand-year period of the apocalypse, toward the end of which Satan will rage even more strongly: "Haec itaque tempore iam venisse." Completely hidden, cloaked in a quotation from Jerome concerning the *brevitas vitae*, the deadline of one thousand years flashes out for a second time: "Truly, our life lasts one thousand years. We have arrived at the last day of the whole epoch (*totius aetatis*). If, therefore, the last hour has arrived, of what use are the fruits of obsessive desire, which as soon as it ends leaves no sign that it ever existed at all? Of what use now are daily luxuries or exquisite linens and royal finery to those who burn in Hell?" (*PL* 133:562–63). At the most, Odo says, one thousand years, and then (*nunc!*) Hell. If any leading figure of the tenth century attempts to enliven the fears of the year 1000, it is the abbot of Cluny.

Indeed, the Cluniac monks could not forget such concerns and thoughts. In his sermon dating from the period 1003–10 and addressed to abbot Maiolus, Aldebald of Saint-Germain d'Auxerre compares the monks of Cluny to the virginal 144,000 elect, who, according to Apoc. 14:4, follow the Lamb, and whose display immediately precedes the announcement of the Final Judgment (Apoc. 14:4ff.). Here we gain insight into the Cluniac self-image at the turn of the millennium. Is the large increase in monasticism in this era itself a sign of the nearness of judgment? Thoughts of this kind were apparently not unusual in Cluniac circles. Abbot Hugo of Farfa, in the introductory poem of his *Liber tramitis*, memorializes the monk John of San Salvator in Montopolo, who brought the Cluniac practices to Italy and gathered them into a book, in order "to shore up the wavering spirit" and to "gradually guide the senses heavenward again." And this was necessary, for

> Finis enim mundi nos fecibus implicat aevi
> Et vetus ecclesiae senium monstratur ubique

In the context of the period around the turn of the millennium, the monastic renewal appears almost as the fruit of the eschatological certainty that in the murky residue of the last age, one was living at the end of time. Abbot Hugo himself speaks words of encouragement to his monks, who fear that they will fail to live up to the example of the holy fathers: if the number of the saints had already been arrived at, the world would have already been destroyed. There is then still a measure of time (*modicum tempus*; see Apoc. 6:11). "Let none of us doubt: all who are worthy will enter the Kingdom of Heaven." The desire for reform on the part of the monks arises out of their millennial expectations.

In the years around 1040, Cluny also occupied itself with an apocalyptically tinged analysis of current events. Radulfus Glaber, that restless and widely traveled historian occupied with the interpretation of apocalyptic signs "concerning the thousandth year of the birth of Christ, our Savior," was for a time a monk at Cluny (1030–35), and he writes for those like himself. At the request of Abbot Odilo, he begins to write his "five books of history." Later, resident at Auxerre (1035–41), a center of eschatological interest, he is unable to escape its intellectual concerns. It is here that he works intensively on his "histories." Perhaps it is also here that they first take on their eschatological tone.

As an example, one need only examine the well-known passage concerning the great famine of the year 1033. The famine rages, *peccatis hominum exigentibus*; it is divine vengeance. However, it deeply affects the monk of Cluny that the people have hardened their hearts, and their senses are dull. The penance of anguished hearts and carnal denial, which is so utterly necessary, is not undertaken. The pain and sorrow and the sobs and tears of penitence are those of the spiritual leaders— monks and a few devout laypeople—alone. Millennial expectations live, then, in the shadow of a heightened consciousness of sin and in the hope inherent in the sense of election on the part of the monks. Since it was thought that famine and the desire to sin are themselves signs of the apocalypse, it seemed that the end was approaching even then. "The order of the times and the elements decays into eternal chaos and sweeps mankind toward its destruction."

> Hear, O Earth, hear, bosom of the great sea!
> Hear, O Man, and hear, all you who live in the sun:
> It comes, it approaches:
> the day of scorn, the hated day, the bitter day.

The psalmody of the office of the dead inspired the monks of Aniane around the turn of the millennium. One of them probably wrote it or at any event transcribed it in the only surviving manuscript. It, too, notes the fear-inspiring signs that will signal those horrific days: the sea will rage and threaten the land. Ships will founder, and foreign goods will not arrive. The people will suffer want. *Surget gens in gentem et regnum contra regnum*. Earthquakes, plagues, famine, and war will arrive. "Vix ulla fides, dividunt dulces scismata fratres." The Antichrist will appear and establish his regime of terror; false teachings will threaten all believers, and false prophets will mislead them, "erigent statuam illi prophano," until finally Christ the Judge descends with his heavenly regiments, "crucis descendet praevio signo."

With only slightly less visibility, Ademar of Chabannes engages in his macro-and microcosmic reading of the apocalyptic signs. Early on he is made apprehensive by a singular, unique, and terrible vision. For half the night he sees a tremendous crucifix in the southern sky. The cross and the body of Christ glow red and bleed as the Crucified One cries bitterly. Such visions are typical of the turn of the millennium. The vision horrifies the observing monk and also moves him to tears. It never leaves his memory. He fears the worst, but apparently he does not confide his experience to anyone. No one else learns what had been revealed to him. But what does the sign mean? This question compels Ademar for the rest of his life, but only later, in his role as chronicler, does he break his silence and attempt an explanation. His vision of Christ weeping on the bleeding cross helps him understand and interpret the calamitous events of which he would later learn, as well as the punishments meted out to those who had caused them. For Ademar locates his vision in the year 1010 and draws a connection between it and the confusing events in al-Hakim's Jerusalem, where heathens, supposedly encouraged by Jews, had destroyed Christ's tomb. Ademar's vision becomes the opening event in a sequence of signs that announce the arrival of drought, flooding, plague, famine, and death, the appearance of heretics (the *nuncii Antichristi*), the decline in belief, and a startling unwillingness on the part of Christians to embrace martyrdom. Ademar's vision appears to him to be so full of meaning that he clearly reckons with apocalyptic events. Perhaps, however, he is not completely sure of himself, since he commits what he has seen to writing only well after the events that his vision was to announce actually occurred.

Ademar the chronicler is certainly not an eschatologist without any sense of hope. Twenty years after he receives his vision, he entrusts the Easter dates for the coming *annus magnus* (1064–1595), together with the letter of Pope John XIX concerning the apostolicity of St. Martial (which Ademar himself had forged!), to a holograph pamphlet, as if the prospect of ensuring the continuing veneration of his monastery's patron saint for the next five hundred years lay particularly close to his heart.

Did Ademar previously lack any apocalyptic fears, even when he originally saw his vision but could not yet interpret it? This is doubtful. What he does fear, however, is illuminated by the relief with which he registers the heavenly punishment meted out to the caliph in his chronicle. God has not yet completely given the Christians over to the Babylonian king. What is occurring is still only divine retribution for sins and not the apocalyptic actions of the Antichrist that will come from Babylon. For famine and death plagued the Saracens, too, and the sword struck against them. The Arabs invaded their land. They captured the "King of Babylon," "qui se contra Deum erexerat in superbiam," disemboweled him, filled the body cavity with stones, weighted his neck with lead, and cast his cadaver into the sea, while his godless soul descended into Hell. The "King of Babylon," his conceit against God, his plunge into the abyss—whoever could read at that time understood the point that Ademar was trying to make. Everything else fit together: the Jews conspiring against Christians, the decline in belief, and the paucity of martyrs. Ademar's implications betray his earlier apprehension of the end times that had for so long forced him to be silent but now guided his pen.

Ademar was certainly aware of the chronological computations of Abbo of Fleury. According to Abbo's calculations, the third year before the thousandth anniversary of Christ's death was the year 1010. Again, two decades later, as the other third year before the thousandth anniversary of Christ's death (as calculated by Dionysius Exiguus) approached, the monk from Limoges, along with countless of his contemporaries who also saw the approaching end of the world, girded himself for a pilgrimage to Jerusalem, from which he would never again return to his homeland, for he died in 1034. Ademar hoped for the future, but the Antichrist, whose coming portended the end of the world, would not have found him unprepared in the present.

As for northern France, Queen Gerberga's inquiry to Adso of Montier-en-Der reveals her curiosity about the coming millennium, or perhaps even acute concern. Adso's response has been frequently analyzed. Current opinion assumes that he calmed the noble lady, saying that the time is not yet come. An "eschatological sense" is foreign to him, and there can be no discussion "concerning an immediate expectation." In this manner, he follows the commentary of Haimo, if not literally then at least substantively. However, it has also been legitimately pointed out that this tenth-century author deviates significantly from his Carolingian source. Whereas Haimo registers temporal uncertainty and imprecision, Adso transports the apocalyptic drama surrounding the Antichrist into the concrete context of tenth-century France and endows it with a principally historical chronology. Nothing better points out the actualizing and "realistic" fundamental tendency of the millennial expectations of the tenth and early eleventh centuries. The belief in the end of the world in the actual year 1000, even as it violates the precepts of Holy Scripture, is only the most precise location of this tendency and the highest flowering of its effect.

We must go still one step farther. In contrast to the current, commonly accepted interpretation of Adso's position, I believe that he tends to view the actual present as the end of time, as that last historical epoch, its length uncertain, before the three and one-half years in which the Antichrist will rule the world. The thought of the end of the world can have little effect on eschatologists trained in the Christian tradition. For them, the end of the world is often only the end of all earthly suffering and a last chance for holy martyrdom, a time of testing and perseverance for the last "chosen." The joy of the chosen will be indescribably immense when the world is destroyed and they are no longer subject to its dangers. Adso, too, subscribes to this view and does not depict terrible futuristic scenarios. In contrast, he mentions the "chosen" of his own time, calmly describing what one "must know" (*debetis autem scire*).

Immediately (*statimque*) after the *consummatio* of the Roman-Christian kingdom, the Antichrist will appear for three and one-half years in order to assemble his sinister regiment. This moment has not yet arrived, but of what consequence is that? Unnoticed until now, Adso parts ways with one of his most important sources, the commentator Haimo. Between the decline of the Roman Empire and the coming of the Antichrist, Haimo had inserted a transitional period of uncertain duration: "non . . . statim venturum [i.e., Antichrist] . . . sed deinde" (*PL* 117:181). Both exegetes, Adso as well as Haimo, find themselves in uncharted territory: neither the first *statim* nor the last *deinde* are found in Paul's text (2 Thess. 2:3). Adso's exegetical "correction" disputes Haimo's transitional period. The coming of the Antichrist has not yet happened. (It would have been apparent, of course, since Enoch and Elijah would have had to appear first.)

Consequently, the Roman Empire, or at least its *dignitas*, must continue to exist. However "destroyed" (*destructum*) the empire may be, it still has a future. It does not occur to Adso to calm a terrified queen by placing the end of the world at a greater distance in time. Calming formulations are missing from his work. He is filled with an ethic of "objectivity" (*certum reddere*), and his work must be exact and applicable. He therefore corrects his source to show the true moment of the Antichrist's *parousia*. Adso likely shares the opinion of those who teach that the last ruler will be a Frankish king who will be the last to rule the *regnum* or *imperium Romanum* in its totality (*ex integro*) before he lays down his scepter and crown on the Mount of Olives, indicating thereby the "end" for which the Antichrist waits. There is nothing inherently fear inducing in this scenario; the statement is full of sublime expectation. The "last of all kings" will also be the "greatest," the fulfillment of all earthly rule. He will guide his kingdom (*imperium* or *regnum*) "fortuitously" until he turns toward Jerusalem to carry out his most significant act.

When will this occur? In what temporal categories does Adso think? His dedicatory letter to the West Frankish queen pleads for the continuation of the *culmen imperii* for her husband and two sons, and he wishes them "the entire *imperium*." Nowhere, neither in the dedicatory letter nor in the following tract, does Adso mention the divided or undivided "Kingdom of the Franks." Instead, he vigorously discusses the "whole" Latin empire, which *ex toto* has not yet declined, since the Frankish kings, including, currently, Gerberga's spouse himself, are preserving its *dignitas*, and under whom it will *ex integro* rise up again. In light of his tract, Adso's wish can only mean that he wishes the queen and her family the final height of earthly rule that would signal the end of time. "If I could effect it, I would have you obtain the whole *imperium*!" For the time being, the rule of Otto I and his decisive victory over the Hungarians lies in the future. Therefore, Adso, and perhaps the rulers themselves, consider the then-living Carolingians as qualified to fulfill the duties of the final emperor. The abbot of Montier-en-Der does not expect a long future. Quite the opposite, he reminds his reader explicitly of the import of the present time: "Knowledge of the Antichrist is of utmost importance in *our* time."

The well-known testimony of Abbo of Fleury must be considered here, since it shows the millennial proclivities of Paris and the attempts of concerned Lotharingian computists to calculate the end of the world (ca. 960–70). The abbot of Fleury claims that the *fama* spread by these computists that the world will end when Good Friday and the feast of the Annunciation fall on the same day has "almost filled the whole world." The letter to the bishop of Verdun cited above confirms analogous concerns. Shortly before this, a sign appeared in the northern sky, which, as the chronicler of Saint-Maximin in Trier noted, "many interpreted as the sign of the Antichrist." The "rumor" of which Abbo speaks is spread among more than just small groups of those who are especially fearful. Although Abbo points out that he has refuted both the Parisian priest and the Lotharingian reckoning, he is so concerned about obsession with millennial fears shortly before the year 1000 that he urgently recommends that the king call a special synod to address them. In spite of Abbo's learned refutation, the anxious questions aroused by these millennial fears belong to those things "which must be corrected in your kingdom." According to him they are not irrelevant.

Abbo's brief remarks illuminate not only the two predecessors he refutes but also three millennially disposed groups which, writing from the 990s, he considered dangerous. They have adherents not only in Lotharingia but, as the notice to the kings makes clear, also over wide regions of France. But we must also ask whether Abbo resolves his pupils' fears of the closely approaching end of the world. He is certainly no "millenarian," since the learned abbot believed that the thousandth year since Christ's birth had already been reached in 979, but he is a Christian and a child of his times. There is a close connection between him and Aelfric of Eynsham. The Anglo-Saxon preached about the approaching end of the world, but he simultaneously forbade any determination of its specific arrival. A prohibition against reckoning and an immediate expectation of the end of the world are in no way mutually exclusive. Abbo could have or may have operated in a similar manner—accepting the rapidly approaching end but eschewing any exact determination of the day and hour of its arrival—although he does not explicate these themes further.

His English pupil Byrhtferth briefly describes the six ages of the world, the last of which is expiring now. "It is not characterized by any specific sequence of generations or periods, but in the weakness of its age it fulfills itself and the whole *saeculum*" (as formulated by Bede). Byrhtferth continues: "John states, 'Post mille annos solvetur Satanas.' The Satanic number 1,000 has been reached according to human numeration. In the present time the Savior has the power to complete the count of years. The number 1,000 is a perfect number (*perfectus*); its completion (*perfectio*) is known only to Him who has made everything according to his will" (Early English Text Society, vol. 177, pp. 238–40). Byrhtferth measures the individual ages of the world exactly, at least according to the Judaic calculation and the Septuagint. In the year 1011 the age of the earth is 4,961 years (according to Judaic calculation) or 6,341 years (according to the Septuagint). In his calculation, though, Byrhtferth explicitly rejects the calming notion that the earth will last 6,000 years, and instead he introduces the notion of the eight days of the earth, whose last is *domes daeg*. With it ends the previously mentioned Satanic year 1000, "all depth and width and length, all kingly rule and injustice, all assault and thievery, unjust courts and treachery." This pupil of Abbo of Fleury, too, does not placate with the promise of a long future but rather teaches that time has reached its fulfillment according to human reckoning. The computist cannot articulate the millennial fears of his contemporaries.

It is in the light of this immediate expectation of the end of the world, more or less strongly held in governing circles, that one must read the "catalinary speech" of Bishop Arnulf of Orléans against the Latin pope, that *horrendum monstrum*, Boniface, and his immediate predecessor, and against "shameful Rome" and the "abandonment" of the true Latin church on the part of almost all churches. "Venerable Father, what do you think this monstrosity is?" "If it is bereft of love . . . it is then the Antichrist, who sits in the temple of God." And the *discessio* described by the apostle Paul happens "not only to the people but even to the churches themselves." "Rome itself, already abandoned, departs from it." "The Antichrist stands before the door: 'Iam misterium iniquitatis-operatur, tantum, ut qui nunc tenet, teneat donec de medio fiat, ut ille perditionis filius reveletur'" (2 Thess. 2:7). With these apocalyptical utterances the bishop captivates the synod meeting in Saint-Basle de Verzy near Reims in order to end the controversy over the Archbishopric of Reims. None of the numerous bishops assembled contradicts him. On the contrary, the defenders of the controversial Arnulf of Reims are convinced, according to his opponent Gerbert, who records the synodal protocols and the quoted sermon from Arnulf. Without the consent of the pope they pass judgment on an archbishop.

The papal legate, Abbot Leo of Saints Boniface and Alexius, is outraged when he later receives the synodal *libellus*, but he can do no better than return the blow in 993 using the same apocalyptic language as his opponent Gerbert. The Antichrists predicted for the end times do not rage in Rome but in France: "in vobis evenit propheta beati apostoli et evangelistae Johannis, qui dicit: 'Multi Antichristi facti sunt; unde scimus, quoniam novissima hora est.' Et quid est Antichristus, nisi contrarius Christi?" (*MGH, SS* 3: 686). "Your Antichrists decry against Rome, [but] the marble statue and the temple of idols is there [i.e., in France]. Let it be far, far away." It is Gerbert himself who is much more the apostate, and his followers, with Bishop Arnulf of Orléans at their head, are heretics, worse even than the Arians. Leo, with a weak argument, attempts explicitly to contradict the accusation that the churches are abandoning Rome, since delegations of fellow believers from Asia, Africa, and Spain had recently arrived in the Holy City. Abbo of Fleury himself, who argued the case of the deposed Arnulf at Saint-Basle, is unaffected by this argument. His demand for a synod to consider the question of the end of the world is a reflection of the Antichrist polemic of the controversy at Reims.

When Gerbert-Sylvester, soon after his death, became identified as a magician and servant of Satan, he was virtually a beast from the apocalypse, "rising up from the abyss shortly after the completion of a thousand years." This legendary figure was not supposed to die as long as he did not celebrate a mass in Jerusalem, but his destiny caught up with him when he celebrated mass at the Church of the Holy Cross in Jerusalem in Rome. Reflected in the legend, not for the last time, is his "ascent" from Antichrist-like Apostate to successor of St. Peter. The Sylvester legend preserves the apocalyptic thematic of anti-Roman polemic before the turn of the year 1000. Only when the situation in Rome itself changed, when Gregory V (996–99) ascended the apostolic throne and Gerbert, driven out of Reims, found sanctuary at the Ottonian imperial court, did the apocalyptic rhetoric fall silent. In his *Histories* of 996–98, Richer of Reims reports extensively on the infamous Synod of Saint-Basle but omits any mention of the anti-Roman invective and its apocalyptic overtones. This lack of reporting on eschatological themes may not serve as an argument that such concerns were not widespread among contemporaries.

One may dismiss all of this as low-grade propaganda, or as a scholarly exercise without basis in actual belief or a real relation with the year 1000, much as the opponents in the Reims controversy dismissed each other; Ferdinand Lot did not dignify the synod at Saint-Basle with a single word. The propagandistic intensity of the synodal *libellus* was heightened not only by the scandalous accusations against the Roman bishop but also by the latent fears of the approaching end of the world, which Gerbert knew well how to exploit. As was later the case in the thirteenth-century political conflict between pope and emperor, in which apocalyptic visionary rhetoric was placed into service as propaganda and influenced prophecies affected by the experience of contemporaries, the accusations against Pope John XV made before the year 1000 were couched in a consistently effective, if waxing and waning, apocalyptic rhetoric of fear.

The same Gerbert who sent apocalyptic signals from France to Rome was not only one of the tutors of the apocalyptically sensitive King Robert of France but also one of the more decisive advocates of the Roman ideal of *renovatio* advanced by Emperor Otto III. His own spiritual characteristics were formed in Catalonia, where the Apocalypse commentaries and illustrations of Beatus of Liebana found a lively resonance. Otto III's eschatology was also influenced by the Sibylline Prophecies, which flourished in Italy and to a lesser extent in France and Germany. Perhaps there is indeed a connection between the discussion of the end of the world and the imperial program of renewal. Is not the young emperor himself an indication that the controversy at Reims entailed more than propagandistic figures of speech? Of course, in his letters Gerbert does not rely upon the approaching end of time to point out the depraved nature of his times but instead relies on a device borrowed from heathen antiquity, *fortuna*, "blind, raging fate," to which he professes to believe that he himself is subject.

Scholars have widely debated whether or not eschatological ideas bloomed in the immediate circles around Otto III. Aside from one exception, explicit examples of belief in the immediate end of the world are lacking. But the number and quality of apocalyptic references connected with Otto are astounding.

Illustrations of Otto as a ruler depict him analogously to the Byzantine emperors as a benefactor or devotee before the Maiestas Domini, the Christ returning on the last day, in a distinct departure from the Carolingian tradition of ruler depiction. His kingship mimics that of Christ in the shadow of the Last Judgment. The Mainz prayer book certainly intended for Otto III shows an impressive illustration, with strong Byzantine influences, of this religious propensity. Otto honors God, the *rex illustrissimus regum*, as the dedicatory poem states, in the bodily position of *proskynesis*, without a crown but with concealed hands. The title of the earthly king practically calls forth the heavenly Parousia (see 1 Tim. 6:14; Apoc. 17:14).

Similarly, as the young Otto prepared himself for his imperial coronation in 996, he wrapped himself in a cloak covered with illustrations from the entire Apocalypse. This is the oldest surviving example of such a cycle of illustrations outside manuscript illumination. The Bamberg Apocalypse, one of the leading examples of Reichenau manuscript illustration and in many respects the trendsetter for new directions in apocalyptic illustration, is probably also dedicated to Otto. The codex contains the oldest depiction of the Antichrist outside the Beatus tradition.

A further incident affects this image. After Otto returned from his puzzling pilgrimage to Gniezno in the year 1000, he celebrated the feast of the Assumption of the Virgin (August 15) in Rome, where processions bearing the Theotokos and an icon of Christ (the famous Acheropita of the Sancta Sanctorum at the Lateran) met one another in a night processional. A violent storm overshadowed the festivities, and the Tiber overflowed, flooding the city—a premonition of impending calamity. An unusually pessimistic hymn affected the mood of the faithful. Roma exclaims that *she* is the whore of Babylon; she bemoans her sins, strikes her breast, and pleads for grace: "Nec procul est opifex gemmam carbone refingens." Of course, it is not the Judge of Earth himself whose proximity is announced but rather his likeness only, which reminds all of the Judgment:

> Vultus adest Domini, cui totus sternitur orbis.
> Signo iudicii vultus adest Domini. (*MGH*, Poetae 5, pp. 465–68)

The city, however, had already been promised comfort: it was "renewed" through the martyrdom of the apostles (*stas renovata*, v. 16). Why, then, the references to the coals of divine scorn and the longing for religious renewal, for the *meretrix nocturna*, for the *iudicium*? The festival of Mary and its liturgy made these superfluous. The poet follows only his own concerns and those of his public. They apparently reflect the mood of the summer of the year 1000. Also, the Assumption processions with Savior icons were imitated outside Rome, in fact throughout the Latin church already in the tenth century, and appropriate pictorial panels begin appearing. Perhaps it was during this time that Romanesque processional icons were translated into altarpieces.

For another example of eschatological fervor during Otto's reign, his adviser and chancellor (994–1002), Archbishop Heribert of Cologne (999–1021), received an edition of Adso's *De antichristo*. This edition soon began to be transmitted as the "original" and therefore had a significant effect.

Further, recently, scholars have suggested that the two *sanctiones* in the diplomata of Otto III (nos. 331 and 347), with their highly unusual references to the Last Judgment, are the product of Otto's own dictation.

However, the strangest example of eschatological thought in the Ottonian milieu is the Ottonian evangelical of Aachen. Its dedicatory illustration, still puzzling to this day, represents the Maiestas Domini, which appears nowhere else in the manuscript. It visually portrays the emperor not only with outstretched hands but also in the likeness of the Christ of the Second Parousia. The dedicatory poem of his prayer book had already portrayed him in this manner literarily. In Otto III, the dedicated, pious disciple who called himself "servant of Jesus Christ" and "servant of the apostles," the Italian anchorites perhaps briefly imagined that they glimpsed the last emperor, as prophesied by the Sibyl. Indeed, the *Vita quinque fratrum* describes Otto in language redolent of the proph-

esied actions of the last emperor: "In the presence of the angels of God, he promised to give up all," abdicate in Jerusalem, and become a monk in the wilder-
ness (ed. J. Karwasinska, *Monumenta Poloniae Historica* 43 [1973], p. 38).

The result of this brief examination of Ottonian sources is somewhat surprising. Of course, nothing in relation to Otto III has concretely demonstrated
that the emperor was affected by an immediate expectation of the apocalypse,
but no other German emperor of the Romans before him, nor anyone after him,
including Frederick II, would avail himself of things millenarian in a comparable way. Perhaps Otto III had, hesitatingly, waited in the expectation of the
end more than has been assumed until now.

Perhaps the religiously sensitive Otto learned to comprehend the nearness
of the danger from the Roman ascetics to whom he was drawn, such as the already familiar Abbot Leo and the monks of Saints Boniface and Alessio, or perhaps from the liturgical readings from the Apocalypse, which were common in
Rome. On the other hand, perhaps his sole influence was Gerbert of Aurillac.
This question must remain unanswered for now.

Nonetheless, the emperor certainly did not bring his views to Italy from
Saxony. The opposite is more likely: it is he who prepared the way for millennial
expectations in his homeland. The intellectual climate of the German northeast
at this time is barely comparable to that of the French or Lotharingian west. It
was at this point that the German northeast began to align itself with the culturally advanced regions of Latin Europe. The example of Bruno of Querfort
(d. 1009) may serve to illustrate this process. This alumnus of the Magdeburg
cathedral school bewailed the terrible contemporary events without attributing
to them any eschatological significance, even though he would have most likely
known of their eschatological implications.

His former classmate, Thietmar of Merseburg, was more direct. When the
apostasy of the Luticians began to incite millennial *desperacio* among his subjects, he attempted to fend it off: "No one . . . shall announce that the Last Judgment is near." As long as the *discessio* (*dissensio*) has not yet come to pass and
the Antichrist has not yet arrived, it should not be preached nor allowed to create unrest among Christians. "No one should dispute that the Last Judgment
will come, but no one should wish for its quick arrival, for it will be terrible
for the righteous as well as the sinners" (*MGH, SS*, n.s., 9:498–500). The
Quedlinburg annals might reveal which group Thietmar felt compelled to admonish, since the annals overflow with the fearful descriptions of signs.

Direct evidence of millennial attitudes in southern Germany has also been
preserved. Notker "the German" of Saint Gall provides an apocalyptic interpretation of Boethius's *De consolatione philosophiae*. The "Roman might" is no longer
sufficient to resist the barbarians. Kings from the north, Odoaker and Theoderic,
begin its *defectio* (= *discessio*), which the Langobards, Franks ("whom we now
call Carolingians"), and Saxons complete. "Sô ist nû zegángen Romanum imperium, ergo Romanorum regnum defecit." What was once prophesied by Paul
is now, in Notker's own time, already halfway fulfilled: now one must only await
the arrival of the Antichrist and his rule. Next will follow the "Day of the Lord"
(*sûonetágo*). Notker does not provide a precise determination of the time of these

events. He follows Haimo's teaching, according to which the Antichrist will come, not "immediately" after the fall of the Roman Empire, but "after." In this sense, he does not rely on Adso. Notker, born ca. 950, is extremely affected by millennial expectations, because of course the fall of the empire has occurred in his own lifetime: "Oportett nos memores esse." Notker's reading of the *De consolatione* informs his apocalyptic sensitivities. Its tone leads one to the expectation of the apocalypse, and it offers intellectual preparation for the Last Judgment.

Of course, it is not only the West Frankish Kingdom in which one finds millennial expectations. Abbo of Fleury represents the forefront of a long tradition to which he was introduced in England. This English tradition stands in close relationship with Continental developments. Eschatology permeates all of Insular Christian theology, and when texts lacked a sufficient eschatological emphasis, Anglo-Saxon exegetes felt compelled to fill in the gaps. One easily recognizes the influence of Gregory the Great and his millennial expectations, and the influence of the Irish is certainly significant as well. Ireland was surely one of the main sources that fed millennial expectations. Exegetes diligently copied certain early Christian apocalyptic texts, and this activity provides at least probable, if not compelling, evidence for a direct connection with contemporary millennial expectations. It appears as if the awareness of the approaching end grew in the tenth century and became more desperate with the aging of the *saeculum*. The Antichrist makes his first appearance in Old English literature at this point, shortly before the turn of the millennium. The sermons contained in the Vercelli Codex, written in the middle of the tenth century, constantly invoke the Last Judgment but barely suggest its *immediate* arrival. In contrast, the slightly younger *Blickling Homilies* never tire of warning, "*Midgards* end is near." The contemporary events are similar to those prophesied in the Bible. The preliminary conditions are almost all fulfilled, and one must now only await the arrival of the Antichrist. Thus states the preacher in the year 971, but at the same time he warns that the exact time of Antichrist's arrival remains unknowable.

The same fears fill Aelfric of Eynsham and compel him to take on the role of the people's instructor and preacher in his native language. He realizes that the people need his Old English homilies, "especially at this time, which is the end of the world" (*Sermones catholici*, ed. Thorpe, vol. 2, p. 298). "For now is the time in which everyone must know better" about that which is to come, especially the myriad unchristian temptations and actions, since "everyone must expect great misery." At one point, Aelfric describes himself and his contemporaries as "we end people of the world (*endemenn*)" (p. 476). Of course, he does not attempt a more precise placement of this eschatological "now." Unlike Wulfstan of York, whom we will discuss below, he does not ascribe it to specific events in the present. A tangible distance remains in his work, despite the extent to which he proclaims that the end of the world is near, and he expressly warns of those who claim that the Antichrist is appearing "even now." "Often people claim, 'Now the day of judgment is at hand,' because the signs which will announce it are fulfilled. But then war follows war, calamity follows calamity, earthquake follows earthquake, one people attacks another, and the Bridegroom still does not come. In this manner will the 6,000 years since Adam end, and still the Bridegroom hesitates. How do we know when He will come? Even as He Himself has said: 'At midnight.' But does not 'At midnight' mean nothing more than that you don't know, and do not expect it? Then He will come" (vol. 2, p. 568). Aelfric's eschatology, deriving from the tradition of Gregory the Great, lacks a high level of concern for the interpretation of contemporary events.

Wulfstan of York, the latest of the Anglo-Saxon clergy we will discuss, is the first to turn the theme of the Last Judgment into a fearful analysis of contemporary events. His well-known *Sermo Lupi ad Anglos* of 1014 may serve as an example. The danger is great, the world nears its end, because before the Antichrist arrives, the signs of evil will increase, just as they are "now." "You must recognize that Satan now (*nu*) has too greatly seduced this people these many years." Wulfstan does not reveal himself to be a chiliast, but he considers the horrors of his times to be signs of the apocalypse, and he lists them all in their blasphemous nature—taxes, rape, escaped slaves, the attacks by the Danes. He thoroughly analyzes Adso's *De antichristo* and is even more concerned than the abbot of Montier-en-Der. Wulfstan exhorts: We have no time left! Each one must examine himself or herself, and do it without delay. Let each one save herself or himself as best she or he can, otherwise we are all doomed together.

The urgency of Wulfstan's appeals increases when he issues them in his native tongue. He is not content merely to translate the *De antichristo*. Rather, he changes or expands it in nuanced, yet revealing ways and in the process turns the tract into a vernacular sermon. Thor and Wotan replace Jupiter and Mercury. The Antichrist is not, as is usually claimed, conceived of a virgin and Satan. Rather, he is the product of an incestuous union between father and daughter. Wulfstan emphasizes the disturbing aspects and bowdlerizes that which should be consoling. The dangerous end times appear to have actually arrived. "Now it is urgently necessary that each messenger of God warns His people again and again (*gelome*)." All must know of the situation: "Since many do not recognize the danger, it is that much more important that preachers announce it, so that when the Antichrist comes, he will find the body of believers prepared." The Archbishop uses this argument to spur on his priests.

"When will the Redeemer come?" "When will God's judgment arrive?" "How many years are left?" These questions tear at the two visionaries [*sic*] of Saint Vaast during the time of Abbot Richard (1011/12). The sense of urgency grew in Flanders as well. Despite the dramatic description of his wanderings in Heaven and Hell, the first visionary monk offers only a reserved "Not yet." The second, however, may read the actual number of years, but he cannot decipher the heavenly inscription (for God alone knows the day of the Last Judgment), and he can only determine that "in a short time" it will come. "In a few years," "the end of these times will be here shortly." "It comes, it comes, the Day of the Lord, like a thief in the night." This visionary speaks with a verse from 2 Peter (3:10), but the doubled *veniet, veniet* has an accelerating affect, and the disturbing chronological description *cito* is his addition. The visions are intended to appeal to hesitating sinners: Repent and do penance! The deadline comes closer with each passing year. The pressure for many of them must have been excruciating. The visionary warnings are intended even for an archbishop of Cologne, perhaps Everger. Through Albuin's plagiarism of Adso we know that Everger's successor, Heribert, was filled with great concern for the Antichrist's arrival, so much so that as he lay dying he commanded that he be placed in front of the consoling image of the Savior. It appears that the visionaries' accounts had the intended effect on one or the other of their high-profile recipients.

Anxiety and fear, then, characterize the era. This fear did not necessarily dissipate upon the expiration of the year 1000. Rather, it remained latent, flaring up from time to time as a dramatically manifested fear of the "mystical" year 1000, as Christian eschatologists repeatedly characterize it. Still, the mystical year of the eschatologists is an unpredictable certainty which may be fulfilled at any time, perhaps even in the actual year 1000. The aging king Rudolf III of Burgundy confessed in 1031 that "because we observe the fall of the world before us, we await with dread the end of all things temporal." His consort, Ermengard, elaborated upon the anxiety with an accounting of the unmistakable signs of the approaching end (*MGH, DD* Reg. Burg., 125 and 127).

What is fear, actually? How does religiously motivated "collective fear" around the turn of the millennium express itself, aside from serving as the occasional motivation for the donation to a church? For theologians and pastors, the expectation of the "imminent" end of the world is self-explanatory: it has its roots in the core of Christian belief. However, how does one express this expectation? What fruits does it bear? How does it affect the religious expression of the laity? Or does the belief in the end of the world remain merely an abstract theological speculation, or a redemptive interpretive model of history for the ruling elite, without any moral catharsis or existential consequence, without any renewed desire for holiness?

IV

Perhaps we have formulated the question incorrectly up to this point. Have we not just discounted the notion of a "paralyzing fear," which deadens all vitality, in favor of the notion of a fear that spurs on and motivates? Beissel would judge this to be false, since it is too modern: "If at the end of the tenth century one had really believed that the Last Judgment was near, one would not have undertaken any more tasks." Ferdinand Lot takes this position as well: "If they [the synods of the year 1000] had been thinking about the end of time, they simply would have let things go."

What we read in the texts, however, is the exact opposite: use the time that remains for pious works! This is almost literally the message of Aelfric and Wulfstan. Aelfric urges, "Flee from evil, and do good!" "Let us use the time we have left, which God has given us!" A Christian should await the end with the highest degree of activity, not in lethargic desperation. Wulfstan himself follows this exhortation. His famous *Institutes of Polity* guide Christians in proper actions, without explicitly appealing to the nearness of the apocalypse: "Therefore we order canons to read this exhortation diligently, ponder it, guard it in their thoughts, and, with God's help, transform it into actions as best they can; then they will earn praise among men and eternal reward with God." A high degree of activity and an expectation of the immediate end are in no way mutually exclusive.

Perhaps we may observe similar beliefs in Leo of Vercelli, especially when we consider the eschatological role ascribed to the Holy Roman Empire. In *DO* 3:324 (999 5.7 for Vercelli) he writes: "ut libere et secure permanente dei ecclesia prosperetur nostrum imperium, triumphet corona nostre militie, propagetur potentia populi romani et restituatur res publica, ut in huius mundi hospitio honeste vivere, de huius vite carcere honestus avolare et cum domino honestissime mereamur regnare." One must do one's best here on earth, in order to inherit the Kingdom of Heaven.

In his *De virtutibus et vitiis*, which he writes for Archbishop Heribert of Cologne, the hermit Albuin includes passages from Adso's *De antichristo*. The message is clear: in the face of the end times, the Christian should increase her or his efforts to live a proper life. The emperor of the Bamberg Apocalypse is accompanied by the "Triumph of the Virtues over the Vices." The Reichenau manuscript illuminator visually portrays the same message that Albuin gives to the archbishop of Cologne. For, however much longer the vice-ridden world may still have in which to turn, may God help the king in war, and "us" in life; Fulbert of Chartres expresses these sentiments in a verse prayer and assumes at least the *possibility* of a quick end.

> Tu qui de nihilo mundum finxisse probaris
> (nam tibi materies nulla coaeva fuit)
> Et nutu facili, noto tibi tempore, solves:
> Tam diuturne dehinc, quam prius extiteras.
> Quantulus his noster modus est, quo saecula volvi
> Cum vitiisque iubes, strenua bella geri
> Regem militibus propriis te semper adesse
> Ad bene certandum nos vegetando proba. (*PL* 141:350)

People were used to the nearness of death. The expectation of the great fire of the apocalypse had been continuously preached, and only in the smallest of ways did this expectation change daily life, the usual economic activities, and the perpetual goals of power politics. Even in the tenth century, it was not the actual end that served to unsettle contemporaries but rather the expectation of the Last Judgment and its punishments. The signs of the end of time announce only the coming of the world's Judge and the necessity for increased efforts. The time remaining in the tenth century was shorter, and therefore more precious, than the time available in the previous century. For those who were conscious of their sins, the pressure increased accordingly. The writer of a letter to Archbishop Sigerich of Canterbury wishes for him the most fortuitous passage of time in the uncertain present and a favorable Last Judgment: "commodissima vacillantis tempora saeculi necne in generalis judicii examine senatorum apostolici prioratus summam" (*Rerum Britannicaum Medii Aevi SS* [Rolls Series] 63, p. 399, ep. 27). One is anxious about the "fleeting nature of time" (*transitorium tempus*).

Each appearance of another eschatological sign reminded one of the dangers and renewed the fear, especially as the millennium after Christ's birth drew to a close. "Numerous people in many places saw fiery aerial battles, which mortally frightened the hearts of those who observed." "The news . . . spreads quickly" (*AASS*, IV, p. 568). As soon as Abbot Ragenard of Rabais learned of the ominous sign, he called upon Abbess Ermengard of Jouarre and discussed the horrible apparition with her. In order to escape the dreaded danger, he urged humbling oneself before the mighty hand of God, and he ordered a day of fasting. On the appointed day the processions from Rabais and Jouarre and a considerable number of the nobility joined at a common meeting place, known since that time as the "St. Agilius Cross." Suddenly the clouds separated, and lightning mixed with stony hail illuminated heaven and earth. All present paled in fear before the face of death. The evil of night covered the middle of the day with the deepest darkness, and all feared sudden death. At the urging of the abbot one of the wisest among them, a man learned in the arts and sciences, appealed to the people: "these horrors are to warn you to repent of the sins you have committed." Nature's rage and the words of the preacher do their work, since otherwise the event would not have found its way into the *Miracles of St. Agilius*. The numerous signs and processions, the fear of death, and the call to penance occurred in response to the threat of the "flames of Styx." The narrative of the miracle may be more recent, but it still reflects the millennial fears of the eleventh century.

The important question is whether the deepened belief in the end's imminent arrival influenced the nature of piety and church reform or whether, in reverse, the new forms of religious expression point explicitly to the apocalypse and the Last Judgment. Repeated reference has been made to the increasing awareness of sin as the spiritual foundation for an actualized awareness of the end of time. Are the changes in religious expression that occurred around the millennium at least partly the result of the "fear" of the end of time? We cannot answer the question conclusively here and now, but several points may be offered toward an answer.

Of course, not every contemporary shared an increased awareness of sin and the belief in the imminent arrival of the Antichrist, and all those who did believe in his quick arrival did not act upon this belief with the same level of intensity and consequence. Even at Cluny, not every monk overflowed with millennial expectations. Many contemporary commentators, such as Atto of Vercelli or Alpert of Metz, remained completely silent concerning the Antichrist. Did they not believe, then, in the imminent arrival of the end?

Another reservation is appropriate here. Silence in the sources alone is not enough evidence to demonstrate a lack of millennial expectation, as I have shown in various instances. We must reckon with transitional forms. And who can determine whether human actions result from motivations steeped in worldly interests or result from attempts to protect Christian faith? Who is able to draw the line between a faith that compels to action and a scrupulous, calculated religious ideology? A Christian simultaneously trusts and mistrusts her or his authorities. Christians must position themselves in life under the influence of uncertain knowledge, faithful certainty, and the holy mysteries of their religion. In other words, they must come to terms with each of these influences, today as during the time of the first millennium.

Among the most thoroughly collected and researched documentary sources are those that refer to "apocalyptic sermons," which are abundant in the area influenced by Cluny. Even when the sources of the tenth century employ older formulations, and thus are affected by tradition, they still reflect the intellectual milieus in which they were created. Abbot Odo's concerns have already been mentioned, and Radulfus Glaber illustrates this point as well, despite what he himself may have thought about the end of the world at various points in his life. The success of the Cluniac monks may be explained, not solely by the perceived value of their prayers, but also by the contents of their sermons and the persuasive nature of their analysis of contemporary events. But we must not overvalue the documentary evidence. Only a few dozen sources offer any appropriate evidence, and they stand against thousands of sources without any recognizable trace of millennial expectation. Critics of the "legend" of the "fear of the year 1000" have long since recognized this and drawn their strongest arguments from it. In so doing, however, they did not investigate to what extent the formulations in the sources accurately reflect the mental and spiritual disposition of those who created them and the complex reasons for their creation. These critics also did not take into account the fact that the earlier, as well as the later, periods of heightened millennial expectations are equally lacking in the sources. The *argumentum e silentio* rests upon shaky ground.

Similar reservations concerning funerary inscriptions are also appropriate. Scarcely any refer to the end of time or the Last Judgment, even though we must assume that the vast majority of, if not all, Christians descended into their graves in expectation of it. However, a reminder of Judgment is hardly necessary in the realm beyond earthly death. The silence of these sources should not irritate us then. References to heightened millennial expectation are equally lacking in synodal statutes. But how would the church have been allowed to conceive of, develop, or defend an "official" plan for the apocalypse when its immediate expectation was magisterially rejected? Yet, Christians have believed repeatedly that they could see behind the mysteries of salvation. Conciliar decrees and synodal pronouncements can inherently reveal little, therefore, concerning the extent, severity, and immediacy of apocalyptic fear. They provide norms for a life that will stand before the Last Judge, but they do not determine the court date.

It was not only the monastic movement that experienced movement toward reform. The church in general enjoyed reforming impulses under the influence of actualized millennial expectation. We must here refer again to the intellectual leaders of the Western Kingdom. The *Dialogus de statu sanctae ecclesiae*, which Heinz Löwe locates in Laon in the 960s, offers a precise analysis of contemporary events, performed using an apocalyptic methodology ("Das Werk eines Iren im Laon des 10. Jahrhunderts," *Deutsches Archiv für Erforschung des Mittelalters* 17 [1961]: 12–90; edition at pp. 68–90). Its author could be Irish, in which case his connection with the tenth-century Irish Antichrist tradition that influenced the Continent would be clear. But Queen Gerberga, the recipient of Adso's *De antichristo*, also resided in Laon on a regular basis. Toward the middle of the *Dialogus*, framed by the question "que episcopo dare liceret et que minime," Theophilus, one of the two participants, offers this commentary: Princes and priests confuse right and wrong. "Ita omnia permixta sunt, ut nihil aliud nisi iuditium Dei supersit." Churches and abbeys are usurped. Bishops, not yet ordained or enthroned, squander the churches' property. "You call them Christians, but in truth they are Antichrists." And what can be said of the laity! They take over the churches and even the altars. They eat and drink the offerings intended for the poor. "Why do you not fear the Lord's judgment? You are not Christians at all. You are like the beast which the prophet Daniel confronted." "Harsh words!" interrupts Eutitius, the other participant, for many high-ranking persons would find the outburst unpleasant, the result of an "excess" of emotion, as well as a departure from the theme. But note how the anonymous author uses exactly this outburst, in which just and unjust distribution of church property is discussed, to remind the reader of the increasing signs of the Antichrist's approach. These practices of distribution are signs with apocalyptic significance. Their correction might ease the apocalyptic pressure, and this task is considered one of the central goals of church reform.

In this context we must pay special attention to Rorico, the bishop of Laon, and his attempts at the renewal of the monastery of St. Vincent. This cloister served as a cemetery for bishops and lay nobility, and it was prepared for canons and members of the Laon church's "family." It was occupied by twelve monks from Fleury and outfitted accordingly. Rorico, for his part, acts "considerans ultimae evocationis sortem ut caeteris mihi quoque imminere" (*PL* 133:951C). This is certainly not evidence of an immediate expectation of the apocalypse. But Theophilus's part of the dialogue suggests the intellectual milieu that prompted Rorico's "reservations" and provided justification for the fight against the Antichrist, who was announcing his arrival. It is noteworthy that Abbot Adso recommended Rorico to Queen Gerberga as a competent, knowledgeable source of wisdom about the Antichrist, someone who is "urgently necessary for our times (*valde necessarium nostra etate*)." The queen's query to the abbot, himself knowledgeable in history, apparently comes from this same milieu.

Abbo of Fleury's *Apologeticus* criticizes the vice of simony and reminds one of the prophecies, false or otherwise, of the Apocalypse. Gerbert (later Pope Sylvester II) also preached against simony and interpreted the signs of the times in an apocalyptic manner. The placing of regions under interdict increased and became established in the two generations around the year 1000, and Ademar of Chabannes did not hesitate to interpret this in light of apocalyptic events. In a sermon he remarked: "all churches of the dioceses of Poitiers and Angoulême are excommunicated at the present time. Their portals are barred, their altars emptied, and no layperson is allowed to enter any church." The streets are strewn with unburied corpses, food for the birds and wild animals. The godless should be forced to stop plundering church property and make peace. "We see that what John says is now coming to pass: 'There was silence in Heaven as the dragon began his fight' [see Apoc. 8:1 and 12:7]. That is, the interdiction causes silence to rule over church services . . . , because the dragon, through his minions, makes war against the poor and the servants of God." Ademar draws together the breaking of the seventh seal and St. Michael's fight against the dragon and considers the latter event fulfilled in the present. Of course, the three authors cited did not explicitly analyze the connection between an actualized sensitivity to the apocalypse and church reform, although Ademar came closest to doing so. Still, it may be helpful to draw even indirect connections between the general feelings of concern and the increased readiness to do good works. The fight against simony and the struggle for peace in the church were really struggles for proper order in the world. The reformer of Laon was not the only one who considered *permixtio* to be a sign of the end of time.

Omnia permixta sunt—again and again chaos, the dissolution not only of ecclesiastical but also of social order, is considered a criterion of the approaching end. Eschatology sensitizes one to the shortcomings of the times, and by categorizing what is to come, it provides ready criteria for order. In his commentary on Apocalypse, Haimo of Auxerre had already developed a schema for order which divides the *ecclesia* into three *tribus: sacerdotibus, militibus et agricultoribus* (PL 117:953B), for each of whom the exegete foresees unique roles. At the turn of the year 1000, it was not only Cluniacs who took up this schema to establish proper order. This functional tripartite division began to establish itself as a framework for structuring society in general. The authors under discussion here ordered society according to the functions of its members: *oratores, bellatores, laboratores*. The origin of this schema is disputed. It may derive from antiquity, it may be, but cannot be proven to be, of Irish origin, or it may be the result of many influences synthesized first in the ninth century. However, this is all irrelevant to our discussion. What is important for our purposes is that especially around the year 1000, this sort of schematic structure became so closely associated with apocalyptic thinking and was reinforced to such an extent that it remained accepted as a model for centuries. For contemporaries, the task was nothing less than the complete reordering of society based upon a new theoretical structure, as an answer to the chaos that enveloped the present. At the beginning of, and in the center of, this task stand three intellectuals who take up the theme of the approaching end: Abbo of Fleury, Aelfric of Eynsham, and Wulfstan of York. Each stands in close connection with the others, and each relies partially on the Platonic tradition, even if the three ultimately differ from one another in their approaches. The eschatological signs of the times and concern for the rapidly approaching end apparently mobilized forces for ordering society anew, even if only to ward off hastily drawn conclusions.

At the same time, there was a sudden and fearful realization that worldly life is "temporal" and fleeting. Instead of one's own affairs, one should contemplate things eternal. The church in the era of reform emphasized the poverty of temporal concerns in the face of the riches of eternity, an attitude fed in part by apocalyptic expectation as expressed around the turn of the millennium and afterward. "Who knows how little time remains until God comes to judge the world!" How could the 7000, even 10,000, years from the creation of the world until its end possibly compare with the boundless Being of God, without beginning and end. It is all just "a brief time" (*tantillum tempus*). For this reason especially, it is important to reflect upon the *novissima* and the *dies iudicii*. Peter Damian expresses these thoughts (*PL* 145:837–38). He himself does not seem to think the "wizened world" has very many years left. He repeatedly reminds the reader: "how short this life is, how loudly does the world announce its destination through ever more definitive signs." "It threatens a rapid end of its course, already frighteningly present to our sight." "People grow enfeebled already in their youth." Only one thing provides comfort: we should "despise that which falls as already fallen" and "diligently hope for that which remains." In the middle of life, the chosen one meditates upon the Last Judgment as if it were already present. He suspends time. He "now considers himself dragged (with Christ) to the judgment seat by the Jews, believes himself already put to the test, and fearfully threatened by the holy questions. . . . thus does he live, a dead man, . . . as if he already lay in the grave." Peter, the anchorite and church reformer, transforms the eschatological tradition into meditation, moral suasion, and mysticism. That which is awaited is already present in prayer. It is a call for withdrawal from the world. Those who have learned to live toward the end of time learn at the same time to despise "temporality" and emphasize spiritual goals: "quam despicienda sint temporalia." Of necessity, that which truly remains and those acts of eternal validity appear in view.

Those alive in the thousandth year after Christ's birth or death built a multitude of new churches. Latin Europe was practically in the grip of a building frenzy. Radulfus Glaber's eulogy is well known: before the thousandth and third year after the Lord's birth, the Christians in Gaul and Italy had renewed their churches. "It was as if the world wanted to shake off its age and clothe itself with the glowing costume of churches." To shake off its age? This often quoted sentence should be read as a variant contemplation of the end of the world.

The adornment of churches and forms of piety changed as well. The later changes are reflected in symbols and cultic objects, no less necessary for the "learned" theologians than for the "simple" masses in order to manifest belief and give it visible expression. We have discussed above the illustrations of the Last Judgment and Apocalypse cycles, which experienced an increase, or perhaps even their beginnings, around the year 1000. We may easily posit a connection between the adoration of crosses and reliquaries and the expectation of the end of time. The topic deserves more attention than has been paid it until now.

As is known from Matt. 24:30, the sign of the Son of Man accompanies and announces the resurrection of the elect for the Last Judgment. This had already been believed to be a cross. The cult and theology of the cross already possessed an eschatological sense, even if it was reflected with varying intensity. The inertia of Christian tradition should in no way be underestimated. Since the antiquity of Christian artistic expression, the jeweled cross (*crux gemmata*) had been understood as representing the Christ of the Second Parousia. We must not discount the idea that this symbolism reminiscent of the approaching end of the world prepared the way for, or partially caused, a new wave of veneration of the cross around the turn of the millennium. Whenever the end of time was contemplated, the glowing cross could not be absent.

In the early Middle Ages, the liturgical *adoratio crucis* of Good Friday found its way from Rome into the Latin West, so its connection of the adoration of the cross with the expectation of the Judgment predates the tenth century. "Domine Ihesu Christe, adoro te in cruce ascendentem. . . . Deprecor te misere mei. Domine Ihesu Christe, adoro te venturum iudicaturum. Deprecor te ut in advento tuo adventu non intres in iudico cum me peccante, sed deprecor te ut ante dimittas quam iudices, qui vives et regnas." Thus ends a prayer known in England since the eighth century, which may have its origins in Spain. Shortly before the turn of the millennium it was taken up anew in the *Regularis concordia*, which is attributed to Aethelwold, and included the newly formulated *adoratio crucis*. The prayer also made its way across Gaul in the tenth century. *Me peccante:* the supplicating monk thought first of his own time, before contemplating the future judgment. Aelfric of Eynsham, Aethelwold's pupil, learned to pray in this manner. His belief in the rapidly approaching end may be the fruit of this schooling. Evidence for the rite of taking down the cross (or crucifix) on Good Friday and assembling it again on Easter, which is later closely connected to the *adoratio*, is available only during this period, leading to the supposition that it was new in the tenth century. Of course, the Carolingians and previous groups had venerated the cross. Already, Rabanus Maurus had entrusted himself to its protection, in order to escape "the avenging flames" of the apocalypse. Rabanus's tract *De laudibus s. crucis*, to name only one popular tenth-century source, was frequently copied and widely known. An analysis of the content and frequency of examples of cross veneration and eschatology during the Carolingian Renaissance reveals a looser connection between them than is evident in the eighth and again in the tenth and eleventh centuries, and this is what is significant.

"Statistics" offers another hint that leads to the tenth century and the turn of the millennium. The evidence for the existence of relics and reliquaries of the cross in the Latin West, present since the fourth century, grows increasingly in the tenth. The sum of references to glyptic or jeweled crosses describes an oscillating line with high points in the middle of the fifth and seventh centuries, after which the number falls off again. It rises rapidly toward the middle of the tenth century, and it reaches its absolute high point around 1060. Cross-shaped reliquaries became popular only around the turn of the millennium. Does the evidently heightened interest in the thematic of the cross, the crucifix, and cross reliquaries reveal a corresponding increase in the level of eschatological expectation? It is around this time that use of the altar cross slowly began to increase, and also when the processional crucifix began to incorporate the corpus of the Savior.

An additional phenomenon is connected here. There is scattered evidence for the creation of large-scale crucifixes during the Carolingian era. By strange coincidence one example, either the original given by Charles the Bald or a reproduction, is extant in St. Peter's Basilica in Rome. It is the crucifix of St. Gero of Cologne, however, which introduces a new epoch of European sacred art. This is the oldest surviving large-scale crucifix that depicts the suffering, crucified

Christ, not the living Godly King victorious over death usually depicted in Latin Europe. This cross begins a long tradition of Ottonian and Romanesque large-scale crucifixes, which, beginning in the tenth century, were customarily placed on triumphal arches. Other crucifixes that began this tradition are Egbert of Trier's crucifix (now lost) and the problematical Benna crucifix, a gold-leaf example with reliquary niches commissioned by Archbishop Willigis of Mainz around 983.

The Son of God does not always hang lifeless on the cross. The Te Igitur prayer from the canon of the Mass became a canonical image and was embodied in the crucifix haltingly in the eighth century, then with increasing frequency around the millennium. The same applies to the image of Christ's removal from the cross, the Deposition, which appeared first in ninth-century Byzantium and parts of the West, but was only expanded into the Latin West in general in the later part of the tenth century. In the last century before the millennium, the church developed a new way of visualizing human suffering and the holy nature of Christ, based upon Carolingian notions of the sacraments, and evinced a heretofore unknown willingness to present them visually to the faithful. This is the difference between the crucifix form of the Ottonian era and the earlier Byzantine form, which seems to be the result of a dogmatic desire to defend against Monophysite teachings. Christ's Passion is emphasized and is thoroughly linked with eschatological expectations.

Around the turn of the millennium, many of these expectations tended to fulfill themselves in various places. The increased need to connect Christ's Passion and the Eucharist with the arrival of the Judgment spread. The concerns about the steadily approaching, unstoppable apocalypse made one search for consolation, for a path of salvation leading away from the danger, and for signs that manifested hope. I do not mean to suggest that fear of the end of the world only now became a sufficient intellectual catalyst for the deepened veneration of the cross or crucifix, or the only reason for the deepened evocation of the crucified Christ; but one must consider the fear of the rapidly approaching end, with the Judgment to follow, and the hope in the salvation represented by a God who took on human form yet triumphed over temptation to be connected. Each is an aspect of the other, and both lead to new expressions of piety. The crucified Christ on the cross, like no other image, reminds one not only of the Christian assurance of salvation but also of the temporal nature of earthly things. The image calls for sacrifice, humility, and commitment, it evokes the way of salvation available to all Christians, and it reminds one of the triumph over death, of the Resurrection, of Christ's return, and therefore the Last Judgment as well. It represents a sensory manifestation of the contemporary expectations of the world's end. This is not to maintain, however, that the image of the *living* Christ on the cross has lost its meaning and is no longer capable of stemming eschatological fears.

At this point we must consider the monks of Cluny again, first Abbot Odo and his *Occupatio*, then Radulfus Glaber. The seventh book of the *Occupatio* is dedicated to the theme of human temptation during one's time on earth. It closes with the quotation cited above concerning the arrival of Behemoth and the present revelation of Christ. The preceding sixth book, however, concerns itself with the cross: "Est ea crux quasi clavis, Pandat ut abdita seclis." The cross even overshadowed the pre-Christian history of the Israelites: "crux agit istud." Episodes from the early history of the Israelites typify Christian life, so it is also true that "scema crucis rebus multam concordat agendis." Birds in flight evoke the form of the cross, and "whoever reaches for the heights climbs in its shape. . . . Each believer must bind his limbs to the cross." The entire Passion of Christ unfolds in the form of the cross. Later, in the seventh book, Odo gives the following advice: "Whoever burns from the venom of the fiery serpent [a metaphor for human temptation] should look upon the cross, whose metallic image he possesses." Odo unites temptation, sin, cross, and the three-dimensional crucifix in his hortatory poem. Gazing upon the crucifix admonishes one to better arm oneself against the dangers of temptation and in this fortification to go strengthened into the Last Judgment. For the abbot of Cluny, the cult of the cross and the immediate expectation of the apocalypse are tightly bound together.

Perhaps building upon the theologians of late antiquity, Radulfus Glaber expands this typology of the Passion in the form of the cross in that he considers the imperial role played in the spread of Christianity and the acceptance of the cross by the believers (especially those of Cluny) as signs of the rapidly approaching end of the world. As Radulfus explains, when Christ hung on the cross, the barbaric east lay behind his head and consequently refused to accept his teachings, but the west lay in Christ's view, and soon became filled with the light of belief. His omnipotent right hand stretched toward the north, which also accepted his message. His left, however, pointed to the south, where his message had no acceptance. This world-encompassing sacred order (salutis . . . dispensatio) in the form of the cross "shows spatially and through piety and righteous judgment that the Creator is omnipotent, purely good, and truthful." It is not for mere mortals to attempt to understand why God made the parts of the world more or less capable of accepting His teachings. But be that as it may, "every day many sons of Adam leave his bosom for the saving protection of the Son of God. And therefore, the more the end of this world threatens, the more that which we have just discussed will occur." Even in this case, the increase of the faithful is a sign of the rapidly approaching end, and it occurs under the image of the cross. It is the duty of the emperor to guard this order of things. So that the emperor may "stand under the life-giving protection of the cross," before his coronation the pope gave the emperor Henry II a golden apple, bound by two jeweled bands and topped by a cross. Henry understood Benedict VIII's admonition and sent the insigne imperiale to the monks of Cluny, because "they tread the pomp of this world underfoot and determinedly follow the cross of the Savior." Even in dying, Radulfus's Abbot Odilo bore witness to his veneration of the cross.

There are further hints of the heightened eschatological significance of the cross and the crucifix around the turn of the millennium, even if they do not reflect as direct a connection with apocalyptic expectations. I can mention only a few here. As already discussed, the visual image of the Last Judgment has a long tradition, with its roots in late antiquity, but around the year 1000 it adopted new elements that, for our purposes, are revealing. Christ's wounds and the instruments of his suffering and, especially, in keeping with Matt. 24:30, the large passional cross were greatly emphasized. The images of the Reichenau School, closely connected with the Ottonian court, show them with special clarity, since they agree partially with the hermit Albuin's description, in which an angel carries the *triumphale signum* before the Lord, who approaches the judgment seat. The Psalter of Aniane (*Audi tellus*) connects the return of Christ with the cross that goes before him (*praevium signum*). Ademar of Chabannes was frightened by a glowing crucifix dripping with blood that appeared to him at night.

Before the millennium, the Cologne cathedral possessed two large-scale crucifixes, that of Archbishop Gero (969–76), now lost, and the remaining one of his second successor, Everger (985–99), who according to the Vision of St. Vaast can apparently not find salvation in the afterlife. Everger's successor, Heribert (999–1021), the recipient of Albuin's tract on the Antichrist and virtue, asked that he be carried before the older cross "in the center of the church." This awe-inspiring crucifix is mentioned by Thietmar of Merseburg, and its commissioner, Gero, placed a splinter of the holy cross and an oblation in its split upper portion. Gero himself asked to be buried beneath this cultic object, in order there to await the heavenly Judge. The Benna crucifix in Mainz from the time of Willigis has already been mentioned. "Its belly is full of reliquaries and precious stones" and was meant to be disassembled. It was mounted only on special holidays or on the occasion of a prince's or king's visit, and then "only high up in the church, on a beam" (probably the triumphal arch).

Bishop Bernward of Hildesheim (993–1022) was another faithful venerator of the cross. He was responsible for commissioning four, perhaps even five, crosses, the largest of which held stones from Christ's tomb. His bronze gates at the church of St. Michael offered an additional crucifixion scene. We may connect Bernward with a manuscript Bible of the Hildesheim cathedral (MS 61). Its only illumination depicts a dedicatory scene dominated by a radiant jeweled cross. The bishop signed documents "dominicae passionis signo manu propria." Bernward lays buried under an additional cross, chiseled into a crypt cover plate of his own design in the St. Michael's church, which is dedicated to the Virgin Mary and the "salvation-bringing, venerable, life-giving cross." He waits there in the special protection of the angel of the Resurrection (Jude 1:9), until that time when he stands face-to-face with his Savior. The new, independently conceived campaign of church construction itself may be seen as a visual typification of the heavenly Jerusalem.

It is not just these isolated examples of cross veneration which allow us to connect Bernward's veneration of the cross with apocalyptic expectations; rather, it is their collective presence, increased through inertia, which bears witness to the heightened consciousness of sin in the bishop of Hildesheim and to his religiosity oriented toward the Last Judgment. The connectedness of "judgment" and "cross," which had manifested itself only sporadically in the past, is actually characteristic of the Ottonian period. The sign of the Son of man that points to the Judgment can be the crucifix itself, as in the St. Vaast visions. The Savior arrives at the Judgment *in cruce praeparatus.* He speaks to the assembled multitudes, saints and angels, and reminds them of his suffering: "As I hung on the cross for you, so now do I appear before you. . . . Observe my wounds!" As he begins to separate the saved from the lost, he changes: "at that point he becomes the great and powerful king."

Other examples of this connection abound. The legend of Pope Sylvester II as magician and partner of the Devil unites three apocalyptic elements in a revealing way: the evocation of the actual year 1000, the Jerusalem pilgrimage, and the cult of the cross. For in the Holy Cross church in Rome, God sent down a lightning bolt that hit the pope, thereby saving his soul, which had been given up for lost. The abbot and archbishop Gauzlin of Bourges commissioned artisans from Italy to paint a crucifix for the monastery of St. Benoît in Fleury. A procession celebrated its completion, and it assumed its place behind the Resurrection altar. Bishop Ulrich of Orléans, one of the pilgrims to Jerusalem in 1033, brought back a large splinter of Christ's cross from Constantinople. One should also mention a contemporary cross, the Viennese imperial cross of King Conrad II, which was constructed to house another splinter of Christ's cross also brought back from Constantinople, and the somewhat older Lothar cross of Aachen. Conrad II's Viennese imperial cross overshadowed the holy lance, which it literally incorporated, to become the most significant reliquary in the treasure hoard of the German kings. The Lothar cross in Aachen may have been a gift of Otto III or the French king Lothar and may have been fabricated in Cologne, but it was certainly constructed before the turn of the millennium. It represents the tradition of the jeweled crosses in its depiction of the heavenly Jerusalem and the announcement of the Second Parousia, but its reverse (that is, the side facing rearward in a processional column) contains the image of the crucified Christ. We have already pointed out the prevalence of millennial expectations in Otto III's circle, and Lothar was the son of Queen Gerberga, to whom Adso dedicated the *De antichristo,* and he was therefore also a member of the family of emperors of the Last Days. A manuscript illumination depicts the Danish king Cnut and his queen, Emma, placing a large cross upon an altar; the only other illumination in the manuscript is a depiction of the Last Judgment. In this case, too, the cross points to the Last Judgment, which the manuscript's royal commissioners are depicted as awaiting. And to introduce a last, later example, the *Cantilena de miraculis Christi* of the early Middle High German poet Ezzo sings of the world's creation and the cross. It was composed for the great pilgrimage to Jerusalem in the year 1064, whose eschatological sense is well documented.

Should one attempt to connect the expectation of the world's end with this new form of reliquary veneration? The cult expanded rapidly during this period shortly before the year 1000, and during this time numerous large and small pilgrimages occurred to reliquaries that had experienced only local veneration in the past. What expectations, what hopes, motivated the pilgrims on their often difficult journeys? Reliquaries became plastic and sculptural after the ninth century and took on the shape of enthroned saints. This fashion expanded rapidly in the tenth century. But why were they so enthusiastically received?

Bernhard of Angers calls one such reliquary sculpture a *maiestas*. The lost figure of Mary of Clermont-Ferrand is the oldest known example, and the Ste.-Foy statuette of Conques is the oldest extant example (984/1005 in its present form). An image of the Madonna is the subject of a newer vision, the vision of Robert, abbot of Mozat. Its commissioner mounted it on a column in the holy of holies of a church, which is decorated to look like the heavenly Jerusalem. The images of the Savior, the Virgin Mary, and the archangel Michael adorn its apse. The figure of Mary rests upon a large plate of jasper, the first foundation of the New City (Apoc. 21:19), appearing like the one who sits on the throne "like the stones jasper and carnelian" (Apoc. 4:3). Before its completion, this figure of Mary was the object of a struggle between flies (the symbol of the Devil and his troops) and bees (representing holy chastity). This scene resonates with the apocalyptic struggle of St. Michael and his forces with the dragon that threatens the pregnant woman. The throne and the term *maiestas* refer to attributes of the Last Judgment. The symbolism of the majestic Mary points, then, to the apocalypse. Of course, Bernhard does not mention a connection between the cultic images and an *immediate* end of the world, but he wrote (around 1013–20) without certain knowledge of the intentions of their artists and commissioners. Learned scholastics observed the veneration of these statues with astonishment, and they were reminded of the idols of antiquity. The Christian images, too, served the function of apotropaic protective gods.

This applies apparently to all these cult figures, independent of their form (enthroned image or statue) and reliquary function. The faithful flock to them for protection. But protection from what? Perhaps Gauzlin of Bourges and Fleury may again provide an answer. As he lies dying, he asks to be carried into the crypt of St. Mary's church of Châtillon-sur-Loire, "whose altar holds a wonderful statue of Mary (*idea*) carved from wood, with a figure (*forma*) of our Savior's Ascension into Heaven. There he threw himself to the floor, as though he already stood before the tribunal of the Just Judge, and entrusted himself and those whom he had governed according to God's will to the prayers of Jesus Christ." After receiving the last rites he was carried back to his sickbed, where he died shortly thereafter. "As though he already stood before the tribunal of the Just Judge"—the cult of the figurines is an association with the Last Judgment.

Even the theologically enlightened Bernhard of Angers, who had dismissed the images at first, murmured a prayer as he approached the *maiestas* of the saints. Half in jest and half in earnest, he uttered a prayer that perhaps reflected the intentions of the others gathered around him: "Saint Foy, a part of whom rests in this image, help me on the Day of Judgment!" Do both image and Judgment, then, belong together more or less from the beginning? Does the historical proximity of the Judgment seek the sensory form and "real" presence of the one who should protect? This question, too, must remain unanswered but should not be prematurely negated.

Apocalyptic expectation and pilgrimage in England had long exhibited a close relationship by the turn of the millennium. One can imagine an Anglo-Saxon pilgrim with the Old English homilies in the famous Vercelli manuscript (Bibl. Capit. CXVII) in her or his hands. Continental Europe followed around the turn of the year 1000. It was at this point that the pilgrimages to Jerusalem and Santiago de Compostela became "events for the masses." Numerous individual pilgrims and massive processions journeyed to the Holy Land during this time (such as in 1026–27). Numerous Holy Sepulchre churches were built in the West during this period, too, a testament to the pilgrimages' effectiveness.

It is again Radulfus Glaber who delivers to us the significant information on this phenomenon. Around the thousandth year after Christ's death, more people make the pilgrimage to Jerusalem than ever before. Astonished, one asks, "What does it mean?" And one learns, "It announces nothing less than the arrival of the rumored Antichrist, who plans to arrive at the end of the world." Radulfus is not at all comfortable with the situation. He is afraid that pilgrimage to Jerusalem contradicts the goals of the Antichrist and leads even the chosen into temptation. Still, he does not doubt that the Righteous Judge will reward the faithful for their troubles. For all these reservations, the interpretation of the pilgrimage as a sign that the Antichrist is approaching "now" arises, not from the criticism of the pilgrimages, but from the attitudes of those who make them. Also, it is not the pilgrims to Jerusalem who are the first to be affected by millennial fears. Rather, it is their predecessors who made shorter pilgrimages to the local reliquaries. The fear of the coming apocalypse makes the pilgrimage to Jerusalem more attractive, and it is not just simple, uneducated people who set out on this difficult journey. Radulfus mentions that Bishop Ulrich of Orléans made a pilgrimage to Jerusalem in 1028. Six years later the chronicler Ademar of Chabannes died there, and in the year thereafter Duke Robert of Normandy died on the pilgrimage and was buried in Nicaea. The example of these three important persons should suffice.

The connection between apocalyptic beliefs and pilgrimage did not end with the thousandth year of Christ's Passion, Resurrection, and Ascension. Its latent effect continued. Some pilgrims from the upper nobility and even bishops set off on a pilgrimage to Jerusalem in the years 1064–65. They were "driven by fear, as if the last day has arrived, since in this year the Easter festival falls on March 27, Annunciation Day, the day to which Christ's Resurrection is attributed [in the old calendars]." This report comes from the earlier *vita* of Bishop Altmann of Passau. Its author considered the frightened pilgrims to be the victims of popular superstitions (*vulgari opinione decepti*). Although he, of course, wrote at a safe distance from that fearful year, he excused no one from the unjustified fear: not the bishop, Gunther of Bamberg; the scholastic Ezzo; Conrad, the (future) provost of Passau; even his own hero, Altmann; or, especially, the person who sent them off, the empress of that region plagued by signs, Agnes of Aquitaine. They all set off on "that troubled way" (*per artam viam*). They left their homeland, families, and riches behind and carried the cross in order to follow Christ. We have no reason to believe that the contemporaries of the turn of the millennium were any less fearful than their grandchildren or, despite their fears, less capable of ordering their affairs in the temporal world and making a career for themselves.

There are other examples of a changing piety. In the Irish eschatological tradition the archangel Michael is the apocalyptic conqueror of the Antichrist.

Latin authors also attribute this role to the warrior angel. Conscious of his sin, Otto III made a pilgrimage to Monte Gargano. The second visionary of St. Vaast received his instruction about the "imminent" arrival of the world's end from Michael. The feast day of St. Michael includes a reading from Apocalypse, uncommon during the rest of the church year. We may draw from this the conclusion that a connection exists between eschatological attitudes around the turn of the millennium and the enlivened cult of the archangel. The conception and image of Michael as the master of the scales of justice when souls are weighed at the Last Judgment began and spread in the ninth century. In this context we may also understand Bishop Bernward's choice of Michael as patron in the founding of his church at Hildesheim.

All that has been described up to this point does not represent a random simultaneity of a number of chaotic, isolated individual events. Rather, all is tied up in a close theological relationship. It would be irrelevant and inappropriate to single out individual elements and ascribe causality to them or to attempt to eliminate some individual developments as irrelevant. The process at work here is the gradual Christianization of the medieval world by means of the outer forms and intellectual means made possible by the Carolingian Renaissance. The tension created by the certainty of the end, threateningly near yet nebulously distant, and by the accumulating epiphanies of the Antichrist is an inseparable aspect of this process. The expectation of the Antichrist corresponds to the increasing awareness of evil in the world.

In the tenth century, diabolical powers gained more and more territory in the imaginations of contemporaries. In fact, the Carolingian and Ottonian eras offer significant reference points for the history of the Devil. Odo's assertion that "Behemoth, the king of evil, makes his joyous entry" is a particularly accurate marker of this religious and intellectual-historical change in Latin Christianity. On his deathbed, his successor, Odilo, defended his soul from the Devil, who wished to claim it: "I warn you, enemy of the humanity whom you seek and whom you can ruin, do not aim your attacks and secret treachery at me. For the cross of the Lord is with me." Satan's diabolical might rose up threateningly in the world, increased its influence, and worked its magical deceit ever more effectively. Every unusual event was attributed to its influence. In art, "demonic figures," especially in the context of images of the world's judgment, became suddenly more and more common. The place of hellish punishments for sinners, the "Stygian" sea of flames, Satan's soul-consuming gullet, the terror-inducing ugliness of evil—all these were depicted visually and began to stir the emotions. More and more visionaries described their descents into Hell or at least glimpses into the hideous abyss. The interest of Adso or his patroness in the Antichrist was nothing more than an aspect of this development. The growing tendency to consider the Devil as real and present manifested itself in the eschatologically determined fear of the coming Judgment and the warning call to penance, since, of course, the world's end was introduced by the triumph of evil.

It is no surprise that, in these circumstances, the sensitivity to the presence of false Christians, who were always considered the multitudinous minor "antichrists" who would precede the great Antichrist of the Last Days, increased. The anonymous monk of Saint-Germain in Auxerre reminded the bishop of Verdun of this when he evoked Augustine's interpretation of Gog and Magog as "inmanissima persecutio haereticorum." Gog is the heresiarch and Magog is his retinue. This *persecutio* by the heretics was to grow toward the end of the world; the contemporaries of the turn of the millennium believed that they were indeed witnessing a growth in the number of antichrists. Heretics appeared in Italy, Sardinia, and Spain. Radulfus Glaber instructs, "This sign fulfills the prophecy of John, since he announced the period of 1,000 years, and that Satan would be unleashed." Ademar considered the heretics of Orléans and Toulouse to be "messengers of the Antichrist," "who pray to the Devil" and "tempt as many men and women in the various countries of the West as they can."

"The Jews recognize their sinful nature late," when the Lord returns "to judge the peoples of the world," states Albuin, who adheres to the chronological events of the Last Days familiar to him through Adso. Only at the last are the Jews to be converted to Christianity. Until then they excitedly await the arrival of the Antichrist. He will be one of their own. He will be born in Babel out of the lineage of Dan and will rebuild the Temple and win his people to his side. They will in turn honor him as the Messiah, even though Enoch and Elijah will turn at least a few of them against him. This was old, accepted knowledge among Christian theologians, current since the patristic era. The presence of Jews around the turn of the millennium was a reminder, then, of the approaching end, and in this heightened climate of fear, anger was easily inflamed against the Jews, those worshipers of the Antichrist. The Antichrist had been interpreted as deriving from the Jewish tradition for many years. Fulbert of Chartres criticized the Judaic teaching that the Messiah will come only on the day of the Last Judgment.

The anti-Semitism of the turn of the millennium received fresh nourishment from the expectation of the Antichrist. The Jews became the veritable pavers of the way for his arrival. When Caliph al-Hakim, the *princeps Babilonis* (according to Radulfus Glaber) or *rex Babilonius* (according to Ademar), attempted to close or even destroy the Church of the Holy Sepulchre in Jerusalem under chiliastic influence in 1009 and began to see himself as the Messiah, Christians believed he was revealing himself to be the Antichrist, and the verdict in the West was fixed: Jews from Orléans had goaded him on, and a false monk had delivered their message to him. The concern that Ademar expressed has already been discussed. Glaber observed that afterward Jews everywhere were persecuted, killed, drowned, or driven to mutual suicide. Today, Glaber's report is usually considered an exaggeration. But, in the face of the dearth of documentary evidence, one must not completely dismiss the idea that the persecution of the Jews during this time—Rouen in 1007, Mainz in 1012 and Rome in 1020—was occasionally motivated by millennial fears. In Rome during that time an earthquake occurred on Good Friday, after the *adoratio Crucis*, because—it was believed—the Jews in the synagogue had denigrated the image of the Crucified One at the same hour. Pope Benedict VIII learned of the event and commanded that the guilty be executed. The uproar abated immediately (Ademar, *Chron.*, 3.52).

V

We have barely touched upon our topic, and yet our discussion already has grown too lengthy. To formulate a brief synopsis, the awareness of the end of time grew increasingly during the Carolingian era, and the tenth and eleventh centuries are characterized by an especially heightened awareness. Commentators repeatedly pointed out how little time remained. The end, unpredictable in advance of its occurrence, will arrive "soon" and "suddenly," and no one can be dissuaded of this certainty. This "certainty" actualized the expectation of the end of time as in no other period since Christian antiquity and led to the investigation and explanation of contemporary "signs" against the backdrop of the apocalypse. Religious expression did not remain unaffected. One may not apply a simple cause-and-effect schema to the anxiety and fear derived from knowledge of the imminent end and contemporary expressions of religiosity. Rather, fear and religious expression fueled a complex system of effects that is more substantial than an "arbitrary," insignificant simultaneity. Analysis of contemporary events, Christian belief, and religious practices influenced each other simultaneously. Their influence upon each other served to strengthen the belief among contemporaries that they were interconnected. Liturgy, artistic expression, forms of religious life, and monastic and church renewal received their impetus from this interconnectedness.

Of all the authors who discounted "millenarianism," or the belief that the end of time is immediately upon them, either by remaining silent on the issue or explicitly discounting it, none completely rejected the fundamental idea that the end will come at some point. What is rejected is its premature announcement and the notion that its arrival may be predicted in advance. Even though the "eschatological ideal of monasticism" was one of the strongest motivations for monastic living and the expectation of the end of time, it was not only monks who were caught up in the belief that the end was near. On the contrary, an abbot like Abbo of Fleury warned against actualizing the end by attempting to fix the time of its arrival, and it was only with the help of a monk that a bishop of Verdun was able to allay his fears of the end of time. Eschatology is not explainable in terms of, nor is it limited to, a particular status. Academics, preachers, artists, simple monks, and influential prelates incorporated the fear of the end, nourished it, and were anxiously affected by it. Still others attempted to minimize the fear and expectation. Even so, certain areas and communities of common discourse exhibited an unusually high sensitivity to fear of the end of time: "Cluny," Aquitania, northern Spain, France, York, and even parts of the Ottonian realm. Lotharingia was perhaps affected earliest, then Italy, and even later some areas of Saxony. What is remarkable is that in all instances, leading intellectual contemporaries grappled with the question. One gets the impression that increasing levels of education, monastic and ecclesiastical reform efforts, and millennial expectations were closely interconnected.

The results of our investigations in no way lead to the spectacle of Romantic, sensational decline, as depicted by Jules Michelet or the historical novelist

Felix Dahn. There was no paralyzing shock, no blinding desperation, and no deadening resignation. Nothing is found like

> Tomorrow at the twelfth hour
> Hurrah! The End will the World devour!

The poetizing professor of history believed that this captured the desperate tone of the year 1000. One may certainly strike the "terrors of the year 1000" from the historical annals, but not the increasing, anxious expectation of an approaching world conflagration or a collective fear fueled by the recognized and acknowledged inability to be certain of its arrival "now." At least some contemporaries were thoroughly affected. Barely an area of religious and intellectual life remained completely unaffected by eschatology. Those who shared this fear were not "merely a few fanatical figures," whose "desperation" concerning "fleeting unpleasantries" made one "hope for miracles." The end of the world and the approaching judgment are universal Christian tenets that, in the decades around the year 1000, became especially actualized against the backdrop of current events. This actualization led to the most disparate of consequences. And, of course, things temporal, the *temporalia*, were judged anew against things "eternal" and found lacking. One would not expect it to have been otherwise among Christians of the year 1000. But the concerns of daily life continued and dulled the millennial fear. They pushed it back or eliminated it completely, and it was renewed again by the concerned preachers.

However, most modern historians who discount the *terreurs* have never concerned themselves with the history of human feeling, and most have not developed an adequate "theory of fear"—an *Angsttheorie*. Those theories that modern historians have developed are usually ahistorical and anachronistic. Even when they addressed this theme and the idea of Purgatory, Jacques Le Goff and Jean Delumeau did not discuss those *terreurs*. Of course, fear, the product of knowledge and ignorance, is not only a phenomenon of the late Middle Ages. Its fruits ripened in the time around the turn of the millennium as well, and it motivated people to conquer their fear with a flurry of activity. Images, sermons, theoretical constructs based on reason, the vision of the Devil, prayers, penance, church construction, and the general renewal itself all bear witness to it.

Fear also serves as its own censor. It is barely thematized in and of itself and is taboo, especially when one allows it to overcome oneself. In the bellicose world of the tenth- and early-eleventh-century nobility, nothing had a more discriminatory effect than the wailing and gnashing of teeth of those in fear's grip. Fear does, however, create for itself specialized release mechanisms, even if they are not identifiable as such. Fear almost demands of reason that reason prove it false and deny that its causes exist. Reason is given the task of conquering fear and sublimating it. The European breakthrough to a system of rational inquiry began in the late ninth century in the West Frankish Kingdom, grew in strength in the tenth, and by the middle of the eleventh century was no longer confinable. This could be the greatest triumph of that fear of the Great Unknown, of the Millennium, the time of whose arrival is concealed. It was in western France and Lotharingia, where the renewed culture of reason developed first, that the fear of the rapidly approaching end of time grew most strongly, and it grew there to a much greater degree than in those areas where this new critical methodology was barely in evidence.

NOTE

Editors' note: This chapter is a translation, by Scott Denlinger and Edward Peters, of the author's seminal article on the apocalyptic underpinnings of the turn of the first millennium, "Endzeiterwartung um die Jahrtausendwende," *Deutsches Archiv für Erforschung des Mittelalters* 45, no. 2 (1989): 385–473. Even though it is now over a decade old, this article still provides one of the best, most wide-ranging introductions to the problem and hence deserves to be accessible to a wider audience. Owing to space limitations, however, we have not included the author's extensive footnotes and scholarly apparatus; for these, the reader must refer to the original. We have, however, parenthetically cited several of the more important primary sources, particularly when those sources receive little or no treatment in the remainder of this volume. Johannes Fried is Professor of Medieval History at the Johann-Wolfgang-Goethe University, Frankfurt/Main.

I

The Apocalyptic
Year 1000
in Medieval Thought

2

Stalking the Signs: The Apocalyptic Commentaries

Guy Lobrichon

"Et vidi angelum descendentem de caelo . . ." (Apoc. 20:1)—this, in essence, is what those scholars living around the year 1000 found in the Apocalypse, just as it is what those of us who happen to peek into that book of the seven seals find even today. While no one will deny that such visionary language is quite familiar, I suspect that it is no easier to decipher now than it was in the era of Pope Sylvester II, Otto III, Abbo of Fleury, and the dissidents of the time.

Since the inter-testamental period, of course, both Jews and Christians have postulated an end of history. Over the centuries, and perhaps even today, Apocalypse 20 has played an essential role in the Christian understanding of the events that are to come in a future—near or far—that remains to be determined. Briefly, this is a drama that unfolds in four acts. In the first act (Apoc. 20:1–3), an angel holding a great chain descends from Heaven, seizes the dragon that is none other than the Devil, and binds him for a thousand years. The second act (Apoc. 20:4–6) sees the ones entrusted with judgment, and also the souls of those who had been beheaded, reign with Christ during the thousand years. At the conclusion of the thousand years, in the third act (Apoc. 20:7–8), the Devil is set free to start a terrifying war, besieging the strongholds of the saints and Jerusalem, the city of the elect. But act 4 (Apoc. 20:9–12) sees the Devil overwhelmed and the appearance of the throne inaugurating the Last Judgment.

Needless to say, the above little summary all too neatly clears up the difficulty that one encounters in reading the text. The scholars of the medieval West understood perfectly well that an alternative reading of the text, combining the first and second acts, is also possible. Their deep desire was for the thousand-year reign with Christ to exactly overlap with the thousand years during which the Devil is bound.

Things are not so simple for those who would read the Apocalypse attentively. Hence, it seems useful to undertake a cursory review of medieval exegesis, focusing upon a rereading of the interpretations that were projected on Apocalypse 20 during the early Middle Ages. Since detailing the vista of practical exercises on the Apocalypse around the year 1000 would prove to be a formidable task, I shall instead give an overview. This essay will zero in on the material that men and women had at their disposal in that remote time and then outline the exegesis in which the scholars of the late-tenth and early-eleventh centuries immersed themselves so as to understand and interpret the Apocalypse, and especially the redoubtable chapter on the Millennium.

Let us begin with a brief—if also somewhat pedantic—exposition of the elementary rules of the medieval hermeneutic, so as to more readily engage the logic of ninth- and tenth-century scholars. For this, it shall suffice to compare three texts of that period. Our authors—a monk and two anonymous writers—sought to calm the distress of their readers; herein we shall judge the degree to which they succeeded. A second facet of my study, touching upon a larger body of sources, will lead toward the deciphering of the strategies they employed and hence divulge and illustrate the indications of a veritable debate under way toward the year 1000. Here we shall see take shape and emerge both a certain urgency to renew the world and also a certain frenzied closure of these new possibilities.

I

The historian can only succeed at wondering about the conventions regarding the production of medieval exegesis, which constitutes a resource nearly completely unknown and unexploited by anyone other than theologians and a mere handful of researchers. But historians should rightly claim exegesis as a part of their "patrimony." These documents can make a weighty contribution and even update to some extent the representations that are usually current in the intellectual and cultural history of the Middle Ages. But heed the dangers and limitations of this documentation! There were a great many commentators on the Bible in the Middle Ages. One must know how to decipher the ponderous style of their Latin and also how to classify all of these men into circles of influence. It takes an iron will not to be misled by these sources.

Beginning with two foundational principles that Christians have used since the end of the first century—the harmony between the Old and New Testaments, and the typology that unites the events and figures of the Jewish and Christian Bibles—certain rules have guided the development of exegesis. Since we shall make use of them again, let me briefly reiterate them:

1. The Bible was the most amazing tool of communication for medieval societies. Even though a sacred book, it was nonetheless copied by the hand of man.

Not only did it contain the language of God, but in the hands of Jews and Christians it remained a code with a practical use for the different "textual communities" that received it. Thus, it was just as useful in learning how to read as in structuring the intellect. By its very nature the Bible was open to different readings by the different groups that used it. This also means that if it is necessary to advance an explication of the Christian doctrine of the "four senses of the Scriptures," the historian is obliged to seek it in the particular standing of the Bible, the tool of communication among each generation, rather than in any fundamental theological structure of the Christian faith. This in itself justifies the historical reading of medieval exegesis.

2. The interpretation of the Bible required *labor*. Even though a sacred book, it contained the Word of God in human languages. Thus, the literal sense was for each and every one the primary sense, both elementary and inevitable. It just as readily supported the task of grammatical analysis as it did a historical interpretation. Whoever omitted that primordial stage would be condemned to understand nothing in the sacred text. Nevertheless, no one— Christian or Jew—had the authorization to cling to the letter of the text. An interpretive effort is required to situate oneself rightly in the vast panorama of the communities of believers, and then it scarcely takes a minimum of experience to spot right away which faith community produced a given exegesis. *Sensus* does not equate to *historia*. The historical meaning is rooted in history. But that first, literal sense is never detached or freed from the other sense—spiritual and allegorical.

3. The interpretation of the Bible took shape in the certitude of the interpretation of human history. Even though a sacred book, it can witness to the ebb and flow of human history. The interpretation of the Bible is, by nature, cumulative; in other words, the history of exegesis advances by accumulation. Each commentator was obliged to become familiar with the survey of the grounds prior to tackling any problems himself. He was not required to repeat all that his predecessors had said; he was, however, obliged to take a position, even if only by his silence on some interpretations acknowledged up to that point. This bears considerable implications for the historian who stumbles into the intellectual landscape of medieval exegesis. Lacking knowledge of what lies below the surface, he risks being allured by the personal preferences of the author upon whom he has fastened. It is as though, in reaction to the powerful allure of the contemporary historian, the commentator on a given biblical book—such as the Apocalypse—chose to surround himself in an obstinate silence and close himself off from the inquiry of the historian or even, on the contrary, inspire all manner of delusions. Nevertheless, exegetical works can begin to speak—and even confess—as soon as one submits them to the trial of comparison. It therefore becomes necessary to equip oneself with a basic kit of possible exegesis; in other words, to plunge into the *longue durée* so as to understand the mechanisms of discernment, discovery, and innovation.

4. The Bible, a book of wisdom, is also the great statute book wherein the wise read the divine law that is fittingly applied to all human deeds. This was

true at least until the twelfth century, when recourse to civil and ecclesiastical law emerged definitively.

Having touched upon these first truths, we can now advance more confidently into the forest of medieval exegesis and return to those on the Apocalypse.

II

Preparing a survey of the exegetical principles of any given time entails three prerequisites. First, one must know how to manipulate the massive *Repertorium* of Friedrich Stegmüller. Second, one must know how to decipher the hieroglyphs of the manuscripts of the given period. Finally, one must not go astray in the common practices of the exegetes of the year 1000.

At the dawn of the eleventh century, the scholars of the medieval West had at their disposal a potent legacy from Christian antiquity: the Fathers had taken up the duty of defusing the anxieties that were born of reading the Apocalypse in the light of Christian history. Their task had been rendered none the easier for their willingness to include the Apocalypse in the biblical canon, despite the reservations of the Greeks of Constantinople. The generation of the year 1000 had at their disposal three other legacies: (1) that of erudites of all stripes, Scots and Irish, who had come from the British Isles; (2) that of the Iberians; and (3) that of the Carolingian Empire. For our purposes, we shall exclude that strange world familiar to us from certain elaborate manuscripts—those of Beatus of Liebana—since the evidence suggests with certitude that they received no attention north of the Pyrenees, despite the fact that there is an unilluminated copy in the library of St.-Amand-en-Pevèle. On the other hand, four works representative of two other exegetical traditions circulated in the mid–ninth century:

1. In the first place, there is the simple, clear, and widely disseminated commentary written by that inspired monk of the British Isles, the Venerable Bede.
2. Next is a seventh-century exegetical compilation that originated in Ireland and covered the whole of the Bible. This work—the *Bibelwerk* unearthed by Bernhard Bischoff, which also bears the title *Pauca problesmata*—was available to scholars in England, in the region around Paris, and in Germania.[1]
3. There was also the lengthy commentary of Ambrose Autpert, composed around 765 at St.-Vincent of Voltruno. This Italian monk, perched on the slopes of the Voltruno, lost himself in banter on moral reform even though there wasn't really an audience in the Benedictine monasteries (and, as for myself, I'll gladly pass over this commentary, too).
4. Finally, there arose at the Carolingian school of Auxerre a monk, Haimo, who composed a powerful synthesis. He followed in the footsteps of his predecessors, especially Ambrose Autpert, whose contributions he incorporated after his own manner.

Then, at the end of the tenth century, the exegesis of the Apocalypse entered into a long period of silence, which was interrupted only toward the year 1000.

Of course, this understanding is rendered tentative by an inventory that is still difficult to reconstruct. It remains to be seen what, in actuality, is contained in the folios dedicated to the Apocalypse in two manuscripts. One of these, from Ripoll (Barcelona Cathedral, 64), seems to preserve many of the works of Haimo of Auxerre. Above all, there are the last several pages of a manuscript that is jealously conserved at Cambridge in England (McClean 5, Fitzwilliam Museum); I have to date been unable to obtain a microfilm. I am most anxious to read this work, which is said to come from Clermont in Auvergne, as I am hopeful that it might possibly be able to cast some welcome light on the famous vision of the monk Robert, which was committed to writing there a bit after 984.[2] It is also necessary to cite the compilations of "Questions on the Old and New Testament," such as that which was undoubtedly copied in the Auxerrois in the tenth century. There one reads (fol. 3r–v) some very interesting responses to questions on the day and hour of the Last Judgment and on the place where the Antichrist will be born:

Tell me, when will the Lord come in Judgment, and at what hour? Response: His Advent will be on an Easter Sunday, in the hour in which he rose again, which is to say in the middle of the night.[3]

Question: Tell me where the Antichrist will be born, and in which city, and also from which people he will come, and for how long he will reign. Response: In the city of Babylon, which renders as "confusion" in our own learned tongue, where Nebuchadnezzar held the Jews in captivity; there the son of perdition, the Antichrist, will be born of the Jewish people, and of the tribe of Dan. He will come to Jerusalem and reign for two years and six months, but Enoch and Elijah will come before him and preach penitence to the people for three years. When this son of the Devil comes, he will apprehend and kill them, and have their corpses cast into the square, and that accursed one will not allow them to be interred. But after three and a half days, they will arise again and, in the sight of all, ascend into Heaven. [Then at the end of two and a half years, fire from Heaven will fell the impious, following which will come a peace of 46 days] for the refreshment of the saints who had fled into the mountains and caves. . . . Once 45 days are completed, the Lord will come in Judgment.[4]

Finally, from an unknown scriptorium, probably in York, there comes a strange work (Cambridge, University Library, Dd.10.16),[5] which draws its inspiration from Cesarius of Arles, Primasius, Isidore, Bede, and above all from the *Problesmata*. Its author, whom I shall call the Anonymous of York, does not reveal much of himself. At the very most, one can wager that he belonged to that illustrious milieu of the monastic cathedrals of Anglo-Saxon England, where despite the reforms under way, the dignitaries were far from living by the rhythms

of the Carolingian monasteries. Our first appraisal of the exegesis of the Apocalypse in the year 1000 bears essentially upon four of the works enumerated above:
Bede, the *Problesmata*, Haimo of Auxerre, and the Anonymous of York.

III

What is the Apocalypse? For us, just as for the medieval commentators, to include those around the year 1000, this question concerns a book situated in
history, written at the end of the first century by one of the Twelve Apostles (it
does not matter which one, since he was the one whom Jesus loved, the one
who rested his head on the breast of Christ during the Last Supper). And what
is this book about? Certainly, it is about, not universal history (this understanding of the Apocalypse appeared only in the twelfth century), but rather Christian history. In effect, the Apocalypse reveals the history of the world, from the
nativity of Christ until the end of time (*a natiuitate Christi usque ad finem mundi*).
Nonetheless, this book resists a simplistic reading. Thus, very early on, scholars armed with a subtle rhetoric were given over to dividing it into reasonably
logical parts. They discovered "recapitulations," repetitions that were so many
different representations of history. Each part, or recapitulation, reprises a cycle
of events from a different point of view. This is an ancient system.[6]

A historical interpretation has thus acquired a certain legitimacy. This comes
straight from the apologists of the third century, but at the beginning of the
eighth century, the Venerable Bede gave it a new life. It seems to me that, from
the eighth and ninth centuries, two concurrent strategies were concocted to
dissolve the phantasms of the Apocalypse. One of these, spearheaded by Bede,
proposes a deliberately historical reading. Still, it reprises each great sequence
as a representation of the history of the church from its origins until the coming of Antichrist and the final destruction. The other, that of the monk Haimo
of Auxerre, dominated the Continent beginning in the mid–ninth century. This
later strategy reveals that the Johannine book cannot be approached historically
but maintains only a spiritual reading emphasizing in particular withdrawal from
the world.

The Anglo-Saxon commentator of the year 1000 returned to the Bedan strategy in a grand manner. Could it be that this backward-looking choice contributed, more surely than Haimo, to diverting the specter of the imminent end of
time? Without doubt, this was Bede's own agenda. It happens that Bede was
not well received on the Continent. His commentary was copied with great se-
riousness in the ninth and tenth centuries, but in insignificant numbers compared to the overwhelming preponderance of Haimo's commentary. Should we
thus believe that the continentals perceived that Bede's strategy was insufficient
to dispel the danger, that they manifested a veritable mistrust in regard to Bede?
However, the intention was the same in the Anglo-Saxon realms, but it was
necessary to multiply the red herrings. Whereas Haimo directed all of his exegesis into an apology that scarcely masks the historical role of monasticism,
the Anonymous of York multiplies his recapitulations.

In regard to Apocalypse 20, Haimo, the Irish compilers of the *Problesmata*, and the Anonymous of York all smoothly unified the first two "acts" that we discussed above. There is no mention of any new earthly Kingdom between the persecution of the Antichrist and the Second Coming, or Parousia; all three identify the age of the church with the millennial reign (e.g., Haimo, *PL* 117:1186B). At the closure of the thousand years, in the third act (which is no more than the second act of Christian history), the Devil is unbound, and thus the persecution of the churches by the Antichrist begins forthwith. The "millennium" of Apoc. 20:4 coincides exactly with the age of the church prior to the final persecutions that, as all know, will last only three and a half years (Apoc. 10:11, 12:6). Following the example of Bede, the *Problesmata*, and the entire common tradition, the Anonymous of York set the scene prior to the Last Judgment ("si autem nouissimo iudicio vidisset, sedes non diceret animas, tunc enim cum corporibus suis erunt," ll. 30–32). There is nothing here beyond the most limited of traditions, beyond that ordinary silence to which we are all accustomed on the part of ecclesiastics concerning the impossibility and uselessness of knowing either the day or the hour.

But in scrutinizing the ecclesiastical millennium from one author to the next, a certain nuance emerges inescapably. Haimo considered that the binding of the Devil began with the Passion (*PL* 117:1182B), while the Insular commentators thought that the major event was the Incarnation. What does this mean? The Carolingian monk speaks of the discretionary power (*potestas*) of Christ (*PL* 117:1181D, where the key to the Abyss is the *discretio* of Christ) and digresses at length on predestination in an echo of Gottschalk's theology, even if his impulses in this direction are more tempered. The Auxerrois most certainly was not ready to follow the lead of Hincmar, and it is uncertain that Haimo consented to the theories of his student Heiric. On the other hand, the Anonymous of York reduced the interval of the Demon, although he avowed that no one can know the lot of God and that of the Devil (fol.101v). The founding of the Kingdom occurs with the descent of Christ in the flesh, prior to the Crucifixion, and from that significant moment on, Christ has the power of constraint—the power of the ban—over the Devil; the Crucifixion only finalizes this power.

There is a second nuance. For Haimo, the Kingdom is the time of the church. The Insular commentators, including the Anonymous of York, working around the year 1000, call it the time of the New Testament. This might seem to be splitting hairs, except that we must recall the extent to which they valued the wisdom of the Bible, which constituted a judicial code ("iudicium per sapientiam scripturarum," to cite the Anonymous of York [fol.101v]). Moreover, at the turn of the year 1000, the Anonymous of York witnesses to a particular consideration, more lively than that of his Irish predecessor, for the totality of the Scriptures, which are a veritable millennial banquet in the here and now. Should we see in this a theme of the Insular societies, an indication of a textual community in the process of formation, which explains why England did not experience the horrors of Continental dissidence? We shall leave this point unresolved and pursue our inventory of the Millennium.

Finally, there is a third nuance. Haimo praised the unabashedly Carolingian theme of the *dilatatio regni,* which encompassed the promise of a kingdom that would buttress all of the faithful and the prediction that it would not cease to expand throughout the world. Conversely, the Insular commentators proposed a collective model closer to the exemplar of the imitation of Christ; hereby they take up the Pauline invitation to "live with Christ." But doesn't this modify somewhat the representation of the church during the ninth century in the Carolingian realms? According to Haimo, the victory of the final act (Apoc. 20:11) is simply no more than that of the imperial church, the *multitudo populi* (*PL* 117:1189B). In the *Problesmata,* it is the victory of the resounding choir of the saints. At York, the Anonymous speaks of the immense "congregation" which henceforth forms the throne.

This brings us to the heart of the problem. These commentators carefully discarded inadmissible exegesis and, in a dense, formal language, pursued their task. The circle of readers of Haimo, of the anonymous Irish composer of the *Problesmata,* and (a narrower circle) of the Anonymous of York steadily challenged any interpretive deviance. The whole business proceeded just as it had been since the days of Jerome and Augustine. Not even the slightest whiff of millenarism rises from these texts, nothing of the beginning of the blessed time after the sealing up of the Antichrist: no controversy at all. Certainly this was repression or, rather, censure. Nonetheless, if the historian knows what to look for, and can read between the lines, he can glimpse another horizon of ideas, more real still. Beneath the appearance of more of the same, there lie many other possibilities that can emerge from the fog. They recombine with other faint, meager, almost imperceptible signs. This calls to mind those psalters of the end of the tenth century that, despite their sumptuousness, testify nonetheless to a double desire on the part of the Fleming Wolbodon, provost of Utrecht and later bishop of Liège (d. 1021),[7] as well as on the part of Abbot Otbert of St.-Bertin. In these, we have, on the one hand, an avowal of a quest for interior conversion and, on the other, the hope of an imminent victory by Christ. These are two indicators of an eschatology that was not as "realized" as is commonly thought, but was well and truly consequent—an expectation of an imminent end that is discretely affirmed but repeated. So, too, this recalls, even more precisely, the traces of that tradition arising from the Apocrypha that one can read in a Burgundian manuscript now in Paris (Paris, BN lat. 614A, fol. 3); these traces blossom in the work of Adso of Montier-en-Der.

IV

As we have seen, two conflicting traditions have existed since the mid–ninth century: the historical tradition of the Venerable Bede, who left the future indeterminate; and the allegorical tradition of Haimo, who preached a realized eschatology accomplished by the redemption on the cross. In effect, these are two strategies of silence that keep the lid quite tight on the pot. Still, we have just seen the outlines of an intermediate tactic adopted around the year 1000 by the Anonymous of York. He employed two effective tools to shake up the earlier edifices, and in the resulting cracks he let a new thought take root. Rather than deliver a single interpretation, he preferred to multiply the possibilities—he admitted, for example, four different interpretations of Apoc. 8:1 (fols. 80v–81r)—even as he covered their tracks. He cloaked matters with ambivalence: at the point where the historical exegesis could admit the present irruption of the Last Judgment (Apoc. 11:15–18), he chose to abandon his readers to their own choice, allowing that this scene might occur either in history or also in the future, at the Judgment (fol. 89v). Better yet, he overwhelmed the historicism of Tyconius and Bede. These latter commentators had carefully avoided identifying any of the "states of the church" with any historical period. Our Anglo-Saxon erudite no longer has states of the soul but deals in ambiguity; he speaks of the African persecutions as though they were those of the Vandals, as well as those that he imagined were even then occurring in the southern Mediterranean.[8]

Hence, this text proffers certain novelties. Prominent among these is a modified representation of the confines of the world: for example, "Asia, figura mundi elevati de peccato Adae ad Deum per Christum." This is new. According to Bede, the Asia of the Apocalypse "signifies the arrogant haughtiness of the earth in which the church is in pilgrimage" (PL 93:135c). Even more soberly, the Insular glossator of the Problesmata simply identifies Asia with the world (Paris, BN lat. 11561, fol. 203v). The soil here is strangely rich. The figure of Asia is wed to the image of the cross, which is itself an image at the center of world history, which the Anonymous of York divides into two ages: before the cross (see his treatment of Apoc. 20:3) and after. This Asia coils about the body of the Crucified One—which abounds in the illuminations of Anglo-Saxon manuscripts—and therefrom draws its redemption. Here it seeks sanctification, whereas in the eighth century it sheltered the forces of evil. This Asia serves as the object of a new manner of viewing things at the threshold of the eleventh century. I cannot help but connect this with the recrudescence of pilgrimages to the Holy Land and perhaps with the appeal that, to follow Hans-Martin Schaller, Pope Sergius IV sent to the Christians in 1010, thereby inaugurating the idea of the Crusade that followed. In this regard, I am struck by the importance given by the Anonymous of York to the concept of vengeance: the divine vengeance that finally comes to pass; the *vindicta*, the blood and the terror, on the evil.

Despite his habitual pessimism, Haimo of Auxerre let a bit of unalloyed optimism show through while treating the Carolingian theme of the *dilatatio regni*. The scope of this idea, as transmitted to our text of the year 1000, was somewhat extended. From all those who had been converted and baptized, the shadows of sin will have dissipated (fol. 104r, on Apoc. 22:5). But even this is still only the faintest whiff of a thought that was never extinguished: that of an earth without evil, of a tranquil millenarianism; a thought that manifests itself, as it was current in the course of the eighth through eleventh centuries, well before Joachim of Fiore, in the idea that there will be forty-five days of peace for the survivors of the cataclysm before the Parousia.

The Anonymous of York was very well able to let escape, just for a moment, the dream of a future peace and an unexpected respite after the great persecution of the Antichrist. Regarding Apoc. 9:5, he evokes a five-year interruption of the persecution. This is a strange temporal determination, such as the commentators rarely authorized. Most certainly, even if their Apocalypse describes great calamities, it ought also to show the indications of successive respites. Better yet, our Anonymous introduced the Last Judgment in his discussion of Apoc. 14:1; this was not in vogue. But he also consented to see in the coming of the Lamb to Mount Zion an aid, *adiutorium*, brought by Christ to the church after the persecution of the Antichrist and well before the Last Judgment. It is this that slips into the possibility of the Millennium.

Certainly, this phase is every bit as important as the period of time that should elapse between the persecution of the Antichrist and the Last Judgment. It remains to be seen whether, in its nuances, it is a period of respite, a breathing space, before the Parousia or a period of blessedness before that same Parousia.

There is a second novelty in the Anonymous of York. The apparently unfailing prestige of monasticism underwent a slight twisting, as though the author surreptitiously intended to distinguish himself from his predecessors, who were all so proud of their monastic privileges. It seems to me that the opposition *ecclesia theorica–ecclesia actualis* does not capture the division between monastic society and lay society. This seems borrowed from the theology of Pseudo-Dionysius and signifies rather the spiritual duality of the church, which is divided between the divine hierarchy and the temporal hierarchy of the church.

There is a third observation: the strong, classical tone of opposition to temporal powers in the Apocalypse takes an unheard-of form in comparison to previous commentaries. Here there is an intermingling of ecclesiastical and lay hierarchies. The twenty-four thrones and the twenty-four elders of Apoc. 4:4 are able to signify, respectively, the order of the *subiecti* and that of the *praepositi*: the lords sit upon their subjects. This is not at all like the ordinary depiction of prelates and subjects. The ecclesiastical hierarchy, ordinal and ordinary, becomes blurred at this moment, only so as to make room for the hierarchies viewed from Heaven. These are, moreover, those of lay society: some are appointed by God and by the church to a specific task, while the others are the subjects. Regarding the commentary on Apoc. 6:6, I am inclined to see the traces of a rediscovery of all before God and on the Day of Judgment: great or small, all have the same reward. The outlines also appear of a fraternal, egalitarian world. The monk of York did not go that far, but it is suggested. It is apparent how, in this communitarian ambiance, the demand for social equality might slip into the picture. Revolution? Mutation? I challenge anyone to find analogous documents for the previous centuries; I have been unable to do so.

Finally, there is a curious notation, quite exceptional in the exegetical literature, on the duties of the prince (fol. 86v, on Apoc. 10:2). Might this not be an indication that this commentary emanated from a princely circle, from a milieu such as that of Aelfric? In this case, the Anglo-French tradition of the Apocalypses could have arisen from a particularly Anglo-Saxon political ideology, which was revisited by the Plantagenets. It was for the king, the princes, the great men, and the lords to arm themselves against perils and make war. It was their duty to protect the "little people" and shelter them from danger in fortified places. As a justification for a sound bipartite social division, this clearly underlay the tripartite divisions of both Aelfric and Adalbero of Laon; it was also an apology for the seignorial system, if not for a new servitude. Certainly, the stress laid so heavily on the duty of preaching rejoins, in effect, the preoccupations of Aelfric.

V

We may bear three striking impressions away from our wanderings through early medieval exegesis of the Apocalypse. The first consists in the acknowledgment that, in this tranquil river of an entirely restrained exegetical tradition, suddenly a patch of "white water" bubbles up around the year 1000. It seems to me rather significant that it emerges in a most peripheral zone of the mainstream (which is distinctly Continental) of commentaries on the Apocalypse: at the point where the imperialism of the collective traditions is the least burdensome or, rather, perhaps, where a certain liberty of tone can best express itself. It remains, therefore, to reconsider the local exegetical traditions and productions, which we know very poorly, and thereby situate more clearly the milieu from whence this curiosity arises.

The nonexegetical documentation invites a second remark, indeed a hypothesis, on the remoteness of the monastic origin in comparison to secular life and ways of thinking, especially in the realm of western France, around the year 1000. It seems that the monks worked toward "de-eschatologization," as opposed to the secular clergy and laity, who all in all lived through it more closely. Around the year 1000 there were plenty of naïfs, or "Judaizers"—such as the count of Sens, whose memory still provoked Raoul Glaber to fury[9]—who were incapable of distinguishing between *spiritualia* and *historia*. There were plenty of stupid prelates who wielded the unbridled anathema, or who tripped themselves up over too literal and obliging exegesis, such as the great Fulbert of Chartres, who botched his interpretation of the rain of blood that fell on the fields in Aquitaine.[10] What did the monks say about the innovations of the pope and the emperor in those times, with the one exalting his throne and the other reserving a seat for himself in every cathedral of his empire? The monks resisted them in celebrating almsgiving and prayer as the surest remedies against the threat and also in pouring increased efforts into an exegesis that was more and more spiritual. The contrast is readily apparent when comparing the two responses to King Robert on the rain of blood: Abbot Gauzlin refused to scrutinize the Bible, while Fulbert turned to a far more shrill literalism. Is it really astonishing, then, that the exegetical renewal at the end of the twelfth century no longer arose from the monks but from the cathedral circles?

Finally, I should make a third point. The trails that the Anonymous of York explores recall to mind the great themes that I have often noticed in the lofty endeavor of the school of Laon at the end of the eleventh century and in the first few decades of the twelfth. The work of the Anonymous of York leads toward that of Anselm of Laon, who echoes several of the better strains of the Anglo-Saxon author. If one can believe that the great innovations of Anselm were aimed at resolving a crisis in the societies of northern France in the final years of the eleventh century and the beginning of the next, should not one wonder if a similar urgency lay at the source of the meditation by our Anglo-Saxon, which has been immured to this day in the thick silence of history? Without doubt, it was but a trial attempt at the resolution of a crisis, and certainly without a future, since in the era of the year 1000 there were plenty of ebbs and flows. Such is amply attested in the chronicles, diplomatic acts, and contemporary liturgies.

NOTES

Editors' note: This paper was originally presented at the "Conference on the Apocalyptic Year 1000" in Boston, Mass., November 4–6, 1996, and has been translated for inclusion in this volume by David Van Meter. Professor Lobrichon is Maître de Conférences at the Chaire d'Histoire de l'Occident Méditerranéen au Moyen Age, Collège de France.

1. On the *Catena patrum de sacra scriptura* of the Carolingian era, see F. Stegmüller, *Repertorium Biblicum Medii Aevi* (Madrid, 1950–80), nos. 10409–411; B. Bischoff, "Wendepunkte in der Geschichte der lateinischen Exegese im Frühmittelalter," in *Mittelalterliche Studien*, vol. 1 (Stuttgart, 1967), pp. 25–73, no. 1.

2. See M. Goullet and D. Iogna-Prat, "La Vierge en majesté de Clermont-Ferrand," *Marie* (Paris, 1996).

3. "Dic mihi quale ueniet dominus ad iuditium aut quale hora? R. Die dominico, ipsa hora qua resurrexit, id est media nocte, in pascha erit aduentus eius." Cf. the Celtic catechism in Vat. Reg. lat. 49, which was studied by A. Strobel, "Die 'keltische Katechese' des Cod. Vat. Reg. lat.49 über das Hebräerevangelium," *Zeitschrift für Kirchengeschichte* 76 (1965): 148.

4. "Interrogation. Dic mihi ubi natus erit Antichristus, in qua ciuitate aut de quale gente erit aut quantum regnabit? R. In ciuitate Babiloniae quae latine confusio interpretatur, ubi Nabucodonosor iudeos captiuabat, ibi natus erit filius perditionis Antichristus de gente Iudeorum de tribu Dan, et ueniet in Iherusalem et regnabit annos duos et menses sex, sed Enoch et Helias ueniet antequam ille et predicabunt ad populum poenitentiae per tres annos. Et ueniente isto filio diaboli, adprehendet illos et occidet illos et iacebunt corpora eorum in platea et non dimittet ille maledictus ut ponant eos in monu- /[3v]-mento, et post tres dies et dimidium, resurgunt et uidentibus cunctis ascendunt in caelum." The forty-six day peace is "pro recuperatione sanctorum quae fugierunt in montibus et in speluncis. . . . Expletos XLV dies ueniet dominus ad iuditium."

5. See Elzbieta Temple, *Anglo-Saxon Manuscripts 900–1066* (London, 1976), nos. 53, 60, 92.

6. See Yves Christe, ed., *De l'art comme mystagogie: iconographie du Jugement dernier et des fins dernières à l'époque gothique: actes du colloque de la Foundation Hardt tenu à Genève du 13 au 16 février 1994* (Politiers, 1996).

7. See K. Reinhardt, "Die Glossen des Wolbodon-Psalter," in *Egbert Erzbishof von Trier, 977–993: Gedenkschrift der Diözese Trier zum 1000. Todestag*, ed. F. J. Ronig, vol. 2 (Trier, 1993), pp. 153–62.

8. On Apoc. 9:12, see fol.85r; on Apoc. 10:11, see fol.87r, l. 24.

9. *Historiae*, 3.6.20; cf. *Chronique de St.-Pierre-le-Vif de Sens, dit de Clarius: Chronicon Sancti Petri Vivi senonensis*, ed. Robert-Henri Bautier and Monique Gilles, with Anne-Marie Bautier (Paris, 1979), p. III.

10. Andrew of Fleury, *Vie de Gauzlin, abbé de Fleury. Vita Gauzlini, abbatis Floriacensis Monasterii*, ed. Robert-Henri Bautier and Gillette Labory (Paris, 1969), pp. 164–67.

3

Adso of Montier-en-Der and the Fear of the Year 1000

Daniel Verhelst

Christianity has repeatedly experienced events that have given rise to eschatological expectations. Over and over again, people have emerged who, with ambitious curiosity, have attempted to evaluate the duration of world history. Likewise, the legend of the Antichrist and the expectation of the end of the world were, at various times in late antiquity and the Middle Ages, perceived by some as a threatening reality. Both of these themes had a traditional basis, passed on from one generation to the next. Cosmic and biological omens, religious commotion, and heresies often triggered such expectations. Hence, annals, chronicles, and hagiographical works tend to give normal cosmic events an apocalyptic twist. When the writers of these works experienced the destruction or the rapid remodeling of a political, economic, social, or cultural situation, they easily resorted to expressions like *mundus senescit* or *mundi termino appropinquante.* Due to a lack of perspective and an overly narrow "biblicism," their diagnosis of the times was rather pessimistic. Disasters were often interpreted as the beginning of the great calamities expected at the end of the world.

Numerous sources bring us into contact with this eschatological anxiety. Though reviewing all this evidence would be too much of a digression to pursue here, we may fairly wonder whether these utterances of fear are attributable to a genuine eschatological awareness or are simply the product of an anxiety psychosis. Based on the available historical documentation, it is extremely difficult to form a safe and correct opinion in the extensive field of collective psychology, where affective motives, convictions, legends, superstition, fear, and love complicate issues. The difficulties connected to the problem of eschatological expectations can be solved only by a thorough analysis and correct value judgment of the source material.

This value judgment, however, is possible only when the vision of contemporaries who were overwhelmed by cosmic, biological, and political powers is taken into account. In the face of all sorts of dangers to body and soul, medieval people must have felt a certain impotence. So impelled, perhaps they spontaneously accepted an apocalyptic mood that obliterated all historical perspective as they projected their current concerns onto the approaching and even already-begun end of the world. Faithful Christians took Christ's teachings about the Last Judgment very seriously, that is, literally.[1] To the faithful, the Parousia meant the final cessation of all misery, to which there was no other possible end. The last sentence of the Apocalypse usually became a sincere prayer: "Etiam venio cito. Amen. Veni, Domine Jesu."

It is precisely this promise that can explain the great interest in the Apocalypse and other eschatological literature during the first millennium.[2] In their exegetical comments, authors could not extricate themselves from the cosmic visions inherent to the apocalyptic genre, and thus these comments contributed to the excessive growth of apocalyptic expectations, against which even Bede had to react.[3] These themes remained principally reserved to the clerics and monks, although they reached into the more educated masses via sermons, mural paintings, and sculpture.[4] The homily in particular must have been an important factor in the spread of such notions, yet traces of a homiletic apocalypticism are confined to a few reactions to sermons that, by means of reckless exaggeration, gave occasion to unjustified calculations and prophecies.[5]

Of course, the unfolding of the Antichrist legend and the simmering of eschatological expectations were not, as it is sometimes claimed, solely to blame for some of the lurid exaggerations proffered by reform-oriented moralists and polemicists, who, naturally, dramatized the situation with a kind of rhetorical abbreviation. Still, such rhetoric must not be minimized and labeled as a purely literary game,[6] even if such a presentation does not conform well to the theological status quo in matters dealing with eschatological knowledge. Such rhetorical devices were taken seriously in the world of the intellectuals themselves and could, through the homily, penetrate into and affect a broader layer of the population, one that was not always able to control its collective imagination. As a result, a series of apocalyptic themes began to appear recurrently in popular lore. For example, the cosmic omens of the world's end were linked in the famous poem *Fifteen Signs*, ascribed to St. Jerome by Bede.[7] Similarly, the Antichrist as an eschatological figure was a cherished motif in medieval literature.

The role of the Antichrist in the final, eschatological drama had already been articulated no later than the middle of the tenth century.[8] At the request of Gerberga, wife of the French king Louis IV d'Outremer, Adso, the abbot of Montier-en-Der, in northeastern France, developed an enduring synthesis of the eschatological vision and tradition: *De ortu et tempore Antichristi*. Written sometime between 945 and 954, it reformulated the nine centuries of eschatological speculation that had surrounded the turning points in the development of the Christian world. His work quickly became the basic text for the legend of the Antichrist, which, after the tenth century and with the infusion of new influences, produced numerous new apocalyptic scenarios and prophecies in Latin literature as well as in the vernacular.

While Adso's letter unquestionably played a very important role in the formation of subsequent legends, it has always evoked questions about its original context and immediate impact. What factual meaning did his treatise have? What was Gerberga's real motivation in requesting the work? Did she merely inquire out of common curiosity, or was her question motivated by a real and pressing feeling of fear? Why did Adso answer in the terms he used? How many others, besides Gerberga, heard his reply, and what kind of an impression did the work have on them?

The prologue and the epilogue, in which Adso dedicates his work to Gerberga, indicate that the queen had made a formal request. The content of that initial request, however, is lost, making it difficult to understand Gerberga's motivation. Did she hear discussion about the Antichrist in the royal court, or did she perhaps want to know more about this terrifying person out of "scientific" interest or apocalyptic anxiety? The text can give no clear answer to these questions, since any position taken by the historian automatically becomes an argument either for or against the existence of Gerberga's apocalyptic anxiety, fear of the Antichrist, and belief in the end of the world. The debate thus infinitely loops back on itself, forming a logical impasse.

We do know with certainty, however, that Gerberga was an educated woman,[9] and that Adso's allusion to her learning does not necessarily have to be considered only a *captatio benevolentiae*.[10] One cannot consider the prologue and the epilogue as a simple dedication to curry favor. It seems unlikely that Adso wrote his treatise without somehow meeting a real need. We could, as a motive for Gerberga's request, posit a certain curiosity about theological problems.[11] If, however, one takes Adso's prophetic visions about the Frankish kings seriously, then Gerberga's question is somehow to be found in the context of Adso's answer. The motive of the request, then, not only lies in the prologue itself but is also implicitly phrased in Adso's treatment of the Antichrist legend.

Adso's answer to the question of the Antichrist's imminent arrival was clearly negative. He could not accept such a notion, although he admitted that the Roman Empire had, for the greater part, been destroyed. Without ignoring this reality, he clung to the conviction that the Roman Empire would not disappear so long as the Frankish kings remained heirs to the imperial title. To justify the continued existence of the fourth world empire, Adso asserted a *translatio imperii*.[12] The Frankish Empire was the direct continuation of the Roman Empire, whose existence, in his own time, rested on the Reges Francorum. The Franks had become the imperial heirs through Charlemagne, and in this manner, their kings ensured the continuity of the Roman Empire, and thus the delay of the Antichrist.

Adso's eschatological hopes for the Frankish royal dynasty apparently were not weakened even by political realities. The last world emperor would also be a Frank and would possess the former territories of the Roman Empire to their full extent. This last emperor would willingly abdicate his crown and scepter in Jerusalem, thus signaling the end of the Roman-Christian Empire. According to Adso, the ideal *imperium* would be created when the universality of the Roman Empire coincided with the universality of Christianity. Christianity was thus given the task of merging its material, corporate body—the church—with the empire; this cooperation would end, with the greatest Christian emperor laying aside his crown, only at the end of time. Since the end of the Roman-Christian Empire no longer depended on coincidence or chance but on an eschatological act of free will by the Frankish emperor, Adso thus condemned all pessimism among the ranks of the powerful. This politically comforting thought of Adso's marked an important elaboration upon the legend of the last emperor (see 2 Thess. 2:2 and 1 Cor. 15:24) that had slowly developed in the Frankish Empire, merging with the legend of Charlemagne.[13] In his prophetic vision, Adso saw the pretended continuity between the Roman and Frankish Empires as a powerful argument against exaggerated eschatological expectations. The *imperium* itself was given a positive eschatological meaning.

However, in spite of Adso's optimistic outlook, it remains impossible to determine whether or not Gerberga's request had been posed out of personal fear or due to unrest among her subjects. It is certain, however, that around the middle of the tenth century an intense eschatological foreboding existed in western Francia and Lotharingia. Abbo of Fleury tells how, in his youth, he had heard a preacher announcing that the world would end in the year 1000, and how, in Lotharingia, a rumor spread that the world would come to an end when the feast of the Annunciation and Good Friday occurred on the same day (March 25), which took place in 992. Abbo, who was a novice in 958, reacted vehemently to such beliefs in his *Apologeticus ad reges Hugonem et Rotbertum*. Adso wrote his own treatise between 945 and 954. Some have sought an explanation for the preponderance of eschatological theory in this period in the monastic revival, because people often turned to the monasteries for answers to difficult problems.[14] Gorze, the head monastery of the Lotharingian reform, with which Adso cooperated his whole life, was already very active in this field. This influence cannot be ruled out, but the other events of the time surely must have played a more important role.

Gerberga did not live in a quiet and peaceful period. To begin with, Louis IV was always having trouble with his dukes. In 945, he was imprisoned in Rouen and turned over to Hugh the Great. Otto I intervened, but it was not until 949 that Louis IV was able to return to his capital city at Laon. Between 947 and 950, the king had to call five times on Otto I, his brother-in-law, for help against Hugh the Great, and Gerberga had to do so once. Moreover, at the beginning of 945, during Liudolf's revolt against his father, Otto I, the Hungarians invaded Bavaria and Swabia. Soon thereafter they swept through Lotharingia, the West Frankish Kingdom, Burgundy, and Italy on their way back to their homelands. Duke Conrad the Red of Lotharingia used the Hungarians against Bruno of Cologne and Reginald of Hainaut, accompanying them as far as Maastricht. Cambrai was sacked and burned. Laon, Reims, and Châlons-sur-Marne were likewise plundered.[15]

It may well be that these very events gave rise to a letter concerning the Hungarians addressed to a bishop of Verdun. Historians have traditionally attributed the letter to Remigius of Auxerre and identified its addressee as Dado of Verdun.[16] However, the known manuscripts contain neither the author's name nor that of the bishop of Verdun. In some of these manuscripts, the place of the name was left blank, and others have only an initial, which varies considerably. R. B. C. Huygens has argued that the letter was written in the second half of the tenth century, and that the bishop of Verdun referred to was Wicfridus (962–72).[17] As this interpretation rests on a possible reading or writing error in the initial only, it seems to me that Wicfridus's predecessor Berengarius (940–60) is an equally plausible candidate. If so, it would mean that the letter was directly related to a current event—the invasion of the Hungarians—which must have left a deep impression upon the people who endured it. The identities of the writer and the addressee can, however, be firmly established only if new evidence surfaces. Despite these uncertainties, this letter is a good source of knowledge about the Hungarians and the reactions that this nation of conquerors elicited. The Hungarians had indeed inspired the conviction among quite a large group of people in western Francia and Lotharingia that the end of the world was near. The author of the letter reacted against such historical interpretations of Ezekiel 38:8 and the link between apocalyptic expectations and the invading Hungarians.[18]

During Louis IV's reign the Normans also caused further uncertainty and unrest. Their invasions undoubtedly created a climate of great anxiety, even if we are to credit A. D'Haenens's opinions on the real extent of their depredations.[19] The alliance of Hugh the Great with the Normans against Louis IV, the imprisonment of Louis, and his son's captivity as a hostage of the Normans hardly helped to relieve the feelings of insecurity among Gerberga's subjects.[20] On the contrary, the Norman military expeditions probably exacerbated the fear and anxiety afflicting the victims of previous invasions.[21]

In light of this, it certainly would not be preposterous to hypothesize that Gerberga's request to Adso was prompted by an apocalyptic unrest that she shared with her subjects. In the letter concerning the Hungarians, as well as in those of Adso and Abbo, the reactions against the fear of the imminent end of the world were similarly reassuring. However, though nobody had anything to fear, not one of these authors denied the *existence* of this fear. On the contrary, they silenced the voice of anxiety by addressing this very fear. Reading Adso's "biography" of the Antichrist attentively, one may conclude that the Antichrist is taken seriously as a real person who is due to appear at the end of the world. Adso was describing a character whose appearance on the scene was still far in the future but whose coming was apparently expected soon by Adso's contemporaries.[22]

Adso clearly believed that one day the real Antichrist would actually come, but when this would happen remained God's secret. This answer in itself should have been conclusive, but Adso was apparently convinced that he could better combat the unrest by expressing, as the believers did, the same conviction in the concrete form of political expectations and desires. This attitude, however, concealed a great danger. By coupling the Antichrist's coming with the collapse of the Frankish Empire, Adso created the opportunity for further speculation and interpretation. His declaration was too closely bound to his time to remain valid and conclusive in the future. His prophetic vision appealed to his contemporaries because it evoked in them, with a certain nostalgia in this period of heavy troubles, memories of the idealized empire of the Franks under Charlemagne, where "real" peace reigned.

However, when the perception of the cohesion and continuity of the Frankish Empire disappeared, a new interpretation of the text was needed to prevent Adso's prophetic vision from becoming a fresh stimulus for new concrete expectations of the Antichrist and eschatological fear. It is in this context that the success of Adso's treatise must be examined and the existence of so many different versions explained. If Adso had stuck to the doctrinal position that nobody needed to worry since the world's fate is entirely up to Divine Providence, his work would have remained nothing more than an exegetical homily urging people to be vigilant and ready for the Lord's Day. Adso's treatise, however, portrays both the Antichrist and the last emperor as two real future characters who would impinge on Frankish political history. In this way, he opened the door to new speculations and supplied new material for a prophetic and eschatological future.

Many historians have not discerned this prevailing tone in Adso's work because they have always approached the treatise with a preconceived opinion. Everyone had to be either in favor of or opposed to the idea of an apocalyptic millenarian movement around the year 1000. At the end of the sixteenth century, Baronius wrote about a rumor concerning the apocalyptic fear,[23] and in 1769 W. Robertson elaborated further upon this fear.[24] Everything that could in some way support this thesis was tracked down and brought together. Michelet adopted those certainties in his *Histoire de France* and described the fear with so much bravura that every liberal reader had to be impressed.[25] The fear of the year 1000, with all its romantic exaggerations, thus entered into popular conceptions, as well as many great works and textbooks.[26] Until the end of the nineteenth century, historians were convinced that the anxiety about the end of the world and of the Antichrist became more and more acute as the year 1000 approached. A climax was reached on the eve of the terrifying year, and the people abandoned hope, awaiting the final hour lost in penitential prayer.[27]

François Plaine started a reaction against this by taking a closer look at the texts used as evidence. Nowhere did he find a text connecting the end of the world with the "year 1000"—999 plus 1—per se.[28] His revision was readily adopted.[29] He was, however, perhaps too overzealous in debunking the myth, for this revision swung the pendulum rather a bit too far in the other direction. People now tended to consider that these rumors had only been the pure fantasy of historians.[30]

Both advocates and opponents, however, have excessively fixed their attention on the rather artificial "year 1000." This is a fatal conceptual illusion, because it posits a relationship that never existed. For the people of the tenth century, the end of the millennium did not, after all, coincide with the "year 1000" in our chronology, since the technicians of the sacred could not unanimously determine the beginning and the end dates of the thousand years.

Dionysius's era system was not generally accepted, and Abbo of Fleury and, later, Sigbert of Gembloux placed Christ's birth twenty-two years earlier than Dionysius did. Even fixing the starting date of the Christian era at the birth of Christ was not universally accepted. Some chroniclers used the *era passionis*, whereby the end of the first millennium only came in 1033. The scholars of the tenth century still had important divergences of opinion about chronology, which explains why, in their works, the end of the first millennium may fall in a stretch of time that runs from 979 to 1033 c.e.[31] During this period, more so than at other moments, some people thought that the end of the world was imminent.[32]

Nevertheless, Adso's treatise has always been rejected by the enemies of the "year 1000 theory" because it was written before the crucial date, and because, they argued, it addressed only a queen's unimportant theological curiosity. Yet, it is clear that there was a lot more to this royal interest than the mere "scientific" answer might first suggest. The reaction contained in the letter about the Hungarians, similar to the responses of Adso and Abbo, forces us to accept that, from the middle of the tenth century, there was a powerful latent anxiety about the end of the world among the clergy and more educated laymen in Lotharingia and the West Frankish Kingdom. This anxiety was prophesied by the Bible and tradition and was expected to herald the coming of the Antichrist. From time to time, under the influence of catastrophe, war, and apocalyptic omens, these eschatological delusions and expectations flared up vehemently.[33]

This collective illusion, present among the clergy and the scholars and passed on to the people, would ensure that even after the year "999 + 1," alarming messages could not help but be noted. It was, in many ways, a self-fulfilling prophecy. In 1009, the destruction of the Church of the Holy Sepulchre took on an apocalyptic meaning.[34] In 1012, a dying abbot had a vision in which the archangel Michael also played an eschatological role, fighting the Antichrist and announcing the end of the world.[35] The mass pilgrimage to Jerusalem in the year 1028 also appeared to some as a sign of the Antichrist's coming,[36] while in 1033 a terrible famine and plague, according to Radulfus Glaber, announced the end of the world.[37] All these occurrences fell within the period of expectation but were not credited as utterances of an eschatological anxiety by historians who, again and again, wanted to see the year 1000 of our calendar as the "glorious morning" of the new millennium.[38]

Eschatological unrest belonged to the irrational elements that undoubtedly weighed heavily in everyday life, but that, for a variety of reasons, we have difficulty today in analyzing. The end of the tenth and the beginning of the eleventh century certainly represented an important turning point, when, under the influence of such great figures as Adalbert, Gerbert, Otto III, Odilo of Cluny, and Fulbert of Chartres, the foundation of a new awakening and a new society was laid. Yet, in the same period obscure, irrational beliefs, such as fear of the Devil and fear of a God who, it was believed, repeatedly announced the end of the world by means of omens, remained strong. Eschatological expectations grew from the basic notion of a disturbed world order and found a place in the fantasy of the community whenever a deep anxiety pressed heavily upon the people. In this way and at that time, both fear and hope were nurtured by all sorts of miraculous omens and the prophetic visions of the men who were counted among the wise.[39] In much the same manner, Adso proclaimed hope when fear was prevalent.

NOTES

Editors' note: This paper originally appeared as "Adso van Montier-en-Der en de angst voor het jaar Duizend," *Tijdschrift voor Geschiedenis* 90, no. 1 (1977): 1–10. It has been translated by An Van Rompaey, Richard Landes, and David Van Meter for inclusion in this volume.

1. W. von den Steinen, *Der Kosmos des Mittelalters: Von Karl dem Grossen zu Bernard von Claivaux* (Bern, 1959), pp. 22, 52–53, 132.

2. D. Verhelst, *De ontwikkeling van Adso's tractaat over de Antichrist: Bijdrage tot de studie van de eschatologische literatuur in de middeleeuwen* (Leuven, 1969); D. Verheist, "La préhistoire des conceptions d'Adson concernant l'Antichrist," *Recherches de Théologie Ancienne et Médiévale* 40 (1973): 52–103; H. D. Rauh, *Das Bild des Antichrist im Mittelalter: Von Tyconius zum deutschen Symbolismus*, Beiträge zur Geschichte der Philosophie und Theologie des Mittelalters, n.s., vol. 9 (Aschendorff, 1973), pp. 98–153; G. Vezin, *L'Apocalypse et la fin des temps: Etude des influences égyptiennes et asiatiques sur les religions et les arts* (Paris 1973), pp. 25–42.

3. Verhelst, "La préhistoire," pp. 82–85.

4. Ibid., pp. 85–87.

5. Abbo Floriacensis, *Apologeticus*, PL 139:471A: "De fine quoque mundi coram populo sermonem in Ecclesia Parisiorum adolescentulus audivi, quod statim finito mille annorum numero Antichristus adveniret, et non longo post tempore universale judicium succederet: cui praedicationi ex Evangeliis ac Apocalypsi et libro Danielis, qua potui virtute, restiti. Denique et errorem qui de fine mundi inolevit abbas meus beatae memoriae Richardus sagaci animo propulit, post quam litteras a Lothariensibus accepit, quibus me respondere jussit; nam fama pene totum mundum impleverat quod, quando Annuntiatio Dominica in Parasceve contigisset absque ullo scrupulo finis saeculi esset."

6. See H. De Lubac, *Exégèse médiévale: Les quatre sens de l'Ecriture*, t. 2, vol. 1, Théologie, vol. 42 (Paris, 1961), p. 532: "Mais on se tromperait sur leur portée si l'on ne voyait pas que, sauf peut-être chez certains ermites, elles constituent alors, plus que jamais, un véritable genre littéraire, adopté par des moralistes, des réformateurs et des polémistes qui dramatisent volontiers la situation."

7. I have noted over 180 manuscripts of the Latin text. Furthermore, there are numerous examples of the French, German, and English versions. See. E. Sommer, "Die fünfzehn Zeichen des Jüngsten Gerichtes," *Zeitschrift für Deutsches Altertum* 3 (1843): 523–30; C. Michaelis de Vasconcellas, "Quindecim signa ante Judicium," *Archiv für das Studium der Neueren Sprachen und Literaturen* 46 (1870): 33–60; G. Noelle, "Die Legende von den fünfzehn Zeichen vor dem Jüngsten Gericht," *Beiträge zur Geschichte der Deutschen Sprache* 6 (1879): 412–75; K. Bartsch and A. Jetteles, "Die fünfzehn Zeichen von den Jüngsten Gericht," *Germania* 29 (1884): 402–4; H. E. Sandison, "Quindecim signa ante iudicium: A Contribution to the History of the Latin Versions of the Legend," *Archiv für das Studium der Neueren Sprachen und Literaturen* 124 (1910): 72–82; W. W. Heist, "Four Old French Versions of the Fifteen Signs before the Judgment," *Medieval Studies* 15 (1953): 187–89, 191–93; H. Eggers, "Fünfzehn Zeichen," in *Die deutsche Literatur des Mittelalters:*

Verfasserslexikon, vol. 5 (Berlin, 1955), cols. 1139–48; R. Mantou, "Le thème des 'Quinze signes du jugement dernier' dans la tradition française," *Revue Belge de Philologie et d'Histoire* 45 (1967): 827–42; B. Lambert, *La tradition manuscrite des oeuvres de Saint Jérôme*, t. 3B, no. 652, Instrumenta Patristica, vol. 4 (Steenbrugge, 1970), p. 540.

8. Verhelst, "La préhistoire," pp. 52–103.

9. R. Holtzmann, *Geschichte der sächsischen Kaiserzeit (900–1024)* (Munich, 1961), p. 228.

10. Adso Dervensis, *De ortu et tempore Antichristi necnon et tractatus qui ab eo dependunt*, ed. D. Verhelst, CCCM 45 (Turnhout, 1976), p. 20.

11. E. Pognon, "L'an mille," in *Mémoires pour servir au temps présent*, vol. 6 (Paris, 1947), p. VII: "Sa dédicace à Gerberge évoque les curiosités théologiques de la reine et non telle ou telle erreur dont elle serait la proie ou qu'elle désirerait voir réfuter." F. Plaine, "Les prétendues terreurs de l'an mille," *Revue des Questions Historiques* 13 (1873): 151.

12. W. Goez, *Translatio Imperii* (Tübingen, 1958), pp. 74–75.

13. Verhelst, "La préhistoire," pp. 100–103.

14. K. Reuschel, *Untersuchungen zu den deutschen Weltgerichtdichtungen des XI. bis XV. Jahrhunderts*, vol. 1, *Gedichte des XI. bis XIII. Jahrhunderts* (Leipzig, 1895), p. 2.

15. Flodoardus, *Annales*, anno 954, *PL 135*, col. 480D: "nimiaque peracta depraedatione, cum praeda magna captivorumque multitudine regnum ingrediuntur Ludowici. Sicque per pagos Veromandensem, Laudunensem atque Remensem, Catalaunensem quoque transeuntes, Burgundiam intrant. Quorum non parva manus tam proeliis quam morbis interiit." Holtzmann, *Sächsische Kaiserzeit*, p. 159.

16. *Epistola R. ad D. episcopum Virduensem*, *PL* 131:936D–968C.

17. R. B. C. Huygens, "Un témoin de la crainte de l'an 1000: La lettre sur les Hongrois," *Latomus* 15 (1956): 225–39.

18. Ibid., p. 231, ll. 94–106: "Ac primum dicendum opinionem quae innumeros tam in vestra quam in notra regione persuasit frivolam esse et nihil veri in se habere, qua putatur deo odibilus gens Hungrorum esse Gog et Magog ceteraeque gentes quae cum eis describuntur. . . . Dicunt enim nunc esse novissimum saeculi tempus finemque imminere mundi, et idcirco Gog et Magog esse Hungros, qui numquam antea auditi sunt, sed modo, in novessimo temporum apparuerunt."

19. A. D'Haenens, *Les invasions Normandes en Belgique au IXe siècle: Le phénomène et sa répercussion dans l'histographie médiévale*, Université de Louvain, Recueil de travaux d'histoire et de philologie, s. 4, 38 (Leuven, 1967), p. 162.

20. Flodoardus, *Annales*, anno 945, *PL 135*, col. 464B.

21. Ruotger, *Vita Brunonis*, 40, ed. I. Ott, *MGH, SS*, rer. Germ., n.s., vol. 10, p. 42, l. 9, to p. 43, l 8: "Imminet regno illi, quod reticendum non est seva clades, Nordmannorum gens, quibus in piratico latrocinio non sunt alii exercitatiores. His ex magna iam parte preda erat populus dissensione et civili pernitie assuetus. Quod illis superfuerat inter se domestica seditione consumpserant. Egit autem provida dispensatio rectoris nostri, qui, quoniam hominem se esse intellexit, humani nihil alienum a se putavit, egit, inquam, ut ad se quasi ad tutissimum portum confugerunt omnes, qui quitem et pacem amarent. Ipsorum etiam barbarorum immanitatem et intolerandam dudum ferociam mitigavit. Siquidem eodem tempore et rex eorum Haroldus cum magna sue multitudine gentis regi regum Christo colla submittens, vanitatem respuit idolorum."

22. A. Vasiliev, "Mediaeval Ideas of the End of the World: West and East," *Byzantion* 16 (1942–43): 479; H. Focillon, *L'an mille* (Paris, 1952), p. 53.

23. C. Baronius, *Annales ecclesiastici*, anno 1001, vol. 11 (Cologne, 1624), col. 2: "idemque non-nullorum vana assertione praenuntiatus mundi postremus, vel ipsi propinquus: quo nimirum revelandus esset ille homo peccati, filius perditionis, dictus cognomine Antichristus. Fuerant ista in Galliis promulgata; ac primum praedicata Parisiis, iamque vulgata per orbem, credita a compluribus, accepta nimirum a simplicioribus cum timore, a doctioribus vero improbata."

24. W. Robertson, *The History of the Reign of the Emperor Charles V*, vol. 1 (London, 1769 [1798]), p. 24: "An opinion which spread with rapidity over Europe about the close of the tenth and beginning of the eleventh century, and which gained universal credit, wonderfully augmented the number of credulous pilgrims."

25. J. Michelet, *Histoire de France*, vol. 2 (Brussels, 1834), p. 301: "Cette fin d'un monde si triste était tout ensemble l'espoir et l'effroi du Moyen Age. Voyez ces vieilles statues dans les cathédrales des Xe et XIe siècles, maigres, muettes et grimaçantes dans leur roideur contractée, l'air souffrant comme la vie et laides comme la mort. . . . C'est l'image de ce pauvre monde sans espoir après tant de ruines."

26. F. Hurter, *Tableau des institutions et des moeurs de l'Eglise au moyen âge*, tran. from German by Jean Cohen, vol. 3 (Paris, 1843), pp. 287–89; C. J. L. Simonde de Sismondi, *Histoire des Français*, vol. 2 (Brussels, 1846), pp. 342–44; C. A. Auber, "De l'an mille et de sa prétendue influence sur l'architecture religieuse," *Revue de l'Art Chrétien* 5 (1861): 48–56; M. Jager, *Histoire de l'Eglise catholique en France*, vol. 4 (Paris, 1863), pp. 311–12; E. Gebhart, *Moines et Papes: Essais de psychologie historique* (Paris, 1896), p. 306; F. Ermini, "La fine del mondo nell'anno mille e il pensiero di Odone di Cluny," in *Ehrengabe für Karl Strecker: Studien zur lateinischen Dichtung des Mittelalters* (Dresden, 1931), pp. 29–36.

27. E. Gebhart, "La Saint-Sylvestre de l'an 1000," in *Au son des cloches* (Paris, 1906), p. 135: "Le dernier jour de l'an 1000, les Romains . . . dirent adieu à la lumière, à l'espérance, à la vie et persuadés que le monde touchait à son heure suprême, de tous les points de la ville sainte, ils s'acheminèrent en pleurant vers la sombre forteresse où, dans une froide cellule, veillaient et priaient les deux vicaires de Dieu, les deux rois de terre, le Pape et l'empereur, Sylvestre II et Otton III."

28. Plaine, "Les prétendues terreurs," pp. 154–64.

29. R. Rosières, "La légende de l'an mille," *Revue Politique et Littéraire*, 2d ser., 1878, pp. 919–24; H. von Eicken, "Die Legende von den Erwartung des Weltunterganges und der Wiederkehr Christi im Jahre 1000," *Forschungen zur Deutschen Geschichte* 23, no. 2 (1883): 305–18; J. Roy, *L'an mille: Formation de la légende de l'an mille, état de France de l'an 950 à l'an 1050* (Paris, 1885); P. Orsi, "L'anno mille, saggio di critica storica," *Rivista Storica Italiana* 4 (1887): 1–56; P. Orsi, *La paure del finimundo dell'anno 1000* (Turin, 1891), p. 32; G. L. Burr, "The Year 1000 and the Antecedents of the Crusades," *American Historical Review* 6 (1900–1904): 429–39; F. Duval, *Les terreurs de l'an mille*, Science et religion, vol. 467 (Paris, 1908), p. 94; F. Lot, "Le mythe des terreurs de l'an mille," *Mercure de France* 201 (1947): 639–55; B. Barbatti, "Der Heilge Adalbert von Prag und der Glaube an den Weltuntergang im Jahre 1000," *Archiv für Kulturgeschichte* 35 (1953): 132–33; G. Fourquin, *Les soulèvements populaires au Moyen Age*, Collection SUP, vol. 12 (Paris, 1972), p. 112.

30. Pognon, "L'an mille," p. VII: "Depuis plus de cinquante ans, les érudits et les historiens sérieux constatent et affirment en toute occasion que le monde chrétien passa sans appréhension particulière du Xe au XIe siècle." P. XIV: "Ainsi

pendant tout le Xe siècle, un seul personnage de nous connu a assigné au monde régénéré par le Christ un terme de mille ans, et rien ne permet d'affirmer qu'il ait effrayé beaucoup de gens, bien au contraire." P. Cousin, *Abbon de Fleury-sur-Loire: Un savant, un pasteur, un martyr à la fin du Xe siècle* (Paris, 1954), pp. 55–56.

31. F. W. N. Hugenholtz, "Les terreurs de l'an mil: Enkele hypothesen," in *Varia Historica aangeboden aan A. W. Byvanck* (Assen, 1954), p. 114.

32. Radulfus Glaber, *Historiae*, IV, praefatio, *PL* 142:669B: "Post multiplicia prodigiorum signa, quae tam ante quam post, circa tamen annum Christi Domini millesimum in orbe terrarum contigere, plures fuisse constat sagaci mente viros industrios, qui non his minora propinquante ejusdem Dominicae passionis anno millesimo fore praedixere; quod utique evidentissime contigit."

33. Focillon, *L'an mille*, p. 53; Hugenholtz, "Les terreurs," pp. 118–20; J. Hourlier, *Saint Odilon, Abbé de Cluny*, Bibliothèque de la Revue d'Histoire Ecclésiastique, vol. 40 (Leuven, 1964), p. 67; G. Duby, *L'an mil*, Collection archives, vol. 30 (Paris, 1967), p. 146. Many authors have accepted the existence of a certain latent fear: E. Wadstein, "Die eschatologische Ideengruppe, Antichrist, Weltsabbat: Weltende un Weltgericht in den Hauptmomenten ihrer christlich-mittelalterlichen Gesamtenwicklung," *Zeitschrift für Wissenschaftliche Theologie* 38 (n.s. 3) (1895): 553; P. Alphandery, *Les idées morales chez les heterodoxies latins au début du XIIIe siècle*, Bibliothèque de l'Ecole des Hautes Etudes, sciences religieuses, vol. 16, no. 1 (Paris, 1903), p. 189; E. Bernheim, *Mittelalterliche Zeitanschauungen in ihrem Einfluss auf Politik und Geschichtschreibung*, vol. 1, *Die Zeitanschauungen: Die Augustischen Ideen, Antichrist und Friedenfürst, Regum und Sacerdotium* (Tübingen, 1918), p. 76; A. Hessel, "Odo von Cluny und das Französische Kulturproblem im Früheren Mittelalter," *Historische Zeitschrift* 128 (1923): 16; Vasiliev, "Mediaeval Ideas of the End of the World," p. 479; P. Vulliaud, *La fin du monde* (Paris, 1952), p. 91; N. Cohn, *The Pursuit of the Millennium: Revolutionary Messianism in Medieval and Reformation Europe and Its Bearing on Modern Totalitarian Movements*, Mercury Books, vol. 23 (London, 1962), p. 34; B. Töpfer, *Das kommende Reich des Friedens*, Forschungen zur mittelalterlichen Geschichte, vol. 11 (Berlin, 1964), p. 20; Rauh, *Das Bild des Antichrist*, p. 164; M. Rangheri, "La 'Epistola ad Gerbergam reginam de ortu et tempore Antichristi' di Adsoni di Montier-en-Der e le sue fonti," *Studi Medievali*, 3d ser., 14 (1973): 695v.; K. Aichele, *Das Antichristdrama des Mittelalters, der Reformation und Gegenreformation* (Den Haag, 1974), p. 15.

34. Willelmus Godelius, *Chronicon*, anno 1010, in *Recueil des historiens des Gaules et de la France*, vol. 10 (Paris, 1874), p. 262B.

35. Hugo Flaviniacensis, *Chronicon*, 2, anno 1012, *PL* 154:237A: "Dico tibi non est amplius; sed hodie relevatum est tibi quam in brevis sit hujus seculi finis, de quo non ulli creaturae, non angelis, sed solius est scire Dei patris."

36. Radulfus Glaber, *Historiae*, 4.6, *PL* 142:681D: "Praetera dum quidam de sollicitioribus qui eo tempore hababantur, consulti a pluribus fuissent quid tantus populorum concursus ad Hierosolymam designaret, olim saeculi inauditus praeteriti, responsum est a quibusdam, satis caute, non aliud portendere quam adventum illius perditi Antichristi, qui circa finem saeculi istius, divine testante auctoritate, praestolatur."

37. Ibid., 4, *PL* 142: 675C, 677D.

38. Thietmarus Merseburgensis, *Chronicon*, 6.1, *PL* 139:1305C: "Post salutiferum intermeratae virginis partum, consummata millenarii linea numeri, et in quinto cardinalis ordinis loco [an. 1004 Febr.], ac in ejusdem quartae inicio

ebdomadae, in Februario mense, qui purgatorius dicitur, clarum mane illuxit seculo."

39. Glaber, *Historiae*, 1. 5, PL 142:628A: "Idcirco ab exordio qui, divina boni Conditoris dispensatione, prolata sunt ei prodigiosa rerum miracula, ac portentosa elementorum signa, nec non et sagacissimorum virorum, tam spem quam formidolositatem incalcatura, divinitus oracula."

4

Thietland's Commentary on Second Thessalonians: Digressions on the Antichrist and the End of the Millennium

Steven R. Cartwright

Elsewhere in this volume, Richard Landes discusses a wide variety of documents from the tenth and eleventh centuries that indicate a concern and expectation during that time about the end of the world, the Last Judgment, the coming of the Antichrist, and either the beginning or the end of the Millennium, depending upon what one believed about the thousand-year reign of Christ. He assesses modern arguments against these expectations, noting that one argument used to deny that they existed is the relative lack of sources exhibiting such beliefs. He also lists many documents indicating that in fact there was an expectation of the end of the world from the mid–tenth to the mid–eleventh century, according to the various theories of how the Millennium should be calculated.

One of these documents, the commentary on 2 Thessalonians by Thietland, second abbot of Einsiedeln (d. ca. 964), provides an additional, and previously unnoticed, witness to the apocalyptic expectations of the mid–tenth century. This commentary, like the rest of Thietland's expositions on the letters of St. Paul, is little known and virtually unstudied, due largely to the fact that it exists in only two manuscripts, Einsiedeln MS 38 and Bamberg Staatsbibliothek Bibl. MS 89,[1] and is only now being edited for publication in the series Corpus Christianorum Continuatio Medievalis by P. Gérard de Martel of Solesmes Abbey.[2] It is significant because of its discussion of the Antichrist, based largely on Book 20 of Augustine's *City of God;* because of its differences from Adso of Montier-en-Der's treatise, although it is contemporary with it; and because of its assertion, contained in a digressing and somewhat literal exegesis of Apoc. 20:1–3, 7, that the Devil will be released at the end of the Millennium, the start of which Thietland dates from Christ's Passion—a distinct departure from the Augustinian denouncement of such anticipations of the end. Coming from the well-read abbot of a prominent, imperially favored abbey, such a prediction is quite important and demonstrates that apocalyptic expectations were not confined to simple and uneducated laymen. The commentary is a kind of *Fachbuch* on the Antichrist, in addition to Adso of Montier-en-Der's treatise on him, once described by Johannes Fried as the only one on this theme in the tenth century.[3]

What can be known about Thietland himself from the available sources is rather sketchy. Several contemporary versions exist of the *Annales* of Einsiedeln, which give both similar and conflicting information. One version, known as the *Annales Sancti Meginradi*, which has been dated to the tenth century, tersely notes that in 945, "Thietland came."[4] A similar notation, "Father Thietland came," is made for the same year in the *Annales Einsidlenses* contained in Einsiedeln MS 319.[5] Two notations, one identical to those already mentioned and the other unique but very important for the authorship of the commentaries, are found in a manuscript that probably originated at Einsiedeln but that later went to the Abbey of Reichenau, with which Einsiedeln had a long, friendly relationship. It contains *Annales* of Einsiedeln in handwriting dated anywhere from the eleventh through the fourteenth century. The first notation, in the eleventh-century hand, contains an entry for 945 reading, as before, "Father Thietland came." The second, written in a fourteenth-century hand, reads, "945. The first Abbot of this place," and contains a marginal note: "Thietland, Abbot of the Monastery of Hermits who made the gloss on the Epistles of Saint Paul."[6] Suzanne Wemple interprets this last entry as meaning that Thietland was working on these commentaries in 945, but the wording does not precisely indicate that.[7] Since the information is contained in an explanatory relative clause, and since the sentence seems to be incomplete, it is hard to know what the annalist had in mind, or when precisely Thietland did his writing.

The last set of *Annales* is contained in another Einsiedeln manuscript, described before the current catalog of Einsiedeln manuscripts was compiled.[8] Parts of the book date perhaps as early as the eleventh century. It contains greater and lesser *Annales*. In the greater annal, Thietland is first mentioned as being named coadjutor of the monastery by Eberhard, the first abbot of Einsiedeln, in 943, two years before the other annals mention his arrival. He is next mentioned as succeeding Eberhard as abbot upon the latter's death in 958, and then as resigning in 964, shortly before his own death. The lesser annal mentions Thietland as coadjutor in 943 and resigning in 960.[9] These are perhaps the most important annals, because they describe Thietland's positions of authority and responsibility, as well as his abbacy.

The monastery itself was founded in 934 when Eberhard, a canon of the cathedral of Strasbourg and a relative of Reginlinde, wife of Duke Hermann of Swabia, came to the site to establish a Benedictine monastery. There was already a group of hermits there, led by Benno, who had arrived in 928. The site at the time was known as Meinrad's Cell, to which Meinrad, a monk of Reichenau, had come as a hermit in 833.[10] Through the generosity of Reginlinde and Hermann, as well as Otto, the Holy Roman emperor, Einsiedeln came to be well endowed with gifts of money and land as well as imperial privileges, some of which came while Thietland was abbot.[11] The monastery very quickly became well known and was even able to attract Gregory, son of King Edmund and brother of King Adelstan of England.[12]

It was also during this time that much of Europe, the region of Swabia around Einsiedeln included, suffered greatly from Arab and Hungarian raids, in addition to feuds between nobles and emperors.[13] The outlook of the period, in the face of continual violence, was pessimistic; there was little hope of peace and justice triumphing on earth and much expectation of even worse things happening, namely, the coming of the Antichrist with all his persecutions.[14] By this point in history the Antichrist tradition had become quite well developed, as Richard Emmerson describes,[15] and the expectation of his arrival weighed heavily on the minds of individuals and on society as a whole. It was in this context that Thietland wrote, and one finds occasional hints of concern about the troubles of his times in his commentaries. For example, in his commentary on 1 Thessalonians Thietland counsels: "They [the Thessalonians] should even be a model for us; that is, if a persecution should happen to us, whether from fellow citizens or from outsiders, that we should take care to endure it patiently according to their example."[16] As we shall see, Thietland expressed concern about the evils in his own society in his commentary on 2 Thessalonians but was intentionally vague in discussing them. He was upset about members of Christian society acting in unchristian ways and feared that they would be among those deceived by the Antichrist. In fact, Thietland slightly alters the Augustinian tradition of the Antichrist that so strongly influences him to reflect his anxiety about the depravity of his time. Thietland was thus aware of happenings in the world around him but expressed little of this awareness openly in his commentaries, as is typical of medieval commentaries, concerned as they are with things eternal. Certainly one can attribute a strong sense of anxiety to Thietland, not only concerning the political and social troubles of his times but also concerning the coming apocalypse, what Ulrich Körtner calls "world anxiety," the belief that the world as we know it is in irreversible decline, leading to the crumbling of trust and confidence in the world. According to Körtner, this anxiety lasted throughout the Middle Ages, and apocalyptic, such as Thietland represents, is the attempt to master this anxiety.[17]

It is clear from the beginning of the commentary on 2 Thessalonians that Thietland wants to get straight into a discussion of the Antichrist. His preface is brief and little different from previous and more widely distributed and therefore probably better known commentaries on this epistle, most notably those of Ambrosiaster (fourth century) and Haimo of Auxerre (ninth century), brief paraphrases of which can be found scattered throughout Thietland's commentary. He notes St. Paul's intentions in writing this epistle: first, to predict, however discreetly and obscurely, the destruction of the Roman Empire; second, to instruct the Thessalonians concerning the coming of the Antichrist; and third, to rebuke and correct busybody preachers who go about proclaiming the Day of the Lord. Thietland notes the apostle's divinely given foresight that heretics would come predicting these very things, and one wonders whether the abbot faced the same phenomenon nine hundred years later. As we shall see, Thietland will return to this topic.[18]

In spite of his desire to discuss the Antichrist, Thietland dutifully and thoroughly expounds according to the moral sense the text of the epistle up to the point where the apostle begins his discussion of future events. He does so carefully and at greater length than any previous commentator, and with a good deal of independence, especially on 1:7b–8, which mentions the impending judgment of God upon the disobedient. Thietland sees in Paul's words a prediction of judgment not only upon pagans, upon those who do not believe, but also upon Catholics who do not live what they believe.[19] Thietland is clearly concerned about the violence and corruption of his time and within his own society, as well as about the violence coming into Christian society from the outside.

This is all preparatory and necessary for Thietland's discussion of the Antichrist to which we now turn. He begins his discourse in his exposition of 2:1–2, where Paul discusses the expected coming of Christ and warns the Thessalonians against those who say that the Day of the Lord is already at hand. Thietland takes up again the subject of heretics who proclaim such things, commenting briefly on each way in which the apostle says they might claim and propagate special knowledge about the end: by predicting future events through the Spirit, through treatises, and through letters. Thietland's attention to this suggests, though does not prove, that he was aware of apocalyptic prophets in his own time proclaiming such things; the attention given by Haimo and Ambrosiaster to this passage, however, leads one to believe that Thietland might simply be following the exegetical tradition of condemning such prophecies. What marks Thietland off from Haimo and Ambrosiaster is his labeling of these prophets as heretics.[20]

In his comments on 2:3, where Paul mentions the *discessio*, the division or rebellion that must precede the Antichrist's coming, Thietland begins to expound anagogically the received tradition on the Antichrist. For patristic and medieval exegetes, Thietland, Ambrosiaster, Haimo, and Adso included, this rebellion is one of the nations against the ancient Roman Empire. Thietland, however, simply states the commonly held opinion without any elaboration on the continuation of the empire by Charlemagne or any other emperor, such as Adso gives; he does not address the questions of whether this rebellion has already occurred and whether the Roman Empire can still be said to exist.[21]

The words "man of sin," also found in 2:3, gave rise among medieval commentators to a discussion of the Antichrist's origin, the question being whether he is conceived by human parents or by the Devil and a whore. This is part of the larger question of the degree to which the Antichrist will imitate, in a diabolical way, the life of Christ.[22] For Thietland, as for Adso, the Antichrist will be a normal human. "He [St. Paul] therefore says he will be a man, that truly the

Antichrist will be a man born from man."[23] Ambrosiaster does not discuss this at all, and Haimo says on this point only that he will be the "son of the Devil, not through nature, but through imitation."[24] In spite of this natural origin for the Antichrist, however, Thietland, like most other commentators, also notes that the Antichrist will be just that—a mirror image of Christ—whatever Christ is, the Antichrist is the opposite. "Just as the fullness of divinity dwells in Christ," Thietland says, paraphrasing Haimo's later comment on the Antichrist seating himself in the Temple of God, "thus also the fullness of deception and malice dwells in him [the Antichrist]."[25]

Thietland's discussion of the Antichrist's self-exaltation, described in 2:4, is typical of most medieval discussions: he will exalt himself not only above the saints but even over the Son of God.[26] His description of Antichrist's seating himself in the Temple follows this and, like much of what follows, is taken from Augustine's City of God, 20.19. Nevertheless, it is interesting because Thietland adapts Augustine's text to reflect his concern for his time. Most medieval commentators, Adso and Haimo included, note that the Antichrist will go to Jerusalem, circumcise himself, and rebuild the Temple.[27] Haimo also notes that the Temple could be the Church, though he does not expand on this except to say that this shows the Antichrist's perverse imitation of Christ.[28] Thietland, following Augustine, says nothing about the trip to Jerusalem and circumcision but expands greatly on the latter option—that the Temple is the Church. He diverges slightly from Augustine when he notes "that by the term 'man of sin' not only should 'Antichrist' be understood but even the entire mass of evil people holding on to his body," and that the Latin text should be rendered to the effect that the Antichrist is the Temple. His divergence is in referring to the man of sin, not mentioned by Augustine, and by making Antichrist's body specifically the multitude of evil people, as opposed to Augustine's reference to those people who belong to the Antichrist.[29]

Thietland's comments on that which detains the Antichrist are paraphrased from City of God and are consequently disappointing compared to Haimo's comments, which emphasize the destruction of the Roman Empire.[30] Augustine refuses to speculate, noting the obscurity of the following passage, that is, the mystery of iniquity. In expounding this passage, Augustine immediately proclaims his own ignorance and his willingness to discuss the opinion of others that the mystery of iniquity that detains the Antichrist was either the destruction of the Roman Empire or the persecution of Christians by Nero. He goes on to note the ancient belief, not expressed by Haimo, Ambrosiaster, or Adso, that Nero might return as the Antichrist. Augustine's response to these opinions on Nero is to wonder at the rashness of those proposing them. Thietland follows this very closely, making few adjustments, showing the strength of the tradition—even the tradition of Nero redivivus.[31]

The abbot, following the patristic and medieval Latin tradition, interprets the text of 2:7b, "tantum ut qui tenet nunc, teneat, donec de medio fiat," not in the sense of restraining, as the Greek text is commonly interpreted,[32] but in the sense of holding power. He continues to follow Augustine's interpretation in City of God, 20.19, and consequently gives a much longer explanation than

Haimo or Ambrosiaster. Thietland's immediate opinion is that this refers to him who holds the kingdom of the Romans: let him hold it until he should be withdrawn from the midst of the peoples, an opinion similar to those expressed by Ambrosiaster and Haimo, though neither Haimo nor Thietland questions or explains what the kingdom of the Romans might now be.[33] Thietland goes farther than Haimo or Ambrosiaster, however, by following Augustine's opinion that the mystery of iniquity refers to "hypocrites and phonies in the church," and therefore he who now holds (or controls?) the faith should hold it until the mystery should be withdrawn from the midst of the faithful. This mystery, he says, is the heretics, the many antichrists, whom St. John describes as leaving the community of the faithful. At this point Thietland departs from Augustine by saying that before the Antichrist appears, "the evil shall be separated from the midst of the good, and shall be joined to his head," a thought to which Thietland will come back in the next section. He then returns to Augustine and states that before Christ comes to judge the living and the dead, the Antichrist will come to deceive the dead in soul.[34]

It is in his comments on 2:8 that Thietland makes a major digression on the Antichrist. He is concerned with the textual problem of whether 2:8 says that the sinful one shall be revealed or loosed, a problem and a verse with which Augustine is not concerned. He initially cites the textual variant that says "revealed," *revelabitur*, but it is clear from his digression that he prefers the alternative version, *solvetur*.[35] To explain this important point, he launches into a lengthy and selective exegesis of Apoc. 20:1–3, 7, in which the Devil is described as being released (*solvi, solvetur*) a thousand years after having been bound by the angel and allowed to lead astray the nations, symbolized by Gog and Magog. Thietland regards this thousand years to have begun with Christ's Passion and thus identifies the appearance of the Antichrist in 2 Thess. 2:8 with the loosing of the Devil at the end of the Millennium, described in Apoc. 20:3. Much of this exposition appears to have been influenced by Haimo of Auxerre's commentary on the Apocalypse, and through Haimo by the commentaries of Primasius and Ambrosius Autpertus, as well as by Augustine's *City of God*.[36]

The digression is important because it allows Thietland to discuss further the separation between the faithful and the infidels, the good and the evil, and also the meaning of the thousand years. For Thietland, there are two sets of nations: the faithful and the infidels. The infidels are symbolized by the abyss into which the Devil is cast; just as the abyss is incomprehensible, so is the great number of the peoples, or nations, to which the Devil goes.[37] The distinction between them, however, is not always clear; "many good people are doers of evil," he says, "and many doers of evil are good." This is a comment made from direct experience. The evil and the good are mixed together in the world, Thietland's own world. The distinction will be made clearer when the Devil is released, for then he will lead astray the nations, in this case, Thietland says, the infidels, for although the Devil will have the power of persecuting the saints, he will not have the power of deceiving them.[38]

According to the text of the Apocalypse, the Devil will be released at the end of a thousand years. Augustine had interpreted this thousand years as the time between Christ's first and second comings when Christ would rule with the saints on earth, though, he said, it should not necessarily be taken as a literal thousand years.[39] Thietland prefers to interpret the thousand years literally rather than spiritually and dates them from the sufferings of Christ, an ancient practice condemned by Augustine[40] but which Thietland nevertheless accepts, following Haimo. He arrives at this number by interpreting the angel who comes down from Heaven to bind the Devil and throw him into the abyss as "the Lord Jesus Christ, an angel of great counsel, who descended from Heaven, appearing to the world through the mystery of the Incarnation."[41] Although it is one thousand and thirty-three years from the Incarnation until this loosing, this does not bother Thietland; the Millennium begins with Christ's Passion, for it is the Passion that binds the Devil. That is, Thietland believed he was living during the Millennium and that the time of the end was near and could be known. The abbot does not openly proclaim that the end is at hand, however. He simply notes that when the thousand years have been completed (i.e., in 1033, some seventy to ninety years in the future), the Devil will be loosed for a brief time, namely three and a half years—a period not found in the Apocalypse text but rather in the Book of Daniel, as well in *City of God*.[42] This is the only reference Thietland makes to the length of persecution, and he, like Augustine, does not mention the forty- or forty-five-day period of repentance and refreshment that others, such as Adso, do.[43]

Thietland's prediction of the end of the Millennium and his use of Haimo in making it raise two questions. First, does his dependence on Haimo in dating and discussing the end of the Millennium make his prediction any less significant for the history of tenth-century apocalypticism? Is Thietland simply repeating Haimo for the sake of following the received interpretation? No, because to begin with, his introduction of Apocalypse 20 into the discussion of 2 Thess. 2:8 is extremely unusual. Thietland believed it was critical to link his interpretation of the Antichrist to the loosing of the Devil at the end of the thousand years and to give a comprehensive view of how the world would end. Placed in the context of his anxiety over the disruptions of his time, Thietland's exegesis of the Apocalypse is even more compelling than Haimo's. In addition, there are significant differences between Haimo's discussion of the Millennium and Thietland's. Thietland does not speak of the thousand years as the whole standing for the part, or as the time of the church, as Haimo does. It is not a symbolic number but an actual number, referring literally to the last age of the world.

Second, there is the question of consistency. How can someone who calls those who preach that the end has come "heretics" himself predict that the end is coming at a certain time? The answer is, in Thietland's view, that these heretics do not realize the divine plan. They are jumping the gun, so to speak, predicting the end far in advance of what St. John foretold in the Apocalypse. Thietland is thus little different from the preacher mentioned by Abbo of Fleury, who, about the same time as Thietland, was predicting that the Antichrist would come in 1033, predicted that the Antichrist would come in the year 1000, still some thirty to forty years away—against those who were saying that the end would come any day. As Richard Landes points out, the Paris preacher was not proclaiming the beginning but rather the end of the Millennium, as was Thietland—and so both can be called Augustinian, for their belief in the present millennium and the coming of Antichrist at the end of that millennium.[44] Both were attempting to allay apocalyptic fears by pushing the event back, as many before them had done, though only by a generation or two, not by hundreds of years; for the Paris preacher and for Thietland, the end was not yet but was unquestionably on the way; there was no agnosticism about when the end would come.

The Devil's loosing allows him to lead the infidel nations, that is, Gog and Magog, astray. In discussing Gog and Magog, Thietland follows the patristic, rather than the Sibylline, version of the Gog and Magog legend. In the former, Gog and Magog are symbols of evil peoples from all over the world who will appear with the Antichrist. In the latter, they are identified with specific, barbarous peoples who will appear before the Antichrist and conquer until defeated by the "last world emperor," a Christian emperor who will maintain order until his abdication, allowing the Antichrist to take over.[45]

Thietland begins his discussion of Gog and Magog by dismissing this latter opinion. Instead, he follows Augustine's interpretation of their names, found in *City of God*, 20.11, though he makes a slight variation in the text. Whereas Augustine and most others after him interpret Gog's name as meaning *tectum*, "roof," or "covered," "secret," and Magog's name as meaning *de tecto*, "from the roof," Thietland interprets Magog's name as meaning *detectum*, "open," "bare," not *de tecto*.[46] It is only a slight variation and does not cause Thietland to vary significantly from Augustine. Augustine offers two opinions of these meanings. One is that the nations are like a house from which the Devil goes forth: Gog is the nations, the house or roof, and Magog is the Devil, going from the house or roof. In the second opinion, both words refer to the nations in whom the Devil is shut up, as if roofed in; but "they shall be from the roof when they break forth from concealed to open hatred."[47] Thietland's interpretations are rooted in Augustine but make a slight, though significant, divergence:

> By Gog, therefore, all evil persons should be understood, in the
> hearts of whom the Devil lies hidden. By Magog the very Devil
> himself should be understood, because it is he who lies hidden in
> the hearts of evil persons. He himself will persecute the saints as
> though going from hiding on to the Day of Judgment. But if perhaps
> this exposition is displeasing, because he says that Gog and Magog
> are nations, it can also be understood differently, that by Gog and
> Magog those evil persons are meant in whose hearts hatred and envy
> lie hidden. They who are against God are savage, even as if Magog,
> that is, going openly, and showing envy.[48]

Thietland thus continues to inveigh against unspecified evil persons. Gog and Magog are thus not outside nations, as Sibylline thought proposes, or "nations," broadly conceived, but evil persons—still general, but more tangible. Thietland does not discuss the destruction of Gog and Magog. It is enough for him to bring them into the discussion of the Devil being loosed, and with him the Antichrist and his persecutions of the church. They represent for him the evil persons of his time who are a sign of the Antichrist's arrival. Thietland's opinion is not far from that of the anonymous writer of the letter concerning the Hungarians, which, according to R. B. C. Huygens and Johannes Fried, was written around 960—about the same time as Thietland's commentary and Adso's treatise on the Antichrist, not to mention Abbo's preacher in Paris.[49]

At this point Thietland returns to the text of 2 Thessalonians. His digression, both from the biblical text and from the Augustinian tradition, allowed him to make veiled comments on his time, though he was circumspect enough not to predict explicitly an imminent end. His position on the Millennium, in spite of Augustine's denunciation of such schemes more than five hundred years previously *and* in the same work from which Thietland derived much of his interpretation, shows the enduring strength of such ideas and the hold they had on people's minds, especially in the tenth century, even among educated clergy. These comments are largely unique among commentaries on 2 Thessalonians. Ambrosiaster and Haimo say little about this one point upon which Thietland diverges, and certainly they, like Adso, make no statements about how soon the Antichrist might come.

On the other hand, they, along with Adso, say much more than Thietland does about the end of the Antichrist. Whereas Haimo and Adso describe his death on the Mount of Olives,[50] Thietland is content simply to interpret "the breath of [Christ's] mouth" as *potentia virtutis suae*.[51] This brevity is probably because Augustine says little about the Antichrist's end in either 20.12 or 20.19 of *City of God*, where he discusses 2 Thessalonians.

Thietland has a more fully developed opinion on the authenticity of the Antichrist's signs and wonders, again paraphrased from Augustine. He notes in his comment on 2:9, "whose coming is according to the workings of Satan, in all power, with false signs and wonders," that the Devil will enter the man of sin and miraculously perform deceptive works. This was another thorny question among medieval commentators, and the opinions offered largely depended on exegetes' views of the Antichrist's upbringing—will he be taught magic as a child, or will he inherit magical powers from his father, the Devil? In the former case, the miracles would not be real, but illusory. In the latter, the miracles would be quite real.[52] Thietland says nothing about the Antichrist's background, but his earlier stated view that the Antichrist will be a man, into whom, he now says, the Devil will enter, helps us understand his view that what the Antichrist performs are false signs and wonders. The faithful, Thietland says, following Augustine, will not be deceived; only those who deserve to be deceived will be deceived.[53] On this larger point, Haimo and Adso agree with Thietland—the Antichrist will be trained by magicians and will perform false miracles[54]—though this view departs from Augustine, who affirms the authenticity of the Antichrist's miracles.[55] Thietland does cite, however, the view of Augustine from *City of God*, 20.19, that just as God's consuming of Job and his family by fire was a true sign, God allows the works of the Devil and gives him the power of performing these works—the permission of "the working of error, that they may believe a lie." Thietland responds by saying that, "nevertheless, in whatever way they happen, they who then will be faithful will recognize," something Augustine does not say.[56] Thietland does return to Augustine's line by stating that God allows the Devil to work miracles and deceive, and that those who are to be deceived have been judged by a secret judgment of God, although Thietland also says that they shall be justified (*iustificabuntur*) at the Last Judgment—an odd statement that Thietland does not clarify and that departs from Augustine, who says they shall be judged (*iudicabuntur*).[57] This is a strange departure, and we must note that in both manuscripts *iustificabuntur* is used without question or correction by scribes.

After this point in the commentary, Thietland mentions the Antichrist no more, holding closely to the perceived intention of the text. His overall presentation of the Antichrist, like Augustine's, is very sketchy compared to Adso's or Haimo's, but this is in keeping with St. Paul's description, itself very vague. Thietland says little or nothing about his political or religious status, about how he will rise or fall, nor does he discuss other themes mentioned by Adso— the ministry of Enoch and Elias, the persecution of Christians, the last world emperor, or the conversion of the Jews—but then, Ambrosiaster and Haimo say little on these subjects either. The abbot sees little point, apparently, in presenting his material in the same way as the others. His was a more evil time than Ambrosiaster's or Haimo's, and though he believes in Christ's ultimate victory over the Antichrist, he strangely dwells little upon it. He is more concerned with talking about the loosing of the Devil and his deception of the evil and unfaithful, even those who are a part of Christian society. With the exception of his millenarian speculation, Thietland's discourse and digression on the Antichrist are strictly within the patristic, specifically Augustinian, tradition. He apparently knew nothing of some of the sources Adso had available to him at perhaps precisely the same time Thietland was writing his commentary. While Thietland's commentary may thus be the less interesting for this and for its extensive paraphrasing of Augustine, it is nevertheless fascinating because of the insights he offers into the moral state of mid–tenth century Swabia and the contemporary expectations of an imminent end. Though Thietland was aware that the Antichrist would ultimately be defeated and that Christ would be victorious, he holds little hope for his own period in history or for his own society. He thus stands out as another example of tenth-century pessimism, in addition to his status as the last Carolingian exegete and a predictor of the Antichrist.

NOTES

This paper was originally delivered at the Twenty-ninth International Congress on Medieval Studies, Western Michigan University, May 5–8, 1994, and has been revised for inclusion in this volume and re-presentation at the "Conference on the Apocalyptic Year 1000," Boston, Mass., November 4–6, 1996. My thanks to David Van Meter and Richard Landes for their generous help and numerous suggestions.

See now Steven R. Cartwright and Kevin L. Hughes, eds., *Second Thessalonians: Two Early Medieval Apocalyptic Commentaries*, TEAMS Commentary Series (Kalamazoo: Medieval Institute Press, 2001); and Charles D. Wright, "The Apocalypse of Thomas: Some New Latin Texts and Their Significance for the Old English

Versions," in *The Apocrypha in Anglo-Saxon England*, ed. Donald G. Scragg (forthcoming). Einsiedeln possesses an abbreviated Latin version of this Apocalypse that is dated to the second half of the tenth century, and it contains two alternative annus mundi calculations dated to 996; one implicitly projects the end of the sixth age to be 1048.

Editors' note: Steven Cartwright is a doctoral associate in history at Western Michigan University.

1. Both manuscripts were cataloged at the end of the last century. See Gabriel Meier, *Catalogus Codicum Manu Scriptorum qui in Bibliotheca Monasterii Einsidlensis OSB servantur*, 3 vols. (Einsiedeln, 1899), 1:28; Friederich Leitschuh and H. Fischer, *Katalog der Handschriften der Königlichen Bibliothek zu Bamberg*, 3 vols. (Bamberg, 1895), 1/1:71. In addition, the manuscripts in the Bamberg Staatsbibliothek originating from the monastery of St. Michelsberg, including no. 89, have been cataloged: Karin Dengler-Schreiber, *Scriptorium und Bibliothek des Klosters Michelsberg in Bamberg* (Graz, 1979), pp. 109–11. Neither Bamberg catalog notes the connection with the Einsiedeln manuscript, and both misidentify the commentaries as being those of either Haimo of Halberstadt or Atto of Vercelli. Heinrich Denifle cites only the Einsiedeln manuscript in his *Die abendländischen Schriftausleger bis Luther über Justitia Dei (Rom. 1, 17) und Justificatio* (Mainz, 1905), pp. 27–28. Friedrich Stegmüller was the first to list the two manuscripts together in his *Repertorium Biblicum Medii Aevi* (Madrid, 1950–61), 5:405–9, no. 8267, where he lists commentaries for Romans, 1 and 2 Corinthians, Galatians, Ephesians, Philippians, 1 and 2 Thessalonians, and Hebrews, this latter being the work of Alcuin. See also Suzanne Fonay Wemple, *Atto of Vercelli: Church, State, and Christian Society in Tenth Century Italy*, Temi e Testi, no. 27 (Rome, 1979), pp. 45–46, where she notes that these commentaries are largely paraphrased from those of Atto of Vercelli (d. 961), and that the commentaries on 2 Corinthians and Galatians are in fact Atto's. She also states, quite accurately, that the commentaries on Philippians and Thessalonians are less dependent on Atto than the earlier ones. Finally, see Rolf Bergmann, "Die althochdeutschen Glossen der Handschrift Bamberg, Staatsbibliothek Bibl. 89," in *Deutsche Sprache und Literatur in Mittelalter und früher Neuzeit*, ed. Heinz Endermann and Rudolf Bentzinger (Jena, 1989), pp. 30–34, who, like the Bamberg catalogers before him, misattributes the commentaries to Atto and makes no mention of the Einsiedeln manuscript.

2. The question of the relationship between the two manuscripts has not been resolved, and it is to be hoped that P. Martel will address it. The textual variants between the two manuscripts are few in number, suggesting that Bamberg Staatsbibliothek Bibl. MS 89 may be a direct copy of Einsiedeln MS 38. But what relationship is there between the monastery at Einsiedeln and the monastery of St. Michelsberg at Bamberg?

3. Johannes Fried, "Endzeitwartung um die Jahrtausendwende," *Deutsches Archiv für Erforschung des Mittelalters* 45, no. 2 (1989): 412; see also chapter 1, this volume. Fried was, of course, unaware of Thietland's commentary, which might also be given this status, even though it lacks the specificity and detail of Adso's work.

4. *Annales Sancti Meginradi, MGH, SS* 3:138.

5. *Annales Einsidlenses, MGH, SS* 3:145.

6. *Herimanni Augiensis Chronicon, MGH, SS* 5:70–71.

7. Wemple, *Atto*, p. 47.

8. Gall Morel, "Liber Heremi," *Der Geschichtsfreund* 1 (1844): 93–147.

9. Ibid., 102, 105, 107, 147.

10. Ibid., 147.

11. Ibid., 102–7.

12. Ibid., 105.

13. See *Annales Heremi, MGH, SS* 3:142; Hans Conrad Peyer, "Frühes and hohes Mittelalter," in *Handbuch der Schweizer Geschichte*, 2 vols. (Zurich, 1972), 1:138, 144.

14. For further discussion of this pessimism, see Heinrich Fichtenau, *Living in the Tenth Century: Mentalities and Social Orders*, trans. Patrick J. Geary (Chicago, 1991), pp. 381–87. Fichtenau gives little attention, however, to the apocalyptic expectations underlying this pessimism.

15. Richard Kenneth Emmerson, *Antichrist in the Middle Ages* (Seattle, 1981), p. 74. For other important studies of the belief in the Antichrist at this time, see Daniel Verhelst, "La préhistoire des conceptions d'Adson concernant l'Antichrist," *Recherches de Théologie Ancienne et Médiévale* 40 (1973): 52–103; and Bernard McGinn, *Antichrist: Two Thousand Years of the Human Fascination with Evil* (San Francisco, 1994).

16. Thietland, Einsiedeln MS 38, fol. 177r: "Debent etiam et nobis forma esse, hoc est ut si nobis vel a civibus vel ab extraneis illata fuerit persecutio, ad exemplum eorum patienter tollerare curemus."

17. Ulrich H. J. Körtner, *The End of the World: A Theological Interpretation*, trans. Douglas W. Stott (Louisville, 1995), pp. 20–22, 56–57, 203–4.

18. Thietland, Einsiedeln MS 38, fol. 182v: "Scripsit thessalonicensibus primam epistolam pro his rebus quas nobis constat esse manifestas, inter quas pauca quidem de adventu Domini nostri Ihesu Christi et futura corporum resurrectione asseruit. At vero scribit etiam eisdem secundam in qua praesertim vigent intentiones. Prima videlicet de regni romanorum destructione; secunda de antichristi adventu et eiusdem interfectione; tertia vero de illorum qui per domos inquiete discurrebant repraehensione atque correctione. Praeviderat namque spiritus sancti gratia revelante, nonnullos hereticos futuros qui dicerent instare diem Domini. Quatenus hac narratione sollicitati ad aliquem traherentur errorem; qua praescribens illis hanc epistolam apertum dedit eis antichristi adventus indicium."

19. Ibid., fol. 183r: "Nota quia duas faciunt distinctiones. Et fortassis de paganis dicunt *qui non noverunt Deum*; de malis autem catholicis, *qui non oboediunt euangelio Domini nostri*, quia ille ignis non solum ulciscetur in eos qui non crediderunt, sed etiam in illos qui non secundum quod crediderunt vixerunt."

20. Ibid., fol. 184r: "*Rogamus*, inquiunt, *vos fratres per adventum Domini Ihesu Christi, et nostrae conversationis in ipsum*. Ad iuratione constrinxerat eos, quia praevidebat nonnullos hereticos futuros qui dicerent instare diem Domini, qua ratione solliciti ad aliquem inlicitum traherentur errorem. Ideoque etiam adventus antichristi manifestum dedit indicum. Sequitur, *Ut non cito moveamini a vestro sensu*. Huius est a doctrina quam a nobis accepistis in vestro sensu non moveamini. Sequitur, *Neque per spiritum*. Hoc est, ab aliquo loquente per spiritum, id est, qui videatur futura praedicere per spiritum, vel diem Domini instare. Sequitur, *Neque per sermonem*. Huius est per aliquem tractatum. Sequitur, *Neque per epistolam tamquam per nos missam*. Hoc propter hereticos dicunt, qui sub praetitulatione sanctorum apostolorum falsas scribeant epistolas." Cf. Haimo, *PL* 117:779BC; Ambrosiaster, *PL* 17:456B.

21. Thietland, Einsiedeln MS 38, fol. 184r: "Hoc est recessio gentium a regno Romanorum." Cf. Ambrosiaster, *PL* 17:456C; Haimo, *PL* 117:779D; Adso, *De ortu et tempore Antichristi*, ed. D. Verhelst, *CCCM* 45 (Turnhout, 1976), 26.110–20.

22. Emmerson, *Antichrist*, pp. 74–83.

23. Thietland, Einsiedeln MS 38, fol. 184r: "*Quia nisi venerit*, inquit, *discessio primum*, hoc est recessio gentium a regno Romanorum. *Et revelatus fuerit homo peccati*, et cetera. Hominem ideo dicit, quia antichristus veraciter erit homo ex homine natus. Peccati vero dicit, quia sicut in Christo habitat plenitudo divinitatis, sic et in illo habitabit plenitudo fallatiae et malignitatis. *Filius perditionis* dicit, ad distinctionem filiorum reconciliationis et hominis, id est Christi." Adso, *CCCM* 45:23.24–26: "Nascetur autem ex patris et matris copulatione, sicut alii homines, non, ut quidam dicunt, de sola virgine."

24. Haimo, *PL* 117:779D: "*Et filius perditionis*, id est filius diaboli, non per naturam, sed per imitationem."

25. Ibid., 780B: "Nam sicut in Christo omnis plenitudo divinitatis requievit, ita in illo homine qui Antichristus appellatur, eo quod sit contrarius Christo, plenitudo malitiae et omnis iniquitatis habitabit, quia in ipso erit caput omnium malorum diabolus, qui est rex super omnes filios superbiae." For Thietland's paraphrase, see n. 23 above.

26. Thietland, Einsiedeln MS 38, fol. 184r: "Ipse autem Antichristus non solum extollet se supra sanctos sed etiam supra ipsum Dei filium, qui dicitur and colitur Deus."

27. Haimo, *PL* 117:780B; Adso, *CCCM* 45:27.142–45.

28. Haimo, *PL* 117:780B: "Vel etiam *in templo Dei*, id est in Ecclesia sedebit, ostendens se tanquam sit Deus."

29. Thietland, Einsiedeln MS 38, fol. 184r–v: "Sequitur: *Ita ut in templo Dei sedeat*. Manifestissime haec de Antichristo dicta intelleguntur. Veruntamen quia sessurus in templo dicitur, incertum est utrum in illa templi quod edificantus est a Salomone sessurus sit ruina an certe in Dei ecclesia. Quapropter nonnulli per illum *hominem peccati*, non solum Antichristum intellegendum, sed etiam omnem malorum multitudinem ad corpus ipsius attinentem decreverunt. Unde rectius putant latine legendum esse sicut in Graeco habetur. *Ita ut in templum Dei sedeat*. Quatenus non ipse dicatur sedere in templo, sed ipse sit templum qui sedeat; et eo locutionis genere dicatur sedere in templum Dei. Hoc est quasi templum Dei, quo nos solemus dicere *sedere in amicum*, hoc est quasi amicis." The above is paraphrased heavily from Augustine, *De civitate Dei*, 20.19, ed. Bernard Dombart and Alphonse Kalb, *CC* 48 (Turnhout, 1955), p. 731.

30. Haimo, *PL* 117:780CD: "*Et nunc quid detineat scitis*, ut reveletur in suo tempore. Dicit: Scitis quid detineat et non demonstrat quid. Quod nihil melius ibi intelligitur voluisse significare quam destructionem regni Romanorum de qua obscure hic locutus est, ne forte aliquis Romanorum legeret hanc epistolam, et excitaret contra se aliosque Christianos persecutionem illorum, qui se puttabant semper regnaturos in toto mundo. Vos *scitis*, inquit, *quid detineat* illum Antichristum, et quid moretur illum, quia necdum destructum est regnum Romanorum, nec recesserunt omnes gentes ab illis. *Ut reveletur*, sive manifestetur ipse Antichristus, *in suo tempore*, id est congruo tempore et a Deo disposito, postquam omnia regna discesserint a Romano imperio."

31. Thietland, Einsiedeln MS 38, fol. 184v: "Hinc beatus Augustinus: Apostolus inquit scire illos dicit, quod illis in hac epistola aperte non ostenderat et ideo nobis manet occultum. Nos propter ea cum labore volumus pervenire ad eius intentionem, sed omnino nequimus. Presertim cum hunc locum obscuriorem subsequentia faciant verba, quibus dicitur *nam misterium iam operatur iniquitatis*. Quid enim voluerit sentire Apostolus, prorsus ignoro. Veruntamen, aliorum opiniones quas vel audire vel legere potui non tacebo. Fuere nonnulli qui hoc apostolum de abolitione aiunt regni dixisse Romanorum, ideoque declinasse aperte narrare, ne forte

calumniam incurreret. Unde nonnulli sunt qui mysterium iam operatur iniquitatis de Nerone dictum putant, cuius opera iam antichristi esse videbantur. Propter quod nonnulli putant eundem resurrecturum et Antichristum futurum; unde etiam nonnulii dicunt quod non sit mortuus, sed potius quando visus est occisus, non sit occisus, sed occulte sublatus, et in eodem aetatis vigore servetur donec in regno restituatur. Horum, ut ipse beatus inquit Augustinus, miranda est temeritas." Cf. Augustine, *De civitate Dei*, 20.19 (*CC* 48:731–32).

32. Horst Dieter Rauh, *Das Bild des Antichrist im Mittelalter: Von Tyconius zum Deutsche Symbolismus*, (Münster, 1973), pp. 59–61.

33. Ambrosiaster, *PL* 17:457A: "Mysterium iniquitatis a Nerone inceptum est, qui zelo idolorum, et apostolus interfecit, instigante patre suo diabolo, usque ad Diocletianum, et novissime Julianum, qui arte quadam et subtilitate coeptam persecutionem implere non potuit; quia desuper concessum non fuerat. His enim ministris utitur Satanas, ut interim sub turba deorum ad seducendos homines unius veri Dei manifestationem illudat, quamdiu steterit regnum Romanum, hoc est, quod dixit: *Donec de medio fiat.*" Haimo, *PL* 117:781B: "Id est hoc solummodo restat, ut Nero, qui nunc tenet imperium totus orbis, tandiu teneat illud, donec de medio mundi tollatur potestas Romanorum. In Nerone comprehendit omnes imperatores Romanos qui post illum imperii sceptra tenuerunt. Ideo dicit: *Donec de medio tollatur*, quia undique ex omnibus gentibus confluebant Romam, et quasi in medio mundi erat, habens in circuitu suo omnes gentes; vel quidquid intra initium et fines continetur, medium potest dici."

34. Thietland, Einsiedeln MS 38, fol. 184v: "At vero quod sequitur, *ut qui tenet nunc teneat donec de medio fiat.* Prorsus inquit ipse de regno Romanorum aestimo dictum, ut sit sensus: Qui tenet nunc regnum Romanorum, teneat donec de medio populorum fiat ablatum. Sunt etiam sicut ipse ait nonnulli, qui illud quod ait: *Nam misterium iniquitatis iam operatur* de fictis et simulatis in aecclesia Apostolum dixisse intellegunt. Et quia hoc misterium nunc quoque manet occultum, idcirco magnopere sanctos admonere curaverit, ut qui tenet nunc fidem tenaciter teneat donec illud iniquitatis mysterium de medio fidelium fiat ablatum. Ad hunc locum videtur attinere illud Iohannis testimonium dicentis: *Filioli novissima hora est*, et cetera [1 John 2:18]. Dicunt namque quod sicut in hac hora novissima ante diem iudicii quam horam ultimam parte saeculi vocat, multi egressi sunt, heretici quos ille multos antichristos appellat, sic etiam ante adventum Domini ad iudicium apparente Antichristo. Mali de medio bonorum segregabuntur, et suo capiti coniungentur. Dicit autem idem beatus Augustinus quia alii sic alii vero sic, singuli pro capite suo hunc obscurum apostolorum exposuerunt. Veruntamen nos scire debemus apostoli fuisse intentionem manifestare quidem quod non sit Dominus prius venturus ad iudicandos vivos et mortuos quam veniat Antichristus ad decipiendos in anima mortuos."

35. Ibid.: "Sequitur: *Et tunc revelabitur ille iniquus.* In quibusdam exemplaribus invenitur *solvetur*, unde ergo revelandus aut solvendus sit videndum est."

36. See notes 37, 41, and 42 below; see also E. Ann Matter, "The Apocalypse in Early Medieval Exegesis," in *The Apocalypse in the Middle Ages*, ed. Richard K. Emmerson and Bernard McGinn (Ithaca, N.Y., 1992), pp. 38–50, where she discusses commentaries on the Apocalypse up through the ninth century and mentions Adso as well. Her point is that these commentaries are concerned more with describing "the integrity and purity of the Church on earth" (p. 49) than with fueling expectations of an imminent end. Thietland, as we shall see, interprets the Apocalypse differently, though he is only expounding a small portion of it, and not the whole.

37. Thietland, Einsiedeln MS 38, fol. 185r: "Quaerendum est quod abyssi nomine intellegi voluerit, videlicet infidelium gentium multitudinem. Quia sicut abyssus, ita et multitudo gentium incompraehensibilis est. Quare ergo mittere in abyssum dicit? Videlicet quia a fidelibus reppulit. Sed numquid non ante in abyssum fuit? Fuit quidem. Sed ideo missus dicitur, quia maiorem nunc in fidelibus [or, *infidelibus?* Bamberg text reads: in infidelibus] potestatem habere invenitur." Cf. Primasius's *Commentarius in Apocalypsin*, ed. A. W. Adams, CC 92 (Turnhout, 1985), 273.33–34: "Utique diabolum misit in abyssum, quo nomine significata est multitudo innumerabilis impiorum"; cf. Haimo, *Expositionis in Apocalypsin B. Johannis, PL* 117:1181D: "Abyssus enim profunda et tenebrosa significat corda impiorum hominum."

38. Thietland, Einsiedeln MS 38, fol. 185r: "Sequitur: *et clausit* [Apoc. 20:3]. Videlicet ut prohibita non tangeret signavit quia occultum ei manere voluit. Quid ad eius pertineret membra? Propterea multi sunt boni malifacti, et multi malifacti boni. . . . *Cum consummati fuerint mille anni, solvetur de carcere suo*, id est dabitur illi potestas, *et seducet gentes* [Apoc. 20:7]. Hic gentes non illos vult intellegi quos superius gentes appellavit, sed infideles, quia etsi habebit potestatem persequendi sanctos, non habebit tamen decipiendi."

39. Augustine, *De civitate Dei*, 20.7, 9 (CC 48:708–12, 715–19).

40. Ibid., 18.53 (CC 48:652).

41. Thietland, Einsiedeln MS 38, fol. 185v: "Angelus iste Dominus est Ihesus Christus magni consilii angelus, qui de caelo descendit per incarnationis mysterium visibilis mundo apparens." The reference to Christ as the angel of great counsel is based on the Septuagint version of Isaiah 9:6 and can be traced through Haimo's commentary (*PL* 117:1181CD) to the *Expositionis in Apocalypsin* of Ambrosius Autpertus (ed. Robert Weber, *CCCM* 27A [Turnhout, 1975], 740.7–8) and to Primasius's commentary (*CC* 92:271.4–6). See also the *Expositio in Apocalypsin* of Caesarius of Arles (*Sancti Caesarii Arelatensis, Opera Omnia*, ed. D. G. Morin O.S.B., 2 vols. [Maredsous, 1942], 2:263.22). The explicit reference to the Incarnation is primarily Haimo's (*PL* 117:1181D: "De caelo descendit, quia homo factus"), though Thietland clearly expands on it.

42. Thietland, Einsiedeln MS, fol. 185r: "Sequitur: *donec consummentur mille anni* [Apoc. 20:3]. Nota quia sic sonare verba videntur, ut quasi post mille annos possit seducere fideles. Sed non est ita, quia donec pro infinito ponitur, sicut multa habes exempla; sive talis esse potest ordo verborum: *clausit et signavit*, donec consummentur mille anni ut non seducat. *Mille annos*. Ultimam hanc saeculi partem vocat, qua erit a Domini nostri passione et nostra redemptione usque ad antichristi adventum. Millenarium ergo numerum pro totius huius temporis posuit perfectione. Sequitur: *post haec oportet eum solvi brevi tempore* [Apoc. 20:3], hoc est trium annorum et dimidii spacio." Cf. Haimo, *PL* 117:1182BC: "Millenarius numerus in Scriptura pro perfectione rei ponitur. . . . Et ideo hic numerus propter sui perfectionem omne significat tempus praesens, a Domini scilicet passione usque ad finem saeculi, et hic totum pro parte positum est, quia mille anni quantumlibet tempus Ecclesiae exprimunt, id est ad regnum Antichristi." Cf. also Ambrosius Autpertus, *CCCM* 27A:741–42.14–31, and Primasius, *CC* 92:272.16–30. On the three and a half years, see Dan. 7:25 and 12:7–12, and Augustine, *De civitate Dei*, 20.13 (*CC* 48:721–23).

43. Adso, *CCCM* 45:29.189. See also Robert E. Lerner, "Refreshment of the Saints: The Time after Antichrist as a Station for Earthly Progress in Medieval Thought," *Traditio* 32 (1976): 97–144.

44. Richard Landes, "Sur les traces du Millenium: La `Via Negativa,'" *Le Moyen Age* 99, no. 1 (1993): 19–20.

45. Emmerson, *Antichrist*, pp. 84–88.

46. Thietland, Einsiedeln MS 38, fol. 185r: "Sed melius locus iste per interpraetationem nominum intellegi potest; Gog namque interpraetatur tectum, Magog detectum." Cf. Augustine, *De civitate Dei*, 20.11 (*CC* 48:720–21).

47. Augustine, *De civitate Dei*, 20.11 (*CC* 48:720–21), trans. Marcus Dods, *City of God* (New York, 1950), p. 729.

48. Thietland, Einsiedeln MS 38, fol.185r: "Per Gog igitur intellegendi sunt omnes mali in quorum cordibus latet diabolus. Per Magog vero ipse diabolus quia qui nunc latet in cordibus malorum. Ipse erga diem iudicii quasi detecto egrediens persequetur sanctos. Sed si cui forte haec displicet expositio quia Gog et Magog gentes esse dicit, potest et aliter intellegi: ut per Gog et Magog ipsi mali designantur, quia in quorum cordibus nunc odium et invidia latet. Qui adversus Dei ecclesiam saeviunt, ipsi etiam quasi Magog, hoc est detecto egredientes, et invidia manifestantes."

49. R. B. C. Huygens, "Un témoin de la crainte de l'an 1000: La lettre sur les Hongrois," *Latomus* 15 (1957): 235–38; Fried, "Endzeiterwartung," pp. 385–86.

50. Haimo, *PL* 117:781C; Adso, *CCCM* 45:29.184–85.

51. Thietland, Einsiedeln MS 38, fol. 185r.

52. Emmerson, *Antichrist*, p. 93.

53. Thietland, Einsiedeln MS 38, fol. 185v: "Verum mendacia sint illa signa, et fantastico more fiant ut videantur signa et non sint an certe veraciter signa sint, et ideo dicantur mendacia, quia ad mendacium pertrahent, hoc est ut ille Deus credatur qui est homo peccati. . . . Item quoquomodo fiant, non alii decipientur nisi qui decipi merebuntur."

54. Haimo, *PL* 117:782A; Adso, *CCCM* 45:24.51–55.

55. Augustine, *De civitate Dei*, 20.19 (*CC* 48:730–33).

56. Thietland, Einsiedeln MS 38, fol.185v: "At tamen sciendum quia ignis ille qui greges Iob puerosque consumpsit, atque turbo qui domum eiusdem concussit, quae corruens oppressit liberos eius (vera signa fuerunt), licet diaboli opera, cui data a Deo potestas haec operandi. Veruntamen quoquomodo fiant, illi qui tunc erunt fideles agnoscerent."

57. Ibid.: "Illud tamen notandum quia ipsi iudicati decipientur, illis tamen Dei iudiciis occulte iustis et iuste occultis, quibus ipse Deus ab initio peccati rationabilis creaturae non cessavit iudicare. Decepti etiam ac seducti iustificabuntur illo ultimo manifestoque Dei iudicio, per Dominum nostrum Ihesum Christum, iustissime iudicaturum iniustissime iudicatum." (Cf. with Augustine, *De civitate Dei*, 20.19 [*CC* 48:730–33].)

5

Avarice and the Apocalypse

Richard Newhauser

Reflecting on the history of the church and the stage of its turmoil in the twelfth century, Gerhoh of Reichersberg (1093–1169) found it necessary to draw on the language of the Apocalypse in describing the conflict between imperial rule and the power of the *ecclesia*. In his major analysis of the stages of development of the church's history, *The Fourth Watch of the Night*, Gerhoh characterized the final, apocalyptic stage in which he himself lived as dominated by greedy behavior. The previous watch was presided over by the popes, from Gregory the Great to Gregory VII, but after that

> more dangerous times began, it seems, because from that point on a new avarice arose in the city of Rome. For previously, the Roman people had the habit of voluntarily pledging feudal loyalty to their pastor with due obedience, but after the contention arose between the priesthood and the kingdom, the citizens of Rome who were followers of the pope did not want to struggle in such a war for nothing but demanded a great deal of money as if it were a kind of salary owed for their military service. . . . Thus, in this fourth watch an avarice enlarged with the greediness for gain rules the whole body of the church from head to foot. . . . Now, however, you would be pouring out a sermon [against this sin] in vain where there is no hearing, in the sight of men who think that gain is a form of piety.[1]

This statement is, in many ways, representative of twelfth-century reactions to the important changes that had taken place in, and were transforming, the economic situation of Europe, in which, as Lester Little has pointed out, gift exchange as the cement of social relations was being replaced by the commodification of liquid capital exchange: feudal obedience, as Gerhoh complains, a system in which loyalty was given freely to those in positions of power, has given way in his age to demands for a salary.[2] Moralists registered this change to a profit economy in which social relationships were becoming commercialized as a disturbance in the ethical continuum by which avarice was often perceived as the dominant vice. Because the use of cash as an agent of exchange allowed more people to manifest the signs of wealth and to desire to be wealthy than had been possible in the early Middle Ages, when only the feudal aristocracy had had access to the immovable wealth in land, the complaints of moralists from the eleventh century onward often contain descriptions of the entire world falling prey to greed. In the context of the eleventh and twelfth centuries, that is to say, complaints about greed proliferated and took on an importance they had only occasionally had before then. And yet, one might ask why the spread of avaricious behavior would qualify, not just as one of the signs of the coming end of the world, but, as in Gerhoh's case and, as will be seen, in that of many earlier writers attracted by the focal point of the year 1000 as well, as perhaps the most significant portent of the approaching apocalypse.

It is clear that before the year 1000, the time of the Antichrist was understood to be a period during which there would be widespread sinfulness in general. It was to be, as Adso, abbot of Montier-en-Der (d. 992), wrote in his letter on the Antichrist, a period in which the wicked would be exalted and the apocalyptic perverter of divinity would teach the "vices opposed to the virtues." Indeed, Adso even refers to the figure of the Antichrist as the "man of sin" in the same work.[3] Albuin (d. 1031 as abbot in Tegernsee), who used Adso's material freely, combined his own tract on the Antichrist with a dossier on vices and virtues. Most of the material Albuin used is presented in different combinations in at least three separate redactions, each addressed to a different recipient: the *Liber scintillarum collectus ab Albuino heremita*, addressed to Heribert, archbishop in Cologne; the *Liber de virtutibus ad Arnaldum, Pariacensem canonicum*; and the *Liber Albuini* addressed to an unknown woman.[4] The last work actually does not contain Albuin's tract on the Antichrist but is given over fully to material on vices and virtues: *caritas, humilitas, obedientia, continentia, de pugna viciorum*, and so on. But even here, Albuin explains his purpose in collecting material from the moral tradition in eschatological terms. It is his wish that the "mater" and "domina" to whom he is sending the work will preserve it like a most precious pearl among her treasures: "If, therefore, you can carry out all the things that you will find written here, I know for certain that you will come safely on doomsday before the seat of judgment of Jesus Christ, and safeguarded from all enemies, you will possess a perpetual crown in Heaven."[5] The coming of the end of days might have been presaged by the rampant spread of vices, but as Albuin shows, and as Johannes Fried has emphasized, the ideal reaction to the knowledge of sin spreading in the world in anticipation of the apocalypse was not to be petrified with fear, or to lose oneself in the perception of social disruptions evoked by millenarian Angst, but to redouble one's efforts, internally and individually, to live a life of virtue.[6] This effort expressed itself in practical and very real terms in the education of those who wrote on apocalyptic matters. In Aquitaine at Saint-Martial, for example, Ademar of Chabannes (989–1034) seems to have worked on the *Psychomachia*, for as Richard Landes has noted, a manuscript of the text shows signs of Ademar's glossing hand and illuminations. A number of years later, Ademar copied the *De octo vitiosis cogitationibus*, mistakenly attributed to Nilus but actually composed of excerpts from the writings of Evagrius, Nilus, and John Cassian. And at the end of his career, Ademar copied Theodulf of Orléans's *De ordine baptismi* and expanded the passage in this text on renouncing the works of Satan by identifying these works with the octad of vices and presenting the opposing virtues as those that the clergy should teach to their flocks, in sacraments and confession.[7] What the effort to live in virtue meant in practical terms, thus, was often a vigilant study of the vices and virtues, a study which made signs of the world's end a matter of contemplative meditation and moderate action, modulating between the hysterical reactions of repenting because the end is just around the corner, on the one hand, and, on the other, of repenting in order to keep the end from turning that corner.

The effort to recognize the vices leading to the apocalypse also meant keeping a sharp eye on the spread of a sinfulness that was understood as turning the world upside down. Chaos as a precondition to the apocalypse was understood in eschatology in its moral and social dimensions; the spread of vice in the church and the dissolution of the social order were taken as equal members in the lists of signs of the approaching end. More than this, the ever-increasing sinfulness of humanity was understood as one of the most important tokens of the decay of the human condition and the imminent destruction of the world. This well-known topic has scriptural precedence, of course, for in 2 Tim. 3:1 one reads: "Moreover, I know this, that in the final days dangerous times will press upon us: there will be people who love themselves, greedy, puffed up, proud, blasphemers, not obedient to their parents, ingrates." The Tiburtine Sibyl added more vices to this list, noting that after the appearance of those who are contentious, the haters of justice, the rapacious, and the greedy, the Antichrist will appear.[8] But the tenth century, under the pressure of the approaching millennium, made of such tropes a *growing* sinfulness of the world, which was interpreted as a sure sign of the hastening end, of the apocalyptic moment's *acceleration*. The critique of everyday reality not only took note of the presence of corruption but also inscribed a conviction that evil was increasing steadily, that immorality was quickly approaching the point of critical mass. "Now barely any tender shoots of *caritas* bloom," one poet of the tenth century put it. "Good qualities sink down, bad ones are on the rise, the vices are repeated. Thus does the Devil's trickery make sport of the appearance of God."[9] One can, thus, understand how in the tradition of 2 Timothy, and comprehended among the catalog of signs of the coming end of the world, the perception of sustained sinfulness might be interpreted as apocalyptic, but what, then, to return to the question posed already, is the *special* relationship between the particular vice of avarice and the apocalypse?

One can begin by noting that the birth pangs of the money economy at the turn of the millennium heightened to a new pitch the consciousness of avarice as the deadliest of the vices. From the vantage point of the monastic chronicler

Radulfus Glaber (ca. 985–ca. 1046), the vice had decimated society as a whole by the late tenth century, and he referred to *filargiria* as a monstrous queen of vices dominating the entire world.[10] The image of avarice in Glaber's work and that of a number of his contemporaries had already begun to reflect the growing consciousness of money and its influence by returning to the Cassianic literal etymology of the vice (*filargyria* being the latinized transcription of a Greek word which means literally the "love of silver"), so that by the early eleventh century avarice was virtually equated with the desire for coin. Peter Damiani (1007–72) noted that when Paul calls avarice idolatry (Col. 3:6), "he teaches in a clearer light that the *avarus* is a servant, not of God, but of coins."[11] By the early eleventh century, then, the critique of avarice encompassed an array of venal behavior much of which was focused on the acquisition of coins.[12] Even such an academic poem as the *Fecunda ratis*, for example, composed by Egbert of Liège around 1025 as a collection of school exercises, echoes the satires of Horace by criticizing a situation in which, "not art, but the goddess Money" is found more excellent than any honor.[13] The interest in ecclesiastical reform that occurred together with the Investiture Contest generated legions of satires censuring the avaricious behavior of the clergy as illustrations of the power of money. In particular, the greed of Rome and of the papacy itself was expressed in the proverbial wisdom that "Roma" was an acronym for *radix omnium malorum avaritia* (the root of all evils is avarice).[14] By the turn of the millennium, the very iconography of the vice and the sinner afflicted by avarice had developed in the visual arts to show a marked tendency to represent greed by the presence of coins or a money bag, generally slung around the neck of the avaricious sinner.[15] Thus, the moral response to the inchoate pressures of a changing economic technology resulted in an emphatic focus on avarice as the source of deviant ethical behavior just when the consciousness of moral theologians was being shaped by the focal point of the millennium and its apocalyptic expectations. Moral thought, in this way, was predisposed to draw a connection between avarice and the apocalypse.

There was certainly further reason to focus on avarice and the end of the world at the end of the tenth century and the beginning of the eleventh in the view of those who saw simony as the destruction of the church—and thus of the primary institution of moral order in the world—since moral theologians frequently listed simony as a progeny of avarice. It is generally true that eschatological vision highlights the failings of the present moment, and at the end of the tenth century the defect of rampant materialism, witnessed particularly in the church, drew all the more alarmed comment. In the area of the old Carolingian Empire, as Henri Maisonneuve noted, the movement of reform, left its mark in acts of the councils of the time in suggested remedies for Christian society among the clergy, monks, and laity. Simony among the clergy is apparently not mentioned often in the councils (though it was specifically condemned in 916 at the council in Hohenaltheim), but one finds various warnings against receiving or demanding payment for giving penance or baptism; in the early eleventh century, the reforming attempts of the preceding century are taken up with great vigor, and from the council of Pavia (1023) and the efforts of Leo IX on, the repression of simony became more severe.[16] Among those who were attuned to the signs of the apocalypse, combating simony and reestablishing order in the church were firmly linked to the question of when the world would end. Among other errors that Abbo of Fleury (945–1004) complains about to Kings Hugo and Robert in his famous *Apologeticus*, for example, one finds a great deal of attention focused on the simony which amounts to the buying and selling of bishoprics: "See, most equitable princes, to where cupidity is leading us, while *caritas* grows cold; from the gifts of omnipotent God, which are received freely, we are made into merchants, and we attempt to sell what we in fact do not own."[17] He continued with little pause to complain of the error that had filled almost the whole world, at least according to some Lotharingians: the stipulation that exactly when the feast of the Annunciation coincided with Good Friday the world would end. Clerical greed is here among the errors afflicting the church, like the attempt to be too exact in reckoning the moment of the apocalypse. Nevertheless, the question of simony is specific only to the clergy, and if one is to discern the relationship between avarice and the apocalypse around the year 1000 in more comprehensive terms, as appears to be called for from writers on eschatology at that time, then the problem of simony may provide supporting evidence for the importance of avarice, like the economic predisposition to see greed as the dominant vice, but not answer completely the question of the particular relationship of greed and the end of the world.[18]

That humanity will become avaricious in the Last Days, and that this fact has a special value in the system of eschatology, belong to the tropes of the signs of deterioration leading to the apocalypse, and such rhetorical forms are notoriously conservative in medieval texts. Even a literary form such as the ecclesiastical charter reveals the view that unbridled avarice is intimately connected with the end of the world. In one charter from Saint-Hilaire in Poitiers written between 997 and the turn of the millennium, for example, Geoffrey, treasurer of the chapter there, complained of the dissipation of ecclesiastical goods, which "we see are plundered in our time, in which greed is on the rise and the end of the world is imminent, and since a briefer life distresses people, a harsher greediness vexes them."[19] One might, therefore, ask if there is a precedent for avarice functioning as such a trope in analyses of time coming to an end, or *a* time coming to an end, that might have served as a model for eschatological thought. There is, in fact, such a precedent in patristic literature, and one can begin to understand the particular function of avarice in the context of apocalyptic expectations by examining the early Christian use of the myth of the golden age and its demise and the reception of these ideas in the Middle Ages.

Not only was the social disruption caused by avarice a contemporary problem for fourth-century writers, but looked at from the vantage point of a Christianity which was quickly becoming the dominant religion of the Roman Empire and from an environment which allowed for leisurely and academic contemplation, the vice could also be seen as having a historical dimension. In the work of Lactantius (ca. 240–ca. 320), rhetorician and teacher of Emperor Constantine's son, cupidity was given a firm place in the Christian mythology of the golden age. Reflections on a former "utopian" state of humanity and the process of its degeneration had, of course, long been common in antiquity. Avarice had frequently served in such considerations as an indicator of the progress of this deterioration, but in Lactantius's thought, in particular his reception of Seneca, the vice plays a much more active role in bringing the *aurea tempora* to an end.[20] Lactantius's remarks on this issue are, in essence, those of a theological apologist; they occur in the context of his attempt to convince the pagan reader of the moral inferiority of polytheism.[21] Historically prior to the Greco-Roman pantheon was an idyllic era characterized by the worship of the one, true God. In this age, the just gave of their reserves generously. No *avaritia* took for itself goods that had been bestowed on all by the divinity; no greed caused hunger and thirst to plague humankind. All things were in abundance for all equally, since the haves gave freely and copiously to the have-nots. Lactantius does not refer explicitly to this period in terms of the biblical account of Eden, but it is clear enough that he has this in mind, along with the golden age of the poets. He is, in fact, the first patristic author to unite these two conceptions.[22]

Monotheism, then, made personal generosity, largess, and above all justice possible among human beings. With the transition to polytheism this situation changed radically, for now social relations began to come under the influence of avarice as humanity gave no more thought to God. Those who possessed something in surfeit not only kept what they had in excess for themselves but also seized things from others for their own treasure. What formerly each individual had put at the disposal of the community was now hoarded up in the homes of a few. This select group claimed the gifts of Heaven for themselves, not out of any philanthropy, but in order to collect all the instruments of greed and avarice so they could enslave the rest of humanity. For this purpose they also created unjust laws in the name of a perverted justice, put themselves in positions of authority over all others, and set about establishing the machinery of oppression to maintain their power. In Lactantius's mythical history of humanity, the tyranny of this overweening individualism, which he describes at one point as a *superba et tumida inaequalitas* and which might be defined in terms of the sin of pride itself, is seen as a direct result of avarice.[23] Personal egotism led in turn to an elitist injustice in society, but behind them both stands an initial act of "rabid and furious *avaritia*."[24]

The golden age was not destroyed once and for all by polytheism. With the resurgence of monotheism, by which Lactantius refers to the genesis of Christianity, at least a *species illius aurei temporis* returned to the earth.[25] This idea of a resurrection of the golden age would not have surprised his pagan audience; Virgil's *Fourth Eclogue* and the *Sibylline Oracles*, both of which Lactantius refers to directly elsewhere, had posited much the same.[26] But by insisting on the ethical function of Christianity as an image of the idyllic time to come, he goes a large step beyond his predecessors. This, of course, has everything to do with his apologetic intention of bringing his audience to an acceptance of the contemporary Christian community, with its inherited social disparity, as nevertheless a model, a type, for millenarian society. Thus, he argues that only through the *iustitia* of Christianity can the social injustice of avarice be undone. Were all humanity to worship the one God, there would be no more wars, dissensions, treachery, frauds, and pillaging; rather, a "pious and religious assembly of those with possessions would support those without them."[27] For Lactantius, in other words, the defeat of avarice is necessarily a simple matter of conversion.

The function of avarice as the vice that led to the destruction of the golden age is, thus, firmly rooted in Lactantius's thought, and it can be seen to have influenced ideas of avarice and the apocalypse elsewhere in patristic and early medieval literature. Ambrose's (ca. 339–397) implicit condemnation of what he took to be the very beginnings of the process leading to private property becomes all the clearer when one takes note of avarice's role in this process. Here, too, the thought of the bishop of Milan shows his critical use of Cicero's De officiis, in particular the Roman writer's statement that striving to increase one's goods is legitimate and avarice is only a perversion of this justifiable desire.[28] For Ambrose, however, the sin has an elementary force; he sees it acting in much the same way as had Lactantius and Seneca, as the cause of the moral decline of the commonwealth and the appearance of private property.[29] And diametrically opposed to his Ciceronian model, Ambrose finds the repercussions of this original sin at work in the very activity the Roman author had justified, for as long as human beings desire to increase their wealth, he says, they have cast off the form of justice and lost the sense of benefiting all. Avarice, in Ambrose's reflection of the golden age mythology, is not a perversion of the desire to increase one's possessions; it is that desire itself.

Early medieval reflection on the golden age mythology and avarice's place in bringing that era to a close remains part of the critique of the times and the perception of humanity's deterioration on the road to its apocalyptic end. Isidore of Seville (ca. 560–636), for example, frequently identified greed as a form of the violent oppression of the poor by the mighty, but this could be seen as much in the corruption of the legal system, in both contemporary and historical terms, as in the open bloodshed of such a literary figure as Achab (1 Kings 21). His view in the Synonyms varies the use of the golden age myth by earlier authors for whom a legal system was the result of primeval greed altogether, but in spite of his reception of Gregorian thought, Isidore's sense of the ubiquitous presence of avarice is no less urgent than what has been observed among tenth-century writers: "Avarice has spread, the law has perished because of the love of cupidity, legal rights have no validity, bribes and gifts have weakened the laws. Everywhere money conquers, everywhere there is a purchasable judgment."[30]

The growth of immorality, the perversion of justice, the spread of oppression, the end of the equality and abundance of nature's goods, and the catalyst for all this—the rise of avarice—these criteria mark parallel situations in apocalyptic thought and the Christian use of the myth of the golden age. For Lactantius himself, not always an original writer but generally a reliable gauge of themes, which resonated for the entire patristic period and the early Middle Ages, the correspondence between avarice and eschatology was apparently evident enough to be reflected in his apocalypticism. His description of the end of the world draws on the same language he uses to describe the end of the golden age, thus encouraging comparison between the present time and the golden one, both having succumbed, or now succumbing, to the sin of avarice:

> Therefore, as the end of the world approaches, the situation of human affairs must change and sink into worse decay while evil prevails, so that our own times, in which iniquity and ill will have grown to the highest degree, can nevertheless be judged as a happy and almost golden time in comparison to the incurable evil of that one. For justice will become so rare, impiety and avarice and covetousness and lust will increase to such a degree, that even if by chance good people should exist, they will be plunder for the wicked.[31]

The vice of avarice, the sin of worldliness par excellence, was uniquely placed to be one of the leading signs of the approaching end of the world in the tenth century not only because of a changing economic situation or a focus on the vices of the clergy but also, rhetorically, because it had already served that purpose in analyses of the end of the golden age and was transmitted as the most significant catalyst for apocalyptic upheaval in patristic thought and early in the medieval period. It is clear that the precise contours of avarice changed in eschatology as the demands on apocalyptic thought were altered, from a tool in the Christian transformation of late antique society to a meditative and social-critical step in the renewal of the church in the tenth century to the critique of a burgeoning mercantilism in the twelfth century. In all of these cases, I would suggest, greed had a preeminent place among the signs of decay because it served as a determining factor in the understanding of humanity's deterioration from the beginning. Avarice had a role in the end of human history, that is to say, because it had played a similar one near the beginning of that history.

NOTES

This essay in its present form reflects my thinking in 1995, when it was written. Some of the material contained in this essay appeared subsequently in the following publication: Richard Newhauser, *The Early History of Greed: The Sin of Avarice in Early Medieval Thought and Literature*, Cambridge Studies in Medieval Literature, vol. 41 (Cambridge, 2000). © Cambridge University Press 2000. Reprinted with permission.

   Editors' note: An earlier version of this paper was presented at the "Conference on the Apocalyptic Year 1000" in Boston, Mass., November 4–6, 1996. Richard Newhauser is Professor of English and Medieval Studies at Trinity University, San Antonio, Texas.

   1. Gerhoh of Reichersberg, *De quarta vigilia noctis*, vol. 11, ed. E. Sackur, *Libelli de lite* 3 (Hannover, 1897), pp. 509–10. See Henrietta Leyser, *Hermits and the New Monasticism: A Study of Religious Communities in Western Europe, 1000–1150* (London, 1984), pp. 55–56; B. McGinn, ed., *Visions of the End* (New York, 1979), pp. 104–5; Peter Classen, *Gerhoch von Reichersberg: eine Biographie mit einem Anhang über die Quellen, ihre handschriftliche Überlieferung und ihre Chronologie* (Wiesbaden, 1960), pp. 292–98.

2. Lester K. Little, *Religious Poverty and the Profit Economy in Medieval Europe* (London, 1978), pp. 19–41.

3. Adso Dervensis, *De ortu et tempore Antichristi*, ed. D. Verhelst, CCCM 45 (Turnhout, 1976), pp. 22–23, 26.

4. See *CCCM* 45:55–89.

5. Paris, BN MS lat. 2780, fol. 69v: "Si itaque poteris omnia perficere, quae hic inueneris scripta, scio pro certo, quod secura uenies in die iudicii ante tribunal ihesu christi et defensa ab omnibus inimicis possidebis perpetuam coronam in coelis."

6. Johannes Fried, "Endzeiterwartung um die Jahrtausendwende," *Deutsches Archiv für Erforschung des Mittelalters* 45, no. 2 (1989): 439 (see also chap. 1, this volume).

7. The MS of Prudentius is Leiden, UB MS Voss. 8° 15, fols. 37–62; the MS of Pseudo-Nilus is BN MS lat. 3784, fols. 122–24; the MS of Theodulf is Phillips MS 1664, fols. 165–66. On Ademar's work on these manuscripts, see Richard Landes, *Relics, Apocalypse, and the Deceits of History: Ademar of Chabannes, 989–1034* (Cambridge, Mass., 1995).

8. Ernst Sackur, ed., *Sibyllinische Texte und Forschungen* (Halle a. S., 1898), pp. 183–85.

9. G. M. Dreves and C. Blume, eds., *Analecta Hymnica Medii Aevi*, vol. 45b (Leipzig, 1915; reprint, New York, 1961), p. 74: "Nulla paene jam virescunt / Caritatis germina, / Bona cadunt, mala surgunt, / Immutantur vitia. / Sic deludit Dei formam / Daemonis versutia." See Dimitri Scheludko, "Klagen über den Verfall der Welt bei den Trobadors: Allegorische Darstellungen des Kampfes der Tugenden und der Laster," *Neuphilologische Mitteilungen* 44 (1943): 25.

10. *Rodulfi Glabri Historiarum libri quinque*, 4.2, ed. and trans. J. France (Oxford, 1989), p. 173. *Filargiria* is, of course, John Cassian's technical term for the vice. The term remained common in the monastic environment even when the understanding of the vice was indebted to Gregory the Great; see Richard Newhauser, "Towards *modus in habendo*: Transformations in the Idea of Avarice, the Early Penitentials through the Carolingian Reforms," *Zeitschrift der Savigny-Stiftung für Rechtsgeschichte* 106, Kanonistische Abteilung 75 (1989): 1–22; and cf. Conrad Leyser, "Cities of the Plain: The Rhetoric of Sodomy in Peter Damian's 'Book of Gomorrah,'" *Romanic Review* 86 (1995): 200 n. 48. On Glaber, see also Richard Landes, "Rodulfus Glaber and the Dawn of the New Millennium: Eschatology, Historiography and the Year 1000," *Revue Mabillon*, n.s., 7 [68] (1996): 1–21.

11. Peter Damiani, *De contemptu saeculi*, 6 (PL 145:256).

12. Besides the important study by John A. Yunck, *The Lineage of Lady Meed*, University of Notre Dame Publications in Mediaeval Studies, vol. 17 (Notre Dame, 1963), see for some later developments in reflections on avarice E. M. Katharina Brett, "Avarice and Largesse: A Study of the Theme in Moral-Satirical Poetry in Provençal, Latin and Old French, 1100–1300" (dissertation, University of Cambridge, 1986).

13. Egbert of Liège, *Fecunda ratis*, 1.1252, ed. E. Voigt (Halle, 1889), p. 103. See Yunck, *Lineage of Lady Meed*, p. 62.

14. See Josef Benzinger, *Invectiva in Romam: Romkritik im Mittelalter vom 9. bis zum 12. Jahrhundert*, Historische Studien, vol. 404 (Lübeck and Hamburg, 1968), pp. 91–93.

15. For early developments in Romanesque sculpture in the Auvergne, see Priscilla Baumann, "The Deadliest Sin: Warnings against Avarice and Usury on Romanesque Capitals in Auvergne," *Church History* 59, no. 1 (1990): 7–18; J. Martin-

Bagnaudez, "Les représentations romans de l'avare: Étude iconographique," *Revue d'Histoire de la Spiritualité* 50 (1974): 397–432.

16. Henri Maisonneuve, *La morale chrétienne d'aprés les conciles des Xe et XIe siècles*, Analecta mediaevalia Namurcensia, vol. 15 (Louvain and Lille, 1963), pp. 7–9, 31–32.

17. Abbo of Fleury, *Apologeticus* (*PL* 139:466): "Videte, aequissimi principes, quo nos ducit cupiditas, dum refrigescit charitas; ex donis omnipotentis Dei, quae gratis accipiuntur, mercatores efficimur, et vendere conamur, quod profecto non possidemus."

18. On the implications of simony for the laity, see Auguste Dumas in *L'Eglise au pouvoir des laiques (888–1057)*, by Emile Amann and Auguste Dumas, Histoire de l'Eglise depuis les origines jusqu'à nos jours, vol. 7 (Paris, 1948), p. 473.

19. Vienne, Arch. Dépt., carton 3, no. 50: "nostris temporibus crescente cupiditate videmus invadi, et seculi imminente fine, cum homines brevior vita perurgeat, atrocior cupiditas p<er>urget." I am grateful to Richard Landes for giving me access to this charter and to Georges Pon for the transcription I have used.

20. Lactantius, *Divinae institutiones* 5.5.8–6.6, ed. P. Monat, SC 204 (Paris, 1973), pp. 152–56. See Seneca, *Epistulae morales*, 90.3 and 90.38, ed. L. D. Reynolds (Oxford, 1965), vol. 2, pp. 332, 342–43.

21. See Vinzenz Buchheit, "Goldene Zeit und Paradies auf Erden (Laktanz, Inst. 5,5–8)," *Würzburger Jahrbücher für die Altertumswissenschaft*, n.s., 4 (1978): 161–85; 5 (1979): 219–35, here esp. 163–64; and Louis J. Swift, "Lactantius and the Golden Age," *American Journal of Philology* 89 (1968): 144–56.

22. Buchheit, "Goldene Zeit," 4, pp. 162–63; Bodo Gatz, *Weltalter, goldene Zeit und sinnverwandte Vorstellungen*, Spudasmata, vol. 16 (Hildesheim, 1967), p. 178.

23. *Div. inst.*, 5.6.4 (SC 204:156). Greed, thus, is for Lactantius the negation of the all-important virtue of *iustitia*, a virtue that leads to *aequitas*, the love of one's neighbor founded on the equality of all human beings. For the idea of justice in Lactantius's thought, see Vinzenz Buchheit, "Die Definition der Gerechtigkeit bei Laktanz and seinen Vorgängern," *Vigiliae Christianae* 33 (1979): 356–74; Albrecht Dihle, "Gerechtigkeit," *Reallexikon für Antike und Christentum*, vol. 10 (1978): 335–36; and P. Monat's introduction to his edition, SC 204:20–33.

24. *Div. inst.*, 5.5.6 (SC 204:152); see also Konrad Farner, *Christentum und Eigentum bis Thomas von Aquin*, Mensch und Gesellschaft, vol. 12 (Bern, 1947), p. 61. Lactantius also considered that the delight in images made of gold, gems, and ivory had led the pagans astray to such a degree that they could not conceive of religion without these precious materials. At this point they were not even serving the gods, but only avarice and cupidity. See *Div. inst.*, 2.6.2–3, ed. S. Brandt, *CSEL* 19 (Vienna, 1890), pp. 121–22.

25. *Div. inst.*, 5.7.1–2 (SC 204:160).

26. See Samuel Brandt's notes to his edition of *Div. inst.*, 7.24.6ff. (*CSEL* 19:659ff.), for the passages in question. But in *Div. inst.*, 5.7.1–2 there are also numerous Virgilian echoes; see Buchheit, "Goldene Zeit," 5, pp. 219–22; Hans Larmann, *Christliche Wirtschaftsethik in der spätrömischen Antike*, Furche-Studien, vol. 13 (Berlin, 1935), p. 84. That Lactantius quoted from the Sibylline Oracles is typical of his reading; he knew no Greek classical prose or poetry, but only oracular literature. See R. M. Ogilvie, *The Library of Lactantius* (Oxford, 1978), pp. 28ff.

27. *Div. inst.*, 5.8.7 (SC 204:166). Compare the list of evils to be corrected here to that which Arnobius, Lactantius's teacher, found to be typical of the evil souls of this world in *Aduersus nationes*, 2.43, ed. A. Reifferscheid, CSEL 4 (Vienna, 1875), p. 83.

28. Cicero, *De officiis*, 1.7.24–8.25, ed. P. Fedeli, (Florence, 1965), pp. 36–37. Note especially the last sentence in 1.8.25: "Nec uero rei familiaris amplificatio nemini nocens uituperanda est, sed fugienda semper iniuria est." How far Cicero is from the thought of an equal distribution of goods in society can be seen in *De off.*, 2.21.73 (ed. Fedeli, p. 144), where he says that there could be no greater pest than this form of social equality.

29. Ambrose, *De officiis ministrorum*, 1.28.137 (*PL* 16:68).

30. Isidore of Seville, *Synonymorum . . . libri 2*, 1.8 (*PL* 83:829). For Isidore's concern with correcting the corruption of judges, see Hans-Joachim Diesner, *Isidor von Sevilla und seine Zeit*, Aufsätze und Vorträge zur Theologie und Religionswissenschaft, vol. 57 (Berlin, 1973), pp. 59–60; Yunck, *Lineage of Lady Meed*, p. 33.

31. *Div. inst.*, 7.15.7–8 (*CSEL* 19:631–32). See Bernard McGinn, *Apocalyptic Spirituality* (New York, 1979), pp. 57–58.

6

Waiting for
the Millennium

Umberto Eco

My presence here is the result of a misunderstanding, and I do not
know if I'll succeed in transforming it into a *felix culpa*. When
Richard Landes asked me to relate more or less what I wrote twenty-
five years ago about millenarism, I believed that this would be a
colloquium on the various problems connected with the expectation
of the year 2000, and so I agreed to say something about the
expectation of the year 1000. Only a few days ago I understood that I
am to speak to people who spend their lives studying just the first
expectation, and I realized that I have nothing new to say to my
fellow medievalists, first of all because my old and modest contributions to medieval studies concerned only the history of aesthetics
and mainly the aesthetics of Aquinas. Thus, please do take my talk,
not as a scholarly lecture, but rather as a collection of personal
remarks about the problem of thinking about the millennium based
on my reading of the commentary on the Book of Revelation by
Beatus of Liebana.

I met Beatus and the series of Mozarabic Beati in the early
fifties, when I tried to understand the general background of the
medieval aesthetic sensibility. In 1972 Franco Maria Ricci, who was
publishing a series of art books—real collector items, each devoted to
a given work of art commented on by a writer (among whom, for
instance, were Jorge Luis Borges and Roland Barthes)—asked me to
suggest to him some visual text that I could introduce, and I decided
that this was my chance to get closer to the tradition of the Beati. We
chose the Beatus by Magius, and I read Beatus's *Commentary* in the
Sanders edition, which was the most reliable at that time. It was the
most boring experience of my life, because Beatus is an unbearable
writer, his ideas are confused, he lacked critical sensitivity and was

unable to make an interpretive decision every time his sources were mutually contradictory—in short, Beatus was certainly one of the less intelligent authors who ever showed up in the course of history. But by virtue of Gresham's Law, his book became a best-seller, a cult book, probably because it was as incoherent and unshaped as the *Rocky Horror Picture Show*.

My reference to a cult movie is not a joke: once I analyzed the reasons by which a book or a movie becomes a cult object, I realized that the essential feature is that it must be out of joint, structurally discombobulated, ramshackle, and generally unhinged. Thus, its readers or spectators can pick up or recall to mind this or that part, without considering the whole. Better still, one can "cut and paste" several parts at a time irrespective of the fact that they are not consistent with the rest.

Thus, I tried to understand why in the eighth century a Spanish monk set out to write a mammoth commentary on a few pages of St. John's Book of Revelation, making it more obscure and ambiguous than it originally was, and why this salmagundi from different sources had an unprecedented success.

At the same time, as soon as I went on to understand something about the history of millenarism, I felt a strange sensation. The 1970s were in Europe the years in which the political springtime of 1968, after a short and very hot summer, entered an ambiguous fall in which the first terrorist movements started to show up, from the Bader Meinhof group in Germany to the Red Brigades in Italy. I knew that the original leaders of the Red Brigades did not come originally from a Marxist background but were on the contrary born Catholic. Thus, in the wake of my reading on the old millenarism I realized that, while writing on the chiliastic tradition, I was also writing about my own times. Let me share, in passing, some of my historical reflections, which are perhaps also introspections.

The Year 1000

We know the old story. Romanticism, which made a specialty of presenting picturesque images of the so-called Dark Ages (strongly spreading about the impression that they kept going until, at least, the times of Notre Dame de Paris), gave us many descriptions of the last night of the first millennium, when crowds packed into the churches, trembling, as they awaited the end of the world. Then, as the Romantic tradition has it, the dawn of the day after breaks, and the world, stunned, moved, exalted, realizes that everything is still in its place. This realization sparks such a burst of energy and optimism that, all at once, the postmillennial rebirth begins. The proof was the famous text by Radulfus Glaber according to which "[a]bout three years after the year 1000 the earth began to be covered by a white cloak of churches." A springtime burgeoning after a long winter. Too beautiful to be true.

Later historians told us that on that famous night nothing happened. Oddly enough, the uneasiness did exist, but both before and after. Personally, I believe that something happened that night, at least here and there among common people, because the image of a dying millennium was too strong to be passed over in silence and indifference and must have fascinated and frightened the popular imagination. But today I am only supposed to share some reflections on Beatus.

The Apocalyptic Web

If the Book of Revelation is such an inexhaustible source of contradictory feelings, of both hope and fear, and if Beatus's commentary is such an untenable mishmash of conflicting points of view, then it seems to me that when speaking of the idea of apocalypse we are not dealing with a unified concept but rather with what I would call the apocalyptic web. This web is made up of many threads, and it is not immediately clear that when one follows one of its possible strands one can also retrieve the others. In attempting to unravel the apocalyptic web, one should choose a thread and follow it all the way to its end; Beatus did not, and was unable to do so.

Even though I am certainly not exhausting the complexity of the web, let me list five main threads that appear over and over throughout the warp and woof of the year 1000:

1. The expectation of the end of the world, of the Last Judgment, and of the Second Coming of Christ (this option being at the same time a reason for both hope and fear)
2. The expectation of the sabbatical millennium
3. The feeling that at the junction between the first and second millenniums something terrible had to happen
4. The philosophical and literary topos of *mundus senescens*
5. The expectation of the coming of the Antichrist

As for point 1 (without even considering the classical trope *bibamus, edamus, et coronamus nos rosis, cras moriemur*), the feeling of the always incumbent end of the world has pervaded the popular imagination even into our own times; otherwise, the troubles provoked by Orson Welles's science-fiction broadcast *Invasion from Mars* would be sociologically inexplicable. People are accustomed to think that all animals are mortal: thus, why should not the world (always considered as a megazoon, a great animal) be mortal as well? St. John's Revelation masterfully plays upon such an archetypal feeling but does not invent it. For instance, the idea of a final *ekpyrosis* existed in the classical Greek tradition as well.

As for point 2, not only the expectation but the action performed in order to enter the sabbatical millennium was particularly strong after the year 1000. Chiliasm is an evergreen fantasy; it is not necessarily linked to apocalyptic expectations, and it has found in the last centuries its own atheistic avatars. In this regard, I think of Marxism and of its Leninist and Maoist versions, not to speak of the various cargo cults in other continents.

As for point 3, the idea that at the junction between the first and second millenniums something terrible had to happen is returning today (and just because it did not happen then) at the junction between the second and the third millennium. This is so even in such patently nonreligious forms as all the fuss over technological and economic collapse swirling around the so-called Y2K problem that may or may not paralyze our computers, and hence those who rely on them.

As for point 4, *laudatores temporis acti* existed before Christianity, and the morbid celebration of decadence is typical of modern and secular culture (think, for instance, of Verlaine's "Je suis l'empire à la fin de la decadence"). The historical or sociological vision of cultural decadence is a common topic of our century as well, from Spengler to the severe analysis of mass civilization by Adorno and the Frankfurt School in general, and from movies like *Blade Runner* to the recurring warnings about the decline of literacy or environmental degradation.

As for point 5, we know that the coming of the Antichrist, or the antitype of an awaited messiah, is a pre-Christian obsession, and that Gog and Magog are not an invention of the New Testament. Well after the year 1000 Roger Bacon identified the Antichrist with the Tartars, and the image of the Enemy haunted even the anti-Semitic thought of the nineteenth and twentieth centuries. The *Protocols of the Elders of Zion* (partly inspired, albeit unconsciously, by the image of the Jew supported by Beatus) promised a new Armageddon that the Nazi chiliasts believed to have won on the battlefields of Dachau and Auschwitz.

Augustine versus Beatus

I said that one must choose among the various threads of the apocalyptic web. Augustine did so with his well-known and celebrated strategic move of projecting back into the past the beginning of the sabbatical millennium, thereby re-routing the road toward the Parousia through the sunnier climes of Hope. The world was not facing its incumbent senescence; it was reaching a supreme state of maturity, ready to welcome the return of Christ in the whole splendor of its ripeness. As for the feeling that the whole of human life is the playground of an eternal conflict, Augustine transformed it into a historical category: the dialectic between the Two Cities is the very essence of the historical development. He was not a victim of the apocalyptic web, because he invented, or fully articulated, a linear vision of human history. Neither Hegel nor Marx (nor, perhaps, Vico) could have woven their philosophies of history without this thread that Augustine unraveled from the apocalyptic web.

But Beatus, and probably his target readers, had no philosophy of history. You must be a great philosophical mind to witness the sack of Rome and to assert that this does not mean the world has reached its final stage. Thus, Beatus (who certainly did not have a great philosophical mind, and not even a small one) not only was unable to unknot but was eager to keep the apocalyptic web in its labyrinthine complexity, and this explains his voracious intention to take into account the whole of the eschatological tradition. I think that this is why his book was so influential and excited both the popular and the cultivated imagination not only during the period from the eighth century to the achievement of the great Mozarabic manuscripts but at least until the accomplishment of the great Romanesque churches with their obsessive celebration of the Last Judgment.

Serial versus Parallel

If we consider the consistent shifts that occurred in fixing both the date of the world's end and the date of the beginning of the sabbatical millennium, we see that, as Richard Landes has remarked, we cannot isolate any linear evolution from the early Fathers to Augustine, or from Augustine to his posterity. It seems that even in the periods in which either the hostility of the church toward chiliasm or the celebration of some *Renovatio* led to an underevaluation of every apocalyptic expectation, a sort of *millenarismus absconditus* was still alive and could not be tamed. The apocalyptic web always encouraged a pessimistic interpretation of every century.

How do we reconcile the Augustinian decision that the Millennium is already upon us with the new apocalyptic and chiliastic speculations following the twin years 1000 and 1033, when the crucial end of a thousand years had expired, and there should be no room for new fears?

We cannot read (according to the contemporary computer and neural sciences) this process as a "serial" one, where every step asks for a binary decision concerning the further one, this choice and the nature of the further step being determined by the previous ones. The apocalyptic and chiliastic process (which implies at least five different issues, as I have proposed before) is a "parallel" or a "new-connectionist" one, where all the elements are working at the same time and a possible structure comes into being only when, by chance or by a decision of the operator, the so-called weights have reached a certain mutual balance. So in different times and places, under the pressure of different historical events, the apocalyptic design found and still finds new configurations, a sort of transitory gestalt, that could be challenged and reshaped in the light of other and new historical events.

The Time of Beatus

Why Beatus at that moment of European history? We know very well that the period in Europe between the seventh and the ninth century was a time of great insecurity. We are speaking of a civilization that had almost forgotten iron; it was, to adapt downward the classical paradigm of the lost golden age, an age of wood. Jacques Le Goff has told us how medieval legends are filled with peasants in despair because they have dropped a sickle down the well, and so the intervention of an angel, or some sort of miracle, was indispensable to recover such an irreplaceable tool. The Middle Ages before the year 1000 were the opposite of a consumer society; everything was of necessity jealously preserved for generations. The land was grudging, ill worked, often in fits and starts, between one devastation and the next. Even natural fertilizer was scarce, since farm animals were few. A certain agricultural nomadism meant that cultivation was more extensive than intensive; the land was not kept up. At once cause and effect, the human labor force that tilled this land was undernourished.

Transportation was difficult; the few surviving roads were unsafe (and many of the Roman roads had returned to forest or heath); the countryside was infested by thieves and armed bands; periodic pestilences decimated the human and animal populations. People never had enough to eat—they ate less than the lumpen proletariat in any other age of European history, and the only possible comparison is with the starving masses of the Third World. At the end of the millennium, Europe numbered only twenty-two million inhabitants, a historical nadir.

We know, as though by heart, the description of these times by Radulfus Glaber:

> The year 1033 after the incarnation of Christ was approaching, the thousandth year since the Passion of our Savior . . . and in the time that followed, all over the terrestrial orb, a great famine spread, and there was the risk that the entire human race might die of it.
> Weather conditions became so unfavorable that no time was suited to sowing any crop, especially because of the floods. Constant rains had soaked the whole earth to such a degree that for three years it was impossible to dig furrows capable of receiving seeds. At harvest time, weeds and harmful tares had covered the whole surface of the fields. . . . Meanwhile, when the wild animals and the birds had been eaten, men, driven by their ravenous hunger . . . had recourse to the roots of the forests and the grasses of the rivers. . . . Finally horror seizes us with the tale of the evils that then reigned over the human race. Alas! Something rarely heard in the course of the centuries: a fierce hunger caused men to devour human flesh. Wayfarers were seized by men stronger than they, their limbs were chopped to pieces, cooked on the fire, and consumed. . . . Others lured children with the sight of an egg or a piece of fruit and, having drawn them to some isolated spot, slaughtered and devoured them. . . . The skin of many people became taut from swelling; the human voice itself became shrill, like the little cries of dying birds.

So, too, it must have seemed in the times of Beatus, who was closely acquainted not only with tuberculosis but also with leprosy, boils, eczema, Saint Lawrence's fire, and Saint Sylvan's fire, and saw around him people with malformed bones, the blind, the lame, hunchbacks, cripples, paralytics, and epileptics.

Thus, the Book of Revelation, with its frightful Horsemen, seemed to the contemporaries of Beatus a chronicle of their present time. The opening of each seal must have appeared to an early medieval listener as the front page of the *New York Times* does to us, with its crashing jumbo jets, terrorism shifting from the Middle East to the Twin Towers, Bosnia massacres, AIDS, and that menace of crazy cattle that has led someone to speak of apocalypse cows. But we read the newspapers and we feel outside the stories they tell; at the time of Beatus, on the contrary, the readers felt themselves to be inside, within the world described by St. John.

Different Interpretations

In such a situation, all the elements of the web can be used and interconnected at the same time: the unquestionable signs of the end of the world, the hope in a sabbatical millennium, the persuasion that the world was irremediably aging, the obsession with the Antichrist, and the permanent persuasion that, if life is not exactly a tale told by an idiot, at least God in his severity wanted it to appear so to our human powerless will. Beatus picked up from the Book of Revelation what met the requirements of his historical uneasiness.

Revelation could have been read the other way round, because it was and it is basically an open text. In his book on apocalyptic movements, Norman Cohn tries to show that the same pattern governs Münzer, the Begards, the Cathars, the communist revolutionary ideology, and the unquestionably apocalyptical references in Hitler's *Mein Kampf*. This is true, in the sense that from time to time in the course of history various groups have set themselves up as chosen, elect, or privileged and theorized a situation of cosmic conflict from which history should emerge transformed.

But the Book of Revelation is so fascinating because it plays on empty oppositions, upon variables that can be bound according to different historical periods and different psychological drives. Beatus did not find in Revelation the roots of enthusiasm that animated other kinds of chiliasm. Such a chiliastic enthusiasm has taken different forms, depending on the kind of guarantee the enthusiast had in mind, this warranty being due to a supernatural vision or to an ideal of power, to an economic need, or to a sense of class solidarity. The very utopia of a holy Jerusalem has, in the course of the centuries, taken on different formats, up to the point when, with Marxist messianism, the celestial city was turned upside down and became a terrestrial one.

Some identified the Beast with the corrupt clergy; others, like certain fellow travelers of the Crusaders (such as Tafur's bands), identified it with the Jews. Nietzsche reread the promise of the Antichrist in his own way, taking the side of the Enemy as the one to whom the plenitude of the next millennium is providentially due. If in John's text the "people" appear as the worshiper of the Beast (ready for the punishment inflicted by the angels), this reading is inverted in the *Manifesto* of 1848, wherein the proletarian masses become instead the protagonists of future history, as they unite all over the world to pronounce their Last Judgment.

The web provided by that terrible little book can lead to the passive expectation of the end as well as to a permanent feeling of hope and to a will toward transformation. The present suffering can inspire either the decision to fight for a different future or the tragic awareness that no rational action can solve the conflict.

Thus, Revelation can also be read in a neurotic way, oscillating between hope and fear without being able to solve this contradiction because the times in which one reads it do not offer a reasonable solution. And that was the way in which Beatus read it, and this is the reason for the irreducible confusion of his reading.

Radulfus

Beatus was not the only one to be caught in the apocalyptic web, as a fly captured by a spider. Radulfus Glaber is another paramount example of a neurotic user of Revelation. He, as we have seen, gives a fairly horrifying description of his times, as though he were awaiting a postponed end of the millennium, but at the same time his chronicle narrates the cultural fervor that opens the new century. Radulfus certainly reflects a sense of optimism linked to many political events of his time, living in years that see the demographic curve on the rise again. However, he is at the same time haunted by a permanent sense of fear. Is this only the persistence of a rhetorical device, or is it a new emergence of uneasiness? Perhaps the most balanced explanation is given by Henry Focillon:

> History involves rational elements and irrational elements. The former include the phenomena of structure, the great political and economic combinations, certain clearly defined movements of thought. The latter lead us into far less clear regions of human life, far less easy to analyze, because the actual values exist in the eternal twilight of the instincts. It would seem that two breeds of men are working at the same time and in the same places, in the most widely different ways.

Radulfus's text reflects this mood: "Satan will soon be unleashed, once the millennium has come," we are told. And Radulfus sees Satan everywhere: several times, at the foot of his bed, as a little black creature. Omens multiply. In the very year 1000 a meteor appears in the sky, foretelling some mysterious and terrible event. Radulfus lives in a state of constant anxiety, with ups and downs. Although he celebrates, three years after the fatal night, the white cloak of churches covering a reborn world, he also narrates the horrible deeds that preceded the year 1033 and says, "It was believed that the order of the seasons and the laws of the elements that until then had governed the world were now fallen again into the eternal chaos, and the end of the human race was feared." But in a few years the situation is reversed: food is plentiful, and Radulfus pours out a description of a kind of new golden age.

A writer who, in the space of a few pages, contradicts himself in this fashion, who laughs with one eye and weeps with the other, is neurotic. But we must decide whether his is a personal or a cultural neurosis, encouraged by the apocalyptic web. In such a permanent redistribution of weights, to use once again the new-connectionist metaphors, no one knows when to tell the interpretive machine to stop; the final gestalt is never reached; one bounces to and fro in the apocalyptic ping-pong.

The Text of Revelation

I think that there are at least two reasons that impelled people to read the Book of Revelation as the source of the apocalyptic web. The first one depends on the book itself and explains part of its mysterious fascination: there must be something in the narrative structure of the book that obliged people not only to read it as a vision but to perform its reading in a visionary mood.

Tyconius has already told us that we cannot read it as a linear sequence of events, since it has a spiral-like structure due to the technique of *recapitulatio*. But there is more to say concerning this spiral-like nature. My hypothesis is that the argumentative structure of Beatus's *Commentary* (as well as the way in which the Mozarabic illuminators translated it into images) was due to the difficulties of rendering in terms of a Greek and Latin visual scene a Hebrew piece of aural literature.

St. John was a Jew writing in Greek while inspired by a Hebrew visionary tradition. His text was read by a Christian world that drew its scriptural tradition from a Hebrew text mainly known through Greek and Latin translations, and hence that approached the text from the point of view of a Greek, or at least Hellenistic, *forma mentis*.

Now, the Greek culture is eminently a visual one. Etymologically speaking, the word *eidos*, "idea," suggests a visual experience. Every "epiphany" of the sacred is eminently visual, as the very word *epiphaino* suggests. The Greeks knew their gods as images, and the role of images in Christian culture is a paramount one. The Hebrew culture was, on the contrary, an aural one. If the Greeks saw their gods, the Jewish people heard his voice. In the Platonic cosmology (Timaeus) the Demiurge creates the world by geometrical figures. In the Bible (and in the Kabbalistic tradition) God creates the world by a series of sounds or letters.

Thus, the Christian culture was split between two conflicting sources of inspiration. When the Christian culture conceives of Holy Jerusalem, it appears as a vision. But, as we have seen in reading Revelation, this vision is not visually represented. It is told. Thus, one of the most influential sources of the Christian visual tradition was verbally expressed. And the same happens with all the biblical descriptions of the Temple or of the Ark, and with the whole vision of Ezekiel, all of which were sources of John's inspiration.

Let us reread the beginning of the vision of Ezekiel, 1:5–18:

> Out of the midst thereof came the likeness of four living crea-
> tures. And this was their appearance; they had the likeness of a man.
> And every one had four faces, and every one had four wings. . . . And
> they had the hands of a man under their wings on their four
> sides. . . . Their wings were joined one to another; they turned not
> when they went; they went every one straight forward. As for the
> likeness of their faces, all four had the face of a man, and the face of
> a lion, on the right side; and all four had the face of an ox on the left

side; all four also had the face of an eagle. . . . And their wings were
stretched upward; two wings of every one were joined one to another, and two covered their bodies. . . . And the living creatures ran
and returned as the appearance of a flash of lightning. Now as I
beheld the living creatures, behold one wheel upon the earth by the
living creatures. The appearance of the wheels and their work was
like unto the color of a beryl; and all four had one likeness; and their
appearance and their work were as it were a wheel in the middle of a
wheel. When they went they went up on their four sides. . . . And
they turned not when they went. As for their rings, they were so high
that they were dreadful; and their rings were full of eyes round about
them four.

If one tries to translate such a vision into a single image, one cannot. Certainly something of the Greek-oriented sensibility inspired the author of Revelation, because he managed to make his vision more visually representable.
Whereas for Ezekiel each of the four creatures had the face of four different
animals, John gives each a face of its own: one of a bull, one of a man, one of an
eagle, and one of a lion. Moreover, for John the eyes are not on the rings of the
wheels but on the wings of the four creatures; indeed, there are no moving wheels
at all.

However, John could not escape the influence of the text of Ezekiel. Before
the presentation of the four creatures, he speaks of a throne whereupon a divine figure is seated. Around the throne stand the twenty-four elders. But when
presenting the four creatures he says that they are "in the midst of the throne
and round about the throne."

Poor Beatus, when commenting on this passage, was driven crazy. How
can it be possible that they stand in the midst of the throne upon which God is
sitting? How can they stand at the same time in the middle and around the
throne? Beatus tries to solve the dilemma by saying that the text is not to be
understood literally but spiritually: if by the throne one means the church, many
persons can stand at the same time within the church, and all together in unity
around the church.

The real embarrassment is the Mozarabic illuminators, who also took into
account the original vision of Ezekiel. In many works of the beati, the elders are
reduced from twenty-four or twelve to eight, for reasons of pictorial composition. But what matters is that the artist is obliged to spatialize, dimensionally,
the description of Ezekiel via John. The four living creatures do not have six
wings, and there is only one central wheel, with eyes, inscribed in a larger one
that is reminiscent of astral symbols.

We are here facing, partly in John and totally in Ezekiel, the example of a
rhetorical figure called hypotyposis, which is realized when the language becomes able to present something to our eyes as if we could actually see it. Alien
as it was from visual representation, the Hebrew culture exploited at its best
the verbal resources of hypotyposis to represent not a still scene but something
in motion, something that could be visually translated only by a movie—and if

you do not want to think of a movie, think of an oneiric experience. The Mozarabic illuminators were obliged to represent it by a still and two-dimensional image, and could not.

The same happened to medieval interpreters when they were confronted by the Temple as represented by Ezekiel. Many of them admitted that the measures of the building were inconceivable in terms of physics, since the doors would have been larger than the walls, and so on and so forth. In fact, it was remarked, Ezekiel did not claim to have seen a building but a *quasi aedificium*, so supporting the idea that his was a dream or that he saw only a ground plan. Even Rashi (Rabbi Solomon ben Isaac), in the twelfth century, complained that nobody could understand "everything concerning the northern outer chambers . . . where they began to the west and how much they extended to the east, and where they began at the inner side and how much they extended outward." Many Christian authors followed this line of thought and declared that the vision of Ezekiel can be interpreted only in its spiritual sense, paying no attention to the letter.

However, in the twelfth century, Richard of Saint Victor, in his *In visionem Ezechielis*, decided that no spiritual sense can be drawn from the sacred text if the literal sense, let us say, does not make sense. The spiritual sense must be based upon the literal one. Without the inalterable evidence of the letter, no further sense can be found. Thus, Richard heroically redid all the calculations, designed many plans and superelevations, decided that when two measures do not coincide, one had to be taken as referring to the whole building and the other only to one of its parts, established the disposition of each room, and tried to change Ezekiel's dream into a finite and readable architectural project. For the medieval mind, the Temple had to be visually understandable, in terms of mathematical *proportio* and *integritas*. Ezechiel was, on the contrary, narrating a metamorphic (and perhaps anamorphic) experience.

To draw a single image from a movie one has to reduce a three-dimensional web into a two-dimensional and linear image. The Mozarabic illuminators did it, and in a way Augustine did the same, from a conceptual point of view. Beatus could not. He succeeded in being contradictory because he took the Book of Revelation, not as a text that describes something according to a given narrative and representative technique, but as a something in itself. He took the text as though it were the world itself, and in that world he got lost, as if he were the visitor of a labyrinth in which he walked along the same path many times without understanding that he had already passed through there.

The World as a Text

When comparing pre-1000 millenarism with the various millenaristic sects and movements of our own millennium, from the Fraticelli to the revolutionary movements of this century, we see a noticeable difference. The later millenarism is an active one: the millennium not only has to be dreamt of but has to be provoked. History must be changed. That means that history is a man-made product, not a natural event.

Beatus could not think that way. The Fathers had conceived of history as a movement from the Incarnation to the Last Judgment and the heavenly Jerusalem, but such a temporal expanse was felt as a period of expectation, not of action. It seems that, after the fall of the Roman Empire and at least for five centuries, people felt that nothing could be done but wait. They dreamt of a Land of Cockaigne—without knowing that 1000 years later their posterity would have it and call it McDonald's (one of the reasons why present ecologists are making their persuasive prophecies on the end of our world). But Cockaigne was precisely the object of a dream because nobody at that time was able to conceive of wealth as something that could be *produced*. As Le Goff recalls:

> The worst aspect perhaps of this reign of hunger is that it is at the same time arbitrary and ineluctable. Arbitrary because it is linked to the whims of nature. . . . At every evil opportunity, an infernal cycle develops. At the outset, some climatic irregularity has as its consequence a poor harvest. The resulting rise in food prices then increases the indigence of the poor. Those who do not die of hunger are exposed to other dangers. The consumption of poor-quality foods—grass or flour not suited for human consumption, spoiled goods—and sometimes even of dirt, not to mention human flesh, which must not be attributed only to the imagination of chroniclers, leads to diseases, often fatal ones, or to a condition of undernourishment conducive to illnesses that undermine and kill the organism. The cycle can thus be summed up: bad weather, famine, high prices, epidemic, and in any case, as was said at the time, "mortality": in short, an increase in the number of deaths.

Since the world was unchangeable, it had only to be read as a text. The idea was an old one, coming from sources such as the *Phisiologus*, but was certainly encouraged by the decision of Augustine: since the Scriptures cannot always be read literally, we have to interpret the objects and the mundane events of which they speak as symbolical or allegorical devices. In order to do so, it is necessary to know the real meaning of every mundane creature. But for Augustine, to read the world was a way to read the scriptural text. For his intellectual posterity, even the scriptural text became a way to read the world, a world that had only to be interpreted, since it was unthinkable to transform it. For Augustine, the reading of the world was a way to show that the scriptural text is highly metaphorical and must not be taken literally. For those who followed him, the hermeneutics of the scriptural text and the effort to understand its symbolic language led to a sort of literalism, in the sense that both the Scriptures and the world formed a sort of homogeneous paste in which the difference between signs and objects was blurred.

See, for example, with what mystical-cartographic punctilio Beatus interprets Revelation 21:13, which says that the heavenly Jerusalem has "on the east three gates; on the north three gates; on the south three gates; and on the west three gates." Everything becomes an allegorizing of the cardinal points, first seeing east as the original provenance of the Jewish people and north as the provenance of the Gentiles; then seeing north as the area of the sinners and south as the area of fervent souls that, "kindled by the warmth of the Holy Spirit, grow in virtue as in a noon light." Moreover, east is the gate by which, proceeding along the strait and narrow path, the "secret joys" are penetrated; north, the gate of those who, plunged into the darkness and ice of their sins, seek the way of penitence; and south the gate of those who palpitate with virtue fed by holy desires and are penetrated in their spiritual intellect by mysterious inner rejoicing.

The twelve gates are also images of the twelve apostles, of the twelve prophets, and of the twelve tribes of Israel. Twelve gates, twelve angles of the gates (a figure that Beatus develops on the grounds of no textual evidence), and twelve foundations make thirty-six, that is, the hours Christ spent in the sepulchre. The city is square to recall the four Gospels, and since its length equals its breadth, Beatus—following the Latin text that speaks of 12,000 by 12,000 stadia—decides to increase 12 tenfold to get 120, which is the number of the souls who received the Holy Ghost (according to the Acts of the Apostles). Then he adds to 120 the 24 elders of the Revelation, thus obtaining 144, which is the length in cubits of the wall of Jerusalem.

The comparisons continue, amid incredible distinctions and hairsplitting, so that everything takes on a meaning—and, if possible, more than one—and nothing remains dumb and inexpressive. We shall see that this kind of symbolical overinterpretation will decline about the third century of the second millennium, but until then, for the medieval mind nothing is insignificant. As the Pseudo–Alanus ab Insulis reminds us:

> Omnis mundi creatura
> quasi liber et pictura
> nobis est in speculum.
> Nostrae vitae, nostrae mortis,
> nostri status, nostrae sortis,
> fidele signaculum.

If later this symbolical attitude became a literary genre, at the time of Beatus it was certainly something more: it was a way of escaping the torments of an unknown and hostile nature. Since it was impossible to transform the world, every evil feature of the real world underwent a sort of redemption and could be accepted at least as the positive "word" of the divine message, so that even pestilence, hunger, disease, war, and death (I mean the real ones)—insofar as they corresponded to those described by the Scriptures—acquired a sense and could even appear as a promise of future events.

Now, the more labyrinthine a text is, the more it is like a web, and hence the more one can interconnect every aspect of it with every other aspect, according to the historical situation one has to portray or foster. To explain the various ways in which the apocalyptic web was used to cope with different historical situations, we must recognize that both the Scriptures and the world were conceived by those early interpreters, not as a text (as the current metaphor suggests), but as a hypertext. In a text one can always try to find a sense. In a hypertext one is encouraged to link together many senses. If the Scriptures are a text, Augustine can decide, as he did in *De doctrina Christiana*, that there must be interpretive criteria and that one cannot accept a given interpretation of a given passage if that interpretation is not reconfirmed by another passage of the same text. With a hypertext such strictures do not exist; on the contrary, one is further and further encouraged to try new connections. The commentator can choose, or meander along, the path of meaning most congruent with his own historical expectation and with a system of associated symbols.

To stop such an interpretive drift we must wait for the more mature rationalism of Aquinas, who makes a hermeneutic move that, at first glance, seemed inexplicable to many modern interpreters. Aquinas seems to say that there is no metaphorical sense in language because even the metaphors are to be taken as instances of literal language. In fact, he turned upside down the current theory of universal symbolism. According to Aquinas, if a writer or an artist uses the image of a goat to represent Christ, this goat is only a semiotic entity. Real goats have not been posited among the mundane furnishing to represent Christ. Goats are goats, not signs: it is the writer who decides to use the image of a goat as a metaphor, but since the sense of this metaphor has been fixed by an iconographical or rhetorical convention, we get it immediately. So we can conceive of that metaphor as something to be intended "parabolically" and the parabolic *sense* "non supergreditur modum litteralem." It is different when the Bible tells us that Moses commanded the waters of the Red Sea to divide. Here we are obviously dealing with an allegory, but the allegory lies not in the words but in the deeds. In short, the sacred text is not a poetic text that uses words "parabolically"; the sacred text is strictly referential. When it mentions an object or a fact, it means that God has governed the course of mundane events so that something really happened, in order to serve as a symbol. God is a fabulous theatrical impresario who has used whole portions of human history to communicate something to us.

Where is the radical innovation? As matter of fact, when Thomas analyzes the ceremonial precepts of the ancient law he behaves exactly like Beatus. But the innovation consists in the fact that the allegorical effort is confined only to the reading of the Scriptures. The real world is different; it has to be investigated in its proper order, which is a natural, as opposed to a symbolical, one. It seems to me that only after the intellectual world was freed from the impulse toward symbolical reading could the new millenaristic movements conceive of nature, even society, as something that can be acted upon and transformed by human initiative.

Conclusion for Today

I should not like to appear as a medieval addict of hallucinogenic overinterpretation, but let me remark that the fascination of the apocalyptic web and of Beatus's hermeneutic is of the same type as that provided today by certain deconstructive theories of reading, which refuse to look in any text for a nonexistent, transcendental meaning and thereby set the interpretive drift free, ad infinitum. Perhaps this remark serves only to shift from the end of the first to the end of the second millennium, thereby calling for a few concluding observations on the latter, since we cannot ignore that we are approaching that date.

I do not want to speculate about the return today of several mystical forms of millenarism, that is, new chiliastic sects, mass suicides, and so on. Scholars working on the chiliastic movements know that these phenomena are not particularly representative of the end of the present millennium. New forms of mysticism cannot but increase in an era of secularization. As Chesterton said, when people no longer believe in God, it does not mean that they believe in nothing; they believe in everything.

Rather, what characterizes the mass expectation of the new millennium is that there is no expectation. Our century, at least in the last two decades, has disposed of the great ideologies of its first half, and without ideology (as well as without messianism) we have little to do for the future. We are certainly troubled by many terrible events, but the whole of our society is convincing us that we must be happy and avoid any fear. Thus, for the coming end of this century great festivities are prepared all over the world. Ecologists are telling us that the earth is going toward its destruction, but an ideal—and habit—of consumption encourage us to identify pillage with happiness.

The apocalyptic web is, as we are seeing, a matter for academic symposia. A new electronic web is, literally, at our fingertips; it is a Whole World Catalogue that tells us that the fact that the world could physically disappear is irrelevant, since it can survive and grow up virtually. The Internet is our heavenly Jerusalem, and we are not supposed to wait frantically for the dawn of January 1, 2000. We suspect that the day after will be like the day before, maybe a little worse, maybe a little better. At the end of this millennium, the only *ekpyrosis* will be represented by the fireworks in Times Square.

This picture does not aim at suggesting any value judgment. I am simply saying that it will be like that. I do not rank among the *laudatores temporis acti*. *Mundus* perhaps *senescit*, but mainly because our life span increases, and the world of the next millennium will be rich in senior citizens as never before in the history of humanity. Nobody would like to have lived at the times of Beatus and Radulfus. Thus, we have no right to complain. At most, we should be terrified by the fact that we keep cool so much.

Every millennium has the apocalypse it deserves.

NOTE

Editors' note: This essay is adapted from the keynote address presented by Professor Eco to the "Conference on the Apocalyptic Year 1000," in Boston, Mass., November 4, 1996. Umberto Eco is Professor of Semiotics at the University of Bologna.

PART II

The Apocalyptic Year 1000 in Medieval Art and Literature

7

Apocalypse and Last Judgment around the Year 1000

Yves Christe

Around the year 1000 (ca. 970–1030), we encounter in the iconography of divine visions, and more particularly in the monumental imagery that was accessible to all, something new: something that betrays at the least some new preoccupations and even a change in attitude with regard to representations of the present or future glory of God. Although the extant documents are rare, dispersed, and often riddled with lacunae, it seems to me that a reexamination of the Last Judgment and the illustrated Apocalypse cycles from these several decades might shed some new light on the matter. In this regard, the sixty-four verses that remark upon the lost decor of Saint-Pierre de Fleury constitute an exceptional testimony in that they reveal a close connection between a depiction of the Last Judgment and some narrative descriptions of the apocalypse. Concurrently, the contemporary cycle preserved in the baptistery of Novara suggests a different approach. Essentially, this cycle was conceived so as to eschew any representation of the end of time and the Last Judgment.[1]

By way of introduction, it may be appropriate to make a few remarks on the Last Judgment according to Apoc. 20:11–15. As I have suggested elsewhere, depictions of the Judgment as described in Apocalypse did not proliferate between the years 800 and 1150; rather they waned almost to the point of disappearing. This phenomenon is all the more curious because in a parallel development, in monumental art as well as in the minor arts, depictions of the Last Judgment according to Matthew 24–25 are regularly attested and even tend to spread. While in group I, as defined by Peter Klein,[2] in the Trier Apocalypse and the tenth-century copy of Cambrai, Apoc. 20:11–15 and 21:1–8 were the object of detailed illustration, in groups

II and III these same verses are practically unknown. The enthroned Christ of Apoc. 20:11 is simply accompanied by *diabolus* and *infernus* bound together in the lake of fire on the same page (fol. 37r) in the Carolingian Apocalypse manuscript of Valenciennes and on two separate pages (fol. 31r and v) in the tenth-century version preserved in Paris.[3] Nevertheless, at this same passage, the Last Judgment of the Bamberg Apocalypse, commissioned by Emperor Otto III, escaped from this disaffection. It is, however, sketched out on the canvas of Matt. 19:28 and 24–25, and no longer on that of Apoc. 20:11–15. Only Satan bound, on the right at the bottom of the page, still evokes the Johannine text. Subsequently, in the eleventh and twelfth centuries, the Judgment according to Matthew regularly replaced that according to Apoc. 20:11–15; the only element retained from the latter text, rather curiously, is the books wherein are written the acts of the dead. These books are often reduced to two, as, for example, in the *Liber Floridus*, where they are referred to by the appellation *Liber vitae et liber mortis* (compare also the capital of the Last Judgment on the tower-porch of Saint-Benoît-sur-Loire, which features the two open books "floating" on either side of Christ enthroned).

This process of substitution, which may reveal a lacuna in the iconographic tradition of Apoc. 20:11–15, can be situated around the year 1000.[4] It is at least from this period that the Judgment according to Matthew, attested in the West for two centuries, overcame and replaced that of Apoc. 20:11–15. Moreover, it is only from ca. 1200—in the Bibles moralisées, in the English Apocalypses, and later in the Neapolitan Apocalypses of the Angevin era—that the Judgment according to the Apocalypse was once again illustrated, after an eclipse of about two centuries.

These remarks, which are made possible today by the catalog of illustrated apocalyptic cycles compiled by Peter Klein,[5] are intended to reinforce the original, even unique, character of the monumental program of Saint-Pierre de Fleury. As a bonus, these observations permit us to better understand another, atypical Last Judgment, which is contained in an illustrated apocalyptic cycle from southern Germany.[6] In this mid–twelfth century manuscript, with a provenance perhaps from Sankt-Blasien in the Black Forest, the whole of chapter 20 of the Apocalypse (including the anonymous saints of 20:4), as at Fleury, finds expression in the image of the Judgment. So, too, again as at Fleury, the retinue of the elect is conflated with the choirs of the saints.

The cycle of Gauzlin is at once well known and misunderstood. It is, indeed, cited nearly everywhere. Nonetheless, it is misunderstood to the extent that the uncertainties that strain the attempts at reconstruction by James, Yoshikawa, and Bautier have diverted criticism away from taking full advantage of its great evidentiary wealth. Whatever the divergences might be, at least two facts shall remain. First, the cycle of Saint-Benoît-sur-Loire comprised a selection of illustrations referring to the entire Apocalypse, or, to be more precise, from chapters 4 to 22, since there is no mention made of the vision between the candelabra and the churches of Asia (these episodes, however, introduce the sculpted cycle of the capitals of the tower-porch). Second, this collection of episodes was organized around, or in the perspective of, the final vision: the Last Judgment of Apoc. 20:11–15 and 21:1–8.

Now, this is very unusual and even contrary to an apparent rule of monumental representations of the Apocalypse, and in particular of the Apocalypse cycles painted between 1000 and 1150. Almost everywhere we look, we observe, first, that no one goes farther than chapter 12 or at most chapter 14, and second that everyone eliminates from the first twelve chapters those periscopes tied directly to the end of time and to the Last Judgment. To put it another way, this is to say that whatever may be the starting point, Apoc. 1:4 or 8:2—the seven Asian churches, the seals, or the trumpets—we skip from Apoc. 6:17 or 7:1 to Apoc. 8:2 or from Apoc. 9:21 or 10:1 to Apoc. 11:19. The immediate consequence is that the seventh seal, the seventh trumpet, and the final vision are never evoked. Neither is the story of the two witnesses, who nonetheless play a primary role in the cycle of Gauzlin.[7]

Hence we note, in almost all Romanesque monumental cycles, a constant desire to "purge" the Apocalypse of those sections treating the Parousia, with the goal apparently being to keep the illustration within the framework of the *tempus ecclesiae*, before the manifestation of the Antichrist. At Fleury, on the contrary, it is these final sections that are privileged. So, too, some of the sections that medieval exegetical tradition had typically maintained in the *tempus ecclesiae*, and sometimes even at its very dawning, are pushed back by Gauzlin to the end of time and conflated with the images announcing the Parousia and the Judgment.

For example, in verses 1 and 2, the powerful angel of Apoc. 10:1 is interpreted, not as a figure of Christ *in suo primo adventu* or as an angelic figure of the Risen Christ, but rather as the messenger of the Judgment. Here, Gauzlin does not take account of the recapitulation *ab Adventu primo* of Apoc. 10:1ff.; instead, he goes even beyond the interpretation of Beatus, for whom the apparition of this angel, a figure of Christ, is a recapitulation *a sola ultima persecutione*. However, it may be that he failed to identify this "very great messenger descended from the heavenly court" with the angel of Apoc. 18:1 who announces the fall of Babylon; but in this case, this angel's presence in a Romanesque monumental cycle would be a *unicum*.[8]

In verses 42 and 43, the sounding of the seventh trumpet (Apoc. 11:15)—otherwise absent from all other extant cycles—is immediately followed by the vision of the Ark in Heaven (Apoc. 11:19). This implies that Gauzlin links the end of the seven trumpets and the final vision, the adoration in Heaven (Apoc. 11:15–18), to the vision of the Ark in the temple, which medieval exegetical tradition normally attaches to the following episode, the vision of the woman and the dragon. Here again, Gauzlin does not take account of the principal recapitulation, *a principio, a nativitate*, of Apoc. 11:19. In so doing, he seems to adopt a solution comparable to that illustrated in the Apocalypses of Trier (fol. 36r), of Cambrai (fol. 26r), and especially of Oxford (fol. 8v), wherein the elders of Apoc. 11:15–18 adore the temple and the Ark in Heaven (Apoc. 11:19) and, according to the Oxford manuscript, in the presence of the angel of the seventh trumpet. Gauzlin refers, therefore, to a division of the text that is the same as that followed in modern editions of the Bible. This division belongs to the beginning of the thirteenth century, but we can find many older attestations, notably in the Apocalypse of Trier before a much later hand (eleventh century?) adduced some corrections.[9]

In verses 44 and 45, immediately after the mention of the seventh trumpet and the Ark in Heaven, "the rulers seated to the right of the Judge, who are worthy to judge the world with him," are more likely the anonymous enthroned ones of Apoc. 20:4 than the apostles, who are the usual judges with Christ. Gauzlin's interpretation might seem natural. Such is not the case, however, since from Augustine at least, these *sedentes* are not the judges of the end of time, *ut quidam heretici putaverunt*, but an image of the prelates through whom, *nunc*, the present church is governed. From Primasius in the sixth century to the Gloss, this affirmation was regularly repeated. Scarcely anyone prior to Haimo of Auxerre, a Carolingian author, contested this reading or recognized in these *sedentes* of the contemporary government of the church any anticipation of the ultimate judiciary college composed of the most eminent saints.[10] Once again, we surprise Gauzlin, in flagrante delicto, eschatologizing the apocalyptic motifs that the most orthodox exegetical tradition had resituated in the present. The illustrator of the Apocalypse of Oxford followed Gauzlin's example. On folio 12r, under the resurrection of the dead, nine anonymous enthroned ones sit on a judicial bench, along the lines of the Trier and Cambrai Apocalypses. Five are crowned, and the other four are tonsured.

Of the seven seals (Apoc. 8:2–11:18), Gauzlin retained only the last three trumpet blasts and the corresponding plagues.[11] The vision of the locust arising from the well of the abyss, that of the liberation of the angels of the Euphrates, and that of the massacres perpetrated by the malefic horsemen were without doubt preceded or introduced by the vision of the eagle of the three "woes" (verses 7–8); although the blasts of the first four trumpets are ignored, the *tituli* accord an important place to the story of the two witnesses (verses 3–6 and 27). Nevertheless, in the framework of chapter 11, a space was reserved for the figure of John measuring the temple (verses 25–26; see Apoc. 11:1). Regarding the fate of the two witnesses, however, Gauzlin did not evoke the figure of the Antichrist.

Gauzlin's choice is singular. In the monumental cycles of the eleventh through twelfth centuries, we never encounter the preaching, death, and ascension of the two witnesses, Enoch and Elijah, nor the image of John measuring the temple. We have already seen that the seventh angel is systematically discarded. If, however, the blasts of the fifth and sixth trumpets enjoyed great favor, that is because the first four were ignored at Fleury. Gauzlin once again privileges the themes with an eschatological character.

We may note the same phenomenon at work regarding Apoc. 19, the vision of the horseman. Rather than represent the triumphal apparition of Apoc. 19:11–16, a vision of the Risen Christ in the exegetical tradition, Gauzlin chose instead the final development of this internal recapitulation, *a passione*. Verses 39–41 essentially evoke the vengeful call to the carrion birds (Apoc. 19:17–18), an image that pertains to the end of time, after a brief recapitulative interlude *a principio–a passione brevius* of Apoc. 19:11–16.[12]

The presence of illustrations of Apocalypse 12 in a cycle centered on the Last Judgment is itself rather astonishing. Two or maybe three scenes were apparently retained. Verses 28–30 combine the flight into the desert—the woman would thus already have been endowed with her wings of an eagle—and the moment when the infant is caught up to God so as to escape the dragon; this is, in fact, how these events are often depicted (Apoc. 12:1–6 and 12:13–16). As for verses 31–32, they treat the combat in Heaven (Apoc. 12:7–12). We should note that in verse 32, Gauzlin has the dragon cast down into Tartarus ("ipsum tartareis tradunt sine margine penis"), an allusion to his definitive end, rather than onto the earth, as is specified in Apoc. 12:9 ("et projectus est in terram").

In the exegetical tradition, the vision of the woman and the dragon is situated, *a nativitate*, at the beginning of the age of the church. The combat in Heaven is not the last battle of Satan against the angels of God but that which followed the Incarnation. Satan cast down upon the earth is thus an image synonymous with that of Apoc. 20:1, where an angel from Heaven (the Risen Christ) arrives to bind him for a thousand years (the age of the Church), so that he might not be as harmful as he would like. This combat continues, and will continue, so long as the church has not arrived at the end of its pilgrimage. As Ambrosius Autpertus reminds us: "Let it not come into the hearts of the faithful to think that this battle occurred in the beginning of time, when through pride the ancient enemy fell from the heavenly fatherland along with his allies, but rather that it occurred from the Passion of Christ in the incipient church, and is now occurring, and will continue until the end of the age, when at last he will be unbound and finished off."[13]

Of this combat, Gauzlin retained only the final phase, the ultimate attack of the dragon and his fall into Tartarus, which is the equivalent of the lake of fire in Apoc. 20:10. If this latest example of "eschatological preference" may be considered legitimate, such is not the case with the assimilation of the birth of the child and the flight of the woman clothed in the sun into the Last Judgment. Moreover, I know of only one other instance where images of the woman and the dragon are associated with a Last Judgment; this dates from ca. 1330 and is on the pediment of the back of the facade of Santa Maria Donnaregina in Naples.[14] As is well known, the woman of the Apocalypse is more of a figure of the pilgrim church which gives birth each day to new *fideles* than a figure of the Virgin, even if in certain aspects she supports a Marian interpretation. Nonetheless, her flight into the desert marks the beginning of the time of the church, and not its end.[15]

For the usual juxtaposition of a flight into the desert after the infant is handed over to God and of a combat in Heaven which ends with the imprisonment of Satan in Tartarus, there is perhaps one other explanation that I shall propose with the greatest caution: that of the use by Gauzlin of an illustration of Apocalypse 12 extracted from a Beatus of group II. This image, which usually fills a double page, in essence reunites all of the elements evoked by the *tituli* of Fleury: at the upper left, the woman about to give birth is menaced by the dragon, which Michael and his angels battle high and to the right, with the infant caught up to God by an angel; at the lower left, the dragon pursues and tries to drown the winged woman; and, most strikingly, at the lower right is Satan with his hordes in a fiery vault. This is, then, an evocation of the thousand-year bondage in Apoc. 20:1, and not of the final punishment. Nonetheless, Gauzlin was able to give it an eschatological translation in his desire to reposition the Apocalypse to the end of time. The influence of Beatus beyond the frontiers of Spain is only rarely attested. The presence of such an exemplar in the library of Saint-Benoît-sur-Loire, even if it is not impossible, is thus very hypothetical.[16]

As Yoshikawa notes, verses 13–24 treat just one vision, that of Apoc. 7:9–17. Bautier, wrongly I believe, did not retain this identification but rather reconstructed here three distinct scenes: an adoration of the Lamb according to chapter 5 (verses 13–16); a vision of the Anonymous according to chapter 4 (verses 17–21); and the image of the martyrs under the altar at the beginning of the fifth seal (verses 22–24). Besides according perfectly with the adoration of the Lamb and the throne by the angels, the living beings, elders, and those who have come from the great tribulation, the solution proposed by Yoshikawa has the advantage of better explaining how a representation of all the saints has taken the place of the elect in the Last Judgment, which we shall consider shortly. Apocalypse 7, in effect, was the principal reading of the mass and the divine office on November 1. We can thus imagine that above the Last Judgment, the heart of Gauzlin's program, there unfolded an adoration of the Lamb standing or seated on a throne, indeed, even an adoration of an "empty" throne as at Pedret, so long as another divine figure, the Anonymous, does not surpass that of the Judge. Restored thusly, the heavenly apparition of verses 13–24 may be classified among the apsidal Romanesque arches, such as that of Saints-Cosme-et-Damien, with the principal accent thus being on the Judgment proper. In verse 14, the expression *conlaudant Dominum*, and the vocative *summe Pater* of verse 17, allow some doubts about this restoration to linger. However, we should remember that it was customary, since the fifth century and the lost apsidal decor of Saint Chrysogone at Rome, to see in the throne a figure of the Father. As for the attitude of the adoring elders in verse 21—"genu flectitur omne"—this echoes Apoc. 7:11: "et ceciderunt in conspectu troni."

The greatest space, however, was reserved for the Last Judgment according to Apoc. 20:11–15; this is the focal point of the entire cycle. This itself is singular, since from the year 1000 the Judgment tends to disappear from the apocalyptic cycles when it was not replaced by an illustration from Matthew 24–25. At the center of the composition, the enthroned Judge (verse 46) was accompanied by those to whom judgment was entrusted; the *tituli* do not identify these co-judges as the apostles. These *rectores residentes* (verse 44) are without doubt the anonymous enthroned ones of Apoc. 20:4, perhaps conflated with the elders since they are mentioned immediately after the vision of the Ark of verse 43. We have seen above that to assimilate the *sedentes* of Apoc. 20:4 with those to whom Christ the Judge will entrust judgment at the end of time stands in contradiction to exegetical tradition. Gauzlin took little heed of this tradition in inaugurating a new iconographic formula destined for a brilliant future. From the second half of the twelfth century, the anonymous enthroned ones, ever more and more numerous and sometimes assimilated to the choirs of all the saints, came to take the place of the apostolic college of judges, first at Santiago de Compostela, in the Portico de la Gloria, then at Chartres, at Saint-Silvain de Levroux, at Paris, Amiens, Bourges, and elsewhere.

Arrayed beneath this scene, the resurrection of the dead in four forms must have been depicted. First would be the bodies regurgitated by Hell (verses 47–48), by the sea (verses 49–50), and by the earth (verse 51–52). The just rising from their tombs in verse 58 became part, no doubt, of the choir of saints, which Gauzlin confounded with the elect. In Apoc. 20:13, it is the sea, earth, and Hades which give up their dead. The sea, as in the Byzantine iconography of the Last Judgment, thus replaced death. I cannot explain this correction/substitution.

The elect enjoyed a favorable treatment. Gauzlin devoted six verses to them (53–58), as opposed to the damned, who received only two (61–62). The elect were arranged into choirs: the holy men (53), the hermits (54), the virgins (55), and the confessors (56). As for the *tyrones* (verse 57), the neophytes, these are almost certainly the martyrs. If we set aside the rather exceptional image in the Psalter of Athelstan, wherein, on folio 2v, the choirs of all the saints surround Christ, pointing out the wound in his side, the Fleury cycle provides us with the oldest attestation of the presence of the choirs of all the saints in a Last Judgment. Even into the twelfth century, it was very rare that the elect, ranged by order, participated in a Judgment. It is only from the thirteenth century, and even more so the fourteenth, that this idea developed, to the point that sometimes the choirs of all the saints were arbitrarily arrayed in nine orders to complement the nine angelic choirs, which similarly, in successive steps, also crept into the skies of the Last Judgment.

Leaving the elect, the vast crowd of all the saints, we come at last to the damned "emitting cries with vain prayers." Verse 62 specifies that they are "excluded from life" *(exclusi vita)*. Thus, they do not participate in the second resurrection, since they are not enrolled in the book of life (Apoc. 20:15). Based on this, we can perhaps restore the open books of Apoc. 20:13, in which the deeds of the dead are inscribed, to the side of the Judge. They are held by two angels on either side of Christ in the Apocalypse of Oxford (fol. 12v), in the Apocalypses of Trier and Cambrai, and in the copies of the *Liber floridus* (e.g., Paris, BN lat. 8865, fol. 42v). They simply float in the space above the shoulders of Christ on the capital illustrating Apoc. 20:11–15 in the porch of Saint-Benoît-sur-Loire.

The end of the poem, lines 63–64, at last introduces the image of Satan, or rather Tartarus, bound in a grotto "which vomits forth flames." This is an allusion to the definitive incarceration of the Devil in the lake of fire (Apoc. 20:10), here perhaps in an exceptional form. Depiction of the "cavern, which vomits forth flames, where Tartarus is bound" is not a normal part of the repertory of the Last Judgment north of the Alps. We find this image only rarely, for example, on folio 12v of the Oxford Apocalypse and, toward the year 1200, in the margin of the Byzantine-inspired Last Judgment in Harrade of Landsberg's *Hortus deliciarum*. This image, however, occurs frequently in Italy, where it enjoyed an astonishing circulation in the fourteenth century. Nonetheless, its first attestation is at Fleury.[17]

The Last Judgment of folios 12r and 12v of the Oxford Apocalypse facilitate a partial reconstruction of that of Fleury. In folio 12v, Christ enthroned is flanked by angels, two of which present the books in which are inscribed the deeds and sins of the dead. In the second register, at the left, the elect, conflated with the choirs of all the saints, are arrayed in six rows, across from a simple lineup of the dead and Satan bound among the flames in a sort of cavern that is fashioned out of a multitude of little heads. On the recto of this same folio, a resurrection of the dead accompanied by extracts from Apocalypse 20, Matt. 25:34, and 1 Thess. 4:16 surmounts, as we have seen, the anonymous *sedentes* of Apoc. 20:4.

Again, the *tituli* of Gauzlin mention, in lines 59–60, the celestial Jerusalem sparkling with gems. It is likewise integrally inserted into the description of the Last Judgment in verses 44–64. In one form or another, the paradise promised to the just is very often evoked by a building: a simple door, a succession of arcades, or sometimes a church or a more complicated, multistoried edifice. It is very rarely, however, that we can recognize in this paradise the heavenly Jerusalem of the Apocalypse. Yet this very image appears to the right of Christ the Judge in the Trier Apocalypse (fol. 39). In the Oxford Apocalypse, although it is not represented in correlation with the Judgment (fol. 12v), it is discretely evoked by the first verse of chapter 21 written at the left in the border of the frame. The occasional spillover of the Judgment of Apoc. 20:11–15 into the beginning of chapter 21 is readily explained by the capitulation of the text in the Middle Ages. Until the beginning of the eleventh century, the first eight verses of chapter 21 were in effect interpreted as the conclusion of the Last Judgment in the majority of the commentaries. After having described the downfall of the impious, it made sense to evoke the joyous fate reserved for the just. Before the Gloss and the intervention of Anselm of Laon, who relied in this matter on the Bedan commentary's scheme of seven *periochas*, our chapter 21 and hence the concluding vision of the Apocalypse began only at Apoc. 21:9.

Since the Apocalypse was rarely chosen as a proof text for the Last Judgment, and since the vision of Jerusalem was excluded from the Judgment owing to the new capitulation of the text beginning in the twelfth century, we can understand the extreme rarity of the formula employed in the paintings of Saint-Benoît-sur-Loire. This formula is another innovation in Abbot Gauzlin's program. We will see the heavenly Jerusalem associated with a Judgment only much later in the background of Heaven in Giotto's frescoes in the Arena Chapel at Padua and in the uppermost register in the back of the facade of the abbatial church of Pomposa.

Taking all of these observations into account, we may wonder at the exegetical trend to which Gauzlin subscribed. It seems clear that he either did not know or rejected the commentaries issuing from the orthodox revisions of the work of Tyconius. This is surprising, since the library of an abbey as important as Fleury ought to have contained a commentary in the style of Bede, Ambrose Autpert, or Haimo of Auxerre. Abbo, Gauzlin's predecessor, moreover gives us to understand that it was in basing his argument on the Apocalypse and on Daniel that he was able to correct the doctrinal errors of certain millenarians; this is an affirmation that can refer only to the symbolic exegesis of Apoc. 20:1–4 and the idea that the reign of a thousand years is to be understood as the indeterminate time of the pilgrimage of the church. Such is what we find in all of the orthodox commentaries, from Augustine or Primasius to Ambrose Autpert or Haimo of Auxerre. This "millennial" reign, the duration of which cannot be calculated, was inaugurated by the angel who descended from heaven to bind Satan (Apoc. 20:1). During the entirety of this time, the church is governed by the anonymous enthroned ones of Apoc. 20:4.

As we have been able to note in the analysis of the different episodes of the cycle of Saint-Pierre, Gauzlin systematically privileged the eschatological interpretation. For him, the entire Apocalypse is a vision of the end of time, a revelation centered upon the ultimate fate of the world and of its inhabitants. The entire text can thus converge on the final revelation, which is the Last Judgment. To accomplish this, Gauzlin openly contradicted some powerful interpretations that orthodox exegesis had progressively advanced since the fifth century: the angel of Apoc. 10:1 becomes a figure announcing the Judgment; the anonymous enthroned ones of Apoc. 20:4 become participants in the Judgment; the Ark in Heaven of Apoc. 11:18 becomes assimilated with a harbinger of the Judgment; the adoration of the Lamb in Apoc. 7:9–17 becomes conflated with a vision of the elect at the end of time. Hence, Gauzlin does not adopt the recapitulative articulations of the complex system "invented" by Tyconius at the end of the fourth century to impede and quash all eschatological perspective. To make the angel of Apoc. 10:1 the messenger of the Judgment is to be oblivious that situated there, after the blast of the sixth trumpet, is an internal, repetitive recapitulation *a principio*. To link the appearance of the Ark in Heaven to the blast of the seventh trumpet is to forget that the episode of the seven trumpets that ends in Apoc. 11:18 is followed by a new period, marked by a return to the beginning of the age of the church, *a nativitate*, inaugurated by the vision of the Ark. What is more, a final interpretation of the adoration of the Lamb (Apoc. 7:9–17) implies a rejection of the internal recapitulation of the seven seals in Apoc. 7:1.[18]

Gauzlin thus situates himself on the margin of exegetical tradition; either he lacked familiarity with it, or he deviated from it in the intention of constructing, using only references to the Apocalypse, an immense tableau of the Judgment and the end of time—a grandiose and complex tableau destined for a rather wider public. Is this merely a willingness to innovate? Is it possible that he made use of the commentary of Cassiodorus, which presents certain affinities with the *tituli* of Fleury? The quaint old secretary of Theodoric saw, above all, in the Apocalypse a vision of the future: *dicit enim Johannes apostolus a Domino Christo visionem sibi de fine saeculi monstratam.*[19] He did not heed the recapitulative articulations of Apoc. 7:1, 8:2, and 10:1, and in the same fashion as Gauzlin, he assimilated the powerful angel of Apoc. 10:1 with a messenger of the Judgment.[20] He interpreted the adoration of the Lamb (Apoc. 7:9–17) as a final vision in the same way as the synonymous vision of Apoc. 14:1–5.[21] So, too, Cassiodorus linked the final adoration of Apoc. 11:15–18 to the vision of the Ark and of the woman.[22]

Even when it was first written, toward the middle of the sixth century, Cassiodorus's *Complexiones in Apocalypsin* were already outdated. In fact, these somewhat confused annotations played no role in the history of the Latin exegetical tradition. Nevertheless, they stand as testimony (in the work of an author who knew of Tyconius and who was by any account a great intellectual of late antiquity) to the resistance to the process of what Kamlah called *Enteschatologiesierung*, which marks the development of the interpretation of the Apocalypse from the fifth century to the eleventh. For reasons that we can only guess, Gauzlin, perhaps without knowing the work of Cassiodorus, expressed the same reticence.

The cycle of the baptistery at Novara is of another spirit entirely. Exposed since 1957, it has been dated to the year 1000 and reveals close iconographic affinities with the porches of Saint-Savin and Saint-Hilaire de Poitiers, both dating to ca. 1080, and the Bamberg Apocalypse. It is composed of eight panels, only seven of which are visible today, engraved in the octagonal tambour of the cupola, which was heightened and vaulted at the end of the tenth century. In the interior, there remain only traces of oscillating wings and, at the summit, a yellow band studded with precious stones that perhaps was part of a ceremonial throne or a plated cross. The limewater inscriptions on a blue-gray base that run along the border of the historiated panels and along the base of the cupola were, unfortunately, neither copied nor photographed during the restorations in the early 1960s. Today they are illegible. Nevertheless, above the eight compartments one can manage to read the adverb CONTINVATIM and, a little farther on, over the altar of the angel with the censer of Apoc. 8:2, SONAT or RESONAT. The cupola, then, would have been occupied by an adoration without respite or repose, die et nocte, as in Apoc. 4–5 or 7:9–17.

The cycle is introduced on the west, across from the entry, by the vision of the angel with the censer standing before the altar (HIC ALTARI DATA SUNT CULTUR . . .). Following this, clockwise from the north to the south, are the blasts of the first five trumpets, always adhering to the same schema. The angel, to the left, occupies a third or perhaps half of the space. He blows into his instrument, which is held horizontally in the face of the plagues that his intervention provokes. The fourth trumpet faces the eagle of the three "woes," which rests upon the sun with its wings closed.

Today the seventh panel is covered by a Last Judgment of the fifteenth century. It would have depicted the liberation of the angels of the Euphrates, pertaining to the blast of the sixth trumpet. Its trumpet-blasting angel was pushed back onto the eighth panel owing to a lack of space; just as at Saint-Savin and elsewhere, it was necessary to squeeze the vision of the liberated angels and of the malefic horsemen into a single compartment. Moreover, the sixth angel turns its back to the woman clothed in the sun (and menaced by the dragon, who is already cast upon the earth), who closes the cycle. Her infant is taken up into Heaven, borne in a sort of box that evokes the crèche of the Nativity, in the direction of the Ark in the temple of Apoc. 11:18. This narrative thus progresses from Apoc. 8:2 to 12:5 (or, more precisely, from Apoc. 8:3 to 9:21 and then from Apoc. 11:18 to 12:5). Omitted are the powerful angel of Apoc. 10:1, the episode of the two witnesses, the blast of the seventh trumpet, and the final adoration.

It is neither for a lack of space nor by whim that the cycle of Novara ends with the image of Apocalypse 12. A century later, the remains of the cycle of Saint-Savin-sur-Gartempe permit us to reconstruct an equivalent program. Here also the blast of the sixth trumpet leads directly to the vision of the woman and the combat in Heaven of Apocalypse 12, which is the end of the narrative. Since we find the same situation at Civate, Bardolino, and Saint-Hilaire de Poitiers, and since it was normal everywhere to omit the blast of the seventh trumpet and not to advance the narrative beyond chapter 12 regardless of the beginning point—Apoc. 1:4 or 8:2—of the particular cycle, we are forced to conclude that the majority of the monumental cycles of the eleventh and twelfth centuries obeyed the same rule. Not only did Gauzlin not conform to this rule, but he did the exact opposite.

While the cycle of Saint-Benoît-sur-Loire is organized around the Last Judgment as a focal point, the other cycles are dominated by a vision that we can qualify as "present" or "current" since it always focuses on Apocalypse 4–5: for example, the adoration of the Lamb at Anagni, the adoration of the throne at Pedret, a Maiestas Domini at Méobecq and also undoubtedly at Saint-Hilaire de Poitiers, a paraphrase of the apsidal decor of Saints-Cosme-et-Damien at Castel Sant'Elia, and Christ accompanied by a triumphal cross, the apostles, and the angelic adorers at Saint-Savin. As we have seen, the narrative generally stops at chapter 12, with the consequence that all that occurs from Apoc. 15:1 to 20:15 is passed over in silence. Beyond chapter 12, only the heavenly Jerusalem of Apocalypse 21–22 receives mention, but this is rarely integrated into a narrative program. It also happens that the adoration of the Lamb of Apoc. 7:9–17 is conflated with that synonymous adoration of Apoc. 14:1–5; as we see in the interior of the cupola surmounting the ciborium of Civate, for example.

The organization of a system so complicated as this aims to reject from the monumental imagery those sections of the Apocalypse that are directly related to the end of time. This phenomenon remained limited to monumental painting, no doubt because it was the medium of a message accessible to all. We note nothing similar in manuscript illuminations, which never present these lacunae.

Because of this phenomenon we can better measure the singularity of the decor at Fleury, where it is the final sections that were systematically developed, even if this meant pushing back to the end of time entire sections of text that the mainstream of exegetical tradition had always maintained in the present. Moreover, it is the Last Judgment of Apoc. 20:11–15, absent almost everywhere else, that dominates the whole.

Unfortunately, monumental cycles from before the year 1000 have not survived; our earliest is that of Novara, which just antedates that of Fleury. Several fragments from the Carolingian epoch have recently been discovered near Brindisi, at Seppanibale, but the lacunae there are such as not to permit the reconstruction of the original program. We find only the vision of the woman and the dragon—the woman is already endowed with wings—and several meager elements of the vision between the candelabra.[23] Hence, we really do not know when the rules that nearly universally govern the cycles of the eleventh and twelfth centuries were first enunciated. This system, however, was already in place by the end of the tenth century. It reflects an understanding of the text which is that of the Tyconian exegetical tradition, and more particularly that of the commentary of Ambrose Autpert composed at Saint-Vincent-aux-Sources-du-Volturne in the second half of the eighth century. It arises not from illustrated models that were transmitted into Italy, France, and Spain but rather from written rules, schemas, and sketches that, it seems, accompanied written annotations and figural elements, and in which different types of illustrations might be mingled. While the cycles of Novara, Saint-Savin, and to some degree Saint-Hilaire de Poitiers belong to the tradition of group II, those of Anagni, Castel Sant'Elia, and Bardolino are of group III. The same is true for the divine vision around which the different episodes that were retained were organized. To follow the evidence from both sides of the Alps, it takes on diverse aspects: for example, the elders are again standing at Anagni and at Castel Sant'Elia, but they are still seated at Pedret.

The rigor of this system, which, as we have seen, became preeminent for two centuries, implies a firm desire on the part of religious authorities to regulate apocalyptic imagery intended for a wide audience. In the eleventh and twelfth centuries the Apocalypse played a large role in the figural decor of edifices of both major and minor importance. To demonstrate this, it will suffice to draw up a list of the cycles discovered since the early 1960s: Novara, in the tambour of the baptistery; Saint-Lizier, in the south apsidiole of the old cathedral; Saint-Polycarpe dans l'Aude, on the vaults and the walls of the nave; Saint-Hilaire de Poitiers, at the base of the apsidal concha; and Santa Maria Gualtieri de Pavie, on the vaults of the nave. Let us add the paintings of Méobecq, which I have restored to this repertoire, as well as the images of the woman and the dragon and of the angel lifting the cover of the pit of the abyss that I believe can be discerned below the Christ on the horse in the crypt of the cathedral of Auxerre.[24]

Thus, it would seem that between the year 1000 and the mid–twelfth century, we predominantly find monumental cycles illustrating the Apocalypse only so far as chapter 12, thereby avoiding at the least the illustration of the material in chapters 15–20. The final sections are regularly and systematically excluded. They are attested together only here and there, almost inadvertently, in monumental sculpture. Since the Last Judgment was at the same time becoming more and more important, we can draw this inference: the Romanesque world was anxious to clearly distinguish between the Apocalypse and the end of the world and between the Apocalypse and the Last Judgment. For fear, perhaps, of an abusive or anarchic use of the revelation of Patmos, or perhaps of an error of the millenarian or adventist sort, the monumental narrative representations were expurgated of their most eschatological characteristics. For some two centuries, an effort to entirely avoid representing the end of time persisted. Just as the narrative seemed to reach the end of time—be it the end of the sixth seal or the end of the sixth trumpet blast—it returned to its beginning owing to the effect of recapitulation.

> Auctor hujus revelationis, a primo usque ad sextum narrando
> perveniens sigillum [or "angelum"]; ordinem narrationis custodisse
> videntur. Sed praetermisso interim sigillo, sub quo novissima
> persecutio et Domini manifestus speratur adventus, ad initiam
> incarnationis Christi redit, eadem aliter diciturus.

This paraphrase from Primasius and from Ambrose Autpert neatly summarizes the problem. Whether the cycle be long or short, every time we reach the sixth step—the sixth seal or sixth trumpet—we return to our point of departure, to the beginning of the age of the church, and are denied an image or allegory of that age's completion. In summary, from Apoc. 6:17 or 7:1, we jump right to Apoc. 8:2; and from Apoc. 9:21 or 10:1, we jump to Apoc. 11:19, accordingly as we retain or not the internal recapitulations *a principio*, introduced by the angel of the rising sun, the angel of the winds, and the angel surrounded by clouds.

This usage, which is in effect a rule established prior to the year 1000, was sedulously respected at Novara and yet was transgressed at Saint-Benoît-sur-Loire. In neither case was this an accident. Gauzlin chose to digress from the received exegetical tradition in pushing the entire Apocalypse forward toward the end of time and conflating it with a vision of the Last Judgment. For his part, the person who designed the decor of the baptistery of Novara went to the other extreme by removing all allusions to the Parousia from the narrative cycle in the tambour of the cupola.

It is essentially clear that this nearly universal refusal to publicly represent, over the course of some two centuries, the most "apocalyptic" sections of the Apocalypse was no accident. It was the consequence of doctrinal decisions undertaken by the highest authorities of the church in an effort to ensure that, in the popular imagination, the Apocalypse was not conflated with the end of time (as it is today!). This impulse toward *Enteschatologiesierung* is all the more striking because we do not observe a parallel impulse in the contemporary illumination of manuscripts. Moreover, since at the same time the monumental cycles of the Apocalypse proliferated, we may conclude that it was deemed necessary to "occupy the terrain," thereby ensuring that the Apocalypse should neither be violated by shortcuts nor fall into the hands of deranged minds. It was decided to "sing" the Apocalypse in a single voice, everywhere in the West, from the year 1000 until at least 1150.

Since these rules were in place by the year 1000, and evident in the baptistery of Novara, we should presume that they were defined some time beforehand, no doubt at Rome, using the exegetical principles that had long been fixed in the orthodox tradition: Primasius, Ambrose Autpert, Haimo of Auxerre, and so on. Thus, orthodox exegesis, already purged of its "adventist" leanings, served as the doctrinal line; the system employed in monumental painting was incomprehensible without recourse to this tradition.

The evidence should necessarily lead us to acknowledge that, from the year 1000, the Apocalypse was utilized to publicly counter eschatological leanings that had doubtlessly become more acute; this is exactly what Abbo tells us had happened in Paris. The monumental cycles reveal this "political" function, which is impossible to explain without the presence of a millenarian danger.

Since I am unaware of any such processes in monumental art prior to the year 1000, I find myself forced to admit, at least provisionally on this precise point, that there was a "mutation." Visions of glory of a synthetic character, which were mostly destined for the apsidal arch or floor, were no longer sufficient. The risk was taken of illustrating a narrative that, regardless of the point of departure (Apoc. 1:12–20, 4:1, or 8:2–5), ignored Apocalypse 15–20 and systematically rejected anything that touched too closely on the end of time within the first twelve chapters.

APPENDIX: THE TEXT OF ANDREW OF FLEURY

Ceterum ipsius aecclesie faciem quibusdam miraculorum Apocalipsis Johannis theologi variari fecit hisque hisque versi exornari:

1. Summus ab eterna delapsus nuntius aula,
2. Temporatestatur divino examine claudi.
3. Olim pro meritis intacti funere carnis,
4. Occumbunt membris pro celsi nomine Regis,
5. Lucida perpetui vocitati lumina regni,
6. Quos ita dextra Patris revocat super atria celi.
7. Signum judicii pandens, haec taliter inquit:
8. "Ve ve terrigenis et toto ve simul orbi!"
9. Panditur atque tetri puteus pregrandis Averni,
10. In terris ex quo diffunditur ista propago,
11. Que rabiem cordis cupiens implere maligni,
12. Non datur ex toto sed partim ledere justos.
13. Ex hinc etheri laudes reboando ministri
14. Conlaudant Dominum nocte dieque pium,
15. Victor quique, sacros referens de morte triumphos
16. Nos dedit excelos mente subire polos.
17. Hic tua, summe Pater, veneratur lucida sedes,
18. Qui celis terras, inclite, consocias,
19. Suscipis inde libens famulorum vota tuorum,
20. Qui tibi celestes dant super astra duces.
21. Huic suquidem vere semper genu flectitur omne.
22. Atque creature agmina stelligere
23. Dictus stellifer Johannes gratia Regis
24. Mirans conspicit hos Christi pro nomine cesos.
25. Corpore virgo, sacer carus Dominoque Johannes
26. Mentis in extasi metitur limina templi.
27. Hi sunt vero due regni celestis olive.
28. Hujus celicolam subductus partus ad aulam,
29. Sic tremebunda fugit tanti terrore draconis,
30. Tercia lucendi quo celi portio defit.
31. Cum quo celestes pugnantes quippe cohortes,
32. Ipsum tartareis tradunt sine margine penis.
33. Eufrates flumen, quos furvo vortice cingit,
34. Nutu divino mittit per secula solutos;
35. Armis insignes, vultu pariterque feroces,
36. Disperdunt populos flammis ac denique ferro,
37. Istud, summe Pater, te permittente potenter,
38. Qui nos pro nostris sic censes tondere actis.
39. Cetibus aligeris divina voce vocatis,
40. Odibiles Christi, celesti cuspide fusi,
41. Spe privata quidem vivendi corpora prebent.
42. Intonat in tectis vox et septena supernis.

43. Archa Dei patuit celebri inspicienda Johanni.
44. Partibus a dextris rectores hi residentes
45. Digne discutiunt summo judice mundum.
46. Majestate potens, qui sic judicat orbem.
47. Agmina millenis semper vexata gehennis
48. Inferus ore vomit, repetendaque corpora mittit.
49. Equor et exesas per tempora loga catervas
50. Rursus subductus tradit pacienter ad auras.
51. Parturit absconsos hominum quoque terra maniplos,
52. Occursu Domini quos offert Leta trementi.
53. Fulgida sanctorum consortia cerne virorum
54. Necne hermitarum, meritum scandantia regnum.
55. Hic et virgineas gaudentes inspice turmas
56. Et confessorum preclaras necne phalanges,
57. Atque triumphantes in Christi laude tyrones.
58. Insonat haecque piis oppressis mole sepulchri.
59. Sanctam Jerusalem gemmis averte choruscam,
60. Virginitate sacer quam vidit mente Johannes.
61. Taliter injusti, quos punit leva Tonantis,
62. Exclusi vita, voces dant cum prece frustra.
63. Tartarus ignivomo constructus carceris antro,
64. Cum mortis rabie dampnatur sic sine fine.

NOTES

Editors' note: This paper was originally presented at the "Conference on the Apocalyptic Year 1000" in Boston, Mass., November 4–6, 1996, and has been translated for inclusion in this volume by Kristin Babock and David Van Meter. Professor Christe is the Director of the Centre d'Etudes du Proche-Orient ancien at the Université de Genève.

1. On the cycle at Saint-Pierre de Fleury, see I. Yoshikawa, *L'Apocalypse de Saint-Savin* (Paris, 1939), pp. 120–61; C. H. Bautier, "Le monastère et les églises de Fleury-sur-Loire sous les abbatiats d'Abbon, de Gauzlin et d'Arnaud (988–1032)," in *Memoires de la Société nationale des Antiquaires de France*, 9th ser., vol. 4 (Paris, 1969), pp. 71–154. The text of the *tituli* reproduced in the appendix is from Bautier. On the cycle at Novara, see U. Chierici, *Il battistero del duomo de Novara* (Novara, 1967); M. B. Mauck, "The Apocalypse Frescoes of the Baptistery in Novara, Italy" (Ph.D. diss., Tulane University, 1975).

2. P. Klein, "Introduction: The Apocalypse in Medieval Art," in *The Apocalypse in the Middle Ages*, ed. R. K. Emmerson and B. McGinn (Ithaca, 1992), pp. 175–77 and 179–83.

3. Valenciennes, BM, MS 99; Paris, BN, nouv. acq. lat. 1132.

4. E.g., the Bamberg Apocalypse and the ivory at Pembroke College, Cambridge.

5. See P. Klein, *Apokalypsezyklen und verwandte Denkmäler: von der Antike bis zum Anbruch der Gotik* (thesis, Bamberg, 1980).

6. Oxford, Bodleian Library, MS Bodl. 352, fol. 12r–12v.

7. Y. Christe, "De l'absence ou des lacunes d'Ap. 15, 1–20, 15 dans les cycles apocalyptiques monumentaux des Xie–XIIe siècles," in *Testo e immagine nell'alto*

medioeveo, Settimane di Studio del centro Italiano di Studi sull'alto Medioevo, vol. 41 (Spoleto, 1994), pp. 801–35.

8. Y. Christe, "Traditions littéraires et iconographiques dans l'interpretation des images apocalyptiques," in *L'Apocalypse de Jean: Traditions exégetiques et iconographiques,* ed. Y. Christe (Geneva, 1979), pp. 111 and 121.

9. Christe, "Traditions littéraires," p. 127, and scenes 1 and 12 of the old enumeration, 11:18, 11:19. In the cycles of groups I and II, in manuscripts as well as on the walls of churches, the ark in the temple in Heaven is regularly associated with the vision of the woman. This association sometimes outlived the Parisian capitulation of the beginning of the thirteenth century.

10. *PL* 117:1001: "In quo numero comprehenduntur omnes patriarchae et apostoli, omnesque qui cum Domino venturi sunt ad iudicium."

11. Verses 9–12 for the fifth seal; verses 33–38 for the sixth seal; and verse 42 for the seventh seal.

12. As brilliantly illustrated on the vault of the axial chapel of the crypt of Saint-Etienne d'Auxerre. See Christe, "De l'absence," pp. 821–22 n. 5.

13. Ambrosius Autpertus, *Expositio in Apocalypsin,* 12, ed. Robert Weber, *CCCM* 27:1.455: "Absit a fidelium cordibus, ut hoc proelium in initio temporis, quando per superbiam antiquus hostis cum satellitibus suis de caelesti patria ruit, factum fuisse existement, sed a passione Christi in Ecclesia inchoatum fuisse, et nunc fieri, et in fine saeculi, quando etiam solutus fuerit, consummari."

14. For a good illustration, see E. Corelli and S. Casiello, *Santa Maria Donnaregina in Napoli* (Naples, 1975), fig. 39. The woman is accompanied, on the left, by St. Michael pushing back the dragon, who vomits his torrents of water, and by another angel on the right, standing to the side of a cross and an altar.

15. Y. Christe, "Traditions littéraires et iconographiques dans l'élaboration du programme de Civate," in *Texte et image: Actes du Colloque international de Chantilly* (Paris, 1984), pp. 117–34.

16. See P. Klein, *Der ältere Beatus-Kodex Vitr. 14.1 der Biblioteca-Nacional zu Madrid: Studien zur Beatusillustration und der spanischen Buchmalerei des 10. Jahrhundert* (Hildesheim, 1976), pp. 114–25, figs. 118–21. Above all, see fig. 121 (New York, Pierpont Morgan Library, m.644, fols. 152v–153, Beatus de Magius).

17. See J. Baschet, "Satan, prince de l'enfer: Le développement de sa puissance dans l'art italien (XIIIe–XVe siècles)," in *L'autunno del diavolo,* ed. E. Carsini and E. Costa (Milan, 1990), pp. 383–96.

18. See W. Kamlah, *Apocalypse und Geschichtstheologie* (Berlin, 1935); G. Kretschmar, *Die Offenbarung des Johannes* (Stuttgart, 1985); and K. B. Steinhauser, *The Apocalypse Commentary of Ticonius* (Frankfurt am Main, 1987). See also G. Lobrichon, "L'Apocalypse des théologiens au XIIe siècle" (thesis, Paris, Ecole pratique des Hautes Etudes en Sciences Sociales, 1979).

19. *PL* 70:1470A.

20. *PL* 70:1410D–1411A.

21. *PL* 70:1410A and 1412D.

22. *PL* 70:1411C.

23. G. Bertelli, "Un ciclo di affreschi altomedievali in Puglia: L'Apocalisse de tempietto di Seppanibale a Fasano," *Arte Medievale,* 2d ser., 2 (1990): 73–97.

24. Christe, "De l'absence," p. 821.

8

The Millennium, Time, and History for the Anglo-Saxons

Malcolm Godden

"And the beast? Where did you see the beast?"

"The beast? Ah, the Antichrist. . . . He is about to come, the millennium is past; and we await him. . . ."

"But the millennium was three hundred years ago, and he did not come then. . . ." "The Antichrist does not come after a thousand years have passed. When the thousand years have passed, the reign of the just begins; then comes the Antichrist, to confound the just, and then there will be the final battle. . . ."

"But the just will reign for a thousand years," William said. "Or else they reigned from the death of Christ to the end of the first millennium, and so the Antichrist should have come then; or else the just have not yet reigned, and the Antichrist is still far off."

"The millennium is not calculated from the death of Christ but from the donation of Constantine, three centuries later. Now it is a thousand years. . . ."

"So the reign of the just is ending?"

"I do not know. . . . I do not know any more. I am tired. The calculation is difficult. Beatus of Liébana made it; ask Jorge, he is young, he remembers well. . . . But the time is ripe. Did you not hear the seven trumpets?"

—Umberto Eco, *The Name of the Rose*

The imminence of the end of the world is one of the most important themes, a framing concept indeed, for Anglo-Saxon writers in the decades surrounding the year 1000. Aelfric proclaims it as the context for his first great collection of homilies around the year 990, and for Wulfstan it is the central focus of his earliest homilies and for his last and most famous, the *Sermo ad anglos*. Yet as for Eco's characters it raised both for them and for their readers complex problems about time and history: where exactly were they in that sequence of historical time from Christ to the end, and was the critical moment a particular spot in historical time or only a state of mind? A peculiar aspect of this issue, though perhaps one that strikes us rather than the Anglo-Saxons themselves, is the grammatical one: what happens when writers try to discuss events of the imminent future in a language whose verbs have no future tense?

Anglo-Saxon writers were acutely aware that when they proclaimed the imminent end they were doing so on the basis of texts that had been used for a similar purpose repeatedly over the last thousand years and more. It was perhaps a unique situation in which the failures and inaccuracies of past exegesis were crucially apparent: just as the early Fathers could look back at the disciples and remark how mistakenly they had interpreted Christ's words when they took him to be prophesying the imminent establishment of the kingdom of God, so Anglo-Saxon writers could in turn look back at their great authorities, such as Gregory the Great, and see how their expectations of an imminent end had proved false; and Anglo-Saxon readers of the eleventh century could in turn see how their own authority figures, such as Aelfric and Wulfstan, had prophesied an imminent end which seemed not to have arrived. While this inevitably gave Anglo-Saxon writers cause for doubt, it did not prevent them from exploiting the possibilities of an impending apocalypse that would make comprehensive sense of the failing world they saw around them.

It is peculiarly hard to discover how seriously Anglo-Saxons took their own predictions of an imminent end. The awareness of living in the last age of the world, in its period of old age, had perhaps been with the Anglo-Saxons almost since their conversion. *The Seafarer* speaks of the lost glories of the past and the present old age of the world, resembling the old age of a man, and the poem *Guthlac A*, which claims to have been composed within living memory of the saint (d. 714), describes the present decline of the world as having been long foretold.[1] One apparent sign of the importance of millennialist ideas in late Anglo-Saxon England is their use in royal charters registering grants of estates. These often begin with a pious explanation for the grant, such as the transience of the world or the evanescence of records, and one common version of this topos is a reference to the approaching end of the world in fulfillment of the biblical prophecies, an end that is offered as an explicit motive for the king to divest himself of material wealth and lay up treasure instead in Heaven.[2] Yet these references to the approaching end seem very perfunctory and are promptly followed by the most detailed and precise listing of what lands, appurtenances, and rights the recipient is to possess in perpetuity, and by prescriptions and curses to ensure the recipient's untroubled retention of the estates into the indefinite future. If such charters begin by asserting that material things will soon become irrelevant to kings, their primary function is nevertheless to ensure the material well-being for the recipients (often religious institutions) through a continuing future.

The temptation to invoke traditional expectations of the end as the year 1000 approached, while recognizing the uncertainty of the prophecies, is evident in the anonymous Blickling homily on Ascension, which announces the current date as 971.

We leorniaþ þæt seo tid sie toþæs degol þæt nære næfre nænig toþæs halig mon on þissum middangearde, ne furþum nænig on heofenum þe þæt æfre wiste, hwonne he ure Drihten þisse worlde ende gesettan wolde on domes dæg, buton him Drihtne anum; we witon þonne hweþre þæt hit nis no feor to þn; forþon þe ealle þa tacno & þa forebeacno þa þe her ure Drihten ær toweard sægde, þæt ær domes dæge geweorþan sceoldan, ealle þa syndon agangen, buton þæm anum þæt se awerigda cuma Antecrist nu get hider on middangeard ne com. Nis þæt þonne feor toþon þæt þæt eac geweorþan sceal; forþon þes middangeard nede on ðas eldo endian sceal þe nu andweard is; forþon fife þara syndon agangen on þisse eldo. þonne sceal[3] þes middangeard endian & þisse is þonne se mæsta dæl agangen, efne nigon hund wintra & lxxi. on þys geare. Ne wæron þas ealle gelic lange, ac on þyssum wæs þreo þusend wintra, on sumre læsse, on sumere eft mare. Nis forþon nænig mon þe þæt an wite hu lange he ure Drihten þas gedon wille, hwæþer þis þusend sceole beon scyrtre ofer þæt þe lengre. þæt is þonne æghwylcum men swiþe uncuþ, buton urum Drihtne anum.[4]

[We learn that the time [of the end] is so secret that no one in the world, however holy, nor even anyone in Heaven, except the Lord alone, has ever known when our Lord would set an end to this world on the Day of Judgment; we know, however, that it is not far distant, for all the signs and portents which our Lord said should occur before doomsday have occurred, except only that the accursed visitant Antichrist has not yet come into the world. It is not long until the time when that must happen. For this world must necessarily end in this age that is present, because five of them have passed. In this age then must this world end and most of it has passed, that is, nine hundred and seventy-one years in this year. These [ages] were not all of the same length, but in this one [sic] there were three thousand years, in one less, in another more. Hence, no one knows how long our Lord will make this one, whether this thousand will be shorter than that or longer. That is unknown to everyone except our Lord.[5]]

The passage is hard to interpret in some places and probably corrupt. Morris interprets the five that have already happened as foretokens, but the number makes it likely that the reference is to the five preceding ages. The statement that there have been three thousand years in this present age is both inaccurate and inconsistent; it is presumably a miscopied reference to one of the earlier ages. The underlying biblical passage is of course the moment when the disciples ask the ascending Christ whether he will now establish the kingdom of Israel, but the homilist promptly converts this into a question about the end of the world. The idea of an imminent kingdom of God on earth is for him a delusion of the disciples, and he imagines them asking what they should really have asked: would the kingdom be established at the end of the world and when would that be? Characteristically, there is a hedging over the timing of the end. Against the assurance that no one in earth or Heaven has known ("wiste") the date of the end, the preacher cannot resist opposing his own "we witan þonne hweþre" ("we [or I] know, however"). The very precision of 971 seems to invite a counting of years rather than decades or centuries. That precision was itself overtaken by the processes of transmission, of course. This is not after all an authorial copy but a version incorporated into a homiliary combining texts by several different writers. The manuscript itself is to be dated roughly around the year 1000[6] and may not be much later than the 971 date (which may in turn be not the author's own date but a scribal revision). Even so, readers cannot have been unaware that the announcement of the critical moment—this year of grace 971—had already been overtaken by time, just as the disciples' own question and Christ's reply were overtaken by the events of Pentecost ten days later.

It is in the homilies of Aelfric and Wulfstan that millennialist issues loom largest among vernacular writings in the period.[7] Their works were widely circulated at the time, and both were concerned to address a wide readership. For both of them, the Millennium was an issue that continued beyond the year 1000 and involved them in constant rethinking and rewriting of their earlier works on the ending of the world. What seems to underlie their discussions is a debate about the nature of time. If they are about to experience the end of time, an end destined since the beginning of time and prophesied since Old Testament days, this strongly asserts a linear notion of temporality; but much of what they say on the subject, and their use of earlier authorities, testifies to a cyclical sense of time, a recognition that apocalypse is always with us; it is a recurrent situation.

A cyclical perception of history is a key feature of Aelfric's writing. In his repeated retellings of Old Testament stories and early Christian history and hagiography, he invites his Anglo-Saxon readers to see themselves as reenacting the experiences of the Israelites or the Christian martyrs; in his exegesis of the Scriptures he continually suggests an identification of contemporary Anglo-Saxons with the first Gentiles. But set against that is a strongly linear sense of history in which all events have their unique place in a coherent design running from Creation and Fall through Incarnation and Redemption to the end of the world and the Last Judgment. It is this linear history that Aelfric proposes as the framing context for his *First Series of Catholic Homilies*, issued within a few years of 990 when he was a monk at Cerne Abbas in Dorset.[8] The opening homily sets forth Redemption history from Creation to the Last Judgment, while the coming of Antichrist and the imminent end of the world are the critical context that Aelfric announces for his work in the Old English preface. After noting the paucity of orthodox teaching for the Anglo-Saxons in the vernacular, he remarks:

> For þisum antimbre ic gedyrstlæhte, on Gode truwiende, þæt ic ðas gesetnysse undergann, and eac forðam þe menn behofiað godre lare swiðost on þisum timan þe is geendung þyssere worulde. (*CH* I:2)

[For this reason I ventured to undertake this work, trusting in God,
and also because people need good teaching most urgently in this
time, which is the ending of this world.]

He goes on to describe in detail the tribulations that will precede the end and
particularly the role and reign of Antichrist, before turning back at the end to
the consequent need for the clergy to speak out. Yet as he develops the description, a time scale stretching some way into the future gradually unrolls. The end
itself, according to Aelfric, will be preceded by a time of tribulations, including
or culminating in the three and a half year reign of Antichrist. The time of tribulations will be a justified punishment for an earlier period of sinfulness, which
is itself still in the future:

> Se Ælmihtiga God geðafað þam arleasan Antecriste to wyrcenne
> tacna, and wundra, and ehtnysse, to feorðan healfan geare; forþan ðe
> on ðam timan bið swa micel yfelnyss and þwyrnys betwux mancynne
> þæt hi wel wyrðe beoð þære deoflican ehtnysse. (*CH* 1:4)

> [The almighty God will permit the wicked Antichrist to perform
> signs and miracles and persecution for three and a half years,
> because at that time there will be such great evil and perversity
> among people that they will be fully deserving of that diabolic
> persecution.]

The birth of Antichrist himself is still evidently in the future:

> Þonne cymð se Antecrist, se bið mennisc mann and soð deofol, swa
> swa ure Hælend is soðlice mann and God on anum hade. (*CH* 1:4)

> [Then Antichrist will come, who will be human man and true devil,
> just as our Savior is truly man and God in one person.]

The importance of verb forms is particularly noteworthy here. The verbs in these
two sentences are all present tense in form, as is standard in Old English references to the future, but the expressions "at that time" and the initial "then" imply
future meaning. So, too, does the use of the *bið/beoð* forms of the verb "to be":
the *bið/beoð* forms in Old English tend to be used for the timeless present and
the future while the *is/sind* forms are used for current time. Though Thorpe's
facing translation renders *bið* as present tense "is" here, Aelfric's careful contrast between the two forms of the verb "to be," *bið* and *is*, should not be overlooked: here he uses *is* for Christ's dual nature, indicating its continued reality
into the present, while using *bið* for Antichrist's dual nature, placing his birth
still in the future.[9] On a literal interpretation, this would seem to place the reign
of Antichrist still some twenty years at least in the future at the time of writing.

It is surely significant that Aelfric not only prefaced his *First Series of Catholic
Homilies* with a warning of Antichrist but also concluded the collection with a
homily on the approaching end of the world, for the second Sunday in Advent. It
is a text that poses surprisingly complex questions of authority, voice, and time

and deserves a closer analysis. The Gospel text for the day, which the homily begins by translating, is Luke 21:25–33, describing the signs in the heavens, earth,
and sea that will precede the coming of the Son of man and the joyous inaugura-
tion of the kingdom of God, apparently (according to a literal meaning) within
the lifetime of Christ's listeners.[10] The primary note of the Gospel text is positive
and comforting, but Aelfric imposes a different emphasis, interpreting the portents as evils and afflictions which proclaim the end of the dying world and supporting that view by adding the series of disasters—wars, earthquakes, plagues,
and famine—mentioned a little earlier in Luke's Gospel; indeed, his words seem
to claim that this was the sense intended by both Luke and Christ. At the outset,
Aelfric identifies Gregory the Great as the source and authority for the subsequent
exposition, and indeed its voice: "Se halga Gregorius us trahtnode þyses godspelles
digelnysse þus undergynnende" (CH 1:608) (the holy Gregory expounded for us
the mystery of this Gospel reading, beginning thus). The lines that directly follow
are indeed virtually verbatim from Gregory and are perhaps to be understood as
a quotation from him, though one that is never explicitly brought to an end. Aelfric
draws much of the subsequent material from the first of Gregory's homilies on
the Gospels, but he also used material from Haimo's homily on the same text
and some additional material of his own.[11] The question of whose voice is speaking, and hence what time scheme is at issue, becomes significant when Aelfric
follows a summary list of the signs with the words:

> Sume ðas tacna we gesawon gefremmede, sume we ondrædað us
> towearde. Witodlice on ðisum niwum dagum arison ðeoda ongean
> ðeoda, and heora ofðriccednyss on eorðan gelamp swiðor þonne we
> on ealdum bocum rædað. (CH 1:608)

> [Some of these signs we have seen happen; some we fear as impend-
> ing. Truly, in these recent times nations have risen against nations,
> and their tribulation has befallen on earth more intensely than we
> read in old books.]

Are these Aelfric's recent times or Gregory's? The wording follows Gregory very
closely, and the reference to recent times is originally his, "in nostris
temporibus."[12] On the other hand, Gregory's codicibus have become more precisely "old books," as if to mark the passage of time since Gregory first spoke
those words. That Anglo-Saxon listeners were to hear Gregory's voice here, or
at least think of his times as included in their own "recent times," was no doubt
confirmed for them by the sentence that follows, citing experience from the
Roman Empire as one of the "recent" portents:

> Oft eorðstyrung gehwær fela burhga ofhreas, swa swa gelamp on
> Tyberies dæge þæs caseres, þæt ðreottyne byrig ðurh eorðstyrunge
> afeollon. (CH 1:608)

> [Often earthquakes everywhere have destroyed many cities, as
> happened in the days of Emperor Tiberius when thirteen cities
> collapsed through earthquake.]

Yet though Gregory does mention the destruction of many cities in other parts of the world, the reference to the thirteen cities and to Tiberius's days is not from him, or indeed from any of the commentaries that Aelfric appears to have consulted. Though his listeners may have heard Gregory's voice here, it appears to be Aelfric's own contribution to cite the events of Tiberius's reign as portents of an imminent end nine centuries later, or at least as a parallel to such portents. Whether the Anglo-Saxon audience heard Gregory's sixth-century voice here or Aelfric's own voice citing ancient tokens, the effect must surely have been to play the sense of imminence against an awareness that imminence is always with us, that the portents of the approaching end have been a persistent feature of the last thousand years. The sense of an ending seems here to refer to an awareness of being in the last millennium rather than the last decade.

Gregory himself goes on at this point to note Christ's reference to signs in the heavens: these have not yet been seen, he says, but they cannot be far off, and he cites as a parallel or precursor the fiery hosts in the sky that he had seen heralding the Lombard invasions of Italy in his own lifetime. Haimo, evidently reworking Gregory two centuries later but adding much additional material, took an opposing view, dropping the reference to the Lombards, adducing the more detailed account of the signs from Matthew's Gospel, and asserting that such signs in the heavens had frequently been seen.[13] Aelfric evidently read both interpretations but chose to follow Gregory in insisting that these signs had not yet been seen, while omitting reference to the portents of the Lombard invasions. It was presumably in silent rebuttal of Haimo that he too cited the Matthew portents but then added a careful explanation that such signs are not to be confused with eclipses of sun and moon and sudden comets, which have often been seen but are natural phenomena, not the portents foretold by Christ. For him the signs in the heavens seem curiously less imminent than they had been for either Gregory or Haimo.

In reading Gregory the Great's homily on the Luke text, Aelfric would have been struck by the strongly topical nature of his interpretation: not just the reference to the Lombard invasions but descriptions in graphic detail of current disasters. Only the day before yesterday, Gregory reminded his audience, trees had been uprooted by a sudden storm, houses destroyed, churches overturned, people overtaken by unexpected death; all this, he told them, showed the hand of God and a foretaste of the horrors of the end.[14] Gregory's reading is strongly located in its own historical moment. Not surprisingly, Aelfric left out such references in his own version, but it is significant that he did not replace them with similar events of his own time (as Wulfstan was to do) but instead opened up the time frame by his reference to still earlier events, the earthquakes of Tiberius's time.[15]

This ambivalent handling of time is particularly evident in the closure of Aelfric's homily, when he quotes from Zephaniah:

> Be ðam dæge cwæð se witega Sofonias, "Se miccla Godes dæg is
> swiðe gehende, and ðearle swyft: biter bið þæs dæges stemn: þær bið
> se stranga gedrefed." . . . Se witega cwæð, þæt se miccla Godes dæg

is swiðe gehende, and þearle swyft. Þeah ðe gyt wære oðer þusend
geara to ðam dæge, nære hit langsum; forðan swa hwæt swa
geendað, þæt bið sceort and hræd, and bið swilce hit næfre ne
gewurde, þonne hit geendod bið. Hwæt þeah hit langsum wære to
ðam dæge, swa hit nis, þeah ne bið ure tima langsum, and on ure
geendunge us bið gedemed, hwæðer we on reste oþþe on wite ðone
gemænelican dom anbidian sceolon. (CH 1:618)

[Concerning that day the prophet Zephaniah spoke: "The great day
of God is very near and very swift. Bitter will be the voice of that day,
when the strong man will be troubled." . . . The prophet said that the
great day of God is very near and very swift. Even if it were another
thousand years to that day, it would not be long, because whatever
ends is short and swift and will be as if it never happened when it is
finished. Even if it were a long time to that day—as it is not—our
own time will not be long, and at our ending it will be decided for us
whether we are to await the general Judgment in rest or in torment.]

In introducing the prophetic text, Aelfric signals an awareness that he is the latest
in a long line of preachers who had announced the imminent end. Both Gregory
and Haimo quote these verses, too, but without comment, and the context focuses
attention on the terrors of the Last Day, not the issue of time. For Aelfric the verses
evidently invoke the whole problem of time. The prophet asserts the imminence
of the end, and yet the prophet was speaking in Old Testament times, more than
a thousand years earlier. The nearness of the end might be merely relative to eternity, and the end might therefore be distant in human terms; but it is not in fact
distant, Aelfric then interjects, and even if it were, the individual end is close. His
somewhat tortuous response expresses neatly the tension between the idea of the
imminent end and the awareness of the repeated cycles of the past.

Aelfric is then ambivalent about the imminence of the promised end. The
homily presents the Anglo-Saxons as living close to a possible end of time. Most
of the portents are past but some are still to come, and the quotation from
Zephaniah can be interpreted as promising a literally imminent end or a relatively imminent one or a personal end; the prophetic texts themselves are ancient and have been spoken and interpreted by other voices in the past; the
portents themselves stretch back over nearly a thousand years.

It was presumably no accident that Aelfric's first major collection began and
ended with powerful accounts of the imminent end of the world, even if, on
more careful reading, both accounts qualify that notion of imminence. And it
should not be forgotten that copies of the collection, with this clear message,
were presented both to Aethelweard, an important ealdorman, and to Sigeric,
archbishop of Canterbury. It is all the more striking that there is so little trace
of the same message in the *Second Series of Catholic Homilies*, produced probably two or three years later in 994 or 995.[16] The preface to this series makes
no reference to the end of the world or Antichrist, though it does include a passing reference to an event that was to succeed the millennium as the great crisis
of the period: the attacks of the Vikings.[17] It seems at first significant that just

as the first series ended with a homily on the imminent end of the world, so the penultimate homily in this collection deals with the coming of the Last Judgment: it is assigned to the feast day of holy virgins and expounds the parable of the five wise and five foolish virgins. But here Aelfric is strikingly dismissive of apocalyptic expectations:

> Oft cweðað men. efne nu cymð domes dæg. for ðan ðe ða witegunga
> sind agane. þe be ðam gesette wæron; Ac gefeoht cymð ofer
> gefeohte. gedrefednys ofer gedrefednysse. eorðstyrung ofer
> eorðstyrunge. hungor ofer hungre. þeod ofer ðeode. and þonne gyt
> ne cymð se brydguma; Eac swilce þa six ðusend geara fram adame
> beoð geendode. and ðonne gyt elcað se brydguma; Hu mage we
> þonne witan hwænne he cymð? (CH 2:xxxix.111–17)

> [Often people say, behold, now doomsday is coming because the
> prophecies that were laid down about it have passed. But there
> comes war after war, tribulation after tribulation, earthquake after
> earthquake, famine after famine, nation after nation, and still the
> bridegroom does not come. Also the six thousand years from Adam
> are completed, and still the bridegroom delays. How then can we
> know when he will come?]

At the outset of his commentary on the parable, Aelfric has emphasized that the interpretations are drawn from Augustine and Gregory and begins his discussion with Gregory's own voice, as if to deny any personal responsibility.[18] Yet though most of the material in the homily is from his two authorities, it is very freely selected and adapted, at times using their words to make rather different points. He is here repeating verbatim the words of Augustine, including the reference to the completion of six thousand years, and must have been fully conscious that erroneous expectations of the imminent end of the world were already a familiar part of the scene five centuries before his own time. Yet there is a striking difference of tone here. He has joined together two distinct passages from Augustine, and the first is used in the Latin text in a much more positive fashion, as evidence of the faithful continuing properly to expect the end up until their deaths; they say these things *fideliter*, Augustine insists.[19] Aelfric uses the point instead to underline the impossibility of knowing when the end will come and to suggest the folly of those who observe such portents. It is a striking repudiation of linear time in favor of a more cyclical sense of history. By this stage in the homily, Aelfric must be understood to be speaking in his own voice, as well as, or instead of, Gregory's or Augustine's, and in appropriating and adapting these dismissive comments about past expectations of the end, he necessarily refers to the expectations of his own time as well, voiced in the charters and earlier homilies and indeed in his own earlier writings. Implicitly, the passage acknowledges the failure or ambiguity of the biblical prophecies: the signs foretold have been seen but still the promised end has not yet come. It is, though, significant that Aelfric does not explicitly identify those failed prophecies and portents as biblical texts and cites against them the authority of Christ's own words in the Gospel parable of the virgins at the wedding feast: the bridegroom will come in the middle of the night, which he interprets not as a specific time but as a time when men do not expect it. Biblical and divine authority are here cited not to affirm the imminence of the end but to affirm its uncertainty, its unpredictability. And this in turn is given the support of Divine Providence: God himself has chosen not to give warning of the end, for the moral benefit of mankind itself:

> Nat nan man þyssere worulde geendunge. ne furðon his agene
> geendunge; Menig man wolde þone maran dæl his lifes aspendan on
> his lustum. and ðone læssan dæl on dædbote. gif he wiste hwænne
> he geendian sceolde; Us is bedigelod ure geendung. to ði þæt we
> sculon symle us ondrædan. ðone endenextan dæg. þone ðe we ne
> magon næfre foresceawian. (*CH* 2:xxxix.207–12)

> [No one knows the end of this world, or even his own end. Many a
> man would spend the greater part of this life in his pleasures and the
> lesser part in penitence if he knew when he was to end. Our end is
> hidden from us, in order that we should constantly fear the last day,
> which we can never foresee.]

Although the time of the end is uncertain, Aelfric writes here as if it would not be in the lifetime of his listeners. He interprets the ten virgins as types of the Christian and their sleep as the universal death which must precede the Second Coming, and he quotes St. Paul to the same effect: the trumpet will blow and the dead will arise uncorrupted, and we will be changed into eternal things in the body as we are now in the soul, he paraphrases.[20] The sudden coming of the bridegroom is to be implicitly understood as the arrival of judgment after a period of death, and he identifies himself and his listeners (*we*) with those who will rise from death.[21]

The preface to Aelfric's next collection, the so-called *Lives of Saints*,[22] makes no reference to the end of the world, or indeed to the Vikings, but two of the pieces do refer in general terms to the present period as the end. In *LS* 13 he discusses Old Testament parallels to the problems of the current time and toward the end briefly refers to the end of the world, implicitly alluding to the apocalyptic words in Mark 13:22 ("tradet autem frater fratrem in mortem, et pater filium"):

> Fela ungelimpa beoð on ende ðissere worulde . ac gehwa mot
> forberan emlice his dæl . . . . Þes tima is endenext and ende þyssere
> worulde . and menn beoð geworhte wolice him betwynan . swa þæt
> se fæder winð wið his agenne sunu . and broðor wið oþerne to
> bealwe him sylfum . and mid ðam geeacniað yfelnysse him sylfum .
> ge on ðissere worulde ge on ðære toweardan. (290–91, 294–99)

Skeat translates:

> There will be many misfortunes at the end of this world, but each
> one must patiently suffer his lot . . . . This time is the last time, and

the end of this world, and men are made unjust amongst themselves, so that the father contendeth with his own son, and one
brother with another, to their own destruction, and thereby add
iniquity to themselves, both in this world and in that which is to
come.

Translated in this way, the passage does seem to suggest that the evils of the
Last Days were already at hand. But the *beoð* of line 295 contrasts with the *is* of
the previous line, and the sense is probably "and people will be made evil toward each other, in such a way that the father will contend with his own son
and brother with brother." If the *is* of line 294 seems to assert the presence of
the end, the *beoð* forms in lines 290 and 295 suggest that the time of apocalyptic sinfulness which precedes and justifies the final tribulations is still in the
indefinite future. Though Aelfric does indeed say that the present time is the
"last time" he remains perhaps deliberately vague whether that term here denotes the final decades or the final thousand years or any period between the
two. The value of the apocalyptic paradigm for him is essentially that it offers a
justifying framework for the experience of misfortune and dissension, which
might otherwise lead men to doubt the justice and benevolence of the Deity and
murmur against him.[23] The end of the world is not here the primary historical
significance that Aelfric proposes for his time. More important is an alternative
historical framework or paradigm that works against the sense of finality here.[24]
Aelfric has already proposed in this text a parallel between the current English
experience of Viking raid and natural disaster and the repeated experiences of
rebellious Hebrews and sinful Ninevites, who suffered the wrath of God but
learned to appease him by timely prayer and repentance. The primary underlying argument is that the prayers of the English monastic order and the reform
of the laity will restore prosperity to England. Cyclical time, in which English
tenth-century experience repeats the earlier stories of Hebrews in the desert,
David and Judea, Jonah and the Ninevites, and allows, as for the earlier societies, the possibility of averting the wrath of God, is actually more important here
than linear time, which relates current tribulation to the unavertable end of time.

   The collection in which this piece appears was dedicated by Aelfric to
Aethelweard and Aethelmaer and must therefore predate the former's death:
Aethelweard disappears from the record in 998 and perhaps died in that year,
certainly within a very few years of that date, and since there are linguistic reasons for dating xiii earlier than many of the other items in the collection, this
piece almost certainly precedes the year 1000.[25] The year 1000 itself passed for
Aelfric without any known discussion of the significance of that date, and when
he returned a few years later to the question of the end of the world, in two texts
dated in the period 1002–5,[26] just before he became abbot of the newly founded
monastery at Eynsham, it is without any suggestion of the imminence of the
end. In the first, a sermon called *In octavis Pentecosten* (Pope, 11), after discussing the principal events of Christ's life and their commemoration by the church,
Aelfric turns to the question of death and the end of the world. He begins by
insisting that no one but God knows when the world's ending will come. He

describes vividly the souls of the departed waiting urgently for doomsday and having to wait until the number which God has ordained from the time of creation is reached. There is a sense of urgency, but it is the urgency of the departed souls, not the author, and there is no suggestion that the end may be near. The other apocalyptic text of this period (1002–5) is Aelfric's *Sermo de die iudicii* (Pope, 18). This is a free-ranging independent homily expounding in turn two scriptural texts on the end of the world, Luke 17:20ff. and Matthew 24:15ff., but in neither case does Aelfric say anything about the imminence of the end.

One other sign of the changing significance of the millennium for Aelfric is the fate of the first–series preface. It survives in fact in only one manuscript, a copy of the two series of *Catholic Homilies* reflecting an early stage of the text, and there is good evidence that Aelfric himself subsequently removed it from this prominent position. The account of Antichrist that forms its centerpiece appears as an independent text in three other manuscripts containing his works, all showing close acquaintance with the later stage of his writings.[27] One of them gives the text in the form seen within the preface, but the other two show an apparently authorial revision to the earlier statement concerning the origins of Antichrist. In place of the words "se bið mennisc mann and soð deofol, swa swa ure Hælend is soðlice mann and God on anum hade," we now find the following words: "he bið begyten mid forlire of were and of wife; and he bið mid deofles gaste afylled" (he will be begotten by fornication from a man and a woman and will be filled with the Devil's spirit). It looks as if Aelfric meant to imply by the original wording that Antichrist would be the offspring of the Devil in the same way that Christ is the son of God, but that on further reflection or reading he altered this to make it clear that Antichrist would be of normal human origin.[28] In the process, Antichrist's birth is placed still more firmly and clearly in the future.

It is possible that this use of the Antichrist account as a separate piece did not preclude its continued circulation as part of the preface to the first series, but it is clear that by the time Aelfric revised and reissued the series, it had been dropped. In the revised version the Antichrist text is reused to form a new conclusion to the homily for the first Sunday in Advent. This is not a very obvious text in which to use the discussion, but the opening does refer to the Second Coming at the end of time, and there is a closing reference to the approaching Judgment. Presumably, this addition meant that Aelfric was no longer using the passage in the preface,[29] and no longer presenting the series as motivated by the imminence of Antichrist. That is perhaps a sign that by that date the imminence was no longer so obvious to him. If his revision of details and subsequent reuse of the account in the Advent homily testify to his continuing interest in Antichrist, his detachment of it from the prominent position in the preface marks a significant shift.

John C. Pope has remarked that "it is hardly safe to suppose that the passage of the millennium brought about a change in Aelfric's attitude towards the imminence of the Judgement."[30] Even so, it remains true that the idea of an imminent end is strongest in the earliest texts, the preface to the first series, and the last homily in that collection, probably written early in the final decade of the millennium. By the end of the second series, he was already dismissing such expectations, and although there are vague references to the ending of the world in the *Lives of Saints* collection, the later texts are striking in their failure to mention it. Yet even the early texts suggest an ambivalence on Aelfric's part, an eagerness to proclaim the nearness of the end alongside an insistence that it could be very distant, and a consciousness that to proclaim the imminent end of all time was to recapitulate the perspectives of the prophets, the disciples, and the fathers of the church.

For Wulfstan, the end of the world was a central concern from his earliest to his latest writings and involved him in an apparently continuous process of rewriting as his ideas developed and situations changed. He produced a series of homilies on the end of the world in the decades surrounding the year 1000.[31] The first homily, on Antichrist, exists in both a Latin and an English version, similar but different in detail. The Latin version describes the future time of tribulations that will last forty-two months, when brother will betray brother to death and many will fall into error because of the great miracles and the torments with which Christians will be afflicted. Twice Wulfstan makes the point that many people will not see the times of Antichrist, but it is important for the clergy to proclaim his coming so that Christians will be prepared. Presumably, he means to imply that some among his readers or listeners will live to see Antichrist, though there is no specific reference to his imminence. At the same time, Wulfstan converts Antichrist into a current issue by also interpreting him as the type of the sinner— Antichrist is anyone who does not act or teach according to Christianity—and by arguing that there already exist parallels to Antichrist, in the form of false Christs and false prophets leading people into error. The English version, essentially a vernacular expansion of the first (1b), repeats and develops these points, though the use of the vernacular creates some uncertainties about tenses. The tribulations associated with Antichrist and prophesied in books are apparently in the future, but Wulfstan offers a personal view that they are imminent:

> And us þincð þæt hit sy þam timan swyðe gehende, forðam þeos
> woruld is fram dæge to dæge a swa leng swa wyrse. (*Homilies*,
> 1b.22–24)

> [It seems to us that it is very close to that time, because this world is
> steadily worsening from day to day.]

He locates himself and his audience at a particular moment toward the end of time: the false Christs prophesied in the Scriptures are now widely visible, but the tribulations that books prophesy are still in the future. The Anglo-Saxons can have the satisfaction of seeing themselves as the fulfillment of the biblical prophecies quoted by Wulfstan.

In the second homily, using Matthew 24 on the tribulations that will precede the end, Wulfstan shows a particular concern for the question of the imminence of the end. He begins by quoting the Latin text of Matt. 24:1–24, on the signs that will precede the end, but adds two further verses, 36 and 42, in which Christ insists that no one but God knows when the end will be:

> Verumptamen diem illam et horam nemo scit, neque angeli celorum nisi Pater solus. Quapropter uigilate, quia nescitis qua hora Dominus uester uenturus sit. (*Homilies*, 2.24–27)

In paraphrasing and discussing the portents, he adds a further one of his own:

> And an þing ic eow secge gyt to gewisse, þæt witod sceal geweorðan godspel gecyþed geond ealle woruld ær worulde ende, þæs þe bec gesecgað, and syððan wyrð se ende swa raðe swa þæt God wile. (*Homilies*, 2.57–60)

> [And one more thing I tell you for certain, that the gospel must assuredly be proclaimed throughout the whole world before the world's end, as books tell us, and afterward the end will be as soon as God wishes.]

Wulfstan presumably knew of at least some of the areas of northern and eastern Europe where the gospel had not yet been preached. As Dorothy Bethurum says, this looks like "a warning against fixing the exact day of the end" (note to 2.57), or at least could have that effect. Yet Wulfstan himself, immediately on paraphrasing the additional two verses from Matthew, on the uncertainty of the end, asserts again a personal conviction that the end is near: "we witan mid gewisse þæat hit þærto nealæcð georne" (2.64) (we know for a truth that it is approaching very close to that time). In the face of Christ's own words, Wulfstan's *witan*, "we know," is curiously strong.

In the third homily, Wulfstan reiterates his conviction that the end is very near, but here his discussion seems to hover between a suggestion that the end is already in some sense present and a sense of its futurity. The sense seems to shift from future to present and back again, and frequently elides the distinction between them. He starts with a reference to the portents of the end that were forecast by the Gospels but are apparently still in the future:

> Ðis godspel segð and swutelað þæt fela fortacna sculon geweorðan wide on worulde, ægðer ge on heofonlicum tunglum ge on eorðlicum styrungum, ær ðam þe se dom cume þe us eallum wyrð gemæne. And witodlice ealswa flod com hwilum ær for synnum, swa cymð eac for synnum fyr ofer mancynn, and ðærto hit nealæcð nu swyðe geome. (*Homilies*, 3.4–9)

> [This Gospel text says and reveals that many portents are destined to occur widely in the world, both in the stars in the heavens and in stirrings on earth, before the judgment which will be common to us all arrives. And truly, just as a flood came in times of old because of sins, so also fire will come upon mankind because of sins, and now that is approaching very quickly.][32]

However, he quickly shifts into an account of the current tribulations and the current sinfulness, for which they are a punishment: "And ðy is fela yfela and mistlicra gelimpa wide mid mannum, and eal hit is for synnum" (9–10) (And therefore there is a multitude of evils and various misfortunes widely among people, and that is all on account of sins). Note the use of *is* rather than *bið*. He does not explicitly identify that sinfulness with the time of corruption that was so often seen as a mark of the approaching end, but that is presumably the tradition in which he is working. In his account of natural calamities, he seems to be arguing that biblical prophecies of the future are being fulfilled now in present time, but the present tenses are ambiguous and presumably were so to Wulfstan's readers:

> And forðy us eac swencað and ongean winnað manege gesceafta,
> ealswa hit awriten is: Pugnabit pro Deo orbis terram contra
> insensatos homines. Ðæt is on Englisc, eal woruld winneð swyðe for
> synnum ongean þa oferhogan þe Gode nellað hyran. Seo heofone us
> winð wið þonne heo us sendeð strynlice stormas and orf and æceras
> swyðe amyrreð. (*Homilies*, 3.34–40)

> [And because of that, many parts of creation also oppress us and
> fight against us, as it is written: "The circumference of the earth will
> fight for God against the foolish." That is, in English, the whole
> world will fight greatly, because of sins, against the proud who
> refuse to obey God. The sky fights against us when it sends us fierce
> storms and severely damages cattle and fields.]

The subsequent references to sun and moon darkening and stars falling are clearly future, using *bið* and a reference forward to Antichrist's time:

> Eac hit awriten is, ðæt sunne aþystrað ær worulde ende and mona
> adeorcað and steoffan hreosað for manna synnum; and ðæt bi Þonne
> Antecrist wedeð Þæt hit bið gelic Þam swylce hit swa sy. Hit is
> gecweden Þæt sunne aðystrað; Þæt is, Þonne God nele cyðan on
> Antecristes timan his mægen ne his mihta swa swa he oft ær dyde,
> ðonne bið gelic Þam swylce sunne sy aþystrad. (3.41–48)

> [Also it is written that the sun will darken before the world's end,
> and the moon will darken and stars fall because of people's sins; and
> it will be when Antichrist rages that it will be as if that is happening.
> It is said that the sun will darken; that is, when God in Antichrist's
> time refuses to show his power and his strength as he often did
> before, then it will be as if the sun is darkened.]

The fourth homily is on the times of Antichrist and draws extensively on the account by Aelfric which appears in the preface to the first series. Wulfstan's opening words assert the imminence of the end but seem to present Antichrist's birth as still in the future, again carefully distinguishing between *is* and *bið*:

> Leofan men, us is mycel þearf þæt we wære beon þæs egeslican timan þe towerd is. Nu bið swyðe raðe Antecristes tima, þaes ðe we wenan magan and eac georne witan, and þæt bið se egeslicesta þe æfre geweard syððan þeos woruld ærost gescapen wæs. He byð sylf deofol and ðeah mennisc man geboren. Crist is soð God and soð mann, and Antecrist bið soðlice deofol and mann. (*Homilies*, 4.3–8)

> [Beloved, there is great need that we should be aware of the terrible time that is at hand. Antichrist's time will be very soon now, as we are able to expect and also know for a fact, and that will be the most terrible time since this world was first made. He will be the Devil himself and yet born as a human person. Christ is true God and true man, and Antichrist will be truly Devil and man.]

Wulfstan seems here to have been drawing on the earlier version of Aelfric's account of Antichrist, since the final words reflect Aelfric's original reading on Antichrist's origins, with the same careful distinction between *bið* and *is:*

> Þonne cymð se Antecrist, se bið mennisc mann and soð deofol, swa swa ure Hælend is soðlice mann and God on anum hade. (*CH* 1:4)[33]

A similar distinction between the Devil who exists in the present and Antichrist who will exist in the future is made at lines 71ff., independently of Aelfric:

> Se sylfa deofol þe on helle is, þæt is se þe þonne wyrð on þam earmsceapenan men Antecriste and bið soðlice ægðer ge deofol ge man. (*Homilies*, 4.71–73)

> [The very Devil who is in Hell is he who then will be in the miscreated man Antichrist, and he will truly be both Devil and man.]

Yet Wulfstan immediately goes on to reassert the nearness of the end.

At some later time, Wulfstan seems to have returned to this homily and reworked it using a variety of additional sources to form the text edited as homily 5, which deals with the tribulations that will mark the end of the world. Wulfstan begins with Mark 13.14–19 and moves on to Paul's epistle to Timothy, on the sinfulness of the Last Days. Here, too, Wulfstan places the birth of Antichrist at some future date: "And mycel is seo þwyrnes þe nu is towerd . . . Þæt Antecrist geboren beo" (great evil is now at hand, . . . that Antichrist will be born [36–37]); "He bið mennisc man geboren, ac he bið þeah mid deofles gaste eal afylled" (he will be born as a human person but will be filled with the Devil's spirit [66]). The latter wording seems to reflect the revised version of Aelfric's short piece on Antichrist rather than the original reading used by Wulfstan in his fourth homily: "he bið begyten mid forlire of were and of wife; And he biþ mid deofles gaste afylled."[34]

As Pope has shown, Wulfstan had also by this stage read Aelfric's *De die iudicii* and drew extensively on that text.[35] He was evidently in close touch with Aelfric's work on the subject and the development of his ideas. This text is firmly dated by Wulfstan as after the year 1000:

Nu sceal hit nyde yfelian swyðe, forðam þe hit nealæcð georne his timan, ealswa hit awriten is and gefyrn wæs gewitegod: *Post mine annos soluetur Satanas*. Þæt is on Englisc, æfter þusend gearum bið Satanas unbunden. Þusend geara and eac ma is nu agan syððan Crist wæs mid mannum on menniscan hiwe, and nu syndon Satanases bendas swyðe toslopene, and Antecristes tima is wel gehende, and ðy hit is on worulde a swa leng swa wacre. (*Homilies*, 5.40–47)

[Now must things become necessarily much worse, since it is coming very close to his time, just as it is written and was long ago prophesied: "after a thousand years Satan will be unbound." That is, in English, after a thousand years Satan will be unbound. A thousand years and more have now passed since Christ was among men in human form, and now Satan's bonds are greatly loosened and Antichrist's time is very close, and therefore things are in the world ever the weaker the longer it goes on.]

(One might note in passing that Wulfstan evidently dated the thousand years from Christ's birth rather than his death; whatever the precise date of this text, Wulfstan himself was long dead by 1033.) But if the thousand years have passed without Antichrist's appearance, this for Wulfstan is confirmation of the imminence of Antichrist's time rather than a reflection on the biblical prophecies.

Wulfstan identifies the period of sinfulness which St. Paul prophesied as a mark of the end of the world with the time now present: "nu is se tima þe Paulus se apostol gefyrn foresæde" (now is the time that Paul the Apostle long ago foretold [15–16]). We might note here his firm *is;* Aelfric had seen that time as still in the future. He goes on to describe in detail the imminent persecutions of Antichrist and his working of false miracles. But the portents that will precede Antichrist's time seem still to be in the future:

And þeodscypas winnað and sacað heom betweonan foran to þam timan þe þis sceal geweorþan. Eac sceal aspringan wide and side sacu and clacu, hol and hete and rypera reaflac . . . and mænigfealde tacna beoð wide gesawene on sunnan and on monan. (5.100–106)

[And nations [will] contend and make war among themselves in advance of the time that this is destined to happen. Also there is destined to spring up far and wide conflict and injury, malice and hatred, and plundering by robbers . . . and manifold signs in the sun and the moon will be widely visible.]

Though it is now past the year 1000, Antichrist is not yet born, and many of the portents of his coming have not yet appeared; the reign of Antichrist is presumably to be thought of as still in the future, even though Wulfstan describes it as "wel gehende."

In commenting on these five early eschatological homilies, their editor, Dorothy Bethurum, remarks that Wulfstan "frequently says that the reign of

Antichrist is in progress."[36] Close attention to his wording suggests that this is far from the case, though the ambiguities of Old English grammar foster an uncertainty that Wulfstan was perhaps happy to exploit. The homilies celebrate a sense of crisis and tension as the end of all things approaches and identify the present time as the time of sin preceding the end that St. Paul had predicted, but the time of tribulation and the reign of Antichrist himself are still in a future that is sometimes almost at hand, sometimes at an indefinite distance.

Perhaps the most important of Wulfstan's writings on the theme is the *Sermo ad Anglos*, a text originally produced in 1014 but substantially rewritten at least twice by Wulfstan, so that three versions survive.[37] In its original form it is a strongly apocalyptic sermon, still announcing the imminent end of the world and the rapid approach of Antichrist's time:

> Leofan men, gecnawað Þæt soð is: ðeos woruld is on ofste, and hit nealæcð Þam ende, and Þy hit is on worulde aa swa lencg swa wyrse, and swa hit sceal nyde ær Antecristes tocyme yfelian swyðe. (*Homilies*, XX[BH].1–6)

> [Beloved, know what the truth is: this world is in haste and it is nearing the end, and therefore things are in the world ever the worse as time passes, and so it must necessarily get worse before Antichrist's time.]

Although this first version carries no dating rubric, the reference to Aethelred's expulsion (which occurred at the end of 1013) shows that it was produced in 1014 or later. As in the earlier sermons, Wulfstan presents his own time as the period of great sinfulness that was destined to precede the end itself. This sin is understood as the justifying cause of the misfortunes and tribulations that mark both the present and the promised future—though Antichrist himself is not mentioned again after the opening line.

Even in the first version there are signs of a different kind of thinking that qualifies the homily's role as a sermon on the millennium. What particularly distinguishes this text as an apocalyptic sermon, and perhaps in the end subverts it, is the focus on England rather than humanity in general. Though the first sentence speaks twice of "this world," in the next Wulfstan focuses on this nation—"deofol Þas ðeode nu fela geara dwelode to swiðe" (the Devil has too greatly led astray this nation for many years now [6–7])—and that is a constant point (9, 11, 40, 47, 49, 55, 65, 73, etc). The examples of tribulations, though often drawing on the biblical tradition, repeatedly relate to current English experience, most notably the murder of Edward the Martyr and the expulsion of Aethelred, and the recurrent "we" and "us" evidently refer to the English, not humanity. This became an increasingly striking feature as Wulfstan revised the sermon, adding references to Viking raids and atrocities and past English history, and eventually a rubric which reflected that focus: *Sermo ad Anglos*. Though the focus on England and the detail of contemporary events add a striking particularity to the sermon, which has often been commented on, the effect is of course to diminish startlingly the universality that is a necessary feature of apoca-

lypse. Despite the opening sentence with its concept of a time of sin and tribulation which is an inevitable feature of the end of the world, the sermon increasingly presents an image of a more local and temporal experience. This is perhaps
to be related to the emphasis on divine punishment as the explanation for the
current tribulations. In earlier texts, Wulfstan (like Aelfric) had suggested that
the tribulations that marked the end were, or would be, justified acts of justice
given the sinfulness that would also mark the end or the prelude to the end;
they fitted into a scheme of divine justice while at the same time being a necessary and destined feature of the end of the world. It is close to a notion that God
had predestined or foreseen the sin to match the tribulation. Aelfric and Wulfstan
see the need for all preachers to warn the people of what is to come, not so that
the tribulations can be avoided but to strengthen the people in their endurance
and their faith. What Wulfstan uses in the *Sermo ad Anglos*,[38] and is to emphasize ever more strongly in revision, is a slightly different notion of a more personal act of punishment and justice; God sends famine and blight and illness
and burning and eventually Viking raids and invasions against the English in
response to their own particular sins and as an expression of anger on his part.
So, far from being an inevitable feature of the promised end (despite the opening words), it is something that can be warded off by timely repentance; God
can be appeased and the tribulations ended. As I have argued elsewhere,[39]
Wulfstan seems here to be drawing on Old Testament models to explain tribulation: the stories of God's anger against Israel for their particular failings. These
work against the apocalyptic model, suggesting a wholly different time scheme
in which the English are placed, a cyclical, rather than a linear, model of time.
The experience of the English is to be understood not in terms of their location
at the end of time but in terms of their reenactment of the recurrent experiences
of the Israelites and subsequently of other nations. The effect of this different
perception of time and place is clearest in the last of Wulfstan's major additions
to the sermon. Toward the end of the original version, Wulfstan urges his listeners to protect themselves lest they all perish, and to repent:

> Ac la, on Godes naman utan don swa us neod is, beorgan us sylfum
> swa we geornost magon þe læs we ætgædere ealle forweorðan. And
> utan don swa us þearf is, gebugan to rihte and be sumum dæle
> unriht forlætan and betan swiðe georne þæt we ær bræcon. (*Homi-
> lies*, XX[BH].117–21)

> [But in God's name let us do what is necessary, protect ourselves as
> well as we can lest we all perish together. And let us do what is
> needful, turn to justice and forsake injustice in some part, and with
> all zeal amend what we previously injured.]

He ends by urging them more specifically to protect themselves from the burning torment of Hell: "utan . . . beorgan us georne wið þone weallendan bryne
helle wites" (127). In the final version of the sermon, he interpolated after the
first exhortation to protection the famous passage about Gildas and the fate of
the Britons: God punished the sins of the Britons by allowing the Anglo-Saxons

to conquer their land and destroy them, and the English need to take note of that precedent. Thus, when the text urges the listeners to protect themselves lest they all perish, this now has to be read not as a universal warning to mankind to repent and save themselves at the Last Judgment but as a specific and temporal warning to the English to repent and save themselves from Viking conquest. Though the sermon still begins and ends like a text on the universal apocalypse, it has changed its nature and its world picture and presented a story that locates the English in the year 1014 not at the end of time but at one point in the recurring cycles of the rise and fall of nations.

A prominent theme of Wulfstan's millennialism is the collapse of kinship loyalty. It evidently draws on the reference to the future persecution of the disciples in Mark 13.12 ("Tradet autem frater fratrem in mortem, et pater filium: et consurgent filii in parentes, et morte afficient eos") or possibly in Luke 21.16 ("Trademini autem a parentibus, et fratribus, et cognatis, et amicis, et morte afficient ex vobis"). But he seems to have recast this topos in a way that reflects Anglo-Saxon social and legal emphasis on the role of kindred in supporting individuals, in lawsuits, and in questions of property. The conflict of father and son and of brother against brother is the main feature of the final corruption cited by Aelfric in *LS* 13, and the future conflict of brothers is cited in Wulfstan's first homily. But in his third homily, he develops this into the notion of a collapse of kinship support: "Ne byrhð se gesibba Þonne gesibban Þe ma Þe Þam fremdan" (Kinsman will not protect kinsman any more than the stranger [54–55]). He extends this idea further in the fifth homily:

> Nis se man on life Þe mæge oððe cunne swa yfel hit asecgan swa hit sceal geweorðan on Þam deoflican timan. Ne byrhð Þonne broðor oðrum hwilan ne fæder his bearne ne bearn his agenum fæder ne gesibb gesibban Þe ma Þe fremdan. (*Homilies*, 5.97–100)

> [There is no one alive who may or can express the evil as it is destined to be in that diabolical time. Then brother will not protect brother at times, nor father his son nor son his own father nor kinsman his kinsman any more than a stranger.]

Once again, in the *Sermo ad Anglos*, Wulfstan uses the motif of the failure of kindred protection, but here it is no longer a predicted feature of future time but a tribulation already experienced:

> Ne bearh nu foroft gesib gesibban Þe ma Þe fremdan, ne fæder his suna, ne hwilum bearn his agenum fæder, ne broðer oðrum. (*Homilies*, XX[BH].56–58)

> [Now very often kinsman has not protected kinsman any more than the stranger, nor father his son, nor at times the son his father, nor brother his brother.]

One might well argue that the shift of tense indicates a belief that the ending has already begun, and that the years since the writing of homilies 3 and 5 and the passage of the year 1000 seem to have brought Wulfstan not to doubt but to an increasing certainty of the imminence of the end. Yet there is no hint here that the motif is a biblical portent of the end, and it may be that what has really happened is that Wulfstan has appropriated a formulation that in earlier texts (his own and Aelfric's and before that the Bible's) had functioned as an expected portent of the universal end of the world but has used it here as part of a different story, of the past and present sins of the English.

The shift of emphasis away from the apocalyptic is also evident in the specific treatment of warfare. In one of his early homilies, Wulfstan seems to identify Viking raiding with the biblical portent of the approaching end, "surget gens contra gentem":

> And ðy us deriað and ðearle dyrfað fela ungelimpa, and ælþeodige
> men and utancumene swyðe us swencað, ealswa Crist on his
> godspelle swutollice sæde þæt scolde geweorðan. He cwæð: *Surget*
> *gens contra gentem, et reliqua.* Ðæt is on Englisc, upp ræsað Þeoda., he
> cwæð, and wiðerræde weorÞað and hetelice winnað and sacað heom
> betweonan for ðam unrihte Þe to wide wyrð mid mannum on
> eorðan. (*Homilies*, 3.20–26)

> [And therefore many misfortunes injure and greatly oppress us, and
> strangers and people from abroad greatly assail us, just as Christ
> said clearly in his gospel it should happen. He said, "Nation shall
> rise up against nation, etc." That is, in English, nations [will] rise up
> and become hostile and fiercely make war and engage in violence
> together, because of the wrongfulness that will exist too widely
> among men in the world.]

Yet when, in the apparently later homily, 5, Wulfstan refers to this same text in very similar words—"And Þeodscypas winnað and sacað heom betweonan foran to Þam timan Þe Þis sceal geweorÞan" (100–102)—he seems to be presenting it as a portent still in the future and makes no connection with current troubles. In the still later *Sermo ad Anglos*, at least in its revised version, the raids, harassment, and invasions of the Vikings become a central concern, but there is no attempt to connect them with the biblical *surget gens contra gentem;* instead, Wulfstan locates the raids within the very different context of historical precedent: divine wrath against the Israelites in the Old Testament and the Britons in English history. The connection between Vikings and *surget gens* dissolves for him, to be replaced by a different kind of parallel, with the past not the future.

Both Aelfric and Wulfstan began their work with the strongest possible sense that theirs was a time of crisis, and in many ways the biggest crisis of them all. Wulfstan repeatedly invokes the Gospels and warns that the coming tribulation will be such as has never happened in all previous time (1b.18–22, 3.10–14, 4.4–6, 5.50–52, 81–86). One cannot help sensing that the main attraction of such ideas was that they dramatized, one might say heroized, the present time and the English scene. Despite their awareness that many earlier ages had been sure that the end was nigh, there is an evident power in the belief that it was their own time after all that had been prophesied down through time, that though the disciples and the Fathers had believed that their times were times of crisis and would see Antichrist and the kingdom of God, it was to be England in their own generation that would see the promised end and be awarded the dignity of experiencing the greatest crisis. Aelfric presents it as the modern equivalent of the heroic days of persecution experienced by the early church. In his homily on the Memory of the Saints, he describes those heroic days, when the faithful suffered from pagan persecutions and then from heretics, and saints were made daily, and then turns immediately to the equivalent of those times in "our days," the ending of the world.[40] In his later homily on the Day of Judgment, commenting on the Gospel verse which promises greater tribulation than has ever been before, he argues that the coming time will be worse than the persecutions of the early church because then miracles were performed by the suffering saints, but in Antichrist's time they will be performed instead by Antichrist and his followers. Wulfstan makes the same point in his fifth homily.[41]

As the millennium passed, however, both were to shift their ground on this. In a late homily, Aelfric again compares the present time to the heroic days of the early church, but now it is the Viking crisis that makes the parallel, not the apocalypse.[42] As we have already seen, Wulfstan does something similar in his rewriting of the Sermo ad Anglos, overlaying the apocalyptic crisis with the increasingly urgent crisis of Viking invasion. And for him it is no longer a matter of the ending of the world echoing the Flood and fulfilling all the biblical prophecies but a matter of invasion repeating a pattern already seen in the Anglo-Saxon invasion of Britain and the Assyrian invasion of Israel. The need for a sense of heroic crisis remains, but cyclical time replaces linear time.

As far as our evidence goes, this millennial expectation was a feature of the learned establishment rather than popular belief. Aelfric's first series seems to have been encouraged by Ealdorman Aethelweard and Sigeric of Canterbury, while Wulfstan's own position as bishop of London and then of Worcester, archbishop of York, and adviser to the king can scarcely have been more central. Warnings of the end are couched in terms of biblical quotations, and when Aelfric reports that many people keep proclaiming that the end is at hand because the portents have been fulfilled, he is actually quoting Augustine rather than independently responding to contemporary excitement. Wulfstan implies that it is the learned who anticipate the end and the unlearned who are slow to believe it: "hit is nyr þam timan þonne ungelærede men gelyfan willan" (it is nearer the time of Antichrist than unlearned people are willing to believe [4.76–77]).

One might have expected a sense of embarrassment over apocalyptic promises to develop after the year 1000, but what one sees rather in the work of Aelfric and Wulfstan is a gradual playing down of the earlier emphases (a shift which in Aelfric's case begins well before the year 1000 and in Wulfstan's case does not appear until well after). Both continued to circulate their earlier apocalyptic warnings but in a different and more muted form. Thus, Aelfric discarded the preface to his first series but reissued the collection with the final apocalyptic homily warning of the imminent end still there, with the Antichrist material from the preface added to the preceding homily, and with a new passage referring to the end of the world added to another homily. Wulfstan revised his *Sermo ad Anglos* and circulated it with a rubric which drew attention not to the millennium but to a later date and the Viking crisis. Nor did their successors lose interest in the apocalyptic homilies. The final homily of Aelfric's first series continued to be copied among his works through the eleventh century and into the twelfth; in the twelfth-century collection found in BL MS Cotton Vespasian D.xiv, it appears immediately after an anonymous piece on the origins of Antichrist and his imminent appearance.[43] The account of Antichrist that he used in his first-series preface and his later homily on the Day of Judgment were also still being copied late in the eleventh century.[44] Wulfstan's five apocalyptic homilies were also copied through the eleventh century and into the twelfth: the twelfth-century manuscript Bodley 343 has a composite homily made up of extracts from Wulfstan's 1b, 4, and 5, followed by the *Sermo ad Anglos* in its early, apocalyptic form.[45] The apocalyptic writings of Aelfric and Wulfstan thus took their place in the long succession of warnings of the end that had passed their date but evidently not lost their interest.

For Anglo-Saxons living in the year 1000, millennialist expectations gave a peculiar pointedness to their own moment in history, as the culminating point of all time, and a seductively justifying context for their sense of contemporary strains. Yet the very texts that they were using in support of those expectations, and the process of adapting and copying earlier texts, fostered in them simultaneously a different and more cyclical sense of history, as a series of repeated crises in which Goths or Lombards were replaced by Anglo-Saxons or Vikings, portents followed portents, and the end of the world was always anticipated but never arrived. And their writings in turn were copied and studied by succeeding generations, as continuing evidence of that recurring anxiety.

NOTES

Editors' note: This paper was originally presented at the "Conference on the Apocalyptic Year 1000" in Boston, Mass., November 4–6, 1996. Malcolm Godden is Rawlinson and Boswell Professor of Anglo-Saxon, University of Oxford.

1. *The Seafarer*, ll. 80–90, in *The Exeter Book*, ed. George P. Krapp and Elliot Van K. Dobbie, Anglo-Saxon Poetic Records, vol. 3 (New York and London, 1936), p. 145; and *Guthlac A*, ll. 37–46, in ibid., pp. 50–51. Both examples are noted by Joseph B. Trahem in his important article "Fatalism and the Millennium," in *The Cambridge Companion to Old English Literature*, ed. Malcolm Godden and Michael Lapidge (Cambridge, 1991), pp. 160–71, at p. 166.

2. See, e.g., documents 480, 482, 489, 501, 502, 504, 518, 632, 636, and 657 (extending over the period A.D. 959–987) in *Codex Diplomaticus Aevi Saxonici*, ed. J. M. Kemble, 6 vols. (London, 1839–48).

3. So punctuated in the standard edition, but it would make better sense to punctuate as "agangen. On þisse eldo þonne sceal . . . ," and my translation follows the latter.

4. *The Blickling Homilies*, ed. R. Morris, 3 vols., Early English Text Society, vols. 58, 63, and 73 (Oxford, 1874–80, 1967), pp. 117–19.

5. Translations here and elsewhere are my own unless otherwise specified.

6. See N. R. Ker, *Catalogue of Manuscripts Containing Anglo-Saxon* (Oxford, 1957), pp. 451–55.

7. There are two valuable discussions of this issue with respect to Aelfric and Wulfstan: Milton M. Gatch, *Preaching and Theology in Anglo-Saxon England: Aelfric and Wulfstan* (Toronto and Buffalo, 1977), esp. pp. 60–117; and Richard K. Emmerson, *Antichrist in the Middle Ages* (Manchester, 1981), pp. 150–55.

8. For the text, see *The Homilies of the Anglo-Saxon Church: The First Part, Containing the Sermones Catholici or Homilies of Aelfric*, ed. B. Thorpe, 2 vols. (London, 1844–46), vol. 1 (henceforth abbreviated as *CH* 1). Both series of *Catholic Homilies* begin with a preface addressed to Sigeric, archbishop of Canterbury from 990 to 994 or 995. On the date, see P. A. M. Clemoes, "The Chronology of Aelfric's Works," in *The Anglo-Saxons: Studies in Aspects of Their History and Culture Presented to Bruce Dickins*, ed. P. A. M. Clemoes (London, 1959), pp. 212–47, at p. 243; and the introduction to *Aelfric's First Series of Catholic Homilies: BM Royal 7 C. xii*, ed. N. Eliason and P. Clemoes, Early English Manuscripts in Facsimile, vol. 13 (Copenhagen, 1966), p. 35.

9. But see the discussion in Bruce Mitchell, *Old English Syntax*, 2 vols. (Oxford, 1985), sections 652–64, for the full complexities of the usage.

10. The text is printed in Thorpe, *Homilies*, 1:608–18, but Thorpe omits most of the opening Gospel text.

11. Gregory the Great, *Homiliae xl in evangelia* (*PL* 76:1077–81); Haimo of Auxerre, *Homiliae de tempore* (*PL* 118:18–25). The sources were identified by Max Förster, "Über die Quellen von Aelfrics exegetischen Homiliae Catholicae," *Anglia* 16 (1894): 1–61, esp. section 57; and C. L. Smetana, "Aelfric and the Homiliary of Haimo of Halberstadt [*sic*]," *Traditio* 17 (1961): 457–69, esp. 467.

12. "Nam gentem super gentem exsurgere, earumque pressuram terris insistere, plus jam in nostris temporibus cernimus quam in codicibus legimus" (*PL* 76:1078).

13. "Signa in sole et luna et stellis, a quibusdam frequenter visa esse referuntur" (*PL* 118:19).

14. *PL* 76:1080–81. See also col. 1080B: "daily the world is assailed by new and increasing evils."

15. Another possibly significant departure from Gregory is Aelfric's interpretation of verse 32, "non praeteribit generatio haec donec omnia fiant" (this generation shall not pass away until all these things happen). Gregory himself has no comment on this difficult verse, but Aelfric suggests it refers to the Jewish race, a point also made by Haimo and Smaragdus.

16. For the text, see *Aelfric's Catholic Homilies: The Second Series, Text*, ed. Malcolm Godden, Early English Text Society, s.s., vol. 5 (London, 1979) (henceforth abbreviated as *CH* 2); on the date see pp. xci–xciii.

17. *CH* 2:1.13–15.

18. The main sources are Gregory, *Homiliae xl in evangelia* (*PL* 76:1118–23), and Augustine, *Sermones* (*PL* 38:573–80). They were identified by Förster, "Über die Quellen," p. 15.

19. "Aliquando autem dicunt sibi homines: Ecce jam dies judicii venit, tanta mala fiunt, tantae tribulationes crebrescunt; ecce omnia quae Prophetae dixerunt, pene completa sunt; jam dies judicii instat. Qui hoc dicunt, et fideliter dicunt, tanquam obviam eunt sponso cogitationibus talibus. Sed ecce bellum super bellum, tribulatio super tribulationem, terrae motus super terrae motum, fames super famem, gens super gentem, et nondum venit sponsus" (*PL* 38:576).

20. CH 2:xxxix.121–27.

21. In this reading, Aelfric is following Augustine and Gregory; but it is striking that whereas Augustine, his main source at this point, acknowledges that the normal interpretation of sleep in the Bible is sin but argues that this is inappropriate in this case and finds one quotation from St. Paul that justifies reading it as death, Aelfric firmly states that "everywhere" in Holy Writ sleep stands for the universal death.

22. *Aelfric's Lives of Saints*, ed. W. W. Skeat, 4 vols., Early English Text Society, vols. 76, 82, 94, and 114 (London, 1881–1900); henceforth referred to as *LS*.

23. Aelfric rehearses a similar line of argument in his earlier homily on society, where the tribulations that mark the end of the world are cited as part of an argument for recognizing the hand of a just God behind the adversities of life (*CH* 2:xix. 253ff.).

24. I have discussed these historical paradigms used by Aelfric and Wulfstan, primarily with reference to the Vikings, in an earlier article, "Apocalypse and Invasion in Late Anglo-Saxon England," in *From Anglo-Saxon to Early Middle English: Studies Presented to E. G. Stanley*, ed. Malcolm Godden, Douglas Gray, and Terry Hoad (Oxford, 1994), pp. 130–62.

25. On the death of Aethelweard, see Simon Keynes, *The Diplomas of King Aethelred "the Unready," 978–1016* (Cambridge, 1980), p. 192. On the linguistic dating evidence, see my article "Aelfric's Changing Vocabulary," *English Studies* 61 (1980): 206–23, at 211.

26. The texts in questions are items 11 and 18 in *Homilies of Aelfric: A Supplementary Collection*, ed. John C. Pope, 2 vols., Early English Text Society, vols. 259–60 (London, 1967–68). For the dates see Pope's introduction to these items.

27. See the critical edition of the first series by Peter Clemoes, "Aelfric's Catholic Homilies, First Series: The Text and Manuscript Tradition" (Ph.D. diss., University of Cambridge, 1956), and the valuable discussion by Emmerson, *Antichrist in the Middle Ages*, p. 151. On the manuscripts in question see Ker, *Catalogue*, nos. 41, 332, and 338.

28. Emmerson gives an excellent account of the differing views on Antichrist's parentage and notes this change but suggests (*Antichrist in the Middle Ages*, p. 151) that Aelfric was concerned only to clarify a view already expressed, if obliquely, in the first-series preface; it does seem to me that a change of view is involved.

29. Indeed, Clemoes argues that the one surviving manuscript of the revised version, which is imperfect at the beginning, probably never contained any prefaces ("Chronology," p. 234 n. 2).

30. Pope, *Homilies of Aelfric*, p. 585.

31. For the text see *Homilies of Wulfstan*, ed. Dorothy Bethurum (Oxford, 1957).

32. Note that *sceal/sculon* has a basic sense of "obligation," "destiny," "necessity," in Old English but is occasionally used in ways very close to that of an auxiliary of the future tense.

33. It does not necessarily follow that Wulfstan was drawing on the preface to the first series; the original reading also appears in one of the separate copies of the Antichrist passage, and in a Worcester MS at that (though later in time than Wulfstan himself).

34. Again, his source may have been one of the independent copies of Aelfric's account rather than the revised version of the *First Series of Catholic Homilies* in which the account is added to the first Advent homily, since two of the independent copies have the revised reading and both have Worcester connections.

35. Pope, *Homilies of Aelfric*, pp. 584–85.

36. Bethurum, *Homilies*, p. 280. See also Stephanie Hollis, "The Thematic Structure of the *Sermo Lupi*," *Anglo-Saxon England* 6 (1977): 175–95, esp. 185.

37. The three versions are edited in Bethurum, *Homilies*, as items XX(BH), XX(C), and XX(EI). On the chronological order and authorial revision of this text, see my article "Apocalypse and Invasion," pp. 143–46, and further references there.

38. Godden, "Apocalypse and Invasion," pp. 146–58.

39. Ibid., pp. 154–55.

40. *LS* 16.189–227.

41. Pope, *Homilies of Aelfric*, 18.345–65; Bethurum, *Homilies of Wulfstan*, 5.57–66.

42. Pope, *Homilies of Aelfric*, 14.128–46.

43. See Ker, *Catalogue*, p. 274.

44. Ibid., p. 401.

45. Ibid., p. 373.

9

The Cult of St. Michael the Archangel and the "Terrors of the Year 1000"

Daniel F. Callahan

The Archangel loved heights. Standing on the summit of the tower that crowned his church, wings upspread, sword uplifted, the devil crawling beneath, and the cock, symbol of eternal vigilance, perched on his mailed foot, Saint Michael held a place of his own in heaven and on earth which seems, in the eleventh century, to leave hardly room for the Virgin of the Crypt at Chartres, still less for the Beau Christ of the thirteenth century at Amiens. The Archangel stands for Church and State, and both militant. He is the conqueror of Satan, the mightiest of all created spirits, the nearest to God. His place was where the danger was greatest.

—Henry Adams, *Mont-Saint-Michel and Chartres*

So, early in this century, Henry Adams began his classic impressionistic masterpiece *Mont-Saint-Michel and Chartres*. To Adams, St. Michael was the symbol of the masculine early Middle Ages, years that found the West under constant attack, when great martial strength was necessary for survival, a period very different from the central Middle Ages symbolized by the Virgin Mary and her radiant Gothic cathedrals.[1]

Today historians continue to recognize the importance of this cult during so tumultuous a period in the history of Western Christendom.[2] The Byzantine East from a very early time had emphasized the archangel's healing ability.[3] In the West, however, it was his martial qualities that made him important. Protector of the Hebrews, as found in the Book of Daniel, he now became the guardian of the Christian people, master of the heavenly forces in his celestial habitat, which necessitated that his cult be practiced on top of hills or mountains.[4]

Of those high places in the West it was Monte Gargano in southern Italy that became especially important, for there he appeared in the early sixth century.[5] After the Lombards became masters of the area, they adopted him as their particular protector, and his cult spread rapidly in Italy in the course of the seventh and eighth centuries.[6] When Charlemagne took the iron crown of the Lombards, he also received the stewardship of their devotion to the archangel, whose cult he and his successors would promote.[7]

In the Carolingian world of the last half of the eighth and the ninth century, a number of currents were meeting to promote and change the image of St. Michael in the West. The Byzantine presentation of the archangel as a militant guardian and patron saint of the Roman Empire, or *imperium Christianum*, found supporters among the Carolingians, especially evident in some of the poems of Alcuin and in a famous piece of Florus of Lyons.[8] Alcuin's pieces also reflect an Insular current that saw Michael as the heavenly messenger who brought souls to Heaven.[9] The same period witnessed the first depictions in art in the West of this archangel as the apocalyptic slayer of the dragon.[10] Yet as in so many other areas of future development, the Carolingians provided a seedbed that would only in later centuries reach fruition and produce a rich harvest. Although the cult of St. Michael flourished and became more complex during this period, it does not seem to have been one of the central foci of Carolingian cultural and liturgical life.[11]

The tenth and eleventh centuries witnessed an extraordinary increase of interest in the archangel in western Europe.[12] During those years such centers as San Michele della Chiusa in northern Italy, St. Michael's of Hildesheim, Michaelsberg in Bamberg, Saint-Michel-de-l'Aiguilhe of Le Puy, Saint-Michel-de-Tonnerre, Saint Michel of Cuxa, among others, were established or renamed. What explains the rapid growth of this cult during the period, especially in the years between 950 and 1050?

Adams was certainly correct in focusing on the militancy of St. Michael as a symbol for this turbulent epoch. Carl Erdmann, in his seminal work on the origin of the idea of crusade, also devoted much attention to the place of this archangel in the Christianization of warfare, in particular the carrying of banners with the insignia of St. Michael by the German imperial forces in the tenth and eleventh centuries.[13] This development of sacred militancy is unquestionably one of the principal reasons for the popularity of the saint.

Another is the increasing prominence given to St. Michael as a personal protector of every Christian soul, the angelic master of the *cura animarum*. Some of this interest stems from the Western discovery of the writings of the Pseudo-Dionysius in the ninth century, with his attention to the hierarchy of spirits and the function of the archangels as messengers.[14] Yet some of it also arises from the Celtic tradition in which during the early Middle Ages St. Michael was seen as a soul mate, one responsible for conducting each person after death to Judgment.[15] Out of this tradition would come the image of Michael with his scales weighing the souls at Judgment, an image that later became so prominent on the western facades of the Gothic cathedrals.[16]

A third aspect of the increasing importance of the archangel in this period is his apocalyptic role, a subject not yet given adequate attention for the tenth and eleventh centuries. Apocalypse 12:7 reads, "And there was a war in Heaven, Michael and his angels fighting with the dragon. And the dragon and his angels fought." The obvious meaning of the passage in its context was the triumph over Satan and his followers before the creation of the earth. But it was also understood to apply to the defeat of this monstrous foe before the Last Judgment.[17] When interpreted in the latter fashion, it recalled Dan. 12:1:

> But at that time shall Michael rise up, the great prince, who stands
> for the children of your people; and a time shall come such as never
> was from the time that nations began until that time. And at that
> time shall your people be saved, every one that shall be found written
> in the book.

The apocalyptic interpretation also included several verses from St. Paul's letters to the Thessalonians:

> For the mystery of iniquity is already at work; provided only that he
> who is at present restraining it [sometimes interpreted as Michael]
> does still restrain, until he is gotten out of the way. And then the
> wicked one [usually interpreted as the Antichrist] will be revealed,
> whom the Lord Jesus will slay with the breath of his mouth [often
> interpreted as St. Michael] and will destroy with the brightness of his
> coming. (2 Thess. 2:7–8)

> For this we say to you in the word of the Lord, that we who live, who
> survive until the coming of the Lord, shall not precede those who
> have fallen asleep. For the Lord himself with the cry of command,
> with voice of archangel, and with trumpet of God [usually inter-
> preted as Michael] will descend from Heaven; and the dead in Christ
> will rise up first. Then we who live, who survive, shall be caught up
> together with them in clouds to meet the Lord in the air, and so shall
> ever be with the Lord. (1 Thess. 4:15–17)

This imagery of Michael's role in the Last Judgment and in the period immediately before it, although found in the early Middle Ages before the tenth century, played a more prominent role in the century before the year 1000 in such works as Adso of Montier-en-Der's popular tract on the Antichrist, the sermon literature of Anglo-Saxon England, and the illustrated manuscripts of Beatus of Liebana's commentary on the Apocalypse, and in numerous frescoes and other forms of ecclesiastical decorations.[18]

How do we account for the growing interest in the apocalyptic Michael? The consensus that has existed for the past century is that there was no heightened sense of apocalyptic expectations around the year 1000, that evidence does not exist to show that the people of the late tenth century had great fear that the world would end at the millennium, and that the so-called terrors of the year 1000 were the product of the Romantic imagination of the nineteenth century. Scientific history demonstrated that Robertson, Michelet, and Gebhart had been led astray by their own imaginations and the ramblings of chroniclers like Radulfus Glaber to produce a picture of the past that never was, be it in 1000 or in 1033, a thousand years after Christ's death.[19]

A few scholars, however, have given some credence to the millennial fears. Henri Focillon, Georges Duby, and a number of students of Anglo-Saxon literature, among others, have taken the material more seriously and, if not returning to the views of the earlier Romantics, have noted the growing eschatological anxiety.[20] More recently, Johannes Fried has made the best case yet for the reality of the heightened apocalyptic fears in the late tenth and early eleventh centuries.[21] Drawing from a variety of disciplines and a number of recent studies, including the two excellent dissertations of Richard Landes and Celia Chazelle, he surveys the situation in many parts of western Europe and finds a pattern of increasing apocalyptic tension.[22]

Beginning to appear is also much additional information about these heightened apocalyptic expectations in the writings of Ademar of Chabannes (ca. 988–1034).[23] In numerous pieces, many of which are unpublished, this monk of Saint-Cybard of Angoulême, who also spent a number of years at the famous cultural center of Saint-Martial of Limoges, bears witness to the intense fears of the end immediately before the year 1033.[24] The preoccupation with signs of the Last Things would ultimately lead him to join the great crowd of pilgrims that Radulfus Glaber records journeying at this time to Jerusalem, where Ademar seems to have died shortly thereafter.[25]

In one of his last sermons before departing for the East, he uses the preface to the Canon of the Mass as a means to consider the nine angelic orders.[26] He tells us that only the names of the three archangels—Michael, Gabriel, and Raphael—are known of the members of the angelic host. Of the three, it is Michael who is his primary object of attention, Michael the leader of the angelic army, Michael who replaced Satan in command after the latter fell.[27] But it is his apocalyptic role that receives the most attention, a description hewing closely to the image that is also found in Adso's tract. He is depicted as the slayer of the Antichrist, the savior of Christendom, and the instrument of the Almighty in checking the designs of Satan at the end of the world.[28] When one recalls Ademar's intense apocalyptic expectations of the early 1030s, it is not surprising that this should be his principal concept of the archangel.

It seems, moreover, to have been the primary image of the archangel for a substantial percentage of Ademar's contemporaries, certainly that found in much of the material that survives. Wherever one looks in western Europe in the period between 950 and 1050, it is this conception of Michael that predominates, and a survey of some of the principal centers of his rapidly growing cult will bear witness to this fact.

As in so many other aspects of the Christian life of the early Middle Ages, Ireland seems also to have been a harbinger in its early interest in the cult of the apocalyptic Michael. A good example is found in an occurrence on the feast of St. Michael in 767. A terrifying thunderstorm created a wave of panic in which the Irish, convinced the Last Judgment was about to occur, begged the archangel to intercede for them.[29]

The presence of Michael in Ireland seems more manifest in a number of ways in the tenth and early eleventh centuries. The archangel was depicted with his scales on a high cross at Monasterboice. He also appears in the concluding portion of the great Irish epic of salvation history, the *Saltaird*, ca. 988. In this work of over 8,000 lines, which seems to have served as one of the foundations for the later medieval interest in the fifteen signs before doomsday, Michael will summon all to the Last Judgment.[30] The growing importance of this archangel for the Irish is additionally confirmed by the fact that sometime in the period between 950 and 1044 the most famous site dedicated to him in Ireland had his name attached to it. The jagged peak jutting 700 feet almost straight up out of the Atlantic twenty miles off the southwest Irish coast became, not simply Skellig, but Skellig Michael.[31]

In Italy in the tenth and eleventh centuries, another mountain, Monte Gargano, continued as the principal center of the devotion to St. Michael in the West. Never before and never again would it have such a distinguished parade of visitors. Spiritual patriarchs such as Odo of Cluny, John of Gorze, and William of Volpiano visited in the tenth century.[32] Pilgrims en route to Jerusalem stopped there.[33] So many Catalans visited in the early eleventh century that one prominent historian has been left very much puzzled by the nature of the attraction.[34]

The pilgrimages of two German emperors to Monte Gargano in the late tenth and early eleventh centuries deserve special attention for what they tell us about the importance and nature of the cult in this period. In early 999, a barefooted Otto III left Rome to make a penitential journey to St. Michael's mountain on the orders of the venerable ascetic St. Nilus.[35] This journey must be viewed in the context of the extraordinary spiritual activity of the last three years of the life of this controversial emperor, much of it lived in the company of a group of formidable ascetics and giving witness to acute apocalyptic concerns.[36] Nowhere is this more obvious than in Otto's veneration of and identification with his illustrious predecessor Charlemagne, whose tomb he opened in 1000.[37] It would seem that Otto and many of his ascetical companions contemplated the Charlemagne legend and legacy in the light of the Last Emperor, whom the Pseudo-Methodius portrayed as awakening and going to Jerusalem to lay down his imperial crown and usher in the Last Days.[38] Moreover, according to an account in the late-tenth-century chronicle of Benedict of Monte Soracte, compiled in a monastery not far from Rome, Charlemagne already had traveled during his lifetime to Jerusalem on pilgrimage and, before leaving Italy, had stopped with his great entourage at Monte Gargano in order to receive the peace of St. Michael.[39] Otto may, therefore, have been as desirous of following in the footsteps of his illustrious model to Monte Gargano as he would later be in expressing a desire to lay down his own imperial crown in Jerusalem and to be buried in Aachen near the tomb of the great Charles.[40]

The theme of the Last Emperor also seems to have influenced Otto's successor, Henry II. Georges Duby has suggested that Henry believed himself to be the Last Emperor, presiding over the end of the world and seeking to restore order to prepare for the Last Judgment.[41] In 1022, during his third and final journey to Italy, Henry visited Monte Gargano and purportedly had a vision in which he was ministered to by the archangel and witnessed the apocalyptic Christ ruling in majesty and surrounded by his heavenly court.[42] Although this episode appears to have been recorded first in a thirteenth-century account from Bamberg, where the emperor is buried, and have been prepared after he had been declared a saint, it does at a minimum testify to the continuing association of Henry II and St. Michael in the minds of the German clerics of that diocese.[43]

A second prominent site for the devotion to St. Michael in Italy in this period was San Michele della Chiusa, in the Piedmont not far from Turin. Here on top of a high peak, reaching 2,800 feet above sea level, St. John Vincentius, a bishop from the area around Ravenna who had become a hermit dwelling on a mountain near Chiusa, built a church ca. 987.[44] The legend about this foundation relates that the saint had a vision in which he saw the top of the neighboring mountain on fire and that the flames stretched to Heaven. For that reason he called it Mount Pirchiriano, from the Greek *pyr kyriou*, the Lord's fire. The account cites Ps. 103:4, "Who makes your angels spirits: and your ministers a burning fire." The archangel also appeared to him in a vision and ordered him to build a church on Mount Pirchiriano. With divine assistance the building was quickly completed, and when Bishop Amizo of Turin (ca. 983–ca. 1002) arrived to consecrate the new structure, those in attendance witnessed the vision of a heavenly fire settling on the mountain. The account cites Gen. 28:17, which follows the dream of Jacob's ladder, on which angels ascended and descended, and concludes, "And trembling he [Jacob] said: 'How terrible is this place! This is no other but the house of God, and the gate of Heaven.'"[45] This theme of the proximity to Heaven will significantly contribute to the future success of Chiusa.

The sanctity of the spot and its location resulted in the establishment of a monastery there ca. 999. A pilgrim from the Auvergne, Hugh of Montboissier, had been ordered to establish a monastery in expiation for his sins.[46] He selected Chiusa, an ideal stopping place for travelers from France who had just crossed the Mount Cenis Pass and were heading south to Rome. Very quickly many donations were received from such visitors.[47]

The first abbot, Advertus, had been head of the renowned reformed Toulousain house of Lezat.[48] He had been closely associated with Abbot Garinus of Lezat, who was also abbot of Saint Michael of Cuxa, a Catalan monastery of much importance dedicated to the archangel in 974.[49] It was Garinus who in the mid-990s established a congregation of Lezat, Cuxa, and several other houses that would have close ties with Chiusa.[50] These Catalan ties are evident in the number of visitors and donations to the Piedmont monastery from Spain and southern France.[51]

Yet not all pilgrims to San Michele della Chiusa came from across the Alps. One of the most prominent Cisalpine visitors and one with an especially strong devotion to the archangel was William of Volpiano.[52] Originally professed a monk at San Michele of Lucedio in the diocese of Vercelli, he would subsequently become abbot of a number of houses in France and Italy, including Saint-Michel de Tonnerre, establish a chapel dedicated to the archangel in the monastery of Saint-Benigne of Dijon, and develop a close relationship with Mont-Saint-Michel when he aided Duke Richard II of Normandy reform a number of Norman houses.[53] That it was the archangel of the apocalypse that he wished to serve is evident in his intense awareness of the proximity of the final days, as seen in a vision of the Last Judgment he had while on pilgrimage to Monte Gargano and Rome.[54]

Germany, like Italy, had two great centers of devotion to the archangel during the Middle Ages. The first was established at Hildesheim by Bishop Bernward in 996, a foundation that enabled the site to become what has been called "the art capital of northern Europe."[55] His devotion to St. Michael is a central theme in his life and an important inspiration for much of his art. Liberally endowing his monastery, he created for it some of the most famous Ottonian artistic works, including the magnificent bronze doors; a historiated column with scenes from the life of Christ; a reliquary containing the piece of the true cross given to him by Otto III in 993 when he left the service of the young ruler as his tutor and became the bishop of Hildesheim; and several extraordinary candlesticks that he had placed in his tomb in the church.[56] Shortly before his death in 1022, Bernward consecrated the church where he would soon be buried in the Benedictine habit he had just received.[57] The apocalyptic motifs in this tomb bear witness to his preoccupation, like that of the two emperors, Otto III and Henry II, he had served so faithfully, with the proximity of the Last Judgment.[58]

Bamberg, in eastern Franconia, contained the other great German shrine dedicated to the archangel Michael. Henry II had established the diocese in 1007 as the ecclesiastical center of Germany and the base of operations for many of his activities.[59] On his fortieth birthday, in 1012, he presided over the consecration of its great cathedral and dedicated the principal altar in the eastern choir to the Virgin Mary and Sts. Michael and George.[60] He himself was a canon there and would eventually be buried in the structure. Bamberg served the emperor as the home of the sacred imperial images, and he bestowed upon it many manuscripts prepared in some of the greatest artistic foci of the empire during the reigns of his predecessor and his own. In particular, the *Gospel Book* of Otto III, regarded by some as the culminating achievement of Ottonian book art; the *Pericopes Book* of Henry II, which Henry Mayr-Harting has called "the apogee of angelic power in Ottonian art"; and the extraordinary *Bamberg Apocalypse*, prepared ca. 1000, a work with intense apocalyptic foreboding that some regard as "the first great German work of art" (all three manuscripts were prepared at Reichenau), were given by Henry to the religious structures of his new ecclesiastical center.[61]

It was in Bamberg in 1015 that Bishop Eberhard established, with the support of the emperor, a new Benedictine house dedicated to St. Michael, Michaelsberg, built on a high hill overlooking the town.[62] In 1021, shortly before leaving on the Italian journey of the following year when he visited Monte Gargano, Henry and a number of churchmen participated in the dedication of the new monastic church of St. Michael.[63] It seems likely that it was at this time that he presented this church with a golden antependium for its main altar, a work that would subsequently be found in Basel.[64] This famous piece depicts Christ with the archangel Michael and St. Benedict standing on his right and the archangels Gabriel and Raphael on his left. Tiny suppliant figures of Henry and his wife, Cunigunde, are at the feet of a stern Christ, who is styled in the apocalyptic inscription above his head as the King of Kings and the Lord of Lords (Apoc. 19:16). A strong sense of the proximity of the Last Days radiates from the art and imagery of Bamberg in this period.

Outside imperial lands the most important center of the cult of St. Michael north of the Alps in this period was Mont-Saint-Michel.[65] Ever since the eighth century, this location off the coast of Normandy had been closely associated with the archangel. In 966 the house became a Benedictine monastery, with special importance to the ducal families of both Normandy and Brittany.[66] Increasing numbers of pilgrims flocked to this site and contributed to the building of the great church of the early eleventh century that Henry Adams celebrated in *Mont-Saint-Michel and Chartres*.

Several descriptions of fire here in the late tenth and early eleventh centuries fit into the pattern of growing apocalyptic fears in western France in the period. Glaber states that a comet presaged the burning of the monastery in 992, and it has been pointed out that Glaber used the episode in conjunction with his material on the approaching millennium.[67] Another account relates a miracle in 1007 in which on a feast day of St. Michael Bishop Norgod of Avranches, looking from a window of his residence, saw the whole mount on fire but not consumed.[68] The description resembles that of Mount Pirchiriano afire at the foundation of Chiusa and is also similar to Ademar of Chabannes's depiction of Mount Sinai aflame about a decade later, one that recalls the theophany of the Old Testament.[69] The Psalms also indicate that God used fire as a weapon. Psalm 82:15–16 states: "As a fire raging in a forest, as a flame setting the mountains ablaze, so pursue them with your tempest and rout them with your storm." The great apocalyptic Psalm 96 on God as the Just Judge, so disturbing to the people of this period, says in verses 3–5: "Fire goes before him and consumes his foes round about. His lightnings illumine the world; the earth sees and trembles. The mountains melt like wax before the Lord, before the Lord of all the earth." But most fundamentally, the fire that Bishop Norgod thought he saw on Mont-Saint-Michel recalls Apoc. 8:8, when, after the opening of the seventh seal, the seven angels begin to sound their trumpets: "And the second angel blew his trumpet and it was as though a great mountain all on fire had been dropped into the sea." No more pertinent image could be found for the mount at this moment in time.

Other apocalyptic signs in France can also be mentioned. The letters of Fulbert of Chartres speak of a rain of blood ca. 1027, especially in western Aquitaine.[70] What Bishop Fulbert does not indicate is that the rain of blood is the first of the fifteen signs of doomsday, with the red drops falling from Heaven and mingling with fire and hail after the first angel sounds his trumpet (Apoc. 8:7). Glaber reports a great glowing dragon traveling through the heavens in the early eleventh century and greatly frightening the people of France.[71] Here again is the drawing on an image from the Apocalypse, 12:3, the dragon about to do battle with the archangel Michael before the Judgment. Ademar of Chabannes, among others, refers to freak lightning storms, another apocalyptic sign (Apoc. 8:5).[72] A vision of St. Michael at Arras in 1011 should also be cited in this context. A mortally ill monk at the monastery of Saint-Vaast had a vision in which the archangel, fighting off attacking demons, led him on a journey through regions of the afterlife and answered his questions about the end of the world and the Last Judgment.[73] The description of the vision is a veritable handbook of apocalyptic imagery.

The signs of the proximity of the end and the growing militancy of the archangel against the forces of darkness are also evident at Mont-Saint-Michel in this period in the changes in the depiction of St. Michael in its manuscripts. In his insightful study *Norman Illumination at Mont St Michel, 966–1100*, J. J. G. Alexander traces the changing image of Michael from that of a prince carrying a staff, scepter, or labarum in his right hand and an orb in the left, in a Byzantine manner dependent on the Book of Daniel, to the warrior with shield and spear or lance piercing a dragon.[74] The earliest representation of this Western tradition is a Carolingian ivory of the early ninth century, but the image becomes increasingly common in the late tenth and early eleventh centuries, as in, among others, the golden antependium of Aachen, the *Bamberg Apocalypse*, several works at Monte Gargano, and the illustrations in the manuscripts at Mont-Saint-Michel.[75]

But of all the areas of the West, the one that shows the keenest awareness of the proximity of the Last Judgment and offers some of the most extraordinary material in its art and writings on St. Michael is Anglo-Saxon England. Surely one of the causes for the intense eschatological apprehensions ca. 1000 is the internal turmoil following the murder of King Edward in 978 and the succession and subsequent weak rule of his half brother Ethelred (978–1016). Even more disturbing were the renewed Viking incursions during this reign, savage attacks often by large numbers that caused the king to turn for support to the vigorous church, whose leaders often bore witness to the effectiveness of the monastic reform of the tenth century.[76] In 1009 at the time of one of the most severe of these attacks, Ethelred utilized the legislative skills of one of his principal advisers, Archbishop Wulfstan of York, and issued an edict seeking heavenly assistance against the invaders and proclaiming a general penance for three days on bread, herbs, and water to be observed before Michaelmas. During this period all were to go to their churches and then with bare feet form processions in which relics would be carried aloft and Christ's mercy invoked.[77] The royal awareness of the importance of the assistance of the archangel was already evident when ca. 1000, he advised his troops raiding the Norman coast to spare Mont-Saint-Michel, "lest they burn a place of such sanctity and religion."[78]

Since there was no site yet in England comparable in importance to any of the great sanctuaries on the Continent dedicated to the archangel (although Saint Michael's Mount in Cornwall was beginning to attract some attention), it is necessary to turn to literature and art from many parts of Britain that give witness to the growing interest in the cult of the archangel and the apocalyptic expectations in the period between 950 and 1050.[79] Although many students of Old English literature have seen the theme of the nearness of the Last Judgment primarily as a topos, appearing in much of the earlier literature in Britain in both Latin and the vernacular, this idea was most prevalent in the writings and the art during the century on either side of the year 1000.[80]

Of all the Old English writings of the period, the sermons of Wulfstan, archbishop of York between 1002 and his death in 1023, reveal the most intense awareness of the proximity of the Last Judgment.[81] Borrowing extensively from earlier writers, Wulfstan, in his most famous piece, "The Sermon of the Wolf to the English" ca. 1014, a work generated by the attacks of the Danes, states, "Beloved men, realize what is true: this world is in haste and the end approaches; and therefore in the world things go from bad to worse, and so it must of necessity deteriorate greatly on account of the people's sins before the coming of Antichrist, and indeed it will then be dreadful and terrible far and wide throughout the world."[82] He expresses a similar thought in another sermon when he refers to a thousand years and more having passed since Christ was with men in human appearance and says that the time of the Antichrist was near.[83] Although many of his pieces treat the power of the Antichrist, they make little reference, to St. Michael, possibly because the sermons focus so strongly on the horrors and destruction of the period that the writer does not wish to undercut their force by considering the instrument of the Antichrist's destruction and the succeeding period of peace.[84]

The archangel's place is more prominent in a number of the other collections prepared at the time in England. He appears, for example, in one of the *Vercelli Homilies*, part of a late-tenth-century manuscript in Old English containing twenty-three sermons and six long poems.[85] Intervening together with the Virgin Mary and St. Peter at the heavenly throne at the Last Judgment, he falls at Christ's feet to plead on behalf of individuals devoted to him.[86] A similar motif appears in several other Old English sermons of the period in which the pleas of Sts. Michael, Mary, and Peter effectively avert the destruction of the world by postponing Judgment Day.[87]

He also appears in several of the *Blickling Homilies*, another late-tenth-century collection of sermons with a very strong eschatological bent and with a sharp sense of the proximity of the Last Judgment permeating many of the pieces.[88] The seventeenth piece in the collection treats the dedication of the St. Michael's church at Monte Gargano and seems drawn from a much earlier Continental source.[89] More Anglo-Saxon in tenor is the treatment of the archangel in a sermon prepared for delivery on Easter and entitled "The End of the World Is Near."[90] Here one finds these words:

> So then on that day [the day before the Last Judgment] shall come St. Michael with a heavenly host of holy spirits, and shall then slay all those accursed folks, and drive them into hell's abyss for their disobeying of God's behests and for their wickednesses. Then shall

all creatures see our Lord's power, though mankind now will not acknowledge or recognize it. Then after these things the seventh day will be nigh at hand. And then Saint Michael the Archangel will command four trumpets to be blown at these four corners of the earth and will raise up all bodies from the dead.[91]

The depiction of the triumph of goodness over the wicked is particularly important in the England of this period with its many millennial fears. Kathleen Openshaw, among others, has written on the vividness of the images of this conquest of evil in the Insular psalters of the tenth and eleventh centuries, especially on Christ trampling on the beasts and the battles of St. Michael.[92] The Benedictine awareness of the need to constantly battle the forces of darkness was also very much sharpened by the tenth-century monastic reform efforts in England and must have contributed to the heightened sacred militancy so evident at this time.

Among the most impressive examples of this emphasis on the triumph over evil around the year 1000 both on the Continent and most especially in Anglo-Saxon England is the depiction of the struggle between St. Michael and the dragon. What is most striking is how often it appears in the period between 950 and 1050 and how lively the depiction has become.[93] What makes these images in Anglo-Saxon England so truly extraordinary ca. 1000 is the presentation of the dragon as a real foe, not some stylized garter snake masquerading as a dragon. Michael faces a ferocious antagonist who will give him as strong a fight as Beowulf faced in his defense of his people.[94]

The ultimate Christian sign of the triumph over the forces of darkness is the cross, especially the glorious rood which will appear at the Last Judgment. In the Easter sermon of the Blickling Homilies, the author, relying on the Apocalypse of Thomas, describes Judgment Day thusly: "And the Rood of our Lord, which now puts to flight accursed spirits on the earth, shall be raised in the course of the stars; and on that day heaven shall be rolled up like a book; and on that day earth shall be consumed to ashes, and on that day the sea shall dry up and all the powers of heaven shall be turned and moved."[95]

In her book Anglo-Saxon Crucifixion Iconography, Barbara Raw examined the importance of the theme of the juxtaposition of the crucifixion and doomsday in Anglo-Saxon art and literature, especially in the century around the year 1000, in a conjoining alpha and omega. One aspect of this examination is a study of the presence of the angels at both events. She cites Carolingian writers, especially Hrabanus Maurus, on the presence of Michael, Gabriel, and Raphael at Christ's death and notes, especially in Anglo-Saxon sermons, the close association of St. Michael and the apocalyptic cross.[96] The cross thus serves as the nexus between Heaven and Earth and enables the believer to reach the next world. As Raw points out, what better gift could one offer to a church than a crucifix?[97]

One of the finest examples of such an offering in this period is the cross depicted in the Liber Vitae of the New Minster of Winchester and donated by King Canute and his wife Emma (Aelfgivu) ca. 1031.[98] The book of life from which the names of the saved would be read at the Last Judgment was also, during the monastic centuries, the name given to the record of the personnel past and present of a monastery and the list of the benefactors of the house. The monastery's *Liber Vitae* was placed on the main altar during liturgical services in order that those mentioned within might profit from the graces resulting from the worship and might be remembered by the heavenly order.

The depiction of Canute's donation and of the expected actions at the Last Judgment are among the most outstanding surviving Anglo-Saxon line drawings and tellingly bear witness to the excellence of the Insular art of the period.[99] The Last Judgment images are presented in a three-level drawing stretching over two folios. That it is St. Michael locking the gates of Hell in the bottom image has long been noted.[100] It seems clear, however, that he is found with St. Peter in the other levels also. Like St. Peter, Michael was one of the protecting saints of the New Minster and was expected to play a central role on behalf of the house and its patrons at the Last Judgment.[101] In the top level Michael with a pearled nimbus and baton is found in his traditional role of the conductor of souls to St. Peter at the heavenly gates. In the middle level, again with a pearled nimbus, he is holding the book of life, while Peter protects a soul by striking with his key a devil carrying the book of the damned.[102] These vivid images were undoubtedly inserted to remind the king and queen of England of the power and importance of the archangel of the Last Judgment at this singular moment in time.[103]

It should be evident by this point that the subject of St. Michael in the Last Days and at the Last Judgment was important in the Anglo-Saxon culture of the century between 950 and 1050, just as it was in many other parts of Europe. This should not be surprising because we are in the heart of the Benedictine centuries when the eschatological perspective is palpable—when the writings of Augustine, Gregory the Great, Bede, Alcuin, and Odo of Cluny, among others, constantly reminded Western man that the Last Things are at hand; when Aelfric of Eynsham around the year 1000 could summarize these perceptions by describing his contemporaries as the endmen. With such a perspective it would have been truly remarkable if the scholars of this period, primarily monks, had not thought much about Apoc. 20:7, "And when the thousand years shall be finished, Satan shall be loosed." Rather than be surprised to find heightened fears of the end between 950 and 1050, it would be surprising if such fears were not found.

The essays in this book call into question the consensus that has existed in Western historiography that the millennial terrors were not real or important. Yet these pieces are but early steps in further exploration. Such topics as Cluniac spirituality, anti-Judaism, the cross, the image of Jerusalem, the Peace of God, the cult of the saints, and ecclesiastical reform, among many, all merit further study from this perspective. The approach, moreover, must be interdisciplinary if it is to bear its full fruit.

The topic of St. Michael and the millennial fears, along with the others just mentioned, warrants such attention because of the importance of the period. In a magisterial article in *Speculum*, Richard Sullivan cited with approval Rob-

ert Fossier's thesis, with its large debt to Georges Duby, that Western civilization saw its genesis during the few decades clustered on either side of the year
1000. Quoting Sullivan:

> He [that is, Fossier] argues that up until about 950 there was little to
> allow one to foresee the birth, let alone the triumph, of a "petite
> Europe occidentale." . . . In the West prior to the mid-tenth century
> nothing meets the eye except ruins and mediocrity. But once into the
> tenth century there was a dramatic reversal which resulted in the
> reorganization of the moribund societies of the West.[104]

Gavin Langmuir, in his collected essays, also has commented on the pivotal
nature of this period and wondered about the reasons for the change in mentality in the late tenth century which resulted in the dramatic improvements obvious by the later eleventh.[105] The observations by Professors Sullivan and
Langmuir are important, and the answers to the questions they raise will be
difficult and complex. Undoubtedly, the role of the millennial expectations must
be considered, especially for a time when the monks dominated intellectual life.

The Benedictine centuries witnessed the rapid growth in the popularity of
the cult of St. Michael, and the monks played an essential role in that ascen-
dancy. Like them, he was a holy warrior fighting Satan and his minions, and
like them, the Last Judgment occupied a central position in his existence. His
cult reflected the significant changes taking place in Western spirituality in this
period. Not only was he a warrior, but he was a soul mate, responsible for bringing each soul before the heavenly throne at the Last Judgment and weighing it.
Henry Adams was right in selecting Michael the warrior as a symbol of the early
Middle Ages, but he did not adequately present the changing picture. There is
much yet to do in understanding these dramatic changes. As with numerous
aspects of the period between 950 and 1050, the cardinal century in the rise of
the West, there are still many more questions than answers.

NOTES

An earlier version of this essay was delivered at the annual meeting of the Medieval
Academy of America in April, 1991, in Princeton, New Jersey. Further research was
undertaken with the assistance of a grant from the University of Delaware during a
stay as a summer visitor at the Institute for Advanced Study in 1992. I wish to
express my gratitude to the institute for its gracious hospitality and to the members
of the staff of the Index of Christian Art for their kind assistance. The first portion of
the present draft was presented in April 1994 at Rutgers University, New
Brunswick, New Jersey, at a meeting of specialists in the Carolingian period. I wish
to thank Professor Karl Morrison for the invitation and Professor Donald Bullough
for his helpful comments. I especially wish to thank Professor Barbara Kreutz for
her careful reading of an early draft.

The only significant change I would make in this piece six years after it was
written would be to examine in more detail the relationship between the growth of
the cult of St. Michael and the origins of the Crusades. The works of Jonathan Riley-

Smith, especially *The First Crusaders, 1095–1131* (Cambridge, 1997), and of others associated with him have raised a number of questions about the roots of the Crusades. I consider some of these problems in my forthcoming *The Making of a Millennial Pilgrim: Jerusalem and the Cross in the Writings of Ademar of Chabannes*.

Editors' note: Daniel F. Callahan is Professor of History at the University of Delaware.

1. The bibliography on Henry Adams and his writings is immense. The standard biography is the three-volume study by Ernest Samuels, recently abbreviated to one volume as *Henry Adams* (Cambridge, Mass., 1989). Some of the most helpful material for understanding the personal background behind the composition of *Mont-Saint-Michel and Chartres* is found in his personal letters of the last years of the nineteenth century and the first years of the twentieth, published in volumes 4 and 5 of the six-volume edition by Ernest Samuels for the Harvard University Press between 1982 and 1988. Also valuable for its insights into Adams the medievalist is *Henry Adams on the Road to Chartres* by Robert Mane (Cambridge, Mass., 1971).

2. There is no satisfactory scholarly single-volume study of the cult of the archangel Michael. Still of much assistance are O. Rojdestvensky, *Le culte de S. Michel et le Moyen Age latin* (Paris, 1922); F. Wiegand, *Der Erzengel Michael* (Stuttgart, 1886); and A. Bialas, *The Patronage of Saint Michael the Archangel* (Chicago, 1954). A font of information is the five-volume collection that commemorates the thousandth anniversary of the establishing of Mont-Saint-Michel as a Benedictine house: J. Laporte et al., eds., *Millénaire monastique du Mont Saint-Michel* (Paris, 1966–73). Also of much value is M. Martens et al., eds., *Saint Michel et sa symbolique* (Brussels, 1979).

3. See W. von Rintelen, "Kult- und Legendwanderung von Ost nach West," *Saeculum* 22 (1971): 71–100, esp. 81ff.

4. On the cult of Michael inheriting traits and places associated with the earlier worship of such gods as Mercury or Wotan, see the comments of M. Martens, "Symbolisme du culte dans sa conjunction du sacre et du profane," in *Saint Michel et sa symbolique*, ed. Martens et al., pp. 122ff.

5. For Monte Gargano, see esp. A. Petrucci, "Aspetti del culto e pelerinaggio di S. Michele Arcangelo sul Monte Gargano," *Convegni del Centro di Studi sulla Spiritualità Medioevale* 4 (1963): 145–80. Still useful is E. Gothein, *Die Culturentwicklung Süd-Italiens in Einzel-Darstellungen* (Breslau, 1886).

6. Petrucci, "Aspetti del culto," pp. 159ff. See also A. Petrucci, "Origine e diffusione del culto di San Michele nell'Italia medievale," in *Millénaire monastique*, ed. Laporte et al., 3:339–54, esp. 346–47.

7. Petrucci, "Origine," pp. 346–47, cites with some approval Rojdestvensky's presentation of St. Michael as "le saint le plus représentatif, sinon le plus populaire, de l'époque carolingienne . . . le symbole adéquat de la civilisation imperiale" (p. 34 of *Le culte*).

8. Among the many pieces by Alcuin on St. Michael one can cite such verses as those found in *MGH, Poetarum Latinorum Medii Aevi*, vol. 1, *Poetae Latini Aevi Carolini*, ed. E. Duemmler (Berlin, 1881), vol. 1, p. 318, item 91, no. 4, on the archangel as "magnus in arce poli [the heavenly Jerusalem] princeps," or p. 345, item 114, no. 2, "Michael, summa in arce minister ades," or p. 307, item 88, no. 12, "Michael aethereus princeps, primusque magister, aeterni regni, summus in arce poli." Even more to the point is the piece by Florus of Lyons (found in *Analecta Hymnica Medii Aevi*, vol. 50, *Hymnographi Latini: Lateinische Hymnendichter des Mittelalters* [Leipzig, 1907], p. 210). The first six lines of the piece are

Clarent angelici sublimia festa diei
Allatura piae dona beata animae.
Hunc etenim Michael, aulae caelestis alumnus,
Conspicuo nobis consecrat ore diem,
Dignatus Petri Paulique invisere sedem
Imperiumque fovens, inclita Roma, tuum.

For more Carolingian sources on Michael and the imperial ideal, see M. de Waha, "Le dragon terrassé, thème triumphal depuis Constantin," in *Saint Michel et sa symbolique*, ed. Martens et al., pp. 58–62.

9. See, e.g., *Versus de patribus, regibus et sanctis Euboricensis Ecclesiae*, ed. and trans. by P. Goodman in his *Alcuin: The Bishops, Kings and Saints of York* (Oxford, 1982), p. 52, ll. 629ff., for the appearance of St. Michael to Wilfrid of York. The archangel announces that Wilfrid will recover from the illness he is suffering but that Michael will return in four years to accomplish his role as the angel of death. Alcuin had drawn this passage from Bede's *Ecclesiastical History*, which had refashioned material in the life of Wilfrid by Eddius Stephanus. See Godman, Alcuin, pp. li–lii and p. 49, note for ll. 577ff.

10. One of the best brief summaries of the history in the West of the depiction of St. Michael fighting the dragon is provided by J. J. G. Alexander in *Norman Illumination at Mont St Michel, 966–1100* (Oxford, 1970), pp. 87ff. "The earliest representation of this type [i.e., Michael fighting the Devil as a dragon] surviving is a Carolingian ivory plaque, now in Leipzig, of the early ninth century and related to the style of the court school of the Emperor Charlemagne" (p. 88).

11. De Waha ("La dragon terrassé," pp. 79–80) is probably closer to the truth than was Rojdestvensky when he indicates that Carolingian imperial symbolism did not count the archangel among its principal motifs and that the cult of St. Michael was likely confined primarily to the great monasteries in Carolingian Gaul, with their imperial religio-political concerns, and was not widely popular among the general populace. I will return to this point in a chapter on the cult of St. Michael in the Carolingian Empire in my forthcoming work *When Heaven Came Down to Earth, Book II: The Cult of St. Michael the Archangel, the "Defensor Pacis," in the Early Middle Ages.*

12. Christopher Brooke, in *The Monastic World, 1000–1300* (London, 1974), p. 210, has noted, "The cult of St. Michael showed its first bloom in the seventh and eighth centuries, then flowered as never before or since in the eleventh and twelfth." He expresses a similar idea in *Europe in the Central Middle Ages, 962–1154*, 2d ed. (London and New York, 1987), p. 167, when he describes Michael as "the fighting archangel, whose cult was flourishing anew in the tenth and eleventh centuries."

13. C. Erdmann, *The Origin of the Idea of Crusade*, trans. and ed. M. Baldwin and W. Goffart (Princeton, 1977), esp. pp. 20–21, 44–45, and 52. St. Michael was expected to raise the banner of the cross on Judgment Day and was thus called the "Bannerer of Heaven." On this point see C. Clement, *Angels in Art* (Boston, 1898), p. 52. See also Petrucci, "Aspetti del culto," esp. pp. 160–72.

14. Pseudo-Dionysius, *De caelestia ierarchia* (*PL* 122:1035–70, esp. 1057–58). G. Duby, in *The Three Orders*, trans. A. Goldhammer (Chicago, 1980), p. 112, states: "An image of paradise thereby came to be rooted in scholarly imaginations, an image that painters worked to represent figuratively.... It helped focus attention on angels, which came to occupy a larger place in pious observances, and assisted Saint Michael in gradually displacing the Savior from the upper chapels to the top level of

the porches. It established a peaceful and orderly setting in which eschatological dreams might unfold. . . . Thanks to knowledge of the works of Dionysius, the Heavenly Jerusalem could truly seem a 'vision of peace,' a model of that order that kings were being pressed to maintain on earth."

15. On Michael as the "psychopomp," the conductor of souls to the next life, in the Celtic tradition, see H. Roe, "The Cult of St. Michael in Ireland," in *Folk and Farm*, ed. C. O'Danachair (Dublin, 1976), esp. p. 252, for examples of prayers and poems from the eighth century invoking St. Michael's aid at the hour of death. Also see her contribution on the cult of the archangel in medieval Ireland in *Millénaire monastique*, ed. Laporte et al., 3:481–87.

16. One of the earliest depictions in the West of Michael with scales is that on a high cross at Monasterboice in county Louth in Ireland from the years between the mid–ninth and early tenth centuries. See Roe, "Cult," p. 254; and P. Harbison et al., *Irish Art and Architecture* (London, 1978), pp. 62–64. Roe suggests an eastern Mediterranean, especially Egyptian, iconographic influence on such a depiction.

17. See the comments of J. M. Ford on this passage and the rest of chapter 12 of Apocalypse in *The Anchor Bible* (New York, 1975), pp. 193–207. Important thoughts on this passage, especially for the Benedictine tradition, are found, for example, in the homilies of Gregory the Great, *PL* 76:1251, and in Bede's commentary on Apocalypse, *PL* 93:167. I thank David Van Meter for the reference from Pope Gregory.

18. Adso Dervensis, *De ortu et tempore Antichristi*, ed., D. Verhelst, *CCCM* 45 (Brepols, 1976), p. 28: "Sive Dominus Iesus interfecerit illum potentia virtutis sue, sive archangelus Michael interfecerit illum, per virtutem Domini nostri Iesu Christi occidetur, non per virtutem cuiuslibet angeli vel archangeli." On the evolution of the idea of the struggle between Michael and the Antichrist before Adso, see D. Verhelst, "La préhistoire des conceptions d'Adson concernant l'Antichrist," *Recherches de Théologie Ancienne et Médiévale* 40 (1973): 52–103. For the sermon literature of England, see below. A clear sense of the growing number of images of St. Michael for this period can be gained from a study of the collection of more than a thousand medieval representations of this archangel, a substantial portion from the tenth and eleventh centuries, at the Index of Christian Art at Princeton University.

19. For a synopsis of the views of the positivist, scientific historians, see F. Lot, "Le mythe des terreurs de l'an mille," *Mercure de France* 300 (1947): 639–55 (reprinted in *Recueil des travaux historiques de Ferdinand Lot*, vol. 1 [Paris, 1968], pp. 398–414); A. Vasiliev, "Medieval Ideas of the End of the World: West and East," *Byzantion* 16 (1942–43): 462–502; and, more recently, D. Milo, "L'an mil: Un problème d'historiographie moderne," *History and Theory* 27 (1988): 261–81.

20. H. Focillon, *The Year 1000*, trans. F. Wieck (New York, 1969), originally published in French in 1952; G. Duby, *L'an mil* (Paris, 1967); and G. Duby, *The Making of the Christian West, 980–1140*, trans. S. Gilbert (Geneva, 1967), esp. pp. 113–15. For England, see, e.g., J. Godfrey, *The Church in Anglo-Saxon England* (Cambridge, 1962), esp. chap. 20, "Homilists and Writers," pp. 331–49; M. M. Gatch, *Preaching and Theology in Anglo-Saxon England: Aelfric and Wulfstan* (Toronto, 1977), esp. the conclusion, pp. 119–28.

21. J. Fried, "Endzeiterwartung um die Jahrtausendwende," *Deutsches Archiv für Erforschung des Mittelalters* 45 (1989): 385–473 (published in the present volume in chap. 1). See also R. Landes, "Sur les traces du Millennium: La 'Via Negativa,'" *Le Moyen Age* 98 (1992): 356–77 and 99 (1993): 5–26.

22. C. Chazelle, "The Cross, the Image and the Passion in Carolingian Thought and Art," 2 vols. (Ph.D. diss., Yale University, 1985); R. Landes, "The Making of a Medieval Historian: Ademar of Chabannes and Aquitaine at the Turn of the Millenium" (Ph.D. diss., Princeton University, 1984). The work of Landes was particularly important. See now R. Landes, *Relics, Apocalypse, and the Deceits of History: Ademar of Chabannes, 989–1034* (Cambridge, Mass., 1995).

23. On the importance of apocalyptic fears in Ademar's writings, see D. Callahan, "Adémar of Chabannes, Apocalypticism and the Peace Council of Limoges of 1031," *Revue Bénédictine* 101 (1991): 32–49; D. Callahan, "The Problem of the 'Filioque' and the Letter from the Pilgrim Monks of the Mount of Olives to Pope Leo III and Charlemagne: Is the Letter Another Forgery by Adémar of Chabannes?" *Revue Bénédictine* 102 (1992): 75–134; D. Callahan, "The Peace of God and the Cult of the Saints in Aquitaine in the Tenth and Eleventh Centuries," in *The Peace of God: Social Violence and Religious Response in France around the Year 1000*, ed. T. Head and R. Landes (Ithaca, 1992), esp. pp. 170–72; D. Callahan, "Ademar of Chabannes, Millennial Fears and the Development of Western Anti-Judaism," *Journal of Ecclesiastical History* 46 (1995): 19–35; D Callahan, "The Manichaeans and the Antichrist in the Writings of Ademar of Chabannes: 'The Terrors of the Year 1000' and the Origins of Popular Heresy in the Medieval West," *Studies in Medieval and Renaissance History* 15 (1995): 163–223; D. Callahan, "When Heaven Came Down to Earth: The Family of St. Martial of Limoges and the 'Terrors of the Year 1000,'" in *Portraits of Medieval and Renaissance Living: Essays in Memory of David Herlihy*, ed. S. Cohn and S. Epstein (Ann Arbor, 1996), pp. 245–58; D. Callahan, *Jerusalem and the Cross in the Life and Writings of Ademar of Chabannes* (forthcoming); R. Landes, *Relics, Apocalypse*; R. Landes, "Paix de Dieu, culte des reliques et communautés hérétiques en Aquitaine en l'an mil," *Annales* 46, no. 1 (1991): 573–93; R. Landes, "Between Aristocracy and Heresy: Popular Participation in the Limousin Peace of God, 994–1033," in *The Peace of God*, ed. Head and Landes, esp. pp. 199–205.

24. Michael Frassetto and I are editing one volume of Ademar's sermons to appear in the *Corpus Christianorum*. A second volume, edited by M. Frassetto and B. Bon, will subsequently appear.

25. "At that time [i.e., ca. 1033] an innumerable multitude of people from the whole world, greater than any man could have hoped to see, began to travel to the Sepulchre of the Saviour at Jerusalem." Radulfus Glaber, *Historiarum libri quinque*, 4.6.18, ed. and trans. J. France (Oxford, 1989), pp. 198–99. On Ademar's death in 1034, see the note by Bernard Itier, a thirteenth-century librarian of Saint-Martial in *Chronicon Bernardi Iterii Armarii Sancti Martialis*, in *Chroniques de Saint-Martial*, ed. H. Duplès-Agier (Paris, 1874), p. 47: "Anno gracie mxxxiiii, obiit Ademarus monacus, qui jussit fieri vitam sancti Marcialis cum litteris aureis, et multos alios libros, et in Jherusalem migravit ad Christum." Itier's reference was probably based on an eleventh-century note added to one of Ademar's manuscripts now found in Leyden, number 15 of the *Codices latini Vossiani*, fol. 141v.

26. Deutsche Staatsbibliothek MS Lat. 1664, fols. 97r–103r. This manuscript, filled with apocalyptic materials, was probably the last Ademar composed before leaving for Jerusalem. The consideration of the nine orders of angelic beings resulted from the reference in the preface to "the angels and archangels, the Cherubim, too, and the Seraphim."

27. Ibid., fol. 99r.

28. Ibid., fol. 100r. In a later sermon, on fols. 112v–114v, one that examines the Lord's Prayer and the prayers immediately following it in the Canon, he states that

the name of Michael is sometimes inserted into the prayer for God's protection that mentions the Virgin Mary, Peter, Paul, Andrew, and even, according to Ademar, St. Martial. The reference to the archangel and the need for peace sought in this prayer prompts, on fols. 113v–114r, dark apocalyptic musings on the terrors of the time and the presence of the Antichrist and his minions.

29. The *Annals of the Kingdom of Ireland*, at the year 767, record: "The fair of the clapping of hands, [so called] because terrific and horrible signs appeared at the time, which were like unto the signs of the day of judgement, namely, great thunder and lightning, so that it was insufferable to all to hear the one and see the other. Fear and horror seized the men of Ireland, so that their religious seniors ordered them to make two fasts, together with fervent prayer, and one meal between them, to protect and save them from a pestilence, precisely at Michaelmas. Hence came the *Lamhchomart*, which was called the Fire from heaven." *Annals of the Kingdom of Ireland by the Four Masters from the Earliest Period to the Year 1616*, ed. J. O'Donovan, vol. 1 (Dublin, 1851), pp. 370–73. The *Annals of Ulster* list the event under 771.

30. "The archangel will call a clear call over the clay of every man, upon Adam's strong seed: all the many will arise." Lines 8229–32 of the *Saltair na Rann* (The Psalter of the Quatrains), found in W. Heist, *The Fifteen Signs before Doomsday* (East Lansing, 1952), p. 12. These lines, along with the other final 376 lines of the piece, are based on the highly popular work of the early Middle Ages *The Apocalypse of Thomas*. On the *Saltair na Rann*, see Heist and the excellent brief articles, with recent bibliography, in J. Strayer, ed., *The Dictionary of the Middle Ages* (New York, 1982–89), s.v. "Saltair na Rann" (by P. O'Neill), "Apocrypha, Irish" (by P. O'Neill), and "Airdena Brátha, Gaelic for the signs of Doomsday" (by M. McNamara).

31. W. Horn et al., *The Forgotten Hermitage of Skellig Michael* (Berkeley, 1990), p. 10.

32. For Odo, see *Vita Odonis* by John of Salerno, bk. 2, chap. 15 (*PL* 133: 69); for John of Gorze, see chap. 25 of his vita by John of Saint-Arnoul of Metz (*MGH, SS* 4:344); for William of Volpiano, see chap. 7 of his *vita* (*PL* 141:855).

33. On the Normans as pilgrims ca. 1016 stopping at Monte Gargano, see book 1 of *Gesta Roberti Wiscardi* (*MGH, SS* 9:241–43). See also the discussion of Petrucci, "Aspetti del culto," 173–4; pp. F. Chalandon, *Histoire de la domination normande en Italie et en Sicile*, 2 vols. (Paris, 1907), 1:48–51. One must also keep in mind the skeptical comments about Norman pilgrims this early at Monte Gargano in E. Joranson, "The Inception of the Career of the Normans in Italy—Legend and History," *Speculum* 23 (1948): 367–68; and, more recently, in R. France, "The Occasion of the Coming of the Normans to Southern Italy," *Journal of Medieval History* 17 (1991): 185–205. Yet the connection between Normandy (albeit not yet the land of the Northmen) and Jerusalem via Monte Gargano and southern Italy was already very old, as is evident in the journey ca. 870 of the pilgrim monk Bernard (the account of which is found in *Itinera Hierosolymitana*, ed. T. Tobler and A. Molinier, vol. 1/2 [Geneva, 1877], pp. 309–20), and unlikely to have been forgotten, as the continuing connection between Monte Gargano and Mont-Saint-Michel suggests.

34. P. Bonnassie, *La Catalogne du milieu du Xe siècle à la fin du XIe siècle: Croissance et mutations d'une société*, 2 vols. (Toulouse, 1975–76), 1:335–36.

35. *Vita de S. Nilo, Acta Sanctorum*, Sept. VII, p. 314, chap. 13, no. 91. The devotion of St. Nilus to the archangel is evident in his giving the name of St. Michael to the cave in southern Italy in which he resided for much of his early ascetic life (ibid., p. 270, chap. 2, no. 13) and to the monastery he established near Monte Cassino (ibid., pp. 303–4, chap. 11, no. 73). Peter Damian, in his life of St. Romuald

(*MGH, SS* 4:849, chap. 25), written much later, in 1042, attributed the penance to Romuald. On the influence of the ascetics on Otto III in this period, see the excellent article, albeit without sufficient attention to the apocalyptic overtones, of J.-M. Sansterre, "Otto III et les saints ascètes de son temps," *Rivista di Storia della Chiesa in Italia* 43 (1989): 377–412. Also valuable are E.-R. Labande, "'Miribilia mundi': Essai sur la personnalité d'Otto III," *Cahiers de Civilisation Médiévale* 6 (1963): 297–313 and 455–76; and B. Hamilton, "The Monastery of S. Alessio and the Religious and Intellectual Renaissance in Tenth-Century Rome," *Studies in Medieval and Renaissance History* 2 (1965): 265–310.

36. Of the many studies of Otto, one of the most sensitive to the apocalyptic currents of the period is M. Ter Braak, *Kaiser Otto III: Ideal und Praxis im frühen Mittelalter* (Amsterdam, 1928).

37. On the opening of Charlemagne's tomb, see Callahan, "The Problem of the 'Filioque,'" pp. 111–16.

38. On the Pseudo-Methodius and the legend of the sleeping emperor, see B. McGinn, *Visions of the End: Apocalyptic Traditions in the Middle Ages* (New York, 1979), pp. 32–36; P. Alexander, *The Byzantine Apocalyptic Tradition* (Berkeley, 1985), pp. 151–84; P. Alexander, "The Medieval Tradition of the Last Roman Emperor and Its Messianic Origin," *Journal of the Warburg and Courtauld Institutes* 41(1978): 1–15.

39. *Benedicti Sancti Andreae Monachi Chronicon* (*MGH, SS* 3:710, chap. 23). On the depiction of Charlemagne in this chronicle, see R. Folz, *Le souvenir et la légende de Charlemagne* (Paris, 1950), pp. 134–37.

40. On Otto's desire in 1001 to go to Jerusalem and lay down his crown, see Bruno of Querfurt, *Vita V fratrum*, (*MGH, SS* 15:720–1, chap. 3). See also the comments of Sansterre, "Otto III," pp. 403–7. On his burial in Aachen, see Labande, "Miribilia mundi," pp. 474–75.

41. G. Duby, *The Knight, the Lady, and the Priest*, trans. B. Bray (New York, 1983), p. 59. Although Duby does not offer abundant evidence to support his statement, he does refer to Henry II wearing at state ceremonial functions a highly decorated cloak covered with symbols of the constellations of the cosmos and his donation of sacred manuscripts and other works of art that reflected his apocalyptic perspective. In this regard, in his earlier volume *The Making of the Christian West*, p. 16, he also mentions the depiction of Henry in a liturgical work illustrated at Regensburg in which the emperor occupies the center of a cruciform image with angels ministering to him and in which Christ, "throned in glory as in the Apocalyptic visions," crowns him. This mystical conception of rule, one might also point out, is seen in his changing of the motto of the empire from Otto III's *Renovatio imperii Romani* to *Renovatio regni Francorum*, a perspective that also reflects Adso of Montier-en-Der's belief that the Last Emperor was to be a Frank ("unus ex regibus Francorum Romanum imperium"; Adso, *Libellus de Antichristo*, ed. D.Verhelst *CCCM* 45 [Turnhout, 1976], p. 26).

42. *Vitae S. Heinrici additamentum* (*MGH, SS* 4:818).

43. On this material and the canonization of Henry and his wife, Cunigunde, see esp. K. Guth, *Die Heiligen Heinrich und Kunigunde: Leben, Legende, Kult und Kunst* (Bamberg, 1986), esp. chap. 5, "Der Mittelalterliche Heinrichs- und Kunigundenkult."

44. The name Chiusa comes from the Latin word *clusa* used to designate a fortified site, in this case one established by the Lombard rulers to protect the valley of Susa from invaders using the Mount Cenis Pass. The literature on Chiusa is quite extensive. One of the best introductions to this monastery and its surrounding area

is G. Sergi, *Potere e territorio lungo la strada di Francia da Chambéry a Torino tra X e XIII secolo* (Naples, 1981). See also G. Tabacco, "Dalla Novalesa a San Michele della Chiusa," in *Monasteri in alta Italia dopo le invasioni saracene e magiare (sec. X–XII)*, Relazioni e comunicazioni presentate al XXXII congresso storico subalpino, IIIe convegno di storia della Chiesa in Italia, Pinerolo, 6–9 sett. 1964 (Turin, 1966), pp. 479–526.

45. See *Chronica monasterii Sancti Michaelis Clusini*, ed. G. Schwartz and E. Abegg, *MGH, SS* 30 (Hanover, 1929), pp. 959–70, esp. chaps. 3–11.

46. The date of the foundation of the monastery of San Michele della Chiusa has been the object of much discussion. For a good synopsis, see C. Lauranson-Rosaz, *L'Auvergne et ses marges (Velay, Gévaudan) du VIIIe au XIe siècle* (Le Puy-en-Velay, 1987), pp. 291–306.

47. See E. De Dienne, "L'abbaye de St. Michel de la Cluse et ses rapports avec la ville du Puy," *Congrès Archéologique de France* 71 (1904): 270–300, for an examination of some of the holdings in France of this house.

48. On the selection of Advertus, see Lauranson-Rosaz, *L'Auvergne*, pp. 295, 299, and 302–3.

49. *Marca hispanica sive limes hispanicus hoc est geographica et historica descriptio Cataloniae Ruscionis et circumjacentium populorum, auctore illustrissimo viro Petro de Marca, archiepiscopo Parisiensi* (Paris, 1688), col. 909. See also on Cuxa Bonnassie, *La Catalogne*, esp. pp. 329–36. On the rapid expansion of the cult of St. Michael in Spain in the tenth and eleventh centuries and the role of Cuxa, see M. Moreu-Ney, "La dévotion à S. Michel dans les pays Catalans," in *Millénaire monastique*, ed. Laporte et al., 3:369–88.

50. Bonnassie, *Le Catalogne*, p. 329.

51. Ibid., p. 330; Lauranson-Rosaz, *L'Auvergne*, pp. 303–5.

52. Radulfus Glaber, *Vita Domni Willelmi Abbatis*, ed. N. Bulst, in John France and Paul Reynolds, trans., *Historiarum libri quinque* (Oxford, 1989), chap. 4, pp. 262–63. On the life and reforming activities of Willam of Volpiano, see N. Bulst, *Untersuchungen zu den Klosterreformen Wilhelms von Dijon, 962–1031, Pariser historische Studien*, vol. 11 (Bonn, 1973).

53. See the valuable essay on William by W. Williams, *Monastic Studies* (Manchester, England, 1938), 99–120 (originally published in the *Downside Review* in Oct. 1934). On William's activities in Normandy, see also D. Douglas, *William the Conqueror* (Berkeley, 1964), pp. 107–9 and 117.

54. On this vision of William ca. 995, see *Chronique de l'abbaye de Saint-Bénigne de Dijon*, ed. E. Bougaud (Dijon, 1875), pp. 136–37.

55. F. Tschan, *Saint Bernward of Hildesheim*, 3 vols. (Notre Dame, Ind., 1942–52), 1:1. See also H. Mayr-Harting, *Ottonian Book Illumination: An Historical Study*, 2 vols. (London, 1991), 1:95–105.

56. On each of these items, see the pertinent material in Tschan, *Saint Bernward*.

57. On the consecration of the church and becoming a Benedictine monk at the end of his life, see the work of his biographer Thangmar, *Vita S. Bernwardi*, chaps. 51 and 53 (*MGH, SS* 4:779–80).

58. In particular, on Bernward's devotion to the cross and its linkage to the archangel and the Last Judgment in the grave motifs and his overall art, see Fried, "Endzeiterwartung," pp. 457–60. See also Tschan, *Saint Bernward*, 1:206–10. Additionally, on the cosmic cross and Bernward, see W. von den Steinen, "Bernward von Hildesheim über sich selbst," *Deutsches Archiv* 12 (1956): 331–35.

59. Thietmar of Merseburg, *Chronicon*, 6.30, ed R. Holtzman, *MGH, SS*, n.s., 9 (Berlin, 1955), pp. 310–11; Guth, *Heiligen Heinrich*, esp. chap. 4, "Lebensformen und ethos," pp. 36–61, and documents, pp. 134–36.

60. Thietmar, *Chronicon*, 6.60 (*MGH, SS* n.s., 9, p. 348). Of special value on the consecration of the cathedral of Bamberg is K. Benz, *Untersuchungen zur politischen Bedeutung der Kirchweihe unter Teilnahme der deutschen Herrscher im hohen Mittelalter* (Kallmünz, 1975), pp. 122–44.

61. Of particular value on Ottonian manuscripts in general, but especially important to this article for its commentary on manuscripts presented by Henry II to Bamberg, is Mayr-Harting, *Ottonian Book Illumination*, esp. vol. 1, chap. 4, sec. 1, "The Gospel Book of Otto III," pp. 157–78; vol. 1, chap. 4, sec. 2, "The Pericopes Book of Henry II," pp. 179–201; and vol. 2, chap. 1, "The Bamberg Apocalyptic Manuscripts of c. 1000," esp. sec. 1 on the *Bamberg Apocalypse*, pp. 11–24, and sec. 4, entitled "The Millennium," pp. 45–48, in which the author takes seriously the importance of the millennial fears of the period. He states at one point on p. 47, e.g.: "Moreover, even if it is true that Otto III's court and the painters of these manuscripts are more likely to have been against than for attaching any significance to the year 1000, we should beware of underrating the millenarianism of the manuscripts in the more general sense of their reflecting a feeling of the imminence of the end of the world. The more emphatically churchmen stressed that men could never know the exact times and seasons ordained by God, the more *strongly* they often felt that they were living in the last days of the world." See also vol. 2, excursus 1, "The Dating of the Bamberg Apocalypse," pp. 214–28.

62. Benz, *Untersuchungen sur politischen Bedeutung der Kirchweihe*, p. 193.

63. Ibid., pp. 191–98.

64. Ibid., p. 196 n. 22; Guth, *Heiligen Heinrich*, p. 96; and Mayr-Harting, *Ottonian Book Illumination*, 1:66.

65. A number of other places of importance dedicated to the archangel were established in this period in France. Among these were Saint-Michel de Tonnerre, founded ca. 980 in the diocese of Langres, and especially the church of Saint-Michel de l'Aiguilhe, consecrated in 961 on the top of a sharp peak jutting straight up about 250 feet above Le Puy. It contains a fresco from this period in the vaulting of the sanctuary with a scene of Christ in majesty accompanied by the archangel. On this fresco, see P. Deschamps and M. Thibout, *La peinture murale en France*, Le haut Moyen Age et l'époque romane (Paris, 1951), pp. 37–39. On this site in general, see X. Barral i Altet, "La chapelle Saint-Michel d'Aiguilhe," *Congrès Archéologique de France* 133 (1975): 230–313.

66. Laporte et al., eds, *Millénaire monastique*, contains many studies of the activities of the pilgrims from many parts of Europe and the radiating influence of the Norman center.

67. Glaber, *Historiarum*, 3.3.9 and 10 (ed. France, pp. 110–13, esp. p. 111 n. 5).

68. Guillaume de Saint-Pair, *Roman du Mont Saint-Michel*, ed. P. Redlich, Ausgabe und Abhandlungen, vol. 92 (Marbourg, 1894), verses 155ff. and 2759ff. For an account of this miracle, see E. Dupont, *Les légendes du Mont Saint-Michel* (Vannes, 1926), pp. 23–29.

69. Adémar de Chabannes, *Chronique*, ed. J. Chavanon (Paris, 1897), bk. 3, chap. 47, pp. 169–70.

70. Fulbert of Chartres, *The Letters and Poems of Fulbert of Chartres*, ed. and trans. F. Behrends (Oxford, 1976), letter 125, pp. 224–27. Here Fulbert explains the rain of blood as presaging a public disaster. See also the letter of King Robert to

Gauzlinus, appendix B, letter 2, pp. 274–75, and the response of Gauzlinus to the king in letter 3, pp. 275–77, which also does not comment on the apocalyptic significance of the event.

71. Glaber, *Historiarum*, 2.8.15 (ed. France, pp. 78–79).

72. Ademar, DS, MS Lat. 1664, fols. 113v-114r. An early winter lightning storm killed a monk of Angoulême. At the funeral, Ademar preached a sermon on the proximity of the Last Judgment and the horrors of the time caused by the Antichrist.

73. The vision was recorded after this period in the prolix and sometimes unreliable chronicle of Hugh of Flavigny, bk. 2, *MGH, SS* 8:381–86. See the comments of M. Baudot, "Saint Michel dans la legende médiévale," in *Millénaire monastique*, ed. Laporte et al., 3:31–32.

74. Alexander, *Norman Illumination*, esp. pp. 85–100.

75. My forthcoming book on St. Michael will examine this evolving iconography in much more detail in its historical context.

76. The influence of the church in England during this period has been well summarized by Simon Keynes: "Indeed, the political insecurity of the time may have led Aethelred and his advisors to apply with renewed vigour the principle that peace should be sought through support of the Church: it can be shown that in the years around 1000 the king was surrounded by men who took the monastic cause to heart" (a statement found in his introduction to J. Backhouse et al., eds., *The Golden Age of Anglo-Saxon Art, 966–1066* [Bloomington, Ind., 1984], p. 15).

77. "The edict when the 'Great Army' came to England (VII Ethelred, probably 1009)," in *English Historical Documents*, ed. D. Whitelock, 2d ed., vol. 1, (London, 1979), p. 447. It is interesting to note the similar use of relics in procession invoking heavenly intervention in the Peace of God movement in Aquitaine in the same period. See my essay in *The Peace of God*, ed. Head and Landes. The invocation of heavenly assistance is also found during Ethelred's reign ca. 1009 in an extraordinary issue of coinage known as the Agnus Dei pennies, which have an image of the Lamb of God on one side and that of the Holy Spirit as a dove on the other. Another eschatological motif issued slightly earlier by Ethelred's moneyers has the hand of God, with an alpha and an omega on either side of it, extending downward from Heaven. On Ethelred's coinage, see R. H. M. Dolley, "An Introduction to the Coinage of Aethelred II," in *Ethelred the Unready*, ed. D. Hill ed. British Archaeological Reports, BS 59 (Oxford, 1978), pp. 115–33.

78. "ne tantae sanctitatis et religionis locum igne concremarent," in William of Jumièges, *Gesta Normannorum Ducum*, ed., J. Marx, Société de l'histoire de Normandie (Rouen, 1914), bk. 5, chap. 4, p. 76.

79. On the growing importance of Saint Michael's Mount, see H. P. R. Finberg, "Culte de s. Michel en Grande-Bretagne," in *Millénaire monastique*, ed. Laporte et al., 3:465.

80. On the proximity of the Last Judgment, see the comments of G. K. Anderson, *The Literature of the Anglo-Saxons*, rev. ed. (Princeton, 1966), p. 343; and, esp. on the doomsday topos, see S. B. Greenfield and D. G. Calder, *A New Critical History of Old English Literature* (New York, 1986), pp. 193–95, 200–202, and 236–38. See also J. Godfrey, *The Church in Anglo-Saxon England* (Cambridge, 1962), chap. 20, "Homilists and Writers", esp. pp. 345–49. On the pervasiveness of the doomsday theme in the Anglo-Saxon sermon literature of the period, see esp. K. Greenfield, "Changing Emphases in English Vernacular Homiletic Literature, 960–1225," *Journal of Medieval History* 7 (1981): pp. 283–97, esp. 284–85. The author notes on p. 285, "In the homilies produced between 1100 and 1225, even those which have

been copied from eleventh-century sources, the pervasive sense of the imminence of doomsday has faded and is no longer used to create a special sense of urgency."

81. See the comments of Gatch, *Preaching and Theology*, esp. pp. 105–14, and of D. Bethurum, "Wulfstan," in *Continuations and Beginnings: Studies in Old English Literature*, ed. E. G. Stanley (London, 1966), pp. 210–46.

82. *Sermo Lupi ad Anglos*, ed. D. Whitelock, 3d ed. (London, 1963), p. 47. The English translation is found in *English Historical Documents*, vol. 1, *English Historical Documents c. 500–1042*, ed., D. Whitelock, 2d ed. (London and New York, 1979), p. 929.

83. *The Homilies of Wulfstan*, ed. D. Bethurum, (Oxford, 1957), sermon 5, pp. 136–37. Bethurum on p. 290 indicates that this piece is Wulfstan's "most completely developed sermon on the Last Days."

84. On Wulfstan as a rhetorician, see Bethurum, *Homilies*, pp. 87–98. For Wulfstan's few references to Michael, see L. H. Dodd, *A Glossary of Wulfstan's Homilies*, Yale Studies in English, vol. 35 (New York, 1908), p. 152, a work based on the Napier edition of Wulfstan's homilies. Bethurum, in the introduction to her edition, pp. 36–43, accepts as genuine only one of the Napier pieces (no. 39) in which there is reference to Michael, although she does admit the possibility that the archbishop commissioned the translation of Adso's *Libellus de Antichristo* in Napier no. 42.

85. This collection has been in Vercelli since the eleventh century. For the homilies, see *Die Vercelli-Homilien: I–VIII. Homilie*, ed. M. Förster (Hamburg, 1932) and; *Vercelli Homilies IX–XXIII*, ed. P. E. Szarmach ed. (Toronto, 1981). See Szarmach's introduction for the history of the manuscript.

86. *Vercelli Homilies*, ed. Szarmach, homily 15, esp. pp. 37–38.

87. For an examination of this topic and related material, see M. Clayton, *The Cult of the Virgin in Anglo-Saxon England*, Cambridge Studies in Anglo-Saxon England, vol. 2 (Cambridge, 1990), esp. pp. 254–57.

88. *The Blickling Homilies of the Tenth Century*, ed. and trans. R. Morris, Early English Text Society, vols. 58, 63, and 73 (London, 1874, 1876, and 1880). On the doomsday terror as a central preoccupation, see M. M Gatch, "Eschatology in the Anonymous Old English Homilies," *Traditio* 21 (1965): 128 and 136. Also see J. E. Jeffrey, *Blickling Spirituality and the Old English Vernacular Homily* (Lewiston, N.Y., 1989), esp. chap. 2, entitled "Morior ergo sum."

89. *Blickling Homilies*, pt. 2, no. 17, pp. 196–211. This piece on the dedication of St. Michael's church at Monte Gargano is very similar to a homily in the collection of Paul the Deacon, *PL* 95:56.1522–25.

90. *Blicking Homilies*, pt. 1, no. 7, pp. 82–97. See the valuable comments on the connection between the harrowing of Hell and the Last Judgment in this piece and other Anglo-Saxon writings in J. J. Campbell, "To Hell and Back: Latin Tradition and Literary Use of the 'Descensus ad inferos' in Old English," *Viator* 13 (1982): 107–58, esp. 133–37.

91. *Blickling Homilies*, pt. 1, no. 7, p. 94.

92. K. M. Openshaw, "Weapons in the Daily Battle: Images of the Conquest of Evil in the Early Medieval Psalter," *Art Bulletin* 75, no. 1 (1993): 17–38. On pp. 32–33, Openshaw notes the likelihood of millennial fears in the monastic scriptoria but only briefly considers the implications. Also valuable for understanding the heightened sense of the struggle against evil in England in the century around the millennium are L. Jordan, "Demonic Elements in Anglo-Saxon Iconography," in *Sources of Anglo-Saxon Culture*, ed. P. Szarmach, Studies in Medieval Culture, vol. 20 (Kalamazoo,

1986), pp. 283–317; and D. Tselos, "English Manuscript Illustration and the Utrecht Psalter," *Art Bulletin* 41 (1959): 137–49.

93. The great increase in the number of images of St. Michael in the tenth and eleventh centuries in Anglo-Saxon England is readily evident in the collection of the Index of Christian Art at Princeton.

94. On the ferocity of the dragon, see P. Tudor-Craig, "Controversial Sculptures: The Southwell Tympanum, the Glastonbury Respond and the Leigh Christ," in *Anglo-Norman Studies*, ed. M. Chibnall, vol. 12 (Woodbridge, 1990), pp. 211–31, esp. 221–24, where a number of places with the image of a real struggle between Michael and the dragon are listed.

95. *Blickling Homilies*, pt. 1, no. 7, p. 90.

96. B. Raw, *Anglo-Saxon Crucifixion Iconography*, Cambridge Studies in Anglo-Saxon England, vol. 1 (Cambridge, 1990), pp. 120–26.

97. Ibid., 63.

98. The cross is gold in color with red pieces attached to each of the four ends and then green caps added. It is likely that the red and green were used on the illustration to suggest the blood-red cross of the apocalypse and the green of life everlasting. On the donation by Canute and Emma, see M. K. Lawson, *Cnut: The Danes in England in the Early Eleventh Century* (London and New York, 1993), pp. 133–37. For an examination of the New Minster *Liber vitae* and its dating, see J. Gerchow, *Die Gedenküberlieferung der Angelsachsen*, Arbeiten zur Frühmittelalterforschung, vol. 20, Schriftenreihe des Instituts für Frühmittelalterforschung der Universität Münster (Berlin, 1988), pp. 155–85.

99. Many distinguished art historians have written about the merits of these pieces. See, e.g., the comments of E. Temple, *Anglo-Saxon Manuscripts, 900–1066* (London, 1976), esp. no. 78, pp. 95–96, with a substantial bibliography included.

100. E.g., H. P. Mitchell, "Flotsam of Later Anglo-Saxon Art," *Burlington Magazine* 42 (1923): 64.

101. Raw (*Anglo-Saxon Crucifixion konography*, p. 18), citing the *Liber vitae*, notes that in the 980s the upper floors of the tower at New Minster were dedicated to the Trinity, the cross, all saints, St. Michael and the heavenly powers, and the four evangelists.

102. On the connection between St. Michael and the book of life, see Dan. 12:1. That the artist does not use a pearled nimbus for St. Michael in all three scenes reveals an inconsistency that is also found in his drawings of St. Peter, who has a pearled nimbus in the top scene but not in the middle. I wish to thank Elizabeth Beatson for discussing with me the possible significance of the pearled nimbi.

103. On St. Michael as the angel of death and of the Last Judgment, see G. Davidson, *A Dictionary of Angels, Including the Fallen Angels* (New York, 1967), pp. 193–95.

104. R. E. Sullivan, "The Carolingian Age: Reflections on Its Place in the History of the Middle Ages," *Speculum* 64, no. 2 (1989): 271.

105. G. I. Langmuir, "Doubt in Christendom," in *Toward a Definition of Antisemitism* (Berkeley, 1990), esp. pp. 113–16.

10

Eschatology, Millenarian Apocalypticism, and the Liturgical Anti-Judaism of the Medieval Prophet Plays

Regula Meyer Evitt

Critical Contexts

Identifying the influence of apocalyptic thinking on medieval liturgical drama is textually complex. As C. Clifford Flanigan has observed, there are few explicit references to the biblical Apocalypse in liturgical texts. When we do find echoic reworkings of the Apocalypse, they appear most often in the unwritten elements which combine to form the liturgy enacted: "the visual elements of a ritual space, what the faithful see as they perform the rites or as they enter a church to do so," "customary (and therefore unwritten) actions and texts, which frequently are to be found only in separate books or which simply had memory as their source."[1] Flanigan identifies the variously troped antiphons and responsories for All Saints' Day and the feast of the Holy Innocents as specific liturgical loci for apocalyptic gestures. He suggests that the liturgical drama that developed from these celebrations offers an even more fluid medium for troping, for elaborating traditional exegesis in order to incorporate a variety of textual influences. Flanigan singles out the *Ordo Rachelis* as an especially liminal dramatic site, one that allows for a fusion of "the tragic temporal and the joyful eschatological themes" which the liturgical incorporation of John's apocalyptic vision of the martyrs into Matthew's narrative of the Holy Innocents affords.[2]

I would like to suggest, however, that the *Ordo prophetarum*, or Prophet Procession, proves an equally intriguing dramatic locus for apocalyptic influences in the liturgy. Prophet Processions are unique among the liturgical dramas in their shared sermon origin—a fifth-century *adversus Judaeos* sermon, *Contra Judaeos, Paganos, et Arrianos*, by Quodvultdeus, bishop of Carthage (ca. 390–453)—and in their consequent association with anti-Judaic polemical literature. For decades historians have acknowledged the Prophet Procession's origin in Quodvultdeus's sermon.[3] However, influenced perhaps by medieval exegetes who attributed Quodvultdeus's work to his contemporary, Augustine, drama scholars have failed to distinguish between the very different constructions of Jews offered by Augustine and Quodvultdeus: the former thoroughly informed by an eschatological attitude; the latter by a blend of eschatological and millenarian impulses. Historians of the drama have overlooked the intimate link between the *Ordo prophetarum*'s depiction of Jews and the competing modes of apocalypticism in its sermon source.[4]

The variegated eschatological threads which run throughout this *adversus Judaeos* polemic in turn focus the liturgical agendas of *Ordines prophetarum* during the twelfth and thirteenth centuries. Almost invariably, these Prophet Processions reach beyond traditional monastic celebratory milieus to focus on the ideological function of Jews for Christianity. The earliest extant *Ordo prophetarum* provides a fine example of this fusion of traditional monastic liturgical materials and polemical literature from the *adversus Judaeos* tradition. Found in a fascicle of a manuscript famous for its tropes and dramatic celebrations, BN MS lat. 1139, which was probably compiled during the years immediately following the First Crusade,[5] this *Ordo prophetarum* begs to be considered in the context of the millennial climate of that period.

Until recently, scholars have followed Jacques Chailley on the provenance and dating of this manuscript. Chailley assumed that the manuscript originated in the Abbey of Saint-Martial de Limoges and dated the fascicle that contains the drama between 1096 and 1099 because it contains a First Crusade song, "Ierusalem mirabilis," which describes Jerusalem as still in the hands of the Muslims.[6] Thus, this Prophet Procession's usual ascription is the "Saint-Martial de Limoges *Ordo prophetarum*." However, as James Grier has argued in his compelling codicological study of Aquitanian *versaria*, both the place of origin and the dating are almost surely off the mark. Grier favors instead a monastery in the Aquitaine—perhaps specifically in the diocese of Limoges—where St. Nicholas and St. Mary Magdalene received special veneration.[7] (In my references to this drama I will, as a result, drop the traditional "Saint-Martial" epithet but retain the "Limoges" marker for the sake of clarity.) He suggests as well that the material in the drama fascicle of BN MS lat. 1139 was probably copied sometime during the first two decades of the twelfth century, observing that a slightly later collection like this could have incorporated "Ierusalem mirabilis" as easily "for the purposes of retrospection" as for a marker of contemporaneity with the crusade.[8] It is in this context that I want to consider the apocalyptic impulses of the Limoges *Ordo prophetarum*: as a retrospective piece concerned with the competition between eschatological and millenarian veins of apocalypticism in southern France during the eleventh century.

Indeed, the millennial eleventh century during which the liturgical drama began to thrive is not as myopically focused on Augustinian constructions of the "end of time" as historians have previously suggested.[9] As Richard Landes argues, at least two veins of apocalyptic thinking compete during this century. Augustinian theology, the one more thoroughly documented by ecclesiastical sources (and, as a result, the more prevalent focus of study among modern historians), has a pronounced eschatological cast that recommends patient expectation of the end of time and is regularly associated with the monastic milieu in which the liturgical drama developed. In contrast, millenarian apocalypticism, with its focus on natural, as well as social, contemporary disasters, immediate conversion of the Jews, and its insistence that the end is not only imminent but will bring with it "une transformation totale de ce monde-ci,"[10] is the popular, more polemical phenomenon. While these two influences are often seen in opposition, occasionally we find an exegetical piece that holds eschatological and millenarian qualities in tension.[11] Quodvultdeus's conversion sermon, *Contra Judaeos, Paganos, et Arrianos*, provides a striking example, drawing on both eschatological and millenarian impulses for its construction of Jews.

The *Contra Judaeos* sermon's dramatic potential was recognized early among liturgists. First appearing as the *lectio* for matins of the Christmas season during the late ninth century, it was used with increasing frequency during the tenth and eleventh centuries.[12] Not coincidentally, this is a period of growing intensity of millennial fears within the cloister and the gradual spread of those fears outside the cloister, "especially," Daniel Callahan argues, "through the agency of the liturgy."[13] Liturgists who draw on Quodvultdeus's sermon shape the *lectio* to just these ends. They excerpt the most incendiary section of the sermon: those chapters (11–16) that describe the testimonial role Jewish prophets play in Christianity's apocalyptic mythos as well as the implicit threat that a contemporary, ostensibly recalcitrant Jewish community poses.

As we will see, the liturgical drama developed in the Limoges diocese from this *lectio*—in keeping with the revisionist historicism practiced in some instances by monastic exegetes at Limoges—at once reproduces and tries to contain its millenarian qualities by emphasizing its eschatological elements. For its portraits of Jews, the Limoges *Ordo prophetarum* draws in part on the relatively temperate, ecclesiastically sanctioned Augustinian anti-Judaism that Quodvultdeus emulates in the frame of his *Contra Judaeos* sermon. However, through its more explicit use of the midsection of Quodvultdeus's sermon, this liturgical drama explores as well the kind of virulent anti-Semitism characteristic of popular polemical sources. In doing so, the Limoges *Ordo prophetarum* creates an inherently paradoxical portrait of Judaism: one that advocates reverence for biblical Jews while simultaneously inventing and then trying to contain fear of contemporary, postbiblical Jews. If we examine closely how liturgists used the sermon source of the Limoges *Ordo prophetarum*, we find a splendid example of monastic authors hedging in echoes of the millenarian with the eschatological. The Limoges *Ordo prophetarum* provides us with an example from the liturgical drama of realized eschatology that functions as a Crusade retro-spective, which enacts what Landes refers to as the almost compulsory, ecclesi-astically sanctioned "optique augustinienne"[14] used to circumscribe millenarian apocalyptic influences in southern France.

Eschatological or Millenarian Portrait? Augustine's and Quodvultdeus's Constructions of Jews

During the millennial eleventh century, Augustine's *Adversus Judaeos* sermon provided the paradigmatic statement of the church's official position on rela-tions between Jews and Christians. Quodvultdeus's sermon, in spite of its vis-cerally anti-Semitic midsection, is routinely attributed to Augustine precisely because it mimics the subject matter and eschatological tenor of Augustine's writings.[15] Indeed, Quodvultdeus was Augustine's disciple, and the latticework of the sermon, with its repeated invocations to the chosen Christian faithful in each section and closing anticipation of Christian hegemony at the end of time, reverberates with eschatological fervor. However, in matters apocalyptic Quodvultdeus does not hesitate, as Landes observes, to diverge explicitly from his mentor's insistent dehistoricization of the apocalyptic.[16] In the *Contra Judaeos, Paganos, et Arrianos,* it is in his portrait of Jews that Quodvultdeus temporalizes, constructing a more contemporary chimeric image of the Jew than the eschatological paradigm of Augustine's *Adversus Judaeos* sermon will allow.

Both Augustine and Quodvultdeus call upon the testimony of the Old Tes-tament prophets to vindicate Christians as the new chosen people. Through this lens of Christian exegetical advance retrospection, the prophets become Jews *in bono* who exist to predict Christ's coming, to affirm his messiahship. Quodvultdeus, however, contrasts these "good" Jews with "stubborn," contem-porary ones, whom he characterizes as insensate, irrational, degenerate Others with respect to their prophet counterparts. The result is a much more chimeric portrait of Judaism: one that constructs contemporary Jews metaphorically as among the pestilences characteristic of millenarian apocalypticism and one that insists on the importance of their immediate conversion.[17]

Degree of intolerance has consistently been a concern among *adversus Judaeos* scholars during this century.[18] Certainly, the rhetoric of the earliest Christian *adversus Judaeos* literature varies considerably in tone, depending on whether the authors are addressing problems of literal Judaizing within their congregations or not.[19] While the ostensible goal of much *adversus Judaeos* literature may have been to convince Jews of the veracity of the Christian faith, in actuality it served to buttress the faith from within, to insist—as Augustine does in his *Adversus Judaeos*—on the empirical truth of its nonrational convictions.[20] However, as is clear from the reception of Quodvultdeus's *Contra Judaeos, Paganos, et Arrianos* sermon, anti-Judaic polemics directed toward an audience literally in contact with a thriving Jewish community that might seem to pose a threat to Christian con-trol can take on the bitter, irrational resonances of anti-Semitic material. This certainly was the case during the eleventh century in Limoges, where ecclesiasts initially engaged in debate, then sought to contain the influence of the local Jewish community through its liturgical constructions of Jews.

Like his patristic contemporaries and predecessors, Augustine was concerned with firmly establishing the identity of Christianity.[21] Not surprisingly, Augustine emphasizes in his *Adversus Judaeos* the importance of textual witness in proving the historicity and veracity of Christianity. He conceives of the relationship between Judaism and Christianity as one that is exegetically problematic; misunderstandings between the two result from heterogeneous interpretive traditions. Jews reject Christianity, Augustine suggests, because they fail to understand even their own prophetic witnesses. They will not recognize the New Testament as sacred Scripture, he emphasizes, until they are able to interpret their own Scriptures (Augustine's Old Testament) "correctly."[22] In the latter part of the sermon, Augustine offers a series of scriptural *testimonia* (a rhetorical gesture duplicated in virtually all the *Ordines prophetarum*) to the truth of the Christian faith, two-thirds of which he draws from the Old Testament to emphasize the anticipation of the new Christian order of the spirit in the voice of the Jewish prophets. From Augustine's perspective, "correct interpretation" clearly requires a christological reading of the Hebraic Scriptures: one grounded in the typological concordance Augustine perceives between the Old and the New Testament, one that assumes that Christianity has displaced Judaism. He works to establish the historicity of the Christian tradition by identifying its roots in Hebraic Scripture even as he argues that the Christian interpretation of these Scriptures necessarily supersedes the Jewish.

Augustine uses an image common to both Old and New Testaments as his central figure for the tension inherent in the supersession he envisions: the olive tree found in Psalms (51:10–11) and Paul's Epistle to the Romans (11:17–30). He opens his sermon with a quotation from Romans describing the olive tree whose original branches, now severed, are replaced by a branch from the wild olive that is newly grafted onto its solid roots.[23] The Jews, he explains, are the branches severed from the fruitful root of the holy patriarchs. The division between Jews and Christians he describes here seems at first glance definitive, a complete separation; it is an understanding of Judaic-Christian relations not extraordinary among the earliest Christian polemical writings. Augustine, however, goes on to qualify this image, warning that even the Christian faithful "who boast against the branches" will find themselves cut off from God. God will, instead, graft those Jews who "do not continue in unbelief" back onto the tree, leaving those "who persist in disbelief" (both Jews and Christians) to be judged.[24]

This passage is suggestive in two essential ways: for its analogy between disbelieving Jews and unfaithful Christians, and for its distinction between those Jews who are irrevocably lost and those who "do not continue in unbelief" and are, as a result, included among the Christian faithful at the end of time.[25] While the highly conventional Pauline image of the olive tree in its biblical context emphasizes the importance of Christian mercy, Augustine gives it an innovative eschatological twist. It is this concern with the eschatological import of the Scriptures that sets his *adversus Judaeos* polemic apart from that of other patristic writers.[26] Augustine is, in fact, the first among Christian *adversus Judaeos* exegetes to insist that contemporary Jews in the Diaspora are not merely being punished for their role in Christ's crucifixion, but that they have a purposive function in God's divine plan, as did the prophets of the Old Testament before them. Both serve as witnesses—either knowing or unknowing—to the truth and historical basis of christological prophecy.

Augustine counts the Old Testament prophets as knowing witnesses who serve as benevolent forefathers in their anticipation of Christ's Incarnation and who, like the Christian faithful, will be rewarded at the Eschaton.[27] Contemporary Jews he describes as "unknowing witnesses" who refuse to convert to Christianity and "remain stationary in useless antiquity."[28] These postbiblical Jews equally fulfill Augustine's typological paradigm. He conceives of them as older brothers who must serve their younger Christian siblings,[29] who, if they do not want to be "cured" by testimonies selected from sacred Scripture, "can at least be convicted by its evident truth."[30] In their very adherence to Old Testament prescriptions, Augustine argues, contemporary Jews witness the historical basis for christological prophecy.[31] Their conversion at the end of time will simply serve as further testimony to the truth of Christianity. For Augustine, both knowing and unknowing Jews, through their function as witnesses to Christianity, exist in eschatological limbo waiting either for Christ's Incarnation or for his return in judgment.

Throughout the sermon, Augustine shifts his audience's focus from the present historical moment to the ultimate fulfillment of history and reintegration of God's theologically fractured creation at the end of time, and he offers advice on the kind and degree of tolerance Christians should exercise in the interim toward Jews.[32] He suggests that the congregation of "beloved" Christians—the new Israelites by virtue of Christ's suffering—may see themselves as prophets when they offer the Old Testament prophecies as evidence of the truth and integrity of their faith to those who disbelieve. Augustine's most potent figure for the concordance he envisions between the two faiths (drawn from Isa. 28:16 and Ps. 117:22) is that of the union of two adjacent walls where "circumcised and uncircumcised meet and unite in the keystone [Christ] . . . as it were, in the kiss of peace,"[33] to form a unified structure. The image underscores Augustine's eschatological vision and serves as a prophecy of the end of time when the remainder of Judaism will conform to the Christian blueprint.[34] Those Jews not initially convinced of Christ's divinity ultimately reunite with the Gentiles and descendants of the apostles who now comprise the true Israel. In this sermon, Augustine calls for the ultimate reentry of Judaism into the Christian faith.

There are then two concurrent impulses in Augustine's sermon: to see Jews as benevolent forefathers who act as knowing witnesses to Christ's Incarnation and prefigure the Christian faithful, or to view them as jealous older brothers, emblematic of disbelief because they initially resist the spiritual inheritance of their younger brothers.[35] Augustine suggests that Judaism may, in effect, be read—interpreted as any biblical text—either *in bono* or *in malo*. It is a highly exegetical construction, one that neatly configures the contemporary Jewish community in terms of a Christian understanding of biblical Judaism. However, because it endows postbiblical Jews with the same kind of iconic, typological status that the

Old Testament prophets have for Christianity, it overlooks the growth and vitality of contemporary Judaism, both culturally and theologically. In its static depiction of Judaism and Jews, it lends itself particularly well thematically to the eschatological context of the Advent liturgy and to later dramatizations of the twofold significance—that tension between anticipation and fulfillment—which comes to characterize the Advent celebration over the next three centuries.

The false attribution of Quodvultdeus's sermon to Augustine and the resulting association of the sermon with an eschatological construction of Judaism are not particularly surprising given Quodvultdeus's apparent familiarity with Augustine's writings. He alludes to one of Augustine's sermons and draws directly from the De civitate Dei for the Sibylline Prophecies of the Incarnation and Crucifixion that end the procession of prophets he develops in the heart of his own sermon.[36] And while the prophecies Quodvultdeus includes do not echo Augustine's choice of Old Testament proof texts, both his selection of prophets (ranging from Old Testament to New, from Jewish to pagan) and the combined focus of their prophecies on Christ's First and Second Comings indicate the extent to which Quodvultdeus shares Augustine's eschatological perspective.

Both Quodvultdeus and Augustine direct their sermons to similar audiences. As with Augustine's Adversus Judaeos, the primary impetus of Quodvultdeus's Contra Judaeos is not conversion but reaffirmation and instruction of the community of the faithful.[37] He develops quite literally Augustine's suggestion that Old Testament Scriptures be used to convince the skeptical or disbelieving. The priest delivering the sermon repeatedly uses the vocative to call upon individual prophets to serve as witnesses to Christ's divinity, inviting them to speak out in the presence of the faithful. He plays, in turn, the role of each prophet by becoming, himself, the mouthpiece for their divine messages: "Dic, Esaia, testimonium Christo," "Dic et tu, Hieremia," "Dic, sancte Danihel," "Dic et tu, Moyses legislator."[38] With each reiterated testimony, the congregation's expectation of the fulfillment of biblical prophecy is further aroused. The implicit emphasis on listening in the repeated figure "Dic . . . Dic et tu" rhetorically anticipates the focus of the sermon's closing eschatological vision of rising above human sensory perception in order to grasp God's divinity.

Yet the two differ dramatically in their constructions of contemporary Judaism. Augustine is convinced of the largely typological function of Jews, both biblical and postbiblical, for Christianity. Secure in his conviction that Judaism will convert en masse at the Eschaton as a testimony to the truth of his faith, Augustine underplays the impact of contemporary Jewish communities on Christian salvation. Quodvultdeus, in contrast, proves more anxious about in malo Jews, more hesitant to dehistoricize contemporary Jews and, as a result, more fearful of Judaism's immediate influence on Christian souls. In his sermon, Jews are not simply metaphorical doubles for Christian disbelief, not merely symbolic of misinformed dissent from within the faith. Rather, Jews not converted before the Eschaton become emblematic of an irrational, immediate, and explosive threat to Christianity. The tenor of Quodvultdeus's conversion rhetoric is consequently much more aggressive. He works to inspire Christian unity, not by modeling the ultimate, eschatological unity of the faith as Augustine does, but by instilling fear of its immediate disunity through his chimeric, potentially demonizing portrait of contemporary Jews.

In stark contrast to the focus on prophetic voices, at the heart of Quodvultdeus's sermon stands the well-known admonishment of contemporary Jews for their obtuseness to christological interpretation and denial of God's son: "You, I say, do I challenge, O Jews, who even to this day deny the Son of God."[39] His initial descriptions of Jews as "prevaricators of the law," "false witnesses," "sons of falsehood," "enemies," and "mockers" of Christ are unexceptional: generalizations typical of typological, eschatological constructions of Jews.[40] However, Quodvultdeus intensifies the rhetoric as he proceeds and bestializes the image of Jew-as-willing-disbeliever by corporealizing that disbelief. Those unwilling to convert he accuses of having goatlike, "exceedingly hard foreheads."[41] Their "alien hands" he insists may yet be restored by the innocent blood they have shed.[42] Mixing metaphors of sensory deprivation, Quodvultdeus describes the "eyes of their hearts" as "thoroughly closed."[43] He claims that Jews are "infused with blindness," "possessed by the devil"—a standard millenarian trope that sets up the analogy between Jews and Antichrist as the Devil's minions.[44] With the relentless monophony that sermons afford, he accuses Jews of crying out for Christ's crucifixion in "insane voices," concluding that their present dispersion is the direct consequence of their sensory and mental disintegration.[45] The rhetoric here is offensive rather than defensive; the accusations and impatience with their failure to convert are immediately grounded in chimeric fear of, rather than nonrational difference with, the Jewish community. In contrast with the predominant eschatological tenor of the sermon, the tone of these accusations is distinctly millenarian.

The portion of the sermon typically excerpted as a *lectio* for Advent preserves, then, in distilled form the eschatological tone of its larger context while foregrounding a chimeric portrait of contemporary Jews. In comparison with Augustine's sermon, which clearly voices the accepted attitude toward Judaism within Christianity, Quodvultdeus produces the sermon with the greatest energy for liturgists who, when they dramatize relations between Jews and Christians in their liturgical celebrations, want to explore a rhetoric of conflict and aggression. The resistance intrinsic to his juxtaposition of eschatologized and chimericized Jew creates a scenario of heightened tension for liturgists who want to emphasize the struggle of conversion in their dramatic celebrations.[46]

It is, however, the eschatological vision that prevails in Quodvultdeus's sermon. In his penultimate section, Quodvultdeus offers his audience, comprising the newly converted, a vision of the eon of the Kingdom which encourages contempt for all that is transitory and joyful expectation of what will come at the end of time:

> XXI. 1. . . . Here falseness, there truth; here perturbation, there true
> enjoyment; here the most excessively bitter taste, there perpetual
> sweetness; here dangerous elation, at that place carefree exulta-
> tion. . . . 3. Here death, there life; here mourning, there rejoicing;
> here all which God created, in that place the self conforming with all,

and in all God. . . . Truly the human tongue does not suffice to
describe it, what mortal sense is not strong enough to comprehend.
4. Let us come there, my brothers, and we will see that which the
eyes here have not seen, there we will hear that which the ears here
have not heard, there we will perceive what the human heart has not
comprehended here.[47]

He describes the experience of the faithful in this world in terms of a dimin-
ished sensory perception that will be redeemed only at the Eschaton: eyes that
cannot see, ears that cannot hear, hearts that cannot fully comprehend until they
exalt in indisputable joy. It is a portrait steeped in the yearning characteristic of
Augustinian eschatological desire.[48]

Ironically, it provides as well a striking echo of his characterization of Jewish faithlessness from the midsection of the sermon, with the distinction, of
course, that Jewish "senselessness" is singled out as willful transgression against
God. No longer directed at a specific ethnic population, the rhetoric of sensory
deprivation can be dechimericized, translated into an expression of universal
faith. The chimeria of anti-Semitism is subsumed within the rhetorical matrix
of Augustine's eschatological *adversus Judaeos* discourse. It is precisely the trick
employed by the liturgists who create the Limoges *Ordo prophetarum* to refocus
the energy of the chimeric through an eschatological lens for their dramatization of the Scriptures of the prophets.

Eschatology and Mysteriology in Amalarius of Metz and the Saint-Martial de Limoges Liturgists

Liturgists in the Limoges diocese seeking a model for infusing the liturgy with
this kind of dramatic energy would have found ample advice in the works of the
influential Carolingian liturgist Amalarius of Metz (ca. 775–850). During the
century that precedes our earliest extant examples of liturgical drama, Amalarius
wrote a series of works that discuss the dramatic potential of the liturgy and
that influenced liturgists throughout Europe well into the millennial eleventh
century: *De divinis officiis, Ecologae de ordine Romano, Liber officialis.*[49]

Amalarius's conception of how the liturgy may be dramatized grows out of
a basic historical tension between contending theological perspectives on liturgical piety: the eschatological and the mysteriological.[50] Liturgical practice with
an eschatological cast focuses on ritualistic presentation and equates the consecrated eucharistic elements with Christ while it emphasizes the singular role of
the celebrant as the instrument through which Christ acts. Liturgical practice
with a mysteriological quality treats the Mass as an opportunity for mimetic
representation and engages in an elaborate re-creation of the life, death, and
resurrection of Christ. It allows the liturgy to serve as a vehicle for popular expressions of devotion such as the millenarian apocalypticism eschewed by
mainstream ecclesiasts. As Cynthia Bourgeault observes, however, in the history of the liturgy, the eschatological and the mysteriological work not hierar-

chically, with the mysteriological displacing the eschatological, but as "competing organizational principles."[51] Indeed, Amalarius's commentaries on the liturgy are innovative precisely because he recommends that the liturgy be dramatized through an unconventional combination of mysteriological and eschatological gestures.[52]

Amalarius was a secular cleric whose new liturgical strategies were intended to reach not merely monastic but lay audiences as well; his mimetic conception of the Mass provides the foundation for an increasingly affective emphasis within the liturgy. It affords within the Mass a space for a millenarian construction of the Apocalypse, one that not only emphasizes Christ's imminent return but also present dangers to the community of the Christian faithful. It establishes a liturgical climate that was ultimately conducive to popular fear of contemporary Jews who continued in their own faith unless forced to convert.[53]

Of works by Amalarius that influenced the liturgical drama, the *De divinis officiis* was clearly known to liturgists at Saint-Martial de Limoges around the millennial year 1033. It would have been available in a collection of manuscripts that Ademar of Chabannes left at his adopted home before his final pilgrimage to Jerusalem in the early 1030s.[54] Interestingly, in a chapter that Ademar wrote as an addendum to Amalarius's *De divinis officiis*, he comments extensively on the import of Jews for the apocalypse, emphasizing Jewish persecution of Christ and the connection between Antichrist and the synagogue. Amalarius's provocative discussion of liturgical practice, reshaped by Ademar's anti-Judaic addendum, testifies to the collocation of the impulse to dramatize the liturgy and the strong anti-Judaic fervor in and around Limoges by the beginning of the eleventh century.

Tensions were high between Christian and Jewish communities throughout Europe after Caliph al-Hakim's destruction of the Holy Sepulchre in Jerusalem in 1009.[55] Rumors of European Jewish complicity in the deed may even have touched off the debates between Christians and Jews in Limoges described by Ademar of Chabannes, in which the Limousin church's *doctores ecclesiae* unsuccessfully attempted to win converts, then unleashed pressure to convert or die, which led to ritual suicide among members of the local Jewish community.[56] Richard Landes argues that church leaders from this region participated in the "mad, apocalyptically inspired attempt to eradicate the Jews" that seized much of Europe around 1010; then they "sought to correct their own impurities"—their failure to conform to the official Augustinian ecclesiastical position on the conversion of Jews—by "redating and retelling the tale" of these forced conversions.[57]

The Limoges *Ordo prophetarum* provides us with liturgical-dramatic evidence of the continuing attempts of church officials in Limoges to "re-enroll their leaders among the ranks of the 'sounder of mind,'" who would toe the official Augustinian line on conversion and ecclesiastically sanctioned Jewish-Christian relations.[58] Mordechaï Breuer has noted the presence of a thriving Jewish community in and around Limoges in the middle of the eleventh century, led by Rabbi Jacob Bonfils, whose most durable legacy, Breuer emphasizes, was his ability to organize individual Jewish communities and to affirm through his *responsa* the juridical independence and autonomy of these communities.[59] Bonfils was known not only for his widespread influence on litigation but also as a "savant" whose contributions to rabbinical literature were profound. In addition to a series of works on ritual law and just processes, he authored a treatise on the most amenable order for synagogue readings of passages from the Prophets. In what is either a striking coincidence or a direct Christian counterpoint to Bonfils's influential liturgical exegesis, the Limoges *Ordo prophetarum* appears within just a few decades of Bonfils's treatise.

If Ademar, in his addendum to *De divinis officiis* in the third decade of the century, in effect "apocalypticized" Amalarius's discussion of the Divine Office, then the Limoges liturgists who created the *Ordo prophetarum* at the beginning of the twelfth century drew on the eschatological qualities of Amalarius's paradigm for dramatizing the liturgy as part of a continued effort at correctives to the earlier apocalyptic fervor. Indeed, as Christine Schnusenberg observes, Amalarius carefully locates his discussion of the representational, commemorative effect of the Mass in an eschatological context. He interweaves the mysteriological and eschatological liturgical focuses, using the eschatological to heighten the effect of the mysteriological in his description of the Mass. His discussion, which focuses in part on the production of prophetic voice, provides an excellent paradigm for the Limoges liturgists who sought to mine the tension between eschatological and millenarian anti-Judaic impulses in their dramatization of the midsection of Quodvultdeus's *Contra Judaeos* sermon while giving the most weight to the ecclesiastically sanctioned eschatological perspective.

The *Liber officialis* offers a discussion of the dramatic function of prophecy which models how liturgists might transmogrify the aggressive, chimeric rhetoric of the prophet section of Quodvultdeus's *Contra Judaeos* sermon into the more temperate Limoges *Ordo prophetarum*. Amalarius pays particular attention to the offices of *lectores* and *cantores* during the Advent season, when readings from the Old Testament form the focus of the Mass—the liturgical locus in subsequent centuries for the *Ordo prophetarum*. Amalarius suggests that the *cantor*, whose function it is to lead the congregation in their singing, can be likened to one of the prophets and the congregation implicitly to the Israelites to whom the prophets appeared.[60] He also emphasizes that the prophetic Scriptures used in the *lectio* are given a special faith-instilling quality when presented lyrically by the *cantor*-prophet.[61] Those without "learned minds,"[62] who cannot be reached through their understanding and who will not recognize the import of the letter of the Scriptures included in the *lectio*, may yet be reached through their hearts with the aid of the *cantor*'s musical gloss of those texts.

Amalarius's comparison of the *cantor*'s voice to a "lofty trumpet" (an allusion to Isa. 58:1) suggests heavenly music, God's word as sounded through one of his prophets. It certainly underscores as well the special efficacy he ascribes to scriptural witness given musical voice. "Auribus cordis," the ears of the heart, is a particularly resonant figure given this context. Amalarius indicates that the truly faithful will hear the voice of the prophets not simply with their ears but in their hearts as well; with this he implies that the expectation and desire invited by the eschatological prophetic readings for Advent must ultimately be spiritually rather than corporeally realized.[63] As we will see in my later discussion of the Limoges *Ordo prophetarum*, Amalarius's description of the *cantor's* role in presenting the Old Testament prophecies, especially in its emphasis on heightening scriptural witness through a musical dialogue between *cantor*-prophet and congregational respondents, offers a remarkably suggestive point of departure for the liturgical prophet processions that follow within the next century and a half. Because of its intricately interwoven simultaneous verbal and musical troping of Scripture, this liturgical drama functions as a kind of musical exegesis, as ritually voiced polemic.[64]

Most tellingly, the language Amalarius uses to characterize the spiritually obdurate among the Christian faithful—"surdus," "obturatis auribus cordis," "torpescit"—echoes that used by Christian *adversus Judaeos* exegetes in the early church to depict Jewish disbelief.[65] Sometimes the echoes are very close indeed. Amalarius's allusion to Isa. 58:1 is, for instance, used by Augustine in his *Adversus Judaeos* sermon to convince the "blind" and "deaf" of heart of the authority of the prophetic witnesses.[66] These verbal consonances between liturgical and polemical literature suggest that the two exegetical traditions work together to shape the theological and cultural milieu for the liturgical *Ordo prophetarum*.

If we compare Amalarius's emphasis on the "auribus cordis" as the means to instill belief in the skeptical with Quodvultdeus's focus on sensory perception as a means for identifying faithless Jews, we begin to understand how the antiphonal voicing Amalarius describes ultimately transforms the verbal texture of Quodvultdeus's sermon and how it can be used by liturgists to control the sermon's millenarian impulses through its strong eschatological bent. The priest who presents Quodvultdeus's sermon recasts his own voice in taking on the role of each of the prophets and speaking their various testimonies. And certainly, in his use of the prophet's voice to articulate "the joy that no human tongue can suffice to express,"[67] he is not unlike the *cantor*-prophet Amalarius envisions, who, through his celestial music, voices the exhilaration that the faithful will feel upon Christ's Second Coming. The potential for dialogue in Quodvultdeus's sermon is evident. His delivery, however, is finally monologic rather than dialogic: imbued with the power to denounce rather than to converse with the faithless, most chimerically represented by Jews. Although the priest's accusations against the Jews invite objections, they allow no forum for a response.

In contrast to the accusatory rhetorical stance that Quodvultdeus deploys, Amalarius suggests that music become the medium through which those worshiping transform simple linguistic utterance into the celestial concordance of diverse prophetic voices. Rather than inviting confrontation, Amalarius's antiphonal liturgical style urges an atmosphere of dramatic reciprocity. However, the conversation he imagines is one among the redeemed. In softer terms—that will ultimately allow the liturgists who create dramatic portraits of Jews to displace their fears of an imminent threat from dangerous, contemporary heretics—Amalarius, too, circumscribes the possibility of a voice of dissent. If Quodvultdeus's accusatory rhetoric prophesying imminent danger has a millenarian quality about it, Amalarius's model of antiphonal communion engenders instead the kind of selfaffirming promise of universal Christian faith characteristic of eschatological prophecy. Amalarius's equation of the voice of prophecy with the inspirational powers of liturgical music allows liturgists to reinvent Quodvultdeus's hyperbolic accusations to form the suggestive liturgical context of prophetic concordance from which the Limoges *Ordo prophetarum* emerges in the early twelfth century.

Eschatology Realized: The Limoges Ordo Prophetarum

During its most glorious epoch, the Abbey of Saint-Martial de Limoges was renowned as a center of learning and cultivation of the arts. Situated at the crossroads of the ancient roads to Lyons, Toulouse, Bordeaux, Saintes, and Bourges, it was a favorite stop for pilgrims on their way to Saint-Jacques de Compostelle,[68] as well as a point of departure for pilgrims "streaming to Jerusalem in the early 1030's."[69] Ademar of Chabannes, who, as we have seen, explored anti-Judaic apocalyptic themes extensively in his sermons and in his responses to the liturgical work of Amalarius of Metz, made Saint-Martial de Limoges his adopted home during the 1020s and 1030s before he, too, left for the Holy Land.[70] The abbey's sojourners served as a fund of knowledge for the *école abbatiale* there. No doubt they brought news of religious communities from across Europe, in turn taking home with them information about the most avant-garde musical styles, liturgical practices, and the more disturbing liturgical themes of their day.

An innovator among its contemporary religious communities,[71] Saint-Martial de Limoges played a leading role in developing new music notation styles, sequences, and tropes in the ninth through eleventh centuries, polyphonic music in the twelfth century, and liturgical dramatic celebrations during the eleventh and twelfth centuries.[72] Callahan emphasizes that the tropes and sequences prepared or used at Saint-Martial de Limoges, especially those from the Easter cycle, provide ample evidence of the anti-Judaic climate that suffused liturgical invention in the Limoges diocese.[73] He suggests, based on the tenor of its liturgical pieces, that the abbey actively cultivated anti-Judaism. Its power as a center of liturgical learning made it a key player in the dissemination of anti-Judaism in southern France.

Of the two earliest versions of the *Quem quaeritis* tropes that have survived, one is to be found in a Saint-Martial de Limoges manuscript devoted for the most part to tropes.[74] It is this trope and the important BN MS lat. 1139 that have given Saint-Martial and the Limoges region its reputation as a center for the early medieval drama. BN MS lat. 1139 is particularly noteworthy for its several liturgical dramatic celebrations. It includes an *Ordo Rachelis*, a *De mulieribus*, the well-known *Sponsus*, and the *Ordo prophetarum* with which we are concerned here.[75] The portion of the manuscript that contains the dramas, folios 32–118, is its oldest fascicle. The compilation itself suggests the work of a redactor who was interested in augmenting regular liturgical materials by bringing together liturgical dramatic celebrations with a reiterated thematic focus: that of the Eschaton.[76] Three of the four dramatic celebrations in BN MS lat. 1139 clearly share this focus: the *Ordo Rachelis*, the *Sponsus*, and the *Ordo prophetarum*. The *Ordo Rachelis* provides a splendid example of how echoes from the Apocalypse that suffuse liturgical antiphons become part of the fabric of liturgical drama as well.[77] The *Sponsus* and *Ordo Prophetarum* offer the best examples of the liturgical confluence of apocalyptic and *adversus Judaeos* discourses.

Both the *Sponsus* and the Limoges *Ordo prophetarum* focus thematically on vigilance for and anticipation of Christ's coming. In the *Sponsus* this is most vividly depicted by the dichotomy between the Wise and Foolish Virgins: the Wise remain alert at all times while the Foolish, apparently, can barely stay awake.[78] The physical lethargy evident in their sleep indicates spiritual torpor as well. Sleep literally limits the Foolish Virgins' ability to *see*, metaphorically to keep their vigil, to watch for Christ's Second Coming. Clifford Davidson describes their deep sleep as "a blindness that may be compared to the blindfold worn by later representations of Synagoga in the visual arts."[79] It has a textual analogue as well in Augustine's description in *Adversus Judaeos* of the unfaithful as blind and deaf. The juxtaposition of sensory and spiritual torpor is central to the *Ordo prophetarum* as well. However, the focus on blindness as the metaphor for spiritual inattentiveness shifts to a concern with deafness. The shift derives precisely from the procession's exegetical origins and central concern with prophecy. Speaking and listening become the remedies for a literal deafness that is also emblematic of spiritual deafness.

The musical infrastructure of the *Ordo prophetarum* itself, in its antiphonal interplay between *cantor* and respondents, emphasizes this exchange between speaking and listening. The *cantor*'s initial invocation similarly combines the two: first, a call to all who are present to sing their praises for God's fulfilled promises; then, a stern warning to those who do not believe in the virgin birth of Christ that they should listen carefully to the prophecies that will follow. The reprimand plays brilliantly on the traditional iconography of the Virgin Mary's conception of Christ. She conceives when Gabriel whispers God's Word in her ear. The implication that the Limoges Jewish community should be similarly inseminated by the "Word" of local ecclesiasts accounts for the strident emphasis throughout the play on establishing a corrected genealogy of the chosen people.

In the opening verses, the cantor singles out Jews for their denial of God's word, admonishes them to "strike away the darkness" that fills their minds, and frames these rebukes with an insistence on Christians' genealogical claim, through David, to being the true chosen people.[80] The tone of this opening passage calls to mind the twofold quality of Quodvultdeus's *Contra Judaeos* sermon. The *cantor*'s call to celebrate the Nativity is ostensibly all-inclusive—"omnes gentes"—and echoes Quodvultdeus's Augustinian eschatological call for the reentry of disbelievers into the community of the faithful. But there is a kind of latent literal brutality in the metaphor "strike away the darkness" that recalls not only the sermon source's aggressive rhetoric of sensory deprivation but also the violent attacks against Jewish communities in Limoges and throughout southern France during the eleventh century. Callahan describes the annual Eastertide custom in Toulouse of giving Jews a *colaphus,* or blow to the face.[81]

Landes observes that early in the century, when the Christian laity began to see itself as a new "Chosen People," it found "the presence of the Jews, with their ancient claims to that title, far less tolerable than it had previously and, particularly in the context of the more militant aspects of the Peace movement, it had fewer scruples about using violence to assert its sense of the right order of things."[82] By the beginning of the twelfth century in the Limoges *Ordo prophetarum*, however, we hear the reverberations of that kind of literal violence deftly contained by decorous metaphor.

In fact, genealogy becomes the primary thematic device in the Limoges *Ordo prophetarum* for containing the millenarian impulse, for transforming it into an eschatologically, ecclesiastically "correct" version of Christian-Jewish conversion relations. The play stages conversations between a *cantor*, who represents the Christian faithful, and a throng of prophets representing Old and New Testament as well as pagan culture. In a sustained antiphonal dialogue (one that recalls Amalarius's key aesthetic suggestion for dramatizing prophetic texts), the *cantor* encourages these *in bono* Jews and good pagans to admonish their willful contemporaries for their egregious errors in faith. Rather than make genealogy a literal battleground between Jews and Christians, the dramatist arrests the linear chronology of the procession, presenting the prophets from this historically diverse spectrum in suspended animation. The prophets emphasize the combined corporeal and spiritual Christian claims to being the new "Chosen People"; they subtly urge their unrecalcitrant contemporaries to concede willingly the transfer of power and divine right in preparation for the Eschaton. The exchange of Quodvultdeus's accusatory rhetoric of sensory deprivation for this rhetoric of anticipation and affirmation is, of course, part of continuing attempts of church officials in Limoges throughout the later eleventh century to encourage Augustinian eschatology over millenarian apocalypticism.

As a tool for containing the millenarian, the revised construction of genealogy is fairly thoroughgoing. All but three of the prophets avow explicitly the Christian genealogical claim to supersession.[83] Moses threatens those who do not listen to Christ as they do to him with expulsion from "his people." In a telling substitution for the "Ecce Virgo" prophecy which Quodvultdeus uses in his sermon (Isa. 7:14), Isaiah's "Virga Jesse" proclamation (Isa. 11:1–2) evokes a rich and prominent iconographic tradition that, rather than emphasizing his mother's virginity, traces Christ's Jewish lineage and the resulting Christian claim to God's covenant. In turn, the *cantor* asks David to speak of his grandson, Christ.

Simeon is quick to describe his acceptance of Christ as Messiah and willingly acknowledges the passing of generations as a transfer of religious covenants. The emphasis on quickly ensuing generations is continued by the simultaneous appearance of Elizabeth announcing with delight her son's in utero leaps of joy and that same son fullgrown, John the Baptist. Even the pagan outsiders Virgil and Nebuchadnezzar underscore the focus on Christians as God's "new progeny," his most recent "offspring."[84] Implicit in the genealogical lineage is God's intentional design for human history with its linear consummation at the Eschaton. The prophets in this drama are incarnations of the biblical texts that witness to Christ's Incarnation; their paraphrased prophecies, in turn, serve as a collection of embodied glosses on Christ's First and Second Comings. Because they appear completely outside their respective historical contexts, they present all of human history in the single continuous present of God. It is history that by divine design is figural and consequently interweaves past, present, and future, eschewing the possibility of present signs of the Eschaton, of apocalyptic imminence.

Sibyl, alone, breaks the pattern of this eschatological genealogy with her threatening closing reminder of the imminent signs of Judgment: the earth dripping with sweat at Christ's second advent. In contrast to the incarnational and genealogical emphases of preceding prophecies, Sibyl offers a vision of the commanding figure of Christ "in carne praesens," returning to judge the world. Her prophecy sustains the memory of the millenarian apocalyptic fervor that characterized liturgical attitudes toward Jews in Limoges at the outset of the century. In its position as closing prophecy, it subtly warns that the celebrated, if somewhat stylized, tolerance of this play's prophets is more a function of liturgical mood than an inherent quality of Christian relations with Jews; that ecclesiastically sanctioned tolerance will almost certainly find its end point within time even as the tone of eschatological affirmation has within this *Ordo prophetarum.*

NOTES

Editor's note: This paper was presented at the "Conference on the Apocalyptic Year 1000" in Boston, Mass., November 4–6, 1996. Regula Meyer Evitt teaches English at Colorado College (Colorado Springs).

1. C. Clifford Flanigan, "The Apocalypse and the Medieval Liturgy," in *The Apocalypse in the Middle Ages*, ed. Richard K. Emmerson and Bernard McGinn (Ithaca, 1992), pp. 333, 334–35.

2. Ibid., pp. 335–37.

3. Quodvultdeus's fifth-century sermon was introduced over one hundred years ago by Marius Sepet as the key source for the liturgical *Ordo prophetarum*, or Prophet Procession. For the sermon, see R. Braun, ed., *Opera Quodvultdeo Carthaginiensi episcopo tributa*, CCSL 60 (Turnhout, 1976). Sepet's groundbreaking work on the prophet drama, "Les prophètes du Christ," has appeared in two editions: serially in five installments in the *Bibliothèque de l'École des Chartes* 27 (1867): 1–27; 28 (1867): 211–64; 29 (1868): 105–39; 28 (1868): 261–93; 38 (1877): 397–443; and as a book, *Les prophètes du Christ: Étude sur les origines du théâtre au Moyen Age* (1878; reprint, Geneva, 1974).

4. For a detailed discussion of *Ordo prophetarum* scholarship since the mid–nineteenth century, see Regula Meyer Evitt, "Anti-Judaism and the Medieval Prophet Plays: Exegetical Contexts for the *Ordines prophetarum*" (Ph.D. diss., University of Virginia, 1992), chap. 2, passim.

5. James Grier, "Some Codicological Observations on the Aquitanian Versaria," *Musica Disciplina* 44 (1990): 30.

6. Jacques Chailley, *L'école musicale de SaintMartial de Limoges jusqu'à la fin du XIe siècle* (Paris, pp. 1960), pp. 109–15, esp. 111; Grier, "Some Codicological Observations on the Aquitanian Versaria," pp. 29–30.

7. "Grier, Some Codicological Observations on the Aquitanian Versaria," pp. 52–56. Grier suggests that because the majority of the texts in the Aquitanian *Versaria* are "suitable for the Christmas season," we should scrutinize closely repeated veneration of saints whose feast days fall outside the Christmas cycle (pp. 52–53). Two saints stand out—St. Nicolas and St. Mary Magdalene—because virtually every *versarium* contains a piece dedicated to one or the other or both (p. 53). Grier argues that we "should seek ultimately a monastery in Aquitaine where, at an early date, one or both of these saints received special veneration" (pp. 54–55). Michael Aubrun points to the diocese of Limoges as a place where parish churches dedicated to these eastern saints became common after the Crusades, after 1100 (*L'ancien diocèse de Limoges des origines au milieu du XIe siècle*, Publications de l'Institut d'Etudes du Massif Central, vol. 21 [Clermont-Ferrand, 1981], pp. 358, 400; cited in Grier, "Some Codicological Observations on the Aquitanian Versaria," p. 54). It may indeed be necessary "to exclude Saint Martial as the place of origin for the *versus* repertory [which includes the drama under consideration]" (Grier, "Some Codicological Observations on the Aquitanian Versaria," p. 55). However, we need not underestimate the influence of liturgists at Saint Martial on musical composition, including the drama, both locally and throughout Europe during the eleventh and twelfth centuries. (See nn. 71, 72, 74 below.)

8. Grier, "Some Codicological Observations on the Aquitanian Versaria," p. 29–30. As I will argue below, the drama provokes a reconsideration of the millenarian apocalypticism popular during the mid–eleventh century. Grier's redating and consequent characterization of other work in the manuscript as potentially "retrospective" underscores my hypothesis, though an earlier date would not necessarily undermine it.

9. Richard Landes, "*Millenarismus absconditus*: L'historiographie augustinienne et le millénarisme du haut Moyen Age jusqu'à l'an mil," *Le Moyen Age* 98 (1992): 355–77; 99 (1993): 5–26.

10. Ibid., 98:357.

11. Ibid., 98:358–62. Although millenarian apocalypticism from the fifth century on has at best an interstitial presence in the sanctioned canon of ecclesiastical exegesis, Landes argues that there is ample evidence for continued interest in it during the centuries on either side of the apocalyptic year 1000.

12. Braun, *Opera Quodvultdeo*, p. xliv. Young, *The Drama of the Medieval Church*, vol. 2 (Oxford, 1933), 125.

13. Daniel F. Callahan, "Ademar of Chabannes, Millennial Fears and the Development of Western Anti-Judaism," *Journal of Ecclesiastical History* 46 (1995): 34.

14. Landes, "*Millenarismus absconditus*," 98:370.

15. See Braun's discussion of the manuscript tradition of this sermon (*Opera Quodvultdeo*, pp. 40–61). Future references to this sermon will be taken from this edition. Augustine's authority was so greatly esteemed that *adversus Judaeos* pieces not written by him were often attributed to him. See Bernhard Blumenkranz, *Die Judenpredigt Augustins* (Basel, 1946), pp. 209–10; Heinz Schreckenberg, *Die christlichen Adversus-Judaeos-Texte und ihr literarisches und historisches Umfeld (1.–11. Jh.)* (Frankfurt am Main, 1982), pp. 352–54, 678.

16. Landes, "*Millenarismus absconditus*," 98:366. Landes describes Quodvultdeus's *Liber de promissionibus* as "une des oeuvres le plus systématiquement apocalyptique dans sa lecture d'événements contemporains" and refers specifically to the section in which Quodvultdeus discusses apocalyptic

promises which have already been accomplished. Landes observes that, in direct contravention of Augustine on this subject, Quodvultdeus identifies the coming of Gog and Magog with the arrival of the Goths and Massagetes during the sack of Rome.

17. See Landes, "*Millenarismus absconditus*," 98:374–75, for a discussion of end-of-time signs, including conversion of the Jews, that constitute the discourse of millenarian apocalypticism.

18. Solomon Katz, "Pope Gregory the Great and the Jews," *Jewish Quarterly Review* 24 (1933/34): 113–36; Blumenkranz, *Die Judenpredigt Augustins*, p. 194. For a discussion of the late Middle Ages and early Renaissance, see Guido Kisch, "Toleranz und Menschenwürde," in *Judentum im Mittelalter*, ed. Paul Wilpert and Willehad Paul Eckert, Miscellanea Mediaevalia, vol. 4 (Berlin, 1966), pp. 1–36.

19. John Chrysostom's sermons provide a case in point. They have been described by some modern historians as "zeal untempered by knowledge" (A. Lukyn Williams, *Adversus Judaeos: A Bird's-Eye View of Christian Apologiae until the Renaissance* [Cambridge, 1935], p. 132) and criticized for their "beastliness" (James Parkes, *The Jew in the Medieval Community* [New York, 1976], p. 19). For the corrective to this view, see Marcel Simon, "Anti-Jewish Polemic, Its Characteristics and Methods," in *Verus Israel*, trans. H. McKeating (Oxford, 1986), pp. 135–55 passim; and Robert L. Wilken, *John Chrysostom and the Jews: Rhetoric and Reality in the Late Fourth Century* (Berkeley, 1983).

20. Robert Chazan, *Daggers of Faith* (Berkeley, 1989), p. 6. "Highly literary and theoretical in character," the polemics represent, as Jeremy Cohen suggests, "adherence to literary genres in vogue" rather than serve as records of actual exchanges between Jews and Christians (*The Friars and the Jews: The Evolution of Medieval Anti-Judaism* [Ithaca, 1982], p. 23). While conversion of Jews was esteemed, it was not the primary function of these polemics. They are written largely in defense of Christianity and intended for a Christian, rather than a Jewish, audience. Many of these works are what we should call, following Gavin Langmuir's distinction, anti-Judaic rather than anti-Semitic. Taken literally, Langmuir argues, anti-Semitism is at best a misleading term ("Toward a Definition of Antisemitism," in *The Persisting Question: Sociological Perspectives and Social Contexts of Modern Antisemitism*, ed. Helen Fein [New York, 1987], pp. 86–127). Rather than lumping all intolerant behavior together under one inclusive rubric, he differentiates between three kinds of verbal assertions: "chimeric," "xenophobic," and "realistic" (p. 90). These three categories are extremely useful because they make possible a qualitative assessment of Christian attitudes toward Jews; they allow us to identify different degrees of and motivations for intolerance and to account for the simultaneous appearance in the later Middle Ages of anti-Judaism and anti-Semitism. For a full discussion, see Langmuir's *History, Religion, and Antisemitism* (Berkeley, 1990), p. 252, in particular his characterization of anti-Judaism as grounded in nonrational difference, anti-Semitism as grounded in irrational difference, and xenophobia as a conceptual middle ground for these opposing constructions of Jews. As Langmuir and Chazan (*European Jewry and the First Crusade* [Berkeley, 1987]) both emphasize, nonrational differences could verge on and sometimes escalate into irrational behavior and ultimately give fuel to chimeric fantasies.

21. Blumenkranz, *Die Judenpredigt Augustins*, p. 179. Still a fledgling religion in Augustine's lifetime in comparison with the antiquity of Judaism, even Christianity's textual tradition was in a state of flux since the authorized canon of its New Testament was not determined until the end of the fourth century.

22. Augustine, *Adversus Judaeos*, 1.2. For the Latin text, see *PL* 42:51–52; for the English translation, see "In Answer to the Jews," in *Saint Augustine: Treatises on Marriage and Other Subjects*, ed. Roy J. Deferrari, trans. John T. Wilcox et al. (New York, 1955), p. 392.

23. Augustine, *Adversus Judaeos*, 1.1 (*PL* 42:51; ed. Deferrari, p. 391).

24. Ibid.

25. As Blumenkranz emphasizes (*Die Judenpredigt Augustins*, p. 195), all the criticisms aimed at Jews apply equally to bad Christians. Indeed, at this point the fear of influence from bad Christians was greater than the fear of influence from pagans, Jews, or heretics. Augustine's concern with "bad Christians" is foremost, Blumenkranz observes, because they pose the greater threat to the integrity of the community of the faithful—the threat that comes from within. The second scenario similarly reveals Augustine's interest in establishing the ultimate integrity of Christianity through the potential assimilation of Jews into the community of the Christian faithful at the Eschaton.

26. For discussion of Augustine's innovative emphasis on the eschatological dimensions of anti-Judaism, see Bernhard Blumenkranz, "Augustin et les juifs; Augustin et le judaisme," *Recherches Augustiniennes* 1 (1958): 235; Chazan, *Daggers of Faith*, pp. 10–11; Cohen, *The Friars and the Jews*, pp. 19–22.

27. Augustine, *Adversus Judaeos*, 6.8 (*PL* 42:56; ed. Deferrari, p. 400).

28. Ibid.

29. Ibid., 7.9 (*PL* 42:57; ed. Deferrari, p. 404). The allusion is to Gen. 25:23.

30. Ibid., 1.2 (*PL* 42:52; ed. Deferrari, pp. 392–93).

31. Cohen, *The Friars and the Jews*, p. 20.

32. Augustine, *Adversus Judaeos*, 10.15 (*PL* 42:63–64; ed. Deferrari, p. 414). Augustine begins his closing remarks to his congregation in this way: "Dearly beloved (*Haec, charissimi*), whether the Jews receive these divine testimonies with joy or with indignation, nevertheless, when we can, let us proclaim them with great love for the Jews. Let us not proudly glory against the broken branches; let us reflect by whose grace it is, and by much mercy (*misericordia*), and on what root, we have been ingrafted."

33. Ibid., 8.11 (*PL* 42:60; ed. Deferrari, pp. 408–9).

34. Blumenkranz, *Die Judenpredigt Augustins*, p. 174.

35. For discussions of Augustine's explication of the parable of the prodigal son in his sermon 163, see Bernhard Blumenkranz, *Les auteurs chrétiens latins du Moyen Age sur les Juifs et le Judaisme* (Paris, 1963), p. 50, as well as Schreckenberg, *Die christlichen Adversus-Judaeos-Texte*, p. 353.

36. *Contra Judaeos*, in Braun, *Opera Quodvultdeo*, pp. 248–49, 253, esp. Braun's textual notes on these pages.

37. Quodvultdeus's sermon is addressed explicitly to catechumens, Augustine's implicitly. See Blumenkranz, *Les auteurs chrétiens latins*, p. 21; Schreckenberg, *Die christlichen Adversus-Judaeos-Texte*, p. 353. Quodvultdeus follows Augustine's pattern of opening and closing his sermon with a call to God's most beloved, his newly chosen people; those Augustine refers to as *charissimi* Quodvultdeus calls *dilectissimi* (*Adversus Judaeos*, 10.15 [*PL* 42:63; ed. Deferrari, p. 414]; *Contra Judaeos*, 1.5 [ed. Braun, p. 228]). At the outset of the sermon, Quodvultdeus admonishes those newly converted to Christianity to guard against sin and to work continually to prepare their souls for the final day of judgment when the Devil will stand as their adversary (secs. 1–4). He warns them, in addition, of the internal threat to their faith of heretics in a direct address to Arians and Manicheans (secs. 6–8) before addressing

the Jews (secs. 11–17). He chides the Arians once more for their disbelief in the Holy Trinity (secs. 18–19) before turning his attention again to the *dilectissimi* (*Contra Judaeos*, ed. Braun, pp. 232–55 passim).

38. *Contra Judaeos*, 11–13 (ed. Braun, pp. 241–44).

39. Ibid., 11.1 (ed. Braun, p. 241).

40. Ibid., 12.1–8 (ed. Braun, pp. 241–42).

41. Ibid., 12.1 (ed. Braun, p. 242).

42. Ibid., 17.7 (ed. Braun, p. 252).

43. Ibid., 17.8 (ed. Braun, p. 251).

44. Ibid., 17.10 (ed. Braun, p. 252). On Antichrist as a Jew, see Callahan, "Ademar of Chabannes," pp. 26–29; and R. Landes, "The Massacres of 1010: On the Origins of Popular Anti-Jewish Violence in Western Europe," in *From Witness to Witchcraft: Jews and Judaism in Medieval Christian Thought*, ed. Jeremy Cohen (Wolfenbyttel, 1996), pp. 79–112.

45. *Contra Judaeos*, 18.1, 18.7 (ed. Braun, pp. 252–53).

46. This was certainly the case in the frontier town of Riga during an early-thirteenth-century production of a *ludus prophetarum*. The dramatized armed conflict between Gideon and the Philistines inspired so much fear among pagan members of the audience (whom local ecclesiasts had hoped to convert) that they fled the performance and had to be coaxed to return. See Regula Meyer Evitt, "Undoing the Dramatic History of the Riga *Ludus Prophetarum*," *Comparative Drama* 25, 3 (1991), pp. 242–56.

47. *Contra Judaeos*, 21.1–4 (ed. Braun, p. 256) (my translation).

48. *Adversus Judaeos*, 7.10 (*PL* 42:59; ed. Deferrari, p. 406).

49. O. B. Hardison, *Christian Rite and Christian Drama in the Middle Ages: Essays in the Origin and Early History of Modern Drama* (Baltimore, 1965), p. 37. A prominent figure at the courts of Charlemagne and Louis the Pious as well as ambassador to Constantinople, Amalarius was also one of the most influential Carolingian scholars of the liturgy. Hardison emphasizes the immediate popular appeal of Amalarius's work, especially the *Liber officialis*, which went through three "editions" between 821 and 835 and circulated widely throughout France and its surrounding regions. Aware that Amalarius's writings were pronounced heretical during his own lifetime (in 838 by the council at Quiercy summoned by Louis the Pious), Hardison suggests that we may nevertheless find the most convincing confirmation of their contemporary popularity in the objections of those opposed to his work. The text of the accusations can be found in *PL* 121:1054, attributed by Migne to Remigius of Lyons. Allen Cabaniss (*Amalarius of Metz* [Amsterdam, 1954], p. 93) has more recently identified the speaker as Florus of Lyons. J. M. Hanssens (*Amalarii episcopi opera omnia liturgica*, vol. [Citta del Vaticana, 1948–50], pp. 83–91) discusses extensively Amalarius's contemporary influence; he offers an overview of the theologians in support of and opposed to Amalarius's work.

50. For a full discussion of this historical tension, see Alexander Schmemann, *Introduction to Liturgical Theology*, trans. Asheleigh E. Moorhouse (London, 1970), pp. 72–115 passim.

51. Cynthia Bourgeault, "The Aesthetic Dimension in the Liturgy: A Theological Perspective for Literary Historians," *University of Toronto Quarterly* 52 (1982/83): 9–10. Bourgeault argues that the widespread critical interest among drama historians during the last decades in the mimetic conception of the Mass has been largely a function of O. B. Hardison's influence, *Christian Rite and Christian Drama*, pp. 35–79 passim. She identifies as a counterpoint to the growing interest in the mimetic,

mysteriological conception of the Mass its more orthodox eschatological roots in the primitive church.

52. Hardison points out that the Solemn Stational Mass, which formed the basis for his allegorical interpretation of the liturgy, was attended by clergy and laity alike on the great feast days of the church (*Christian Rite and Christian Drama*, p. 41). His description of the appeal of Amalarius's writings suggests a popular audience quite different from the cloistered, learned monastic communities described by Jean Leclercq in, for example, *Contemplative Life* (Kalamazoo, 1978), or *The Love of Learning and the Desire for God: A Study of Monastic Culture* (New York, 1974). This more secular congregation anticipates the "populum Christianum" imagined as the audience for the dramatized Mass by Amalarius's eleventh-century disciple, Honorius of Autun, in his *Gemma animae*, written ca. 1100 (see Young, *Drama of the Medieval Church*, 1:83). Even Hardison, however, acknowledges the eschatological emphasis of the ninth-century Mass and identifies elements of it at work in the "Introit" described by Amalarius in the *Liber officialis (Christian Rite and Christian Drama*, pp. 44, 48–49). For an important alternative reading to Hardison's primary focus on the mysteriological, see Christine Schnusenberg, *Das Verhältnis von Kirche und Theater* (Frankfurt am Main, 1981), p. 143. She underscores Amalarius's balanced interest in both the mysteriological and the eschatological elements of the liturgy.

53. The mysteriological elements of Amalarius's description of the liturgy (his mimetic conception of the Mass) played an important role in later dramatizations of Christ's Passion, where anti-Semitic representations of Jews as torturers and crucifiers of Christ are at their most virulent. The eschatological elements of his description were most influential for early dramatizations of the liturgy (like the *Quem quaeritis, Ordo prophetarum, Ordo stellae*) that celebrate Christ's Incarnation.

54. Callahan, "Ademar of Chabannes," pp. 20–21.

55. For further details, consult Radulfus Glaber's *Quinque libri historiarum*, 3.7.24–25, in *Rodulfi Glabri Opera*, ed. John France (Oxford, 1989), pp. 132–36. Though Glaber is considered by many the "gossipmonger" of medieval historiographers, Landes makes a splendid contextual case for taking seriously his "lurid account of European-wide pogroms aimed at a final solution to the Jewish presence in this world, in which all but a tiny remnant of Jewry was obliterated" ("Massacres of 1010," p. 81).

56. Callahan, "Ademar of Chabannes," pp. 23–24; Landes, "Massacres of 1010," pp. 79–89, esp. 83 and 89.

57. Landes, "Massacres of 1010," p. 103. Landes describes Ademar's "late addition," which "suggests that in his initial account Ademar had tried to gloss over the excesses of the actual incident, toning it down so that the Christians treated the Jews according to the rules" (p. 85): a revision of dates in the chronicles "permitted (or reminded) him to place the effort to convert the Jews *before* the destruction of the Sepulcher" so that the "news from Jerusalem and the accusations of Jewish complicity could not have motivated efforts to convert the Jews, and the violence that anger at such news might have provoked would not have played a part in the pressures put on the community," a "narrative deception" ultimately unraveled by Ademar's final addition to the account of the ritual suicides (p. 86).

58. Ibid., p. 103.

59. Mordechaï Breuer, "Un grand talmudiste à Limoges au XIe siècle: Rabbi Joseph Bonfils," *Bulletin de la Société Archéologique et Historique du Limousin* 119 (1991): 61–62.

60. Amalarius of Metz, *Liber officialis*, in *Amalarii Episcopi Opera Liturgica Omnia*, 3 vols., ed. J. M. Hanssens (Citta del Vaticana, 1948), 2:292–93.

61. Ibid., 2:295.

62. Ibid.

63. Three centuries later Bernard of Clairvaux makes explicit the link between Amalarius's understanding of the impact of Old Testament prophecy on the community of the faithful and the eschatological quality of Advent. His description of the threefold significance of Advent has the same Augustinian echoes as Amalarius's conception of the efficacy of prophecy: "Triplicem enim eius adventum novimus: ad homines, in homines, contra homines." Christ's literal birth in the historical past, his perpetual presence in the hearts of humankind, and his coming as judge at the end of time (sermon 7, *PL* 183:45a).

64. Medieval exegetes from Boethius on understood the process of interpreting Scripture as fundamentally related to that of making music. On "the metaphysical importance of organized sound" in the Middle Ages and for a thorough introduction to how words and music work together in the liturgy and its drama, see John Stevens, *Words and Music in the Middle Ages* (London, 1986), pp. 372–409, 268–371. See as well Giles of Rome's commentary on music as exegesis in the Song of Songs in *Medieval Literary Theory and Criticism, c. 1100–c. 1375: The Commentary Tradition*, ed. and trans. A. J. Minnis and A. B. Scott (Oxford, 1988), pp. 243–46.

Hugh of St. Victor draws a particularly striking analogy between textual and musical harmonics in his *De scripturis et scriptoribus sacris*, a treatise on how to read sacred Scripture. He begins by identifying what he perceives to be the three essential levels of interpretation: *historia, allegoria,* and *tropologia.* He emphasizes that readers need not be discouraged if they cannot find all three senses in each text they examine. The task is often difficult, sometimes even impossible (*PL* 175:12). Hugh goes on to explain that not seeing all three senses does not necessarily indicate that they are not there. He does so through a remarkable comparison of the interpretive resonance of the biblical text and the harmonic reverberations of a *cithara* (*PL* 175:12–13). The *cithara* analogy is a favorite of Hugh's. See A. J. Minnis's discussion of Hugh's use of it in the *Didascalicon* (in *Medieval Theory of Authorship* [London, 1988], p. 46). Scripture as a whole with its individual verses is like the *cithara* with its multiple strings. The music of the whole will depend on two things: where the individual strings are connected (or how they reverberate in harmonic concordance when one is plucked) and how the musician "frets" them.

If we apply this analogy to reading the Bible, then scriptural exegesis as Hugh conceives it derives its meaning from an interplay between text and reader that is much like that between *cantor* and respondents during a liturgical celebration. The *cantor* presents his scriptural text musically only to have the respondents complete its sense. To present the Scriptures musically is, in effect, to manifest aurally levels of scriptural interpretation. In this way, the singing that forms the core of all liturgical drama becomes itself an interpretive act. The liturgical drama's "aesthetic" is, as a result, quite apart from our twentieth-century concept of drama as a form of entertainment (a concept that necessarily distinguishes between artists and audience). Even as this drama essentially incorporates its audience by making the chanting congregation its "actors," so it consolidates both celebration and interpretation of Scripture by dramatizing biblical narrative with an eye toward prevailing church doctrine. Through its emphasis on the ritual experience of *adversus Judaeos* exegesis, it literally gives voice to the tropes of these texts in a way that even the imagined dialogues between Jews and Christians cannot.

65. Some contemporaries responded less than enthusiastically to Amalarius's analogy between *cantor* and Jewish prophet. In *Les auteurs chrétiens latins*, p. 155, Blumenkranz describes the following marginalia by a contemporary in a manuscript of one of Amalarius's liturgical works: "L'auteur de quelques note marginales sur le manuscrit d'une oeuvre liturgique d'Amalaire prétend avoir vu Amalaire au milieu des Juifs pendant l'office solennel. Les notes datent de 835 à 838." Nevertheless, Amalarius's emphasis on the eschatological import of the Advent liturgy grew increasingly popular in the centuries that followed. Among theologians of his time Amalarius was "a recognized Judeophile" (see Bernard S. Bachrach, *Early Medieval Jewish Policy in Western Europe* [Minneapolis, 1977], p. 88). That is to say that his attitude toward Judaism was considerably more tolerant than that of some contemporaries. Archbishop Agobard of Lyons, who lobbied extensively for the right of Christians to convert Jewish-owned pagan slaves to Christianity without the owners' permission, embodies the kind of opposition Amalarius might have encountered. For an overview of the contrast between Agobard's more stringent anti-Judaism and the policies of the Carolingian Empire under Louis the Pious embraced by Amalarius, see Bachrach, *Jewish Policy*, pp. 98–102, as well as Manfred Kniewasser, "Bischof Agobard von Lyon und der Platz der Juden in einer sakral verfassten Einheitsgesellschaft," *Kairos* 19 (1977): 203–27. Kniewasser offers an important corrective to Bachrach's discussion of the conflict between Agobard and Amalarius as one between "church" and "state." These terms, he argues, are recent ones and largely inapplicable before the French Revolution (p. 203). Kniewasser describes early medieval society as a "sakralen Universal und Einheitsgesellschaft" (p. 203) that is at once worldly and spiritual and in which "der Ort der Juden kaum präsentisch sein und nicht präsent werden [konnte]" (p. 203). For a more detailed discussion of the two kinds of anti-Judaism represented by Amalarius and Agobard, and for further explanation of the early medieval understanding of contemporary Jews as fixed emblems of their Old Testament ancestors, see the next section of this essay.

66. Augustine, *Adversus Judaeos*, 7.10–8.11 (*PL* 42:51–64; ed. Deferrari, pp. 391–414).

67. Quodvultdeus, *Contra Judaeos*, 21.1–4 (ed. Braun, p. 256).

68. Monique Langlois and Michel Duchein, "Notice historique sur l'abbaye de Saint-Martial de Limoges," in *L'art roman à Saint-Martial de Limoges* (Limoges, 1950), p. 12. For liaisons between Saint-Martial de Limoges and the religious communities in Cluny, the Iberian Peninsula, Fleury-sur-Loire, and St. Gall see Chailley, *L'école musicale de Saint-Martial de Limoges*, pp. 30–58.

69. Callahan, "Ademar of Chabannes," p. 22.

70. Ibid., p. 21. The link between Ademar and the liturgists who were developing new liturgical materials for Saint-Martial de Limoges is explicit. Although Ademar was officially a monk at Saint-Cybard of Angoulême, he was residing at Saint-Martial during the height of the monastery's involvement in antagonism against the local Jewish community and studying, as Landes observes, with his uncle Roger, "the cantor of that wealthy and illustrious monastery" ("Massacres of 1010," pp. 5–6).

71. Jacques Chailley, "Le drame liturgique médiéval à Saint-Martial de Limoges," *Revue d'Histoire du Théâtre* 7 (1955): 127, calls it "un des centres les plus importants de la lyrique latine paraliturgique."

72. William L. Smoldon, *The Music of the Medieval Church Dramas*, ed. Cynthia Bourgeault (London, 1980), pp. 66–67; Chailley, *L'école musicale de Saint-Martial de Limoges*, pp. 183–319 passim, 363–66.

73. Callahan, "Ademar of Chabannes," p. 32.

74. Smoldon, *Music of the Medieval Church Dramas*, p. 67. This trope (which can be found in BN MS lat. 1240, fol. 30v) has been dated to 933–36. Chailley, "Le drame liturgique médiéval à Saint-Martial de Limoges," pp. 130–36, discusses both the trope and its manuscript. The Saint-Gallen version has been dated ca. 975.

75. The order is manuscript order: *Ordo Rachelis*, fols. 32v–33r; *De mulieribus*, fol. 53r; *Sponsus*, fols. 53r–55v; *Ordo prophetarum*, fols. 55v–58r. Chailley observes ("Le drame liturgique médiéval à SaintMartial de Limoges," p. 130) that while the manuscript was apparently compiled by two hands, this part was compiled in the Limousin for "une abbaye clunisienne indéterminée," but not necessarily expressly for Saint-Martial. He divides it into three smaller sections: (*a*) fols. 32–77, *versus, tropes, drame liturgiques*; (*b*) fols. 79–82, *tropes, proses*; (*c*) fols. 93–116, *proses*. He emphasizes that the manuscript has "une homogénéité de plan et d'époque qui nous permettra de considérer l'ensemble de cette partie sans y intercaler de subdivisions internes" (*L'école musicale de Saint-Martial de Limoges*, p. 110).

76. Flanigan, in "The Fleury *Playbook*, the Traditions of Medieval Latin Drama, and Modern Scholarship," in *The Fleury Playbook: Essays and Studies*, ed. Thomas P. Campbell and Clifford Davidson, Early Drama, Art, and Music Monograph Series, vol. 7 (Kalamazoo, Mich., 1985), introduces the idea of examining the celebrated Fleury *Playbook* (that portion of Orléans, Bibliothèque de la Ville MS 201 that contains the verbal and musical texts for ten plays) as a deliberate selection of texts by its redactor, which, "teaches us about at least one twelfthcentury scribe's under-standing of the nature and character of drama" (p. 2). He argues against attributing a similar impetus to other manuscripts containing plays on several subjects (see his discussion of the Hilarius, Hildesheim, and *Carmina Burana* collections) because their redactors "apparently believed that musicdrama belonged generically with lyric poetry in a category consisting of sung and performable texts" (p. 11). BN MS lat. 1139 (in contrast to all of the above) is essentially a liturgical collection: a troper. I am not arguing that the redactor's choices suggest anything about his awareness (or lack of awareness) of what might constitute the generic criteria of drama for the eleventh century. However Flanigan's observation about the possibility of deliberate choice on the part of a redactor surely is applicable to matters other than genre; I am applying it here to thematic content.

77. I will discuss the eschatological tone of the *Sponsus* and *Ordo prophetarum* in more detail below. Let me briefly touch on the *Ordo Rachelis* here. The liturgical context of the *Ordo Rachelis* is the feast of the Holy Innocents on December 28, which commemorates Herod's slaughter of the Holy Innocents as described in Matt. 2:16–18 and their ultimate reunion with Christ in Heaven (the eschatological emphasis). John Stevens, *Words and Music in the Middle Ages* (Cambridge, 1986), p. 355 suggests of the Fleury *Ordo Rachelis* that the slaughtered children "are not only little Jewish two-year-olds but also the Innocents of Revelation 14: 1 ff., the 144,000 virgins who follow the Lamb singing 'a new song' in the Heavenly City." The biblical text Stevens cites is the liturgical epistle for this celebration and would have been part of the liturgical context of the Saint-Martial de Limoges *Ordo Rachelis*.

The Saint-Martial de Limoges version is considerably shorter than the slightly later and more extended treatment of this theme in the Fleury *Ordo Rachelis*, which Flanigan describes as "the culmination of this kind of interpretative interplay between the story of the innocents, the text of the Apocalypse, and the ever-shifting perspectives of the Christmas liturgy" ("The Apocalypse and the Medieval Liturgy," p. 337). However, the liturgical responsory with which the Saint-Martial de Limoges

Ordo Rachelis begins, "Sub altare Dei audivi voces occisorum" (for matins of the feast of the Innocents), suggests in compressed form the same gathering of the souls of the Innocents under God's heavenly altar: "vidi sub altare Dei animas sanctorum, propter verbum Domini quod habebant, et clara voce dicebant." (See Smoldon, *The Music of the Medieval Church Dramas*, p. 135, or Young, *Drama of the Medieval Church*, 2:109, for the text of the responsory.)

78. Young, *The Drama of the Medieval Church* 2:366.

79. Clifford Davidson, "On the Uses of Iconographic Study: The Example of the *Sponsus* from St. Martial of Limoges," *Comparative Drama* 13 (1979): 308.

80. Young, *Drama of the Medieval Church*, 2:138–39 (my translation).

81. Callahan, "Ademar of Chabannes," p. 24.

82. Landes, "Massacres of 1010," pp. 17–18.

83. The three are Jeremias, Daniel, and Habakkuk (Young, *Drama of the Medieval Church*, 2:139–40). In those cases in which the composer-author of the Limoges *Ordo prophetarum* modifies the group of prophecies he draws on from the *Contra Judaeos* sermon, he does so with an eye to further underscore what I call the "eternal now" of this drama: the figural function of the prophets and the transchronicity of their prophecies. He recasts his exegetical material in a liturgical mold that emphasizes its focus on the continuum between Old Testament prophets, the contemporary faithful, and the final judgment. The exegetical and liturgical dovetail nicely in this respect. Augustine's desire to understand human history typologically, that is, from what he would cast as the perspective of God's timelessness, is not unlike the liturgical impetus to enter into the divine present.

84. Young, *Drama of the Medieval Church*, 2:139–42.

II

Visualizing the Millennium: Eschatological Rhetoric for the Ottonian Court

Susan E. von Daum Tholl

Ottonian iconography, like Ottonian culture and politics, had strong precedent in the Carolingian realm. The manner in which this art presents its message, however, differs from its earlier counterparts. This essay will discuss the visual rhetoric used by Ottonian artists to convey a message of transcendence, atemporality, and eschatological events, while reinforcing the significance of strong imperial rule as the turn of the millennium approached. On the one hand, eschatological events are gracefully but graphically depicted; on the other, the emperor enthroned as a sign of unbroken rule is associated with the visions.

Both style and iconography are crucial as connotators of rhetoric, the signifying aspect of ideology. Both must be formally addressed in order to derive the connotational effectiveness of the message. Ottonian use of reductive compositions, privileged framed fields, and ubiquitous gold grounds, combined with hierarchic figures, inescapable eye gaze, and authoritative gesture, creates a rhetorical system that projects beyond the immediate, temporal realm. Analysis of this rhetoric leads to synthesis and apprehension of a fuller message—a truer one that suggests profound millennial awareness.

Two types of Ottonian illumination relate to this discussion: innovative visionary compositions that enhance the apocalyptic literature they accompany; and depictions of the emperor that are essentially secular and not referential to the religious texts in which they are found. These imperial portraits are scattered and unexpected epiphanies, visual commemorations of rule that parallel appearances of the emperor himself on the royal *iter*, journeys of the court through the realm. Ottonian artists employed rhetorical

formulas and iconographic referents to Roman imperial portraiture to com-
memorate enduring empire in the person of the emperor. These images were
not intended as propaganda for the masses, since only a very thin upper crust
would have been privy to them. Nevertheless, it seems that such imperial portraiture did serve a specific function in the face of the millennium. By making
present an image of strong, continuing imperial rule, the established rhetoric
may have memorialized the belief that the world would not end as long as rule
descending from Rome remained unbroken.

Twentieth-century historians have traditionally (and reasonably) rejected a
hyperbolized, Romantic view of *les terreurs de l'an mil*.[1] Certain tenth-century
authors have been cited as debunking the notion that the apocalypse was near:
Adso of Montier-en-Der, who wrote that the world would not end so long as the
Roman Empire endured in the Frankish kings, and Abbo of Fleury, who claimed
to have resisted the notion that the Antichrist would come when the year 1000
was over.[2] But these same authors implicitly convey a curiosity about the Parousia
that was prevalent in the tenth century. Given the knowledge of Bede's Easter
tables since Carolingian times,[3] and the fact that by the late tenth century no
monastery or cathedral chapter was without such tables—consulted yearly—
arguments that the calculation of time anno Domini was confused or not well
known should be reconsidered.

Any discussion of apocalyptic curiosity or expectation around the year 1000
is served by a close examination of a group of manuscripts dating from 998–
1002 that reflect eschatological interest and are known to have been in Otto III's
library.[4] Deliberate selection of texts, visual rhetoric, and painting style are all
culturally referential signifiers that should be questioned for what they can reveal about the hopes and fears and curiosity of the ruler at the turn of the millennium. As the tenth century came to a close, the interest in eschatological
iconography intensified. Examples of so-called visionary images multiplied, and
even the types of the texts copied and illuminated for Otto III betray a preference for the visionary books of the Bible.

As noted by Florentine Mütherich,[5] Otto's library included four commentaries on books of the Hebrew Bible: on Isaiah (Staatsbibliothek Bamberg, Bibl.
76), the Song of Songs, Daniel, and the Wisdom of Solomon (Bamberg,
Staatliche Bibl., Bibl. 22).[6] These selections from the Bible are telling. Isaiah,
the greatest of the prophets, appeared at a critical time in Israel's history: the
collapse of the Northern Kingdom and the siege of Jerusalem in the second
half of the eighth century B.C. The book of Daniel, whose popularity peaked
between 200 B.C. and A.D. 100, serves as a Hebrew Bible counterpart to the
Apocalypse, with which it has literary parallels. The Wisdom of Solomon and
the Song of Songs are poetic projections into an ideal world. Like the Apocalypse, each of these texts relies on dreams and visions as literary devices, and
as a result, the skepticism of the modern eye may be blinded to the full
significance of a program that singled them out for copying. Significantly, the
illustrations for these books are unprecedented,[7] and what the illuminators
chose to depict argues for eschatological interests and perhaps apocalyptic
concerns.

Besides decorated initials, each commentary contains two facing miniatures. Both are full-page illuminations, with the recto page also constituting the initial page that opens the text. The end of the Daniel commentary is marked by an added image.

The Isaiah commentary is illustrated with the call of the prophet and his vision of the Lord sitting upon a throne (Isa. 6:1–7).[8] Christ appears seated on a gold orb set against a thick gold mandorla that emits forked rays of light. The vision is seen against a green oval field centered on the purple page; the whole composition is framed with a slender gold molding. Christ is adored by six seraphim, one of whom uses tongs to lift a burning ember from an altar below to purge the unclean lips of the prophet. The centered figure of Christ, isolated by the surrounding realm of gold, serves to ground the lyrical movement of the winged angels. The stylized forks of radiating light create a transition between the stasis at the vortex and the rhythmic energy of the angels. The geometric frame and matte purple parchment support and anchor the composition at its periphery. The artist has constructed the vision from opaque planes, frontality, and centeredness that isolate and stabilize the divine presence. This is juxtaposed with the mutable lyricism of the lesser (angelic) realm.

The two Bamberg Song of Songs miniatures show a procession of the faithful to the cross, led by a personification of Ecclesia, with cross-staff and banner. The faithful include crowned figures without halos; nimbused saints in quotidian dress of tunics, stockings, and mantles; tonsured monks; and vested clerics. Female saints lead the procession. The movement starts with initiation at the center of the image, where St. Peter baptizes a neophyte as three catechumens (?) look on. It curves outward and clockwise ending with Ecclesia, who operates conceptually to unite the church with Christ by offering a chalice to the lead female saint at her right, as she gestures to the cross at her left. Christ wears the eastern colobium and hangs limply on a double-armed, patriarchal cross; blood and water pour from his wounded side. Peter Klein's analysis of the signs of Christ's Passion that were incorporated by Reichenau artists into representations of the Second Coming helps to associate this image with the apocalyptic tradition.[9] The miniature relates the sacramental life of the church, grounded in baptism and the Eucharist, with the redemptive death of its founder, from whose wounded side blood and water spill. The life of the church (first militant and then triumphant) is joined to Christ, as is the Bride of the Song of Songs to her Beloved. The authority of the rhetoric depends on the conflation of Christ's wedding with his church and the visionary moment of the Second Coming. For its very limited Ottonian audience, this image would have been persuasive of love, not fear of the Last Days. Intimate union with Christ is reinforced by word and image on the facing (recto) page, where Christ appears enthroned in majesty within a mandorla formed by the initial "O" opening the Latin text: *Osculetur me osculo,* "Let him kiss me with kisses" (Cant. 1:1). A new visualization of a typological relationship is established in this pair of miniatures— one that relates the intimacy of wedded bliss with the apocalypse.

This imagery stands outside time. Humanity's movement from unbelief to initiation, from earthly life in the sacraments to Heaven, from the temporal to the eschatological, is telescoped. The circularity of the procession to the cross signifies continuity of the redemptive act. The centeredness of the facing initial page has a centripetal effect that draws the peripheral units of the composition to itself in a single moment.

Color plays a part. The amorphous, absorptive sea of blue against which the procession winds toward the great cross contrasts with the thick, opaque gold ground that encodes the *maiestas* page. As in many Ottonian miniatures, this gold ground is more than a mere indicator of costly production and powerful patronage. The opacity of the metallic field is a conceptual operative, signifying the authoritative immediacy of the visionary event. The gold ground stays the action and demands an experiential response from the viewer. Its immediacy and directness cannot be ignored and constitute a verifier of the truth of the vision.

The illumination of the dream of Nebuchadnezzar on the verso page before the opening of the Daniel commentary (Staatsbibliothek Bamberg, Bibl. 22, fol. 31v) is an unusual composition that shows the shining colossus, both strong and weak—an allegory of world history that anticipates the first apocalypse in Dan. 7:2–8. During the mid–tenth century, an illustrated version of Jerome's commentary on Daniel was added to the Apocalypse commentary of the eighth-century Spanish monk Beatus of Liebana. A visual tradition resulted that associated Nebuchadnezzar's clay-footed idol with the fallen colossus that was Rome for readers of the Johannine Apocalypse. The colossus becomes a parallel of the apocalyptic Whore of Babylon, the personification of the fallen Roman Empire, a haunt for demons, whose passing was mourned by all the kings of the world who had had relations with her (Apoc. 19:11–20).

The end of the Daniel commentary is signaled by a contrasting depiction of rule, a miniature of Christ as sign of the indestructible empire.[10] This image is a key to the eschatological question. If strong earthly rule can be associated with the eternal rule of Christ, there need be no concern that "empire" (i.e., Christian empire) will ever cease to exist, and the appearance of the Antichrist in the Last Days ceases to be an issue. The final image in the Bamberg Daniel commentary points us toward the rhetoric of Ottonian ruler images.

The Ottonian use of ruler imagery may be read as a witness to successful rule that will endure uncompromisingly. As imperial rhetoric, Ottonian ruler portraits complement the need to recalculate time in order to stave off the Parousia. In books made for the Ottonian emperors and court, portraits of rule contain clear, contemporary references to current imperial politics. The portrait of rule in the Gospel Book of Otto III (Munich, Bayerische Staatsbibliothek, Clm. 4453, fols. 23v–24r) covers two facing pages and presents a basic, formulaic type of composition that is also an "insider's view" of an important political program. The composition, which had parallels in Roman and late antique images of conquered nations offering homage to the emperor, reflects a text by Gerbert of Reims, whom Otto III named as pope (Sylvester II), that describes the provinces paying homage to Otto.[11] Here the four lands are inscribed Slavinia, Germania, Gallia, and Roma. Slavinia represents a new conquest in the East that was brought under Ottonian rule in the tenth century; Germania represents the locus of Charlemagne's tomb, opened by Otto III in the year 1000; Gallia represents the land where Otto III was around the year 1000; and Roma, who leads the procession, is a Tyche-like personification of the center of the world. All four offer homage to a rigid, frontal, iconic figure that personifies authority. Here, as in all ruler imagery, the disposition of the visual components is in terms of emphasis: the dominant or center image in the composition is key to message reception. Attributes such as Otto's eagle-headed staff refer to the Augustan Age of Roman peace. The formulaic composition, with nations in submission, is itself a rhetorical device that has a long tradition and is a remembrance of late antique compositions, where it was used on triumphal arches and ivory diptychs.[12] The configuration is adopted into Christian art as iconography of the Magi adoring the child Jesus.[13]

Byzantine artistic impulses in Ottonian art have long been acknowledged, but little attention has been paid to the connection between the visual rhetoric used in Ottonian and Byzantine portraits of rule. Henry Maguire has discussed the literary rhetoric that gave rise to "an elaborate display of conventional ideas" in Byzantine imagery. He points out that a type of Byzantine panegyric that praised the emperor as a "diagram of supernatural qualities" led in the East to highly abstract compositions.[14] The Ottonians adopted similar diagrammatic formulas that presented the ruler stripped of incidental detail. In accordance with a mid-eleventh-century panegyrist, Psellos, the eastern emperors were depicted as stable in character and judgment, "unmoved by the excesses of emotion . . . rigid, calm and serene."[15] The absence of emotion was viewed by the panegyrist as a sign of the emperor's divine status. Psellos called this type of imperial portrait "an image (*eikon*) of the signs of God." In the Ottonian West, the rhetoric of detachment renders figures immobile and immutable by stark gazes, rigid frontality, and simple, closed contours containing broad planes of pure colors. The reduction of detail contributes to an atemporality that is reinforced by thick and impermeable gold grounds. The artist achieves a tension between the immediate physical presence and the remoteness of an abstract concept of rule. The aura created by both painting style and composition enhances a surrogate presence of the type that antique imperial cults equated with the person himself. Rhetoric that denotes a dispassionate "realm apart" is key to our understanding of the typical Ottonian emperor enthroned as found in the Gospel Book of Otto III, in a fragment from a *Registrum gregorii* now in Chantilly, and in a portrait on a double leaf intended for another manuscript but later inserted as a frontispiece into a copy of Josephus's *De bello Judaico* in Bamberg.

Ottonian portraits take a rhetorical cue from their Byzantine counterparts. Familiar and legible eastern rhetoric is borrowed to present the western emperor as an icon of strong rule, which serves as a sign of God and replaces other, eschatological signs. The significative language of the Byzantine East seems to have been absorbed into Ottonian imagery in a more subtle and profound way than we have previously acknowledged.

These epiphanies of Ottonian rule are not text referential; they are ideological signifiers, whose forms are carefully selected and serve to concentrate the viewer's attention. They make present, as well as document, a rule that descends continuously from Rome,[16] using imagery that presents an allegory of peace in which the emperor inherits the temporal power of Augustus and participates in the celestial power of Christ. They authoritatively convey an aura which, to cite Walter Benjamin, "is a unique manifestation of something remote, no matter how close it may be."[17]

Privileging the idea of rule over the individual is exemplified by the Chantilly emperor "portrait," in which the depiction of power and rule follows the same basic formula as in the Gospel Book of Otto III.[18] But precisely *who* is represented here is problematic: a dating based on style puts the image in the early 980s, a time when Otto II was already dead and Otto III was still a small child.[19] So, in its generic depiction of empire, the Chantilly leaf spans two reigns and may be read as signifying unbroken rule. A similar confusion exists over the identity of the youthful ruler represented in the Bamberg Josephus frontispiece, which bears the inscription *Hein(n) - (rich)us* above the figure in white lettering that matches the inscribed names of the nations on the facing page. If the youthful emperor shown is indeed Otto, as Schramm maintained,[20] then the inscription must have been added later. If, as Carl Nordenfalk suggested, the inscription is contemporaneous with the image, it could refer to Henry the Quarrelsome, the uncle of Otto III who kidnapped the child-emperor and for a time made his own claim as regent.[21] Nonetheless, this controversy as to the identity of the image underscores the fact that the youthful, beardless emperor in the Bamberg Josephus frontispiece (and in the Chantilly leaf) transcended portraiture and served as a generic image of rule.

Ottonian ruler imagery also shows a bold and validating interaction with the divine.[22] Once Ottonian rule was associated, even visually, with the eternal rule of Christ, the eschatological continuity of the "empire" (i.e., Christian empire) was effectively asserted. The audacious rhetoric in the image of Otto III in majesty in the Aachen Gospels makes this point. Here, Otto (like Christ) bridges the heavenly and earthly realms as he is supported by an atlante figure personifying Terra and is crowned by the Hand of God emerging from the heavens. He sits within a mandorla in a frontal, emblematic pose that recalls a Christ in majesty or the epiphany-type of Ascension image.[23] The four beasts of the Apocalypse, which also symbolize the Evangelists, flank him and support a scroll unfurled across the emperor's chest, separating the heavenly and earthly realms.[24] In the Aachen image, Otto visually assumes the place of Christ in Majesty as he mediates between Heaven and Earth. As a type of figure ascending, he also identifies with the apotheosis or divinization of the emperors of Rome. The burnished gold ground functions conceptually to imply atemporality and sends a message of unquestionable authority ordained by God for all time. In the Aachen miniature, unbroken imperial rule serves the same eschatological purposes as recalculating the time to stave off the end of the world.

One collateral issue is worthy of note. Otto III possessed a life of St. Silvester, written at Nonantola about 820 and decorated with gold initials. Mütherich has pointed out that, due to its decoration, this ninth-century life of Silvester was more than a routine library copy.[25] According to legend, when

Silvester I was elected bishop of Rome, within a year of the peace of the church in 313, Constantine the Great conferred on him and his successors in the see of Rome primacy over all other bishops and temporal dominion over Italy. This purported act not only distinguished the see of Rome, of course; it also testified to the emperor's ability to convey such status. The legends surrounding Silvester were, no doubt, familiar to an emperor who owned a copy of the saint's life and who named his new pope, Gerbert of Reims, Silvester II. The memory of Constantine's imperial power may have served Otto when he named Gerbert on April 2, 999. In any case, the new pope would have celebrated his first name day on December 31, 999.

The *Bamberg Apocalypse* witnesses to eschatological awareness around the year 1000. The inclusion of signs of the Passion in representations of the Second Coming in Reichenau manuscripts has been discussed by Peter Klein and seems to support an Ottonian concern with the millennium of the Passion.[26] This brings the events of Jesus' death within the scope of eschatological rhetoric. Imperial imagery interjected into the *Bamberg Apocalypse* provides another document of the emperor's presence, perhaps essential in a book that graphically depicts those eschatological events that unbroken imperial rule assimilates. But the Bamberg ruler has no direct function in relation to the text of the Apocalypse. Thus, Klein has interpreted this imperial image as a depiction of Otto's triumph over those nations who give homage, while the virtues triumphant over the vices are at his feet. The emperor thus becomes an "excellent representative of triumphant virtue." Klein noted that the triumph was made even bolder because during Otto's pilgrimage to Poland in the year 1000, he adopted the audacious title Servus Jesu Christi, as did the popes, and thereby presumptuously became the lay vicar of St. Peter.[27] It would seem that the facing pages in the *Bamberg Apocalypse* typically display Otto's hubris and only peripherally (if that) relate to the call to repentance that pervades the text of the Apocalypse. Here, the imagery serves as an imperial statement, similar in iconography and meaning to that in the Chantilly "portrait," the Bamberg Josephus, and the Gospel Book of Otto III. In each of these examples, the priority of ideology to image replaces the more usual subordination of image to text.

It is thought that the *Bamberg Apocalypse* pages were originally placed at the front of the book, as planned by Otto III, the youthful, beardless emperor who is depicted (at least by type) here.[28] Otto died in 1002, and the manuscript was completed by Henry II, who is normally shown older and with a beard. Presumably, when Henry's artists completed the book, the emperor image was moved to the middle of the book to diminish its prominence, since it no longer depicted the reigning emperor. Ironically, however, the image of Otto gained potency by this rearrangement of leaves, since it now immediately follows the final image of the apocalyptic Christ of the Apocalypse. Leafing through the book, the reader arrives at the final apocalyptic image, the Christ of the Second Coming. As if in antidotal fashion, the very next depiction projects the formulaic rhetoric of imperial authority in an unbroken descent from Rome.

In sum, each of these Ottonian portraits of rule are secular images in books of Scripture. They employ similar, formulaic compositions and prioritize imperial ideology over scriptural text. These miniatures raise the emperor image to a mythological level. The mythological image is structuralist, in that the individual is decentered; he is not the object but rather signifies a message that is expressed to a collective consciousness, microcosmically represented by the court but in essence comprising all those subject to his rule. The message commemorates imperial strength and bolsters the belief that such uninterrupted authority overrules eschatology.

NOTES

Editors' note: This paper was originally presented at the "Conference on the Apocatlyptic Year 1000," Boston, Mass., November 4–6, 1996. Susan von Daum Tholl is Associate Director of Library, Emmanuel College, Boston, Massachusetts.

1. See Richard Landes, "Lest the Millennium be Fulfilled: Apocalyptic Expectations and the Pattern of Western Chronography, 100–800 C.E.," in *The Use and Abuse of Eschatology in the Middle Ages*, ed. W. Verbecke, D. Verhelst, and A. Welkenhuysen (Louvain, 1988), pp. 137–211.

2. Henry Mayr-Harting cited Adso of Montier-en-Der's *Liber de Antichristo*, written for Otto the Great's sister Gerberga between 949 and 957, and a letter of Abbo of Fleury to the Capetian kings in 998; see Henry Mayr-Harting, *Ottonian Book Illumination*, vol. 2 (London, 1991), p. 46.

3. Wesley Stevens, "Cycles of Time: Calendrical and Astronomical Reckonings in Early Science," *Time and Process: Interdisciplinary Issues*, vol. 7 of *The Study of Time*, ed. J. T. Fraser and Lewis Rowell (Madison, Conn., 1993), pp. 27–51.

4. Florentine Mütherich, "The Library of Otto III," *Bibliographia* 4, no. 2 (1986): 11–25. See also Mayr-Harting, *Ottonian Book Illumination*, 2:45–48.

5. Mütherich, "Library of Otto III," pp. 11–25.

6. Percy Ernst Schramm and Florentine Mütherich, *Denkmale der deutschen Könige und Kaiser* (Munich, 1962), p. 156, no. 109. Excellent color reproductions from the Song of Songs (fols. 4v–5r) can be found in Mayr-Harting, *Ottonian Book Illumination*, 2: pls. II, III.

7. Mayr-Harting recently attempted to piece together precedents for various parts of these images *Ottonian Book Illumination*, 2: 31–43. Whereas he is surely correct in saying that Ottonian artists knew various earlier monumental works and Carolingian compositions, the fact remains that these Ottonian compositions are innovative and show that the artists were concerned with forward-looking subject matter.

8. The text of Staatsbibliothek Bamberg, Bibl. 76, is laid out on 143 folios; the illuminations are found on fols. 10v–11r. For a reproduction, see Mayr-Harting, *Ottonian Book Illumination*, 2: fig. 22.

9. Peter Klein, "Zum Weltgerichtsbild der Reichenau," *Studien zur mittelalterlichen Kunst, 800–1250: Festschrift für Florentine Mütherich zum 70. Geburtstag*, ed. K. Bierbrauer, P. Klein, and W. Sauerländer (Munich, 1985), pp. 117–19.

10. Mütherich, "Library of Otto III," p. 13. On the issue of Christomimetes, see Robert Deshman, "Otto III and the Warmund Sacramentary: A Study in Political Theology," *Zeitschrift für Kunstgeschichte* 34 (1971): 8 and 15; Robert Deshman, "*Christus Rex et magi reges*: Kingship and Christology in Ottonian and Anglo-Saxon Art," *Frühmittelalterliche Studien* 10 (1976): 384–85.

11. Gerhart B. Ladner, *L'immagine dell'imperatore Ottone III*, Unione Internazionale degli Istituti di Archeologia Storia e Storia dell'Arte in Roma (Rome, 1988), pp. 20–21.

12. E.g., the fourth-century arch of Galerius at Saloniki and the Barberini Diptych in the Louvre (ca. 525–50), where the frontal figure of Justinian on horseback appears above the nations giving homage. On the latter, see Kurt Weitzmann, ed., *The Age of Spirituality: Late Antique and Early Christian Art, Third to Seventh Century* (New York, 1979), pp. 33–35, no. 28.

13. The imperial, two-page ensemble in the Gospel Book of Otto III has a compositional parallel in the Adoration of the Magi from the Pericopes of Henry II, where the three kings bearing gifts appear within a draped architectural setting on the verso page and move toward the Madonna and child on the facing recto (Munich, Bayerische Staatsbibliothek, Clm. 4452, fols. 17v–18r); see Mayr-Harting, *Ottonian Book Illumination*, 1: figs. 108–9.

14. Formulaic, frontal presentations of the Byzantine imperial couple would be set against a solid gold ground, with a half-figure of Christ Emmanuel emerging from the heavens to crown them. See Henry Maguire, *Art and Eloquence in Byzantium* (Princeton, 1981), p. 13; Henry Maguire, "Style and Ideology in Byzantine Imperial Art," *Gesta* 28, no. 2 (1989): 217–31.

15. Cited in Maguire, "Style and Ideology," p. 224 nn. 33 and 34.

16. It has been suggested that the companion miniatures of the emperor enthroned and the nations offering gifts in the Gospel Book of Otto III present an allegory of peace in which the emperor descends ideologically from Augustus and Christ. See Konrad Hoffmann, "Das Herrscherbild im 'Evangeliar Ottos III' (Clm. 4435)," *Frühmittelalterichen Studien* 7 (1973): 332–34.

17. Walter Benjamin, *Das Kunstwerk im Zeitalter seiner technischen Reproduzierbarkeit*, Suhrkamp 28 (Frankfurt, 1972), p. 53 n. 7.

18. Chantilly, Bibliothèque Condé, MS 15654, and Staatsbibliothek Bamberg, Class. 79. See Schramm and Mütherich, *Denkmale*, pp. 147–48, no. 82, and pl. 82, and p. 155, no. 107, and pl. 107.

19. Mütherich points out that the inscription *Otto imperator augustus* at the left and right of the figure's head would not have referred to Otto III until the year 996 (Schramm and Mütherich, *Denkmale*, pp. 147–48, no. 82). Peter Klein calls this a posthumous image of Otto II ("L'art et l'idéologie impériale des ottoniens vers l'an mil: L'Evangéliaire d'Henri II et l'Apocalypse de Bamberg," *Les Cahiers de St.-Michel de Cuxa* 16 [1985]: 197). On the other hand, Gerhart Ladner interpreted the changes in the appearance of the ruler, from Chantilly leaf to the Gospel Book of Otto III, as the result not only of a change in style but also of an evolution in the person. The later imagery becomes more reflective of the enormous tension that existed in the brief life of Otto III (Ladner, *L'immagine*, pp. 48–54; Gerhart Ladner, "Die Papstbildnisse des Altertums und des Mittelalters," *Monumenti di antichita cristiana*, ser. 2, vol. 4 [Vatican City, 1984], pp. 335–43).

20. Schramm and Mütherich, *Denkmale*, p. 155, no. 107.

21. Carl Nordenfalk, "Archbishop Egbert's *Registrum Gregorii*," in *Studien zur mittelalterlichen Kunst, 800–1250*, ed. Bierbrauer, Klein, and Saverländer, pp. 91–92.

22. As in the Aachen Gospels (Aachen, Domschatz, fol. 16r).

23. This type of Ascension was popular from early Christian times and is found, for example, in the Rabbula Gospels of A.D. 586; see C. Cecchelli, G. Furlani, and M. Salmi, *The Rabbula Gospels* (Olten and Lausanne, 1959), fol. 13v.

24. Kantorowicz likened this banderole to the veil of the Tabernacle, symbolic of the sky separating the heavens from the earth. According to Bede, the veil of the sanctuary dividing the Temple symbolized the twofold church: pilgrims on earth and saints and angels above. See Ernst Kantorowicz, *The King's Two Bodies: A Study in Medieval Political Theology* (Princeton, 1957), p. 69.

25. Mütherich, "Library of Otto III," p. 17.

26. Klein, "Zum Weltgerichtsbild der Reichenau," pp. 117–19.

27. Klein, "L'art et l'idéologie," pp. 202–5.

28. Klein, "L'art et l'idéologie," pp. 206–7 n. 129.

PART III

Historiography of the Apocalyptic Year 1000

12

The Fear of an Apocalyptic Year 1000: Augustinian Historiography, Medieval and Modern

Richard Landes

In the 1901 issue of the *American Historical Review*, George Lincoln Burr published an article in which he summarized for American historians a new consensus among their European colleagues that there were no apocalyptic expectations associated with the arrival of the first millennium since the Incarnation.[1] This position represented a complete reversal of the previous view. In the mid–nineteenth century, many historians, led by Jules Michelet, had drawn a dramatic picture of mass apocalyptic expectations climaxing in the year 1000. For Michelet, the liberating power of this eschatological fervor—arousing hope in the oppressed and terror in the oppressors—was the key to the transformations of eleventh-century France.[2] Other historians of the period readily embroidered on this theme of Apocalypse and Revolution, although in time the emphasis shifted from revolutionary hope to paralyzing terror.[3]

However, shortly after the Paris Commune in 1871, a powerful reaction set in among both ecclesiastical and the increasingly "professionalized" secular historians, who categorically rejected these "terrors of the year 1000" as a Romantic legend. There was, these historians argued, simply no evidence to support such a picture of an entire society quaking in fear at the approach of a date which, they contended, few contemporaries even knew about.[4] On the contrary, nothing distinguished the year 1000 from any other in the sources. This revisionist position became an integral part of European and, through Burr, of American historiography by the early twentieth century. By the mid–twentieth century, a historian could merely note in passing that this "myth has been effectively banished from serious historical writing," without even citing a reference.[5]

This exclusion of 1000 is true not only among generalists but also among specialists of the eleventh century who deal with topics where apocalyptic tensions might be relevant. For example, no discussion of the meaning of the year 1000 accompanies studies of Otto III that commonly refer to him as "L'empereur de l'an mil" and describe him as an unbalanced religious mystic,[6] extensive discussions of the sudden rise in popular and elite heresies in the first decades of the eleventh century,[7] or analysis of the Cluny of "l'an mil," whether looking at the central role of the Book of Revelation in the self-imagery of the monks[8] or trying to understand the motives of the aristocrats who donated so much land to Cluny from the 980s to the 1030s.[9]

In effect, the historiography of the tenth and eleventh centuries leans, uncritically or even unconsciously, upon the late-nineteenth-century rejection— the "anti-Terrors" school—of the excesses of the Romantics toward the rather hairy problem of apocalypticism. In what other area of historical research do modern scholars still base their approach on an argument first made over a century ago in a strongly polemical and politically charged atmosphere and grounded in a historical method and a knowledge of the phenomenon that have subsequently lost their luster?

In this essay, I shall trace the cultural process whereby I think the year 1000 took on its apocalyptic significance and the peculiar effects this process had not only on our documentation but also on the manner in which historians have interpreted those documents. My argument, however, is certainly not that we should return to the "Romantic" vision, which was deeply flawed in its conception of how apocalyptic expectations work. In that sense, both Romantic and Positivist historians (with the possible exception of Michelet) overemphasized the importance of fear and relief as the defining emotions of apocalypticism. Rather, I would suggest, the more significant and creative emotions at work in apocalypticsm have always been hope and disappointment.

The Nature of Apocalyptic and Millennial Expectation:
On the Persistence of the Irrational

As a social phenomenon, apocalypticism defies all expectations of fundamentally "rational" behavior. One might think, rationally, that those who "fall for" a prophecy or prediction that the end is near would simply repudiate and walk away from such nonsense once the predicted date had passed uneventfully. Far from facing reasonable facts, however, and acknowledging the failure of their apocalyptic expectations, many, if not most, believers in a specifically imminent end in fact redate and reformulate their failed prophecies in order to preserve and extend them.[10] Far from being susceptible to rational argument, committed apocalyptic believers are impervious to disconfirmation, even after the most egregious failures.[11] They respond to the passing of their Doomsdate by recalculating, reformulating their expectation, and redoubling their efforts to convince others of its truth. This "irrational" response derives from one of the most frequently overlooked aspects of apocalyptic expectations. For many believers, the time that they spend await-ing the end is a time not merely of fear and trembling but also of great hope and anticipation. None other than Michelet captured this powerful mood in his ex-pression "l'effroyable espoir du Jugement Dernier."[12]

Hope, then, is the key to understanding the apocalyptic mind-set. The medievals, of course, knew this. The divine oracles, said Radulfus Glaber, had been pronounced to inspire "as much hope as terror."[13] The problem, of course, is that apocalyptic hope is most often the currency of those who are oppressed, not the powerful. As a result, these hopes rarely express the attitudes we find in the writ-ten sources, which reflect the views of the *potentes*, the dominant aristocratic elite; and at the same time such hopes find their greatest audiences among the *pauperes*, the powerless masses, who do not leave us, at least in the Middle Ages, ample documentary evidence of their thoughts and deeds. When, however, on the rare occasions that we can track the voices of popular apocalyptic fervor, they often express desire for violent vengeance against the *potentes*. Such sentiments emerge in a text from the year 1011 on Doomsday: "then will end the tyranny of kings and the injustice and rapine of reeves and their cunning and unjust judgments and wiles. Then shall those who rejoiced and were glad in this life groan and lament. Then shall their mead, wine and beer be turned into thirst for them."[14] Dooms-day may be a "day of wrath" feared by some who prayed for its delay; but to others it was a longed-for "day of pleasure" whose advent they prayed would be hastened

Belief in such a "day of wrath, day of pleasure" has always been encouraged by the church. Indeed, as Hans Käsemann has reminded us, for Christendom "apocalyptic is the mother of theology."[15] We can thus fairly conjecture that, in the early and central Middle Ages, the date of the coming Eschaton was of some interest even to the rural population, who might not otherwise be sensitive to such learned notions as linear time. Indeed, the evidence suggests that the church offered the populace a promise of eschatological release from the sufferings of this world throughout the Middle Ages.[16] Numerous documents, including sev-eral tenth-century ones, point out that the bishop's particular task was to distrib-ute the meat of apocalyptic hope and fear to his congregation.[17]

Although, of course, any reconstruction of the attitudes of commoners is inherently speculative, we shall see that the peasantry (and some clerics for that matter) clearly got quite excited when prophetic figures announced the Apocalypse for the near future. By way of prelibation, let us recall that Bede complained bitterly of the rustics importuning him about how many years remained in the millennium.

Clerical Hostility to Chiliasm and the "Consensus of Silence"

This brings us to the nub of the problem of early medieval apocalypticism, namely, the relationship between the largely antiapocalyptic clerical elites who produce our sources and the rest of the population, both clerical and lay, whose voice rarely appears in the texts. Few Christian teachings more directly concerned and excited the commoners than chiliasm, with its promise of a time of heavenly peace, dreamlike prosperity *here on earth*, and a justly ferocious punishment for sinners, particularly those who have abused their power by oppressing the poor and defenseless. Chiliasm has, thereby, always had a distinctly political character. As a result, ruling groups invariably opposed it, often violently wiping out any traces.[18] More than with any other form of Christian belief, then, the historian needs to consider the apocalyptic, and especially chiliastic, tendencies of the *pauperes* independently from what the clerical elites taught (or said they taught) to their "flocks."

All this goes a long way toward explaining official ecclesiastical attitudes, both toward apocalypticism in general and toward chiliasm is particular. On the one hand, eschatological beliefs lay at the origin and the core of Christian belief, and the sacred texts from the Gospels to Revelation all announced the coming promises of God, and especially Christ's return. Indeed, it was incumbent upon the bishop to warn his flock and prepare them for the Day of the Lord, lest he be held responsible for their lack of preparedness, and often enough, priests played a prominent role in apocalyptic and other revolutionary religious movements.[19] On the other hand, as Christianity developed an institutional superstructure that copied and identified with that of the Roman Empire, the disruptive nature of its own—historically anti-Roman—eschatological tradition grew increasingly less tolerable. From nearly the first, Christian leaders did their best to contain the ill effects of a too-passionate and too-immediate sense of the end, and by the time that Christianity officially converted to Roman imperialism in the early fourth century, most of its chiliastic past had been systematically erased from the record. The Greeks even tried to eliminate the Book of Revelation from the Christian canon altogether.[20]

In the West, prominent figures like Jerome and Augustine did their best to delegitimize most forms of apocalyptic expectation and the chiliastic hopes it often inspired, in part by pointing to the absence of any valid text that might hold out such "carnal" promises. After them, ecclesiastics all but banished chiliasm from official Christian theology: no one was to write about it as a valid option, and neither should anyone encourage it by identifying current historical events with the obscure prophecies of that most bothersome of chiliastic texts, Revelation. Does that mean that apocalyptic speculation and hopes for a coming Millennium died out in Latin Christendom?

Rather, the evidence suggests that medieval writers avoided the subject of the Millennium whenever and wherever possible; that for every open and explicit denunciation of apocalyptic chiliasm, clerical writers used dozens of euphemisms: *false* prophets, *false* Christs, Judaizers, *delirantes*, fears that "the world was returning to its original chaos."[21] The reasons for this reluctance can and should be explored and debated at length; but the fact of it is inescapable to anyone who chooses to look at, rather than turn away from, the evidence. Here, I want to look at two elements that contribute to the relative silence on apocalyptic phenomena in our texts: the theological agenda most forcefully articulated by Augustine and the psychological tendency to revisionism that affects both our sources and ourselves.

The exegetical legacy of Augustine banned all chiliastic or apocalyptic speculation from orthodox theology. Rather than awaiting a Millennium of perfect peace on earth still to come, Christians were living in the invisible Millennium, as imperfect in its terrestrial manifestations as it was perfect in its celestial ones, already in progress since the Ascension of Christ in A.D. 33. Henceforth, chiliasm deserved mention only as a condemned popular belief: Julian of Toledo (687), Bede (724), Remi of Auxerre (ca. 940), and Byrhtferth (1011) all openly speak of the "vulgar" belief in the Millennium, to which they oppose their Augustinian teachings.[22]

This does not mean that all clerics always adhered to the austere agnosticism of Augustine on so crucial a question as the timing of the end. On the contrary, some striking evidence suggests that the temptation to see in current events the signs of the end was endemic, that clerics themselves were susceptible to chiliastic longings. However, the fact remains that every apocalyptic expectation that we deal with in our sources was demonstrably wrong, since the world did not end. Thus, whatever indiscretions clerics, even bishops and historians, might have committed in the heat of the moment, when the apocalyptic fever passed, Augustinian agnosticism reasserted itself in the cold light of the morning after. It was in this embarrassed, revisionary moment that most of our *learned* sources were composed. They are understandably loath to give details on moments of contra-Augustinian historico-exegetical activity. Such revisionism is further emphasized by the fact that very few texts survive to our day that were not copied and preserved by monastic institutions whose decisions were made long after any apocalyptic moment had passed. Thus, despite limited success in the oral (and lay) world in the face of apocalyptic signs and wonders, Augustinian agnosticism had signal success in the clerical, written world of postapocalyptic revisionism.

The Approach of the Year 1000: Evidence for Apocalyptic Concerns

The most famous and popular text of the mid–tenth century, Adso of Montier-en-Der's *Libellus de Antichristo* was, according to Daniel Verhelst, written at a time of apocalyptic crisis.[23] A contemporary letter from the bishop of Auxerre to the bishop of Verdun deplored the chiliastic response of the masses that saw in the Northmen and the Magyars the forces of Gog and Magog.[24] Adso tried to reassure his audience that the end had not yet come and thus invoked a politically conservative strategy of postponement: the imperial exegesis of 2 Thessalonians. According to this tradition, which dated back to the second Christian century, Antichrist could not come as long as the Roman Empire, or rather its Frankish rump, still existed.

Of course, the mid–tenth century was hardly a good time to invoke the Roman Empire as a bulwark against the forces of chaos and evil. Even Adso had to admit that "we see the Roman imperium almost completely destroyed." Nevertheless, he insisted, "as long as there were kings of the Franks who *ought to be king* [i.e., Gerberga's husband, the Carolingian Louis IV, and his line], the dignity of the Roman kingdom has not entirely perished."[25]

This was a perilous reassurance indeed. By linking his antiapocalyptic exegesis to imperial developments, Adso could only intensify speculation.[26] Within Adso's own lifetime, two major changes in the imperial situation occurred: in 962 a Saxon, Otto I, was crowned in Rome; and in 987 the last Carolingian king, Louis VI, died, replaced not by a relative but by a new dynasty. Obviously, Ottonian loyalists would argue that their emperor maintained the Roman dignity; and Otto III certainly made dramatic efforts to both "revive" the empire and link his own rule to that of Charlemagne's at the approach of the year 1000. In France, where the Capetian kinglets had replaced the Carolingians, and the king, Robert II, was in a state of excommunication in the year 1000, no such argument was possible. As we shall see, the difference between an acephalous, disorderly France and an imperially dominated Germany and Italy had a significant influence on manifestations of apocalyptic expectation at the turn of the millennium.

In addition to exegetical texts concerned with apocalyptic matters, clerics of the tenth century produced a number of liturgical texts with strong eschatological elements. In general the musical and poetic creativity of the tenth century (and beyond) found apocalyptic themes particularly inspiring.[27] Perhaps the most dramatic poem, an alphabetic acrostic about the end of the world, appears on the flyleaf of a liturgical manuscript from Aniane, written in a mid- to late-tenth-century hand. The same text reappears in a deluxe edition at Fécamps ca. 1040; and the similarities to the immensely popular thirteenth-century Dies Irae are notable enough to suggest a continuing tradition of this poem in various forms from the latter tenth century onward.[28] Other poetry, both vernacular (Muspilli) and Latin (like the Aniane poem, written in the margins of manuscripts), emphasize the terrors of Antichrist's advent.[29]

The most curious and predictable material, however, comes from the patterns evident in the history of computing the sabbatical millennium. As Bernard Guenée has noted, the end of the tenth century marks the beginning of a period of "computistical fever" within monastic culture, an "obsessive concern for chronology" that lasts two centuries.[30] In the early tenth century, Helpericus of Auxerre wrote a short and very popular treatise on computus in which he paid particular attention to the calculation of the current year anno Domini, and subsequent copyists took care to update the calculations to their own time.[31] Although not as explicit as the updates of Isidore's *Chronicle*, which concluded with the number of years remaining in the Millennium (as reckoned in *Annus Mundi* II),[32] such texts could also serve as apocalyptic countdowns.[33] Nor did one need to engage in elaborate calculations to know the date and count the years remaining. They were, as we have seen, in Bede's Easter tables, which, by the late tenth century, every significant monastery or church would have had.[34] At the approach of the millennium, at least the learned of Europe knew a great deal about the date anno Domini.[35]

Moreover, the acute awareness of the date that so many manuscripts indicate, even the mistakes, often focused specifically on the year 1000. Normally, for example, one began or ended an Easter table, no matter how short, with a nineteen-year cycle. Since 1000 fell in the middle of the cycle 988–1006, one would not expect to see it either begin or end such tables if it were a neutral date. Yet a number of tables either begin or end with the years 999, 1000, or 1001.[36] Such abnormal procedures are not explicitly apocalyptic, nor do I think they necessarily indicate some kind of eschatological expectation. Quite the contrary, those written after 1000, like Byrhtferth, emphasize its passage.

In some cases, one can detect the presence of a countdown. For instance, a scribe from the cathedral school at Angoulême, confronted with an annalistic list that only went to 989, noted the final eleven years of the millennium in sequence, adding the computistical data for these years and concluding not with the numeral M but with the word MILLE written in capitals.[37] As for the Angevin annalist who (perhaps before, perhaps after, 1000) identified the year 968 or 969 as the year *mille anni a nativitate Christi*, his error may have been from stupidity or from cleverness,[38] but either way, it offers unquestionable evidence for a fixation on this particular date.

This focus on the end of the millennium also accounts for the renewed interest in the Annus mundi chronology, which had passed the eschatologically significant year 6000 two centuries previously and had since then largely been neglected by Latin historians. A scribe at Notre-Dame de Paris noted, in a manuscript composed around 1000, that the date annus mundi of the Incarnation had two variants: 4955 according to the Hebrews (instead of 3952) and 5199 according to the Septuagint. This shifted attention from the implicitly apocalyptic year 1000 *era Incarnationis* to an alternative chronology, which, with his "mistake" of over 1000 years in the Hebrew count, he rendered only slightly less apocalyptic. His year 6000 would come in A.D. 1045![39] Ademar of Chabannes similarly shifted his chronology from anno Domini to annus mundi.[40] Further, a scribe from the monastery of Massay in the Berry noted opposite the year 1000 in his Easter tables: "A severe famine. There are 6201 years from the beginning of the world."[41] Such efforts to draw attention away from apocalyptic chronology fell flat, however: not until the early twelfth century would the *era mundi* return to the center of European historiography.[42]

Unable to replace anno Domini, chronographers turned their attention to undermining its accuracy. Thus, although Dionysius Exiguus's calculations of anno Domini had gone unchallenged since he published them in 525, they were "corrected" twice between 983 and 990. For Abbo of Fleury, 1000 was really 1021, and for Heriger of Lobbes, 1000 was 992.[43] We shall return to Abbo's work in its context below, but it is worth remarking here on the similarity between these kinds of small adjustments and those with which the Byzantine chronolographers met their millennial date, A.M. 1 6000. According to the various Eastern traditions, that year came in 492, 500, 502, and 508.[44] However, unlike the Byzantine historians of the seventh millennium, whose work acknowledged the passage of the year 6000 with great reluctance,[45] the historians of the year 1000 were singularly fascinated by the passage of the year 1000. The continuator of the *Annales Hildesheimenses*, writing in the late 1030s, noted for the year 1000: "With Otto III ruling, the thousandth year passing the number of established reckoning according to that which is written: 'The thousandth surpasses and transcends all years.'[46] Other annalists and historians note the passage of the year 1000 more laconically, but even this is unique to this date. "A thousand years from the birth of Christ."[47] "This was Gerbert at whose time the thousandth year from the Incarnation of the Lord was completed."[48] "Meanwhile, the thousandth year from the Incarnation of the Lord was fortunately (feliciter) completed, and this was the twelfth year of the archbishop."[49] As with the curious Easter tables, no other year receives this kind of attention from Christian historians East or West.

Abbo of Fleury and the Apocalyptic Year 1000

Nowhere is the combination of computistical-chronological and apocalyptic concerns more evident than in the work of Abbo, scholasticus, then abbot of Saint-Benôt of Fleury sur Loire (ca. 945–1004). In a letter to the kings of France dated ca. 994–996, Abbo recalls several incidents of apocalyptic rumors circulating in earlier years:

> Concerning the End of the World, as a youth I heard a sermon preached to the people in the Paris church to the effect that as soon as the number of 1000 years was completed, Antichrist would arrive, and not long after, the Last Judgment would follow. I resisted as vigorously as I could to that preaching, citing Revelation and Daniel. Then my abbot of blessed memory and keen mind rejected another error which grew about the End of the World; and after he received correspondence from Lotharingians, he ordered me to answer. For a rumor had filled almost the entire world that when the Annunciation fell on Good Friday, without any question, it would be the End of the World. Concerning the beginning of Advent, which happens each year before Christmas, there were also grave errors, some beginning it after December 29, others before, while Advent never has more than four weeks, even if only [a week of] a day. And since from these various divergences conflict grows in the church, a council should be called so that all those who live in her should know what your diligence grants, that He wishes to have us unanimous in His house."[50]

This passage, which concludes a letter of utmost importance for Abbo, by means of which he was seeking royal support in a desperate conflict with his bishop, offers a host of information about apocalyptic concerns in the generation before the year 1000.[51]

The encounter in Paris ca. 965–970 reveals the presence of the *augustinisme chronologique,* which had, in the Bedan/Carolingian world, replaced the sabbatical millennium as the clerical means for postponing the Eschaton. This preacher is not a chiliastic rabble-rouser but a cleric most probably preaching in the cathedral itself[52] and espousing an Augustinian eschatology. For him the year 1000 does not bring the beginning of the Millennium but its end: the release of Antichrist (Rev. 20:7) and the Last Judgment shortly thereafter. This is considerably *more* Augustinian than the almost exactly contemporary belief expressed in the Blickling Homilies, which, in giving the date as A.D. 971, emphasized that the sixth and final age was almost finished, thereby invoking the coming sabbatical millennium.[53]

Why then, would this conservative Parisian cleric invoke the Eschaton in the year 1000? The answer comes in the next incident Abbo reports: the apocalyptic rumor from Lotharingia that, he claimed, had "filled almost the entire world." This computus-based calculation predicted the end when the Passion and the Annunciation coincided on Friday, March 25, the very date of the creation of Adam, of the Annunciation, and of the Passion.[54] This coincidence occurred three times in the final generation before 1000: in 970, 981, and 992. Apparently this rumor had already become serious at the approach of the first date, 970. To the west of Paris, in Anjou, an annalist not only dated the year 1000 to this same period but also reported prodigies for the year 965 that have more than a hint of apocalypticism: "fire from heaven throughout the kingdom, demons appearing."[55]

What occurred in Paris in Abbo's youth, then, was not a battle between Abbo and a lone chiliast whom he soundly defeated. Rather, it was a conflict between a monk and a cleric (a canon, if this took place at the cathedral) over how to calm an apocalyptically agitated crowd. The cleric, using a common Carolingian technique, invoked the year 1000, not to stir them up, but to urge patience (at this point, for another thirty years).[56] The dispute was a reprise of earlier debates between far-sighted, conservative theologians and their short-sighted, traditional colleagues. We can detect these debates occurring during the final century of every millennial date as a once antiapocalyptic chronology inexorably mutates into its opposite, and the dating shift became a necessity.[57] Opposing the Carolingian *augustinisme chronologique* of the Parisian preacher, the true Augustinian Abbo argued on the basis of Daniel (according to Jerome's exegesis) and Revelation (according to Augustine's) that man simply cannot know the time of the end.

What is most striking about this debate, therefore, is not its content but that it occurred in public. Although Abbo may have been both theologically and historically correct, that hardly means that he carried the day.[58] In fact, seen in this light, the debate constitutes exactly what Daniel Milo assumed never happened when he speculated on the unlikely success of the *ecclesiasticas doctrinas* in swaying a crowd:

> One can hardly imagine the ignorant masses of "believers"
> accepting, even understanding, the Augustinian exegesis in seeing
> the year 1000 appear on the calendar; symbolic, allegoric, and
> anagogic readings of the Scriptures would at that point have had an
> opacity which pushed the limits of fraud. "Luckily" for the church,
> one might say, the potential terrorized were completely ignorant of
> the approach of the funereal date, and especially of its passage
> without results.[59]

Milo has intuitively expressed a key insight, and only his misconception of the situation has prevented him from following it to its logical conclusion: the populace would have no patience for Augustinian eschatology. Indeed, if Augustine had already tried these arguments with an apocalyptic bishop to no avail,[60] how could they work against illiterate peasants? Indeed, it was precisely because Augustinian eschatology was so useless in the face of an apocalyptic movement that, alongside this all but "official" position, clerics readily revisited the older, less austere (and more dangerous) teachings like the sabbatical millennium.

If Abbo's battle against the Parisian cleric went perhaps less well than we modern historians might imagine, perhaps the case against the Lotharingian computists went better. After all, the case was clear: the coincidence had happened numerous times since the Passion without eschatological results. Again, the logic is more convincing to those of us who have seen *many* more such coincidences pass, whereas the evidence suggests that even after all three dates before the year 1000 had passed inconclusively (we shall return to the final two), March 25 retained its apocalyptic fascination for at least another three centuries. When the coincidence next occurred, in 1065, a huge pilgrimage, led by the bishop of Bamberg, set off for Jerusalem, "deceived by the vulgar belief that that day would bring the Last Judgment."[61] For Lambert of Saint-Omer in the early twelfth century, the date had become a veritable vortex of cosmic time: in his calendar, the eighth of the Kalends of April (March 25) was the date of (1) the creation of Adam, (2) the binding of Isaac, (3) the crossing of the Red Sea, (4) the Annunciation, (5) the Passion, and (6) the Battle of Armageddon.[62] In 1250, the myth continued to inspire apocalyptic behavior. Matthew Paris laid down his pen that year, expecting the Lord's advent on the first Passion of March 25 that fell in a jubilee year.[63]

Matthew's embarrassing adherence to this medieval superstition offers us a key here. To scoffers, the apocalyptic thinker would have replied that this is the first time that it occurs in conjunction with some imminent chronological coincidence. Thus, for the people of the late tenth century, the proximity of the year 1000 would have given these computistical rarities their apocalyptic power. The passage of 970, then, would hardly have put an end to this kind of speculation; on the contrary, each successive date would have carried still greater weight among apocalyptic hopefuls. This is, after all, the classic pattern among those disappointed by failed prophecy—redate, and intensify commitment.

At this point, we must turn to an aspect of Abbo's computistical work that anti-Terrors historians have willingly cited but never connected to the passage in question. A year after the second apocalyptic date, 981, Abbo published his correction of anno Domini. His studies indicated a significant mistake: Christ was born twenty-one years earlier than Dionysius thought. And so, writing in 982 by this mistaken system, Abbo argued that the real date was in fact 1003. Significantly, Abbo based his correction, not on chronological data, but directly on the logic of eschatological expectation for when the Passion fell on March 25 (the previous year), seeking thereby to hoist these apocalyptic computists with their own petard. According to the current *era incarnationis*, only the Incarnation fell on March 25, not Good Friday. Indeed, the only possible year the Passion could have fallen on that date was A.D. 12 according to Dionysius; hence, the Incarnation (thirty-three years earlier), occurred twenty-one years before A.D. 1, and likewise, the year 1000 had already occurred in 979.[64]

Abbo's renewed concern with the Passion of March 25, and indeed his use of this date in order to correct the current, unanimously accepted calculation of the Incarnation, suggest that the apocalyptic expectations of 970 had revived in 981. It was that very strength that called for a dose of stronger medicine, one that addressed the real problem in this apocalyptic speculation, namely, the approach of the year 1000. Abbo's response, his effort to postdate a millennial year, goes back at least to Augustine.[65] The Angevin annalist who placed the year 1000 in 968/969 (if he wrote his entry around the same time as Abbo was making his calculations), may well have had similar intentions.

Like all the previous efforts, however, neither Abbo nor the Angevin annalist had any success convincing their contemporaries that the millennium had already passed. None of these corrections succeeded even in their monasteries of origin;[66] and these erudite dissensions aside, all of England and Carolingian Europe followed the same date anno Domini, the one they found every year in their Easter tables. Rather than a time of uncertainty and doubt about the date anno Domini, the turn of the millennium marks the complete victory of Dionysius Exiguus's calculations as the standard European usage.[67] Indeed, Radolphus Glaber, the Cluniac historian of the next generation, not only reflected the broad consensus of his day but may have even had Abbo and Heriger in mind when he wrote that "although in the Greek and Hebrew versions of the Old Testament the number of years which have passed since the moment of creation is different [i.e., A.M. I and II], we can be certain [of] the year of the Incarnation of Our Lord," which he then dated according to Dionysius Exiguus.[68]

If Abbo failed to quiet apocalyptic expectations for the second Good Friday to fall on March 25 (981), and if, in fact, the closer to the year 1000 that this magical coincidence fell, the more potent it became, then the final occurrence would have been the worst: 992. Circumstances probably did not help, since the collapse of the Carolingian dynasty (according to Adso, the last barrier to the Antichrist) in 987, a notable appearance of Halley's comet in 989,[69] and the traitorous defeat of the last Carolingian in 991 would all have contributed to an apocalyptic mood. Indeed, two collections of original charters from institutions supposedly favorable to the Capetians offer some interesting reactions to these events.[70] Beginning in January of 992, the charters of Nouaillé date King Robert's first year of rule to 991, that is to say, not to the time of his coronation (988), but to the time of Charles's dastardly capture.[71] At the same time and for the first time, the scriptorium introduced the apocalyptic preamble "Mundi terminum adpropinquante . . . ," which its scribes used repeatedly in subsequent charters. At Saint-Hilaire in the final years of the millennium, a charter laments how "with the end of the world at hand, since men are driven by a shorter life, a more atrocious cupidity consumes them."[72]

This is striking: most allusions to a looming end of the world in charters and other literature formulaically add that men responded with fear and piously mended their ways. Here, on the contrary, we find a kind of fin de siècle mentality attested to nowhere else in the literature of the period. Whether one wishes to take this apocalyptic cupidity as an insight into the mentality of some of the castellans and their warriors in these closing years of the millennium or not, it certainly deserves more attention than it has received.[73]

Rather than fade away, then, the evidence suggests that the anxiety caused by each apocalyptic March 25 *gained* in strength in the final generation of the millennium; and its final passage in 992 would merely have primed the population for the advent of the millennium in eight years. This could explain why Abbo wrote his coda on apocalyptic movements to the king in 994, at a time when he was fighting for survival against powerful enemies and serious charges.[74] By invoking his past opposition to such movements, Abbo played his trump card. He did not rehearse in his letter the arguments he had then used, not because, as anti-Terrors historians confidently assert, they were irrelevant, but because they were by then well known and widely circulated in church circles; the formal eschatological position of the church dated back to Augustine, and it had repeatedly, at the approach of a target date, returned to its former prominence.[75] Rather, just as Augustine would have wanted it, discretion was the order of the day.[76] With his laconic closing remarks Abbo underlined both his importance in this ecclesiastical victory of "true" Augustinian eschatology and his importance in the ongoing war against apocalyptic expectation, whose greatest challenge loomed ahead in the year 1000. What better way for a beleaguered churchman to conclude a letter seeking royal support in his hour of need; and what more striking example of the king's support could Abbo request than his closing plea for a council, called to restore church unity in matters of liturgy and computus?

The Apocalyptic Years 1000: Millennium of the Incarnation and Millennium of the Passion

We have a particularly explicit treatment of apocalyptic hopes and terrors linked to the year 1000 in the history of Christendom from 900 to the present written by the Cluniac monk Radulfus Glaber. In two passages, Glaber tells us that the central organizing principle of his work was the passage of the millennium. In his preface, dedicated to Odilo and the monks of Cluny, he proposed to tell of the "many events that occurred with unusual frequency about the millennium of the Incarnation of Christ our Savior."[77] In his *Vita Willelmi*, written around the same time, he reveals that this concern was not a personal eccentricity, but the overarching historical vision of his mentor, the great Cluniac reformer William of Volpiano (d. 1031): "For at [William's] command I had already described the major part of those events and prodigies that had occurred around and during the thousandth year since the Incarnation of the Savior."[78] Most strikingly, at the end of Book 2 (which traces the history of the West Franks from 900 to 1000), Glaber discusses the appearance of popular heresies around 1000 and links them explicitly to the fulfillment of prophecies in Revelation: "All this accords with the prophecy of St. John, who said that the Devil would be freed after a thousand years [Rev. 20:7]; but we shall treat of this at greater length in our third book."[79]

This is in fact perhaps the single most anti-Augustinian passage in the historiography of the early Middle Ages; it at once embraces the *augustinisme chronologique* described above (this is at the end of the 1000 years in Revelation) and contravenes Augustine's explicit prohibition on interpreting the Book of Revelation in historical terms. Not until the later eleventh and twelfth centuries would such tendencies to historicize apocalyptic prophecies become part of the historiographical tradition in the West.[80] Glaber's remark, however, coming at least two generations earlier, is all the more striking because it is written so long *after* the events in question: in the two to three decades since 1000, Glaber and his Cluniac mentors had plenty of time to see that the Antichrist had not come and gone in three and a half years. Here Glaber expresses the endemic tendency of apocalyptic believers to extend their expectation after prophecy has failed. Apparently he went too far for his mentors, for despite his promise to treat the period after 1000 (Book 3) in the light of this apocalyptic exegesis, Glaber did not cite Revelation again or make any further explicit reference to this passage on the year 1000.[81]

The years after the passage of 1000 are unusually rich in distinctly apocalyptic incidents: prodigies near Orléans, a terrible famine, a supernova spotted the world over in 1003–6,[82] and, in 1009–14, more prodigies and disasters, a rain of blood, and the slaughter of Jews in response to al-Hakim's destruction of the Holy Sepulchre in Jerusalem.[83] One might reasonably conjecture that, after 1000, people's attention turned to 1003–4. After all, if as the Anglo-Saxon and Parisian homilists predicted and Glaber insisted afterward, the year 1000 saw the release of the Antichrist, then one should expect his defeat three and a half years later.[84] Perhaps the Romantics were not wrong, then, to interpret the strikingly new and optimistic strain in some of the ecclesiastical historiography of that moment as relief. Glaber, writing three years after the millennium, records that Europe shook off the past (*rejecta vetustate*) and covered itself with a white mantle (*candida vesta*) of churches,"[85] while Thietmar of Merseburg spoke of a new dawn illuminating the world (*saeculo*) in 1004.[86]

However we wish to view the interpretations of contemporaries during the years after the year 1000—be they conservative clerics or raving apocalyptic prophets—it becomes quite clear that the next major redating was the millennium of the Passion. This was not merely convenient redating; it was the proper date according to the *augustinisme chronologique* of clerics like Thietland of Einsiedeln. Again, we turn to Glaber, who, in the opening passage of his fourth book of *Histories*, written after the death of his mentor, William of Volpiano, and shortly after the passage of the year 1033, noted: "After the many prodigies that had broken upon the world before, after and around the millennium of the Lord Christ, there were plenty of able men of penetrating intellect who foretold others, just as great, at the approach of the millennium of the Lord's Passion, and such wonders were soon manifest."[87]

The apocalyptic significance of this date then becomes the main theme of the book which centers on a devastating three-year famine that drove people to fear the end of the world, followed by a dramatic turnabout in 1033–34, when God and nature smiled upon humanity with clement skies and abundant harvests. This, in turn, provoked a wave of popular assemblies throughout France at which wildly enthusiastic participants believed they were forming a covenant with God to bring his peace to earth. The same year also saw an unprecedented mass of pilgrims on the road to Jerusalem, which prompted some contemporaries to speculate further on the approaching end.[88]

Nor does Glaber's evidence stand alone on this issue. A number of other texts indicate a sharpening of eschatological anxieties in the period just before the millennium of the Passion, some dealing specifically with the year 1033:[89] a rain of blood in Aquitaine in 1028 (by Jerome's chronology, one year before the millennium of the Passion) elicited a remarkable correspondence about its significance among Duke William, King Robert, Fulbert of Chartres and Gauzlin of Fleury.[90] At least four texts testify to radical Peace councils attended by large crowds in 1032–33.[91] The most extensive corroboration of Glaber's account of the final years of the millennium of the Passion, however, comes from the independent writings of Ademar of Chabannes, Glaber's colleague from Aquitaine: the death of great and pious men,[92] the famine and anthropophagy,[93] the apocalyptic preoccupations,[94] the Peace councils,[95] the constantly swelling mass of pilgrims to Jerusalem,[96] which, in its peak year of 1033, included even Ademar himself.[97] Finally, both these writers' testimony to the redating of apocalyptic expectations to the millennium of the Passion receives eloquent confirmation from a later-eleventh-century hagiographical report:

> With Robert holding the right of kingship among the Merovingians [sic], also known as the Franks, after the turning of a thousand years from the Passion of the Lord, with that millennial year completed, when the observance of Lent had been completed, and Good Friday had come, fiery armed troops were seen in the sky in many places, prodigious to behold, terrifying the hearts of those who gazed in amazement. Immediately, the rumor (an evil that moves faster than any other) reached the ears of many.[98]

The text goes on to describe a classic ecclesiastical response to widespread panic at such terrifying prodigies: relic delations and public penitential processions. Certainly, then, this text attests to the pressures that popular apocalyptic agitation exerted on ecclesiastics at the advent of a millennial year.

The Anti-Terrors School and *Augustinisme Historiographique*

At the end of this incomplete survey of the evidence for an apocalyptic year 1000, we come to an interesting irony. While Christians in the ninth and tenth centuries incorrectly invoked Augustine as they interpreted the signs and wonders at the approach of an apocalyptic year 1000, modern historians all too often unwittingly implement Augustine's teachings when they systematically reject the apocalyptic interpretation of the texts that generation produced.

Modern historians, in fact, have shown themselves to be a far more receptive audience for orthodox Augustinianism than the men and women we study. Thus, the anti-Terrors school has an aggressive naiveté in its approach to the texts, indignantly dismissing the possibility that the clerics who composed our sources might be under discretionary pressure, and reaffirming as an article of faith that there can be no "conspiracy of silence." However, in order to do so they must take the texts literally and not probe for allusions and hidden meaning. To dig for an archaeology of responses that lie buried beneath these literate and revisionary products "would be personal presumption and inexcusable temerity."[99] Thus, they take at face value the decidedly theological and polemical testimony of the great minds who were correct to caution against apocalyptic beliefs (Augustine, Bede, Adso, and Abbo) and dismiss the possible appeal that these men's opponents (e.g., Hesychius, the preacher in Paris) may have had for throngs of people who—unlike us—did not know that the year 1000 would not be the end.

This modern penchant for the revisionist Augustinians produces a rhetoric and argumentation very close to that of Augustine's own attacks on millenarianism. In his various writings, especially in Book 20 of the *City of God*, Augustine systematically dismantled the millenarian position by (1) reducing the number of proof texts acceptable for discussion to the minimum, a list already reduced by previous censure (*douze textes—pas un de plus*); (2) disposing of all but one of the remaining texts for not explicitly mentioning the belief in question (*donc, à écarter du débat*); (3) reversing the meaning of the most revered millenarian text: Rev. 20:1–9 (*Abbo n'est donc pas troublé par ce phénomène*);[100] and (4) having done so, covering with ridicule all those who chose to believe such superstitious nonsense, for which no textual support existed (*un dégoût qui submerge tout*).[101] Perhaps the most striking illustration of this unconscious Augustinianism is the notable discomfort historians of the anti-Terrors school display when confronted with genuinely apocalyptic passages directly linked to the year 1000. Some are capable of reporting the exact opposite of what the text says,[102] evidence of a singular ability to "read out" any apocalyptic significance. Others deny the very existence of a particularly problematic text, evincing a tendency to depreciate and exclude whenever possible. And when representatives of this school actually confront such texts, they resort to technicalities and exegetical gymnastics to dismiss their significance,[103] participating in a rhetoric of indifference that they draw directly from the posturing of their sources.[104] When confronted with too much evidence to wave aside, one can always trivialize it as commonplace: after all, apocalyptic beliefs were merely the "banal doctrine of the church," and in the Middle Ages, they were as common as lice.[105]

To reiterate, I am not arguing that we should reintroduce the Romantic notion of the "terrors of the year 1000." In fact, with the outstanding exception of Michelet, these earlier historians seem to have misconceived the impact of apocalyptic expectations as badly as their detractors;[106] and to the extent that subsequent historians reacted against their simplistic vision of fear and paralysis followed by relief and revitalization, they were correct. The analysis offered above seeks less to reinstate *les terreurs de l'an mil* as previously conceived than to reintroduce apocalypticism, variously understood, into our consideration of the developments in the period surrounding the year 1000: the hopes and fears of the two apocalyptic millennia—of the Incarnation and the Passion.

Let us conclude, then, with a brief list of the elements of that larger picture in turn-of-the-millennium western Europe that deserve an eschatological rereading:

1. *The Peace of God*: The movement's very name, given by contemporaries, suggests messianic hopes of a transformation of this worldly society into a realm of Peace and Justice.[107] Its dynamics often followed a classic millenarian pattern: divinely wrought disaster, followed by collective public penance, crowned with redemption and a new society. Its brief but intense period of dominance correlates closely to an apocalyptic chronology of the year 1000: it came in two waves, each a decade before the two millennia.[108] Characteristically, Michelet pointed to the Peace councils of the period as examples of millennial hopes at work, while later historians pointed to them as proof of the absence of a paralyzing terror.[109]

2. *Popular heresies*: Historians of the subject almost never raise the issue of apocalyptic expectations when dealing with the unusual rise of "popular" heresy around the year 1000, partly from a tendency to see either Manichean or apostolic beliefs at the core of these communities. At least in the latter case, this should not exclude apocalyptic beliefs, since both Jesus and his disciples lived in a world shaped by an imminent expectation of the end.[110] Indeed, one might even define "apostolic Christianity" as the sectarian response of apocalyptic believers at once disappointed in their initial hopes (Jesus as triumphant Christ/Messiah) and fervent in their expectation of his return (the Second Coming)—precisely the situation of those popular heresies that appeared in such unusual numbers in the years between 1000 and 1033.[111] And whatever these dissenters believed, ecclesiastical writers like Radulfus Glaber and Ademar of Chabannes unquestionably saw their appearance as signaling the time of the Antichrist and felt justified in contravening all precedent in exterminating them physically—perhaps another consequence of the *augustinisme ecclesiastique* of a William of Volpiano.

3. *Anti-Jewish violence*: Because Christian eschatological scripts cast Jews in a number of key roles, both negative (the Antichrist will be a Jewish "false messiah" and his first disciples will be Jews) and positive (a remnant of the Jews will see the light and convert to Christianity), unusual activity in Christian-Jewish relations often marks the intensification of apocalyptic expectations among Christians. In the early years of the eleventh century, we have an unusual number of cases of forced conversion and mass violence against the Jews. Many of these come in the wake of the destruction of the Holy Sepulcher in 1009 by the Abbasid caliph, al-Hakim, a deed that provoked widespread apocalyptic reactions in the West and that ecclesiastical authorities blamed on the Jews.[112]

4. *Mass popular movements*: The marked rise in pilgrimages, particularly to Jerusalem, the proliferation of saints' relics and the forms that their veneration took, the various forms of public worship, from mass penitential processions

to liturgical drama, all indicate a marked increase of interest in, and commitment to, Christian religiosity among the populace. Whether directly apocalyptic in inspiration (the pilgrimage to Jerusalem, the penitential processions) or the result of ecclesiastical efforts to channel such sentiments into more normative channels (relic cults, liturgical dramas,) this heightened activity deserves particular attention.[113]

5. *Political and religious reform*: The two generations around the millennium saw some unusually pious behavior from both secular and religious leaders: an unusual number of kings, dukes, counts, bishops, and abbots became saints, or, short of that, were remembered for their exceptionally pious acts: pilgrimages, charity, donations to the church, retirement to a monastery. The extraordinary behavior of Otto III and Gerbert around the year 1000 deserves to be seen as an intensified recapitulation of the behavior of Charlemagne and Alcuin around the year 6000. Given the topos that the approaching end should encourage those with the means to give generously of themselves, and the characteristic effort of religious and political elites to dampen more revolutionary sentiments by offering serious reforms, such behavior would seem to have a strong component of apocalyptic concern. After all, not only would unrepentant lords—lay and ecclesiastical—fare ill at the Last Judgment, but even before that, to those convinced that the end was nigh they would appear as agents of Antichrist.[114]

6. *Transformations in the conception of Christ*: Many historians have noted the dramatic new emphasis on the human Jesus at the turn of the millennium. He becomes an intensely historical figure—preaching, prophesying, suffering on the cross. The apostolic hagiography of the day, the enthusiasm of pilgrims for walking in his footsteps, even the first appearance of the relic of the "Holy Foreskin"—all attest to the emphasis on Jesus' human nature. More strikingly, both Radulfus Glaber and Ademar of Chabannes report visions of the Crucified One pouring out rivers of tears, an image unmatched for its emotions even in the most Gothic or Baroque portrayals. Since apocalyptic omens surround both of these visions and the interest in a historical Jesus can, at least in part, be attributed to the completion of one thousand years from the Incarnation, these remarkable shifts in Christian religiosity should be considered in the context of the "terrible hopes" of the year 1000.[115]

Once one turns, therefore, from the "terrors of the year 1000" to the hopes, fears, disappointments, and reprieves of two "millennial generations," a different picture emerges. This analysis, of course, does not have to exclude other elements from the picture, other factors and forces at work that may have little or nothing to do with any kind of apocalyptic activity—climatic change, technology, demography, the behavior of Europe's neighbors. However, that explanations which cite those factors should exclude apocalyptic seems as ill-advised an approach to the problem as a monolithic eschatological one. Even economists realize that demonstrating opportunity is insufficient cause: people must be motivated to act, to change, to try new things and create new possibilities. And in most cases, their motivations are not consonant with their achievements: most results are unintended consequences. Therefore, for all its ephemeral volatility, its protean qualities, its documentary disguises, the phenomenon of apocalyptic expectations and chiliastic enthusiasms belongs within the purview of historical analysis of the millennial generation. Otherwise, we fail to appreciate the hearts and minds of people who lived, not in our "Middle Ages," but in their *Last Age*.

NOTES

This chapter builds on earlier work on apocalyptic expectation in the patristic and early medieval periods: "Lest the Millennium Be Fulfilled: Apocalyptic Expectations and the Pattern of Western Chronography, 100–800 C.E.," in *The Use and Abuse of Eschatology in the Middle Ages*, ed. W. Verbeke, D. Verhelst, and A. Welkenhuysen (Leuven, 1988), pp. 141–211; "Millenarismus absconditus: L'historiographie augustinienne et le millnarisme du Haut Moyen Age jusqu'en l'an Mil," *Le Moyen Age* 98, nos. 3–4 (1992): 355–77; 99, no. 1 (1993): 1–26. I wish to thank David Van Meter, Fred Paxton, Philippe Buc, Bernard Bachrach, Amy Remensnyder, Tom Head, Conrad Leyser, Steven Fanning, and many others for their conversation on these matters and their feedback on earlier drafts of this work. I also want to thank the Boston University Humanities Fellows Seminar and Patrick Geary and the UCLA Center for Medieval and Renaissance Studies for the opportunity to present earlier drafts of this work and benefit from valued criticism.

Editors' note: Richard Landes is Associate Professor of History and Director of the Center for Millennial Studies at Boston University.

1. George Lincoln Burr, "The Year 1000 and the Antecedents of the Crusades," *American Historical Review* 6 (1901): 429–39.

2. Jules Michelet, *L'histoire de France*, vol. 2 (Paris, 1835), 132, cited from Claude Mettra, ed., *Le Moyen Age* (Paris, 1981), pp. 229–35.

3. See Christian Amalvi, "L'historiographie française face à l'avénement d'Hugues Capet et aux terreurs de l'an mil: 1799–1987," *De l'art et la manière d'accommoder les héros de l'histoire de France: Essais de mythologie nationale* (Paris, 1988), pp. 115–45.

4. Dom Franois Plaine, "Les prétendues terreurs de l'an mille," *Revue des Questions Historiques* 13 (1873): 145–64, H. von Eiken, "Die Legende von der Erwartung des Weltunterganges und der Wiederkehr Christi im Jahr 1000," *Forschungen zur Deutschen Geschichte* 23 (1883): 303–18; Jules Roy, *L'an mille: Formation de la légende de l'an mille* (Paris, 1885); Christian Pfister, *Etudes sur le règne de Robert le Pieux (996–1031)* (Paris, 1885), pp. 320–25; Pietro Orsi, *L'anno mille: Saggio di critica storica* (Turin, 1887); Burr, "The Year 1000 and the Antecedents of the Crusades"; Frederic Duval, *Les terreurs de l'an mille* (Paris, 1908); [L. F.] duc de La Salle de Rochemaure, *Gerbert-Silvestre II: Le savant, le faiseur de rois, le pontife*, vol. 2 (Paris, 1914), 507–26; Ferdinand Lot, "Le mythe des Terreurs de l'an mille," *Mercure de France* 300 (1947): 639–55, reprinted in *Recueil des travaux historiques de Ferdinand Lot*, vol. 3 (Geneva, 1970), 398–414; Edmond Pognon, *L'an mille* (Paris, 1949), pp. viii–xv; Edmund Pognon, *La vie quotidienne en l'an mille* (Paris, 1980), pp. 7–16; A. A. Vasiliev, "Medieval Ideas of the End of the World: West and East," *Byzantion* 16 (1942–43): 462–502; Bruno Barbatti, "Der heilige Adalbert von Prag und der Glaube an den Weltuntergang im Jahre 1000," *Archiv für Kulturgeschichte* 35 (1953): 127–41; more recently, Daniel Le Blevec, *L'an mil*

(Paris, 1976), pp. 1–10; Pierre Riché, "Le mythe des terreurs de l'an mille," in *Les Terreurs de l'an 2000* (Paris, 1976), pp. 21–30.

5. David Knowles, *The Evolution of Western Thought* (Baltimore, 1962), p. 79; cf. Robert Lerner, "The Medieval Return of the Thousand-Year Sabbath," in Richard Kenneth Emmerson and Bernard McGinn, eds., *The Apocalypse in the Middle Ages* (Ithaca, NY: 1992), p. 51.

6. Alain Ollivier, *Otton III, empereur de l'an mille* (Lausanne, 1969); E.-R. Labande, "*Mirabilia mundi*: Essai sur la personnalité d'Otton III," *Cahiers de Civilisation Médiévale* 6 (1963): 297–313, 455–76; *E.-R. Labande*, "Essai sur les hommes de l'an mil," in *Concetto, storia, miti e immagini del medio evo* (Florence, 1973), pp. 135–82. Labande cites at length the one historian who does give the apocalyptic dimension a significant place—Menno Ter Braak, *Kaiser Otto III: Ideal und Praxis im fürhen Mittelalter* (Amsterdam, 1928)—but never raises this aspect of Ter Braak's argument. Cf. J. Fried's treatment, "Endzeiterwartung um die Jahrtausendwende," *Deutsches Archiv für Erforschung des Mittelalters* 45, no. 2 (1989): 427–33 (chap. 1, this volume). On the dramatic visit to Charlemagne's tomb, see the analysis of the sources in Heinrich Beumann, "Grab und Thron Karls des Grossen zu Aachen," in *Karl der Grosse: Lebenswerk und Nachleben*, vol. 4, ed. L. Braunfels (Dusseldorf, 1967), 8–39.

7. See Malcolm Lambert, *Medieval Heresy: Popular Movements from the Gregorian Reform to the Reformation* (Cambridge, 1992); Janet Nelson, "Society, Theodicy and the Origins of Heresy: Towards a Reassessment of the Medieval Evidence," in *Schism, Heresy and Religious Protest*, ed. D. Baker, Studies in Church History (Oxford, 1972), pp. 65–77; Talal Asad, "Medieval Heresy: An Anthropological View," *Social History* 11 (1986): 345–62.

8. Through their virginity the monks are identified with the virgins of Revelation; their renunciation is a "visible sign of a present spiritual eschatology." See Dominique Iogna-Prat, "Continence et virginité dans la conception clunisienne de l'ordre du monde autour de l'an mil," *Comptes Rendus de l'Académie des Inscriptions et Belles-lettres* [1985], pp. 127–46; see also his *Agni immaculati: Recherches sur les sources hagiographiques relatives à Saint Maïeul de Cluny (954–994)* (Paris, 1988).

9. Barbara Rosenwein, *Rhinoceros Bound: Cluny in the Tenth Century* (Philadelphia, 1982), pp. 34ff., 101–12; Barbara Rosenwein, *To Be the Neighbor of Saint Peter: The Social Meaning of Cluny's Property, 909–1049* (Ithaca, 1989), pp. 35–48; Constance Bouchard, *Sword, Miter, and Cloister: Nobility and the Church in Burgundy, 980–1198* (Ithaca, 1989), pp. 38–46. Bouchard, despite focusing on personal crises and fear of death—and hence, obviously, judgment—never raises the matter of the last one. Neither of Rosenwein's arguments—not the earlier "anomie" nor the more recent "social networking with intercessors"—necessarily excludes the influences of an anticipated and delayed apocalypse; to the contrary, they could work quite well with such an interpretation.

10. The classic work on the subject is by Leon Festinger et al., *When Prophecy Fails: A Social and Psychological Study of a Modern Group That Predicted the End of the World*, 2d ed. (New York, 1964).

11. Stephen O'Leary, *Arguing the Apocalypse: A Theory of Millennial Rhetoric* (New York, 1994), pp. 20–61; Frank L. Borchardt, *Doomsday Speculation as a Strategy of Persuasion* (Lewiston, 1990), pp. 216–23.

12. Michelet, *Histoire de France*, cited from *Le Moyen Age*, p. 230; see also Henri Desroche, *Sociologie de l'esperance* (Paris, 1973), esp. pp. 18–38.

13. Radulfur Glaber, *Historiarum*, 1.5.26.

14. *Byrhtferth's Manual*, ed. S. J. Crawford, Early English Text Society, vol. 177 (Oxford, 1972), p. 242, ll. 3–9.

15. Hans Käsemann, "Die Anfänge christlicher Theologie," *Zeitschrift für Theologie und Kirche* 57 (1960): 180.

16. For the early Middle Ages, see Martin of Braga, *De correctione rusticorum* (ca. 574), esp. nos.14–19, ed. A. F. Kurfess, *Aevum* 29 (1955): 181–86.

17. Hesychius (ca. 418) to Augustine (Augustine, *Epistulae*, 198); the bishops at the Council of Trosly (909), *Conciliorum collectio*, 18.264–66, ed. G. D. Mansi (Florence and Venice, 1758–98) (see also Fried, "Endzeiterwartung," p. 410); Anglo-Saxon Homilies, e.g., Wulfstan's opening passage to his *De Antichristo*, 1a, ed. Dorothy Bethurum, *The Homilies of Wulfstan* (Oxford, 1952); Ademar of Chabannes (ca. 1032) speaks of giving a sermon at the funeral of a monk struck by lightning on the theme of how such signs indicate the imminent Day of Judgment calling the faithful to terror-filled repentance (Phillips 1664, fol. 113v, cited by D. Callahan, "The Problem of the Filioque," p. 124).

18. Kenelm Burridge, *New Heaven, New Earth* (New York, 1969), p. 34.

19. See, e.g., the remarks of Rodney Hilton, *Bond Men Made Free* (New York, 1973), chap. 3.

20. See P. Fredriksen, "Apocalypse and Redemption in Early Christianity: From John of Patmos to Augustine of Hippo," *Vigiliae Christianae* 45, no. 2 (1991): 171 n. 22.

21. "Estimabatur enim ordo temporum et elementorum, preterita ab initio moderans secula in chaos decidisse perpetuum atque humani generis interitum." Glaber, ad an 1033, *Quinque libri*, 5.4.13.

22. On Julian and Bede, see Landes, "Lest the Millennium Be Fulfilled," pp. 171–78.

23. Adso, *Deortu et tempore Antichristi*, ed. D. Verhelst, *CCCM* 45 (Turnhout, 1976). Anti-Terrors historians consider the nonpolemical tone of this letter, "addressed to the theological curiosities of the queen rather than to refuting some error that had seized her in its grip," a "devastating silence that voids all relevance of this letter for the argument about the year 1000" (Pognon, *L'an mille*, p. xiv; similar arguments from Plaine, "Les prétendues," p. 152; Roy, *L'an mille*, p. 187; Lot, "Le mythe," p. 400).

24. "Ac primum dicendum opinionem quae innumeros tam in vestra quam in nostra regione persuasit frivolam esse et nihil veri in se habere, qua putatur Deo odibilis gens Hungrorum esse Gog et Magog ceteraeque gentes quae cum eis describuntur.... Dicunt enim nunc esse novissimum saeculi tempus finemque imminere mundi, et idcirco Gog et Magog esse Hungros, qui numquam antea auditi sunt, sed modo, in novissimo temporum apparuerunt." Analyzed and edited by R. B. C. Huygens, "Un témoin de la crainte de l'an 1000: La lettre sur les Hongrois," *Latomus* 15 (1956): 224–38 (citation from p. 231, ll. 94–106).

25. Adso, *Libellus*, p. 26, ll. 113–20.

26. For the spectacularly successful posterity of Adso's text see R. Konrad, "*De ortu et tempore Antichristi*": *Antichristvorstellung und Geschichtsbild des Abtes Adso von Montier-en-Der* (Munich, 1964); and Verhelst's edition, pp. 3–18.

27. See N. Bridgman, "Les thèmes musicaux de l'Apocalypse: Leur signification spirituelle et leur interpretation dans les miniatures," in *Musica e arte figurativa nei secoli X–XII*, Centro de studi sulla spiritualità medievale (Todi, 1973), pp. 197–222; Nicole Sevestre, "La tradition melodique du *Cantus sibyllae*," in *La representation de l'antiquité au Moyen Age* (Vienna, 1982), 269–83; Gunilla Björkvall, "*Expectantes*

Dominum: Advent, the Time of Expectation, as Reflected in Liturgical Poetry from the Tenth and Eleventh Centuries," in *In Quest of the Kingdom: Ten Papers on Medieval Monastic Spirituality*, Bibliotheca Theologiae Practicae, vol. 48 (Uppsala, 1991), pp. 109–34; Regula Meyers Evitt, "Anti-Judaism and the Medieval Prophet Play: Exegetical Context for the *Ordines Prophetarum*" (Ph.D. diss., University of Virginia, 1992).

28. The poem was analyzed and edited by Paulin Blanc, "Nouvelle prose sur le Dernier Jour, composée avec chant noté, vers l'An Mille. . . ," *Mémoires de la Société Archéologique de Montpellier* 2 (1850): 451–509; C. Pfister dismissed it as isolated and undatable, *Etudes sur le règne de Robert le Pieux*, p. 325; most anti-Terrors historians do not even mention this text; cf. Fried, "Endzeiterwartung," p. 416. Second copy located by Michel Huglo: BN lat. 1928, fol. 178, Fcamp c. 1040).

29. On Muspilli, see F. von Leyen, *Deutsche Dichtung des Mittelalters* (Frankfurt, 1962), pp. 58–60; partial translation in Bernard McGinn, *Visions of the End Apocalyptic Traditions in the Middle Ages* (New York, 1979), pp. 80–81; B. Bischoff discusses two marginalia written ca. 950 in a Norman manuscript: "Vom Ende der Welt und vom Antichrist: Fragment einer Jenseitsvision (Zehntes Jahrhundert)," in *Anecdota Novissima: Texte des vierten bis sechzehnten Jahrhunderts* (Stuttgart, 1984), pp. 80–82.

30. Bernard Guenée, *Histoire et culture historique dans l'Occident médiévale* (Paris, 1980), p. 152.

31. Helpericus, *Liber de computo*, PL 137:17–48; see also A. Cordoliani, "Les traités de comput du Haut Moyen Age (526–1003)," *Bulletin du Cange* 17 (1943): 62–63; and P. McGurk, "Computus Helperici: Its Transmission in England in the Eleventh and Twelfth Centuries," *Medium Aevum* 43 (1974): 1–5.

32. See Landes, "Lest the Millennium Be Fulfilled," pp. 168–71, 187–96.

33. See the concerns on calculating the date anno Domini in Regino of Prüm, discussed by Arno Borst, *The Ordering of Time* (Chicago, 1993), p. 48.

34. See the long list of manuscripts in Charles W. Jones's edition of the *De temporum ratione* in CCSL, 123B, including his remarks on the number of worn fragments that bear eloquent witness to how often and hard ecclesiastics used these tables (p. 241).

35. G. L. Burr, ("The Year 1000," pp. 436–37) refers to A. Giry and A. Vasiliev's remarks on the erratic use of anno Domini (by the popes until 1431): "The data show us clearly that about the year 1000 Dionysius' era had by no means spread all over Western Europe and was not yet in popular use" ("Medieval Ideas," p. 477).

36. See, e.g., Vat. Reg. lat. 1127, fol. 10v, from 990 to "MILLE"; St. Gall 902, 817–999; St. Gall 387, 1001–1129. This list is purely provisional, based on a very small sampling of manuscripts; I suspect that attention to such matters would uncover far more.

37. Vat. Reg. lat. 1127, fol. 10. This is an unusual annal, not done in the margins of Easter tables but an independent list of dates with no computistical data included until the final addition.

38. Halphen thought it was so careless an error that he did not even include the text in his edition, preferring to append a dismissal of this mistake in a note to a different year (see Louis Halphen, *Recevils d'annales angevines et vendômoises* [Paris, 1903], p. 58 n. 2, p. 116 n. 6). And yet, this note was copied by the compilers of the *Annals of Vendôme* (later eleventh century) and *St. Florent de Saumur* (early twelfth); and cases of intentional error are hardly out of the question for both apocalyptic and antiapocalyptic calculators (see Landes, "Lest the Millennium Be Fulfilled," pp. 174, 190).

39. "Anno a creato mundi 4955 iuxta hebreos natus est secundum carnem dominus noster iesus christus, iuxta alios vero 5199" (BN lat. 17868, fol.2r [dated by the hand to ca. 1000]).

40. See Richard Landes, *Relics, Apocalypse, and the Deceits of History: Ademar of Chabannes, 989–1034* (Cambridge, Mass., 1995), p. 6.

41. *Annales Masciacenses* (*MGH, SS* 3:170).

42. On the return of the universal chronicle in the twelfth century, see A.-D. van den Brincken, *Studien zur lateinischen Weltchronistik bis in das Zeitalter Ottos von Freising* (Dusseldorf, 1957), chaps. 6–8.

43. On Abbo's computistical work, see A. Cordoliani, "Abbon de Fleury, Hériger de Lobbes et Gerland de Besançon sur l'ère de l'Incarnation chez Denys le Petit," *Revue d'Histoire Ecclésiastique* 44 (1949); 464–69; W. Van der Vyver, "Les oeuvres inédites d'Abbon de Fleury," *Revue Bénédictine* 47, no. 2 (1935): 150–58.

44. Landes, "Lest the Millennium Be Fulfilled," p. 163; and Venance Grumel, *La Chronologie*, pp. 73–97, in *Traité d'études byzantines*, eds. Paul Lemerle et al. (Paris, 1958), pp. 73–97.

45. See John Malalas, *Chronographia* (*PG* 97:354, 579–80, 632), with comments in Landes, "Lest the Millennium Be Fulfilled," p. 163 n. 107. See *Chronicon Paschale*; with comments by G. Podskalsky, "Représentation du temps dans l'eschatologie impériale byzantine," in *Le temps chrétien de la fin de l'antiquité au Moyen Age: IIIe–XIIIe siècles* (Paris, 1984), pp. 439–50; and J. Beaucamp, "La *Chronique Pascale*: Le temps approprié," in ibid., pp. 451–68.

46. *Annales Hildesheimenses,* 3, preface (*MGH, SS* 3:91–92).

47. *Annales sancti Florentii Salmurensis* and *Annales Vindocinenses* of Anjou, ad an. 969.

48. *Annales Pragenses,* ad an. 999 (*MGH, SS* 3:120) (contemporary hand).

49. Adam of Bremen, *Gesta Hammaburgensis ecclesiae pontificum*, 2.40 (*MGH, SS* 7:320) (late eleventh century).

50. Abbo of Fleury, *Apologeticus ad hugonem et rodbertum reges francorum*, London, BM 10972, fol. 22v; *PL* 139: c. 471–72C; dated before 996 by A. Vidier, *L'historiographie à Saint-Benoît-sur-Loire* (Paris, 1965), pp. 105–7; to 994–95 by M. Mostert, *The Political Thought of Abbo of Fleury* (Hilversum, 1987), pp. 48–51.

51. Anti-Terrors historians dismiss it as an irrelevant digression, so lacking in details about how Abbo refuted these challenges that it indicates a subsidence of apocalyptic beliefs at the approach of the year 1000: "The [apocalyptic fears] preoccupied only a small number of weak minds avid for wonders. Otherwise, how can one explain that after these admirable proofs of zeal for the purity of the faith [ca. 970], the abbot of Fleury would have kept a culpable silence precisely at a time when the poison of such doctrines supposedly multiplied . . . hence one can conclude that these [earlier] efforts remained without apparent results" (Plaine, "Les prétendues," pp. 454–55; see also Pognon, *L'an mille*, p. xiii; even Georges Duby, *L'an mil*, Collection archives, vol. 30 [Paris, 1967], p. 36). Most recently, Mostert has characterized the passage as so unrelated to the rest of the letter that it might be called an "author's interpolation" (*Political Thought*, p. 51 n. 38).

52. If it were any other church, Abbo would have likely written *quodam ecclesia.*

53. See Blickling Homily 11 (Ascension Day), ed. R. Morris, *The Blickling Homilies* (London, 1967), p. 119.

54. On the patristic and Carolingian origins of this calculation, see David C. Van Meter, "Christian of Stavelot on Matthew 24:42, and the Tradition That the World Will End on a March 25th," *Recherches de Théologie Ancienne et Médiévale* 63

(1996): 68–92. See also Eduard Weigl, "Die Oration 'Gratiam tuam, Quaesumus, Domine': Zur Geschichte des 25. März in der Liturgie," *Liturgisches Jahrbuch* 3 (1923): 57–73.

55. "Hoc anno, iv idus maii, in maxima parte hujus regni, in omnibus fere villis in quibus ecclesiae sunt, caelestis ignis sine vento et tonitru ac turbine, non hominem neque pecus ledens, cecidit et in quibusdam locis daemones in forma luporum, ad imitationem capraearum balantes, apparuerunt et nocte auditi sunt.— Finis chronicae Frodoardi" (Halphen, *Receuils d'annales angevines*, p. 58). None of this appears in Flodoard, only one of whose manuscript copies includes anything similar: "Mira et inaudita inundatio pluviae et fragor tonitrui ac coruscatio fulgoris decima Kalendas Augusti accidit" (*MGH, SS* 3:407, addition of codex 2, BN lat. 5354, Limoges, mid–eleventh century).

56. Jerome mentions some chronographers who, in the apocalyptic aftermath of the fall of Rome in 410, date the end to 430 years after the Passion (i.e., some fifty years away), *In Ezechielem*, 4.4 (*PL* 25:46B); Landes, "Lest the Millennium Be Fulfilled," p. 159.

57. Compare Eusebius's introduction of A.M. II and Lactantius's emphasis on no more than 200 years (A.M. I); Jerome and Augustine insisted on A.M. II just as Hilarianus announced 101 years to go (A.M. I); Bede introduced A.D. and A.M. III just as Fredegar counted 63 years left (A.M. II), the Carolingian annalists were working with A.D. when Beatus counted 14 years left; and so on (see the extended treatment in Landes, "Lest the Millennium Be Fulfilled," pp. 149–56, 169–70, 174–78).

58. The copy of Abbo's letter made at Fleury in the eleventh century contains marginal indications of the content: at the conclusion one finds the clearly post facto reflections: "Error finis mundi" and "De resta observatione adventus domini post posito errore" (London, BM 10972, fol. 22v). For the modern anti-Terrors school, Abbo's victory is self-evident: "en quoi [his attack on the preacher] il réussit pleinement" (Plaine, "Les prétendues," p. 153).

59. Milo, "L'an mil," p. 263.

60. Augustine had urged Hesychius to read Jerome on Daniel as an antidote to apocalyptic expectations in the aftermath of the fall of Rome; but Hesychius rejected the exegesis out of hand (letter included in Augustine, *Epistulae*, 198).

61. *Vita Altmanni*, 3 (*MGH, SS* 12:230).

62. *Liber Floridus*, fols. 2r, 27v.

63. Matthew Paris, *Chronica Maiora*, ad an. 1250, ed. F. Madden, Rerum Britannicarum Medii Aevi Scriptores, vol. 44 (London, 1869), 3:97–98.

64. The only alternatives were A.D. 1 and 91.

65. At the fall of Rome, and later in his *City of God*, Augustine had ridiculed those who had believed in a passed date (Landes, "Lest the Millennium Be Fulfilled," pp. 154–56); in 5970 A.M. I (470 C.E.) a chronicler updated Hilarianus's chiliastic chronography and demonstrated that the year 6000 (A.M. I) had already occurred two years earlier (*MGH, AA* 13:415–17; Landes, "Lest," p.162); in 681 Julien of Toledo attempted to prove that the year 6000 had already passed six years earlier in 675 (*De comprobatione sextae aetatis*, 3.10, ll. 100–148, ed. J. Hillgarth, CCSL 115.

66. See A. Cordoliani, "Les manuscrits de la bibliothèque de Berne provenant de l'abbaye de Fleury au XIe siècle: Le comput d'Abbon," *Zeitschrift für Schweizerische Kirchengeschichte* 52, no. 22 (1958): 148. The subsequent historiography at Fleury indicates that even his greatest admirers had rejected Abbo's system: Aimo, writing in the *Miracula s. Benedicti* shortly after Abbo's death, dated the

terrible and recent flood to "A.D. 1003, the sixteenth year of the reign of Robert with his father, and the seventh of his monarchy" (3.9; ed. M. de Certain, (Paris, 1858), pp. 150–53). See also Helgaud, *Epitome vitae Rodberti pii regis*, 22, ed. Robert-Henri Bautier and Gillette Labory (Paris, 1965), p. 110.

67. A. Giry, *Manuel diplomatique* (Paris, 1894), pp. 89–90.

68. Glaber, *Historiarum*, 1.1. When he wrote this preface, he was at Cluny in the later 1030s; but his use of A.D. dated back to the mid-1020s.

69. Cited in *Annales divionenses*, MGH, SS 5:40; and *Annales Quedlinburgenses*, MGH, SS 3:68; Thietmar of Merseburg, *Chronicon*, 4.10; see also P. Moore and J. Mason, *The Return of Halley's Comet* (Cambridge, 1984), p. 46.

70. These originals are therefore not subject to manipulation by twelfth-century cartulary compilers, who tended to eliminate "unnecessary" (not to mention embarrassing) preambles. (See Alexandre Bruel, "Note sur la transcription des actes privés dans les cartulaires antérieurement au XIIe siècle," *Bibliothèque de l'Ecole des Chartes* 36 (1875); and Giry, *Manuel de diplomatique*, pp. 29–33, with an example of a de-eschatologized formula from Saint-Maixent (pp. 32–33 n. 5); A. Richard, ed., *Chartes et documents . . . de l'abbaye de Saint-Maixent*, vol. 1, Archives historiques du Poitou, vol. 16 (Poitiers 1886), p. 46.

71. For the symbolic significance of such a system, see Richard Landes, "L'accession des Capétiens. Une reconsidération selon les sources," in *Religion et Culture autour de l'an mil: Royaume capétien et Lotharingie* (Paris, 1990)," 151–66; 160–61. Monsabert erased the negative meaning by noting that the charter was dated to January 992, first year of Robert's reign, "est prise de son . . . couronnement à Reims, le 29 mars 991 [sic! for the date of Charles's betrayal at Laon]." See Dom P. de Monsaber, ed., *Chartes de l'abbaye de Nouaillé de 678–1200*, Archives historiques du Poitou, vol. 49 (Poitiers, 1936), p. 118 n. 2.

72. ". . . et seculi imminente fine, cum homines brevior vita perurgeat, atrocior cupiditas purget." L. Rédet, ed., *Documents pour l'histoire de l'église de Saint-Hilaire de Poitiers (768–1300)*, Mémoires de la Société des Antiquaires de l'Ouest, (Poitiers, 1847), no. 65, p. 74; datable by the treasurer Geoffrey (end of the 990s) and by the hand.

73. "[T]his [apocalyptic] preoccupation may have surfaced in certain circles at the approach of the year 1000 . . . but it had no influence on the acts of our dukes of Aquitaine . . . and [especially not] at Saint-Hilaire, where the most elevated teaching took place . . . and where we find no trace of a belief of the end of the world in its charters" (A. Richard, *Histoire des comtes de Poitou*, vol. 1 [Paris, 1903], pp. 191–92). Nouaillé, Saint-Maixent, and Saint-Jean-d'Angély were all prominent ducal monasteries.

74. On the situation, see most recently Jean-Pierre Poly, "Le sac de cuir: La crise de l'an mil et la premiere renaissance du droit romain," in *Droits savants et pratiques françaises du pouvoir (Xie–XVe siècles)*, ed. J. Krynen and A. Rigaudière (Bordeaux, 1992), pp. 48–62.

75. For an example of this process, see the wide dissemination around 1000 of Julian of Toledo's antiapocalyptic treatise, *Prognosticon de futuri saeculi*, largely drawn from Augustine's writings (discussed in Landes, *Relics, Apocalypse, and the Deceits of History*, chap. 4).

76. Abbo, in fact, opens his letter to the king, not with the normal salutations, but with a pointed reminder: "Saepe contingit ut, dum nimius insurgentium calamitatum horror mentem fatigat, ipso horrore non ea quae dicere debuerat turbatus animus expediat, sed fantasmate cogitationum aliorsum raptus, quae

tacenda erant dicat at quod est consequens quae dicenda taceat" (Abbo, *Apologeticus*, London, BM 10972, fol. 15v; *PL* 139:461B [text in italics missing from *PL* edition].

77. Glaber, *Historiarum libri quinque*, 1.1, ed. John France (Oxford, 1989), p. 2; written ca. 1035–40 as a revision of his original (now lost) preface to the then-dead William of Volpiano.

78. Radulfus Glaber, *Vita Guillelmi Divionensis*, 28; *PL* 142 718; Neithard Bulst, "Rodolfus Glabers Vita domni Willelmi abbatis. Neue Edition mach einer Handschrift des ll. Jahrhunderts, (Paris, BN lat. 5390)" in*Deutsches Archiv* für Erforschung des mittelalters 30 (1974): 485; Glaser (France), pp.294–97). This text is not considered by most anti-Terrors historians.

79. Glaber, *Quinque libri*, 2.12.23.

80. McGinn, following the consensus of earlier scholarship, dates this develop-ment to the end of the eleventh century and the works of Rupert of Deutz (*Visions of the End*, p. 96).

81. Note that in the context of his millennial theme, Glaber tells us of a serious falling out that he had with William of Volpiano, just as he was composing the third book (*Vita Guilllelmi*, 13, [France] p. 294, see below). Note also that this passage and the equally apocalyptic one on the year 1033 happen to be part of the two lost segments of the autograph manuscript (Glaber [France], pp. lxxxii–lxxxvi).

82. For 1003, the *Annales sancti Benedicti floriacensis* report the prodigies (BN lat. 5543, fol. 22; *MGH, SS* 2:255; *PL* 139:583); also *Miracula s. Benedicti*, 3.9; ed. de Certain, pp. 150–53. In 1005–6 a devastating famine afflicted much of western Europe, associated with apocalyptic portents in several texts: *Annale Sangallienses* by Hepidannus: "Ecce fames qua per secla non saevior ulla" (*MGH, SS* 1:81); *Annales Leodinienses* and *Laubienses, MGH, SS* 4:18; *Annales Quedlinbourgenses*, ad an. 1009, *MGH, SS* 3:80; *Annales Hildesheimenses*, ad an. 1006; Glaber, *Quinque libri*, 2.9 (five years, ca. 1001–6); Hugh of Flavigny (based on Glaber); *Chronicon Turonensis*, ad an. 1006; Sigebert of Gembloux, ad an. 1006. In May of 1006, a new star was sighted in the heavens (supernova of 1006), at the same time a chaplain of the emperor converted to Judaism (Albert of Metz, *De diversitate temporum*, 1.6–7; 2.22–33, *MGH, SS* 4:704, 720–23; *Annales Leodinienses* and *Laubienses, MGH, SS* 4:18; *Annales Mosomagenses, MGH, SS* 3:161; *Annales Beneventani, MGH, SS* 3:177; probably Glaber, *Quinque libri*, 3.3.9; *Chronicon Venetum, MGH, SS* 7:36). See B. Goldstein, "The Supernova of A.D. 1006,"*Astronomical Journal* 70 (1965): 105–11.

83. A rain of blood was seen on Palm Sunday, 1009, and the sun turned a horrendous color of red and failed to shine for three days, followed by a plague and death (*Annales Quedlinburgenses, MGH, SS* 3:80). In November 1009, the chiliastic Muslim caliph al-Hakim (inspired by the supernova of 1003–6) destroyed the Holy Sepulcher in Jerusalem, provoking an apocalyptic reaction in the West, including violent anti-Jewish outbursts (Glaber; Ademar; *Annales Lemovicenses*, ad an. 1010; *Annales Beneventani*, ad an. 1010, *MGH, SS* 3:177); see R. Landes, "The Massacres of 1010: On the Origins of Popular Anti-Jewish Violence in Western Europe," in *From Witness to Witchcraft: Jews and Judaism in Medieval Christian Thought*, ed. Jeremy Cohen (Wolfenbüttel, 1996), 79–112. Between 1012 and 1014 various prodigies and natural disasters provoked the expulsion of the Jews from Mainz and led some to believe that the world was "returning to its original chaos" (*Annales Quedlinburgenses, MGH, SS*, 3.82–83; see also Alpert, *De diversitate temporum*).

84. This reading would find support in Augustine's discussion of whether the three and a half years would come before or after the thousand years (*De civ. Dei*, 20.13).

85. Glaber, *Historiarum*, 3.3.13, ed. France, p. 116. As Thomas Head points out, the adjective Glaber used here was not *albus* but *candidus*, a term with considerable apocalyptic resonance, especially from Cluny (T. Head and R. Landes, introduction to *The Peace of God: Social Violence and Religious Response in France around the Year 1000*, ed. T. Head and R. Landes [Ithaca, 1992], pp. 11–12); cf. Anti-Terrors historians' emphasis on Glaber's optimism as a disproof of apocalyptic (hence gloomy) expectations: e.g., John France, *Rodulfus Glaber, opera*, p. lxvi.

86. "Post salutiferum intemerate virginis partum millenarii numeri linea consummata et in quinto cardinalis ordinis loco et in eiusdem quarte ebdomade inicio clarum mane illuxit seculo" (Die Chronikdes Bischofs Thietmar von Mersebury und ihre Korveier Überarbeitung (Berlin, 1957) 6.1; ed. Walther Holtzmann p. 243 and n. 7).

87. Glaber, *Historiarum*, 4.1.

88. Ibid., 4.4–6.

89. It should be noted that although 33 had become the most widely accepted date for the Crucifixion, a strong case could have been made for any year from 29 to 33 from the chronographical traditions of the day (see Landes, "Lest the Millennium Be Fulfilled," pp. 196–97, n. 226).

90. Edited together by Robert Henri Bautier in *La vie de Gauzlin par André de Fleury* (Paris, 1975), pp. 159–67. Although Fulbert and Gaulin cite previous cases in the historical record to predict coming difficulties and encourage people to reform their ways, neither makes any reference to the fact that a rain of blood constitutes the first of the "Fifteen Signs before Doomsday" (see analysis of J. Fried, "Endzeiterwartung," pp. 381–84; Landes, *Relics, Apocalypse, and the Deceits of History*, chap. 9).

91. Poitiers (St. Maixent, 1032); Vich (1033); Autun (1033); Amiens-Corbie (1033); Beauvais-Soissons (1024–36); see Hartmut Hoffmann, *Gottesfriede und Treuga Dei* (Stuttgart, 1964), pp. 33–40, 54–69. On the date of Amiens-Corbie, which unfolded in explicitly apocalyptic circumstances, see David C. Van Meter, "The Peace of Amiens-Corbie and Gerard of Cambrai's Oration on the Three Functional Orders: The Date, the Context, the Rhetoric," *Revue Belge de Philologie et d'Histoire* 74, nos. 3–4 (1996): 633–57.

92. Alphonse V, king of Leon (May 5, 1027), Richard, duke of Normandy (August 23, 1027), William, count of Angoulême (April 6, 1028), Fulbert, bishop of Chartres (April 10, 1028), William V, duke of Aquitaine (January 31, 1030), Robert II, king of France (July 20, 1031).

93. See excerpts from his sermons written contemporaneously in Léopold Delisle, *Notice sur les manuscrits autographes d'Adémar de Chabannes* (Paris, 1895), pp. 293–96. On the famine, there is further corroboration in Andrew of Fleury, *Miracula s. Benedicti*, 6.10, ed. de Certain, p. 233.

94. On Ademar's apocalyptic concerns, see Landes, *Relics, Apocalypse, and the Deceits of History*, chaps. 5–6, 11–12, 15; Daniel Callahan, "The Peace of God, Apocalypticism, and the Council of Limoges of 1031," *Revue Bénédictine* 101 (1991): 32–49.

95. Most of Ademar's final work gives the detailed minutes of debates at Peace councils in Aquitaine from 1029 to 1032–33. Historians regularly quote the decisions as reflecting some of the most radical measures adopted at such councils (e.g., on interdict, see Edward Krehbiel, *Interdict: Its History and Its Operation* [Washington, 1909], p. 17). Ademar describes how the disasters of the early 1030s, compounded by a public excommunication (interdict), led to "cuncti principes eorum inter se

invicem justitiam et pacem foederent in manibus episcoporum" (Delisle, *Notice*, p. 296).

96. *Ademari Cabannensis Chronicon*, ed. P. Bourgain (*CCCM* 129; Turnhout, 1999), 3.69.

97. "Hic est liber sanctissimi domni nostri MARCIALIS Lemovicensis, ex libris bonae memoriae Ademari grammatici. Nam postquam idem multos annos peregit in Domini servicio ac simul in monachico ordine, in ejusdem patris coenobio, profecturus Hierusalem ad sepulchrum Domini, nec inde reversurus, multos libros in quibus sudaverat eidem suo pastori ac nutritori reliquit, ex quibus hic est unus" (Leiden, Voss. 80 15, fol. 141v, written ca. 1050). Ademar was still in Angoulême in 1032.

98. *Miracula sancti Agili abbatis*, 1. 3, ed. *AASS*, August 6, p. 588. The date is uncertain since the incident is also dated to the reign of Robert II (d. 1031); but in any case, the fixation on a millennial date is beyond dispute: "post mille a passione Domini volumina annorum. Ipso milenarii impleto anno, cum peracta quadragesimali observatione, sanctae Parasceves dies advenisset, visae sunt multis per loca multa in aere igneae acies, prodigioso visu corda se intuentium perterrentes. Extemplo fama (malum, quo non aliud velocius ullum mobilitate viget) multorum perculit aures."

99. Plaine, "Les prétendues," p. 157.

100. For an example of the boldness with which Augustine reversed the previous understanding of Revelation, see his remarks on the millennial kingdom of peace as a "kingdom at war with its enemies" (*De civ. Dei*, 20.9).

101. All the citations in italics are from Lot, "Le mythe."

102. De La Salle de Rochemaure describes Andrew of Fleury's account of the famine of 1031–32 in the Loire valley as "un malheur tout local circonscrit à la Bourgogne" (*Gerbert-Sylvestre II*, p. 509).

103. In his notes to Glaber's *Historiarum libiquingue* Pognon has numerous passages to explain away: here Glaber speaks of the year 1000 and prodigies (preface) "but not the end of the world" (*L'an mille*, p. 267 n. 4); there he links prodigies and the end of the world (1.5) "but no mention of the year 1000" (p. 169 nn. 39–40); here Glaber cites Rev. 20:4 about Satan unleashed at the end of one thousand years in the year A.D. 1000 (2.12), "but he makes no mention of the end of the world[!?]" (p. 271 n. 68); finally, Glaber puts prodigies, the end of the world, and the one thousand years together (4.4–6), "but it is the year 1000 since the Passion" (p. 274, n. 142, p. 275, n. 153).

104. Lot's explanation for the disappearance of apocalyptic preambles from Cluny's charters ca. 984 is that "the scribe who liked them died or changed jobs and his replacement preferred others" ("Le mythe," p. 649).

105. Giry considers apocalyptic preambles "nothing more than the banal expression of the Christian doctrine on the proximity of the end of the world" (Giry, *Manuel de diplomatique*, (p. 544). Töpfer also considers such sentiments too banal to include in serious historical analysis (*Volk und Kirche zur Zeit des beginninden Gottesfriedensbewegung im Frankreich* [Berlin, 1957], pp. 81–83), a point F. Paxton paraphrased by calling apocalypticism "as common as lice" in the Middle Ages ("History, Historians and the Peace of God," in *Peace of God*, ed. Head and Landes, p. 28), an image taken up by J. Nelson to criticize my suggestion that the Peace had a significant chiliastic dimension in her review (*Speculum* 69 [1994]: 165).

106. See also J. Fried's discussion of this issue ("Endzeiterwartung," pp. 470–73).

107. David Van Meter has treated this topic at some length in regard to the Peace of Amiens-Corbie in "The Peace of Amiens-Corbie"; David Van Meter, "St. Adelard and the Return of the 'Saturnia Regna': A Note on the Transformation of a Hagiographical Tradition," *Analecta Bollandiana* 113, nos. 3–4 (1995): 297–316.

108. Roger Bonnaud-Delamare's dissertation on the Peace of God placed the movement specifically in the context of the apocalyptic expectations surrounding the two years 1000 ("L'ideé de la Paix au XIe siècle" [diss., Ecole des Chartes, 1941], pp. 74–86), briefly reasserted in his "Les fondements des institutions de paix au XIe siècle," in *Mélanges d'histoire du Moyen Age dédiés à Louis Halphen* (Paris, 1951), pp. 19–26.

109. Cf. "Ces excessives misères brisèrent les coeurs [des guerriers] et leur rendirent un peu de douceur et de pitié. Ils mirent le glaive dans le fourreau, trembants eux-mêmes sous le glaive de Dieu. . . . c'est ce qu'on appela la paix, plus tard la trève de Dieu" (Michelet, *Le Moyen Age*, p. 231); with "Le monde de l'église, est il inquiet? Dans son ensemble, il ne parait guère. . . . Les conciles sont fréquents. En France ils se succèdent: Charroux (989), Narbonne (990), au Puy-en-Velay (990), Anse (994), Poitiers (1000)" (Lot, "Le mythe," p. 646).

110. See most recently, R. Landes, "La vie apostolique en Aquitaine au tournant du millennium: Paix de Dieu, culte de reliques et communautés 'hérétiques,'" *Annales* 46, no. 3 (1991): 573–93; and Malcolm Lambert, *Medieval Heresy*, 2d ed. rev. (London, 1992), chap. 1.

111. For a discussion of the apocalyptic undertones of the heresy at Arras, see David Van Meter, "Eschatological Order and the Argument for Clerical Celibacy in Francia around the Year 1000," in *Medieval Purity and Piety: Essays on Medieval Clerical Celibacy and Religious Reform*, ed. Michael Frassetto (New York, 1998), pp. 149–75.

112. In particular, see Lea Dasberg, *Untersuchungen über die Entwertung des Judenstatus im 11. Jahrhundert* (Paris, 1965); Hans Liebeschtz, *Synagoga und Ecclesia: Religionsgeschichtliche Studien über die Auseinandersetzung der Kirche mid dem Judentum im Hochmittelalter*, 2d ed. (Heidelberg, 1983); and R. I. Moore, *The Formation of a Persecuting Society* (Oxford, 1987), pp. 27–45, 147–52. Specifically on the incidents of 1009–10, see J. Fried, "Endzeiterwartung," pp. 469–70; Landes, "The Massacres of 1010"; Daniel Callahan, "Ademar of Chabannes, Millennial Fears, and the Development of Western Anti-Judaism," in *Journal of Ecclesiastical History* 46(1995): 19–35.

113. B. Töpfer, "Reliquienkult und Pilgerbewegung"; Ludwig Schmugge, "'Pilgerfahrt macht frei': Eine These zur Bedeutung des mittelalterlichen Pigerwesens," *Römische Quartalschrift* 74, nos. 1–2 (1979): 16–31.

114. For a survey of religio-political reform activity around the year 1000, see John Howe, "The Nobility's Reform of the Medieval Church," *American Historical Review* 93 (1988): 317–39; for the apocalyptic element in church reform, see Fried, "Endzeiterwartung," pp. 438–70.

115. On Ademar's and Glaber's reports of visions of a weeping Christ on the cross, see Landes, *Relics, Apocalypse, and the Deceits of History*, chap. 14. On the "Holy Foreskin," which first appears in the mid–eleventh century, see G. Chapeau, "Les grandes reliques de l'abbaye de Charroux: Etude d'histoire et d'archéologie," *Bulletin de la société des Antiquaires de l'Ouest*, ser. 3, 8 (1928): 101–28. On the weeping Christ on the cross, see the remarks of Duby, *L'an mil*, pp. 222–26; Stephen Nichols, Jr., *Romanesque Signs: Early Medieval Narrative and Iconography* (New Haven, 1983), pp. 110–19; Fried, "Endzeiterwartung," pp. 451–61.

13

Eschatological Imagination and the Program of Roman Imperial and Ecclesiastical Renewal at the End of the Tenth Century

Benjamin Arnold

As a system of belief, medieval Christianity was assertively soteriological and eschatological in its teaching. The church was much concerned with the science of personal and collective salvation, soteriology. Less coherent were its teachings about eschatology, the collapse of human history and of the Church Militant at the end of time, to be consummated in the Last Judgment.[1] Aptly enough, the theological handbook of the Christian church terminates with the apocalyptic end of time described in the Book of Revelation. In the Middle Ages, this surrealistic work was usually ascribed to the pen of St. John the Apostle in his old age, as a result of visions experienced while supposedly in custody upon the isle of Patmos.[2]

The books of the Bible running from the Hebrew prophets in the Old Testament to the Gospels and Epistles in the New, to say nothing of the Book of Revelation as such, are well stocked with speculative eschatological passages. They have provoked an enormous literature from the time of the church fathers onward, some of it determined to establish the exact nature and, even worse, the exact date of the end of human history. Rigorist churchmen condemned such excesses. Bishop Augustine of Hippo hoped to master the incautious spirits in this field through a long exposition, Book 20 in thirty chapters in his *De civitate Dei*, the section devoted to the Last Judgment. Actually, Augustine's conclusions were not designed to soothe the listener into complacency either:

Antichrist will persecute; Christ will judge; the dead will rise again; the good and the evil will be separated; the earth will be destroyed in the flames and then will be renewed. All those events, we must believe, will come about; but in what way, and in what order they will come, actual experience will then teach us with a finality surpassing anything our human understanding is now capable of attaining.[3]

In other words, St. Augustine considered that attempts to calculate the program and date of the Last Judgment against the years of human history were misguided, but he did not deny the reality of the apocalypse either.

Scholars of today who investigate such sources stemming from late antiquity and medieval times legitimately distinguish between eschatology (i.e., orthodox theological science speculating about the culmination of the world's history) and unruly debate about an imminent apocalypse, with or without a millenarian interlude consisting of the reign of the saints on earth.[4] Augustine was quite alive to such distinctions. According to the American scholars Richard Emmerson and Ronald Herzman, "Augustine was opposed not to apocalyptic lore nor to expectations of the end, but to chiliasm, literal interpretations of the apocalyptic numbers, and other naive applications of the esoteric symbols of the Apocalypse to contemporary personages and events."[5] So the Latin church was not in principle opposed to scholarly interpretation by respectable theologians, but another problem perceived by medieval churchmen was that popular misconceptions of biblical eschatology excited a desire for millenarian and apocalyptic information as well.[6] This may help to explain why, in the tenth century, Adso of Montier-en-Der thought he was required to answer such questions in the celebrated *De ortu et tempore Antichristi,* addressed to Queen Gerberga of France.[7] Eschatological speculation was thus a proper pursuit for educated churchmen living at what was conceived to be near the end of time. But when would time end?

It is perhaps not too much to claim that everyone in medieval Europe, however tenuous the understanding of the Bible by an illiterate mass may have been, sensed through the religious culture that the world would end spiritually in the Last Judgment and physically in some violent act of fiery annihilation. As the Second Letter of St. Peter (3:10) announced: "the heavens shall pass away with a great noise, and the elements shall melt with fervent heat, the earth also and the works that are therein shall be burned up." This is so strongly apocalyptic that thoughts about the interim reign of Antichrist as discussed by Adso of Montier-en-Der, inspired to some extent by a long tradition from writers such as Haimo of Auxerre, the Venerable Bede, and Jerome, may even have come as a relief. The principal proof text was provided by Paul of Tarsus's Second Letter to the Thessalonians (2:1–12) a short prophecy of the Son of Perdition's seizure of the Lord's sanctuary, his reign of evil, his subsequent annihilation by Christ, and the end of the world at the Day of the Lord. Later commentators equated the satanic figure with the Antichrist, although biblically that name is used only in the Letters of St. John.[8]

To the medieval mind, eager for eschatological certainty, the strongest hint was dropped by the apostle Paul's words in verse 3: "for that day shall not come, except there first come a falling away" (*discessio* in the Vulgate text). What was this *discessio,* or falling away? According to Adso, basing himself upon previous commentary: "All nations were subject to the Romans and served them as tributaries."[9] The *discessio* is the loss of such sway to the Roman name, in other words, the disintegration of the Roman Empire. But had this potentially fatal event really taken place in human history or not? Rome itself had fallen to the Goths in 410 C.E., yet the world had survived, permitting a change in emphasis upon what constituted "Roman" and, in consequence, *discessio* from it. It was thought that Antichrist was still waiting in the wings, but Adso was by no means the only tenth-century churchman frightened of him. Abbot Odo of Cluny (927–42) had discussed the subject in his *Occupatio,* and according to the analysis by Steven Cartwright,[10] Abbot Thietland of Einsiedeln's *Exposition on Second Thessalonians* may well turn out to be as forceful as Adso's letter to Queen Gerberga. Thietland's text was written at about the same time as Adso's. As Johannes Fried has pointed out, Odo of Cluny was very successful in stirring up anxiety about the impending apocalypse.[11]

In carefully argued work upon shifts in early medieval methods of annual and cyclical computation, Richard Landes has shown how patterns combining biblical text with varying interpretations of Roman and sub-Roman history served both to postpone the medieval learned world's attention upon the actual end of time and to refocus the debate about meaningful dating. For our purposes, the most significant shift occurred in the eighth century when the Carolingian realm abandoned anno mundi dating in favor of the anno Domini method recommended by Bede.[12] This had the advantage of diluting fears of a millennial, possibly apocalyptic, year 6000 anno mundi that, as Landes points out, "could have fallen on any of several dates between 799 and 806."[13] With the restoration just then of the Roman imperial name in the West by means of Charlemagne's coronation, the immediate threat of the Pauline *discessio* and its consequences could be postponed speculatively at least until Christ's own millennial anniversary, sometime around 1000 C.E. (dating from his birth) or 1033 C.E. (dating from his crucifixion).

The cultural success of the postponement exercise can be demonstrated from Notker the Stammerer of St. Gallen's biography of Charlemagne written in the 880s. The text's opening conjoins the neo-Roman emperor's charisma with the historiographical and religious theory of a divinely commissioned final empire, which was designed to preside over Christian society until the end: "He who ordains the fate of kingdoms and the march of the centuries, the all-powerful Disposer of events, having destroyed one extraordinary image, that of the Romans, which had, it is true, feet of iron, or even feet of clay, then raised up, among the Franks, the golden head of a second image, equally remarkable, in the person of the illustrious Charlemagne."[14] The imagery derives from the Book of Daniel.

One effect of adopting anno Domini dating was inevitably to revive millennial speculation in the tenth century, since the year 1000 C.E. was drawing nigh. As Abbot Abbo of Fleury attests in a very well known passage, "When I was a young man I heard a sermon about the End of the world preached before the people in the cathedral of Paris. According to this, as soon as the number of a thousand years was completed, the Antichrist would come and the Last Judgment would follow in a brief time."[15] One of Adso of Montier-en-Der's contributions was to tackle the problem in a more political sense: "The Apostle Paul says that Antichrist will not come into the world unless first comes the falling-away. . . . This time has not yet come, because, though we see the Roman empire destroyed in great part, nevertheless as long as the kings of the Franks who hold the empire by right shall last, the dignity of the Roman empire will not totally perish, because it will endure in its kings."[16] Adso's theory depends to some extent upon the current theory of translatio imperii, or transfer of the empire to the Franks. Crudely stated, the fourth and last of the empires outlined in the Book of Daniel, held in medieval historiography to be that of the Romans, could be transferred by celestial command to other authorities not specifically Roman in origin.[17] So the Frankish Charlemagne, after his coronation as western emperor in 800 C.E., had been entitled emperor "governing the Roman Empire."[18] So, too, the Roman name was similarly adapted in Adso's sense to the kings of the East Franks not long after the Saxon king Otto the Great was crowned emperor in Rome in 962 C.E. But it is clear that Adso had in mind the original line of neo-Roman rulers of the Franks, the Carolingians still ruling in West Francia in the tenth century.

Adso's ideas were nevertheless convertible currency. In her Gesta Ottonis, the Saxon nun Hroswitha of Gandersheim explained how "the King of kings, who alone reigns forever, by His own power changing the fortunes of all kings, decreed that the distinguished realm of the Franks be transferred to the famous race of the Saxons,"[19] another move in the great game of translatio imperii. In 966 the imperial chancery itself combined the correct signals by entitling the new emperor "August Emperor of the Romans and the Franks."[20] Like Adso, Hroswitha knew that a Roman imperium should include authority over several nations: Otto I, as "mighty sovereign of the empire of the Caesars," surpassed all previous emperors, and "many nations dwelling far and wide reverence thee."[21]

It may sound as though these tenth-century sources were gradually converging toward a consensus that the translatio to the Franks and the Saxons would postpone the dreaded Pauline discessio outlined in 2 Thessalonians more or less indefinitely. But scholars today such as Daniel Verhelst, Johannes Fried, and Kevin Hughes have pointed out that behind the conservative structure of Adso's text, the whole question of the end of time was perilously politicized by tying it so closely to the fortunes of Frankish rule, either in its western (or "French") guise or in the neo-Roman imperial mode after 962.[22] In other words, this was the last possible translatio of all, and should the Frankish political experiments falter or fail, then the discessio was inevitable and Antichrist would arrive to do his worst. It is significant that texts of the oracles of the Tiburtine Sibyl, which go back to the fourth century and contain explicit, detailed, and frightening prophecies about the reign of Antichrist, were being reedited and circulated in the tenth century.[23] The story in the oracles is similar to Adso's account of the reign of Antichrist.

In his edition of Adso of Montier-en-Der's *De ortu et tempore Antichristi*, Daniel Verhelst has addressed questions of the diffusion of such eschatological knowledge in the tenth century. Adso's colleague Gerbert of Aurillac not only understood his exposition on the *discessio* of 2 Thessalonians 2 but also used it to effect in 991 at the Council of St. Basle de Verzy when the French clergy impeached Archbishop Arnulf of Reims for his improper elevation to the see.[24] In order to attack papal authority, which was supporting the archbishop, Gerbert drafted Bishop Arnulf of Orléans's speech in which he stated that Rome's feeble papal rule permitted the Pauline *discessio* "not only of peoples but also of churches."[25] Gerbert accurately cited the sees of Alexandria, Antioch, Constantinople, and those in Muslim Spain as having been lost to the Roman obedience. Obviously, all this is quite unfair to the papacy, which had never been in a position to oppose in any realistic sense the advance of the Islamic caliphates or the Byzantine patriarchate. To sharpen the point, some of the bishop of Orléans's words chosen for him by Gerbert are actually a free rendering from the crucial *discessio* passage (Vulg. 2 Thess. 2:7): "*Iam misterium iniquitatis operatur, tantum, ut qui nunc tenet, teneat donec de medio fiat, ut ille perditionis filius reveletur.*"[26] According to Carl Erdmann,[27] Gerbert must have changed his mind about the current *discessio* that had induced him in 991 to the sensational proclamation that "Antichrist seems to be at hand."[28] This was a useful insult against the Roman See, which was supporting Arnulf of Reims, but once the papacy was itself reformed by Otto III's installation of Gregory V in 996 and of Gerbert himself as Sylvester II in 999 as popes, then the significance of the *discessio* and the purpose of reversing it became much more apparent. As pope, Gerbert appears to have stuck to his interpretation of *discessio* voiced in 991— "not only of peoples but also of churches"—which was broader than Adso's concept of a political and national *discessio* from the Roman Empire. Although the evidence is opaque, Gerbert is often credited in modern historiography with the conception of a reform program that was preventive in style, to include the Apostolic City and See of St. Peter (scene of so many instructive martyrdoms), the Catholic church as a whole, the Ottonian Empire with its diverse *gentes* (peoples), and accessible pagan peoples ripe for conversion within one *renovatio imperii Romanorum*, "the renewal of the Empire of the Romans." Erdmann showed how Gerbert was already familiar with the idea of equating the Christian church as a universal community with the ecumenical pretensions of imperial rule into one *imperium christianum*, and the concept can be found in Adso as well.[29] It has antecedents in what Alcuin of York told Charlemagne in a memorandum of 798, just on the eve of the *translatio* of the Roman Empire to the Franks: that the realm committed by God to the Frankish king and his sons to govern was the *imperium christianum*.[30]

Whatever the nuances of Gerbert's thought as detected by Erdmann, modern scholarship has voiced quite varied opinions as to how far Gerbert was truly responsible for his pupil Otto III's sponsorship of Roman renewal under papal and imperial aegis, confirmed by the adoption of the imperial seal legend (by April 998) of *renovatio imperii Romanorum* with a portrait of Charlemagne himself.[31] Johannes Fried has demonstrated that Otto III was also surrounded by apocalyptic imagery.[32] Certain clauses of diplomas that may have been dictated by the emperor in person show an awareness of eschatological teaching in their references to the Last Judgment, when Christ would return to punish the world with fire.[33] It is significant that Otto III's counselor and chancellor from 994, Heribert, who was archbishop of Cologne from 999 to 1021, possessed a version of Adso's *De ortu et tempore Antichristi* prepared for him by the monk Albuin of Gorze.[34] It is often held that the Heribert referred to in a royal diploma of 992 as "my dearest teacher and chaplain" was this Heribert, but in 1966 Josef Fleckenstein pointed out that the evidence is quite unsafe.[35] It is also probable that Albuin's version of Adso's text entered Heribert's library after his return to Germany as Cologne's pastor. But this need not render impossible Heribert's knowledge, like Gerbert's, of Adso's eschatological theories during the 990s, when they had their formative didactic influence upon the young emperor.

Leaving aside for the time being the question of the eschatological influence of Otto's counselors upon his mentality, what Gerbert may well have done for his pupil is to have broadened the scope of *renovatio* to include every Christian endeavor appropriate to conserving the Roman name against the threat of *discessio*, enterprises solidly demonstrable from Gerbert's writings. For example, he hinted at ideal emperorship by praising Otto for uniting the learning of Greece and Rome, celebrating the ruler's potential for restoring Rome's universal light made so illustrious in the life and works of Boethius.[36] In other words, the torch of the Last Roman is proffered to the new imperial Wunderkind. In the dedication to the emperor of his treatise *Libellus de rationali et ratione uti*, Gerbert showed how the Roman Empire ought to be considered the same as the realm of the Ottonians, even being improved for including peoples, notably the Slavs, not to be found under Roman rule in antiquity: "Ours, ours is the Roman Empire. Italy, rich of fruits, Gaul and Germany, teeming with fighting men, and even the mighty kingdoms of Scythia [i.e., the Slav lands] impart to us their strength."[37] It is often noted how this passage is extremely reminiscent of the contemporary illustration in the Gospel Book of Otto III that shows the emperor receiving tribute from Italy, Gaul, Germany, and the Slav territories.[38]

The ambitious scope of what was to be restored in the imperial *renovatio* seems to have taken some of Otto III's contemporaries by surprise. Bishop Thietmar of Merseburg complained that "in his desire to renew in his own time the old customs of Rome now mostly defunct, the emperor did many things which were understood in very different ways."[39] The passage is itself an important testimony to widespread knowledge of the *renovatio* in an era of constipated communications. Although the bishop cites a rather trivial example—Otto's adoption of the imperial custom of dining alone at a table set above the others—the "many things" about which we do possess information fit a pattern for reversing the eschatological dangers of a *discessio* from the Roman name as discerned by Gerbert since 991 at least.

These "many things" and their significance were discussed exhaustively by Percy Ernst Schramm in his *Kaiser, Rom und Renovatio*, first published in 1929, and by subsequent historians of the Ottonian thought-world: the emperor's insistence upon residing in Rome; his journey as *servus Jesu Christi*, servant of

Jesus Christ, to extend the authority of the Roman church to Poland; plans and measures for the conversion of Hungary, Scandinavia, and Russia to Roman obedience; and the cult of Charlemagne, the emperor whose restoration of the Roman imperial name in the West in 800 C.E. had allayed suspicions of an imminent advent of Antichrist after six thousand years of human history. In other words, Otto III's "many things" were rational acts of Christ's terrestrial deputy, and it is in this image, in a semidivine Parousia, that the emperor is so startlingly portrayed in Liuthar's Gospel Book presented to the ruler.[40] As Karl Leyser wrote of this:

> The exaltation of the king came to entail ever greater expectations of righteousness and imposed gigantic duties. In the imperial Gospel Book at Aachen, Otto III appears crowned by the hand of God and seated in a mandorla normally reserved for the enthroned Christ. The Gospels, which in the form of a scroll he seems at once to receive and to dispense, represented a form of divine investiture. Nowhere is Christocentric kingship depicted so uncompromisingly as in this painting.[41]

In the eschatologically charged circumstance of the chronological approach to 1000 C.E., it is probable that the example of Charlemagne appealed strongly to the *sapientia* of Otto III testified by Gerbert of Aurillac. Just as Charlemagne's imperial coronation in 800 C.E. had supposedly postponed the threat of the Pauline *discessio*, so the "many things" planned or carried out by Otto III were designed to avert it once more. Bishop Leo of Vercelli, an enthusiast for the *renovatio*,[42] explained that Otto III was, "according to the will of Jesus Christ, August Emperor of the Romans and most devout augmentor, *dilatator*, of holy churches."[43] As Schramm pointed out, it is likely that the bishop relied upon Augustine's *De civitate Dei* (5.24), which states that the ultimate felicity and success that can ever be attained by a Christian emperor is the expansion, as *dilatator*, of the church.[44] The point to make here is that one of Otto III's "gigantic duties," *dilatatio* of the Roman name, provoked a courageous attitude to the dangers of *l'an mil*. Church and empire were entrusted to pope and emperor for reform and renewal, as Leo of Vercelli indicated in the preamble of an imperial grant to his own bishopric: "so that the church of God may always be free and secure, our empire may prosper, our Crown and its warriors may triumph, the power of the Roman people may be spread far and wide, and its republic may be restored."[45] Another example of reform in such a sense concerns right order in Christian society as understood by the ruling elites. By means of a capitulary likely to have been issued at Pavia in 998,[46] Otto III and his advisers endeavored to repress all serfs back into their proper hereditary servitude to their lords, against the social mobility apparent in the Lombardy of their day.

Before turning to the final crisis of Otto III's reign, with its explicit apocalyptic resonance, we need to examine an extremely significant aspect of Roman *dilatatio* that contrasts completely with the ecclesiastical *discessio* that had been discerned by Gerbert of Aurillac in 991. This consists of the missionary activity of Otto III's contemporaries, especially of two men well known to the emperor, the

Czech Adalbert of Prague and the Saxon Brun of Querfurt.[47] News of the martyr-dom of Bishop Adalbert during a mission to the Prussians in 997 was clearly a decisive influence upon Otto III's conception of his religious mission as protec-tor of the church by means of the imperial office granted to him by God. It partly inspired the emperor's famous journey to Poland in 1000 C.E. to collect the relics of the martyr and to preside over the establishment of the new archbishopric of Gniezno awarded to Adalbert's half brother as the first incumbent.

This is the best-documented event illustrating one purpose of the *renovatio imperii Romanorum*, the conversion of the pagans. It united the idea of the ever-lasting *pax Romana* and the salvatory New Law of Christ with the ingathering of the nations to the Lord's Tabernacle as adumbrated in certain passages of Scripture such as Isa. 2:2–4, 25:6–12, and 66:18–24. As Ps. 86:9, cited in Apoc. 15:4, expressed it: "All nations whom thou hast made shall come and worship before thee, O Lord; and shall glorify thy name." In cultural terms, the rulers of the Poles and Hungarians were ready to receive some of the aims of the *renovatio*. The Polish leader Boleslav I Chrobry and the Hungarian prince Vjak, baptized as King Stephen I, became associates of the Ottonian dynasty. Boleslav Chrobry was proclaimed Otto III's *amicus et socius* (friend and ally), and accompanied the emperor from Gniezno to Aachen, where the relics of Charlemagne were honored. By 996 Vjak had married Otto III's cousin Gisela, sister of Duke Henry of Bavaria, who succeeded Otto as King Henry II in 1002.

Other missions undertaken at this time proved much more arduous: to the Magyar Széklers in what is now Rumania, to the Slav Liutizi east of the Elbe, to the Prussians on the Baltic, and to the Pechenegs on the steppes south of Kiev. It is known that an interest was taken in the conversion of Scandinavia, and Brun of Querfurt actually sent a missionary bishop to Sweden. Pope Sylvester II wrote to the rulers recently converted to Christianity: King Olaf Tryggvason of Nor-way, Prince Vladimir of Kiev, Prince Boleslav of Poland, and King Stephen of Hungary.[48]

Ekkehard Eickhoff has steered the various arguments about the political and religious inspiration for these missions in northern and eastern Europe back to regarding them as Rome directed and functionally connected with Otto III's patronage of the Basilian monastic movements, an interest he inherited from his parents.[49] Both Adalbert of Prague and Brun of Querfurt spent time as Basilian monks in Otto's favorite Roman monastery, SS. Alexius and Boniface,[50] and another Basilian, Gregory of Cassano, had already been appointed Otto III's confessor and first abbot of Burtscheid, just outside Aachen, by the ruler's mother, Empress Theophanu.[51] Yet the sources are not really explicit enough to allow us to regard the new missions as the politico-religious department of the *renovatio*. As the career of Brun of Querfurt reveals, the missionaries could pursue their aims without direct support from the court. But it was clearly in the spirit of Otto III's *renovatio* that Sylvester II conferred the pallium of a mis-sionary archbishop upon Brun in the fall of 1002, a few months after Otto's death. Unusually, the commission was not tied to a specific cathedral town. Brun was entitled "archbishop of St. Adalbert" in reference to Otto III's inspiration for an invigorated missionizing program in eastern Europe. The actual consecration took place, conventionally enough, at King Henry II's court in 1004. The Prussians martyred Brun in 1009.

The careers of Adalbert of Prague as missionary, Otto III as sponsor of *renovatio*, Sylvester II as pope, and Brun of Querfurt as roving archbishop are representations of the upsurge in Christian *dilatatio* perceived toward the end of the tenth century. It is recorded as the conversion of pagan peoples to the soteriological and eschatological faith of Christ: the Russians, the Icelanders, the Norwegians, the Poles, and the Magyars. Only Russia eluded the Roman rite in favor of Constantinople's ecclesiastical supremacy, but the papal and imperial courts in the West still hoped to recruit Russia to Roman obedience and sent ambassadors for the purpose. It is not known if pope and emperor knew of the conversion of Iceland in 999 or 1000.[52] An Icelandic source written down much later, the sibylline *Völuspà*, is held by some scholars to date from the conversion years, as a literary conflation of pagan and Christian ideas explicitly concerned with the eschatological punishment of the world for its wickedness.[53] If it really did originate at this time, then it is a fine testimony to the eschatological zeitgeist of the approaching millennium experienced from Rome to the farmhouses of Iceland.

In his well-known diploma rejecting the Donation of Constantine, not exactly as a forgery but as a document irrelevant to his own rights,[54] Otto III proclaimed Rome to be "the capital of the world, and we assert that the Roman church is the mother of all churches." Knut Görich has returned to the question of exact meaning in Otto III's *renovatio*,[55] but it is obvious that the city was, in some sense, axiomatic to the emperor's concept of *renovatio*. It is not so clear what the Roman nobles, clergy, and people thought of the ideals of the *renovatio*, with its ecclesiastical, imperial, and eschatological dimensions. After all, the pope was from West Francia, the emperor was a Saxon, his chancellor was from Lotharingia, and the Basilians were chiefly Greek. Rome was developing a popular tradition of riots against outsiders, and to this Otto III and Sylvester II fell victim early in 1001. Pope and emperor were expelled from the city, and the current *dilatatio* of the Roman name was brought to an abrupt conclusion.

According to a famous passage in Thangmar's *vita* of Bishop Bernward of Hildesheim, who was visiting the emperor at the time, Otto III did have the opportunity to harangue the Romans about how cruel it was to be rejected by those whom he had most cherished, and for serious purposes: "I led you into remote parts of my empire in which your fathers, when they ruled the world, never set foot [probably referring to Roman clergy who accompanied him to Poland], that I might spread your name and glory to the ends of the earth."[56] Here is the theory of Roman *dilatatio* expressed with a vengeance, and according to Thangmar, the emperor in his speech, whatever dialect he may actually have been speaking, used the equivalent of the very verb *dilatare* for "to spread." But Rome itself now primed the time bomb of *discessio*, which Otto III himself was tempted to ignite in revenge.

Outraged by his rejection by the Romans, Otto III temporarily reconsidered his role as Roman emperor in Christian salvation history by abandoning the *renovatio* and contemplating a possibly apocalyptic scenario. Brun of Querfurt, who was in Italy at the time, reports how the emperor retired to Ravenna to consult the eremitical reformer Romuald.[57] After heart-searching and penances, Otto came to the following conclusion: "From this hour I promise to God and his saints: after three years, within which I will correct the mistakes of my imperial rule, I will give up the realm to someone better than I am and, giving away the money that my mother left to me as an inheritance, will follow Christ in destitution, and with all my soul." The text suggests that the emperor proposed to found a monastery in St. Adalbert's countryside, that is, in Sclavinia "on Christian ground upon the border with the pagans," a project with obvious missionary intent.

But Romuald, as rigorous with his disciples as any Zen master, disapproved of the three-year interim as perilous to the soul and body. The hermit correctly prophesied that if Otto III undertook a proposed campaign of revenge against the rebellious Romans, then he would die within the year. Under such pressure, the emperor appears to have modified his intentions. Brun's record quotes further discussion among Romuald's disciples to the effect that Otto III decided to renounce the empire, to travel to Jerusalem, and to disappear as a monk into an unknown hermitage.

This extraordinary scenario surely reflects another lesson from Gerbert's and Heribert's understanding of Adso's ideas. Do not Adso's words foreshadow Otto's intentions because the emperor had heard of similar things from his teachers?

> Some of our learned men say that one of the kings of the Franks
> who will come in the last time will possess anew the Roman Empire.
> He will come at the last time and will be the last and the greatest of
> all rulers. After he has successfully governed his empire, at last he
> will come to Jerusalem and will put off his scepter and crown on the
> Mount of Olives. This will be the end and the consummation of the
> Roman and Christian empire. Immediately, according to the opinion
> of Paul mentioned above, they say that the Antichrist will be at
> hand.[58]

In order to set his house in order first, Otto III planned to restore his own and the pope's rightful authority by a military assault upon Rome, but death overtook him in January 1002. In any case, it seems unlikely that the apocalyptic theme in his mind during his visit to Ravenna would have survived a restored program of *renovatio* directed from reoccupied Rome. After all, the successful negotiations confirming ecclesiastical organization and a Christian kingdom in Hungary, a profitable exercise in Roman religious *dilatatio* if ever there was one, had already taken place from Ravenna. The emperor had also taken advantage of his proximity to Venice to visit the republic and to renew its alliance with his empire.[59] Upon the emperor's death, the program of *renovatio* had to be abandoned for the time being, although Sylvester II did write back to the doge of Venice and to the patriarch of Grado about reforming the church in their territories.[60]

The functions of the *renovatio* and the *dilatatio* of the Roman name as preventive measures against some Pauline *discessio*, Antichrist's advent, and an imminent apocalypse in the uncertain years round about the millennial anniversary were well understood in the educated milieu of the time. Bishop Thietmar of Merseburg mirrored Adso's exposition almost exactly. We hear that when the Saxon frontier was again threatened in 1018 by military operations of the Slavs who were in theory subjects of the Roman Empire, the bishop warned his readers that this *discessio* was precisely not the signal for the arrival of Antichrist and the Day of Judgment forecast by St. Paul.[61] Thietmar had regretted the loss of Otto III and so had Brun of Querfurt, who, in spite of some criticisms, had praised the dead emperor as "father of monks, mother of bishops, son of humility and mercy."[62] Thietmar called upon the God of the Apocalypse, Alpha and Omega, the Lord as creator and judge in the Book of Revelation, to be merciful to the young emperor's soul. But it is obvious that the bishop was relieved that 1000 C.E. was safely in the past, praising the piety and good sense of the new East Frankish ruler Henry II. Adapting some words from Persius's Third Satire, he hailed the reign as a bright new day for the world.[63]

It is remarkable how churchmen such as Adso of Montier-en-Der and Thietland of Einsiedeln (writing ca. 950), Gerbert of Aurillac (writing in 991), and Thietmar of Merseburg (writing in 1018) can be shown to have shared convergent approaches to the eschatological Pauline text at 2 Thess. 2:1–12. It is sometimes thought that the more cautiously expressed views of Abbo of Fleury were out of step because he opposed "with what force I could" the belief that "as soon as the number of a thousand years was completed, the Antichrist would come and the Last Judgement would follow in a brief time."[64] But Abbo was a skilled theologian who knew very well that the Last Judgment was on the agenda. He is asking for a properly Augustinian deference to such texts from Scripture as Matt. 24:35–36 and Mark 13:31–32: "Heaven and earth shall pass away, but my words shall not pass away. But of that day and hour knoweth no man, no, not the angels of heaven, but my Father only." Abbo's approach combines the eschatological imagination with a distaste for chiliasm, an attitude translated into politics at the court of Otto III and Sylvester II.

In their similar eschatological attitude, Adso, Gerbert, and Thietmar held that the Roman name and Roman authority, imperial and ecclesiastical, stood for postponing the Last Days outlined by St. Paul in 2 Thessalonians 2. Adso and Thietmar even employed the same turns of phrase in their texts: "Romanum imperium ex maxima parte destructum" (the Roman Empire demolished for the greatest part), and "Romanorum consuetudinem iam ex parte magna deletam" (Roman custom for the great part destroyed).[65] But now the reigns of the Frankish and Saxon rulers, adorned since 800 C.E. with the neo-Roman imperial title, delayed the *discessio*, the Antichrist's advent, and the apocalypse because, as Christ's vicar and terrestrial image, an emperor was cosmic lord with latitude for maneuver in Christendom's salvation history. In Otto III's case, we know that at his imperial coronation in 996, he wore a mantle adorned with a representation of the apocalypse, and some idea of its appearance can surely be gathered by comparison with Henry II's robe, preserved in the treasury of Bamberg cathedral, which depicts the solar system and the constellations.[66] Thietmar of Merseburg thought of Henry II as a preserver of the Roman name in a favorable light but did warn his readers: "No one should question the coming of the Last Day or wish for its swift arrival either, because it is to be feared by the just, and much more so by those worthy of punishment."[67]

About 1030, the Hildesheim annalist recorded: "Millesimus exsuperat et transcendit omnia annus" (the thousandth year surpasses and transcends all others),[68] referring explicitly to the activities of Otto III's reign, when it had passed. But the problem remained that another potentially apocalyptic date was fast approaching, 1033 C.E. or thereabouts, as the millennial anniversary of Christ's Passion. In his *Histories*, the Burgundian monk Radulfus Glaber threw his audience into a new anxiety by suggesting that the western emperor of the time, Conrad II (1024–39), had achieved his authority over the Roman Empire with demonic assistance: "Know that it was by my (Satan's) aid and help that Conrad was recently created emperor. You know very well that no emperor has been able so quickly to subjugate to his rule the whole of Germany and Italy."[69] This peculiar opinion did not achieve widespread acceptance. In the very year 1033, the imperial chancery proclaimed the opposite: "And now by God's grace our imperial power is established and strengthened more and more in the realm."[70]

Satan's emissary the Antichrist may have been awaiting an eschatological opportunity through the criminality of Conrad II, but the majority view in the surviving sources indicates that the western Roman Empire was on course for another *renovatio* under an emperor whose biographer Wipo compared more than once to Charlemagne.[71] Adopting a new seal legend, ROMA CAPVT MVNDI REGIT ORBIS FRENA ROTVNDI, a truly universal claim upon cosmic authority inherited from the Caesars, Conrad II's *renovatio* seems to us somewhat less religious in tone than Otto III's, concerning, for example, the practical extension of Roman law.[72] Like Otto III, Conrad II had difficulty in keeping the Romans under control and once asserted with some irritation, "If Italy hungers for law, then, God willing, we shall satiate her well enough with laws."[73]

Conrad II's seal legend as a historical statement within imperial and ecclesiastical politics resembles Otto III's regard for Rome and is similarly tinged with eschatological intent: "To make a historical statement is to make an eschatological one, because historical events and patterns in the Middle Ages are always understood within the larger philosophy of Christian history that sees history as essentially teleological, to be judged by its ending, from the perspective of eschatology."[74] Papacy, Roman *imperium*, and the city of Rome were perpetual guardians of Christian order, their roles divinely commissioned to last until the eschatological consummation of human history at the Last Judgment.

I hope to have demonstrated that the explicitly eschatological, even apocalyptic, imagination at work in the imperial court around the year 1000 C.E. was very close to this "perspective of eschatology" as reflected in the works of authors such as Adso of Montier-en-Der, Gerbert of Aurillac, and Thietmar of Merseburg. Such churchmen were speculating within a very long eschatological tradition that was to have an enormous developmental future in Latin Christian culture and theology. Between 950 and 1050, eschatological imagination, as well as the deeds of Otto III at a particular time, had renewed influence in reestablishing Antichrist as a realistic figure to be feared and expected by the Church Militant;[75] in advertising the role of the western Roman emperors in delaying the historically awaited *discessio* from Rome supposedly prophesied by St. Paul in 2 Thessalonians; and in promoting the ideals of a reformed papacy as experienced under Gregory V, Sylvester II, and Benedict VIII as a foretaste of the great days to be inaugurated in 1046, in its guardianship of the moral health of Christian society,[76] another antidote within the scheme of salvation history to the dreaded reign of Antichrist.

NOTES

Editors' note: This paper was presented at the "Conference on the Apocalyptic Year 1000," Boston, Mass., November 4–6, 1996. Benjamin Arnold is Professor of Medieval History at the Universtiy of Reading.

1. On the subject see Nikolaus Wicki, Bernard McGinn, and Gerhard Podskalsy, "Eschatologie: Lateinisches Mittelalter, Ostkirche/byzantinischer Bereich," in *Lexikon des Mittelalters*, ed. Robert-Henri Bautier et al., vol. 4 (Munich and Zurich, 1989), pp. 4–10; Richard Landes, "*Millenarismus absconditus*: L'historiographie augustinienne et le millénarisme du haut Moyen Age jusqu'à l'an mil," *Le Moyen Age* 98 (1992): 355–77.

2. John Sweet, "Revelation, The Book of," in *The Oxford Companion to the Bible*, ed. Bruce Metzger and Michael Coogan (New York and Oxford, 1993), pp. 651–54.

3. Henry Bettenson, trans., *Augustine: Concerning the City of God against the Pagans* (Harmondsworth, 1972), p. 963.

4. Richard Landes, "Lest the Millennium be Fulfilled: Apocalyptic Expectations and the Pattern of Western Chronography, 100–800 C.E.," in *The Use and Abuse of Eschatology in the Middle Ages*, ed. Werner Verbeke, Daniel Verhelst, and Andries Welkenhuysen (Leuven, 1988), pp. 205–8, explains the distinctions needed in defining eschatology, apocalypticism, millenarianism, and apocalyptic millenarianism. See also Robert Lerner, "The Medieval Return to the Thousand-Year Sabbath," in *The Apocalypse in the Middle Ages*, ed. Richard Emmerson and Bernard McGinn (Ithaca and London, 1992), pp. 51–71.

5. Richard Emmerson and Ronald Herzman, *The Apocalyptic Imagination in Medieval Literature* (Philadelphia, 1992), p. 3.

6. Robert Lerner, "Refreshment of the Saints: The Time after Antichrist as a Station for Earthly Progress in Medieval Thought," *Traditio* 32 (1976): 97–144; Guy Lobrichon, "Conserver, réformer, transformer le monde? Les manipulations de l'Apocalypse au Moyen Age central," in *The Role of the Book in Medieval Culture*, ed. Peter Ganz, vol. 2 (Turnhout, 1986), pp. 75–94; E. Ann Matter, "The Apocalypse in Early Medieval Exegesis," in *Apocalypse*, ed. Emmerson and McGinn, pp. 3–50.

7. *Adso Dervensis: De ortu et tempore Antichristi necnon et tractatus qui ab eo dependunt*, ed. Daniel Verhelst, *CCCM* 45 (Turnhout, 1976), pp. 20–30.

8. Sweet, "Antichrist," in *Oxford Companion to the Bible*, ed. Metzer and Coogan, pp. 30–32.

9. Adso, *De ortu* (*CCCM* 45:26); translated in Bernard McGinn, *Visions of the End: Apocalyptic Traditions in the Middle Ages* (New York, 1979), p. 86.

10. See chap. 4 in this volume.

11. Johannes Fried, "Endzeiterwartung um die Jahrtausendwende," *Deutsches Archiv für Erforschung der Mittelalters* 45, no. 2 (1989): 414; see also chap. 1 in this volume.

12. Landes, "Lest the Millenium Be Fulfilled," pp. 174–303; and R. Landes, "Sur les traces du Millennium: La 'Via Negativa,'" *Le Moyen Age* 99 (1993): 7–26.

13. Landes, "Lest the Millenium Be Fulfilled," p. 196.

14. Lewis Thorpe, trans., *Einhard and Notker the Stammerer: Two Lives of Charlemagne* (Harmondsworth, 1969), p. 93.

15. McGinn, *Visions*, p. 89.

16. Ibid., p. 86. See Gian Andri Bezzola, *Das Ottonische Kaisertum in der französischen Geschichtsschreibung des 10. und beginnenden 11. Jahrhunderts*, Veröffentlichungen des Instituts für Österreichische Geschichtsforschung, vol. 18, ed. Leo Santifaller (Graz and Cologne, 1956), pp. 55–64, on which rulers Adso may have had in mind.

17. See Werner Goez, *Translatio Imperii: Ein Beitrag zur Geschichte des Geschichtsdenkens und der politischen Theorien im Mittelalter und in der frühen Neuzeit* (Tübingen, 1958), pp. 74–104.

18. Engelbert Mühlbacher, ed., *Die Urkunden der Karolinger*, 2d ed., *MGH, Diplomatum Karolinovum* (Berlin, 1956), 1 from no. 197 (801) to no. 218 (813).

19. Quoted in Boyd Hill Jr., ed., *Medieval Monarchy in Action: The German Empire from Henry I to Henry IV*, Historical Problems: Studies and Documents, vol. 15, ed. G. R. Elton (London and New York, 1972), p. 121.

20. Theodor Sickel, ed., *Die Urkunden Konrad I. Heinrich I. und Otto I.*, 2d ed., *MGH, Diplomatum Regum et Imperatorum Germaniae* (Berlin, 1956), 1 from no. 318 to no. 329 (966).

21. Hill, *Medieval Monarchy*, p. 119.

22. See, e.g., chaps. 1 and 3 in this volume.

23. McGinn, *Visions*, pp. 43–50, 294–97.

24. Adso, *De ortu*, VII–VIII.

25. *Gerberti acta concilii Remensis*, ed. Georg Waitz, *MGH, SS* 3:676: "Fit ergo discessio secundum apostolum, non solummodo gentium, sed etiam ecclesiarum"; see Percy Ernst Schramm, *Kaiser, Rom und Renovatio: Studien zur Geschichte des romischen Erneuerungsgedankens vom Ende des karolingischen Reiches bis zum Investiturstreit*, 3d ed. (Darmstadt, 1975), p. 123; Karl Ferdinand Werner, "Arnulf, Bischof von Orleans," and "Arnulf, Erzbischof von Reims," in *Lexikon des Mittelalters*, 1:1019–20.

26. *Gerbertis acta* (*MGH, SS* 3:676).

27. Carl Erdmann, "Das ottonische Reich als Imperium Romanum," *Deutsches Archiv für Erforschung des Mittelalters* 6 (1943): 412–41, reprinted in his *Ottonische Studien*, ed. Helmut Beumann (Darmstadt, 1968), pp. 174–203, which edition I cite here. See esp. pp. 192–95.

28. *Gerberti acta* (*MGH, SS* 3:676): "Antichristus instare videtur."

29. Erdmann, "Das ottonische Reich," pp. 193–94; and Adso, *De ortu* (*CCCM* 45:26).

30. Ernst Dümmler, ed., *Epistolae Karolini Aevi*, vol. 2 (*MGH, Ep.* 4), no. 148.

31. Tilman Struve, "Otto III, Kaiser, deutscher König," in *Lexikon des Mittelalters*, 6:1568–70; Schramm, *Kaiser*, pp. 116–33; Bezzola, *Ottonische Kaisertum*, pp. 65–104; Mathilde Uhlirz, "Das Werden des Gedankens 'Renovatio Imperii Romanorum' bei Otto III," in *I problemi comuni dell'Europa post-carolingia*, Settimane di Studio del Centro Italiano di studi sull'alto medioevo, vol. 2 (Spoleto, 1955), pp. 201–19; Johannes Fried, *Der Weg in die Geschichte: Die Ursprünge Deutschlands bis 1024*, Propyläen Geschichte Deutschlands, vol. 1 (Berlin, 1994), pp. 582–602.

32. Fried, "Endzeiterwartung," pp. 428–32.

33. *Die Urkunden Otto des III.*, 2d ed., *MGH, Diplomatum* (Berlin, 1957), 2/2, no. 331 (999) for Farfa Abbey; no. 347 (1000) for the imperial chapel at Aachen. See Hartmut Hoffmann, "Eigendiktat in den Urkunden Ottos III. und Heinrichs II.," *Deutsches Archiv für Erforschung des Mittelalters* 44 (1988): 398–99.

34. Fried, "Endzeiterwartung," p. 430; Adso, *De ortu* (*CCCM* 45:55–74).

35. Josef Fleckenstein, *Die Hofkapelle der deutschen Könige, MGH, Schriften* 16 (Stuttgart, 1966), no. 2, p. 80.

36. Fritz Weigle, ed., *Die Briefsammlung Gerberts von Reims, MGH, Die Briefe der deutschen Kaiserzeit* 2 (Berlin, Zurich, and Dublin, 1966), pp. 223–25 (no. 187); Karl Strecker, ed., *Die lateinischen Dichter des deutschen Mittelalters, MGH, Poetarum latinorum medii aevi* 5 (Dublin and Zurich, 1970), pp. 474–75.

37. Francis Tschan, *Saint Bernward of Hildesheim: His Life and Times*, rev. ed. (Notre Dame, 1950), p. 105.

38. Henry Mayr-Harting, *Ottonian Book Illumination: An Historical Study*, pt. 1, *Themes* (London and New York, 1991), p. 159 and pl. XX. See pp. 157–77 for the Gospel Book's relation to the *renovatio*. See also chap. 11 in this volume.

39. Werner Trillmich, ed., *Thietmar von Merseburg: Chronik*, Ausgewählte Quellen zur deutschen Geschichte des Mittelalters, vol. 9 (Darmstadt, 1974), pp. 162–64 (Book 4, chap. 47).

40. Mayr-Harting, *Book Illumination*, p. 59. On this image and its implications, see Johannes Fried, *Otto III. und Boleslaw Chrobry: Das Widmungsbild des Aachener Evangeliars, der 'Akt von Gnesen' und das frühe polnische und ungarische Königtum*, Frankfurter Historische Abhandlungen, vol. 30 (Stuttgart, 1989).

41. Karl Leyser, *Rule and Conflict in an Early Medieval Society: Ottonian Saxony* (London, 1979), p. 78.

42. Schramm, *Kaiser*, pp. 119–31; see Roland Pauler, *Das Regnum Italiae in ottonischer Zeit: Markgrafen, Grafen und Bischofe als politische Kräfte*, Bibliothek des Deutschen Historischen Instituts in Rom, vol. 54 (Tubingen, 1982), pp. 33–45.

43. *Die Urkunden Ottos III., MGH*, no. 324 (999); translated in Mayr-Harting, *Book Illumination*, 2:50.

44. Schramm, *Kaiser*, pp. 119–31.

45. *Die Urkunden Ottos III.*, no. 388 (1001).

46. *Constitutiones et acta publica, MGH* 1, no. 21; see Giovanni Tabacco, *The Struggle for Power in Medieval Italy: Structures of Political Rule*, trans. Rosalind Brown Jensen (Cambridge and New York, 1989), pp. 199–201.

47. G. Labuda, "Adalbert Vojtecht," in *Lexikon des Mittelalters*, 1:101–2; and F. Lotter, "Brun von Querfurt," in ibid., 2:755–56; see also Reinhold Wenskus, *Studien zur historisch-politischen Gedankenwelt Bruns von Querfurt*, Mitteldeutsche Forschungen (Münster and Cologne, 1956), p. 5.

48. Harriet Pratt Lattin, *The Letters of Gerbert with His Papal Privileges as Sylvester II* (New York, 1961), p. 60, nos. 12, 22, 25, 34.

49. Ekkehard Eickhoff, "Basilianer und Ottonen," *Historisches Jahrbuch* 114 (1994): 10–46.

50. Bernard Hamilton, "The Monastery of S. Alessio and the Religious and Intellectual Renaissance of Tenth-Century Rome," in his *Monastic Reform, Catharism and the Crusades, 900–1300*, Variorum Reprints: Collected Studies (London, 1979), p. 97, pt. III.

51. Eickhoff, "Basilianer," p. 35.

52. On which Margaret Cormack gave a talk at the 1996 Boston "Conference on the Apocalyptic Year 1000."

53. Jònas Kristjánsson, *Eddas and Sagas: Iceland's Medieval Literature*, trans. Peter Foote (Reykjavík, 1988), pp. 40–44; on the conversion period, see Jesse L. Byock, *Medieval Iceland: Society, Sagas, and Poetry* (Enfield Lock, 1993), pp. 138–43.

54. *Die Urkunden Ottos III.*, no. 389 (1001); see Horst Furhmann, "Konstantinische Schenkung und abendländisches Kaisertum: Ein Beitrag zur Überlieferungsgeschichte des Constitutum Constantini, I und. II," *Deutsches Archiv* 22 (1966): 63–178; and Kurt Zeillinger, "Otto III. und die Konstantinische Schenkung: Ein Beitrag zur Interpretation des Diploms Kaiser Ottos III. für Papst Silvester II.," in *Fälschungen im Mittelalter*, pt. 2, *Gefälschte Rechtstexte: Der bestrafte Fälscher*, MGH, Schriften 33/2 (Hanover, 1988), pp. 509–36.

55. Knut Görich, *Otto III. Romanus Saxonicus et Italicus: Kaiserliche Rompolitik und sächsische Historiographie*, Historische Forschungen, vol. 18 (Sigmaringen, 1993).

56. Tschan, *Bernward*, p. 110.

57. Reinhard Kade, ed., *Brunonis Vita quinque Fratrum*, MGH, SS 12/2:718–21; see Giovanni Tabacco, "Romuald von Camaldoli," in *Lexikon des Mittelalters*, 7:1019–20; and Schramm, *Kaiser*, pp. 179–82. I would like to thank Patricia McNulty for her advice on Brun's text.

58. Adso, *De ortu* (CCCM 45:26); translated in McGinn, *Visions*, p. 86.

59. Wolgang Giese, "Venedig-Politik und Imperiums-Idee bei den Ottonen," in *Herrschaft, Kirche, Kultur: Beiträge zur Geschichte des Mittelalters, Festschrift für Friedrich Prinz*, ed. Georg Jenal, Monographien zur Geschichte des Mittelalters, vol. 37 (Stuttgart, 1993), pp. 219–43.

60. Lattin, *Letters of Gerbert*, pp. 350–52, 384–85.

61. Trillmich, *Thietmar*, p. 446.

62. Kade, *Brunonis Vita quinque Fratrum*, p. 724.

63. Trillmich, *Thietmar*, pp. 166, 242.

64. McGinn, *Visions*, p. 89.

65. Adso, *De ortu* (CCCM 45:26); and Trillmich, *Thietmar*, p. 162. I owe this observation to Professor Richard Landes.

66. *Miraculis S. Alexii*, MGH, SS 4:620; see Renate Baumgärtel-Fleischmann, "Der Sternenmantel Kaiser Heinrichs II. und seine Inschriften," in *Epigraphik 1988*, ed. Walter Koch, Abhandlungen der Österreichischen Akademie der Wissenschaften, Philosophisch-Historische Klasse, vol. 213 (Vienna, 1990), pp. 105–25.

67. Trillmich, *Thietmar*, p. 446.

68. Georg Waitz, ed., *Annales Hildesheimenses*, MGH Schol., 8 (Hanover, 1878 [reprint 1990]), pp. 27–28.

69. John France, ed., *Rodulfus Glaber: The Five Books of the Histories*, Oxford Medieval Texts (Oxford, 1989), pp. 178–79.

70. Harry Bresslau, ed., *Die Urkunden Konrads II.*, 2d ed., MGH, Diplomata 4 (Berlin, 1957), no. 198.

71. Harry Bresslau, ed., *Die Werke Wipos*, 3d ed., MGH, Scriptores Rerum Germanicarum in Usum Scholarum (Hanover, 1915), pp. 20, 28–29; Karl Schmid, "Zum Haus- und Herrschaftsverständnis der Salier," in *Die Salier und das Reich*, vol. 1, *Salier, Adel und Reichsverfassung*, ed.Stefan Weinfurter, (Sigmaringen, 1991), pp. 21–54; Hartmut Hoffmann, *Mönchskönig und "rex idiota": Studien zur Kirchenpolitik Heinrichs II. und Konrads II.*, MGH, Studien und Texte (Hanover, 1993), p. 8.

72. Bresslau, *Die Urkunden Konrads II.*, MGH, p. XXVI and no. 275; Schramm, *Kaiser*, pp. 284–86.

73. Bresslau, *Die Werke Wipos*, p. 54.

74. Emmerson and Herzman, *Apocalyptic Imagination*, p. 101.

75. See Richard Emmerson, "Antichrist as Anti-Saint: The Significance of Abbot Adso's *Libellus de Antichristo*," *American Benedictine Review* 30 (1979): 175–90.

76. Benedict VIII (1012–24) at least raised hopes of reform in conjunction with Henry II; see John Kelly, *The Oxford Dictionary of Popes* (Oxford and New York, 1986), pp. 139–41.

14

"Satan's Bonds Are Extremely Loose": Apocalyptic Expectation in Anglo-Saxon England during the Millennial Era

William Prideaux-Collins

The year 1000 holds a particular place in the historiography of medieval apocalypticism. Romantic historians of the nineteenth century spoke of the "terrors of the year 1000" and painted a lurid portrait of a Europe gripped by widespread panic as the millennium neared. Later scholars, reacting against the obvious exaggerations of this interpretation, dismissed it as a "myth" based upon insufficient evidence. In the opinion of these "anti-Terrors" scholars, the approach of the year 1000 troubled neither the clergy nor the general populace, apart from a handful of fanatics.[1] This counterargument in support of a nonapocalyptic millennium remains the reigning consensus.[2] Like their Continental peers, scholars of Anglo-Saxon England have also proceeded from the premise that an apocalyptic year 1000 was a myth. Although acknowledging the presence of apocalyptic rumblings, scholars have generally argued that most Anglo-Saxons, or at least those of consequence, remained indifferent to the millennium and were disinclined to engage in rash speculation regarding the nearness of doomsday.[3] In their view, virtually all of the upper clergy were strictly orthodox in their interpretation of eschatology and thus were not particularly troubled by apocalyptic fears surrounding the year 1000.[4] As for the lesser clergy and laity, they either shared the indifference of the upper clergy or, alternatively, did, in fact, hold millenarian expectations but their beliefs were of only marginal significance.[5]

Scholars have considered the issue of Anglo-Saxon apocalypticism something of a closed case: the turn of the millennium was not a period of significant apocalyptic anxiety and the year 1000 represented for the Anglo-Saxons an eschatological nonevent. For this reason, the subject has been little studied and even less debated.[6] I believe, however, that the approach with which Anglo-Saxon scholars have analyzed the documents of this era bears reconsideration. Contrary to the prevailing consensus, the documentary evidence suggests that the year 1000 was hardly a banal and eschatologically inert date for the Anglo-Saxons. Rather, I would argue that the years surrounding the millennium witnessed not only heightened apocalyptic anxiety, aroused by a belief in the profound eschatological significance of the year 1000, but also a corresponding interest in biblical prophecy and various chronology-based doomsday prediction schemes.

This picture of late Anglo-Saxon apocalypticism does not, however, readily emerge from our sources. We must recognize that the Anglo-Saxon clergy were not of one mind regarding the apocalypse. In our documents we find the clergy alternating between two distinct, and fundamentally irreconcilable, positions: one argued that by observing prophesied signs and/or recognizing the eschatological significance of chronological dates, it was within the power of men to discern the approach of doomsday. Exemplifying this position, Archbishop Wulfstan II of York claimed that the signs of the Last Days were being presently fulfilled and that the millennium heralded the imminent arrival of Antichrist. The other, more properly orthodox, position forbade speculation concerning the time of doomsday, insisting that "it is not for you to know the times or the seasons which the Father hath put in his power."[7] Unequivocally supporting this position, Byrhtferth of Ramsey opposed all efforts to reckon the date of the apocalypse, particularly by means of chronological schemes. In terms of Anglo-Saxon apocalypticism, Wulfstan and Byrhtferth represent two opposing ends of a spectrum. The eschatological interpretations of other clergy occupied an ambiguous middle ground between these two positions. For example, Aelfric of Eynsham asserted that the world was in its waning days—citing the fulfillment of biblical prophecy as proof—yet, conversely, he elsewhere denounced those who would interpret earthly calamities as signs of the approaching apocalypse.

These conflicting attitudes regarding doomsday reflect a dilemma faced by any clergy in a time of heightened apocalyptic expectation. A debate between Augustine of Hippo and Hesychius, bishop of Salona, in 418–19, provides insight into the nature of this dilemma.[8] In his letter to Augustine, Hesychius argues that "the signs which were given in the Gospel and in prophecy" were, as God intended, comprehensible to mankind and thus would "show forth the coming of the Lord," if not the precise time of his arrival.[9] Armed with this knowledge, Hesychius believed that he had an obligation to proclaim to the faithful the news of Christ's return: "by noticing and believing the existing signs of the coming, it befits me to hope for it and to distribute this food to believers that they may hope for the coming of Him who said: 'When you shall all see these things, know ye that it is nigh, even at the doors.'" Hesychius believed that the signs of the times confirmed that this event was imminent, declaring that "we know that the coming is at hand" because "all the signs which the Gospel describes . . . have in large measure been accomplished."

In his reply, Augustine attacked Hesychius's blatantly apocalyptic contentions by arguing that all men, including the apostles, were completely ignorant concerning the "times and the seasons" of the Second Coming, and he chastised those "who would dare to teach or presume to know what neither God the Master taught the disciples by whom He was questioned face to face, nor the holy great doctors have been able to teach the Church."[10] Augustine then presented a lengthy repudiation of various prediction schemes based on biblical prophecy. In the concluding chapters of his letter, Augustine argued against predicting an imminent Second Coming because, if Christ delays, one "may think that the Lord's coming is not so much delayed as nonexistent."[11] Rather, he councils that the faithful may hope for Christ's swift return but must admit their ignorance and resign themselves to patiently await this event, whenever it may come.

The conflict between orthodox agnosticism and apocalyptic expectation evident in the Augustine-Hesychius debate recurs in the commentaries of Anglo-Saxon clergy written around the millennium. Like Hesychius, several Anglo-Saxon clerics, including figures no less prominent than Aelfric and Wulfstan, claimed that the signs of the Last Days were being fulfilled in their own times and felt similarly compelled to warn the faithful of the approaching apocalypse. Yet we also see evidence of a concerted effort to uphold the Augustinian position. The eschatological doctrine of Augustine was well known to the Anglo-Saxons directly through works such as *De civitate Dei* or, more significantly, via Bede's widely disseminated *De temporum ratione*.[12] As we shall see, the proponents of orthodoxy turned repeatedly to Augustine's antiapocalyptic arguments in order to suppress doomsday anxiety and discredit various prediction schemes.

In our surviving documents, the orthodox antiapocalyptic position, the position of Augustine, predominates; the voices of Hesychian expectation seem more muted. Faced with this contrasting picture, scholars have chosen to emphasize the prevalence of antiapocalyptic pronouncements; less frequent instances of open speculation regarding the imminence of doomsday are generally marginalized or dismissed outright. The consensus supporting a nonapocalyptic year 1000 rests upon this assessment of our sources. However, this interpretation has, I believe, created a skewed picture of the prevalence and significance of apocalypticism at the turn of the millennium. Let us turn to the methodological assumptions that underline this current interpretation.

First, the paucity of references to the apocalyptic significance of the year 1000 in the documents of this era has been generally viewed as evidence that the millennium aroused little concern among the Anglo-Saxon people, clergy and laity alike.[13] However, this interpretation does not take into consideration the singularly biased nature of our sources. Virtually all written documents from this period were produced by a small elite of learned clergy who not only would have been well aware of biblical admonitions against apocalyptic speculation but would have also been, to varying degrees, familiar with the antiapocalyptic arguments of Augustine. Orthodox doctrine, as prescribed by the Bible and patristic tradition, specifically prohibited speculation concerning biblical prophecy or the eschatological significance of particular chronologies. Thus, one should expect that these clerical authors, out of a desire to maintain orthodoxy, either would remain silent regarding any eschatological significance attributed to the millennium or would, conversely, actively attempt to discredit apocalyptic predictions focused on that date.[14] Our written documents suggest only that a majority of the educated upper clergy, with noteworthy exceptions, held an antiapocalyptic attitude toward the year 1000 and eschatological speculation in general. It is, however, unsafe to assume that these documents necessarily reflect the beliefs of Anglo-Saxons outside this small clerical elite: the laity and lesser clergy.

Second, scholars have seemed willing only to accept direct evidence—overt speculation or expressions of apocalyptic concern—as indications of the existence of anxiety regarding the millennium. Little consideration has been given to the possibility that the frequent admonitions against apocalyptic speculation found in our documents may represent a conscious reaction against contemporary apocalyptic sentiments. In the years surrounding the millennium, we find prominent clergy setting forth explicit and often quite specific refutations of various forms of apocalyptic speculation, including millenarianism. Indeed, not since Bede had Anglo-Saxon clergy shown such a keen interest in upholding eschatological orthodoxy.[15] I would suggest that, like Bede, commentators of the millennial era responded to heightened anxiety by making a concerted effort to quell apocalyptic fears and discourage speculation concerning the date of doomsday.

Last, although admonitions against apocalyptic speculation may be a common feature of the eschatological commentaries of this era, they may not always provide definitive proof of the orthodoxy of the authors who penned them. However, scholars generally argue that Anglo-Saxon clergy showed little inclination to speculate as to the nearness of doomsday, citing as evidence their frequent quotation of biblical passages that forbade such practices.[16] This contention is undermined by the fact that a number of commentators openly disregard their own prohibitions. The author of Blickling Homily 11 engages in speculation concerning the fulfillment of biblical prophecy and the amount of time that had elapsed in the sixth—and final—age of the world, yet brackets this commentary with biblical passages, namely Acts 1:7 and Mark 13:32, which declare that the time of doomsday is known only to God.[17] In a similar manner, Aelfric claimed that the fulfillment of prophesied signs foretokened the imminent end of the world, and Wulfstan made the further assertion that the year 1000 held profound apocalyptic significance, yet each cites biblical admonitions against speculation.[18]

The fact that Aelfric, Wulfstan, and the author of Blickling Homily 11, cite passages such as Acts 1:7 shows that they were well aware of orthodox prohibitions against speculation. However, to varying degrees, they all choose to disregard them. Although these commentators do not violate the letter of these prohibitions by predicting an exact date, they clearly violate their spirit by making the claim, based solely on human reckoning, that Doomsday will occur within the near future. Thus, we find in these documents not pervasive orthodoxy but rather apocalyptic expectation and an inclination toward speculation, despite the prohibitions.

To facilitate the reader's understanding, I will define the following terms as used in this essay.[19] "Eschatology" indicates a belief in the end of time and a conception of God's ultimate judgment of mankind. "Apocalypticism" is the belief that Judgment Day is imminent and that one is living very near or in the Last Days; this belief does not require that believers predict a specific date for the end. I define "millenarianism" narrowly as the belief that the year 1000 held profound eschatological significance or, more specifically, marked the date of the arrival of Antichrist. This belief was based on a literal, and therefore unorthodox, reading of Augustine's interpretation of Apoc. 20:1–7.[20] "Sabbatical millennialism" is the belief that the fallen world would exist for only six "days," totaling six thousand years, after the creation and that upon the arrival of the six-thousandth year, a seventh "day" would dawn inaugurating the thousand-year reign of Christ and the saints over an earthly kingdom of peace and plenty.

Blickling Homily 11 provides the first evidence during the late Anglo-Saxon period of apocalyptic speculation focused on the millennium.[21] The author of Blickling Homily 11 begins his commentary regarding the impending apocalypse by paraphrasing Acts 1:7 but then promptly violates this admonition by openly speculating as to the time of Antichrist's appearance: "Nevertheless we know that it is not far off, because all the signs and fore-tokens that our Lord previously said would come before Doomsday are all gone by, except one alone, that is, the accursed Antichrist, who, as yet, has not come hither upon earth."[22] Though clearly interested in the fulfillment of signs, the author apparently believed that chronology, specifically the current date, also provided a significant indicator of the nearness of Antichrist's reign.[23] He writes: "Yet the time is not far distant when that [Antichrist's arrival] shall also come to pass; because this earth must of necessity come to an end in this age which is now present, for five of the six [ages] have come to pass in this age; wherefore this world must come to an end and the greatest portion has elapsed, even nine hundred and seventy-one years, in this (very) year."[24] However, after making these openly apocalyptic claims concerning the decrepit state of the world's final age, the author seems to back away from these assertions by stating that all prior ages had varied in length and that the duration of the final age was "wholly unknown to every one except our Lord alone (Acts 1:7)."

In Blickling Homily 11 we find elements of both Hesychian speculation and Augustinian restraint. By emphasizing the author's appeals to orthodoxy, one could argue, as has Milton Gatch, that the author was conservative in his eschatological views. Gatch contends that the mention of the year 971 was no more than a casual and innocuous reference to the current Christian year. He has thus concluded that in the Blickling Homilies "there is no evidence of untoward eagerness to predict the date of the denouement."[25]

However, if we look beyond the author's professions of orthodoxy, we see that he showed a marked interest in apocalyptic speculation. The author first asserts that doomsday "is not far off" because all the signs heralding this event had been fulfilled, except the appearance of Antichrist. In order to estimate the time frame in which this final sign would be fulfilled, he relied not on biblical prophecy but rather on a chronological scheme based upon an unorthodox interpretation of the Augustinian "millennium."

In keeping with Augustinian tradition, the author states that the end of the sixth age would inaugurate the reign of Antichrist.[26] However, his commentary suggests that he interpreted the millennium in a chronological sense. The author refers to the current date anno Domini precisely because it provided an indication of the amount of time remaining in the final millennium. By his reckoning, as of the year A.D. 971 the "greatest portion" of the sixth age had already elapsed and thus the reign of Antichrist was "not far distant." This estimation rests on the implicit assumption that the final age would endure approximately a thousand years. If, in fact, the author believed that the sixth age would last substantially longer than a thousand years or was of truly unknowable length, such an assertion makes no sense. The author's conjecture confirms that he understood the "millennium" as a chronological period of estimable length.

More important, can it be only coincidence that the author declares the final age very near its end less than three decades before the millennium, a date to which contemporaries attributed great eschatological significance?[27] Given his chronological interpretation of the millennium, it seems unlikely that the author viewed the year 1000 with indifference. Granted, he did not claim that Antichrist's reign would begin in that year. He may have refrained from making an exact prediction because he believed that the date was known only to God. Alternatively, he may have wished to avoid violating, in writing, the oft-repeated prohibition against date setting. In any case, he does make allusions to a profoundly apocalyptic time frame in which this event would occur: the final age was in an advanced state of decrepitude as the year 1000 approached, and all the signs except the arrival of Antichrist had come to pass. The lack of specificity in the author's speculation reflects not indifference but rather uncertainty and expectation concerning the millennium. This reading casts doubt on Gatch's contention that Blickling Homily 11 provides evidence that "there was not evidently a millenarian expectation focused on the approach of annus domini 1000."[28]

Blickling Homily 11, then, provides interesting evidence that the millennium aroused apocalyptic expectations among the Anglo-Saxon clergy. However, in this regard, the eschatological homilies of Archbishop Wulfstan surpass Blickling Homily 11 in significance in two important respects. First, Wulfstan was the most apocalyptic commentator in all Anglo-Saxon history. He repeatedly asserted that biblical prophecy was being fulfilled, showed a preoccupation with the figure of the Antichrist, and attached profound eschatological significance to the year 1000. Second, whereas the author of Blickling Homily 11 was anonymous, Wulfstan was arguably the most prominent ecclesiastic of his era.[29] If a person as well educated and influential as Wulfstan could be gripped by the apocalyptic implications of the millennium, it seems improbable to suggest that those of lesser status and training would be more restrained in their speculation.

Like Hesychius, Wulfstan was convinced that the signs of the impending apocalypse could be discerned in his own times and that he therefore had a duty to ready the faithful for the coming tribulations: "preachers above all ought to warn all so that when that Antichrist will come, who is the son of perdition, he will find the Christian people prepared."[30] In a series of homilies on eschatology, written in the years surrounding the millennium, Wulfstan relates the various signs that he believed heralded the imminent arrival of Antichrist.[31] In *Secundum Lucam*, Wulfstan, paraphrasing Matt. 24:21, explains that before the arrival of Antichrist, the enmity and tribulation in the world would be worse than it even had been before. He then asserts that present times resemble those described in Matthew 24: "it is in the world ever worse and worse as we ourselves know full well."[32] More significantly, Wulfstan viewed the ravages of the Vikings as the fulfillment of the prophecy of Matt. 24:7: "barbarous men and foreigners greatly trouble us, just as Christ in his gospels truly said must happen. He said: 'surget gens contra gentem, et reliqua.'"[33] By linking current events to biblical prophecy in this fashion, Wulfstan had reached the conclusion that the reign of Antichrist was "now very quickly approaching."

Wulfstan presents similar observations in *De Anticristo*, a homily on the nature of Antichrist and the terrors of his impending reign. In it, he openly declares that Antichrist had already begun to work his evil upon the world. Again Wulfstan turns to biblical prophecy to support this claim: "there are many of his [Antichrist's] limbs ["lima," members or agents] whom one can now see everywhere and recognize through their evil, just as it is read in the Gospel: 'Surgent enim pseudocristi.' Everywhere it happens that false liars rise up and are plausibly deceitful; and those injure many and lead them to error."[34] As this passage shows, Wulfstan believed he was witnessing the fulfillment of prophecy of Matt. 24:24 in his own times, which in turn led him to declare with even greater urgency that the arrival of Antichrist was "extremely near."[35]

Yet these homilies pale in comparison to the apocalypticism of *Secundum Marcum*. Wulfstan, as he did in his earlier homilies, makes a linkage between biblical prophecies and troubles of his own times. He relates that Paul's prophesies regarding the signs of the Last Days ("endenyhstan dagum") were presently occurring: "Lo, it must of necessity grow worse in the world because of people's sin because now is the time of which the apostle Paul foretold long ago."[36] After citing the litany of human misdeeds foretold by Paul in 2 Tim. 3:1–5, he states: "And let him understand who is able, now is the time that this world is disturbed with numerous crimes and manifold evil, and it is therefore widely worse in the world."[37] Wulfstan continues by quoting Matt. 24:12, in Latin and English, and comments that "neither does one love God as they should . . . but evil increases all too widely."[38]

The general argument set forth in these passages is in keeping with *Secundum Lucam* and *De Anticristo*. In each, Wulfstan asserts that various observable signs, such as earthly calamities and the growing wickedness of mankind, fulfilled specific biblical prophecies regarding the Last Days. However, in *Secundum Marcum*, Wulfstan presents an additional and fundamentally different argument to support his predictions concerning the imminence of doomsday, one based on a wholly unorthodox interpretation of Christian chronology:

> Now it must of necessity become much worse, because it is now
> quickly approaching his [Antichrist's] time, just as it is written and
> was prophesied long ago: "Post mille annos soluetur Satanas" [Apoc.
> 20:7]. That is in English, after a thousand years Satan will be un-

bound. A thousand years and even more have now passed since
Christ was with men in human form and now Satan's bonds are
extremely loose, and Antichrist's time is very near, and therefore the
world is ever weaker the longer it endures.[39]

Not only does this passage attest to the intensity of Wulfstan's apocalypticism
but, more significantly, it provides explicit evidence that Wulfstan was a chronologically based apocalyptic thinker. He had committed the fundamental error
that lay at the very heart of millenarianism: the literal interpretation of the "thousand years" of Apocalypse 20. Wulfstan's reasoning was as simple as it was unorthodox; the reign of Antichrist must be imminent because, according to the
Christian calendar, the stated period of a thousand years from the time of Christ
had just elapsed.

The importance Wulfstan attributes to chronology in *Secundum Marcum*
reveals that his apocalyptic expectations were aroused not only by the fulfillment
of signs but also by the timing of these events. According to Wulfstan's interpretation, the fulfillment of prophetic signs was inexorably linked to the current chronological date. If, as he believed, the year 1000 heralded the imminent
reign of Antichrist, then the signs that biblical prophecy foretold would accompany his arrival must occur around this date and at no other time. Indeed,
Wulfstan's apocalyptic expectations seem to have, in large part, stemmed from
his literal interpretation of Apocalypse 20. Viewed from Wulfstan's millenarian
perspective, the various crimes and calamities of his troubled times assumed
apocalyptic significance precisely because these events were occurring around
the year 1000.[40]

It is possible that, prior to the millennium, Wulfstan had interpreted Apoc.
20:7 in a strictly literal sense: the reign of Antichrist would begin in the year
1000. However, in *Secundum Marcum*, written several years after the millennium, he tacitly acknowledges that the year 1000 did not witness the appearance of Antichrist and states that various signs that would occur "right before
the time [of Antichrist]" had not yet been fulfilled.[41] Yet the fact that Antichrist
had failed to manifest himself in the millennial year does not seem to have less-
ened Wulfstan's conviction that his reign was imminent.[42] The wretched and
ever worsening state of the world provided manifest evidence that the Last Days
were in progress. The current date indicated that the culminating event of this
final period of tribulation—the reign of Antichrist—was "very near." Thus, in
Secundum Marcum, Wulfstan interprets the year 1000 not as the inception date
of the reign of Antichrist but rather as a profoundly significant milestone in the
unfolding of the apocalyptic scenario set forth in biblical prophecy.

Despite the explicit evidence provided by *Secundum Marcum*, Anglo-Saxon
scholars seem reticent to acknowledge that Wulfstan was indeed a millenarian.
The prevailing consensus on this subject largely reflects the views of Dorothy
Bethurum, the editor of *The Homilies of Wulfstan*. Bethurum viewed millenarianism as a "superstitions belief" held only by the "illiterate" and "ignorant" and
thus seemed keen to dissociate Wulfstan, the distinguished archbishop, from
such misguided speculation. To this end she sought to portray Wulfstan's lit-

eral interpretation of Apoc. 20:7 as something of an aberration, by noting that he was "indefinite as to the exact time, except for one passage" and had himself cited a biblical admonition against date setting (Matt. 24:36).[43]

Citing the relative paucity of references to Antichrist in Wulfstan's later writings, Gatch suggests that after his brief flirtation with millenarianism, "Wulfstan was forced to alter his eschatological expectations after 1000."[44] However, this contention cannot be reconciled with the blatant apocalypticism of Wulfstan's most famous work, Sermo Lupi ad Anglos. In this sermon, written in 1014, Wulfstan presents a highly apocalyptic interpretation of the crimes and calamities afflicting the English people. For Wulfstan, the increasingly woeful state of the world presaged the imminent arrival of Antichrist: "Beloved men, realize what is true: this world is in haste and the end approaches . . . and so it must of necessity deteriorate greatly on account of people's sin before the coming of Antichrist."[45] Wulfstan believed that the manifold woes that he described in Sermo Lupi— Viking attacks, the growing wickedness of the English people, and disasters such as pestilence and famine—all held apocalyptic significance.[46] Indeed, many of these events fulfilled specific biblical prophecies that Wulfstan had cited in his earlier eschatological homilies. In Secundum Marcum, he describes various signs that would occur "right before" the arrival of Antichrist: "brother will then neither defend brother (Mark 13:12) . . . fighting and infamy shall break forth . . . devastation and famine, burning and bloodshed . . . sedition and pestilence."[47] However, in Sermo Lupi, Wulfstan described these events in the past tense: "kinsman has not protected kinsman," "there has been devastation and famine, burning and bloodshed . . . sedition and pestilence."[48] By his own reckoning, Wulfstan placed his present times (ca. 1014) at the very threshold of the reign of Antichrist.[49] Thus, Sermo Lupi confirms that even fourteen odd years after the millennium, Wulfstan still held fast to his belief in an imminent apocalypse.[50]

Blickling Homily 11 and Wulfstan's homilies provide direct and compelling evidence that the millennium had aroused apocalyptic expectations among the Anglo-Saxon clergy, including one of its most prominent members. Moreover, we see that some of these clergy, perhaps more than our surviving documents reveal, showed a keen interest in both biblical prophecy and the eschatological significance of chronology. However, like Hesychius some five centuries before, the apocalyptically minded commentators of late Anglo-Saxon England would not go unchallenged. Two clerics, Aelfric of Eynsham and Byrhtferth of Ramsey, responded to these apocalyptic sentiments by reiterating the orthodox position on eschatology. Armed with computus and Augustinian doctrine, they sought to ease apocalyptic anxieties and discourage speculation concerning the time of the end. The antiapocalyptic commentary put forth by Aelfric and Byrhtferth bears closer consideration because it offers intriguing insights into the beliefs and expectations of the doomsayers of the millennial era.

Scholars generally regard Aelfric of Eynsham, the foremost homilist and theologian of his era, as a steadfast proponent of orthodoxy on all issues of theology, including eschatology.[51] However, Aelfric's commentaries show that his attitudes concerning the apocalypse were neither clear-cut nor consistently orthodox. In his works, one finds both declarations of impending doom as well as appeals to the antiapocalyptic doctrine of Augustine. Although Aelfric appears to have shifted to a more orthodox, and hence less apocalyptic, position rather early on in his career, he never fully abandoned his belief that the world would not long endure.

I believe Aelfric's ambiguity concerning doomsday stemmed from a conflict between two firmly held convictions. On the one hand, Aelfric was committed to promoting the orthodox interpretation of eschatology. He was well versed in the Augustinian eschatological doctrine, both directly and via Bede, and thus knew that both biblical and patristic opinion admonished against any speculation regarding the time of the Last Judgment. However, like Hesychius, Aelfric himself expressed the belief that doomsday might well be at hand and that he had an obligation to prepare his people for this event. Aelfric's shifting and often contradictory views regarding apocalyptic signs and the imminence of doomsday are most evident in his *Catholic Homilies*, issued in two series early in his career.[52] In the preface to the first series, Aelfric strikes a rather Hesychian tone, explaining that he composed his homiliary out of a desire to educate the English in proper "evangelical doctrines," lest they fall prey to the great persecutions and deceptions of the impending reign of Antichrist. As he relates, "men need good instruction especially at this time which is the ending of the world."[53]

Aelfric continues this apocalyptic theme in the concluding homily of the first series, *Dominica II in adventum Domini*. In drafting this homily, Aelfric closely followed *Homiliae xl in evangelia*, Gregory the Great's exegesis of the apocalyptic prophesies of Luke 21.[54] After noting that these prophesies were Christ's "words to his disciples concerning the signs which will happen before the end of the world," Aelfric paraphrases Gregory's commentary on Luke 21:10–11:

> Some of these signs we see accomplished, some we fear are yet to
> come. Verily in these new days nations have arisen against nations;
> and their affliction on earth has happened greater than we read in
> old books. Oft an earthquake in divers places has overthrown many a
> city, as it happened in the days of Tiberius, that thirteen cities fell
> through an earthquake. With pestilence and with hunger we are
> frequently afflicted.[55]

By adapting *Homiliae xl* in this manner, Aelfric created a sermon more urgently apocalyptic than Gregory's original. As had Hesychius, he aroused anxiety among his audience by declaring that the signs which Christ had foretold were presently discernible. However, having thus aroused expectations, Aelfric appeared eager to suppress any undue speculation concerning other signs. Still quoting Gregory, Aelfric ends his commentary on apocalyptic portents by relating that "we have not yet seen the signs in the sun, in the moon, and in the stars."[56] Interestingly, Aelfric here inserts his own cautionary comments regarding astronomical signs:

> We read in astronomy, that the sun is sometimes darkened by the
> intervention of the lunar orb, and also the full moon suddenly
> becomes dusky, when it is deprived of the solar light by the shadow

of the earth. There are also some stars beamed with light, suddenly rising, and quickly departing, and they by their uprise ever indicate something new: but in the evangelical prophecy, the Lord meant not these signs but the awful signs which will proceed the great day.[57]

Using his knowledge of astronomy, Aelfric wished to disabuse his audience of any notion that natural celestial phenomena held any apocalyptic significance. Yet, in the passage that follows thereafter, Aelfric again sought to create a sense of impending apocalypse. He relates that the aforementioned heavenly signs would occur "straightway after the great tribulation" and, returning to Gregory, that "when many of the before-said signs have been fulfilled, there is no doubt that the few which are remaining will also be fulfilled."[58] In this homily, we find a curious mix of apocalyptic urgency and Augustinian restraint. Aelfric inspired a sense of hope and fear by declaring that some of the signs of the Last Days were being fulfilled in "these new days." Yet he also seemed intent on curbing further speculation concerning terrestrial and heavenly signs, lest it give way to false predictions. His descriptions of earthly tribulations, though provocative, were quite vague. Unlike Wulfstan, he avoids linking prophesied signs with contemporary events.[59] Aelfric's inserted lecture on astronomy served a similar function. Thus, Aelfric seemed intent on creating a restrained sense of apocalyptic expectation among his audience—one that would inspire piety but not provoke outright panic.

In *Dominica II*, Aelfric's attitude toward speculation regarding prophetic signs seems rather conflicted. However, in later works, Aelfric moved away from this ambiguous position toward an explicit denunciation of apocalyptic speculation. In his homily *Natale Sanctorum Virginum*, presented in the second series of his *Catholic Homilies*, Aelfric argues vehemently against any efforts to predict the time of doomsday and refutes, nearly point for point, his earlier statements concerning the fulfillment of prophetic signs that he himself made in *Dominica II*.

Aelfric's selection and adaptation of the source material for *Sanctorum Virginum*, Augustine's *Sermo XCIII*, suggest that his intended purpose in crafting this homily was to discourage apocalyptic speculation.[60] Drawing selectively from *Sermo XCIII*, an exegesis of Matt. 25:1–13, Aelfric creates a commentary more explicitly antiapocalyptic than Augustine's original. Quoting Augustine, he attacks the notion that current calamities foretold an imminent apocalypse: "Men often say, 'Lo, now Doomsday comes,' because the prophecies are gone by, which were made concerning it. But war shall come upon war, tribulation upon tribulation, earthquake upon earthquake, famine upon famine, nation upon nation, and yet the bridegroom [Christ] does not come."[61] Passing over a section of *Sermo XCIII*, Aelfric next succinctly paraphrases Augustine's more verbose refutation of chronologically based doomsday predictions: "In a like manner, the six thousand years since Adam will be ended and the bridegroom will tarry." He then presents a standard Augustinian reply to all questions regarding Christ's Second Coming: "How can we then know when he will come? As he said himself 'at midnight.' What is 'at midnight' but when you know not and you expect him not, then he will come." Like Bede before him, Aelfric turned to the antiapocalyptic arguments of Augustine to aid him in discouraging both speculation concerning prophesied signs and efforts to calculate the date of doomsday.

Aelfric's comment that "the six thousand years from Adam will be ended" bears closer examination because it suggests that he was attempting to discount claims that the world would end in or around the year 1000.[62] At first glance, Aelfric's statement that the six-thousandth year since Adam would not mark the date of the Last Judgment seems a poor counterargument against apocalyptic speculation. By Jerome's reckoning, these six thousand years were completed in A.D. 800 and, according to Bede's *De temporum ratione*, the passage of this date would not occur until A.D. 2048.[63] Aelfric, a skilled computist, would have surely known that the year 6000 held no eschatological significance at the time in which he wrote *Sanctorum Virginum*.[64]

Why then did he include a reference to this date? Perhaps Aelfric was simply reproducing the commentary of Augustine, with little consideration as to its contemporary relevance. However, Aelfric was quite selective in his use of Augustine's *Sermo XCIII*, and thus I would suggest that he chose this passage because it provided a potent refutation to claims that the six-thousandth year since Adam would occur around the time of the millennium. Apocalyptic predictions based on the reckoning of this date were by no means new in Aelfric's time. In the early eighth century, Bede confronted persons who made similar claims concerning the year A.D. 800 (the six-thousandth year according to Jerome). In his letter to the monk Plegwin, Bede attacked contemporaries who argued that the six-thousandth year since Adam marked the date of the world's end.[65] Aelfric's efforts to refute such calculations confirm that this belief, known as sabbatical millennialism, had survived into his day.[66]

Sabbatical millennialism would have been even more applicable to the year A.D. 1000 than to A.D. 800. The logic being that if each age, and certainly the final age, was roughly a thousand years long, then the birth of Christ would have occurred at the beginning of the sixth millennium and thus the world would end approximately a thousand years later, at the end of the sixth age. Viewed in this context, Aelfric's puzzling reference to the six-thousandth year becomes more explicable. By asserting that Christ would not return in the six-thousandth year since Adam, Aelfric was attempting not only to discredit chronological speculation in general but also, more significantly, to strip the year 1000 of its eschatological significance and thus diffuse apocalyptic expectations focused on this date.

Aelfric's efforts to discourage apocalyptic speculation were not confined to his *Catholic Homilies*. In the years surrounding the millennium, Aelfric produced several works that served this purpose. His *De temporibus anni* was one such work. In it, Aelfric skillfully used Bedean commentary to disabuse his audience of the notion that terrestrial and heavenly phenomena could be interpreted as apocalyptic signs. For instance, Aelfric sought to correct popular misconceptions concerning falling stars: "Some men say that stars fall from heaven; it is not stars that then fall, but it is fire from the sky which springs from heavenly bodies as do sparks from fire. . . . They all [the stars], for the most part, are fast in the firmament, and will not fall thence, while this world stands."[67] By explaining that falling stars were in actuality only sparks of heavenly fire, Aelfric sought to discourage any speculation that streaking lights in the night sky were portents of the end of the world, as foretold in biblical prophecy.[68]

Similarly, Aelfric describes the natural events that occasionally caused the sun and moon to darken.[69] As we have seen, Aelfric used this same commentary in *Natale Sanctorum Virginum* to explain to his audience why these celestial events should not be confused with the prophetic signs described in the Gospels. This fact strongly suggests that Aelfric's reiteration of this explanation in *De temporum ratione* served the same purpose. In the closing section of this work, Aelfric makes explicit the antiapocalypticism underlying many of his comments. He explains that "the thunders of which John wrote in Apocalypse are to be understood in a spiritual sense" and thus should not be confused with earthly thunder.[70]

In the works of Aelfric's later career, one finds further evidence of a shift toward a more conservative and orthodox position regarding the apocalypse. In later reissues of his *Catholic Homilies*, he deleted the preface to the first series—with its references to Antichrist and impending doom—thus removing the sense of apocalyptic urgency that had previously framed the homiliary.[71] The two commentaries on eschatology written by Aelfric after the millennium, *De die Iudicii* and *In Octavis Pentecosten*, display none of the apocalypticism of earlier homilies such as *Dominica II*.[72] In *De die Iudicii*, Aelfric presents a detailed exegesis of the apocalyptic prophesies of Luke 17 and Matthew 24 and yet, significantly, makes no attempt to link these prophesies with current earthly calamities. He places the events of the Last Days firmly in the future and states unequivocally that doomsday will arrive without warning and that no man can know the time of its coming. *In Octavis Pentecosten*, which focuses on the soul and the Day of Judgment, Aelfric similarly emphasizes the folly inherent in all human efforts to reckon the time of the apocalypse: "The day of the world's end does not come according to any person's decision but through the foresight alone of Him who created all things."[73] Aelfric based this homily on Julian of Toledo's *Prognosticon futuri saeculi*, a rigorously Augustinian commentary on eschatology that counseled that worldly events could not be interpreted as signs of the approaching apocalypse.[74]

These later works are significant for two reasons. First, they indicate that after his early flirtation with Hesychian speculation, Aelfric had by his later career adopted a much more Augustinian position concerning the interpretation of biblical prophecy. Second, the fact that even after the year 1000 Aelfric felt compelled to reiterate biblical and patristic admonitions against speculation suggests that the passage of the millennium had not defused all expectations of an imminent apocalypse. However, despite his firm commitment to eschatological orthodoxy expressed in *Natale Sanctorum Virginum* and works written thereafter, Aelfric did not entirely abandon his belief that the world was in its waning days. In his *Lives of the Saints* he writes that "this is the last time and the ending of the world."[75] Similarly, in a letter to Wulfstan concerning clerical reform, he asks rhetorically, "if the herald remains silent, who will announce the coming judge?"[76] Although these sentiments are more muted in their apocalypticism than the proclamations of impending doom found in *Dominica II*, they do suggest that, throughout his career, Aelfric was himself never able to fully resolve the tensions between Hesychian expectation and Augustinian agnosticism.

Unlike Wulfstan and Aelfric, Byrhtferth of Ramsey is seldom mentioned in discussions of Anglo-Saxon eschatology. Rather, he is famous for his *Manual*, the most extensive work on science and computus produced in the late Anglo-Saxon era.[77] However, what is not generally acknowledged is that Byrhtferth was a staunch proponent of eschatological orthodoxy committed to discouraging use of computus as a tool for reckoning the time of doomsday. Indeed, in his *Manual*, Byrhtferth presents the most thorough refutation of chronology-based prediction schemes since Bede's *De temporum ratione*.

Byrhtferth's keen interest in upholding the orthodox interpretation of chronology stems from his association with Abbo of Fleury, a master computist and avowed opponent of apocalyptic speculation. Circa 965–70, Abbo denounced a preacher who predicted that Antichrist would arrive in the year 1000.[78] Some years later, he attempted, unsuccessfully, to undermine predictions that the world would end when the Passion and the Annunciation coincided on Friday, March 25, by recalculating the date anno Domini.[79] Abbo came to Byrhtferth's monastery at Ramsey in 986, bringing with him numerous works on computus, and established a school in which he instructed novices, Byrhtferth among them.[80] Years later, in his own rather mediocre work on computus—the *Manual*—Byrhtferth showed that he had learned well the antiapocalyptic methods of his master.

In the concluding section of his *Manual*, Byrhtferth presents a veritable arsenal of antiapocalyptic computus. Employing methods learned from Abbo and Bede, he sought to discredit chronologically based doomsday predictions. Of these schemes, Byrhtferth devotes most of his commentary to the refutation of sabbatical millennialism. Judging from Byrhtferth's comments, these efforts were well warranted: "Many people suppose that this world shall last for six thousand years, because God Almighty created all things in six days."[81] Byrhtferth also expressed concern that many clergy, particularly uneducated priests, held unorthodox views regarding chronology. In his discussion of the "arrangement" of six ages of the world, Byrhtferth remarks that he wished to instruct the clergy on this subject: "in order that less ignorant clerks may have the truth of these mysteries, so as to be able to follow it without a veneer of falsehood."[82] Since the fifth century, the greatest "falsehood" associated with the six ages had been sabbatical millennialism.

Guided by Bede's *De temporum ratione*, Byrhtferth sought to undermine this belief by reiterating orthodox doctrine regarding the six ages. He began by explaining that "these same ages did not consist of equal numbers (of years)." To demonstrate this fact, Byrhtferth presented both the "hebraica veritas" and Septuagint calculations of the lengths of the five previous ages.[83] Regarding the sixth and final age, he relates that it "is not fixed by any series of generations or times" and "is very uncertain as to its end."[84] Byrhtferth's Bedean commentary

on the six ages offered an effective refutation of the chronological interpretations underlying sabbatical millennialism. Not only did the two chronologies
show that the various ages were not, as sabbatical millenarians often supposed,
roughly a thousand years long, but more significantly, they placed the six-thousandth year since Adam alternatively in the past or in the remote future.

To a similar end, Byrhtferth sought to discredit the literal interpretation of
Genesis 1 and 2 Pet. 3:8, which formed the basis of sabbatical millennialism.
He relates: "But as to this number, wise scholars have expounded it in another
way . . . these six days signify that we must spend this life in toil."[85]

Here again Byrhtferth cites orthodox doctrine to demonstrate to sabbatical
millenarians the error of their beliefs; the six days were symbolic and thus could
not be interpreted as literal thousand-year "days" in a six-thousand-year "week."

Apart from sabbatical millennialism, which had a considerable pedigree,
Byrhtferth also encountered a doomsday prediction scheme particular to his era:
millenarianism. His refutation of this belief was direct and explicit: "St. John
has said: 'After a thousand years Satan will be loosed.' This thousand is already
accomplished according to human numeration, but it is in the power of the
Savior, when he shall bring it to an end."[86] In this passage Byrhtferth is, in effect,
pointing out to millenarians the indisputable fact that the chronological year
A.D. 1000 had come and gone and Antichrist had not arrived. He then further
emphasizes the folly of millenarian predictions by repeating the often cited
admonition that the date of doomsday was beyond human reckoning. To further discredit millenarians, Byrhtferth notes that "the number one thousand is
perfect" and thus could not be interpreted literally.[87]

Writing a decade after the millennium, Byrhtferth, in a very real sense, had
time on his side. Time's passage had proven the millenarians dead wrong in
their predictions. Byrhtferth exploited this fact to full effect by directly attacking the validity of the literal interpretation of Apoc. 20:7, the very foundation of
millenarianism. However, this approach becomes effective only after the year
1000 had passed. Byrhtferth could employ a highly effective argument; namely,
that the year 1000 had passed and the end had not come. Thus, cold hard facts,
rather than Augustinian doctrine, offered the most effective argument against
millenarianism.

NOTES

I wish to thank Richard Landes and Robin Fleming for their encouragement and
helpful criticism of this essay.

Editors' note: An earlier version of this paper was presented at the "Conference
on the Apocalyptic Year 1000" in Boston, Mass., November 4–6, 1996. William
Prideaux-Collins is a private scholar.

    1. Ferdinand Lot, "Le mythe des 'Terreurs de l'an mille,'" *Mercure de France* 300
(1947): 639–55.
    2. See Richard Landes, *Relics, Apocalypse, and the Deceits of History: Ademar of
Chabannes, 989–1034* (Cambridge, Mass., 1995), pp. 16–19.
    3. L. Whitbread contends that millenarianism "made no great impression on

the Anglo-Saxon mind"; see his "The Doomsday Theme in Old English Poetry," *Beitrage zur Geschichte der Deutschen Sprache und Literatur* 89 (1967): 478. Milton M. Gatch argues that "there was not evidently any millenarian expectation focused on the approaching annus domini 1000"; see his "The Unknowable Audience of the Blickling Homilies," *Anglo-Saxon England* 18 (1989): 113; see also Milton M. Gatch, *Preaching and Theology in Anglo-Saxon England: Aelfric and Wulfstan* (Toronto, 1977), pp. 78–79. Joseph Trahern largely reiterates Gatch's views regarding millenarianism in "Fatalism and the Millennium," *The Cambridge Companion to Old English Literature*, ed. Malcolm Godden and Michael Lapidge (Cambridge, 1991), pp. 160–70. Dorothy Whitelock, seemingly giving more credence to millenarianism, remarks that instances of prohibitions against doomsday predictions "suggest that there were in England, as abroad, people who had expected the world to end in 1000"; see her *Sermo Lupi ad Anglos* (Exeter, 1966), p. 47 n. 7.

4. Dorothy Bethurum contends that "learned" clergy heeded biblical and patristic prohibitions against making doomsday predictions; see her *The Homilies of Wulfstan* (Oxford, 1957), pp. 278–79.

5. Gatch argues that both the English church and the "audience" of sermons held no expectations concerning the millennium ("Unknowable Audience," p. 113). Bethurum states that the year 1000 was "undoubtedly" the focus of apocalyptic predictions but dismisses millenarianism as a "superstitious fear" held by "not very learned priests and an illiterate public" (*Homilies*, p. 278).

6. Scholarly discussion of Anglo-Saxon apocalypticism ca. 1000 has been largely confined to short passages and footnotes. The brief comments by Whitelock, Whitbread, Bethurum, and Gatch represent the lion's share of commentary on this subject. Malcolm Godden has in some respects addressed this deficiency in his article "Apocalypse and Invasion in Late Anglo-Saxon England," in *From Anglo-Saxon to Early Middle English: Studies Presented to E.G. Stanley*, ed. Malcolm Godden, Douglas Gray, and Terry Hoad (Oxford, 1994), pp. 130–62. See also chap. 8 in the present volume. However, previous studies have given scant consideration to the relationship between chronology and apocalyptic expectation and have either ignored or downplayed the significance of the millennium as an eschatologically charged date.

7. Acts 1:7. This and similar passages are frequently found in Anglo-Saxon commentaries on eschatology.

8. For a discussion of this debate, see J.-P. Bouhot, "Hesychius de Salone et Augustin," in *S. Augustin et la Bible* (Paris, 1986), pp. 229–50; and Paula Fredriksen, "Apocalypse and Redemption in Early Christianity: From John of Patmos to Augustine of Hippo," *Vigiliae Christianae* 45, no. 2 (1991): 160–61.

9. *Epistola* 197.5 (*PL* 33:903); translation of letters by Sister Wilfrid Parsons, *Letters*, vol. 4 (165–203), *Fathers of the Church, a New Translation*, vol. 30 (Washington, D.C., 1955).

10. *Ep.* 199 (*PL* 33:902).

11. *Ep.* 199 (*PL* 33:925).

12. In *De civitate Dei*, Book 20, Augustine refutes various schemes for predicting the date of the Last Judgment, including speculation based on the literal interpretation of the "thousand years" of Apoc. 20:1–7. J. Ogilvy notes that *De civitate Dei* "was one of the most popular, if not the most popular, of Augustine's works among the English"; see his *Books Known to the English, 597–1066* (Cambridge, Mass., 1967), p. 82. In the final chapters of *De temporum ratione*, Bede reiterates many of Augustine's antiapocalyptic arguments and admonishes that although it is proper for the faithful to hope for the imminent return of Christ, "they act danger-

ously if any presume to think or predict that this is near or far away." He then quotes a section of Augustine's rebuttal of Hesychius from Ep. 199; see *Bedae venerabilis opera*, ed. C. W. Jones, *CCSL* 123B, p. 537.

13. Bethurum contends that Anglo-Saxon documents "fail to reveal any emphasis on the year 1000," citing as evidence the disappearance of apocalyptic references from charters written near the end of the tenth century (*Homilies*, pp. 279–80). Whitbread argues that if the approach of the year 1000 had truly troubled the Anglo-Saxons, the Anglo-Saxon Chronicle would have alluded to the imminence of doomsday in the years prior to the millennium ("Doomsday Theme," pp. 478–79).

14. This conspicuous silence can be seen most clearly in the *Anglo-Saxon Chronicle*. An entry for 973 comments regarding King Edgar's consecration: "Then . . . had passed away ten hundred years, all but twenty-seven" since the birth of Christ. Yet no eschatological significance was attributed to this date or to the year 1000 itself. See *Anglo-Saxon Chronicles*, ed. and trans. G. N. Garmonsway (London, 1990), pp. 118, 133. Aelfric and Byrhtferth of Ramsey (who specifically discredits millenarianism) defended the orthodox position by denouncing chronological speculation. As I hope to demonstrate, it seems unlikely that the authors of the *Anglo-Saxon Chronicle* and other documents were unaware that some, perhaps many, attributed eschatological significance to the year 1000.

15. Like commentators ca. 1000, Bede denounced those who made chronologically based predictions and sought to discredit his apocalyptic opponents with computus and Augustinian doctrine; see Richard Landes, "Lest the Millennium Be Fulfilled: Apocalyptic Expectations and the Pattern of Western Chronography, 100–800 C.E.," in *The Use and Abuse of Eschatology in the Middle Ages*, ed. W. Verbeke, D. Verhelst, and A. Welkenhuysen (Leuven, 1988), pp. 174–78.

16. For examples of this argument, see Gatch, "Eschatology in the Old English Homilies," *Traditio* 21 (1965): 130–31; Bethurum, *Homilies*, p. 280.

17. *The Blickling Homilies*, ed. R. Morris, Early English Text Society, vol. 58 (London: 1874), pp. 116–17. The commentary of the eighth-century monk Beatus of Liebana offers an interesting parallel to that of Blickling Homily 11. By his own calculations, Beatus reckoned that "only 14 years" remained in the sixth age of the world. After presenting this blatantly apocalyptic prediction, Beatus paid lip service to biblical orthodoxy by citing Acts 1:7 and Mark 13:32; see H. A. Sanders, *Beati in apocalypsin libri duodecim*, Papers and Monographs of the American Academy in Rome, vol. 7 (1930), IV, 16, pp. 77–80. Juan Gil argues that Beatus's citation of these passages provided a "smokescreen" of orthodoxy; see his "Los terrores del ano 800," in *Acta del Simposio para el estudio de los codices del 'Comentario al Apocalipsis' de Beatus de Liebana* (Madrid, 1978), p. 225. Also Landes, "Lest the Millennium," pp. 192–94.

18. Gatch notes that Aelfric showed a keen interest in promoting orthodox doctrine on eschatology (*Preaching and Theology*, chap. 7). However, Aelfric's speculation regarding apocalyptic signs in an early homily violates Augustinian prohibitions with which he was undoubtedly familiar. Despite Wulfstan's openly apocalyptic commentary on Apoc. 20:7, Bethurum suggests that his citation of a biblical prohibition against speculation (Matt. 24:36) attests to his orthodoxy (*Homilies*, 2, pp. 121/57–62; 5, 136/40–45, 137/1–2; 280.

19. For further discussion of some of these definitions, see Landes, "Lest the Millennium," pp. 205–6.

20. Augustine argued that the thousand-year binding of Satan described in Apocalypse 20 represented the invisible "millennium" of the church (i.e., the faithful

would reign "with Jesus for a thousand years") that began with the incarnation of Christ and would end with the release of Antichrist. Significantly, he declared that this perfect number signified a "totality" of time and thus could not be interpreted as a literal thousand years (*De civitate Dei*, 20. 7–9). However, millenarians interpreted Augustine's scheme in a literal sense, claiming that A.D. 1000 marked the end of the "millennium" and the beginning of the reign of Antichrist. Richard Landes has termed this interpretation "chronological Augustinianism" (*Relics*, pp. 291–92). For recent discussions of Augustine's eschatology, see Landes, "Lest the Millennium," pp. 156–60; Robert Markus, *Saeculum: History and Society in the Theology of St. Augustine* (Cambridge, 1970), pp. 22–71.

21. For background on the Blickling Homilies, see N. R. Ker, *Catalogue of Manuscripts Containing Anglo-Saxon* (Oxford, 1957), no. 336.

22. Morris, *Blickling*, pp. 116–31.

23. Reaching a similar conclusion, Elizabeth Jeffery comments that the author employed a "chronological proof based on the medieval division of the world into six ages"; see her *Blickling Spirituality and the Old English Vernacular Homily* (Queenston, 1989), p. 79.

24. Morris, *Blickling*, pp. 116/30–34, 177/1–2. J. E. Cross argues convincingly that p. 116/35 of Blickling Homily 11 should read "for five of these [ages] are past in this age" rather than "five of these [foretokens]"; see "On the Blickling Homily for Ascension Day (No. XI)," *Neuphilologische Mitteilungen* 70 (1969): 233.

25. Despite the author's comments concerning the impending arrival of Antichrist and his linkage of this event to the waning of the sixth age, Gatch asserts that the author was disinterested in speculation and attributed little or no eschatological significance to the present date ("Eschatology," p. 135; "Unknowable Audience," p. 113).

26. Significantly, the author does not claim, as did sabbatical millenarians, that the sixth age would be followed by the thousand-year reign of Christ on earth. The author's knowledge of the six ages strongly suggests that he was familiar with *De temporum ratione*, in which Bede vehemently denounces sabbatical millennialism. Apparently heeding Bede, the author adopted what he believed to be the more properly orthodox Augustinian interpretation of the six ages.

27. Wulfstan declared that the year 1000 heralded the imminent arrival of Antichrist. Byrhtferth of Ramsey dismissed apocalyptic predictions focused on this date. On the Continent, ca. 965–70, Abbo of Fleury wrote of hearing "a sermon about the End of the world. . . . According to this, as soon as the number of one thousand years was completed, the Antichrist would come and the Last Judgment would follow in a brief time." *Apologeticus* (*PL* 139:571); translated by Bernard McGinn in *Visions of the End: Apocalyptic Traditions in the Middle Age* (New York, 1979), pp. 88–89.

28. Gatch, "Unknowable Audience," p. 113.

29. For discussion of Wulfstan's career and influence in ecclesiastical and secular affairs, see Dorothy Bethurum, "Wulfstan," in *Continuations and Beginnings: Studies in Old English Literature*, ed. E. G. Stanley (London, 1966), pp. 210–46.

30. Bethurum, *Homilies*, 1a, p. 115/52–53. Wulfstan makes a similar statement in the Old English version of this homily (1b), where he speaks of the clergy's "duty to warn the sacred flock" (pp. 117–18/32).

31. Bethurum suggests, on admittedly tentative evidence, that Wulfstan's eschatological homilies were written in the order 2, 3, 1a, 1b, 4, 5 (*Homilies*, p. 282). Gatch supports this conclusion (*Preaching and Theology*, p. 236 n. 3).

32. Bethurum, *Homilies*, 3, p. 123/12–14.

33. Ibid., p. 124/21–23.

34. Ibid., 1b, pp. 116/13–14, 117/15–17. Wulfstan makes the same claim in the Latin version of this homily (1a, p. 113/8–10).

35. Ibid., 1b, p. 117/22–23.

36. Ibid., 5, p. 134/14–16.

37. Ibid. p. 135/23–26.

38. Matt. 24:12; Bethurum, *Homilies*, 5, p. 135–36/27–30.

39. Bethurum, *Homilies*, 5, p. 136/40–47.

40. An interesting parallel can be seen in Radulfus Glaber's *Historiarum quinque libri*, written ca. 1035–40. After discussing the emergence of heretical movements in Italy and Spain, he comments, "All this accords with the prophecy of St. John, who said that the Devil would be freed after a thousand years." *Rodulfi Glabri Historiarum quinque libri*, ed. and trans. John France (Oxford, 1989), p. 93.

41. Wulfstan relates that various earthly tribulations and celestial signs had not yet come to pass. Also, Wulfstan's comments suggest that he believed that Antichrist had not yet been born: "Antichrist will be the worst of all the children born in the world." The ambiguity of Old English tenses and the context of this comment (a discussion of the nature of Antichrist) make it unclear whether Wulfstan wished his audience to believe that the arrival of Antichrist lay, at the very least, a generation in the future (i.e., he must first be born and mature naturally before beginning his reign); Bethurum, *Homilies*, 5, pp. 136/38–39, 140/97–107, 141/108.

42. The uneventful passage of the year 1000 did not necessarily quash millenarian expectations. Radulfus Glaber continued to attribute apocalyptic significance to the passage of the millennium nearly forty years after this date; see n. 50.

43. Bethurum, *Homilies*, p. 280.

44. Gatch suggests that Wulfstan's millenarian convictions waned after Antichrist failed to manifest himself in or immediately after the year 1000 (*Preaching and Theology*, pp. 113–14).

45. Bethurum, *Homilies*, 20(EI), p. 267/7–11.

46. For a more extensive analysis of the apocalypticism of this homily, see Stephanie Hollis, "The Thematic Structure of the 'Sermo Lupi,'" *Anglo-Saxon England* 6 (1977): 175–95.

47. Bethurum, *Homilies*, 5, p. 140/98–104.

48. Ibid., 20(EI), p. 269/55–59, 61–65. Godden has noted the significance of this shift in tense in regard to the Mark 13:12 passage ("Apocalypse and Invasion," pp. 146–47).

49. Godden reached the same conclusion: "Wulfstan locates the text internally, at a moment when the signs of the approaching end are all around him and the reign of Antichrist is almost upon him" ("Apocalypse and Invasion," p. 147).

50. Godden offers a similar assessment: "Although the millennium is now well past, the apocalyptic expectations of this version [of *Sermo Lupi*] are if anything more intense." However, I do not agree with Godden's argument that Wulfstan's increasing reference to the Vikings as divine punishment for the nation's sin in the subsequent versions of *Sermo Lupi* indicate a "diminishing concern with apocalypse" ("Apocalypse and Invasion," pp. 147, 152).

51. See Gatch, *Preaching and Theology*, chap. 7; and Lynne Grundy, *Books and Grace: Aelfric's Theology*, King's College London Medieval Studies, vol. 6 (Exeter, 1991), chap 5.

52. The dating of both the first and second series of the *Catholic Homilies* is a matter of debate. K. Sisam argues that the first series dates to 990–91 and the second to 992 in "MSS. Bodley 340 and 342: Aelfric's Catholic Homilies," in *Studies in the History of Old English Literature* (Oxford, 1953), pp. 156–60. P. Clemoes argues for the dates 989 and 992, respectively, in "The Chronology of Aelfric's Works," in *The Anglo-Saxons: Studies in Some Aspects of Their History and Culture Presented to Bruce Dickens* (London, 1959), pp. 243–44. Malcolm Godden argues a later dating, 993–94 and 995, respectively, in *Aelfric's Catholic Homilies: The Second Series Texts*, Early Engish Text Society, s.s., vol., 5 (London, 1979), pp. xci–xciii (hereafter referred to as *CH* 2).

53. Preface, *Homilies of the Anglo-Saxon Church: The First Part, Containing the Sermones Catholici or Homilies of Aelfric*, ed. B. Thorpe, 2 vols. (London: 1844–46), 1: 2. I use Thorpe's translations of these homilies.

54. Gregory the Great, *Homiliae xl in evangelia* (*PL* 76:1077–81). Aelfric cites "the holy Gregory" as his source. Aelfric also consulted Haymo of Halberstat's homily based on Gregory's original, see Max Forster, "Über die Quellen von Aelfrics exegetischen Homiliae Catholicae," *Anglia* 16 (1894): 1–61; and C. L. Smetana, "Aelfric and the Homiliary of Haymo of Halberstadt," *Traditio* 17 (1961): 467.

55. *Dominica II*, *CH* 1, xl, p. 609/23–29.

56. Aelfric chose not to reiterate Haymo's claim that celestial signs had been frequently observed and rather followed Gregory's less apocalyptic commentary; compare Haymo's *Homiliae de tempore* (*PL* 118:18–25) and *Homiliae xl* (*PL* 76:1078).

57. *CH* 1, xl, pp. 611/29–33, 611/1–5. Neither of the two versions of this homily that Aelfric consulted, Gregory's original or Haymo's, contains this discussion on astronomy. However, Aelfric presents similar commentary in his *De temporibus anni*, ed. Heinrich Henel, Early English Text Society, vol. 213 (London, 1942), pp. 21, 71.

58. *CH* 1, xl, p. 610/13–16.

59. Aelfric deletes Gregory's comment: "Before Italy was handed over to be struck by pagan swords, we saw fiery flashes in the sky," *Homiliae xl* (*PL* 76:1078). He may have wished to avoid arousing speculation concerning the renewal of Viking raids, in 980, and an ominous event described in the *Anglo-Saxon Chronicle* in 976: "This same year a cloud as red as blood was seen, frequently with the appearance of fire. . .it took the form of rays of light of various colours" (Garmonsway, *Anglo-Saxon Chronicles*, p. 122).

60. Augustine, *Sermones* (*PL* 38:573–80). Aelfric credits the "wise Augustine" as his source (*CH* 2, xxxix, p. 327/25). On Aelfric's use of this sermon in *Sanctorum Virginum*, see Forster "Über die Quellen," p. 15; and *Homilies of Aelfric: A supplementary Collection*, ed. John Pope, 2 vols., Early English Text Society, vols. 259–60, (London, 1967), 2:782.

61. *CH* 2, xxxix, p. 330/111–15. Aelfric adapts this passage from *Sermones* (*PL* 38:576). Interestingly, Aelfric substitutes "oft" for Augustine's "aliquondo."

62. *CH* 2, xxxix, p. 330/115–17. "Six thousand years . . . will be ended" seems to me the most appropriate translation of this passage. Augustine writes "transierunt" but implies speculation about a future event. More important, Aelfric knew of Bede's calculations, based on "hebracia veritas," which placed the year 6000 far in the future. To state that this date had already passed would be an implicit rejection of Bede's calculations.

63. Bede presents both calculations in *De temporum ratione* (*CCSL* 123B:463–64).

64. Aelfric was quite familiar with Bede's works on computus and cited them frequently in his *De temporibus anni*, pp. liii–lvi.

65. *Epistola ad Pleguinam*, in *Bedae Opera de Temporibus*, ed. C. W. Jones (Cambridge, Mass., 1943), pp. 305–15. Aelfric's comment concerning the six-thousandth year echoes Bede's: "I warn you, dear brother, lest you, seduced by the vulgar opinion, should hope that the duration of this world will be only 6000 years." Also see Landes, "Lest the Millennium," pp. 174–78.

66. Aelfric was not alone in his desire to discredit sabbatical millennialism. Byrhtferth of Ramsey claimed that "many people" held this belief and similarly employed Augustinian arguments to discredit it; *Byrhtferth's Manual*, ed. S. J. Crawford, Early Enlish Text Society, o.s., vol. 177 (London, 1929), p. 235.

67. Henel, *De temporibus anni*, pp. 66–67. Aelfric's source was Bede's *De natura rerum*, wherein he refers to this belief as "falsa autem opinio et uulgaris," p. xxv, I.

68. For the apocalyptic significance of falling stars, see Matt. 24:29, Mark 13:25, Luke 21:25–33, Apoc. 6:13, 12:4.

69. Henel, *De temporibus anni*, pp. 20, 21 n. 6. Aelfric source was Bede's *De temporum ratione*, vii. Darkening of sun and moon as apocalyptic signs: Matt. 24:29, Mark 13:24.

70. Henel, *De temporibus anni*, p. 82. Reference to thunders: Apoc.. 10:3–4.

71. The preface's commentary on Antichrist appears in three later manuscripts associated with Aelfric. However, the full preface appears as such only in MS Gg. 3, 28, issued around 1000, which itself was a copy of an early edition of both series of the *Catholic Homilies*, completed ca. 993–94. On Aelfric's use of the preface material, see Pope, *Homilies of Aelfric*, pp. 34–35, 53–55, 62–66, 71–73. Also see Ker, *Catalogue*, nos. 15, 41, 332, 338.

72. These homilies were both composed ca. 1002–5; see Pope, *Homilies of Aelfric, De die Iudicii*, vol. 2, xviii, pp. 584–612; *Sermo ad populum, In Octavis Pentecosten Dicendus*, vol. 1, xi, pp. 407–53.

73. Pope, *Homilies of Aelfric*, xi, 430/277–79

74. *Prognosticon futuri saeculi (CCSL* 115:11–126). Aelfric drew from his own compilation of excerpts from this work. For a discussion of Aelfric's use of *Prognosticon*, see Gatch, *Preaching and Theology*, pp. 96–101, 129–46. On Julian's antiapocalyptic commentary, see Landes, *Relics*, pp. 92–93.

75. *Aelfric's Lives of the Saints*, ed. W. W. Skeat, Early English Text Society, vols. 76, 82, 94, 114 (London, 1881–1900), I, p. xiii.

76. "Aelfric's First Old English Letter for Wulfstan," in *Councils and Synods with Other Documents Relating to the English Church*, vol. 1, *871–1204*, ed. D. Whitelock, M. Brett, and C. N. L. Brooke (Oxford, 1981), pt. 1, no. 46, p. 260.

77. On Byrhtferth, his *Manual*, and his use of sources, see Cyril Hart, "Byrhtferth and His Manual," *Medium Aevum* 41 (1972): 95–107.

78. In his *Apologeticus*, Abbo writes that he "opposed this sermon with what force I could from passages in the Gospels, Apocalypse and the book of Daniel" (translated by McGinn, *Visions*, pp. 88–89).

79. This coincidence occurred in 970, 981, and 992. Abbo's recalculation, published in 982, added twenty-one years to anno Domini and thus, by his reckoning, invalidated predictions based on the standard calendar. However, Abbo's calculations received no acceptance; see Landes, "Millenarismus absconditus: L'historiographie augustinienne et le millenarisme du Haut Moyen Age jusqu'en l'an mil," *Le Moyen Age* 98 (1992): 19–25.

80. Abbo resided at Ramsey from 986 to 988, teaching from works on computus by Bede, Dionysius Exiguus, Isidore of Seville, and Jerome; see Hart,

"Byrhtferth," pp. 95–96. Byrhtferth openly acknowledged his debt to Abbo: "the wise Abbo . . . by whose benevolence we have gained knowledge of this subject [computus]"; see G. F. Forsey, "Byrhtferth's Preface," *Speculum* 3 (1928): 552.

81. Crawford, *Manual*, p. 241.

82. Ibid., p. 235.

83. Ibid.

84. Ibid., p. 239.

85. Ibid., p. 241.

86. Ibid.

87. In an earlier section, Byrhtferth presents "the account of this number given by Abbo." He included a diagram that demonstrated the "perfect" nature of the number 1000 (Henel, *De temporibus anni*, pp. 232–33).

15

Apocalyptic Moments and the Eschatological Rhetoric of Reform in the Early Eleventh Century: The Case of the Visionary of St. Vaast

David C. Van Meter

At this point in the "new historiography" of the apocalyptic year 1000, if one may speak so confidently, it is no longer sufficient for historians to merely root around in the documents for evidence of eschatological tensions and millennial rhetoric. Once we have learned what to look for, the evidence proves to be rather plentiful: we find set before us a veritable millennial banquet of texts, each begging to be sampled first. Now we face the rather more stimulating challenge of discerning the broader patterns that shall tell us something about how and why, if at all, such apocalypticism and millennial rhetoric exerted some meaningful influence on the course of those events and processes, great and small, that are the stuff of history.

In particular, we are beginning to appreciate more readily the overwhelming importance of considering genre, audience, and context—social, ecclesial, and political—in analyzing the expressions of apocalypticism in our sources. By way of example, Guy Lobrichon reminds us, in his contribution to this volume, of the enormity of the gap between the monastic milieu from which most of our documentation emerged and the secular world in which the most historically interesting apocalyptic anxieties would have played themselves out around the year 1000. The very point of medieval, Benedictine monasticism, after all, was flight from the world in order to merge one's very self-identity with the Johannine vision of the virgins of the Apocalypse,[1] and thereby enjoy a highly spiritualized pre-liberation of the New Jerusalem.[2] Monastic life was thus, by its very nature, intensely eschatological. Monks even enjoyed a certain ongoing but rigidly disciplined flirtation with the apocalypse itself, by virtue of the ebb and flow of the liturgy, climaxing in those seasons of intense expectation and longing for the New Advent of Christ which punctuated the more placid periods of recognizing the ongoing millennial reign of the saints with Christ in the memorial feasts of ordinary time.[3]

Comparatively rare, however, are those moments around the year 1000 in which we see ecclesiastical thought on the end of time neatly packaged for secular consumption and, presumably, action. Famous examples, already discussed elsewhere in this volume, include Adso's letter to Queen Gerberga, Abbo's apology to Kings Hugh and Robert, and the correspondence on the rain of blood in Aquitaine. What links these texts is their conservative, erudite, and invariably de-eschatologizing tone. Indeed, it remains a staggering and even somewhat amusing irony that a great many historians have looked at these very documents, which explicitly proffer and unabashedly discuss evidence of apocalyptic anxiety, and thence have come away with the odd conclusion that there were, in fact, no significant apocalyptic anxieties around the year 1000.

Placed in their proper context, however, these texts speak less about a stalwart antiapocalyptic agenda on the part of their ecclesiastical authors than they do about the invariably pointed purposes of any given millennial rhetoric.[4] At the most basic level, each of these texts avowedly applies Christian doctrine to the task of answering a very specific question: does this sign, or that chronographic computation, tell us that the end is very near? To this question, there can be only one doctrinal answer, founded upon Christ's own repeated admonition (e.g., Matt. 24:36, 42) that the time of the end is inscrutable: No! More broadly, however, the inherently politicized context in which these texts originated leads one to wonder whether or not the authors were in fact leery about sharing the intense eschatological experience, and even apocalyptic rhythms, of the liturgy with the outside world? In fact, my own readings have suggested that the eschatology that one most often finds in any sort of politicized text, ranging from letters to kings to hagiographies treating on political matters, is most often of the realized sort. In this period, in which the various binary and ternary constructions of the social order proved to be potent topoi in the trenchant debates that raged over the questions of monastic immunity and exemption, the monastic pretenses of occupying an elevated position in the Johannine paradigm of the millennial reign of the saints, assumed distinctively polemical overtones.[5] One might fairly conclude that the abbots and bishops who were the most caught up in the debates and struggles surrounding the various reform programs fought to preserve something of a monopoly on eschatological conceptualizations.

But what of those moments in which the abbots assumed the role of rabble-rousers, if you will? Would they have stooped to using eschatological rhetoric as a tool to shape public opinion, both within the cloister and among the laity? Certainly this is what the abbots and bishops who spearheaded the Peace of God movements and the various local and regional reform impulses must have done on at least several occasions.[6] Indeed, it is precisely the rabble-rousing, implicitly eschatological aspect of Cluniac activism that Adalbero of Laon lampoons in his image of the monks and their followers in his famous satire of King Robert's topsy-turvy reign.[7] We should expect that, in such circumstances as these, the ecclesiastical rhetors would have laid aside their erudition and placid tones. But would they have also laid aside the doctrinal, antiapocalyptic argumentation that so often assumes almost genre-like proportions in their exegetical and hagiographical works? If so, what rhetorical novelties did they introduce to frame, circumscribe, and rationalize these hypothesized dalliances with the apocalyptic present? What were the results of their apocalyptic arguments?

In this paper we shall reconsider, in light of these musings, a fairly well known, yet vastly underexploited, apocalyptic text from around the year 1000: the letter of Richard of St. Vanne describing the two otherworldly visions of a monk of St. Vaast in Arras. Specifically, we will examine the manner in which this letter functioned as millennial rhetoric aimed at persuading a specific audience—monks who were resisting the efforts of an outsider to reform them—to adopt a clearly articulated program of action.

Richard of St. Vanne and the Apocalyptic Visionary of St. Vaast

In Book 2 of his *Chronicon*, Hugh of Flavigny includes a very lengthy circular letter written by Richard of St. Vanne in ca. 1012 and addressed to the entire community of the faithful. [8] In this letter, Richard, who was at that time struggling to restore discipline to the wayward monastery of St. Vaast, [9] announces that one of the monks of St. Vaast had recently experienced two visionary journeys to the otherworld, during the course of which the archangel Michael had entrusted him with a number of revelations that promised to cast some interesting light on the sayings of the prophets as well as the apostles and the evangelists. He goes on to explain that while he felt some apprehension about publishing these dramatic and even frightening revelations, he nonetheless clearly perceived that they represented a part of the divine plan for the salvation of many. The central message of these revelations, repeated over and over again in this letter, was that the Second Coming of Christ and the Final Judgment were at hand, and that within but a few years humankind was to experience the long-anticipated "Day of Wrath." Not one either to mince his words or to turn his back on an opportunity to promote his cause, Richard parlayed this visionary message of imminent apocalypse into a harsh and at times detailed condemnation of his potential foes—to include the count of Flanders and monasteries that were resisting reform—as well as an implicit call for all Christendom to repent and reform. In so doing, he introduced Flanders to the political power of apocalyptic rhetoric.

According to Richard's testimony, one of the monks of St. Vaast fell ill and very nearly died in April of 1011; indeed, his soul was carried off to the otherworld. Although he ultimately recovered from this illness, he suffered a similar near-death experience in August the following year.[10] While his soul was out of its body on both occasions, it visited those places of purgation and refreshment that await the dead. These two visions recorded at the behest of Abbot Richard advance several interesting innovations in the Christian conceptualization of the topography of the otherworld, but it is not our purpose to examine these here.[11] Rather, we shall turn at this point to the soul's other activities in the otherworld: with the archangel Michael as its guide, the soul of the monk of St. Vaast was given a detailed tour of the eschatological future.[12]

In his perceptive essay on the divine comedy in the Middle Ages, Aron Gurevich notes that one of the most significant cultural effects of visionary literature in the early Middle Ages was that it facilitated a shift in the way that most Christians conceptualized the resolution of the problem of theodicy, leading them away from the historical focus on the settling of divine accounts in the Last Judgment at the end of time and toward an infinite series of "personal eschatologies," or smaller judgments that lay in the near future for each and every person.[13] That is to say, in large measure through the publication of otherworldly visions which describe scenes of purgation and refreshment in lurid and often frightening detail, such church luminaries as Gregory the Great, Bede, and Hincmar of Reims, to name but a few, underscored in a visual and palpable manner the notion that every individual faces an immediate and personalized, albeit interim, Judgment of his or her sins upon death. Perhaps this shift reflects a pastoral concern that the concept of the Last Judgment was rather too remote and abstract—under normal circumstances—to exert a great deal of moderating influence on a person's behavior in the present. Similarly, one can imagine that it must have been eminently more satisfying to imagine that one's departed kinfolk were already resting in the cool meadows of refreshment and, conversely, that those former enemies and oppressors who had departed from this life were already being torn into pieces by grinning devils brandishing fiery pincers, rather than sleeping peacefully in the grave while awaiting the blast of the final trumpet. In any event, the vast majority of extant medieval visions utterly disregard the Last Judgment and focus instead on exactly such fantasies of immediate retribution and reward.[14]

Yet the visions of the monk at St. Vaast dwell at great length, and in considerable and imaginative detail, on the scenario and the actors of the Second Coming and the Last Judgment. Indeed, the greater portion of the first vision is, in fact, devoted to presenting a vivid and literal account of the apocalyptic scenario in very rudimentary Latin. While the second vision expends considerably more effort in describing the postmortem punishments that await various sinners, it also contains a startling and thoroughly unprecedented revelation about the timing of the apocalypse. In deviating so dramatically from the topoi and the conventions of what was by 1012 a more or less fixed literary genre, surely Richard's account of these visions functions as something of a galvanometer that permits us to measure the unusual intensity of the current of apocalyptic expectations that coursed through the Low Countries around the year 1000.

The monk of St. Vaast received his visions at a time of comparatively acute apocalyptic anxieties in western Europe.[15] In part, these anxieties were generated by the apparently widespread belief that the thousandth anniversaries of the Incarnation and the Passion were particularly propitious times to expect the Second Coming.[16] Indeed, the observant among the faithful were quick to notice a great concentration of potentially apocalyptic signs in the years following 1000. The most dramatic of these were of a political nature. A giant dragon was seen hovering in the sky in 1002,[17] and then Otto III—the emperor of the Romans who had painstakingly claimed for himself the legacy of Charlemagne and, according to some historians, postured as the emperor of the end time—died without an heir while besieging a rebellious Rome, prompting some, no doubt, to wonder if this might not herald the long-anticipated *discessio* predicted by St. Paul.[18] To follow Adso of Montier-en-Der's more recent exegesis of this tradition that the Roman emperors were the barrier to the final *discessio*, such a sign in connection with the death of Otto might readily be equated with the unleashing of the Antichrist and the unbinding of Satan.[19] That Otto's successor, Henry II, did not receive the imperial dignity for over a decade, until 1014, must certainly have encouraged such a line of speculation. Then, in the midst of this gap in the continuity of the Roman Empire as it was conceived in the Ottonian tradition, a Muslim ruler—al-Hakim, the caliph of Cairo—raised himself up as the Mahdi, or the hidden Imam. He began forcing the conversion of Christians and Jews and in 1009 attacked the Holy Sepulchre in Jerusalem. To the shocked Christians of the West, such behavior could all too readily be associated with the prophesied actions of the Antichrist himself.[20]

The natural world, too, seemed to have slipped into a state of disorder and even dissolution presaging the end. The first ten or so years after the turn of the millennium were marked by a variety of signs and wonders, including extreme famines and mortality in some parts of Europe, and even the appearance of a brilliant supernova in 1006.[21] Those among the Flemish literati who were familiar with the Pseudo-Bede's discussion of the so-called fifteen signs of the end, of which the very first was to be the raising of the sea and rivers, must have been particularly distressed by the flooding of rivers in northern France and the Low Countries in 1003, and then the great maritime inundations that occurred along the coast of Flanders beginning in 1014.[22] Another distressing, potentially apocalyptic omen appeared as well just beyond the borders of Flanders: near Mons, a therapeutic fountain dedicated to St. Waletrude turned to blood in ca. 1011.[23]

So, too, we should note that yet another apocalyptic date may have had even more to do with the anxieties manifested in the visions of St. Vaast than the year 1000 per se. As we are well aware, Abbo of Fleury mentions an odd belief, emanating from some monastery in Lorraine, that the world would come to an end when Good Friday falls on a March 25. I have recently traced the origins of this belief as far back as the mid–ninth century, to the Matthew commentary of Christian of Stavelot, who provides a detailed exegetical rationale for what ought to be termed "Paschal eschatology."[24] Christian's exegetical scheme, which in fact seems to originate from the interplay between the liturgy and especially developments in the cult of the archangels, allowed in various permutations for the potentiality of the end of the world during the Paschal vigil in a year in which

Good Friday fell on March 25, as well as in a year in which Easter Sunday fell on March 25. It seems quite reasonable to suspect that Christian's scheme underlies a number of reported outbreaks of apocalyptic anxiety, including the episode of the pseudoprophetess Thiota at Mainz in the year 847, and the dates that Abbo mentions in his *Apologia*. Similarly, Easter fell on March 25 in the year 1011; this apocalyptic date may well have fueled the anxieties recorded for the prior year by the pseudo–William Godellus.[25] For our purposes, we should note that it was just a little over a month after the passage of that eschatological Easter that the monk of St. Vaast is purported to have had his first vision of the apocalyptic future.

The monks of St. Vaast were certainly not immune to an intensely anxious longing for the literal unfolding of the apocalyptic scenario. At some point in the very early years of the eleventh century, a monk of St. Vaast who was possessed by a remarkable concern for the precise reckoning of the time wrote the following entry in the margins of the computistic table that Richard was later to export to St. Amand when he began reforming that house in 1013, whence they became known as the *Annales Elnonenses*:[26]

> In the one-thousandth year of the Incarnation of the Lord, in the thirteenth indiction and epacts 12, concurrents 1, paschal term 9, on Good Friday the 29th of March, while Christians were celebrating the sacrosanct mystery of his Passion and Redemption, there was a great earthquake. It was not like one as often occurs . . . but rather the whole magnitude of earth shook everywhere with a general and vast tremor, so that that which had been promised before by the mouth of Truth might be made manifest to everyone. With these and other signs that had been predicted having been completed by divine operation, hence our hope is made more certain in the sight of all regarding those that remain to be completed in due order.[27]

If Richard had, perchance, been seeking an audience that was receptive to apocalyptic arguments and blandishments, it would seem that he found it among the monks of St. Vaast.

The visions of the monk of St. Vaast vividly reflect this climate of apocalyptic anxiety in the very eschatological themes that they draw upon and paraphrase. Indeed, many of these themes were already quite familiar to the literati of the eleventh century. Michael the Archangel describes for the soul the imposture of the Antichrist and the divine mission of Enoch and Elijah to witness against him in terms that echo Gregory the Great's *Moralia in Job*.[28] There follows a reminder, drawing directly from 2 Pet. 3:12–13, that upon the death of the Antichrist, the earth shall burn and then the Savior shall come, whereupon there shall be a new heaven and a new earth. Purely literary sources also served as proof texts for the visionary. Awed by the immensity of the impending Judgment, the soul utters a lament that would seem to have been inspired by the corpus of Carolingian poetry on the theme of the Day of Wrath: "Quid o miseri, miseri, cum supervenerit districti et novissimi iudicii Dei inrecuperabilis hora et impenitens dies illa? Dies irae, dies illa calamitatis et miseriae, dies magna et amara valde!"[29]

The Visions at St. Vaast as Apocalyptic Rhetoric

Rather than dwelling at length on the sources and employment of the eschatological themes in the visions of the monk of St. Vaast, however, our purposes
will be better served by examining the manner in which Richard's letter em-
ploys these visions as the foundation for a powerful and specifically apocalyptic
rhetoric. Among the other eschatological themes, these visions present an utterly unprecedented revelation that seems aimed at convincing the audience of
this letter that the end of the world is at hand. But, as Stephen O'Leary has argued, apocalyptic rhetoric is above all a discourse of action, rather than a manifestation of irrationality and hysteria. The apocalyptic rhetor, if he is successful
in convincing his audience of the veracity of his conclusion that the end is indeed at hand, is often able to contribute directly to the mainstream of social
thought.[30] Indeed, accompanying Richard of St. Vanne's frightening and yet
hopeful news concerning the imminence of the end, there are several other
revelations that suggest the courses of action that various members of the audience should undertake in order to ensure their own salvation.

O'Leary's work on apocalyptic rhetoric provides us with a useful theoretical framework for analyzing the visions contained in Richard's letter. The first
and perhaps most important element that distinguishes apocalyptic rhetoric
from more general eschatological discussions is an urgent sense that the end is
temporally near.[31] We should note that Richard's letter accomplishes this by
narrating a direct revelation of the monk of St. Vaast.[32] On its second journey to
the otherworld, the soul was conveyed to a small building, emanating brilliant
rays of light, situated between two lofty peaks. Contained therein, according to
Michael the Archangel, was "the most secret secret of heavenly mysteries." The
soul, overwhelmed by joy and anticipation of the savory sweetness of this mystery, went inside and with great difficulty read the words, which echo 2 Pet. 3:10,
"The day of the lord will come, it will come like a thief." Below this was written,
apparently in roman numerals, the number of years remaining until the Second Coming of the Lord. The soul could not read this number with any certitude but readily understood that there were only a few years remaining in this
age. The angel confirmed this, gravely admonishing the soul that "today it was
revealed to you how in a short while will be the end of the world. This is known
to no creature, nor to angels, but only by God the Father."

Now, to follow O'Leary, once a rhetor has postulated that the end is near,
he faces the challenge of demonstrating by what authority he knows this.[33]
Richard's letter takes great care to establish its authority at several levels. As we
have just seen, Richard claims that his knowledge that the end is near is the
product of a divine revelation, confirmed by the presence of the archangel
Michael. But he goes even further and, in what represents a fascinating example
of the perceived power of the written word in the early eleventh century,[34] attempts to establish several layers of pseudotextual authority for this apocalyptic
prediction. To begin, the knowledge of the end is conveyed to the soul not orally
but rather as a result of *reading* or rather attempting to read God's own secret

calendar. The soul gains access to the chamber in which this calendar is kept, moreover, only by using the Word of God as a key.[35] Finally, Richard discards a salient topos of visionary literature: normally, in this genre, the visionary orally relates his recollections of his travels in the otherworld at some time after his return. Perhaps Richard did not wish to entrust the import of his message to the perceived incertitude and vagaries of oral transmission based upon memory, for he invents a unique device by which he claims these visions were revealed. In his letter, he asserts that the soul, while it was struggling to depart from the body throughout the course of its visionary experiences, continued to animate the dying monk's tongue, which uttered not only the words of the soul but those of the otherworldly figures that it encountered as well. Hence, Richard claims that even the text of the visions represents an exact and certain transcript of the soul's conversations and impressions in the otherworld, as recorded exactly by a notary who had been assigned to remain by the languid body.[36] Thus, Richard founds his prediction that the end is near upon what he asserts is the sound textual authority of a verisimilitudinous revelation.

Finally, according to O'Leary's model of apocalyptic rhetoric, the rhetor must leave his audience with a clear sense that there is an absolute distinction between good and evil, which is on the verge of becoming manifest.[37] Indeed, the two visions of the monk of St. Vaast give the reader a rather clear glimpse, by way of foretaste, of who shall be the winners and the losers in the impending separation of the sheep from the goats. Most of the goats are admittedly rather stock figures, such as adulterers, whores, and false priests. But in railing against the hidden figures of evil who are about to be unmasked, Richard also names names, to include some of the great potentates and institutions in the region. Given that Richard wrote his letter in the immediate aftermath of his efforts to install Gerard as bishop of Cambrai, over the strenuous objections of Walter of Lens, it is little surprise that we find that both Seiherus, who is labeled a "son of the Devil," and his brother, the elder Walter, have a great many special torments reserved for them.[38] But although we might expect to find members of the family of the obstreperous castellan of Cambrai among those marked out for both purgatorial and eternal torments, some of the other names proffered by Richard are altogether astonishing. In the most interesting of these cases, moreover, their chief "evil" seems to have been their status as the obstacles to Richard's own ambitions to further the cause of monastic and ecclesiastical reform in Flanders. In taking up these nominations for damnation, our analysis of Richard's apocalyptic rhetoric must merge briefly with a cursory awareness of the contemporary currents of politics in Flanders and the diocese of Arras-Cambrai.

The Apocalyptic Suasion to Reform at St. Vaast

Through the first decade of the eleventh century, the Abbey of St. Vaast was caught up in a vicious and highly politicized struggle for exemption from the bishops of Arras-Cambrai.[39] In the course of this struggle, the exemptionist abbot

Fuldrad became aligned with Count Baldwin IV of Flanders, who looked to expand his own sphere of interest to the east, at the expense of the empire. Indeed, the bishops of Arras-Cambrai only succeeded in breaking the exemptionist
movement at St. Vaast when Baldwin overextended himself in a conflict with
Henry II over Valenciennes, and the German ruler used Baldwin's defeat as the
opportunity to buttress the position of the bishops. Specifically, in 1008 Bishop
Erluin of Arras-Cambrai appointed Richard of St. Vanne as the abbot of St. Vaast.
Richard, it must be remembered, stands out among the great monastic reform-
ers of the early eleventh century because his program tended to eschew the idea
of monastic exemption and stressed instead the submission of the monks to
the authority of the local ordinary.

Richard had enjoyed a considerable measure of success in his efforts to
reform St. Vaast prior to 1012. Although evidence, which we shall shortly review, suggests that he did not yet enjoy the favor of Count Baldwin, he took
immediate steps to win at least the count's quiescence regarding his early
changes at the monastery. Most notably, he imported one of Baldwin's distant relatives and a respected aristocrat, Frederick, the former count of Verdun,
who had assumed the monastic habit at St. Vanne and was a close friend of
Richard, to serve in the capacity if not actually the office of prior.[40] Nonetheless, while his piety and exhortations won over many of the monks, others
obdurately continued to resist the reforms. Similarly, most of the monastery's
lay vassals and knights, who had formed the backbone of Fuldrad's resistance
against the bishops of Cambrai, had little desire to surrender all or part of their
benefices to the abbot. Thus, in 1012 the situation at St. Vaast remained tense,
and the status of the reforms precarious.

One of the dominant themes of the visions recounted in Richard's letter of
1012 is that the monastery of St. Vaast has been sundered into two camps, the
one of good and the other of the Devil. Some of the members of the camp of
good are identified by name and include Richard himself, of course, as well as
Frederick and a certain Robert. Indeed, the visionary goes out of his way to flat-
ter Richard while at the same time wryly commenting on his foreign origins.
Michael the Archangel speaks of the embattled abbot in words echoing the Lord's
salutation of Nathanael (John 1:47): "He is truly an Israelite in whom there is
no guile."[41] Interestingly enough, the soul of the monk that experienced the
visions is not at all certain of the status of its own salvation.

As to the other camp, Richard's letter explains that the Devil raged like a
lion among the brothers and the vassals of St. Vaast.[42] Some of the damned are
identified by name: Albric, as well as two renegade monks named Gotmund and
Baldwin. Many more are referred to rather more elliptically: the recently departed
father of one of the monks, a monk who was currently ill, an elderly monk who
had just died, and so on. From the tone of the letter, not to mention the comparative size of the lists, it would seem that the Devil's camp far outnumbered
that of Richard, and posed a very serious threat. The soul makes clear the extent
of the enemy's power by revealing that less than a week before its first vision, a
boy—perhaps an oblate whom Richard had won over—had been murdered in

his sleep by one of the monks. But not all of the monks carried their resentment of Richard that far. Most, it seems, were to be condemned simply for not obeying their abbot and murmuring against him.[43]

But this letter functioned not as a jeremiad in which Richard, through the voice of the visionary, gave vent to his anxieties and frustrations regarding St. Vaast; rather, it constituted an urgent appeal for the monks to reform before the Day of Wrath. Michael the Archangel explains to the soul that in order to obtain indulgence and ensure their salvation, the brothers must simply confess to their abbot and henceforth adhere to him in genuine obedience. The alternative is clear, as the angel explains: "Many say, 'We serve the Lord,' but they serve the Devil. They must make a true confession of their sins, whatever they have done. I tell you, if they do not do this, then you shall quickly see a great Judgment."[44] We cannot, of course, be certain how these visions were received at St. Vaast. Nonetheless, it may not be mere coincidence that it was toward the end of 1012 or early in 1013 that Richard succeeded in appointing a prior—a monk named Poppo from St. Verdun (and later the abbot of Stavelot-Malmédy)—who in short order regained possession of most of the goods of the monastery that remained in the hands of knights.[45] In 1013, Richard of St. Vanne was comfortable enough with the status of St. Vaast that he departed to undertake the process of reform elsewhere in Flanders. Indeed, the author of the Gesta episcoporum Cameracensium may have associated Richard's successful reform of St. Vaast with the visions that occurred there when he wrote of the monastery, that it "rejoices in the religion of monks and is illuminated from Heaven by many prodigies of great wonders."[46]

Since the days of St. Augustine, the authorities of the church have tended to actively discourage, and at times even harshly repress, apocalyptic speculation. This is no surprise, since by its very nature apocalyptic expectation has nearly always constituted something of an implicit—and at times explicit—repudiation of the institutions and ideologies of political and religious authority.[47] In 1012, Richard of St. Vanne was a prominent figure within the church and, as abbot of St. Vanne and St. Vaast, the bearer of considerable titular authority. But the monks and vassals of St. Vaast, and even the count of Flanders, refused to fully acknowledge—and at times openly challenged—Richard's authority as abbot. Hence, Richard found himself confronted by a very real need, which was awkward in the extreme, to assert his own authority by subverting to some degree the institutions and ideologies that stood behind the status quo at the monastery of St. Vaast and, even more broadly, the monasteries across all of Flanders. He needed, quite simply, to shake things up a bit. To do so, he employed a time-proven technique, and one that was particularly well adapted to the psychological climate of the early eleventh century: he claimed that the end was nigh, and the passing of the old powers was at hand; he urged his charges and potential patrons to join him in welcoming the dawn of a glorious new era. Fine and persuasive rhetoric it was, and perhaps even a daring display of political legerdemain on the part of one who presumably knew better.

But we must ask ourselves, did this virtuoso display of apocalyptic rhetoric do more harm than good? Did Richard let the apocalyptic genie out of the bottle that Augustine had so carefully corked up some six hundred years before? We might note in passing, and only by way of suggesting the outlines of future research, that the citizens of Arras seem to have taken note of Richard's claims that the Second Coming was at hand. In 1013, the city embarked upon a remarkable festivity of piety that was centered on the relics of the saints—some familiar and true, and yet many more newly discovered just for the occasion. For two or three years this went on, producing a multitude of miracles and attracting an influx of sick people, tourists, and pilgrims.[48] But, as the work of Richard Landes has demonstrated, the combination of apocalyptic anxieties and relic cults proved to be a volatile mixture around the year 1000 and gave rise in some instances to new expressions of piety that were not always suitably orthodox.[49] Looking back at Richard of St. Vanne's apocalyptic rhetoric of 1012, and the ensuing orgy of relic hunting and miracles in 1013, one may fairly wonder if Richard contributed to the climate that produced the famous outbreak of "heresy" at Arras, against which Bishop Gerard was to fulminate in 1022 and again in 1031?[50]

NOTES

Editors' note: David Van Meter is a private scholar and a 1997 graduate of the Ph.D. program in History at Boston University.

1. Dominique Iogna-Prat, "Continence et virginité dans la conception clunisienne de l'ordre du monde autour de l'an Mil," in *Académie des Inscriptions et Belles-Lettres, Comptes rendus des séances de l'année 1985, Janvier–Mars* (Paris, 1985), pp. 136–37; Dominique Iogna-Prat, "Entre anges et hommes: Les moines 'doctrinaires' de l'an mil," in *La France de l'an mil*, ed. R. R. Delort (Paris, 1990), pp. 256–59.

2. Unsurpassed on the eschatological nuances of monastic spirituality is Jean Leclercq, *The Love of Learning and the Desire for God*, trans. C. Misrahi (New York, 1961).

3. See Leclercq, *Love of Learning*, pp. 248–50; Gunilla Björkvall, "*Expectantes Dominum*: Advent, the Time of Expectation, as Reflected in Liturgical Poetry from the Tenth and Eleventh Centuries," in *In Quest of the Kingdom: Ten Papers on Monastic Spirituality*, ed. Alf Härdelin, Bibliotheca Theologiae Practicae, Krykovetenskapliga studier, vol. 48 (Uppsala, 1991), pp. 109–32.

4. See Stephen D. O'Leary, *Arguing the Apocalypse: Toward a Theory of Millennial Rhetoric* (Oxford, 1994).

5. David C. Van Meter, "Eschatological Order and the Argument for Clerical Celibacy in Francia around the Year 1000," in *Medieval Purity and Piety: Essays on Medieval Clerical Celibacy and Religious Reform*, ed. Michael Frassetto (New York, 1998), pp. 149–75.

6. See especially David C. Van Meter, "The Peace of Amiens-Corbie and Gerard of Cambrai's Oration on the Three Functional Orders: The Date, the Context, the Rhetoric," *Revue Belge de Philologie et d'Histoire* 74 (1996): 633–57.

7. Van Meter, "Eschatological Order," pp. 159–60 n. 43.

8. Hugh of Flavigny, *Chronicon* (*MGH, SS* 8:381–91). While historians of the late nineteenth century tended to disparage Hugh of Flavigny as a credulous witness and hence an unreliable source, Hubert Dauphin has painstakingly qualified and in some regards corrected that misperception in *Le Bienheureux Richard, Abbé de Saint-*

Vannes de Verdun (d. 1046) (Louvain, 1946), pp. 18–26. In particular, he has shown that Hugh was habitually scrupulous in transcribing the texts of the letters that he included in the *Chronicon*.

9. For the background of the highly politicized and arduous reform of St.-Vaast, see David C. Van Meter, "Count Baldwin IV, Richard of Saint-Vannes and the Inception of Monastic Reform in Eleventh-Century Flanders," *Revue Bénédictine* 107 (1997): 130–48.

10. For an interesting attempt to compare medieval visions to modern near-death experiences, see Marc Van Uytfanghe, "Les *Visiones* du très haut Moyen Age et les récentes 'expériences de mort temporaire': Sens ou non-sens d'une comparison," *Sacris Erudiri* 33 (1992–93): 135–82.

11. The most recent treatment of these visions is C. Carrozi, *Le voyage de l'âme dans l'au-delà d'après la littérature latine (Ve–XIIIe siècle)*, Collection de l'Ecole Française de Rome, vol. 189 (Rome, 1994), pp. 396–412. On the visionary literature, see Michel Aubrun, "Caractères et portée religieuse et sociale des 'Visiones' en Occident du VIe au XIe siècle," *Cahiers de Civilisation Médiévale* 23 (1980): 109–30; Peter Dinzelbacher, *Vision und Visionliteratur im Mittelalter*, Monographien zur Geschichte des Mittelalters, vol. 23 (Stuttgart, 1981); Aron Gurevich, "The 'Divine Comedy' before Dante," in *Medieval Popular Culture: Problems of Belief and Perception*, trans. János M. Bak and Paul A. Hollingsworth (Cambridge, 1988), pp. 104–52; Jacques Le Goff, "Les rêves dans la culture et la psychologie collective de l'Occident médiévale," in *Pour un autre Moyen Age* (Paris, 1977), pp. 299–306. For a summary list of visions that have been published, as well as a general discussion of the visionary genre and its uses and limitations as a source, see Peter Dinzelbacher, *Revelationes*, Typologie des sources du Moyen Age Occidental, fasc. 57 (Turnhout, 1991).

12. Johannes Fried discusses the importance of these visions as evidence of a general apocalyptic mentality in the Low Countries, without addressing their context (and, in fact, wrongly attributing them to two separate monks) in "Endzeiterwartung," pp. 436–37. Hubert Dauphin, on the other hand, accurately sees in the visions an admission that Richard's reforms at St. Vaast were ill-received by many of the brothers, without taking up what are, as he admits, "les révélations touchant l'avenir" (*Bienheureux Richard*, pp. 180–82). One should note that Michael was typically viewed as the angel of prophetic visions; see Valerie J. Flint, *The Rise of Magic in Early Medieval Europe* (Princeton, 1991), p. 171.

13. Gurevich, " Divine Comedy," pp. 119–21.

14. Ibid., p. 144.

15. See esp. Fried, "Endzeiterwartung"; Daniel Verhelst, "Adso van Montier-en-Der en de angst voor het jaar Duizend," *Tijdschrift voor Geschiedenis* 90 (1977): 110–23. On the eschatological significance of 1033, see F. W. N. Hugenholtz, "Les terreurs de l'an mil: Enkele hypothesen," in *Varia Historica aangeboden ann Professor Doctor A. W. Byvanck* (Assen, 1954), pp. 110–23. For a discussion of the "millennial generation" that emerged as a result of this mental climate of apocalyptic expectations, and particularly the biography of one of its most productive intellectuals, see Richard Landes, *Relics, Apocalypse, and the Deceits of History: Ademar of Chabannes, 989–1034* (Cambridge, Mass., 1995).

16. So says Abbo of Fleury, in counseling King Robert on the errors to be avoided in his realm, when he brings up the example of a preacher in the cathedral at Paris who predicted that the world would end at the millennium; *Apologeticus ad Hugonem et Rodbertum reges Francorum* (PL:471–72). On the eschatological underpin-

nings of Christian chronography and its relation to millenarian outbursts through the year 1000, see Richard Landes, "Lest the Millennium Be Fulfilled: Apocalyptic Expectations and the Pattern of Western Chronography, 100–800 C.E.," in *The Use and Abuse of Eschatology in the Middle Ages*, ed. Werner Verbeke, Daniel Verhelst and Andries Welkenhuysen (Leuven, 1988), pp. 137–211; Richard Landes, "*Millenarismus absconditus*: L'historiographie augustinienne et le millénarisme du haut Moyen Age jusqu'à l'an Mil," *Le Moyen Age* 98 (1992): 355–77; and Richard Landes, "Sur les traces du Millennium: La 'Via Negativa' (2e partie)," *Le Moyen Age* 99 (1993): 5–26.

17. The earliest source for the dragon is the *Gesta ep. Camer.*, 1.114 (*MGH, SS* 7:451). Radulfus Glaber describes the dragon as appearing in 1003 and hence removes it from the context of Otto III's death; *Historiarum libri quinque*, 2.8.15 (hereafter cited as *Historiarum*); the edition cited is John France, ed. and trans., *Rodulfi Glabri, "Historiarum libri quinque"/Rodulfus Glaber, "The Five Books of the Histories"* (Oxford, 1989), pp. 78–79 (hereafter cited as *Histories*). Sigebert of Gembloux transcribes this same event, using the *Gesta ep. Camer.* as his source, although under the year 1000 (*MGH, SS* 6:357), and hence also separates it from Otto III's death. Hugh of Flavigny abbreviates Glaber's description while relocating it to the context of Otto's death in 1002 (*MGH, SS* 8:368). Arnulf of St. Emmeran also saw a giant, airborne dragon while traveling in Pannonia around 1030; for his account, see *De miraculis S. Emmerammi libri duo* (*PL* 141:1039–42); for an indepth discussion of Arnulf's vision and his initial apocalyptic interpretation of it, which was later subsumed within a nonapocalyptic mode of remembering, see Patrick J. Geary, *Phantoms of Remembrance: Memory and Oblivion at the End of the First Millennium* (Princeton, 1994), pp. 158–76.

18. On the theory of the continuity of the Roman Empire, see W. Goez, *Translatio imperii: Ein Beitrag zur Geschichte des Geschichtsdenken und der politischen Theorien im Mittelalter und in der frühen Neuzeit* (Tübingen, 1958), pp. 74–104. On the tradition that the continuity of the Roman Empire prevents the arrival of the Antichrist, see H. D. Rauh, *Das Bild des Antichrist im Mittelalter: Von Tyconius zum deutschen Symbolismus* (Münster, 1973), pp. 58–63; F. Paschoud, "La doctrine chrétienne et l'idéologie impériale romaine," in *L'Apocalypse de Jean: Traditions exégétiques et iconographiques, IIIe au XIIe siècle*, ed. Y. Christe (Geneva and Paris, 1979), pp. 31–72; and chap. 13, by Benjamin Arnold, elsewhere in this volume. On the eschatological aspects of Otto III's imperial ideology, see esp. Fried, "Endzeiterwartung," pp. 427–33; Peter Klein, "L'art et l'idéologie impériale des Ottoniens vers l'an mil: l'Évangéliaire d'Enri II et l'Apocalypse de Bamberg," *Cahiers de St.-Michel de Cuxa* 16 (1985): 177–207; Menno Ter Braak, *Kaiser Otto III: Ideal und Praxis im frühen Mittelalter* (Amsterdam, 1928).

19. *Adso Dervensis: De ortu et tempore Antichristi necnon et tractatus qui ab eo dependunt*, ed. Daniel Verhelst, *CCCM.* 45 (Turnhout, 1976). An English translation is provided by Bernard McGinn in *Apocalyptic Spirituality: Treatises and Letters of Lactantius, Adso of Montier-en-Der, Joachim of Fiore, the Franciscan Spirituals, Savonarola* (New York, 1979), pp. 81–96. For discussions of the text and its sources, see R. Konrad, *De ortu et tempore Antichristi: Antichristvorstellung und Geschichtsbild des Abtes Adso von Montier-en-Der* (Kallmünz, 1964); Paul Alexander, *The Byzantine Apocalyptic Tradition*, ed. D. de F. Abrahamse (Berkeley, 1985), pp. 105–9; Bernard McGinn, *Visions of the End: Apocalyptic Traditions in the Middle Ages* (New York, 1979), pp. 82–84.

20. Karl Grund, *Die Anschauungen des Rodulphus Glaber in seinen Historien*

(Greifswald, 1910), pp. 51–53; Landes, *Relics, Apocalypse*, pp. 40–44, 304–5, 337.

21. On the famine, see, e.g., *Annales s. Martini Tornacensis*, anno 1006 (*MGH, SS* 15.2:1297), which draws from the discussion of a famine at Ghent in ca. 1012 in the *Vita s. Macharii altera*, chap. 26 (*MGH, SS* 15.2:680); *Annales Leodinienses* and *Laubienses* (*MGH, SS* 4:18); *Anglo-Saxon Chronicles*, anno 1005; *Annales Sangallienses* (*MGH, SS* 1:81); *Annales Hildesheimenses*, anno 1006 (*MGH, SS* 3:93); Glaber, *Historiarum*, 2.9.17 (*Histories*, pp. 80–83); Sigebert of Gembloux, *Chronicon*, anno 1006 (*MGH, SS* 8:354). On the supernova, see Albert of Metz, *De diversitate temporum*, 1.6–7, 2.22–23 (*MGH, SS* 4:704, 720–23); *Annales Leodinienses* and *Laubienses* (*MGH, SS* 4:18); *Annales Mosomagenses* (*MGH, SS* 3:161); see also B. Goldstein, "The Supernova of A.D. 1006," *Astronomical Journal* 70 (1965): 105–11. The rain of blood took place on Palm Sunday in 1009 and was followed by yet another local famine; *Annales Quedlinbourgenses* (*MGH, SS* 3:80). On the potential apocalyptic significance of natural disorders, see Guy Lobrichon, "L'ordre de ce temps et les désordres de la fin: Apocalypse et société, du IXe à la fin du XIe siècle," in *Use and Abuse of Eschatology*, ed. Verbeke, Verhelst, and Welkenhuysen, pp. 221–41; Michael Barkun, *Disaster and the Millennium* (New Haven, 1974).

22. Pseudo-Bede, *Excerptiones patrum* (*PL* 94:555); see also William Heist, *The Fifteen Signs before Doomsday* (East Lansing, 1952), pp. 24–26. On the flooding of rivers in 1003 and the maritime inundation of 1014, see the *Annales Blandinienses*, ed. Philip Grierson, *Les Annales de Saint-Pierre de Gand et de Saint-Amand* (Brussels, 1937), pp. 23–24.

23. *Gesta ep. Camer.*, 3.8 (*MGH, SS* 7:468–69); Sigebert of Gembloux, *Chronicon*, anno 1011 (*MGH, SS* 6:354).

24. David C. Van Meter, "Christian of Stavelot on Matthew 24:42, and the Tradition That the World Will End on a March 25th," *Recherches de Théologie Ancienne et Médiévale* 63 (1996): 68–92.

25. See ibid., pp. 89–90.

26. On the early textual history of these annals, see Grierson, *Les Annales*, pp. LV–LVII.

27. *Annales Elnonenses*, anno 1000, ed. Grierson, *Les Annales*, p. 153.

28. These same themes were also taken up in the early eleventh century by Burchard of Worms, in his *Liber Decretorum*, 20.94–97 (*PL* 140:1053–54).

29. Hugh of Flavigny, *Chronicon* (*MGH, SS* 8:388). On the impact of such poetry around the year 1000, see Fried, "Endzeiterwartung," pp. 406ff.

30. O'Leary, *Arguing the Apocalypse*, pp. 14–17.

31. Ibid., pp. 61–62.

32. Hugh of Flavigny, *Chronicon* (*MGH, SS* 8:390).

33. O'Leary, *Arguing the Apocalypse*, p. 51.

34. See Brian Stock, *The Implications of Literacy: Written Language and Models of Interpretation in the Eleventh and Twelfth Centuries* (Princeton, 1983).

35. Hugh of Flavigny, *Chronicon* (*MGH, SS* 8:390).

36. Ibid., 8:381, 391.

37. O'Leary, *Arguing the Apocalypse*, pp. 34ff.

38. Hugh of Flavigny, *Chronicon* (*MGH, SS* 8:389).

39. See Van Meter, "Count Baldwin IV."

40. Frederick was the eldest son of Godefrey of Verdun and Mathilda of Saxony, who was the widow of Baldwin III and hence the grandmother of Baldwin IV; see Dauphin, *Bienheureux Richard*, pp. 58, 182.

41. Hugh of Flavigny, *Chronicon* (*MGH, SS* 8:385–86).

42. Dauphin, *Bienheureux Richard*, p. 181; Hugh of Flavigny, *Chronicon* (*MGH, SS* 8:389).

43. Hugh of Flavigny, *Chronicon* (*MGH, SS* 8:385–86).

44. Ibid., 8:385.

45. Everhelme, *Vita s. Popponis*, chaps. 18–20 (AASS OSB, saec. VI-I, pp. 578–80); Dauphin, *Bienheureux Richard*, p. 183.

46. *Gesta ep. Camer.*, 2.14 (*MGH, SS* 7:459).

47. Landes, "*Millenarismus absconditus*," pp. 362–63; Landes, "Lest the Millennium," pp. 156–60; O'Leary, *Arguing the Apocalypse*, p. 54.

48. *Gesta ep. Camer.*, 2.13, 3.4 (*MGH, SS* 7:459, 467).

49. Richard Landes, "La vie apostolique en Aquitaine en l'an Mil: Paix de Dieu, culte des reliques, et communautés hérétiques," *Annales ESC* 46 (1991): 573–93; Richard Landes, "Between Aristocracy and Heresy: Popular Participation in the Limousin Peace of God, 994–1033," in *The Peace of God: Social Violence and Religious Response in France around the Year 1000*, ed. Richard Landes and Thomas Head (Ithaca, 1992), pp. 184–218. See also Malcolm Lambert, *Medieval Heresy: Popular Movements from the Gregorian Reform to the Reformation*, 2d ed. (Oxford, 1992), pp. 9–32.

50. On the 1022 incident, see *Acta synodi Artebatensis* (*PL* 142:1269–1312); on the 1031 incident, see Gerard's letter to Abbot Leduin of St. Vaast, *Gesta ep. Camer.*, 3.32 (*MGH, SS* 7:478–79). On dating and full bibliography, see Lambert, *Medieval Heresy*, pp. 22–25; Jean-Pierre Poly and Eric Bournazel, *The Feudal Transformation, 900–1200*, trans. Caroline Higgitt (New York, 1991), pp. 276–77. On the eschatological undertones, see Van Meter, "Eschatological Order," pp. 159–66.

PART IV

Tools and Sources

16

The Astronomical Situation around the Year 1000

Bradley E. Schaefer

Since the heavens are the abode of God, what better place is there for him to display his messages to humanity? The celestial vault is untouched by humans, so the author of any sign in the sky is unambiguously divine. The skies are full of activity, from passing storms to streaking meteors to wandering planets, any of which may be omens.

Humanity has a long record of reacting strongly to heavenly spectacles. Constantine the Great saw a cross in the sky before the climactic battle at the Milvian Bridge and interpreted it as a sign from the Christian God. With his scientifically derived foreknowledge of a lunar eclipse, Christopher Columbus impressed the awestruck Jamaican natives to supply his shipwrecked crew with desperately needed food for the many months before rescue ships arrived. In an ironic turnabout, Tecumseh used his own foreknowledge of a solar eclipse to confirm the prophetic powers of his brother, and hence cemented a confederation of Indian tribes in the Ohio River valley in 1806. Comet scares in 1795, 1857, and 1910 created popular panic due to the supposed end of the world.[1] Again, Nat Turner based the timing of his slave revolt in 1831 on the "divine sign" of a solar eclipse.[2] The list goes on: throughout history, astrology in various forms has affected decisions both large and small.

Celestial events can be regarded as omens for many reasons. Eclipses and meteor showers impress any observer with the awesome nature of the spectacle itself. Astrological theory can attach importance to certain specific planetary configurations. Tradition associates both comets and meteors with death. The Christian Bible and the Islamic Koran associate solar and lunar eclipses with Judgment Day.

Judgment Day is fundamental to Christian theology, and there are some biblical grounds for anticipating its imminent arrival. It is natural to think that such a momentous event will be heralded in the skies. For a variety of reasons, medieval Europeans were expecting Judgment Day to arrive around the end of the first Christian millennium. Hence, any study of the apocalyptic year 1000 should include a survey of the astronomical situation during that period.

Inventory: 950–1050

Many celestial phenomena can be identified as signs from God. The century that centered on the changing millennium had many astronomical events of note. These can be known in modern times either by reliable back-calculations of orbits or from the descriptions of contemporary chronicles. This section will detail the important sky events from the years 950 through 1050, primarily from the perspective of a European observer.

A total solar eclipse is perhaps the most awesome spectacle in the heavens. The darkened sky has the ominous overtone that the life-giving sun may never return. These two factors have resulted in solar eclipses having the power to frequently change the course of history.[3] The paths of the Sun and Moon in ancient times are reliably known, so modern researchers can be confident concerning the details of solar eclipses around the change of the millennium.[4] Total solar eclipses visible from Europe, excluding northern Scandinavia, occurred on December 22, 968 (Ireland, France, Italy, and the Balkans), on July 20, 996 (Baltic states to Ukraine), and on January 24, 1023 (Ireland, England, and Norway). Less spectacular, annular eclipses occurred on May 17, 961 (England and Norway), May 8, 970 (Greece and Ukraine), October 21, 990 (southern Scandinavia, the Baltic states, and Ukraine), March 18, 1010 (Spain, France, and Italy), June 29, 1033 (France, Switzerland, and the Balkans), August 22, 1039 (France and Sicily), and November 22, 1044 (Spain, Sicily, and Greece).

The visual and symbolic impact of a lunar eclipse is significantly less than that of a solar eclipse, but the frequency of the lunar phenomena results in both types of eclipses causing comparable numbers of history-changing events.[5] Between two and five lunar eclipses occur each year, although typically only one of them will be both an umbral eclipse and visible from a given location. Given this frequency of occurrence, I will list here only those umbral eclipses with a magnitude greater than 0.5 that were easily visible from Europe in the years 990–1010.[6] Total lunar eclipses were visible on April 1, 991, September 26, 991, January 30, 994, July 14, 995, May 14, 998, November 6, 998, March 12, 1001, March 1, 1002, April 12, 1009, and October 6, 1009. Partial eclipses with a magnitude greater that 0.5 were visible on April 12, 990, October 6, 990, May 24, 997, November 17, 997, June 14, 1006, and April 23, 1008.

Sunspots are magnetically confined cool regions on our Sun's surface. Large sunspot groups may cover a few percent of the visible disk and are easily visible to the naked eye provided that the Sun is somehow dimmed.[7] This dimming might arise from either dust storms or volcanic eruptions, or near sunset on any hazy day. Sunspot numbers follow a roughly eleven-year cycle, with an average of a few visible groups at any time down to no sunspots detectable for many months at a time. While European observers rarely noted sunspots, Chinese observers frequently noted them and recorded them as omens for the emperor. There are 157 recorded Chinese sightings before the discovery of the telescope, of which only one (March 3, 974) is recorded for our century of interest.[8] Drawing from back-calculations, however, the years of maximum sunspot activity during the period would have been 950, 963, 974, 986, 994, 1003, 1016, 1027, and 1038.[9]

Aurorae appear as beautiful arcs, rays, and curtains of multicolored, ghostly lights that dance and dart about in the sky. The cause is charged particles streaming from the Sun into the upper reaches of the Earth's atmosphere. The Sun emits bursts of particles during solar flares, and so the frequency of aurorae follows the same roughly eleven-year cycle as the sunspots. The particles spiral down along the lines of the Earth's magnetic field, which is why the auroral rate is the highest at the far northern and southern latitudes. At the peak of a sunspot cycle, northern Europe may have a display on the majority of nights, while southern Europe will get a show perhaps once a year. Extensive searches for mentions of auroral events in medieval European chronicles have been conducted,[10] from which we may note that aurorae were reported in 953, June 955, January 957, February 962, 965, May 12, 966 or 971, 971, 971 or 972, 975, 978, October 28, 979, ca. 988, October 21, 992, December 26, 992, March 29, 1000, December 14, 1001, December 19, 1002, 1005, October 31, 1008, 1010, September 29, 1014, 1032, September 1034, April 6, 1039 or 1040.

Supernovae are stars that explode to form neutron stars or black holes, a cataclysm that usually emits more light than a whole galaxy. Any supernova that occurs near Earth will usually appear as a very bright star visible for a year or two as it fades back into obscurity. Eight supernovae have been recorded in historical sources, primarily in oriental dynastic chronicles. Interestingly, one of the brightest came to its peak brightness in late May of 1006. Scholarly interpretation of the few records suggests that the peak brightness may have been either somewhat brighter than Venus or equal to the brightness of the quarter Moon,[11] although my own recent analysis of the reported heliacal rise and set dates strongly suggests that the fainter end of the range is correct.[12] The supernova was first discovered by the Chinese on May 1, 1006, and was observed for up to two years in China, Japan, Korea, Iraq, Egypt, and Europe. Since the supernova was deep in the southern sky (declination -37°), it was totally invisible from any site north of latitude 53°. For most of Europe, then, the supernova appeared as a very bright star cutting low across the southern sky on summer evenings in the year of 1006. Anyone with even a modest familiarity with the sky would easily have noticed the new star, although it would have ceased being spectacular by the year 1007. Despite lying just outside our inventory period, mention must be made of the most famous supernova, the Crab Supernova, which appeared on July 4, 1054 and which peaked a bit brighter than Venus.[13] Speculation has been advanced that this new star was associated with the Second Coming,[14] but this idea presents some difficulties.[15]

Novae are another class of cataclysmic explosions, although in this case the eruption involves only the surface of a white dwarf star. Novae are much fainter and more numerous than supernovae. They appear as transient stars that are visible for several months. A total of sixty-seven novae have been reported in the years before the discovery of the telescope; of these, two occurred during our inventory period: February 8, 1011, and January 15, 1035.[16]

Comets are large balls of frozen gases mixed with some meteoritic gravel. When the orbit of a comet takes it into the inner solar system, the Sun's heat boils the ices, which fall behind to form the characteristic tail. If a comet passes close to the Earth or is large (bigger than a few kilometers in diameter), then the nucleus of the comet can appear as bright as Venus and the tail can apparently stretch across the heavens. In Europe, comets were often associated with portents of wars (e.g., the Norman invasion of England) and the deaths of kings (e.g., Julius Caesar). In the century centered on the year 1000, sixty-one comets were recorded in the old chronicles.[17] Widely observed comets were discovered on August 3, 975, August 13 ,989 (Halley's comet), February 23, 998, February 12, 1014, August 3, 1018, and September 20, 1034.

As the ices of a comet are boiled away by the Sun, the trapped meteoritic gravel is released to follow an orbit similar to that of the parent comet. Should the Earth happen to pass through the orbit of a young comet, this debris will pelt the atmosphere like a blast from a shotgun. Each rock will be visible for perhaps a second as a meteor, while the parallel paths of all the rocks will make all of the meteors appear to radiate out of one point in the sky. The Earth passes through many such cometary debris clouds each year, with the densest swarm producing around fifty meteors per hour that are visible to the eye under good conditions. However, once in a great while the Earth will pass through an exceptionally rich cluster and a meteor storm or shower will result. These are spectacular events with up to a thousand meteors visible at any instant, so that one might well think that the sky is falling or adopt some other apocalyptic interpretation. Meteor storms reported in European and Arab chronicles were observed in the year 952/53 in Egypt and in August or September 1026 in Baghdad.[18]

Bolides are extremely bright meteors, or rocks passing by the Earth that fall into our atmosphere. The light is created by the glow from the tremendous heat generated by the great speed of the meteor. Meteors brighter than the full Moon will be visible from any specific site roughly once in every millennium, or once a year from a continent the size of Europe.[19] Such a bolide might easily conjure up visions of the apocalypse during its brief passage across the sky. From the historical sources, we may conclude that the years from 991 to 1034, and particularly from 991 to 1002, saw a higher-than-normal rate of reported bolides.[20] This increase is also apparent in the Chinese bolide records.[21]

A planetary conjunction occurs when two planets pass close to each other as they wander along the ecliptic. Such events look impressive if the planets are bright and the grouping is close. In addition, there might be astrological significance associated with either a conjunction or other configuration. These events are frequent, with typically half a dozen pairings between the five bright planets each year, although many of these are not visible due to their proximity to the Sun. So, too, there are typically five Moon/planet conjunctions each month. Multiple conjunctions are also frequent enough that a simple inventory over a century would be long and useless. However, a search for planetary massings in the decade around the year 1000 reveals three events of potential interest. The first occurred on New Year's Day of the year 1001, when the Sun, Moon, and all of the planets except Saturn were within 30° of each other near the modern constellation of Sagittarius.[22] The second event occurred on August 14, 1007, when the Sun, Moon, and all five planets were within 20° of each other near the star Regulus in Leo. Finally, on October 24, 1008, the Sun, Moon, and all the planets except Saturn were within 35° of each other near the modern constellation of Virgo.

Discussion

The above inventory shows that celestial spectacles occurred frequently around the year 1000. For example, in the decade from 1000 to 1009, a European observer could have been astounded by two total lunar eclipses, two partial lunar eclipses, six major aurorae, one exceptionally bright supernova, a bumper crop of bolides, and three planetary massings. The inventory is incomplete due to poor records, so the final tally of astronomical wonders was likely to include several events in any given year.

With this high rate, any seer or mystic can always find some convenient sign in the sky to support an apocalyptic prophecy. That is, any one who searches the heavens for a divine message need not wait long. Similarly, any modern historian who seeks some astronomical phenomenon to connect with an apocalyptic account will inevitably be able to find some match, whether correct or not.

This conclusion can be extended to modern researchers who seek to find a celestial event to correspond with some other cultural or religious symbol. In such a case, that researcher may confront many sky phenomena that could plausibly be advanced as the origin of the symbol. The best-known example of this is the Star of Bethlehem, which has variously been identified with a comet, a nova, a supernova, a triple conjunction of Jupiter and Saturn, and the stationary point of Saturn.[23] Another classic example is the origin of the "star and crescent" symbol, which has been tied to battles or visions in 340 B.C., A.D. 610, 1079, 1453, and 1922, even though the symbol was already in widespread use in the Middle East in the third millennium B.C.[24] A lesser-known example is the attribution of a star pair on a Byzantine gold coin of Constantine IX to the Crab Supernova in 1054, even though the symbol is more likely to have arisen from propaganda surrounding the Great Schism.[25]

Hence, while some classes of celestial events may plausibly have historical associations with catastrophic interpretations, nevertheless the perceptions of real people are more important than what was or was not in the sky. All study of the apocalyptic year 1000 must accordingly be based on written history, while astronomy can only provide a tool for comparison or possibly verification.

NOTES

Editors' note: This paper was originally presented at the "Conference on the Apocalyptic Year 1000" in Boston, Mass., Nov. 4–6, 1996. Dr. Schaefer is Professor of Astronomy and Physics at Yale University. His research interests lie in supernovae and gamma-ray bursters and in the calculation of the visibility of celestial events in those situations that have had an impact on history.

1. See O. Gingerich, *The Great Copernicus Chase* (Cambridge, 1992); D. Olson, "Comet Panics, Daytime Visibility of Venus, and Napoleon's Star," *Bulletin of the American Astronomical Association* 25 (1993): 1334.

2. B. E. Schaefer, "Solar Eclipses That Changed the World," *Sky and Telescope* 82 (May 1994): 36–39.

3. Ibid.

4. T. R. Oppolzer, *Canon der Finsternisse* (New York, 1887); H. Mucke and J. Meeus, *Canon of Solar Eclipses, −2003 to +2526* (Vienna, 1983).

5. B. E. Schaefer, "Lunar Eclipses That Changed the World," *Sky and Telescope* 84 (May 1992): 639–42.

6. B. L. Liu and A. D. Fiala, *Canon of Lunar Eclipses, 1500 B.C. to A.D. 3000* (Richmond, 1992).

7. B. E. Schaefer, "Visibility of Sunspots," *Astrophysical Journal* 411 (1993): 909–19.

8. K. K. C. Yau and F. R. Stephenson, "A Revised Catalog of Far Eastern Observations of Sunspots (165 B.C. to A.D. 1918)," *Quarterly Journal of the Royal Astronomical Society* 29 (1988): 175–97.

9. D. J. Schove, "The Sunspot Cycle, 649 B.C. to A.D. 2000," *Journal of Geophysical Research* 60 (1955): 127–46.

10. See U. Dall'Olmo, "An Additional List of Auroras from European Sources from 450 to 1466 A.D.," *Journal of Geophysical Research* 84 (1979): 1525–35.

11. D. H. Clark and F. R. Stephenson, *The Historical Supernovae* (Oxford, 1977).

12. B. E. Schaefer, "The Peak Brightness of Historical Supernovae and the Hubble Constant," *Astrophysical Journal* 459 (1996): 438–54.

13. Clark and Stephenson, *Historical Supernovae*.

14. P. de Vicci, "A Coinage of Astronomical Significance," *Numismatist* 107 (1994): 956–61.

15. B. E. Schaefer, "The Crab Supernova in Europe: Byzantine Coins and Macbeth," *Quarterly Journal of the Royal Astronomical Society* 36 (1995): 377–84.

16. Clark and Stephenson, *Historical Supernovae*.

17. I. Hasegawa, "Catalog of Ancient and Naked Eye Comets," *Vistas in Astronomy* 24 (1980): 59–102.

18. U. Dall'Olmo, "Meteors, Meteor Showers and Meteorites in the Middle Ages: From European Medieval Sources," *Journal for the History of Astronomy* 9 (1978): 123–34.

19. See C. W. Allen, *Astrophysical Quantities* (London, 1976).

20. K. L. Rasmussen, "Historical Accretionary Events from 800 B.C. to A.D. 1750: Evidence for Planetary Rings around the Earth?" *Quarterly Journal of the Royal Astronomical Society* 32 (1991): 25–34.

21. X. L. Liu, "Statistical Analysis of Chinese Historical Records of Fireballs," *Chinese Astronomy and Astrophysics* 11 (1987): 312–19.

22. While such an event would not have been seen in the sky, an astrologer's calculations could have revealed its existence.

23. B. E. Schaefer, "Astronomy and the Limits of Vision," *Vistas in Astronomy* 36 (1993): 311–61.

24. B. E. Schaefer, "Heavenly Signs," *New Scientist* 132 (1991): 48–51.

25. Schaefer, "The Crab Supernova."

17

Selected Documents on Eschatological Expectations and Social Change around the Year 1000

David C. Van Meter

I. Apocalyptic Expectations, ca. 950–1050

Document 1. Thietland of Einsiedeln on the binding of Satan for one thousand years, in Apocalypse 20:3 (Einsiedeln MS 38, fol. 185r). Composed in the mid–tenth century.

There follows "so that he shall no more seduce the nations." He calls the nations those whom he wishes to be understood by the name of the nations, that is to say, the faithful. There follows "until a thousand years are fulfilled." Note that these words seem to indicate that after a thousand years he will be able to seduce the faithful. But it is not until he is placed there indefinitely, as many examples pretend, or rather the order of the words should then be "he closed it and sealed it until a thousand years are fulfilled, so that he might not seduce. . . ." He calls the thousand years the final portion of this age, and he looks for it from the Passion of our Lord and our redemption to the advent of the Antichrist. Therefore, he posited the millenarian number for the completion for all of this time.

Document 2. A letter on the Hungarians that speaks of widespread millenarian reactions among the population; R. B. C. Huygens, "Un témoin de la crainte de l'an 1000: La lettre sur les Hongrois," *L'Atomus* 15 (1957): 232.

First it is to be said that the opinion, which persuaded many people in your region and ours, is frivolous and without any merit: that the Hungarian people, hateful to God, are Gog and Magog and the other races described along with them, concerning which it is especially said that "You will come out of your places in the North. . . . after many days you will be visited, in the latter years you will go to the land which is restored from the sword" (Ezek. 38:15, 8). They said that this is the last time of the age, and the end of the world is near, and therefore Gog and Magog are the Hungarians, who were never before heard of but have now, at the end of time, appeared.

Document 3. Abbo of Fleury on apocalyptic expectations prior to the year 1000; *Apologeticus ad Hugonem et Rodbertum reges Francorum* (PL 139:471–72). Composed ca. 994.

Also, regarding the end of the world, as an adolescent I heard a sermon preached before the populace in the church at Paris: the Antichrist should arrive straightway, with the number of one thousand years having been completed, and the universal judgment should follow not long after that time. I resisted this prophecy, to the extent that I was able, from the Gospels and the Apocalypse and the Book of Daniel. Then my abbot, Richard of blessed memory, with a keen mind warded off an error that arose regarding the end of the world. After that, he ordered me to respond to a letter that he received from the Lotharingians; for the rumor had filled nearly the whole world that when the Annunciation fell upon Good Friday, it would without doubt be the end of the world.

Document 4. From the *Chronicle* of the Pseudo–William Godellus (*RHF* 10:262). Composed in the early twelfth century.

In the year of the Lord 1009, with the permission of God, the unclean Turks invaded the lands of Jerusalem and captured Jerusalem, and they possessed the glorious sepulchre of Christ the Lord. This happened under Kings Basil and Constantine of the Greeks, under Emperor Henry of the Romans, and in the eleventh year of King Robert of the Franks. In that same year, many Jews were baptized on account of fear. In the year of the Lord 1010, after the report of this had been heard in many places in the world, fear and sorrow occupied the hearts of many, and many suspected that the end of the world approached. Those who were of sounder mind concerned themselves, by salubrious council, even more attentively with the correction of their own lives.

Document 5. Richard of St. Vanne's description of the second vision of the otherworld experienced by a monk of St. Vaast in 1012 (Hugh of Flavigny, *Chronicon*, in *MGH, SS* 8:390). Composed in ca. 1012.

The angel said to him, "This very thing that you see, soul, is the most secret of the secrets of heavenly mysteries." The sign of the word of God released the seal, and going even nearer, a little door was seen to open; from it issued such a great smell and fragrance of lilies and roses that it might overpower the most precious species and kinds of all aromas. That soul, eager to fulfill his desire for this inestimable heavenly vision and peace, and the inestimable joy of perennial happiness, said, "Lord Saint Michael, how great is the good of all felicity!

How marvelous is this undiscovered sweetness!" The angel said to him, "Approach, soul. Follow me, come and look and read." Eager for these things, the soul said, "Lord, I am unable to read." Again the angel said, "Soul, behold and read." And the soul said, "I am unable, lord, unless you say it aloud." With the light of the eyes being applied a little more perspicaciously, before the great clarity with which they completely shone forth, he was thus scarcely able to read the inscriptions that were contained there: "The day of the Lord will come, it will come quickly like a thief."[1] He said, "What, lord, what will the sinners do then? Rather, how many years remain for this last age to await the arrival of the Judge of all?" The angel said, "Soul, read that which follows, and know those things that are to be marveled at by all who contemplate them." And the soul, seeing the letters that expressed numbers, but not being able to calculate a number from them, nonetheless understood that a modest time remained. He said, "Indeed, lord, the years are few." And the angel said, "I tell you, it is no longer. But today it was revealed to you how in a short while will be the end of the world. This is known to no creature, nor to angels, but only to God the Father.

II. Signs and Wonders

Document 6. Anselm of Liège on the eclipse of December 22, 968; *Gesta episcoporum Leodiensium* (*MGH, SS* 8:202). Composed in the mid–eleventh century.

The emperor had reached the boundaries of Calabria, and his army was arrayed throughout the fields, when an unexpected failure of the sun struck everyone with unbridled terror. I heard Bishop Wazo, when he was very old, describing how when he was still young he saw, as the sun was gradually failing, the day darkening as though it were evening, and how, as though it were already night, the herds of cattle left the pastures for the stables and the birds sought their nests. Our soldiers who happened to be there were incredibly terrified and thought that none other than the Day of Judgment was at hand. These strong warriors—who had deprived many cities of their best men, and who had subdued many rebellious peoples by the sword—became so afraid of this strange night with its reddish stars that they sought out various hiding places as though their lives depended on it. Thus, some ignominiously stowed themselves away in wine vessels, others in chests, and still others under wagons—may whosoever values life be able to find a refuge on account of this strange night!

The prudent bishop was stupefied by these things—not by the eclipse of the sun, the perfectly natural explanation of which he well knew—but by the irrational terror of such brave men. He suspected that their enemies in battle would much less fear them if word were to get out that they had been so frightened by a natural phenomenon. Thus, while everyone hid in his own fortress from such a slight danger of what he thought to be death, the bishop went around and zealously accused them all of cowardice and reminded them of their inborn virtue. Arguing rather infamously, he asked why those who were born of great ancestors, no one of whom ever succumbed to any difficulties whatsoever, and who themselves were accustomed to frequently overcoming hardships, could be so easily shaken in the minds by this natural failure of the sun? He said: "You strongest of warriors, who in the face of a thousand perils have so often seized famous victories for your name, I ask you to get up! Do not be afraid, but get up! Find once again your manly vigor, which you have lost while ignobly sleeping! It should be shameful to fear natural changes of the elements. There is nothing to fear in this; no blood drips from the wound inflicted by the right hand of the enemy. A harmless darkness has enfolded the air; soon, you will see, it shall grow bright, with the light having been restored." At length, with these words the lulled breasts of such great heroes were purged of empty terror. Not long afterward they perceived the lucid orb of Phoebe's lamp reform in its own shape;[2] they saw again the day, the failure of which they had shortly before watched with terrified hearts. Since then, their horror of these things is made a butt of jokes.

Document 7. Description of an earthquake on Good Friday in the year 1000, as recorded at St. Vaast in the margins of an Easter table; *Annales Elnonenses,* ed. Philip Grierson, in *Les Annales de Saint-Pierre de Gand et de St. Amand* (Brussels, 1937), pp. LV–LVII, 153. Composed in the early eleventh century.

In the one-thousandth year of the Incarnation of the Lord, in the thirteenth indiction and epacts 12, concurrents 1, paschal term 9, on Good Friday the 29th of March, while Christians were celebrating the sacrosanct mystery of his Passion and Redemption, there was a great earthquake. It was not like one as often occurs . . . but rather the whole magnitude of earth shook everywhere with a general and vast tremor, so that that which had been promised before by the mouth of Truth might be made manifest to everyone. With these and other signs that had been predicted having been completed by divine operation, hence our hope is made more certain in the sight of all regarding those that remain to be completed in due order.

Document 8. Sigebert of Gembloux on the year 1000 (*MGH, SS* 6:353–53). Composed ca. 1100–1106.

In the one-thousandth year of Jesus Christ, according to the computation of Dionysius, many prodigies were seen. There was an extremely great earthquake, and comets appeared. On the 14th of December, at around the ninth hour, what seemed to be a burning torch, with a long trail like a flash of lightning, fell to the earth from a fissure in the heavens with such splendor that not only those who were in the fields but also those indoors were struck by the light which burst forth. While this fissure in heaven was gradually vanishing, there was meanwhile seen a figure like a dragon, with a growing head and dark blue feet.

Document 9. The building of a heavenly city, as recorded in the *Annals of Saint-Benoit-sur-Loire* (*MGH, SS* 2:255).

In the year of the Lord 1003, there was a longer winter than normal, and the rains were quite severe. In many regions, the rivers overflowed their banks beyond measure . . . such that it was believed to be the Deluge. In that same year, near Orléans . . . a great many people reported seeing a ghostly city being built, from the third hour of the day until the ninth hour. It was surrounded by fields and streams with mills and completely filled with knights and supplies.

Document 10. A dew of blood and a darkening of the sun in 1009, as recorded in the *Annales Quedlinbourgenses* (*MGH, SS* 3:80).

On Palm Sunday, in a number of places drops of blood fell onto people's clothing. On Saturday, April 29th, the sun, having been altered by a horrible vapor and an astonishing hue so that it appeared bloody and smaller, struck terror into the eyes of those looking at it; after showing these signs for two days, on the third day it regained nearly all of its own light. A grave pestilence and mortality followed.

III. Relic Delations, Public Penance, and Apocalyptic Anxieties

Document 11. The *Miracula s. Agili* (*AASS OSB* 2:326–27). Composed in the eleventh century.

God, whose mercy fills the earth, watches over his sons with blows, because they will not be corrected by kindnesses. He is seen to hold out threats and reveal wraths, so that through the manifested dangers of present furor his merciful patience might liberate them, whom He does not wish to perish by death, from the eternal flames and lead them back to life.

We have an example of this inscrutable piety, revealed just before our times. When Robert was holding the right of kingship among the Merovingian realm, which is also designated by the other name of Francia, and after the passage of a thousand years since the Passion of the Lord, in that very year of the millenary fulfillment, when the observation of Lent was done and the day of holy preparation—that is, the day of the Crucifixion of Christ—had arrived, long columns of fire were seen high in the air in many places and by many people. This prodigious vision terrified the hearts of those who contemplated it. Immediately this rumor—and disaster thrives with a rapidity that nothing else exceeds[3]— reached the ears of the multitudes, of whom it is said there are as many tongues in them as their feathers. When the most prudent man Rainard, who was then the abbot of this house, learned of this harbinger of disasters, he summoned Abbess Ermengarde, who was presiding over Joire, and discussed the horrific vision with her. In order that they might evade those perils that they feared, he urged that they humble themselves in common counsel below the potent hand of God, and so he set a day of fasting. On that appointed day processions from the monasteries of Rebais and Joire came together at that place which, on account of the tokens of the virtue of God, henceforth deserved to be called the Cross of St. Agile. Great crowds of not ignoble laymen came together there as well. They began to sing out the penitential melody of the seven psalms, along with the names of the saints, and suddenly clouds blackened the sky and lightning flashed incessantly and hail the size of stones fell, and pallid terror reigned in the image of death.

Thus, when in the middle of the day the black night—victorious in all directions—had spread the densest darkness, everyone it seemed suddenly expected a quickly arriving death. By the order of the abbot and the wise men, a certain man who was especially imbued with talent in the liberal arts made a speech to the people, saying that the terror of the present commotion admonished them to do penance for their sins, and that henceforth, avoiding sin and offering alms to paupers with a tender mind and open hand, they might redeem the bond of their debts.

Document 12. From the *Acta s. Veroli*, patron of Chatillon-sur-Seine (*AASS*, June 4, 313–14). Composed ca. 1040–50.

Recently [i.e., the early 1030s], with our sins demanding it, and with the just judgment of the Omnipotent permitting it, a twin plague wore down the people through nearly all the regions of the quadripartite globe. Such an immense drought struck that all hope for the crops in the fields began to be lost. Also, such an immensely destructive plague raged that if anyone found himself unharmed in the afternoon, he believed that the advancing twilight would not see him; rising in the morning, moreover, he despaired to make it to the evening; and every person thought that he was to be killed by a sudden death.

Thus, the clergy serving the athlete of God Verolus gathered and spoke to each other in these words: "We see, Brothers, that through our scandalous behavior the entire age is put into peril in a twofold manner; a scourge is consuming nearly the entire human race, while a drought is wasting the fruits of our labors. Both plagues are so intolerable that a means or path of avoiding either is scarcely able to be discovered. Even if anyone avoids the moment of present death, he will not avoid the famine that is to come. But you know that our present protector has always heard those, distressed at heart, who beseech him with devout mind, and he has opportunely dispensed a plenitude of assistance. Because of this it seems necessary to us that the body of the holy man be removed from the apse, in which place it rests, and be honorably stationed in an open place outside the town. Naturally, hearing of this, great throngs of afflicted commoners will gather from all sides to seek his aid; they will beseech his mercy with prayers, they will honor his magnificence with odes and gifts, and thus, perhaps, they will rejoice to succeed in winning escape for themselves and for us." With everyone approving of this opinion, the consensus was reached that this was the best plan.

Therefore, the tomb of the holy man is opened; the holy corpse, having been elevated, is carried out of the church, or rather *castrum*, and is fittingly stationed in a pavilion next to the basilica of the nourishing martyr Mammes. The populace, recognizing that this had been brought about for their own safety, came flying eagerly from nearly all of the country. Bringing with them such gifts as each was able, they gave them to the saint, and they ardently surrounded him with hymns and devout prayers. The venerable father, having received these with a pious ear, took care to reveal how highly he was valued by God. For just as once before Pope Gregory the Great, having instituted sevenfold litanies, allayed a plague of the groin [i.e., the bubonic plague]; so, too, our Verolus, with the pestilence of the aforesaid disease having been driven away, with merits to be marveled at made the lingering mortality cease as soon as possible. And as Elias, who was later seized up above the stars by a flaming chariot, by prayer alone returned the rain that had been denied for three and a half years, so, too, our father, with the dry land sufficiently inebriated by a sweet bounty of heavenly rains, restored abounding verdure to the now drooping crops. . . .

Indeed, it is strictly by the benign piety of the Lord that we deserve to have this patron, in whose daily merits and intercessions we perceive the present gift of the Lord to be among us. . . . What, therefore, remains for us to do? Let us look for his refuge when we are vexed by any tribulation; let us implore that his aid be there for us. And let us turn our vows and prayers to the most pious father, because, with our sins demanding it, we presently perceive the scourge of divine indignation more frequently than normal: indeed, according to the prophecy of the Lord,[4] we discern that nations rise up against nations, and kingdoms against kingdoms; we are shaken by the blows of earthquakes, and we are put to the trial by the anguish of famine and pestilence; we fail before the dismay of heavenly terrors; and beyond these things, we are devastated by the rapacity of plunderers. First, let us beseech him that he will correct the depraved morals that have earned this; next, that he shall mitigate the just wrath of the Almighty, drive away the diseases, shut up the famine and the scourge, bear away discord and all things that will be harmful, and confer peace and everything that will be useful. If, with corrected morals, we shall have invoked his clemency, we shall without any doubt be able to obtain it, with the help of the Lord Jesus Christ, who lives and reigns forever with the Father and the Holy Spirit.

Document 13. From the *Miracula s. Adelardi (AASS,* Jan. 1, 119). Composed ca. 1055.

At that time it happened that many troubles seized upon Corbie, but even more so the kingdom of the Franks. For at Corbie, the principal temple of St. Peter was inflamed with fire by the envy of the devil, and almost all of Gaul was delivered over to the peril of famine. King Robert was administering on his own behalf in the kingdom of the Franks, and Abbot Richard on behalf of Christ at Corbie, both auspiciously, except when the fire dominated the one, and the famine atrociously tyrannized the other for seven years. To be sure, hunger dismissed so many people to death that the Fates seemed to break the threads of life not with the thumb but with the sword.[5] Moreover, this pestilence of the dying, along with too many others, particularly vexed the regions of the people of Amiens.

Compelled by this need, they decided to quickly provide a remedy for themselves, that is to say, to placate God, whom they had offended with evils in many ways, with some goods. It seemed that this vengeance had come upon them from heaven since they had not preserved peace, which the Lord especially loves and orders to be loved. Indeed, those of the kingdom of the Gauls, more than the rest of nations, always desired by their very nature to exercise madness of wars. But what now? It was not necessary to wish to die in war, since they were dying in heaps by the sword of famine and pestilence. The world is unable to bear the wrath of the Judge; it enters into counsel with the men of Nineveh. Peace and justice combine together; any moment now it seems fitting that the *Saturnia regna* return.[6] There remained but one desperate plan: to beseech the intercessory prayers of the saints for placating the wrath of the heavenly Judge. The relics were beseeched; the relics were gathered together at a central place, and there an inviolable pact of peace was confirmed. Thus, the men of Amiens and Corbie assembled along with their patrons and decreed a complete peace, that is for the entire week, and unanimously promised by God that each year they would return to Amiens on the day of the festival of St. Firminus for the purpose of confirming it. They bound themselves to this promise by a vow, and bound in turn this vow with an oath. There was, moreover, this counterpromise, that if anyone should dispute among themselves, they should not vindicate themselves by plunder nor arson until on an ordained day, in front of the church, there should be made a peaceful declamation before the count and bishop.

Document 14. Sigebert of Gembloux on the year 1033 (*Chronica*, anno 1033, ed. *MGH, SS* 6:357). Composed ca. 1100–1106.

There was an eclipse of the sun around midday on June 29. The bishops of Francia imposed such a decree upon the peoples subject to them. One of them said that a letter had been sent to him from heaven, admonishing that peace on earth be renewed. He communicated this matter to the rest and gave them these mandates to be conveyed to the populace: let no one bear arms or seek to recover what had been plundered, and let whoever is in any way the avenger of his own blood or that of any kinsman be compelled to indulge the attacker; let all observe a fast of bread and water on Fridays, and on the Sabbath abstain from meat and gravy; and let them, content with this fast alone for the remission of all sins, understand that no other penitence is to be assigned to them; and let them affirm with a sacred oath that they will observe these mandates. Let whosoever refuses to do so be deprived of Christianity; and let no one visit him when he is dying or bury him. Also, they gave numerous other unbearable commands, which seem onerous to repeat.

While many who were eager for new things embraced the novelty of the mandates all too willingly, Gerard of Cambrai—who alone among the Lotharingians was subjected to the ecclesiastical jurisdiction of the Franks—would be swayed to accepting them by the urging of no one but rather rebutted each and every point. He said that the race of men was divided in a threefold manner since the beginning into those who pray, warriors, and farmers; and that the one required the help of the two, and the two of the one. Therefore, arms ought to be borne, and plunder returned through the authority of the law and grace; the avenger of the injured or the murdered ought not to be angered by constraining but, according to the Gospels, was to be reconciled with him; a single fast was to be imposed upon all on Fridays and Saturdays, since there is not just one capability among all, nor should all be content with a single fast, since there is not just one means of doing penance among all. It would not be useful to affirm these mandates with an oath or, rather, to worsen the violation of the oath with perjury; it would be detestable if those speaking against these things were to be excommunicated, or if visitation of the sick or the burial of the dead were to be denied. Let the authentic decrees of the fathers suffice, and let the means of penitence consistently accord with the omissions.

NOTES

1. 2 Pet. 3:10.
2. See Virgil, G. 1, 459; Aen. 4.6.
3. Virgil, Aen. 4.165 ff.
4. Matt. 24:7.
5. Martial 11.37; Statius, Theb. 1.632–33.
6. Virgil, Ecl. 4.6.

Index